Border Fury

Border Fury
England and Scotland
at War, 1296–1568

John Sadler

PEARSON
Longman

Harlow, England • London • New York • Boston • San Francisco • Toronto
Sydney • Tokyo • Singapore • Hong Kong • Seoul • Taipei • New Delhi
Cape Town • Madrid • Mexico City • Amsterdam • Munich • Paris • Milan

PEARSON EDUCATION LIMITED

Edinburgh Gate
Harlow CM20 2JE
United Kingdom
Tel: +44 (0)1279 623623
Fax: +44 (0)1279 431059
Website: www.pearsoned.co.uk

Hardback edition published in Great Britain in 2005
This paperback edition published 2006

© John Sadler 2005, 2006

The right of John Sadler to be identified as author of this work has been asserted
by him in accordance with the Copyright, Designs and Patents Act 1988.

ISBN-13: 978-1-4058-4022-4
ISBN-10: 1-4058-4022-6

British Library Cataloguing in Publication Data
A CIP catalogue record for this book can be obtained from the British Library

Library of Congress Cataloging-in-Publication Data
A CIP catalog record for this book can be obtained from the Library of Congress

10 9 8 7 6 5 4 3 2 1
10 09 08 07 06

Printed and bound in Malaysia

The Publisher's policy is to use paper manufactured from sustainable forests.

For Katherine

Contents

List of Illustrations

4. James IV
5. James V
6. Mary, Queen of Scots
7. Stirling Castle
8. Caerlaverock Castle

Maps

Acknowledgements

Thanks are due to the following whose generous assistance has made the writing of this book possible. First to my agent Duncan McAra for his unstinting encouragement and support over many years; to Casey Mein, Benjamin Roberts and Viv Church at Pearson for their support, encouragement and unfailing courtesy, and also to Ann Hall for the indexing.

In addition, thanks are due to Dr David Edge at the Wallace Collection, Ailsa MacTaggart of Historic Scotland, Shona Corner of National Galleries of Scotland, Dr Richard Britnell of Durham University, Professor Anthony Pollard at Teeside University, Joe Ann Ricca of the Richard III Foundation, Charles Wesencraft, who has shed interesting new light on the battle of Otterburn, the members of The Steel Bonnets Living History Society, the staff of the Border History Museum at Hexham, the Royal Armouries Leeds, staff of English Heritage at Aydon, Prudhoe, Carlisle and Berwick, of Historic Scotland at Hermitage and Smailholm, and of The National Trust for Scotland at Bannockburn Visitor Centre.

Lastly and, as ever, especial thanks are due to my wife Ruth for her continued patience and for understanding the stresses of an author struggling to cope with the day-to-day demands of home and 'day' job!

Any errors, omissions or inconsistencies are, of course, entirely my own.

John Sadler

The publishers are grateful to the following for permission to reproduce copyright material:

The Scottish National Portrait Gallery for six plate section images of royal personages, © National Galleries of Scotland; The Royal Armouries for use of seventeen plate section images of arms and armour, © The Board of Trustees of the Armouries; the Historic Scotland Photographic Library for use of their image of Stirling Castle, © Crown copyright reproduced courtesy of Historic Scotland.

In some instances we have been unable to trace the owners of copyright material, and we would appreciate any information that would enable us to do so.

Timeline

1286 – death of Alexander III of Scotland

1292 – John Baliol ascends Scottish throne

1296 – beginning of the Wars of Independence, capture of Berwick and battle of Dunbar

1297 – battle of Stirling Bridge, Wallace appointed Guardian

1298 – Wallace defeated at Falkirk

1302 – battle of Courtrai in Flanders, French Chivalry defeated

1304 – siege and capture of Stirling

1305 – capture and execution of Wallace

1306 – Bruce murders John Comyn, is crowned King of Scots, defeated at Methven by Alymer de Valence

1307 – death of Edward I of England, accession of Edward II, civil war in Scotland between Bruce and Comyn factions

1308 – battle of the Pass of Brander

1314 – battle of Bannockburn

1315 – Scots unsuccessfully besiege Carlisle

1320 – Declaration of Arbroath

1322 – battle of Boroughbridge, execution of the Earl of Lancaster

1326 – Edward II is dethroned by Isabella and Mortimer

1328 – Treaty of Northampton, in France last of the Capetin Kings dies, Valois dynasty established

1329 – death of Robert I, accession of David II

1330 – Edward III executes Mortimer, assumes full control

1332 – the Disinherited, battle of Dupplin Moor

1333 – battle of Halidon Hill, Edward Baliol briefly in power in Scotland

1338 – the Hundred Years War between England and France begins

1340 – English win major naval victory at Sluys, land campaigns ineffective

1341 – David II returns from exile in France

1342 – English intervene in civil war in Brittany, longbow tactics win battle of Morlaix

1346 – battle of Crécy in Picardy and Scots defeated at Neville's Cross, David II taken prisoner

1348–9 – outbreak of the Black Death in England, later the 'English Disease' spreads to Scotland

1356 – battle of Poitiers, Edward the Black Prince captures the King of France

1357 – David II returns to Scotland

1366 – English intervention in Spain, battle of Najera

1369 – resumption of Anglo-French hostilities

1371 – death of David II, Robert Stewart becomes King Robert II and founds Stewart dynasty

1376 – death of the Black Prince

1377 – death of Edward III of England

1385 – Richard II invades Scotland

1388 – battle of Otterburn, death of 2nd Earl Douglas

1390 – death of Robert II, accession of Robert III

1399 – Richard II deposed, usurpation of Henry Bolingbroke (Henry IV of England)

1402 – battle of Homildon

1403 – Percy Rebellion in England, battle of Shrewsbury and death of Hotspur

1406 – capture of Prince James of Scotland, death of Robert II, Duke of Albany as regent

1411 – battle of Harlaw near Inverurie

1415 – the English capture Harfleur in Normandy, battle of Agincourt

1420 – Scots under Buchan serving in France

1421 – Franco-Scots defeat English at Beauge

1423 – English defeat Franco-Scots at Cravant

1424 – English defeat Franco-Scots at Verneuil

1429 – Joan of Arc defeats English at relief of Orleans and battle of Patay

1431 – Joan of Arc burnt as a witch

1435 – end of the Anglo-Burgundian alliance

1436 – murder of James I

1449 – English defeated at Formigny

1453 – Percy/Neville dispute, Talbot defeated and killed at Castillon

1455 – James II subdues Douglases at battle of Arkinholm, Yorkists and Lancastrians clash at St Albans, start of the Wars of the Roses in England

1458 – battle of Blore Heath, Lancastrians defeated but Yorkists flee after Rout of Ludford Bridge

1460 – James II killed at siege of Roxburgh but fortress falls and is slighted

1460 – in England battles of Northampton and Wakefield, death of the Duke of York

1461 – battles of Mortimer's Cross, 2nd St Albans and Towton, Yorkists triumphant

1461 – Margaret of Anjou surrenders Berwick to the Scots, attempts to barter Carlisle, Lord Montagu relieves the city

1461–4 – war in Northumberland

1464 – battles of Hedgeley Moor and Hexham, executions of Somerset and other Lancastrians

1470 – in England 'Re-adeption' of Henry VI, Warwick triumphant

1471 – battles of Barnet and Tewkesbury, deaths of Warwick, Edward of Lancaster and Henry VI

1475 – Edward IV invades France

1482 – Gloucester invades Scotland, recovers Berwick, James III favourites purged at Lauder

1483 – Gloucester usurps the throne of England as Richard III

1485 – Richard III defeated and killed by Henry Tudor (Henry VII) at Bosworth

1488 – rebellion in Scotland James III defeated and murdered at Sauchieburn

1487 – Henry VII wins battle of Stoke

1497 – James IV of Scotland besieges Norham

1504 – marriage of James and Margaret Tudor

1513 – campaign and battle of Flodden, death of James IV

1523 – James V executes Johnnie Armstrong and other borderers

1536 – religious controversy in England, the beginnings of the reformation, dissolution of the monasteries and the Pilgrimage of Grace

1542 – James V launches abortive attack on England, defeat of Solway Moss, death of James, infant Mary becomes Queen of Scots

1544 – 'The Rough Wooing', Henry VIII seeks control of Scottish affairs, the Scots reformation gathers pace, Hertford (later Duke of Somerset's) invasion, destruction of Leith

1547 – reign of Edward VI of England, campaign and battle of Pinkie

1553 – Mary Tudor on the throne of England, Marie de Guise regent in Scotland

1558 – death of Mary, accession of Elizabeth I

1561 – Mary returns to Scotland, protestant lords in ascendancy

1562 – Mary and Moray defeat the Catholic faction of Huntly at battle of Corrichie

1567 – Mary flees to England

1568 – Treaty of Berwick

1572 – in France the protestants in Paris are massacred on St Bartholomew's Eve

1575 – Raid of the Reidswire

1577–80 – Drake circumnavigates the globe

1585 – murder of Lord Francis Russell

1588 – defeat of the Spanish Armada

1596 – The 'Bold' Buccleuch rescues Kinmont Will Armstrong from Carlisle

1603 – on the death of Elizabeth James VI of Scotland becomes King James I of England

Chapter 1

Flowers of the Forest

*Here are two people almost identical in blood . . . the same in language
and religion; and yet a few years of quarrelsome isolation – in
comparison with the great historical cycle – have so separated their
thoughts and ways, that not unions nor mutual dangers, not steamers
or railways, nor all the king's horses and all the king's men seem able to
obliterate the broad distinction.*

R.L. Stevenson, *Essays of Travel*

There stands, in the market place of Selkirk, in the county of that name
a fine bronze statue by Thomas Clapperton. The figure of a fifteenth-
century borderer, albeit looking more like a Prussian cuirassier, holds aloft
a captured English banner. Legend relates that of an eighty-strong company from the town which served on the fatal field at Flodden. Only one,
a man named Fletcher, returned alive, his trophy the flag of the Macclesfield
contingent, led by Sir Christopher Savage. Casting the hard-won spoils in
front of his fellow citizens in the market place, the lonely survivor inspired
the tradition of the Common Riding, an annual event where local horsemen parade the banners of trade and guild around the burgh before sym-
bolically throwing them down.

The disaster at Flodden in 1513 has been the inspiration for a vast liturgy of romantic verse. The ballad 'Flowers of the Forest' recorded by Scott,
though of no great antiquity in his day, captures the tone of lament:

We'll hear nae mair lilting, at the eve milking;
Women and bairns are heartless and wae;
Sighing and moaning on ilka green loaming,
The flowers of the forest are a' wede awee.[1]

The sighing and moaning is almost certainly apocryphal; the borderers suffered few casualties on the field, led as they were by Lord Hume who cannily resisted his doomed monarch's desperate pleas for his division, blooded but by no means decimated, to come to the aid of their fellows. Hume may or may not have previously reached an accommodation with his English counterpart Lord Dacre, but their actions would certainly suggest an understanding based on ruthless pragmatism. Whichever national army triumphed, fire and sword would likely descend on the other's border country. Besides, a true borderer, whilst he might die for profit or family honour, saw little advantage in dying for his country.

The Bishop of Durham, writing shortly after the battle, supplies a far more grittily realistic assessment of (in this case) English borderers, though his observations could be just as easily applied to their Scottish contemporaries:

The borderers . . . be falser than Scottes, and have doon more harm at this tyme to our folkes than the Scottes dyd . . . I wolde all the orsemen in the bordours were in Fraunce with you for there schulde thay do moche good, where as here they doo noone, but muche harme, for, as I have wretyn byfore, thay never lyghted from thayr horses, but when the battaylis joynyd than felle thay to ryfelying and robbying aswelle on our sideas of the Scottes, and have taken moche goods besides horses and catelle. And over that thay tooke dyverse prisoners of ours, and delyveryd theym to the Scottes, so that our folks as moche feare the falsued of thaym as they do the Scottes.[2]

It is likely that the sixteenth-century inhabitants of Selkirk, or any other of the border towns on both sides of the line, would have had no difficulty in recognising themselves from that less-than-flattering description.

Being of mixed Anglo-Scottish descent, like so many who live in the border region, I may lay claim to a degree of impartiality. My first memories of the border dales are of camping trips with my father when I was a boy. We travelled in an ageing Series II Land Rover, whose uncompromising suspension gave a fair impression of a medieval cart. The border hills are narcotic in effect – once they're in your blood, they are there for good; once you begin to delve into their human past, you're hooked.

Tramping up Broad Law, Windygyle or The Grey Mare's Tail, usually in the lashing rain, left an indelible impression, not just of cold and wet but of belonging, being accepted into a landscape unchanged and unchanging. Camping by Meggat or Uswayford was to open a window on a past whose echoes were all around, the landscapes soaked (usually in the most literal sense) in romance, from Arthur to Hotspur and Marmion.

The very names resonate with conflicts past: Bloody Bush, Mainslaughter Law, Foulbogskye, Woden Law, Wolf Rig, Shield on the Wall, Morebattle, Gallowhill and the Ninestanrig where wicked Lord Soulis, the Bluebeard of Liddesdale, whose atrocities finally stretched the understanding of his neighbours, met a very unpleasant end:

They rolled him up in a sheet of lead,
A sheet of lead for a funeral pall;
They plunged him in the cauldron red,
And melted him, lead and bones and all.[3]

Between *Bond* books I read the Reverend Borland's Edwardian *Border Raids and Reivers*, a racy account of the riding surnames in the sixteenth century and became acquainted with Johnnie Armstrong of Gilnockie, Kinmont Will Armstrong, the 'Bold' Buccleuch and Auld Wat of Harden, along with a host of others.

As a student I devoured *The Steel Bonnets* by George MacDonald Fraser, probably the best single-volume history of the subject and which, published in the mid-Seventies, spearheaded a revival of interest in the reivers. The author's approach is very much 'warts and all' – he strips away the 'Young Lochinvar' gloss of the nineteenth-century romantics to show the life of the riding names as it was: very nasty, usually very poor and generally very short.

I was also of a school generation that was still likely to be inspired by Bruce and the Spider, Percy and Douglas and the other paladins of the age. This solid grounding, even if rooted in a jingoistic and frighteningly 'incorrect' era, led to a lifetime's interest. That two nations, like Montagu and Capulet, with so much in common, spent so much time at war, no mere skirmishing either but bloody and relentless conflict, replete with ample atrocities, is the story of the 'three hundred years war'. A war that has left a lasting divide in the hearts and minds of many, fuelled by the stylish propaganda of Scott and the other romantics, together with the less subtle appeal of the more recent 'Braveheart' mythology.

More recently, as one of those 'anoraks' whose concept of leisure is to dress in period costume and refight, though usually without bloodshed, historic battles (in my case those of the English Civil Wars under the aegis of the Sealed Knot Society), I am frequently reminded of the depth of feeling these encounters still engender, especially, it has to be said, on the Scottish side. I recall a very warm afternoon in June 1993, marching as part of the 'Scots' army down the main street of Linlithgow, a wise choice for the Scots were amply supplied with ale from the taverns lining the way, the 'English' markedly were not. These welcome libations were accompanied by martial exhortations and helpful advice on how to deal with those 'English bastards'. This phenomenon does not occur as one moves to campaign further south.

The border is not a paper frontier. At several crossing points, perhaps most noticeably the Tweed at Coldstream, you are aware of an immediate cultural shift. The buildings on the Scottish side with their crow stepped gables exhibit a totally different architectural heritage, displaying far more French influence than English.

Even the term 'border' is open to debate. Most would regard the border country as comprising the two most northerly counties of England, Northumberland and what is now Cumbria, formerly Cumberland and Westmorland, together with the southerly Scottish counties of Berwick, Selkirk, Roxburgh and Peebles, with possibly Dumfries.

This great swathe of country running from the Solway in the west to the North Sea in the east takes in a wide mix of landscapes, a region moulded by the shifting glaciers of the last ice age which persisted until some 15,000 years ago. When the great thaw finally triumphed, the hills and valleys were humped and scored, nearly four-fifths soon covered in primeval forest, or wild wood, of oak, ash, elm and beech, teeming with game.

The colder shores of the North Sea have some of the finest beaches in Britain, bounded by a lowland plain from the coal measures of south-east Northumberland to the Tweed valley and the Merse, arguably the most fertile farmland in Europe. The broad sweep of the River Tweed now marks the border in the east, from the frontier bastide at Berwick past great fortresses such as Norham, formerly part of the Bishopric of Durham, and the crumbled motte at Wark.

Once inland the country begins to rise. The upland valleys of Coquetdale, Redesdale and North Tynedale wind up to the wild sweep of the Cheviot hills. This rolling sea of wind-tossed tussocks and peat hags signally failed to impress Tudor travellers like John Leland, writing in the 1530s – 'craggi and stoni montanes'[4] – a sentiment echoed by Camden, 'lean, hungry and waste'.[5] The view from the present visitors' car park atop Carter Bar on the line of the A68 offers, at least on a clear day, a panoramic sweep of the middle marches territory, looking over the sculpted rise of the hills towards Jedburgh and Kelso.

On the Scottish side the southern uplands confront the Cheviots traversed by Liddesdale and Teviotdale, former haunts of the mosstroopers, Armstrongs, Elliots, Bells and Croziers. The grim fortress of Hermitage still lowers over Liddesdale, perhaps the single most potent monument to centuries of strife. West of the Cheviot is Bewcastle Waste, with the shattered bulk of the castle still standing. The border does not truly run east west but more south west to north east, on the English side guarded by the impressive bulk of Carlisle Castle. North of the Solway lie Eskdale and Annandale, formerly the Scottish West March, with the threap of the 'Debatable Land' lying between the two.

No two locations can really be said to be alike. The fertile reaches of the Till, winding past Etal and Ford, the river valley settled since antiquity, present a wholly different aspect to the upper reaches of Coquetdale where the hills crowd the narrowing glen and the thunder of artillery frequently creates a suitably warlike backdrop. The still mighty border fortresses, maintained and manicured, cannot entirely be compared with Bewcastle or Thirlwell, isolated, hacked and overgrown.

The visitor who searches for reminders of the border wars will not be disappointed. The forbidding nature of much of the country and the continued predominance of agriculture, a relatively sparse and stable population have combined to leave much of the landscape unchanged. Now there are roads where formerly there were none, even in Liddesdale and Teviotdale, which for centuries remained remote, inaccessible fastnesses, where the natives were far from friendly, 'the beautiful valleys full of savages'[6] as both were described. Much of the forestation has now gone, replaced by cultivation, and several of the towns on the Scottish side have a more recent industrial heritage based on the mill trade.

To glean an impression of the border country as it stood for most of the long years of the border wars we must imagine a landscape where barely any roads, or at least roadways we would now recognise as such, existed. Natural forest of oak and scrub alder covered much of the ground and a good deal of the land between was wet and generally impassable, the mosses impenetrable to all but those who knew the hidden pathways.

Castles, tower houses and peles still abound, such as Smailholm near Kelso, almost impossibly romantic in its cliff-top setting, and Hollows Tower near Canonbie, now restored and often incorrectly identified with Johnnie Armstrong. The battlefields at Heavenfield, Flodden, Otterburn, Hedgeley Moor and the Reidswire are marked for the visitor; others – Carham, Homildon, Ancrum Moor, Pinkie, Haddon Rigg – require more sleuthing.

From Berwick to the Solway is no more than 70 miles as the crow flies. The line of the border is nearer 120 miles, with the hump of the Cheviot massif rising to 2,500 feet at the highest point. By the mid-thirteenth century the governance of the region on both sides of the line became the function of the march wardens, indentured servants of their respective crowns whose role was to control the unruly inhabitants and defend their section of the frontier. This could, and not infrequently did, extend to a more proactive role. Warden raids or 'rodes' could be large-scale affairs with hundreds, sometimes thousands, of light border horses stiffened with a levy of foot 'loons' or garrison troops carrying out a wide sweep through the opposing march. Teviotdale and Annandale were both frequent targets.

The English East March comprised the districts of Norhamshire, Islandshire, Glendale and Bamburghshire. Norham, 'the Queen of Border Fortresses', was part of the County Palatine and thus a fief of the Prince Bishop, while the coastal flank was anchored on the great fortress of Berwick. Originally Scotland's premier port and a flourishing royal burgh the town changed dramatically in character and appearance after the savage English assault of 1296, becoming a military outpost and a bone of contention between the two nations until it finally changed hands for the last time in 1482.

Lord Hunsdon, the military governor and East March Warden during Elizabeth's reign,[7] estimated the extent of his wardenry as 24 miles long and 16 miles broad, extending from the North Sea to the Hanging Stone in the foothills of the Cheviots. The Tweed provided the natural frontier, with Berwick, Norham and Wark as the principal fortresses and though Berwick was provided with splendid new walls in the latest Italianate style, the other holds were left to deteriorate during the sixteenth century as their importance declined.

Norham retains its imposing presence despite the ravages and thefts of time[8] but Wark is almost totally decayed; only the remains of the motte survive. Though formidable in flood, the Tweed was usually easily fordable, with some seven or eight crossing places between Berwick and Norham. The Till bisects the March from north to south, with castles at Etal and Ford. The east coast was the favoured invasion route for armies forging north or south. William the Conqueror set the pattern in 1070 when, supported by a fleet hugging the coast, he launched a punitive raid through the Lothians to chastise Malcolm Canmore.

The English Middle March encompassed the high ground of the Cheviot and Carter Bar whilst also taking in mid Northumberland. The warden was based at Alnwick, dominated by the great stronghold of the Percys, with his lodging in the Abbey. The upland dales of Coquetdale, Redesdale and North Tynedale fell within his jurisdiction, together with their quarrelsome inhabitants. Each of the valleys had its own distinct character, with Coquetdale being decidedly less lawless than the other two, though much harried by riders from Liddesdale and Teviotdale. The upper reaches of the valley were guarded by the castle at Harbottle, another bastion that was allowed to fall into ruin as the sixteenth century progressed. The mosstroopers came by the Bowmont Water and over Cocklaw, following the reivers' trails, spreading fire and pillage in their wake.

The English West March covered both Cumberland and Westmorland – now, since the dead hand of central bureaucracy did away with the latter, the confines of Cumbria. Westmorland played a relatively minor role in border strife. Kendal was a thriving wool town, Appleby Castle a Clifford hold. Carlisle was the principal city in the west; the great, red sandstone mass of the castle, stark, square and utterly uncompromising had been built as a challenge to the Scots and remained so, defying several determined sieges. The land frontier of the march ran for some 20 miles, bounded in the west by the waters of the Esk and towards the Middle March by the Liddel. The land was open moor rather than border hill country, the barren reaches of Bewcastle Waste a favoured reivers' haunt.

The ravaged remains of the castle do not reflect its importance, with other holds at Askerton, Naworth and Thirlwell.[9] The warden maintained his office at Carlisle where he was aided by his deputy and a constable. The city was a local metropolis with, perhaps not entirely unsurprising, a brisk trade in stolen beasts and gear!

On the Scottish side the East March comprised the county or sheriffdom of Berwick, facing the English garrison in the town and separated from Haddingtonshire by the swelling Lammermuirs. The formidable hold of Hume Castle seemingly impregnable on its sharply rising bluff commanded the Merse, a palpable expression of the family's power in the march, the wardenship being virtually a hereditary office.[10] On the coast some seven miles east of Cockburnspath lay Fast Castle, the remains of which still perch dizzily above the North Sea like a northern Tintagel, the cold breakers hammering the sheer cliffs below. The pleasant and picturesque fishing village of Eyemouth previously stood as a Scots bastion against English Berwick some eight miles distant – the French maintained a fort on the coast until slighted after a treaty concession in 1561. The inhabitants of both eastern marches are perceived as less belligerent than their upland neighbours from whose rapacious inroads they suffered equally.

The sheriffdoms of Roxburgh, Selkirk and Peebles together with the 'County of Liddisdail' made up the Scottish Middle March. From the banks of the Tweed above Carham to the Hanging Stone the district abutted the English East March; from there westward to Kershopefoot along the barren rise of the Cheviots it adjoined the middle and then finally, for the last seven miles, the West March. Peebles, another busy wool town, stood largely aloof on the north-west periphery, though some of its gentry, notably the Tweedys and the Veitches, were inveterate and bloody in their feuding. Hawick was, as it remains, the principal town of Teviotdale, though sharing its prominence with Jedburgh, Kelso and Selkirk. Liddesdale was sufficiently lawless to merit its own law officer or keeper who resided at Hermitage – his was not an enviable commission.

The Scottish West March, encompassing the Stewartries of Kirkcudbright and Annandale with the Sheriffdom of Dumfries, ran from Kershopefoot to the wild fastnesses of Galloway, slashed with pleasant river valleys, Niddsdale, Annandale, Eskdale, Ewesdale and Wachopdale. Dumfries itself, the seat of the warden, his deputy and a sheriff, was another bustling wool town located at the navigable mouth of the Nith. This was Maxwell country and

Lord Maxwell exercised his sway over the area from his stronghold at Caerlaverock on the banks of the Solway.[11] Annan was something of a poor relation. The strength of the valley was the Johnstone seat at Lochmaben, girded about with an elaborate system of earthworks, of which very little now remains. The castle was important enough to warrant its own captain or keeper. Eskdale was guarded by the tower at Langholm; few traces survive. The feud between Maxwell and Johnstone which culminated in a savage mêlée at Dryfe Sands near Lockerbie in 1593 is an epic in itself, the fight probably the bloodiest family or 'clan'[12] battle ever fought.

It is difficult to attempt any accurate assessment of the population of the Anglo-Scottish border at any particular point in history and all estimates are conjectural. What can be said with some degree of certainty is that in England the population rose steadily from the Domesday record in 1086 until the close of the thirteenth century, perhaps threefold, so that the total was between 5 or 6 million by 1300. The climatic shifts of the early fourteenth century and the famines which followed failed harvests in 1315, 1316 and 1317 may have engendered a mortality rate as high as 15 per cent. From 1348–9 the grim spectre of pestilence drastically increased the mortality rate, perhaps killing off almost half the population. Thereafter, like Banquo's ghost, plague stalked the land to erupt periodically.[13] Recovery was slow and even in the mid sixteenth century it is unlikely that the population of England exceeded 3 million people.

Domesday did not extend beyond the frontier of the Tyne, thus depriving us of that initial yardstick. The 1377 poll tax returns indicate that Northumberland contained some 16,800 taxpayers (it has to be said the census was far from popular and figures may thus be wildly inaccurate), but if we accept the figure as broadly correct then the total population may have been around 35,000, a reasonable figure allowing for the recent havoc of the black death. The three border counties were undoubtably far more sparsely populated than their southerly neighbours, though Yorkshire was far larger than Northumberland, with a population five times greater, with an average density of 37 persons per square mile as against a mere seventeen persons per square mile in Northumberland.[14]

D.L.W. Tough, writing in the 1920s, attempted to reach a figure for the population of the three English marches by looking at the surviving muster rolls for 1584 and assuming that these represent the bulk of 'fencible' males, i.e. those eligible for military service between the ages of 16 and 60.

He compared these figures with similar returns in the nineteenth century and attempted a calculation based on the census data from 1841 and 1881, which indicates that fencibles represented about 250 per 1,000 head of population, one in four. To achieve a figure for the late sixteenth century he increased the multiple to five, wisely to allow for a higher disaffection rate and greater mortality in border strife. He thus arrived at a total figure for the marches of some 120,000 souls.[15]

Comparative data for the Scottish side is not available, so any estimate is even more rule of thumb. It may generally be supposed that the Scots marcher population was somewhat smaller – none of the towns corresponded in size either to Newcastle (say 10,000 inhabitants) or Carlisle (perhaps half that). With the dissolution of the monasteries in the 1530s and the consequent 'privatisation' of the coal trade monopoly the church had enjoyed, Newcastle underwent an economic boom in the mid-sixteenth century, a level of industrialised growth that was not paralleled elsewhere in the borders. The smaller towns on both sides of the line, Alnwick, Morpeth, Hawick, Jedburgh, Kelso, Selkirk, may have housed perhaps 1,200–1,500 inhabitants. As we know, Berwick was a military outpost whose complement may have comprised, say, 2,000 military and support personnel, with a further 1,500 or so civilians, undoubtably a decline since the town's prominence as a Scottish port was destroyed.

Although the line of the frontier was generally agreed after 1257 there were still isolated pockets of ground where no consensus as to title existed. These 'threaplands' were claimed by both but governed by neither, a haunt for outlaws and thieves. Of these pockets the most prominent was a stretch of land perhaps four miles wide and twelve miles long that ran northward from Gretna, almost to Langholm and as far east as the wild fastness of the Tarras Moss, the empty quarter that guarded the entrance to Liddesdale and known as the 'Debatable' Land. No writ or rule of law ran here, despite frequently strenuous efforts by both governments to draw a viable line. Badlands in the fullest sense of the word, where those who had made even Teviotdale or Liddesdale too hot could seek a kind of desperate refuge among their own kind, a thieving elite, invariably with a price on their heads and usually with blood on their hands.

Topography clearly played an important part in determining the history of the border region, but in order to glean an understanding of how events unfolded after 1296 and continued to 1603, we need to consider, at least in outline, that which went before, how the line of the border became fixed and something of the history that caused the line to become established where it did.

The Celtic tribes who inhabited what is now the borders region of England and Scotland prior to and during the Roman occupation would have had difficulty in recognising the later boundaries. What is now Northumberland, latterly the Celtic fief of Bernicia, was home to the Votadini. North and west, on what is now the Scottish side, lived the Damnonii; to the west of them lay the lands of the Selgovae. Imperial expansion under a series of energetic governors in the late first century AD into the north of England, the kingdom of the Brigantes, peaked after the appointment of Julius Agricola in AD 77. An ambitious and aggressive career soldier who had served under Suetonius Paulinus in the savage campaign against the Iceni and their warrior queen Boudicca, Agricola planned to subjugate the lands of the Celtic tribes in central and northern Scotland, thus carrying the eagles to the very rim of the known world.

Having tightened his grip on Brigantia he constructed a series of forward strong points between the Forth and the Tay, anchored on a major legionary fortress at Inchtuthil at the confluence of the Islay and Tay. From AD 79 he campaigned annually in Caledonia, seeking a decisive engagement against the native tribes. Five years later they finally obliged him, making a stand at Mons Graupius[16] which may have been fought on the slopes of Bennachie by Inverurie, north west of Aberdeen. He won a spectacular if somewhat empty victory, soon followed by his recall to Rome, certainly not in disgrace but perhaps not in triumph. Inverurie was a long way from the Capitol Hill and the game, quite simply, was not worth the candle.

Hadrian, as every schoolchild knows, was the one who built the wall, the 'limes' or frontier between 'us', Rome and civilisation, and 'them', the hordes beyond. The great wall with its chain of forts, mile castles and turrets, the northern flank of the empire whose southern boundaries rested on the Euphrates, was largely completed by AD 128. It remains one of the greatest monuments of antiquity, a massive and awe-inspiring statement of imperial power and logistical capacity. In AD 140 the frontier was shifted north to the shorter Forth–Clyde isthmus – the Antonine Wall, a lesser work in timber and earth which took five years to complete. Overrun in the reign of Commodus, the northern defence was soon abandoned and Hadrian's earlier wall rebuilt after a thorough slighting by the locals.

As imperial power waned in the fourth century the increasingly beleaguered Roman administration was forced onto the defensive as raids by
Saxon and Irish pirates intensified along the coasts and the northern tribes
became belligerent. In AD 367 concerted action by a major barbarian
coalition overran the faltering defences completely. The province was split
into two and then four administrative regions; defence of the north rested
with the impressively labelled Duke of the North based at York (Eboracum).
When the Emperor Honorius wrote to the towns of Britain in 410
advising them to shift for themselves he was probably merely confirming
a situation that had persisted for some time, successive pretenders had
whittled down the garrisons of the province to launch bids for the purple,
most famously in the case of Magnus Maximus in AD 383.

The last of the dukes of the North may have been named Coelius,
whom the Welsh Annals called Coel Hen and whom we now know better
as 'Old King Cole'. Coelius appears to have been able to maintain garrisons throughout the north, the rump of such imperial forces as remained
supplemented by native militias or foederati. Since the disaster of AD 367
it appears to have been policy to plant regular soldiers, much like district
officers in the British empire, to administer friendly tribes beyond the wall,
creating a Romanised buffer against the wilder peoples to the north.
These late imperial frontiersmen along with Coelius himself seem to
have, in several instances, fostered lines of native princes who thus claimed
their descent and their cultural heritage from Rome. With the death of
Old King Cole, his single dominion disintegrated into a group of prin-
cipalities – no less than eight native dynasties claimed to be descended
from him.[17]

For a time in the sixth and seventh centuries these Romano-British
kingdoms of the north exercised a powerful influence, to the extent that it
has even been suggested that Arthur may have been a northern rather than
a southern warlord. After the great barbarian tide that swept Roman Britain in AD 367 had been repulsed (or bought off), Count Theodosius who
had restored such order as could be restored insisted the towns look to
their own defences and ensure their walls were refurbished and maintained.
This was undoubtably excellent advice in a period of such upheaval and
appears to have been well heeded by the citizens of Carlisle (Luguvallium).
Here the city fathers kept the Roman administration going for generations
after the collapse of imperial control, maintaining walls, roads, aqueducts

and drainage, keeping alive the spirit of Roman and classical civilisation – 'Romanitas'.

In AD 573 a major and locally decisive battle was fought near Carlisle at Arthuret when the Christian Britons of York triumphed over the pagans of the north west. From this victory emerged the powerful Celtic kingdom of Rheged, which under its greatest ruler, Urien, stretched from Stranraer to Rochdale and which, for a period, an almost mystical twilight, acted as a buffer against Anglian expansion from the east.

The Anglo Saxon Chronicle tells us that the first Saxon ruler of what was to become Northumbria arrived in AD 547 – Ida, Prince of the Angles, who ruled for 12 years. The Celtic kingdom of Bernicia which he came to control probably comprised the bulk of what is now Northumberland and into the Lothians. Ida's accession to power may not necessarily have resulted from military conquest; it is by no means impossible that his warband came as mercenaries and assumed authority either through a carefully staged coup or through dynastic marriage. By AD 590, however, the expanding Anglian kingdom was coming into conflict with Rheged and the other remaining Celtic realms. Urien led an alliance of princes against Ida's aggressive successor, Fflamddwyn, winning a major engagement at Argoed Llwyfein and driving the Saxons eastward, penning the battered survivors in their coastal holds. Urien then laid siege to Lindisfarne (Metcaud) and was poised to achieve total victory when, with the blind, internecine squabbling that so continually hamstrung the Celts, he was assassinated by Morcant, his rival.

With the death of Urien his great coalition fell apart and the Angles were spared destruction. Even though his son Owain again defeated and this time killed Fflamddwyn, the inexorable rise of what was to become Northumbria under Aethelfrith, ('the artful dodger'), heralded the doom of the Celtic states. Around 600 Aethelfrith defeated the Britons from the Lothian Kingdom of Manau Goddodin at Catreath (Catterick?). Three years later he smashed a new challenge from the remaining Celts allied to the Scots of Dalriada under their king Aedan Mac Gabran at Degsastan, a battle which may have taken place near the Pass of Soutra.

Aethelfrith's Christian successors, Edwin, Oswald and Oswy, despite defeats from the Welsh and the Mercians under the formidable leadership of the pagan Penda, finally triumphed over both and extended the northern boundaries of Northumbria to the Tay. The northward drive of the Anglian Kingdom was halted decisively at Nechtansmere in 685 when King Ecgfrith and his army were cut to pieces by a confederation led by the Pictish leader, Bridei mac Bile.[18]

Beginning in the fateful year 793, Northumbria and later Scotland were beset by internal Viking raids. These intensified after 865 when the Norsemen exploited one of the many feuds in Northumbria to effect a more permanent conquest. This led to the partition of the old kingdom, with a new Viking state centred on York and the English, as we may now call them, forced back upon Bamburgh, the old seat of Northumbrian power. The Scots too suffered, though united as a kingdom under Kenneth MacAlpin, few of his successors died in their beds. Constantine I fell in battle against the northmen and Constantine II (900–940) suffered a major reverse against Raghall of York at Corbridge in 914, though with tidy irony he met the Norseman again four years later, also at Corbridge, and this time emerged triumphant.

Resistance to the Vikings in England had been spearheaded by the dynamic kings of Wessex. Alfred's grandson Athelstan extended his power northward, rolling up the Norse enclave at York. So powerful was this resurgence that Constantine formed a great coalition, drawing in the Britons of Strathclyde in the west and the Norsemen from York and Dublin. The clash, a mighty one, took place on the field of Brunanburh, possibly on Humberside. Constantine's army was shattered and the rise of Wessex was unchecked. Malcolm I (943–964) found it expedient to agree terms with Edmund of Wessex, whereby he was able to secure Cumbria, effectively on lease from the English crown. In 973 King Edgar of England was ceremoniously rowed along the Dee in a barge oared by six client kings, among them Kenneth II of Scotland (971–995).

The unhappy reign of Ethelred (known to history as the 'Unready' though this was more likely 'Unraed' or 'Ill Advised'), provided fresh opportunities for Malcolm II (995–1034). For several decades the Scots had been steadily chipping away at Northumbrian power in the Lothians. King Kenneth's homage to Edgar was likely the consideration for the ceding of the whole of the region to Scotland. The West Saxon kings had broken the rump of the old kingdom of Northumbria into three smaller fiefdoms with earls of Cleveland and York. Oswulf the earl of the northern fragment was succeeded by earl Waltheof who succeeded in reuniting the separate holdings into one. Militarily, however, he was not a success. The

Danes sacked Bamburgh in 993 and this humiliation was compounded when Malcolm II launched a campaign against Northumbria in 1006. The earl's son Uhtred was made of sterner stuff, however – he raised the siege of Durham and harried the Scots northward.

Having replaced his incompetent father, Uhtred's star appeared to be firmly in the ascendant as he also received a grant of the earldom of York, making him the king's most powerful subject in the north. He pursued Malcolm north of the Tweed and re-imposed Northumbrian control of the Lothians. He also campaigned in the west, raiding into Cumbria, but suffered a reverse at Brough-under-Stainmore. Married to a daughter of King Ethelred, Uhtred's position was severely weakened by the triumph of Cnut the Dane who had finally defeated Ethelred's son Edmund Ironside in 1016. The Scandinavian monarch was clearly nervous at having so over-mighty a subject presiding in the north, especially one who had supported his late rival's cause, and he connived at Uhtred's murder.

Despite killing the earl Cnut never gained full control of the country north of the Tees, where loyalty to the House of Bamburgh persisted. The southern portion of the former kingdom was entrusted to men of proven loyalty, firstly to the colourful swashbuckler, Eric of Hlathir ('Bloodaxe'), and then to the formidable Earl Siward, 'Siward the Dane'. The emasculated northern rump of Northumbria was ruled by Edwulf Cadel, Uhtred's younger and considerably less dynamic brother. Malcolm saw his chance and stepped up the pressure north of the Tweed once more. In desperation Edwulf sought to buy off the King of Scots by once again ceding the Lothians. This craven surrender produced a howl of protest from the church in Northumbria orchestrated by Bishop Aldhun, enraged at the massive loss of ecclesiastical revenues.

In 1018 King Malcolm, with his ally and liegeman Owen of Strathclyde, confronted Edwulf's host at Carham on the Tweed. Details of the battle which ensued are at best sketchy, but we know that the Northumbrians were routed with considerable loss, including, it is said, eighteen leading members of the clergy. The significance of the fight is that the Lothians were lost to the English and the Tweed came to form the border with the Scots in the east, though it was some time before this became fixed.[19]

Malcolm II was succeeded by his grandson Duncan I (1034–1040). Duncan was not the rather kindly, harmless old duffer portrayed in *Macbeth* but a much younger and more aggressive ruler whose zeal for battle was matched only by his disastrous incompetence. His six-year reign was marked by a series of stinging reverses; his attempt on Northumbria was bloodily repulsed by Siward, now controlling the earldom in its entirety. Duncan's death, in his last ill-judged fight against the earl or mormaer of Moray, Macbeth, provided Siward with fresh scope for aggression when he sponsored the cause of Duncan's illegitimate son Malcolm.

Macbeth's seventeen-year rule was not the span of a tyrant but of a competent and largely successful ruler who even found sufficient leisure to undertake a pilgrimage to Rome. In 1054 Siward's campaign on behalf of Malcolm pushed Macbeth back north of the Tay. At Lumphanan three years later Macbeth fell in battle. Even so Malcolm was not yet king. The immediate succession fell on the dead usurper's stepson Lulach and it took Malcolm another year to encompass his death by ambush.

By then Siward was dead, his earldom entrusted by Edward the Confessor to the younger brother of Harold Godwinson (the future Harold II), Tostig, who having been ousted by his disgruntled subjects, appealed in 1065 to Malcolm, now secure as Malcolm III (1058–1093), for military aid. Tostig's defeat and death at Stamford Bridge and the Norman triumph at Hastings both failed to cure the fissiparous tendencies of the northerners. This chronic instability gave scope for Scottish aggression and Malcolm invaded on no less than five occasions, in 1061, 1070, 1079, 1091 and lastly in 1093 when he came once too often and was slain in battle at Alnwick.[20]

Before turning his attention southward the king had consolidated his grasp on the northern reaches of his rule by marrying Ingibjorg, widow of the powerful Norse Earl Thorfinn of Orkney. When she died in 1069 he married Edgar the Atheling's sister Margaret. This trend was continued in a flurry of dynastic marriages up to 1113, as Scottish kings and nobles sought to cash in on alliances with either the old House of Wessex or the Norman invaders.

In 1070 Malcolm invaded Cumbria, his aim appears to have been to create a buffer state or pale as far south as Lancashire in the west and the Tees in the east. Inevitably these inroads produced a savage backlash. William the Conqueror, even if he found administering the turbulent north of his new domain a tiresome and frustrating chore, was not about to allow such flagrant aggression to go unchecked. He launched a major invasion of the Lothians, with a powerful force of mixed horse and foot, supported and provisioned by the fleet sailing up the east coast. This was undoubtedly the most potent 'English' army to take the field and Malcolm wisely adopted fabian tactics, pursuing a policy of scorched earth to deny sustenance to the invader whilst avoiding battle. At Abernethy on the Tay a concord was arrived at whereby Malcolm did a form of homage to William as his overlord, 'made peace . . . and gave hostages and was his man'.[21] This echoes Kenneth's earlier submission to the West Saxon kings and it is highly unlikely Malcolm intended anything other than a temporary expedient. In 1079 he crossed the border once again, seeking to exploit renewed disturbances in Northumbria and once again the counter stroke was swift and vigorous, with Malcolm being compelled to consolidate the earlier agreed terms, this time at Falkirk.

He did not, however, come away empty handed for his influence as far south as the Tyne was recognised. The Conqueror's son, Robert Curthose, tacitly acknowledged the fact by founding the 'New Castle' by the Tyne as a frontier garrison. In spite of this success Malcolm did not abandon his hopes of extending the Scottish pale to the Tees. In 1091 he laid siege to Durham, provoking the by now customary retaliation against the Lothians. Worse, the Normans began work on a great castle at Carlisle, threatening any claims he might have in the west. His final expedition ended in death and with him fell his eldest son by Queen Margaret.

Malcolm III was not immediately followed by a son but by his brother Donald Ban (1093–1097). His short reign was followed by those of Edgar (1097–1107) and Alexander (1107–1124). All this time Malcolm's youngest son by Margaret, David, had been living as a favoured client of the English court of Henry I, the young man's brother-in-law. The Scottish prince was, in his youth, regarded as the very epitome of chivalry and the king's favours extended to the granting of the lucrative earldoms of Huntingdon and Northampton. The border regions of England, at the same time, were becoming more feudal, with permanent Norman settlement in both Northumberland and Cumberland consolidating the king's authority north of the Tees.

David, having been active in the affairs of Scotland for some time, came to the throne as David I in 1124, and despite being in his middle years his vigorous rule continued until his death in 1153. It is perhaps not surprising that his reign witnessed a rash of Norman innovations. Motte and bailey-type fortifications began to appear,[22] Norman knights and adventurers sought his patronage. The age was viewed, with hindsight, as a time of prosperity. The growth of urban centres was recognised by the creation of a number of Royal Burghs, including Berwick, and there was a marked upsurge in monasticism with a spread of new abbeys including the splendid Cistercian foundation at Melrose.

The death of Henry I of England, and the bitter and protracted civil war which developed between his daughter, Matilda, and Stephen of Blois, provided David with an opportunity to resurrect his father's great dream of a Scots pale in northern England. His great raid or chevauchee of 1138, however, ended in disaster as the Battle of the Standard near Northallerton.

Internal unrest marked much of the shorter reign of Malcolm IV (1153–1165). He was particularly discomfited by rebellions in the west, the most serious being that of Somerled the 'Lord of the Isles', a Norse-Hibernian chieftain who enjoyed the virtual status of a free prince. The long-oared Hebridean galleys carried Somerled's wild kerns to the banks of the Clyde and Renfrew in 1164 where they were checked and routed by a body of mailed knights, leaving their lord slain upon the field. By 1157 Malcolm was forced to formally vacate any claim to Cumberland and Westmorland and acknowledge Henry II as his feudal superior. Henry went so far as to demand knight service from his Scottish vassal during a campaign in Aquitaine in 1160.

Malcolm was succeeded by William II (1165–1214), 'William the Lion', an energetic and aggressive soldier but one who, like Malcolm III, came to serious grief at Alnwick in 1174 when he was taken in a surprise attack on his siege lines.[23] The king's capture was a serious blow and in the same year he was obliged, among other humiliations, to agree to the terms of the Treaty of Falaise when he renewed his predecessor's submission and did homage to Henry 'for Scotland and for all his other lands'.[24] This pernicious matter of vassalage would return to darken Anglo-Scots relations until the death of Henry VIII, notwithstanding the fact that Richard I of England, 'Lionheart', formally relinquished his claim to feudal superiority by means of a formal quit claim in 1189. Lionheart's motives were purely financial – he needed the agreed fee of 10,000 merks.

It was during William the Lion's long reign that the expression 'Kingdom of Scots' first appears and relations with the southern kingdom appeared to improve during the relatively peaceful and prosperous years of the thirteenth century. Alexander II (1214–1249) married Joan, the daughter of King John and Margaret, daughter Henry III was wed to Alexander III (1249–1286).

Matters were by no means entirely harmonious however. Alexander II was leading expeditions into northern England whilst still in his teens – he mounted no less than five major incursions between 1215 and 1217. John retaliated in the by now time-honoured way, leaving a trail of devastation through the Lothians, with Berwick, Roxburgh, Dunbar and Haddington all in flames. The reign of Alexander III, who ascended the throne as a minor, latterly the curse of Scottish medieval kingship, came, in the light of subsequent turmoil, to be seen as a 'golden age' of peace and plenty. Presiding over his council in Edinburgh in the late winter of 1286 the forty-four-year-old king might have looked back upon the thirty-six years of his kingship with some satisfaction. The realm had enjoyed both peace and plenty. In the north and west he had scored a signal coup in 1266 when the King of Norway had ceded Man and the Hebrides to him, the first King of Scots to enjoy such a total hegemony along his western seaboard. His relations with England were cordial, but though like his forbears he had sworn fealty to Edward I, the terms were loaded with ambiguity: 'I become your man for the lands which I hold of you in the Kingdom of England for which I owe homage, saving my kingdom.'[25]

His kingdom was in fact enjoying something of a boom in trade with its North Sea partners; the great herds of sheep grazing the southern uplands produced a fine wool that found a ready market in Flanders. Hides, timber and fish were also exported from Stirling, Leith, Haddington, Roxburgh and above all Berwick, the nation's busiest port. Such was the volume of trade with the low countries that Fleming merchants and artisans had their own centre in Berwick, the Red Hall, whilst the White Hall in the Seagait was used by Germans from Cologne. Scotland traded extensively with the Hanseatic League. The Flemings, as a condition of their tenure, had undertaken to defend their hall against the English if called upon to do so. An obligation thus entered into with the utmost seriousness.

Though Alexander II had first married an English wife, she was not the mother of his son. When she died he married again, this time looking to a French bride, Marie de Couci. Alexander III had three children by Henry III's daughter Margaret but within a decade of her death in 1275 all three had followed her to the grave. The king's heir therefore was his infant granddaughter, the frail and distant 'Maid of Norway', formally recognised in 1284. He naturally had high hopes of his young, French wife Yolande of Dreux; though in his middle years, the king was a vigorous man with by all accounts a most active libido; besides, it was his duty to produce a strong male heir.

Monday the 18th of March was a wild and stormy day in late winter. Once the business of the day was done and the wine flowed around the council chamber the king expressed his intention to ride to his royal manor of Kinghorn where the queen was lodged. His councillors expressed reservations – the night was filthy and the Forth stood between the king and his consort. Fuelled by wine and lust, doubtless tempered with a sense of duty, Alexander remained adamant. With a tiny retinue he undertook the crossing as the cold wind whipped the waters of the Firth and the late winter dark descended. It was pitch black by the time the royal party disembarked at Inverkeithing. Refusing the Baillie's warnings and calling for local guides the king, with but a pair of squires as escort, rode off along the wild and storm-tossed coast. Somewhere in the blundering dark Alexander became separated from his companions. Exactly what transpired will never be known but the following dawn his broken body was found sodden and sprawled on the foreshore. Scotland was without a king.

Notes

1 Scott, Sir Walter, 'Flowers of the Forest', *Minstrelsy of the Scottish Border* p. 84.
2 MacDonald, Fraser G., *The Steel Bonnets*, London 1971 p. 21.
3 Scott, *Minstrelsy*, 'Lord Soulis' p. 403.
4 Quoted in MacDonald Fraser p. 34.
5 Ibid p. 34.
6 Ibid p. 34.
7 Henry Carey, Lord Hunsdon (1525–1596), most probably an illegitimate son of Henry VIII. He was a long-serving East March Warden and a good servant to his half sister Elizabeth, particularly during the crisis of the rebellion of the Northern Earls in 1569. His two sons also served on the marches, the younger Robert Carey with considerable panache and distinction.
8 Norham began, like most castles, as a motte and bailey construction and was taken by the Scots in 1136 and in 1138. The present, stone edifice was begun in the reign of Henry II; the actual construction was undertaken by Bishop Hugh of Puiset and the castle remained part of the County Palatine for most of its history. The great bulk of the keep remains mightily impressive, being heightened from the original three storeys to five in 1423. See Long, B., *Castles of Northumberland*, Newcastle 1967 p. 142.

9 Built from plundered Roman masonry Thirlwell, which is mentioned in the 1541 survey, occupies a strong position covering the Irthing Gap. The Thirlwall family were distinguished in the early years of the border wars. Most of what remains is probably early fourteenth century and the site has recently been restored and opened to the public, see Long, p. 161.

10 Virtually nothing of the original castle remains; the building which now crowns the site is but a hollow eighteenth-century folly.

11 Caerlaverock, idyllically situated by the banks of the Solway, was rebuilt in the later thirteenth century after the earlier site, traces of which have now been excavated, was abandoned due to the rising water level. The red sandstone castle remained the seat of Lord Maxwell and its triangular shape is particularly distinctive, with much original work surviving in the walls and the massively fortified gatehouse. Longshanks laid siege to the place in 1300 and the event is now commemorated annually by re-enactors. Medieval siege engines such as would have been deployed against the walls in 1300 have been reconstructed on the site.

12 Border families are not referred to as clans; that description has been reserved for the highlanders. The borderers are more properly called 'names' or 'graynes' – the 'riding names' a collective for those families most active in raiding. Dryfe Sands was a savage affair that spilled into the streets of Lockerbie. Many casualties were caused among the fleeing footsoldiers by downward cuts from the pursuing horse – 'Lockerbie Licks' as these ghastly wounds were thereafter known.

13 The plague did in fact have three forms. The bubonic, where bacilli were transmitted to humans by fleas from infected rats and which attacked the lymphatic glands – death usually ensued within 3–5 days – was largely seasonal as the fleas were more active in warm temperatures and the disease was not contagious between humans. The pneumonic, which attacked the lungs and was invariably fatal, was not affected by seasonality and remained highly contagious. The septicaemic was, mercifully, more rare but so virulent that death ensued within hours (see Lomas, R., *County of Conflict, Northumberland from Conquest to Civil War*, East Lothian 1996 pp. 70–1.)

14 Lomas p. 70.

15 Tough, D.L.W., *Last Years of a Frontier*, Oxford 1928 p. 26.

16 Tacitus, our main authority for Agricola's campaigns, is vague about geography, though he took evidence first hand from the great general in retirement. (Agricola was, in fact, his father-in-law.) He had no first-hand knowledge of the terrain and the exact location of the battle of Mons Graupius has eluded scholars and archaeologists.

17 Roxburgh Castle, which was a prominent medieval hold and which features frequently in the chronicles of the border wars, may, it has been argued, mask the remains of an earlier, possibly iron age construction re-fortified in the late Roman period and modified into a cavalry fort. This seductive thesis has been

extended to suggest Roxburgh may have been a northern Camelot. Readers are referred to Alistair Moffat's *Arthur and the Lost Kingdoms*, London 1999 pp. 232–59.

18 Also referred to as the battle of Dunnichen Moss which was fought on the 20th May of that year. The events of the campaign may have been commemorated on the reliefs depicted on the Aberlemno Stone, unearthed from Aberlemno churchyard. The victory has been hailed as 'the most decisive battle in Scottish history', see Lynch, M., *Scotland: A New History*, London 1991 p. 13.

19 The site of this fateful encounter lies a quarter of a mile or so east of Wark on the flat and fertile flood plain of the Tweed. The ground is clearly visible from the present B6350 which bisects the field, although there is no public access. There is no commemorative marker and the OS map incorrectly identifies the date as 1016. This was by no means the last time that the vicinity would echo to the clangour of arms. The Augustinian cell of the Black Canons of Kirkham was wasted by Wallace's raiders in 1297. In 1370 a lively skirmish between Scots under the redoubtable Sir John Gordon and an English force under Sir John Lilbourne occurred half a mile or so west of the settlement. At the end of a hard-fought mêlée the Scots had the best of the day with Lilbourne and a number of the English being taken captive.

20 A memorial, erected by the Duchess of Northumberland in 1774, marks the spot where, it is said, the King of Scots met his sanguinary end. He is actually said to have fallen by a spring, latterly known as 'Malcolm's Well', and credit for the slaying is given to the Constable of Alnwick, Eustace de Vesci.

21 Quoted in Lynch p. 75.

22 A motte and bailey castle was the form of defence first introduced by the Normans in the campaign of 1066. It consisted of two wards, both on raised earthern embankments and surrounded by a timber palisade. The lower or outer ward was the more extensive and held all of the domestic buildings, barracks, stables, kitchens, chapel and the lord's hall. The inner, much smaller ward comprised a conical earthwork topped by a timber tower, intended as a final refuge if the lower, outer ward fell to an attacker. These castles were built almost to a pattern and were relatively easy to throw up. Their purpose was to create a fortified base from which mounted knights could control a territory and which was capable of being defended by a small garrison.

23 The capture of the Scottish king involved the English relief force, comprised entirely of mounted knights, undertaking a night ride from Newcastle and approaching Alnwick at dawn, their arrival masked by an early morning mist. They immediately spurred into the attack on spotting the royal banner. William and his mesnie or household knights were caught completely off guard and scattered, the king left unhorsed and captive on the field.

24 Quoted in Lynch p. 86.

25 Ibid p. 89.

Chapter 2

Sinews of War

But that the Scot in his unfurnish'd kingdom,
Came pouring like the tide into a breach,
With ample and brim fullness of his force;
Galling the gleaned land with hot assays,
Girding with grievous siege castles and towns;
That England being empty of defence,
Hath shook and trembled at the ill neighbourhood.

William Shakespeare, *Henry V* (I:II)

In 1181 Henry II of England, founder of the great Angevin Empire and notorious as the instigator of Archbishop Becket's murder, made statutory provision for the arming of the nation. The Assize of Arms specified the arms and armour to be carried and worn by each degree in society from the knight to the commoner. This legislation was revised by Henry III in 1242, then substantially modified by his son Edward I, 'Longshanks', forty years later. The king, mustering a host at York and Northampton in that year, provided that all who held land to the value of £20 or more, be they gentlemen or yeomen, could commute their feudal service by means of a cash subsidy, a form of war tax.

In 1295 Longshanks went further, ordering that all who were found to hold property worth £40 or more should be prepared and ready, on three weeks' notice, to fight as paid soldiers of the crown. Each was to provide his own arms and equipment according to his rank. This system, an early variant of conscription, was employed the following year for the Scots campaign and proved less than popular. The lure of glory and the guarantee of wages (not necessarily reliable) appears to have been an insufficient incentive to tempt the chivalry of England into the hostile reaches of the northern kingdom.

Edward I expanded the role of the Royal Household as the primary state engine of war, the only military elite that represented a form of standing army. The Household acted as more than simply a kernel of dedicated professional warriors bound to the king's service; its function extended to the administrative and logistical. Later in the fourteenth century in the reign of Longshanks' grandson, the Royal Household, in recognition of the growing tactical significance and capital cost of ordnance, assumed control of the Tower arsenal.

After Edward I, in the reign of his son, Edward II, a king unhappily noted more for his defeats than his triumphs, further efforts were made to improve the quality and composition of the crown forces by requiring both magnates and towns to muster suitably furnished heavy infantry ('the foot') in addition to their established obligation to supply cavalry ('the horse'). Such a levy was called out to march to the relief of beleaguered Norham Castle, the 'Queen of Border Fortresses', in 1319. The unsettled conditions in the northern marches meant that there was a continued reliance on locally raised militias including men at arms, archers and light cavalry ('hobelars').

A contemporary chronicler has left us with this stirring vision, fit for the pages of Scott or Malory, of the English host on the march northwards from Carlisle in the campaign of 1300:

> *There were many rich caparisons embroidered on silks and satins; many a beautiful pennon fixed to a lance, many a banner displayed. The neighing of horses was heard from afar; the mountains and valleys were covered with packhorses and wagons with provisions, tents and pavilions.*[1]

In practice the east coast route, along the line of Dere Street, the old Roman road, was the favoured path for the English invader, used by Longshanks in the Falkirk campaign of 1298 and followed by his son on the way to his nemesis at Bannockburn. The advantages of using Dere Street were that it was flatter than the west coast route and the fleet could more easily keep station with the army – this was essential for adequate supply and re-victualling. Even with this precaution the army of 1298 ran dangerously short of supplies; an unfortunate combination of empty bellies and full wine casks led to an unseemly fracas between the English foot and Welsh archers. The supply situation became so dire that the king was on the point of bowing to the ignominy of retreat when intelligence arrived of the Scots mustering at Falkirk, preparing to accept trial by battle, and thus, perversely, saving the English from a humiliating reverse.

In Scotland the pace of military development was somewhat slower. In the course of the twelfth and thirteenth centuries Scottish kings had attempted to impose a system based on feudal service; knight service is referred to in charters from the period, smaller estates were granted to mounted men at arms or sergeants. In return for the regular supply of galleys and rowers to propel them, manors or fiefs were parcelled along the west coast.

At the same time the distinctive motte and bailey type of castles begin to appear in Scotland, constructed originally, as earlier in England, in timber. The thirteenth century witnessed much rebuilding in stone. Scottish armies of the late thirteenth and fourteenth centuries might comprise a variety of troop types: mounted knights of Anglo-Norman descent, spearmen from the central lowlands, wild Picts and Gallowegians from the Norse Hiberian realms of highlands and islands, with a sprinkling of hardened Flemish or other continental mercenaries.

Professor Barrow, distinguished biographer of Robert Bruce, citing the apparently well-informed chronicler of *The Life of Edward II*, records that such was the magnitude of the royal baggage train snaking its way towards Stirling in the hot June of 1314 that the column of wagons, had they been lined up one behind the other, would have stretched for over twenty miles!

We may therefore summon up an impression of an Edwardian army on the march which is somewhat less heroic than the poet might have us believe. The knights, divided for the 1300 campaign into four divisions, would not mount their precious destriers until taking the field; they would rather amble on lighter palfreys whilst grooms led the valuable chargers. Most armour and trappings would be stowed in the pack or baggage train, colours would be muted rather than flamboyant, the whole seeming more like a migration. The foot, clad in a riot of gear (there being no standardisation of kit), would slouch in uncomfortable columns, clouded by the vast quantities of dust stirred by their betters, ill shod, generally ill provisioned and frequently unwilling.

Here and there we might see a well-drilled troop of continental mercenaries marching more in step or specialist troops such as engineers, their
carts loaded with timbers and tools. The army was a sprawling host that
required an array of trades to keep it functioning – carpenters, wheelrights,
farriers, armourers, bowyers, fletchers, surgeons and sutlers, with a motley
trail of wives and whores plodding in its wake. Add to this unwieldy herds
of beasts and flocks of sheep, driven by drovers and churning the way still
further, and we have a huge column stretching for mile upon mile, the very
sight of which must have terrorised local inhabitants for whom the passage
of a medieval army could only spell ruin.

We should not be tempted to forget that the majority of the medieval
population lived in relative isolation in hamlet and steading, so the spectacle of such a veritable horde filling the landscape from horizon to horizon
with the vast accompanying din, deafening the silent countryside, would
create a terror of biblical proportions. In the majority of instances such
terror would have been an entirely appropriate response. Despite the number
of full-scale invasions and counter-invasions mounted by both English and
Scots, the more usual form of warfare featured infinitely smaller mounted
columns, raiders rather than invaders, relying on mobility and surprise
rather than numbers. It is unlikely that a beleaguered peasantry would be
able to draw much solace from such alternative tactics.

Behind the army in the field stood a complex logistical effort that sorely
taxed the resources of the medieval state. To underpin every campaign it
was necessary to establish a series of forward supply dumps – Berwick in
the east and Skinburness near Carlisle in the west, which were victualled
from the sea. These supplies were usually collected by the royal prerogative
of 'prise', a form of compulsory purchase, guaranteed, at least in theory, by
promissory note. The ships that were employed to transport the supplies
were often equally unwilling, being private merchantmen pressed into the
royal service.

In order to provide a reliable supply of trained fighting men Edward III
considerably developed the contract system whereby the monarch as commander in chief entered into formal engagements, indentured contracts
in writing, with experienced captains who were then bound to provide
an agreed number of men, at established rates for a given period. The
protracted and widespread campaigning in France made the reputations
of famous captains such as Knollys and Chandos. Frequently scions of the

nobility acted as the principal or main contractor and sub-contracted knights, men at arms and archers in turn. From the 1330s the practice of recruiting mounted archers developed and grew – this arm combined the missile power of the archer with the mobility of light cavalry, precursor to dragoons in the age of pike and shot.

Later, in the mid-fifteenth century, the end of the Hundred Years War and the final demise of English hopes resulted in large numbers of unemployed soldiery crossing the Channel, frequently seeking new opportunities in the swelling armies of the great magnates. As the land drifted towards misrule and violence under the weak governance of a feeble king, border lords such as the Nevilles and Percys began increasingly to rely on their swords, and those of their retainers, to settle disputes. It became common practice for landowners to bind their mesnie knights to their service by the provision of annuities. Humphrey Stafford, 1st Duke of Buckingham who died in 1460, had a total of ten knights and twenty-seven esquires in his service. One of the former, Sir Edward Grey, was granted a life annuity of £40 in 1440; lesser men received payments of between £10 and £20 per annum.

In addition to these professional retainers a lord, when setting off on campaign, could call upon his tenantry, whose muster could be swelled by a scattering of landless or simply frightened men who craved the relative security of a great man's badge or livery. Thus the pernicious system of 'livery and maintenance' came into being. As the baronial armies grew in size and in temerity the rule of law diminished accordingly. A surviving indenture from 1452, entered into between Walter Strickland, a knight of Westmorland, and his lord, the Earl of Salisbury, lists the complement which the former could provide: billmen, 'horsed and harnessed' – seventy-four; bowmen, likewise arrayed – sixty-nine; dismounted billmen – seventy-six; and dismounted bowmen, seventy-one – a by no means unimpressive total of 290.[2] In most foot companies of the fifteenth century it would appear that archers were the predominant arm, outnumbering men at arms by anything from three to one to ten to one.

When Sir John Paston was preparing to sail for Calais he requested that his brother recruit four archers, '. . . Likely men and fair conditioned and good archers and they shall have four marks by year and my livery'. In short these were to be permanent retainers with an annual salary. A particularly skilled archer belonging to a lord's household retainers might command as high a wage as a knight. In 1475 Edward IV was raising an army to intimidate France and his magnates contributed to the muster as follows: Duke of Clarence ten knights, a thousand archers; Duke of Gloucester ten knights, a thousand archers; Duke of Norfolk two knights, three hundred archers; Duke of Suffolk two knights, three hundred archers; Duke of Buckingham four knights, four hundred archers.[3]

The king still had the power to issue what were termed 'commissions of array' which empowered his officers to call up local militias, who, at least in theory, were to be the best armed and accoutred men from each village in the county. This system was much open to abuse, a tendency Shakespeare was later to parody in *Henry V*, [Falstaff] – 'If I be not ashamed of my soldiers I am a soused gurnet I have misused the king's press damnably' (IV:I).

Letters from the contemporary Stonor correspondence which relate to the Oxfordshire half hundred of Ewelme, comprising some seventeen villages, show that the catchment yielded eighty-five soldiers, seventeen of whom were archers; Ewelme itself fielded six recruits:

> *Richard Slyhurst, a harness and able to do the King service with his bow, Thomas Staunton* [the constable] *John Hume, whole harness and both able to do the king service with a bill. John Tanner, a harness and able to do the King service with a bill. John Pallying, a harness and not able to wear it, Roger Smith, no harness, an able man and a good archer.*
> [Those without armour are described as 'able with a staff'.][4]

Surviving muster rolls from the later period also provide an insight into the local levy. One held at Bridport in Dorset on 4th September 1457, before the Kings Officers, reveals that a man was expected to possess a sallet, jack, sword, buckler and dagger. Some two or three of those paraded carried bows and a number of arrows. Other weapons noted included poleaxes, glaives, bills, spears and axes, staves and a miscellany of armour.

The Italian, Dominic Mancini, has left us with a vivid eyewitness account of the appearance of the troops Gloucester and Buckingham brought into London in 1483 to supply the 'muscle' behind Richard's usurpation.

> *. . . There is hardly any without a helmet, and none without bows and arrows; their bows and arrows are thicker and longer than those used by other nations, just as their bodies are stronger than other peoples', for they seem to have hands and arms of iron. The range of their bows is no*

less than that of our arbalests; there hangs by the side of each a sword no less long than ours, but heavy and thick as well. The sword is always accompanied by an iron shield . . . they do not wear any metal armour on their breast or any other part of their body, except for the better sort who have breastplates and suits of armour. Indeed the common soldiery have more comfortable tunics that reach down below the loins and are stuffed with tow or some other soft material. They say the softer the tunics the better do they withstand the blows of arrows and swords, and besides that in summer they are lighter and in winter more serviceable than iron.[5]

Until the close of the fifteenth century the armoured knight was still regarded as the prime arbiter on the battlefield, notwithstanding the havoc caused amongst mounted chivalry by massed archery and on occasion by bodies of pikemen and spears (Courtrai, 1302, and Bannockburn, 1314). The longbow was a highly specialised weapon and not one that was ever used in significant numbers by continental armies. By the late fifteenth century, Swiss halberdiers and pikes had hacked down some of the pride of European knighthood, as at Sempach in 1386 and later against Charles the Bold of Burgundy in his doomed campaigns. It was not until the handgun came into widespread use that the long supremacy of the mounted gentleman finally came to an end.

The roots of knighthood lay in the mist-shrouded past. Chivalry was a creation of the early middle ages which, on paper at least, provided a code for the behaviour, on and off the field, of the military elite. The profession of arms was the only career open to a man of good family and he trained assiduously from an early age, usually being placed in the house of another noble to receive his training among other young men of his class, squires, (from *ecuyer*, bearers of the shield or *ecu*).

Edward I regarded his Scottish wars as insurrections and those opposing him as rebels and traitors. This left little room for chivalry, as the king's harsh conduct towards the defeated after the storming of Berwick would amply testify. Throughout the period, however, it was felt that there was a general decline in knightly virtues, a pernicious trend much bemoaned by contemporary writers, though vestiges did remain. In his work 'Le Jouvencel', the chronicler Jean de Beuil, writing *c.* 1466, gives an insight into the mind of the fifteenth-century gentleman:

What a joyous thing is war, for many fine deeds are seen in its course, and many good lessons learnt from it . . . You love your comrade so much in war. When you see that your quarrel is just and your blood is fighting well, tears rise in your eyes. A great sweet feeling of loyalty and pity fills your heart on seeing your friend so valiantly exposing his body to execute and accomplish the command of our Creator. And then you prepare to go and live or die with him, and for love not abandon him. And out of that there arises such a delectation, that he who has not tasted it is not fit to say what a delight is. Do you think that a man who does that fears death? Not at all; for he feels strengthened, he is so elated, that he does not know where he is. Truly he is afraid of nothing.[6]

The employment of massed archers, Englishmen or Welsh in the English service, was for generations a battle-winning tactic as the results of encounters such as those at Dupplin Moor, 1332, or Halidon Hill in 1333, Neville's Cross 1346 or Homildon in 1402 show. The potency of massed archers had signally contributed to the numerous victories in the French wars at Crécy, 1346, Poitiers, 1356, Najera, 1366 and, perhaps most famous of all, Agincourt in 1415. Even as late as 1487 at Stoke Field, the Earl of Lincoln's lightly clad Irish kerns were mown down by the Tudor's longbowmen, but none of the major clashes in the period was determined solely by archery – battles were won by the skilful deployment of the various arms, by the co-ordination of horse and foot. The infantry, certainly in England, were typically divided into small platoons of twenty under a vintenar; five of these shrunken platoons formed a company under a centenar and ten such companies formed a battalion under the command of a millenar.

The opening showers of arrows would, nonetheless, have been an almost unbearable test for the forces being assailed – even the knights and better armoured men at arms were not immune from hurt. On or before 'Palmsunday Field', Towton, near Tadcaster fought in 1461 during the Wars of the Roses in England, both Lords Clifford and Dacre were fatally struck down when they unwisely removed their bevors to take (doubtless much needed) refreshment. It has been calculated, again with reference to Palmsunday Field, that if each archer loosed forty-eight arrows, over a million shafts with a total weight of some 40 tons would have been expended in that engagement alone.

The Scots continually fought at a disadvantage. True, they had the benefit of interior lines, but as the poorer nation they suffered a constant deficit in terms of both heavy cavalry and missile troops. The response to this, first seen on the field of Falkirk in 1298 under William Wallace, was the hedge of spears, the 'schiltron' or 'schiltrome'. The term appears to mean something akin to a 'shield wall' as might have been deployed in the Viking era, but under the leadership and inspiration of the Guardian it became a mobile formation, bristling with steel. The idea of the phalanx of pikemen was hardly a novel concept – Alexander's phalangists had helped him overcome the might of Persia and win victories throughout the breadth of Asia Minor.

The schiltron was formed by a line of spears several ranks deep bending at the flanks till they met in what was then a circular formation. The points were thrust outwards to form a formidable barrier which, unless breached, could resist any assault by the horse. Unsupported cavalry recoiled before the schiltron in the opening moves at Falkirk and again on the first day of Bannockburn. The numbers employed were variable but each formation seems to have formed a tactical unit with a commander who most likely remained in the centre with the reserve, which was fed in to the lines as casualties mounted.

Pike tactics were developed to a fine art by the Swiss who relied upon a formidable mix of momentum and discipline. Their victories were facilitated by a clever use of terrain, concealing the troops in dead ground or woodland until contact was imminent, then sweeping forward with great elan to, quite literally, steamroller the opposing forces, who, if they received the charge whilst static, would be swept away, trampled or impaled. The Swiss recognised that the formation had to both keep moving and avoid prolonged exposure to the fire of missile troops to which they could not respond.

This was the main weakness of the schiltron, as the events on the field at Falkirk showed. If immobile and unsupported by horse or archers to keep enemy missile troops at bay, the formations were horribly vulnerable. Wallace had to endure the agony of watching his men shot down in droves by relentless longbows, so weakening the strength of each unit that they were inevitably overcome when the horse swept down upon them once again.

The dire lessons of this bloody debacle were not lost upon Bruce, who, at Bannockburn, in the advance of the second day, ensured that the formations retained their momentum, attacking in echelon so that each division in turn crashed into the enemy with sustained impetus, a tactic favoured by the redoubtable Swiss. Later commanders, however, disregarded or failed to appreciate the lessons of Bannockburn where Keith's light horse rode down the few archers Edward managed to deploy. In later battles, particularly Dupplin Moor, Halidon Hill and Neville's Cross, lumbering columns of spearmen were decimated by archery from the flanks.

In the preparation for James IV's ill-starred campaign of 1513, French officers attached to the king's staff sought to instil up-to-date Swiss pike tactics into the Scottish levies. Even had this training been effective and the Scots had had time or the will to reach the high standards of professionalism already attained by the Swiss, whose mercenary prowess had become the arbiter on the battlefields of North Italy, the fatal topography of Flodden would still have defeated them. Later in the sixteenth century the power of both field artillery and hand guns made themselves felt – gunfire finally defeated the Swiss at Bicocca in 1522 and Scottish pikes were similarly mown down at Pinkie a quarter of a century later.

In the later battles of the period knights and men at arms dismounted to fight on foot; horses were sent to the rear, to be mounted only when the enemy was in rout – pursuit of a beaten foe was both rigorous and merciless, the slaughter indiscriminate. A wealthy captive from the ranks of the nobility could be the makings of a yeoman's fortune, but a lowly farmer had little or no commercial value.

Light horse or 'prickers' were used for scouting and reconnaissance, but once battle was joined, there was little direct control that a commander could exercise. Armies were marshalled into three divisions or 'battles' – the van, or vaward, main battle and the rear, who deployed for combat in line, the knights and men at arms with archers to the fore standing beneath the unfurled banners of their captain or lord. On the march the army advanced in columns, conforming to the three divisions.

In the sixteenth century the same order of march prevailed, though 'battles' were now being referred to as regiments and the foot were divided into companies of around one hundred strong under a captain, assisted by a petty captain and a senior NCO described as a 'wiffler' or, more recognisable to us, a sergeant. The company was an independent tactical unit, with its own flag or ensign, a fifer or drummer, and comprising both pikes and missile weapons. Brigades, under a great captain, were formed of a fluid number of companies, rather along the lines of the Spanish Tercio.

The line of march had to be refined to allow for the movement of the great guns and the army was preceded by a screen of light horse who also acted as flankers and rearguard. The foot marched with bodies of pikemen interspersed with bodies of shot, the guns trundled along the flanks of the foot with the cavalry moving beyond. The horse were likewise divided into companies of a hundred riders.

War is and has always been a hazardous business. In the medieval period a commander had limited forces at his disposal, a defeat in the field was likely to be fatal to his cause, and quite likely to his person. Communications were dependent upon gallopers and, where possible, signalling with flags, supply and victualling were a constant headache and treachery waited around every corner. In a number of battles fought in the border wars English generals stood on the defensive, adopting the harrow or 'herce' formation with dismounted battalions of men at arms alternating with wedge-shaped formations of archers. The missile power of the long-bow, the discipline and cohesion of the foot, had combined to produce a series of stunning victories over both the hasty elan of French chivalry and the lumbering might of the schiltron.

Once battle commenced it is probable that a commander could do little to influence events. Nonetheless for purposes of morale a leader was expected to display both valour and prowess. Bruce's triumph over his impetuous challenger de Bohun in front of the lines at Bannockburn was a tremendous boost to his beleaguered men, particularly the Highlanders to whom such a Homeric display was the very epitome of valour.

Good intelligence was, as always, vital – all armies fielded scouts or 'scourers'; bad intelligence could be fatal. As we have seen Edward was preparing to abandon the campaign of 1298 when his scouts brought him word of the proximity of Wallace's army. Although armies tended to deploy in linear formation with opposing divisions aligned, this could go awry, depending upon weather and terrain. Troops being struck by arrows from the flanks tended to bunch together in the centre to try to escape the deadly shafts; of course all this achieved was to present a better target, the ruin of the Scots' pike columns at Dupplin Moor. A commander with an eye for ground might try to deploy an ambush party for a flank attack, as the English commander did at Neville's Cross, hiding Edward Baliol's mounted reserve in dead ground – the charge of the 'disinherited' on the flank of the wavering Scots proved decisive.

Sometimes the trick might backfire, however. Henry Percy 'Hotspur' decided to maximise the element of surprise by mounting a night attack at Otterburn in 1388. The fitful moonlight and lack of proper reconnaissance played into the hands of the Scots. Darkness prevented the English from using their bows and a flank attack led by Douglas won the day, even at the cost of his own life.

Medieval captains were usually literate and familiar with their trade. Many would have read the classical authors, such as the late Roman theorist, Vegetius, whose 'Epitoma Rei Militaris' was revised in the fifteenth century by Christine de Pisan who also wrote 'Livre des fais d'armes et de Chevalerie'. This was translated and popularised by Caxton as 'The Book of the Fayttes of Armes and Chyvalrye'. A modern writer has, however, summed up the likely approach of most professional soldiers and even though he is writing with reference to the Italian mercenary condotierre, his remarks ring true for most armies of the period: 'The fifteenth-century captain learnt the art of war as an apprentice to an established condotierre, not from books. He may have been gratified to learn from one of the humanists in his entourage that his tactics resembled those of Caesar in Gaul but it is unlikely that he consciously intended to be so. It was not a study of the Roman republican army which produced a revival in infantry but the practical necessities of fifteenth-century warfare.'

We should not forget that despite the supposed influence of chivalry, 'frightfulness', the deliberate harrying of an enemy's lands and civilian population, was an accepted tactic: conquest by terror and waste. As a form of economic warfare this was undoubtably effective, destroying the enemy's crops and indeed the tools needed to produce them. Such tactics also struck at the social order. Good 'lordship' was an essential element in the baron's relationship with his tenants; if this was damaged or destroyed the lord's position became increasingly tenuous. Plunder was a prime incentive to medieval soldiers and such robbery also reduced the economic wealth of the enemy.

Atrocity breeds atrocity. The Scots were the first to taste Longshanks' ruthlessness with the fall of Berwick in 1296. Wallace and later Bruce retaliated by striking into the English border counties. In the wake of the

English debacle at Bannockburn this pressure was increased to the extent that the Scots were able to levy large amounts of blackmail from the northern shires, converting frightfulness to commercial advantage. Jean II, King of France, after signing the humiliating treaty of Brétigny in 1360, explained his willingness to agree to such terms in the following manner:

> *Because of the said wars many mortal battles have been fought, people slaughtered, churches pillaged, bodies destroyed and souls lost, maids and virgins deflowered, respectable wives and widows dishonoured, towns, manors and buildings burnt and robberies, oppressions and ambushes on the roads and highways committed. Justice has failed because of them, the Christian faith has chilled and commerce has perished, and so many other evils and horrible deeds have followed from these wars that they cannot be aid, numbered or written.*[7]

The continental system of 'lances' was not used, it appears; companies were led by their captains and formed according to their weapons. Banners were important as both morale boosters and as rallying points in the heat of battle. In the fifteenth century the use of liveries did produce some degree of uniformity amongst companies of retainers. The soldier wore a tunic or tabard over his armour or jack bearing his lord's badge. In the case of the Percys, for instance, this was a livery of russet, yellow and orange bearing the Percy lion rampant on the shoulder. Conversely this could also cause confusion and, as in the mist shrouding the Wars of the Roses battle of Barnet in 1471, where Lord Montagu's men mistook the Earl of Oxford's star and stream for King Edward IV's sun and stream, disaster.

The Tudor period witnessed a series of reforms instigated by Henry VIII, a monarch besotted by the lure of martial glory, though ironically the greatest fight of his reign, at Flodden in 1513, was won by the Earl of Surrey and Lord Howard, his son, whilst the king was posturing in France.

The pace of military development was quickening in the long slaughter of the Great Wars in Italy and a flush of new manuals appeared. The Henrician reforms split his soldiers into a number of defined classes:

- Heavy cavalry – these were the mounted shock troops, akin to the French 'Gendarmerie'. Men and horses were armoured, riders carried sword and lance.

- Light cavalry of 'demi-lances' – these wore only three-quarter armour with plate greaves or shoes ('sabatons'). Instead they took to wearing stout horsemen's boots, the leather reaching to mid thigh and thus affording a fair measure of protection against a cut. As the mounted horseman gave way to pike and shot, a tactic derived from German mercenary light cavalry or 'reiters' came into use whereby the horse would ride up to the bristling hedge of pikes and by rote discharge successive pistol volleys into the tightly packed ranks, an elegant if somewhat ineffective movement known as the 'caracole'.
- Very light horse – these were scouts and skirmishers who carried a light lance or sword. From mid century onwards one or two brace of wheelock pistols and a carbine came to form standard gear for light horsemen.
- Handgunners and bowmen (now lumped collectively as the 'shot') – generally these were unarmoured beyond an open helmet and a padded jack.
- Pikemen and billmen – the 'puissant pike' with its eighteen-foot shaft was coming to supplant the venerable bill. Those who 'trailed' the pike usually wore a half armour and protective headgear.

As the century progressed all ranks began wearing a combed or pointed form of kettle hat called a morion which might have a high protective comb along the ridge (a 'combed' morion) to deflect a blow to the skull. The horse wore a variant with hinged protective cheekpieces called a burgonet – the 'steel bonnet' of the reivers. The growing effectiveness of firearms contributed to the decline of full body armour. Henry's Provost Marshall Lord Audley observed that:

> I would wish that no shot should have armour upon him but a morrionn or skull upon his head, for there can be no shot neither archer nor arquebus server [musketeer] being well armed [armoured].

In Longshanks' day the mounted knight relied mainly upon chain mail for bodily defence, together with a flat-topped helmet with narrow eye slits ('the sights'), the cheek pieces perforated for limited ventilation, with arming cap and a mail hood or 'coif' worn underneath. His mail would consist of two garments: a long-sleeved, thigh-length shirt called a hauberk, and leg defences or hosen. Mail is both flexible and, when compared with plate, quite light; it may not, however, resist a point and a crushing blow may still cause fractures even though it does not sever the links.

As the need for greater protection grew it became common place, following continental fashion, for the horseman to secure additional protection in the form of a poncho-like garment reinforced with steel plates to back and breast. Shoulder defences or ailettes were also added often bearing the wearer's heraldic device. Shields, shaped like the base of an iron and curved to conform with the contours of the body, were also still carried.

The increasing use of the longbow after 1300 spurred the need for further improvements – mail could not resist the deadly bodkin point and gutter-shaped plate defences to the arms and legs were introduced, strapped on over the mail. As the fourteenth century progressed a more shaped and pointed helmet with a gracefully curving ridge replaced the squarer great helm. This, the basinet, could be equipped with a visor, sharply pointed to improve deflection; it is often referred to as a 'pig face'. The flowing outer cloth garment, the surcoat, was shortened and made more fitting to become the jupon. Solid plate defences to the chest and back replaced the earlier and flimsier fashion and the knight of the period, when fully armoured, thus had three full layers of protection – over his shirt and hose, a padded arming doublet with mail and then plate armour.

In terms of distinguishing English and Scots the chivalry of both sides would wear similar armours. The fourteenth century graveslab of Brice Mackinnon on Iona shows an effigy wearing a basinet over a coif with a mail collar or pisane. He also wears a pleated fabric outer garment or aketon which was waxed and stiffened, stuffed with rags or tallow, to provide protection and, though less effective than plate, was considerably cheaper and lighter. He is armed with a hand and a half sword which has a distinctive lobated pommel.

The later image of Sir Gilbert de Greenlaw at Kinkell near Inverurie also shows the knight, who was a lowland casualty in the battle of Harlaw in 1411, bearing a similar blade with the rather fine, downswept quillons that became a feature of the final sixteenth-century development of the Scottish 'great' sword or *claidheah-mohr*. Sir Gilbert's armour is typical of the early fifteenth-century style – he wears an open basinet, a mail reinforced arming doublet with plate defences worn over. The separate pieces that together made up an armour were, where necessary, hinged on the outside but always buckled from the inside; for obvious reasons the buckles were never exposed, being too easy to sever. By this time both the jupon and the shield had become redundant, the plate giving sufficient protection. The sword belt hangs across the hips over the lower belly and thigh defences ('fauld').

The latter half of the fifteenth century saw the final flowering of the armourer's art, fine plate armours that could even resist the clothyard shaft. Italian harnesses of the period were skilfully crafted to maximise deflection, defences for vulnerable areas at the shoulder, elbow and knee were strengthened, fashioned ribs on exposed parts were constructed to deflect a killing thrust. German armourers further developed this concept into the angular perfection of the Gothic style with its emphasis on uncompromising lines swept by heavy fluting. A harness of this period might weigh 60 lb or so and would not greatly inhibit the mobility of a robust man, trained since boyhood to move and fight in armour. The medieval knight, even when fighting on foot, as he most often did during the Wars of the Roses, bore a lesser burden of weight than the 'tommies' going 'over the top' in the mud of Flanders four-and-a-half centuries later, gasping under their 80 lb of rifle and pack.

The Italian and German styles came together in Flanders, which was a flourishing centre of manufacture where Italian armourers working there produced a hybrid style that featured the flexible, fluted plates of the Gothic combined with the more rounded pauldrons and tassets of their native land. Such armours were sold in quantities in England and feature on numerous funerary monuments.

For head protection the stylish sallet form of helmet was popular from the mid fifteenth century onwards. The rear of the elegantly curved brim was swept downwards into a pointed tail to provide extra deflection to the vulnerable areas at the back of the head and neck, usually furnished with a hinged visor. Protection to the throat was afforded by a separate piece, the bevor, which strapped around the neck. Although knights were able to move relatively freely even in full plate, thirst and head exhaustion were constant threats, even in winter campaigning.

The increasing dominance of hand-held firearms in the sixteenth century did not completely eclipse the armourer's art. Some harness was made to be shot proof though the increased weight confined its use to mounted troops. The foot engaging in 'push of pike' or melee still needed plate defences at least to the upper body, whilst gentlemen frequently retained full harness and the century saw a final flowering of magnificently engraved and gilded parade armours.

Dressing for battle was best achieved at leisure, as a contemporary account from *c.* 1450 quite clearly shows:

> *To arme a man. Ffirste ye must set on Sabatones and tye hem up on the shoo with smale poyntis that woll not breke. And then griffus* [greaves] *and then cuisses and ye breche of mayle. And the Tonletis* [Tonlet – Fauld]. *And the Brest and ye Vambras and ye rerebras and then gloovis. And then hand his daggere up on his right side. And then his shorte sworde on his lyfte side in a round rynge all nakid to pull it out lightli. And the put his cote upon his back. And then his basinet* [bascinet] *pyind* [pinned] *up on two greet staplis before the breste with a dowbill bokill* [double buckle] *behynde up on the back for to make the basinet sitte juste. And then his long swerd* [sword] *in his hande. And then his pensil* [pennon] *in his hande peynted of St George or of oure ladye to bless him with as he goeth towarde the felde and in the felde.*[8]

Whilst knights and men at arms would wear full harness, archers tended to favour padded 'jacks' or 'brigandines'. These were fabric garments reinforced with plates of steel or bone riveted to the leather or canvas, sometimes just stuffed with rags. Much lighter and cheaper than plate, these afforded surprisingly good protection and were sometimes finished with sleeves of mail. Though archers generally did not wear leg protection, billmen and men at arms might wear full or part leg harness. A man's equipment would reflect the status of his lord, quite frequently augmented by his dexterity at looting dead or prisoners so that more seasoned campaigners probably boasted greater protection, in an eclectic array of pieces and styles. The foot relied for headgear on a steel sallet or the 'kettle' hat, a forerunner of the steel helmets worn by British soldiers in both world wars of the twentieth century.

One of the most popular knightly weapons of the age was the fearsome poleaxe, a heavy axe blade on a stout ash shaft, four to six feet in length, a hefty 'beak' or hammer head on the reverse of the blade and the head tapered to a wicked spike. This tool was designed to defeat the armourers' art by 'opening up' an armoured opponent, like a rather crude but deadly can opener. Popular in the tourney and for judicial duelling, the blade was protected by steel strips or languets which sought to frustrate an attacker's attempt to strike off the head. The halberd, made famous by the Swiss, was also popular, heavier than the poleaxe with a cleaver-like blade and short double-headed spear point.

By this time the crude peasants' bill had been refined into an elegant killing implement or 'glaive', with a long head tapering to a point, the blade furnished with a hook and a handy spike on the back edge. James IV, together with many of those who fell around him, was bloodily hacked down by the ubiquitous bill. The horseman's lance, carried couched under the arm, was used for thrusting. The hold meant that the weapon angled across the chest and effective use required extensive training and constant practice. For foot combat the shaft was frequently cut down in length.

The medieval sword reached the peak of its development at this time prior to its eclipse in the next century by the more stylish rapier. Blades were designed for both cut and thrust, long and elegantly tapering with a full grip that could be held one or two handed, in section not unlike a flattened diamond; simple quillons, curved or straight, a wheel, pear or kite shaped-pommel. The first six inches or so of the blade below the quillons, the 'ricasso', was often left blunted to facilitate a double-handed spear-like thrust. The foot carried a simpler, lighter and considerably less expensive sidearm, a short single-edged sword with the quillons curved around the hilt to provide a crude knuckle guard. By this time, as the knightly shield had disappeared, archers engaged in siege operations would use a heavy wooden shield or pavise and the simple round target or buckler, made of steel, with a central grip was used primarily for parrying and for a deft blow to the opponent's face if the opportunity offered.

Gentlemen and commons alike carried daggers, the former tending to favour the rather stylish rondel, not unlike the much later Scottish dirk in dimension and appearance with a tapering triangular section blade, hardwood grip, disc guard and pommel. A favoured method of dispatching an armoured foe was a lethal thrust through the narrow eye slit above the visor. Once felled to the ground a man's chances of survival were drastically reduced, as he was hacked, trampled or stabbed – not even the finest plate could offer much real protection.

Another weapon which featured in both foot and mounted combat was the war hammer, a variant of the battle axe and mace with a wooden or steel shaft two-and-a-half feet in length, a pick head with a stubby hammer on the reverse. The enigmatic English usurper Richard III is said to have fought his last fight at Bosworth in 1485 wielding a war hammer, to considerable effect, in the press of his enemies.

Many Scottish armies, from Bannockburn to Pinkie, deployed High-landers. For generations the Lords of the Isles were virtually independent rulers. Donald of the Isles, in the early fifteenth century, treated with Henry IV as a free prince. Donald's defeat at Harlaw in 1411 hastened the ruin of the lordship. These fierce and proud Norse/Celtic warriors from Galloway, the Western Highlands and the isles fought in their traditional attire and with their own weapons under the leadership of their chiefs. United by blood and honour, skilled in raid and foray, their fighting skills honed by endemic clan warfare, they were fearsome opponents. The six-teenth-century Scots historian, John Mair, has left us a fine description of a contemporary clansman and we may assume that this appearance had not much altered from the preceding centuries:

> From the mid leg to the foot they go uncovered; their dress is, for an overgarment, a loose plaid and a shirt, saffron dyed. They are armed with a bow and arrows, a broadsword and small halbert. They always carry in their belt a stout dagger, single edged but of the sharpest. In time of war they cover the whole of their body with a coat of mail, made of iron rings and in it they fight. The common folk amongst the Wild Scots [Highlanders] go out to battle with the whole body clad in a linen garment sewed together in patchwork, well daubed with wax or with pitch, and with an overcoat of deerskin.

We have already seen how the deployment of the longbow came to domin-ate battlefield tactics from the end of the thirteenth to the beginning of the sixteenth century. The term longbow, or long bow as first used, came into being only during the sixteenth century; the plain expression 'bow' or 'livery bow' was more common in the fifteenth.

Retained or liveried archers normally carried their own weapons, but in the course of the French wars, the Office of Ordnance began issuing standard bows on campaign to make up for those lost or damaged, so that many bows were manufactured to a standard or government pattern, like the soldiers musket and rifle of later generations. Yew was the pre-ferred timber, though ash, elm and wych-elm were also used. The bow was usually between five feet seven inches and six feet two inches in length, the cross section corresponding to a rounded 'D' with a draw weight of 80–120 lb (a modern target bow has an average draw of around 45 lb).

Arrows were made from a variety of woods. Roger Ascham, Elizabeth I's tutor and a noted authority from the sixteenth century, advocated aspen as the most suitable, though ash, alder, elder, birch, willow and hornbeam were also utilised. The shafts were generally around two feet six inches in length, the fletching made from grey goose feathers. Arrowheads came in a variety of forms: flat hammer headed, barbed or wickedly sharp needle points or bodkins to punch through plate. Arrows were described as 'livery' (being issued to retainers), 'standard' (made to a universal specification) and 'sheaf' (as they came in bundles of twenty-four).

The bow was tipped at each end with cowhorn, grooved to take the linen string. When not in use the weapon was carried, unstrung, in a cloth bag. To draw, the archer gripped the bow with his left hand about the middle, where the circumference was around four-and-a-half inches, then he forced the centre of the bow away from him to complete the draw, using the weight of his body to assist the draw rather than relying on the strength in his arms alone. Such expertise required constant training, and practice at the butts was compelled by statute. Long-range shooting was preferred and the bow was effective at over two hundred yards, a distinct improvement on the later matchlock musket, which was seldom effective beyond fifty paces. A leather or horn 'bracer' was strapped to the wrist to protect the archer from the snap of the bowstring.

Properly deployed the longbow was an effective battle-winning weapon. Many of those who fought in the wars between England and Scotland would have seen service in the French wars. Time has dulled the memory of the arrow storm's ferocity but few who survived can ever have forgotten. The arrow wound did not have the merciful numbing of a high-velocity bullet and the majority of the rank and file had little real defence.

Crossbows, which existed throughout the period, had by the fifteenth century become both powerful and sophisticated, so much so that they required a rather complex arrangement of pulleys and cords operated by windlass to span. The draw weight might thus be as great as 1,000 lb, enough to punch the bolt through several files of soldiery. The great disadvantage obviously was the very slow rate of fire and the crossbowman, when on the field, generally needed a heavy wooden shield or pavise to cover him whilst he went through the cumbersome process of loading. Though favoured on the continent, crossbows were little used in England.

Although traditional siege engines whose design remained unchanged from classical times, the ballista and the mangonel dominated siege warfare during the earlier period, but by the fifteenth century artillery was steadily growing in importance. The ballista was, in effect, a giant crossbow which hurled a bolt or occasionally stones at the enemy's ramparts. It was intended as an anti-personnel weapon, flensing unwary defenders from the walls and used to cover an assault or escalade.

The mangonel, descended from the aptly named Roman onager or 'wild ass' on account of its savage kick, was a throwing engine that used a skein of ropes tightened under considerable pressure to propel a beam, the extremity of which was fitted with a cup holding a projectile. When released the beam snapped upright against a cross member, thus hurling the missile, usually a stone or lead shot.

Perhaps most fearsome of all was the mighty trebuchet, a high-trajectory sling which could send a stone ball weighing two or three hundred weight crashing against the defender's walls. A reconstructed example stands outside Caerlaverock Castle, near Dumfries, a replica of the engine Longshanks deployed in earnest in the siege of 1300 when Lord Maxwell commanded the garrison.

Four years later, when baulked by the resolute defenders of Stirling for three long months in the late spring and early summer of that year, Edward had his engineers build a truly massive trebuchet, named the 'warwolf', his lesser engines having failed to make an impression. By the time the trebuchet was ready the garrison were so reduced by hunger that they were on the point of capitulation and had sought terms. Age, however, had not mellowed the king nor diluted his propensity for savagery. He curtly refused terms and advised he intended to hang and disembowel the defenders to a man. Even when prevailed upon to show some clemency he insisted the wretched men should spend an extra, nerve-wracking day behind their crumbling walls whilst his giant engine battered the masonry and the king noted its effectiveness.

Sieges could be protracted and gruelling for those both without and within. Few were decided by the fury of the escalade. Berwick was, in

1296, particularly unlucky to be an exception. Untried for many years the town's makeshift defences proved a paltry obstacle to Edward's seasoned veterans. The ease of the storming did not benefit the luckless citizens who were then subjected to three days of slaughter and pillage. In addition to the use of siege engines, mining was a much-used tactic and heavy wooden beams used as rams, protected by a movable timber gallery, could be wheeled against weakened masonry or vulnerable gateways once the defending ditch had been filled in.

It was, however, the use of cannon which fatally altered the balance of power between those who built walls and those who sought to knock them down. By the mid-fifteenth century heavy siege pieces were being used on the Anglo-Scottish border. James II of Scotland was a particular enthusiast. By a cruel irony he was supervising the laying of the guns before the walls of Roxburgh Castle in 1460 when, in the course of a ceremonial salute to honour the arrival of his queen, one of the monsters burst and his thigh was smashed by shrapnel, killing him. In April 1464, King Edward IV was preparing to march into Northumberland to confront diehard Lancastrians who were holding, in loose alliance with Scotland, the key border fortresses of Alnwick, Bamburgh and Dunstanburgh. He made ready his siege train, which was to include 'the great ordnance of England' – the bombards 'Dijon', 'London', 'Newcastle', 'Edward' and 'Richard Bombartel'. Notwithstanding this great weight of shot the Yorkists were reluctant to reduce any of the castles by bombardment as these were the backbone of the English border defences. In the final siege of Bamburgh in May 1464, the Earl of Warwick threatened to hang a defender for every shot he was obliged to expend against the walls.[9]

'Bombard' appears to have been a generic description applied to any large siege gun; there was no standardisation of calibres at this time. These larger pieces were fired from ground level and from behind a hinged timber shutter, rather like a large version of the archer's mantlet, that provided some cover for the gunner and matrosses – their calling was distinctly hazardous even safe from enemy action. Most guns loaded at the breech, having a removable breech-block, shaped not unlike a beer mug; by the 1460s trunnions were coming into use and even the heavier pieces were being equipped with serviceable if crude gun carriages. Elevation was achieved by the use of wedges.

The transportation of these monsters was a major difficulty. Large teams of draught horses or oxen were needed. A section of pioneers would almost certainly be added to the complement, theirs the unenviable task of levelling and filling the generally appalling roads. Larger guns were still manufactured on the 'hoop and stave' principle, though casting in brass and bronze was becoming commonplace.

A survivor from this period, and still to be viewed in Edinburgh Castle, is 'Mons Meg' which may be considered typical of the heavy guns of the period. Cast in Flanders around 1460, the barrel length is thirteen feet two inches with an enormous bore of nineteen-and-a-half inches. This beast could hurl a stone ball weighing 549 lb and the shot is said to have carried for two miles. So heavily did such guns weigh that a crane was needed to lift the barrel on and off the carriage.

An even larger gun was cast by the renegade Hungarian master Urban for Sultan Mehmet II. The smith had previously offered his services to the Byzantine emperor who had declined on the grounds he could not afford so expensive a project. The gun which Urban cast for the Turk measured twenty-six feet eight inches in length and could send a 12 cwt ball over a mile. Ironically the weapon was used to batter the walls of Constantinople in the great siege of 1453.[10]

The period also witnessed the growing importance of the handgun, which at this time was nothing more than a small cannon lashed onto a timber stock, or fitted with a rude socket. The handgun or 'hagbutt' was aimed by being held underarm, or lifted over the shoulder and pointed in the general direction of an enemy. The weapon was then discharged by applying a slow match to the touch hole. The weapon was unreliable and exceedingly slow. The great advantage it possessed over the elegance and efficiency of the longbow was that it could be fired by more or less anyone after only minimal training. The years of constant practice at the butts and the high level of physical strength and stamina required to draw the bow were not necessary.

Gunpowder or 'serpentine' was milled from a mix of sulphur, saltpetre and charcoal. At this time the science of gunnery was in its infancy and the powder was more finely milled than would be the case in later centuries. It was by no means consistent in quality or reliable in operation; slow burning at best, the ingredients were often likely to separate in the course of transportation.

The ignition system was improved by the introduction, mid century, of the matchlock which was to remain in service for well over a century. A piece of slow match, already lit, was held in a set of jaws or serpentine and a measure of fine priming powder was used to fill the pan. When the trigger mechanism was depressed, the serpentine was lowered onto the pan, whose cover rotated in the same moment. The match ignited the primer and that, in turn, set off the main charge. Wind and rain could, of course, significantly impede or utterly frustrate firing.

As we have seen, by the latter part of the fifteenth century dominance in the centuries-old competition between those who built castles and those who sought to knock them down had swung dramatically in favour of the latter. Developments in fortified architecture had not yet caught up with the science of gunnery, though the concept of the artillery fort was literally just around the corner. In about 1480 the burghers of Dartmouth caused a small but potent fort to be erected covering the Haven, complete with a range of gun ports. The trend therefore was to move away from building castles as fortified residences for the baronage and gentry towards more specialised defences with no domestic function. In Scotland James III contemplated a chain of artillery forts on the banks of the Forth Estuary, though in practice only one of these, at Ravenscraig in Fife, ever proceeded to completion.

At the start of the period Edward I had ushered in a great era of castle building in terms of both activity and innovation. The chain of fortresses he built in Wales employed what were termed concentric defences. Hitherto castles had relied upon a stout curtain wall with a massive keep or donjon within. The concentric system, gleaned from the crusades, preferred to create a series of strongpoints, circular towers, studding the walls with several lines of defence – walls within walls, the inner levels topping the outer. This gave the defenders several lines of defence and the attrition of attacking would wear down the besiegers' resources and morale. It also meant that a concentric castle could be held, often against impressive odds, by a very small garrison.

The earliest example of this style in Scotland is to be found at Kildrummy near Alford in Aberdeenshire where the curtain wall is furnished with four strong towers. A fortified gatehouse was later added by Longshanks' chief military engineer, the Savoyard, James of St George. As the conflict continued, a series of great castles was built along both sides of the border. In the English marches, Berwick a fortified town or 'bastide', Norham, Wark on Tyne, Bamburgh, Dunstanburgh, Warkworth, Alnwick, Naworth and Carlisle. Facing these on the Scottish side, Tantallon, Dunbar, Fast Castle, Jedburgh, Roxburgh, grim-visaged Hermitage in Liddesdale, a newer and larger castle at Caerlaverock on the Solway Firth.

On both sides of the line as warfare became endemic in the fourteenth century gentlemen rebuilt or fortified their residences. A good example is Aydon, near Corbridge in Northumberland, where the Reymes family in the course of the early wars of independence added a substantial stone curtain wall to their fortified manor house, finished with several strong towers. The era of the border reiver in the sixteenth century saw the development of the Scots' tower house and the distinctive English 'pele' or bastle.

The late fifteenth century ushered in an era of profound change in naval architecture which saw a move away from the cumbersome 'round' ship of the earlier medieval period towards the sleek warships of the Elizabethans. The merchantman of the day, only twice as long as it was broad, fat bellied, slow to steer with fixed square mainsail, was the jack of all trades; for the conversion to man o' war timber 'castles' were fitted fore and aft. Tactics were usually restricted to grappling and boarding, missile power being provided by archers. Even ramming was near impossible and just as perilous for the aggressor. By the fifteenth century the earlier medieval vessel the 'cog', which had been fitted with a steering oar, was replaced by the more sophisticated 'nef' steered by rudder.

By the thirteenth century the use of crossbows as on-board missile weapons was commonplace in the Mediterranean, while regular contingents of retained marines were also in evidence. However, both these trends were slower to catch on in northern waters. As fleets engaged, with limited manoeuvring, lime was used to blind opponents and soap was employed to render the enemy's decks slippery and treacherous underfoot; thereafter it was a case of grapple and board.

At sea, as on land, guns made a difference. There are references dating as far back as the early 1400s to ordnance aboard ships but naval gunnery was of only limited importance during the latter years of the century. Initially light pieces were mounted in the twin castles, principally as anti-personnel devices rather than as a means of disabling or sinking. To carry the weight of even lighter pieces the timber castles had to be sturdier than before; soon they were rising to several tiers and carrying over prow and stern, bristling with cannon, the armament carried round the internal elevation so that between decks could be swept of enemy boarders, 'ships of forecastle'.

Ships of the day feature in the many invasions and alarums of the period, though full-scale sea battles were relatively rare. One such occurred during the swashbuckling days of Warwick's captaincy of Calais in 1458. As castellan of this most important outpost the earl commanded a small fleet, five 'ships of forecastle', three carvels and four pinnaces. On 28th May, hearing of a superior Spanish squadron with some sixteen of the larger ships being sighted in the Channel, he immediately left port, his tiny fleet crammed with archers and billmen. Coming upon the Spaniards strung out in line the next morning, Warwick ordered the attack. With much, probably ineffectual, cannonading the squadrons collided, longbowmen loosing into the tightly packed ranks crowding the enemy decks. The battle lasted for most of the day and though he lost eighty-odd men the honours went to the earl, some two hundred Spanish being reported dead and six substantial vessels taken. As one survivor enthused: 'As men say, there has not been so great a battle upon the seas these forty winters.'[11]

We know that Richard III made extensive use of warships during his campaign against the Scots in 1482 and appears to have been successful in a naval engagement against a Scottish squadron.

Time and much romantic fiction have cast a shroud of pageantry over the harsh realities of medieval combat, but the truth is somewhat less comforting. Though lacking the scale and devastation of modern wars, devoid of the horrors of machine guns and high explosive, warfare in the middle ages was every bit as frightful.

We have seen that most battles began with an archery duel, regular volleys of arrows thudding into the packed ranks, causing fatalities and savage wounds; though the better protected men at arms might suffer less, the ordinary rank and file must have dreaded the hissing rain of death. It is unlikely that this preliminary phase of the combat would last that long, the files thinned and disordered. Once the order to advance was given the men would move forward, not at a particularly fast pace for it would be necessary to maintain as much cohesion as possible. Much would depend upon visibility and the nature of the ground – there are numerous examples of lines advancing in a mistaken belief of the enemy's location.

Once battle was joined in earnest the combat became an intensely personal affair, a hacking, stamping melee of bills, polearms, sword and axe. Men, half blind in armour, soon assailed by raging thirst and fatigue, would swiftly become disorientated. Few would be killed by a single blow, but a disabling wound, bringing the victim to ground, would expose him to more and fatal blows, most likely to the head or the dagger thrust through the visor, a horrible, agonising and by no means speedy end.

Once one side broke, leading to a rout, casualties would begin to mount. Armoured men fleeing towards their horses tethered a distance away in the baggage park would be easy meat; the less encumbered foot might run the quicker but many would fall. Mounted pursuers would swoop on the frantic stragglers, sword and lance doing fearful execution. Abbot Whethamstede, who may have been an eyewitness, graphically chronicles the fate of some of Warwick's men fleeing from the disaster at the second battle of St Albans in 1461.

> *The southern men, who were fiercer at the beginning, were broken quickly afterwards, and the more quickly because looking back, they saw no one coming up from the main body of the King's army, or preparing to bring them help, whereupon they turned their backs on the northern men and fled. And the northern men seeing this pursued them very swiftly on horseback; and catching a good many of them, ran them through with their lances.*[12]

This carnage was repeated on many fields in the Scottish wars, Halidon Hill and Homildon being just two examples.

A fourteenth-century work, 'The Vows of the Heron', describes how the man at arms' bravado rapidly diminishes the closer to contact he comes:

> *When we are in taverns, drinking strong wines, at our sides the ladies we desire, looking on, with their smooth throats . . . their grey eyes shining back with smiling beauty nature calls on us to have desiring hearts, to struggle awaiting* [their] *thanks at the end. That we would conquer . . . Oliver and Roland. But when we are in the field, on our galloping chargers our shields round our necks and lances lowered . . . and our enemies are approaching us then we would rather be deep in some cavern.*

A recently excavated mass grave on the site of the battle of Towton, 1461 has provided a grim insight into the sheer nastiness of fifteenth-century warfare. Thirty-seven skeletons were unearthed. Most of these had suffered a series of horrific head injuries, puncture wounds and calamitous fractures, with evidence of specific dagger thrusts to the back of the skull, almost surgical in lethal intent, either the *coup de grâce* on a wounded victim or perhaps a deliberate execution. In either event the victim's head protection would have had to have been removed.

By our standards medical services were rudimentary and unreliable. The perceived presence of evil humours was the source of much bleeding of patients, quacks cast horoscopes and prescribed bizarre potions, wounds were cauterised with hot pitch. However, the use of forms of anaesthesia, derived mainly from herbs, was not unknown and surgical techniques were perhaps more advanced, at least in the hands of competent practitioners, than may be imagined. One of the dead from Towton recently exhumed from a grave pit on the site showed evidence of a prior and massive facial injury which had been skilfully repaired. Nonetheless throughout the period northern European medical services lagged far behind those available both to Byzantine and to Islamic armies.

Whilst armies did not possess a medical corps per se, each contingent would have surgeons and doctors in its train and these, like other specialists, would sign contracts of indenture; sieges were often concluded with arrangements for the care of the wounded and a valuable prisoner had no value if he succumbed.

As we have seen most fatal injuries were caused by blows to the head, as the mute remains from grave pits testify, the bodies of the English dead from Otterburn, whose remains were found beneath the nave of Elsdon church in the nineteenth century, from Visby in Sweden (1361), and from Towton. Slashing and stabbing wounds, though ghastly, were not always fatal and more victims probably recovered than might be expected. Complications such as peritonitis or blood poisoning, however, were invariably fatal – many injured would be left lying on the field exposed to the rigours of climate and the tender mercies of scavengers. A contemporary account from a European traveller, Gerhard von Wessel, recorded the return of Edward IV's battered army from Barnet in 1471: '. . . many of their followers were wounded, mostly in the face or the lower part of the body, a very pitiable sight.'[13]

Campaigns of the period tended to be highly mobile and of relatively short duration, which was undoubtably a major blessing for the participants for, in medieval wars as a whole, far more men died of disease, particularly dysentery, than from enemy action. Henry V's tattered band that stood at Agincourt was but a pale shadow of the host he had brought from England, the ranks thinned dreadfully by dysentery, rampant in the foetid confines of the siege lines around Harfleur. The king himself later died from the disease, the final triumph within his grasp, leaving an infant to rule, with all the tribulations that followed.

The late middle ages has been referred to as 'The Golden Age of Bacteria'; bubonic plague visited these shores some thirty times between 1348 and 1485, a dozen of these outbreaks were on a national scale. French mercenaries in the service of Henry Tudor were blamed for introducing the 'sweating sickness' that killed off two mayors and six aldermen of London within a handspan of days in 1485.[14]

Notes

1 Prestwich, M., *Armies and Warfare in the Middle Ages*, London 1996 p. 2.
2 Oman, Sir Charles, *The Art of War in the Middle Ages*, London 1924 Vol. 2 p. 408.
3 Wise, T., *The Wars of the Roses*, London 1983 p. 22.
4 Ibid p. 27.
5 Ibid p. 27.
6 Boardman, A., *The Medieval Soldier in the Wars of the Roses*, London 1998 p. 173.
7 Traquair, P., *Freedom's Sword*, London 1998 p. 289.
8 Oakeshott, R. Ewart, *A Knight and his Weapons*, London 1964 p. 51.
9 'Edward' is featured in an inventory of 1475 – the master of ordnance John Sturgeon handed into store at Calais 'divers parcels of the King's ordnance and artillery including a bumbardell [bombard] called The Edward'. See Blackmore, H.L., *The Armouries of the Tower of London Ordnance*, HMSO 1976 p. 33 and also Haigh, P., *The Military Campaigns of the Wars of the Roses*, London 1995 p. 83.
10 Runciman, Sir Stephen, *The Fall of Constantinople*, Cambridge 1965 pp. 77–8.
11 Kendall, P. Murray, *Warwick the Kingmaker*, London 1957, p. 44.
12 Riley, H.T. (Ed.), *Registrum Abbatis Johannis Whethamstede*, 1872 Vol. 1 pp. 388–92.
13 Bartlett, C., *The English Longbowman 1330–1515*, London 1995 p. 51.
14 Thrupp, Sylvia L., *The Problems of Replacement Rates in Late Medieval English Population*, ECHR 2nd Series 18 (1965–6).

Chapter 3

Under the Hammer

For those Scots,
I rate 'em as sots,
What a sorry shower!
Whose utter lack
In the attack
Lost 'em at Dunbar

Contemporary doggerel[1]

It was in 1291, according to the annals of Waverley Abbey, that Edward I of England 'Longshanks'[2] informed his council that he intended to assume direct rule of Scotland, to reduce the kingdom to a mere province, much as he had with the Welsh. There were precedents for such centralised control; the Kings of Wessex had exercised sway over the lesser princes of Scotland and Wales. Did Edward therefore see himself as a successor to Athelstan or perhaps a new King Arthur, whose cult was already flourishing? It may be, however, that the king merely intended to gather up the reins of power to ensure a smooth transition whilst the interregnum lasted, as a prudent overlord might be expected to do.[3]

Though by no means young the king was still a formidable ruler: 'His physique had deteriorated little even in his sixties. His hair might have been white, but his glance was as keen as ever, he was upright in stance, and could still mount a horse unaided.'[4] His youth had been marked by a predeliction for violence and a threat of cruelty ran throughout his campaigns. He had squared up to his father's rebellious barons, led by his uncle Simon de Montfort, and had utterly destroyed the baronial army in a bloodbath at Evesham. He had been active on crusade and his long reign (he came to the throne on the death of Henry III in 1272) had seen a number of major changes to the law and constitution. Pious, a good and devoted husband, skilled diplomat, accomplished soldier and constant lawgiver, yet he could be imperious, devious and untrustworthy, and his relations with both magnates and clergy were not always cordial.

The conquest of Wales, sealed by the construction of a ring of mighty fortresses, had been thorough and complete, the principality reduced to an occupied territory. He had quarrelled with Philip IV of France over Gascony, a simmering dispute that erupted into armed confrontation in the 1290s. The cost of the king's wars was a constant drain on the Exchequer and the huge financial burden imposed by the expenditure on the Welsh castles ensured Edward could never repeat the process of building such commanding fortresses in Scotland. For the Scots this was providential; the king, in his Scottish campaigns, was obliged to rely on the occupation of existing, native strongholds bolstered by outposts hurriedly thrown up in timber and earth.

Prior to 1291 there appears to have been no suggestion that Edward had any ambitions towards Scotland. Alexander III was his brother-in-law, having married Edward's sister Margaret in 1251, and their relationship was entirely amicable. Indeed the English king seems genuinely to have shared Alexander's grief over the loss of both his sons – the younger boy, David, had died in 1281 aged only eight and Alexander, the elder, had barely made it out of his teens when he too died three years later. His daughter, Margaret, had been married to Eric II of Norway in 1281 and had departed sorrowfully for her short life in Bergen, which she found cold and depressing. She was not destined to see her native land again, dying a mere two years after her marriage, leaving an infant daughter. This sickly child, named after her mother and clearly no more robust, was the last of the Canmore line and now became Queen of Scots. To ensure a smooth transition in the event of his death (which in 1284 Alexander had reason to hope might lie some years distant), the king, at Scone, had formally confirmed the child as his successor.[5] He would also have reason to hope that his marriage to the young Yolande of Dreux, solemnised on the 14th October 1285, ending a decade of widowhood, might produce another male heir.

The king's untimely death following so soon upon his marriage confirmed the popular and pessimistic view that a day of judgement was at
hand, that what would be seen in retrospect as a golden era came violently
to a close:

> *Quehen Alysandyr our King was dede*
> *That Scotland led in lure and le*
> *Awaye was sons of ale and brede*
> *Of wyne and wax, of gamyn and gle*
> *Our gold was changed into lede*
> *Chryst born into vyrgynte*
> *Succour Scotland and remede*
> *That stad in perplexite.*[6]

A kingless kingdom with a distant heir, a distant, sickly, infant female heir
to boot, was ripe for civil war as contending factions prepared to scrabble
for power. It seemed obvious that a strong external hand was needed to
pick up and hold the reins of government, albeit to be held in trust for the
child queen in Norway. There was a further complication in that Yolande
of Dreux now claimed to be with child. Obviously if this were indeed
so and she was to bear a son then he might expect to be favoured. The
interim administration was placed in the hands of half a dozen elected
custodians[7] or 'guardians' – these represented or were intended to represent 'the community of the realm of Scotland': two bishops, Glasgow and
St Andrews, two leading barons, the earls of Buchan and Fife, with two
drawn from the ranks of the lesser nobility, John Comyn of Badenoch and
James the Steward.

In the south-west two powerful magnates were already squaring up to
each other: Bruce 'the Competitor' (grandfather of King Robert I and,
despite being nearly eighty, extremely active in his own cause) and John
Baliol.[8] In the unquiet aftermath of the king's death, Bruce moved swiftly
to consolidate his power in the west, seizing the royal castles of Dumfries,
Wigton and Baliol's hold at Buittle. He also entered into an accord or
'band' with various other magnates: his son, the earl of Carrick, Angus
MacDonald, 'Lord of the Isles', the earls of March, Menteith and Dunbar
together with James the Steward and a brace of Irish peers, Richard de
Burgh, the 'Red' Earl of Ulster (destined to be King Robert I's father-in-

law) and Thomas de Clare. The Band of Turnberry was ostensibly related solely to dealing with matters in Ireland but was, in reality, the affirmation of a powerful Bruce affinity. The agreement did contain an expression of loyalty to both Edward I and 'whoever' became ruler of Scotland.[9]

The Guardians realised they needed the steadying influence of a strong external arbitrator to curtail the incipient violence simmering in the west. There were two obvious candidates. The first was Eric II, the father of the young queen and king of Norway. Eric was, however, distracted by a dispute with Denmark and the favoured choice was inevitably Edward I of England. In the circumstances this was a perfectly logical conclusion. Longshanks had experience of acting as an arbitrator in the difficult area of disputed kingship. Unfortunately the Scottish emissaries found the king on the point of departure for Gascony where the deteriorating situation, as he advised, required his full and immediate attention.

Matters therefore were to be left in the hands of the Guardians who took steps against the Competitor's aggression. Faced with such resolve his challenge quickly cooled. The queen, as it transpired, was not pregnant and so the infant Margaret, the 'Maid of Norway', remained the most viable candidate. Upon his return from France in 1289 Edward proposed a dynastic union between the Maid and Edward of Caernarvon, the Prince of Wales. At a stroke Edward I would have united the whole of mainland Britain as a Plantagenet empire.

In that November the pre-nuptial negotiations began in earnest at Salisbury and an early draft of the proposed treaty, whilst not directly mentioning the marriage alliance, did provide for Edward's intervention in Scotland as mediator and 'honest broker' when matters of such weight as surpassed the competency of the Guardians arose. Eric II had stipulated that his daughter's rights as to sovereignty should not be interfered with. As the two young people were blood relations[10] a papal dispensation was needed before any marriage could be finally agreed. In 1290 the Scots Parliament sitting at Birgham approved the draft treaty though the union could not be solemnised until 1298 when both children were of age.

Significantly the question of sovereignty in Scotland was not directly addressed but the Scots were clearly concerned to ensure that their independence was not infringed; the existing border was to be maintained, no new castles were to be constructed and the rights of the Scottish clergy was to be preserved without infringement. The Prince Bishop, Anthony Bek,[11] acted as Edward's chief negotiator. In July the Scots agreed a final draft, ratified by Edward at Northampton on 28th August. The treaty stated quite emphatically that Scotland was to remain 'separate and divided, and free in itself without any subjection to England and divided by its proper frontiers and marches as in the past'.[12] The administration of the realm was to remain wholly unfettered by English intermeddling and the regalities were to remain at Scone pending the Maid's anticipated coronation.

If Edward had intentions to bring Scotland directly under his sway then these were far from obvious. The fact that he clearly placed greater emphasis upon matters in Gascony would tend to suggest that he did not, at that time, have ambitions in Scotland. However, with the marriage treaty now sealed he had no need for haste – with a Plantagenet as her consort the young queen would soon find herself under the powerful influence of her father-in-law. In the king's mind therefore the establishment of Plantagenet rule was possibly already a matter of fact.

Edward now wrote to the Guardians intimating he had appointed Bek[13] as his lieutenant in Scotland. The term was perhaps ambiguous; was the Prince Bishop merely an ambassador or a viceroy? The intention was that Bek would hold the administration of Scotland on trust jointly for both Margaret and Caernarvon. On 4th June Edward appointed Walter de Huntercombe as custodian of Man on the basis that the Earl of Ulster had offered the place to the English crown.

Later that month Bek was empowered to admit the fissiparous Islesmen into the King's peace.[14] None of this appeared to augur well for the Scots' continuing independence and the Guardians must have been rendered un-easy. They presently had other concerns, however, for the Maid of Norway never saw her throne. In the autumn of 1290, whilst still in Orkney, the unfortunate child sickened and died. There was now no clear heir to the vacant throne and the spectre of civil war emerged, like Banquo's ghost, from the shadows.

On 7th October Bishop Fraser of St Andrews wrote to the king with the dire news and in fear of civil strife. The magnates, including Bruce the Competitor, had gathered at Perth to await the arrival of the child queen. The Bishop urged Edward to come north to the border with the English host as a deterrent to rival factions, particularly those of Bruce and Baliol.

The king was soon presented with another loss when, on 28th November, Eleanor of Castille, his wife of thirty-six years, also died. Edward was wracked with grief. The great warrior king turned his back on affairs of state whilst he tried to come to terms with his loss.

It was not until early in the new year that Bishop Bek presented the suggestion to the Guardians that Edward should decide upon the matter of the succession in his capacity as feudal superior. In the meantime Bruce proposed an allegedly ancient and highly dubious process referred to as 'the Appeal of the Seven Earls of Scotland', a form of collegiate election. Cannily the Competitor also hastened to confirm his loyalty to Edward. The Scots Parliament most likely found that an arbitration by the King of England was the best means of avoiding internecine conflict. Edward was widely regarded as a leading jurist and the legal procedure which followed marked the beginning of the 'Great Cause' – the dispute over not only who should be King of Scots but whether that king owed homage to the King of England as feudal superior.

The hearings lasted for a full eighteen months, with the court actually in session for a third of that time. Edward ordered that a full record be kept – he did not intend that posterity should accuse him of any partisan leanings. The proceedings were convened at Norham on 10th May 1291, with John of Caen maintaining the record.[15] In his opening address Robert Brabazon, Chief Justice of the King's Bench, required the Scots present to formally recognise Edward as overlord. This request undoubtably caused consternation and yet from the king's point of view was entirely logical – for him to arbitrate according to feudal custom, his right to act in that capacity had to be accepted by all parties to the dispute. Robert Wishart, Bishop of Glasgow, might have protested at this point and the hearing was adjourned for the Scots representatives to consider their position.

On 2nd June the court reconvened and the Scots, probably orchestrated by Wishart, argued that they could not respond as, being without a king, who could offer homage if any were due? A clever response and one which did not please the English king. The obvious alternative for him was to wring the necessary undertaking from each of the rival candidates – whoever was successful his oath would bind the Guardians. From Edward's point of view the position was not satisfactory – the fact of the matter was that he had not received a clear recognition of his feudal superiority from the community of the realm and the notion of English overlordship was by no means universally accepted as he may have imagined. The reply given to Edward stated that the community '. . . have no knowledge of your right, nor do they ever see it claimed and used by you or your ancestors; there-fore they answer you . . . that they have no power to reply to your state-ment, lacking a lord to whom the demand ought to be addressed . . . for he, and not they, will have power to reply and to act in the matter'.[16] This was carefully worded defiance.

In spite of any reservations Edward seamlessly assumed control of key royal castles. Again there was sense in this for an English presence would deter rival factions. He was also nominally a competitor – even though he sat in judgement, he had not conceded his own, albeit more remote, claim.[17] The Guardians could hand bastions to the King of England in his guise as a candidate and other claimants could do so in acknowledging Edward as their feudal lord.

With the matter of his overlordship still undefined Edward opened the main court hearing at Berwick in August, with his final judgement not handed down until 17th November 1292. The weight of legal argument was considerable. Both Bruce and Baliol, as leading contenders, were per-mitted teams of forty representatives or auditors each whilst Edward retained twenty-four. After exhaustive deliberation Edward decided upon Baliol. In law this decision was inexpugnable – his claim was undoubtably the strongest – and on 19th November the king instructed that possession or seisin of the realm be given to him.[18]

John Baliol was now to be crowned King of Scotland, having recog-nised Edward as his sovereign lord. On 26th December he performed homage for the realm of Scotland. At the coronation Anthony Bek was in attendance whilst John of St John acted as proxy for the infant Earl of Fife. The seal used by the Guardians, now discharged, was formally broken up and the fragments sent to Edward in recognition of his rights. Scotland now had a king but he was not his own man. This act of submission has earned King John almost universal opprobrium from subsequent writers yet, at the time, he really had no alternative. Other competitors, notably Bruce, had shown indecent haste to offer their allegiance to the English king and there was ample precedent; Malcolm Canmore had sworn fealty to William I and the oath had been renewed from time to time by his successors.

It also appeared that Edward was content to allow the governance of Scotland to remain in the hands of the king and his ministers and to refrain from intermeddling. Even as feudal superior it was assumed Edward was still bound by the guarantees stated in the Treaty of Northampton. On 7th December, before Baliol had even sworn the oath, a Berwick burgess, Roger Bartholemew, appealed to Edward against three judgements found against him in the Guardians' courts. On hearing the appeal the king upheld two and overturned one. The decision sent ripples of alarm back to the Scottish Parliament but Edward made it plain he would continue to hear cases on appeal as he saw fit, even summoning the King of Scots as a party to proceedings if appropriate. As though to underline his own inferior status Baliol agreed to the annulment of the Treaty of Northampton on 2nd January 1293.

If Edward was technically correct in exercising his powers as overlord he showed a total lack of understanding of the Scots and of how fiercely they valued their independence. By the end of the year he had indeed summoned King John to appear before the English courts. The matter was an action brought by MacDuff, a younger son of Malcolm Earl of Fife, alleging false imprisonment and theft of his inheritance. If this was not sufficient provocation then in the following summer Baliol, together with eighteen Scottish magnates, was summoned to perform military service against Philip IV.

Such summonses were by no means unprecedented. Edward had previously requested knight service of Scottish nobles in the Welsh wars as a condition of their homage for lands they held in England.[19] From Edward's perspective Baliol's position was now the same, though service was now due for the kingdom of Scotland. Malcolm IV had served Henry II on the same terms in 1159. In the event a general muster proved unnecessary when the Earl of Warwick defeated the Welsh rebels in March 1295.

Fresh disturbance arising in Wales frustrated Edward's plans to campaign against Philip but the fact he had demanded service from Baliol undermined the latter's position in Scotland. King John's inability to stand up to the King of England had begun to anger the representatives of the community who, at a Parliament convened in Stirling in July 1295, appointed a council of twelve, four bishops, four earls and four barons, to better advise the king or rather afford him that measure of backbone which appeared to be lacking.

The council were undoubtably the driving force behind overtures for a treaty of mutual support to be entered into with Philip IV. The delegation which travelled to France to negotiate comprised the bishops of St Andrews and Dunkeld, John de Soules and Ingram de Umfraville. The terms of the accord were agreed on 23rd October and included provisions for mutual defensive and offensive action. As an incentive there was the offer of a marriage alliance, King John to marry Jeanne de Valois, the king's niece. Even accepting the difficulties of his position there has to be some question as to Baliol's suitability for kingship. Furthermore there is doubt as to whether he was imbued with any great desire for the role. Later, in comfortable captivity, he is said to have admitted to Bek, his host that: 'When he possessed and ruled the realm of Scotland as king and lord of the realm, he found in the men of that realm such malice, deceit, treason, and treachery, arising from their malignity, wickedness, and stratagems, and various other execrable and detestable actions.'[20]

To anyone as literally minded as Edward this was treason. Baliol had yet to appear to respond in the MacDuff case and he had failed to hand over the three key castles demanded as a surety for his non-attendance. In law Longshanks was now justified in resorting to force of arms. As proof of his resolve he appointed Bek and Earl Warenne as his deputies for all of the counties north of the Trent; Warenne was also given custody of Berwick (still in Scottish hands at this point) and Bruce, the Earl of Carrick, clearly no supporter of Baliol, was entrusted with Carlisle. On 16th October Edward I as feudal superior formally demanded the surrender of the fortresses of Berwick, Roxburgh and Jedburgh. He also confiscated Baliol's lands in England. In December the king sent out writs summoning the host to appear at Newcastle by 1st March 1296. A state of open war was now imminent.

The Scots responded with defiance. Early in 1296 a general muster or 'wapinschaw' was proposed and the host called out for 11th March at Caddonlea near Selkirk. A wave of anti-English sentiment swept the country. English clergy were ousted and merchants harassed. At Berwick some sailors were said to have been murdered. Through his arrogance and high-handedness Edward had produced a degree of political unity in Scotland not seen since the appointment of the Guardians. The Bruce faction and the other pro-English magnates had no popular support; the political revolution of July 1295 illustrates just how determined the Scots had become to assert their independence.

The army which Edward I mustered to deal with his troublesome vassal was undoubtably a large one. His expenditure incurred in raising and maintaining forces amounted to the very considerable sum of £21,443.12s.0d.,[21] although this figure also included the costs associated with the troops then operating in Gascony. On 23rd January he had requested sufficient funds from the Exchequer to recruit 1,000 men at arms and a staggering 60,000 foot. If this were not enough the Red Earl was commanded to provide a further 400 men at arms and 30,000 foot (in fact the Irish who mustered at Roxburgh on 13th May were barely ten per cent of this requirement.[22]

On 5th March the English army marched north out of Newcastle. Edward had arranged for the collection of the sacred banner of St John of Beverley to provide the requisite spiritual uplift. The Scots, wary of the size of the host coming against them and equally wary of the king's formidable military reputation (in fact the last pitched battle in which Edward had led had been Evesham in 1265), had opted for a defensive strategy based on holding the border line itself. James the Steward held Roxburgh whilst William Douglas commanded at Berwick.

The Scottish army was most assuredly not led by King John, now relegated to the role of hapless spectator. Command was in the hands of a general staff comprising seven earls: John Comyn of Buchan, Alexander Stewart of Menteith, Malise of Strathearn, Malcolm of Lennox, William of Ross, John Strathbogie of Athol and Donald of Mar. Prior to what would now be termed a pre-emptive strike the army moved into Annandale, Bruce's confiscated estates having been passed to Buchan. On 26th March, advancing in three columns, the Scots entered the English west march. From the outset this war was marked by a degree of merciless savagery that was to become all too familiar to marchers on both sides.

The land around Carlisle was thoroughly wasted and the city itself imperilled when a Scots spy managed to start a fire within the walls. The flames spread to a dangerous extent but the women took position on the ramparts whilst their menfolk fought the blaze. Two days later the Scots withdrew. Beyond burnt thatch and empty byres the raid had achieved nothing; moreover it had provided the moral justification Edward needed to assume the offensive.

It was also on 28th March that the English crossed the Tweed and appeared before the walls of Berwick. The castle was formidable and Douglas was no mean soldier. However, the walls of the town comprised a hastily repaired timber palisade with earthen ramparts and ditches. Despite the paucity of their defences the townsfolk remained defiant in the face of Edward's formal demand for a surrender. Their replies were at best pithy, enlivened by obscenities and familiar gestures. Such conduct might provide inspiration for contemporary film makers but it was not the stuff of chivalry and such brimming overconfidence in the face of so potent an invader was to prove fatal.

> *King Edward wanne thu havest Berwick pike the*
> *Wanne thu havest geten dike the.*[23]

With due formality thus concluded the English host moved to leaguer the walls. In accordance with custom the king dubbed a number of new knights. The associated cheers and flaunting of banners persuaded the fleet lying in the Tweed estuary that an escalade was in progress and several vessels moved in to support. This proved unfortunate. The first ship ran aground and was promptly set on fire by the defenders, the crew cut down to a man, while the second was also engulfed in flames but the sailors managed to get off in the boats.

First blood to the townsmen, but they did not have long to savour the success. A general assault from the landward side swiftly exposed the inadequacy of the wooden palisade, which was overcome, and the defenders pushed back into the narrow streets amidst scenes of frightful slaughter. Edward's men at arms, experienced in the Welsh and Gascon wars, had been quick to spot a weakness in the makeshift ramparts, 'where the townsfolk had made a path along the fosse, [the English] entered pell mell with those on horseback, whoever could get in first'.[24]

Resistance collapsed. Only a squad of determined Flemings, no more than thirty strong, held out in the Red Hall until it was burnt down around them. The attackers generally suffered few casualties although the young Richard of Cornwall, a son of the king's uncle, was amongst them, having unwisely lifted his helm to obtain a better view of the progress of the assault and receiving a fatal bolt for his pains. Although the women and children who survived the initial holocaust were permitted to depart, a significant proportion of the male population was left dead in the ashes, an atrocity which the Scots were never to forget. The castle surrendered on terms but the intransigent Douglas was to remain a captive.

Despite the fall of Berwick, Northumberland was not to escape unscathed. On 8th April, Ross, Menteith, Athol and Comyn of Badenoch launched a raid from Jedburgh against Redesdale, Coquetdale and Tynedale. The attack was stopped at Harbottle where the Umfraville castle resisted two days of assault but the Scots proved themselves the equals of the English in terms of frightfulness – 'They imbued their arms, hitherto unfleshed, with the blood of infirm people, old women, women in child bed, and even children two or three years old, proving themselves apt scholars in atrocity, in so much so that they raised aloft little span-long children pierced on pikes.'[25]

Having achieved no more with their second raid the Scots withdrew, falling back through Lothian and Teviotdale, gathering their resources to attempt to relieve the siege of Dunbar being undertaken by Earl Warenne. The castle was in the ownership of Patrick Dunbar, Earl of March, an English sympathiser serving with Edward at Berwick, but his defiant countess, a patriot, had taken advantage of his absence to open the gates to a Scottish force. Undeterred by the prospect of facing the relieving army, which appeared around noon on 27th April, Warenne drew up ready to accept battle, leaving a masking force to contain the defenders. The Scots appeared over the brow of Spottismuir and Warenne, whose men were mainly mounted, moved forward to seek contact at the crossing of the Spot Burn which ran along the anticipated front line of both armies. The Scots mistook this manoeuvre for flight and whooped down for the chase. Warenne's charge smashed home, scattering the Scots and capturing most of their leaders. The fight dissolved into a rout and the Scottish army disintegrated.

For the hapless King John this reverse, following upon the fall of Berwick, proved fatal. The English advance was now unopposed and Baliol was made to savour the full weight of his humiliation at Montrose, his coat of arms torn from him and flung to the ground, earning him the enduring sobriquet of 'Toom Tabard' – in the words of the chronicler Wyntoun:

This Johun the Balliol dispoyilyeide he
Off al his robis and ryalte.
The pellour that tuk out of his tabart,
Tuyme Tabart he was callit efftirwart;
And all other insignyis

That fel to kynge on any wise,
Baythe septure, suerde, crowne and rynge,
Fra this Johun, that he made kynge,
Hallely fra hym he tuk thar,
And mad hym of his kynrik bare.[26]

Scotland was now no longer a kingdom, it was to be an English province, administered by a crown officer with vice regal powers. Warenne was to be governor and the relics of kingship, the Stone of Destiny and the Black Rood of St Margaret were to be carried off to England as the spoils of conquest. A timid approach from the Earl of Carrick was met by a snarling royal rebuke[27] and the king is credited with a short, telling summary of his feelings towards Scotland when finally handing over the reins of government to Warenne: 'A man does good business when he rids himself of a turd.'[28]

Before Edward left all men of rank were obliged to swear an oath of allegiance at Berwick, the 'Ragman Roll'. The name of Malcolm Wallace of Elderslie is not on the roll, nor is that of his younger brother William; the estate of the elder brother was not a large one and William as the junior had no lands of his own. It is quite likely that Edward had never heard the name of William Wallace. If he had not then he would be hearing it a great deal in the following year.

In the year 1136 the knight Walter Fitzalan entered the retinue of the anglophile David I. Within his own affinity was one Richard Wallace or le Waleis ('the Welshman'). Richard's great-great-grandson, William, was the second son of Malcolm Wallace of Elderslie, near Paisley. He had his older brother, another Malcolm, possibly a younger called John and two sisters. Wallace's earliest biographer was the poet Blind Harry, who died around 1385 but who likely relied upon more contemporary sources now lost. Blind Harry's version of his hero's life is written on an epic scale as befits his subject and may tend to sensationalise certain events. The young William may have been intended for the priesthood; he was quite probably educated at Dundee where he made the acquaintance of John Blair, a Benedictine, later to become his chaplain in the field and first biographer (also a prime source for Blind Harry).

It is not possible to determine the exact year of William's birth though it is certain he was still a young man, possibly very young, in 1297. Wallace erupts onto the political scene in May of that year with the slaughter of the hated William Heselrig, the English sheriff of Lanark. This may have been a calculated act of terrorism designed to unsettle the invader or an act of vengeance for the death, at Heselrig's hands or by his order, of the hero's lover, Marion Braidfute. She perished horribly with her family and retainers when the sheriff, frustrated in his efforts to capture the daring young outlaw, ordered her house to be burnt down.

> *Gathering together a band of desperate men, he fell by night on the sheriff and his armed guard, hewed the sheriff into small pieces with his own sword and burned the buildings and those within them . . . For the first time one of the high officials of the hated conquerors had been slain and a ripple of jubilation spread throughout the oppressed.*[29]

It would be tempting to see this murder of Heselrig as the spark that ignited rebellion but this is likely too fanciful. There were stirrings of unrest throughout the realm but Wallace could not, at this early stage, be said to be the natural focus. He was an outlaw, a landless son of minor gentry, he had no network of grand alliances or affinity within the magnates. He was beyond doubt a born leader, a doughty fighter and a savage opponent. Physically strong, morally resolute, he did not shirk frightfulness. He was a dark warrior in a dark time.[30]

Warenne was the king's lieutenant, assisted by Hugh Cressingham as treasurer and Walter of Amersham as chancellor, with the chief justiciar being William Ormsby. There is evidence that Warenne was less than zealous in his duties, preferring the relative comfort of his English estates. He was also ageing and his reactions during the coming conflagration were at best sluggish and lacking in that dash and elan he had displayed at Dunbar.

As Wallace's guerrilla campaign began to gather momentum several of the nobility raised the banner of rebellion, Bishop Wishart, the Steward and Robert Bruce. There is no suggestion that this rising was inspired by or co-ordinated with Wallace's actions. Warenne's grandson Henry Percy (whose estates at this time were confined mainly to Yorkshire) and Robert Clifford from Cumberland[31] were instructed to raise a force of marchers to deal with this uprising of nobles. The two English knights marched their forces into the Scottish west march and by the end of June had penetrated as far as Ayr. This prompt riposte seems to have cowed Bruce and the

Steward, who promptly negotiated terms for submission at Irvine without striking a blow.

Undeterred by this craven collapse Wallace and his growing band of bandits cum guerrillas were sallying out from their lair in Selkirk Forest to wage war on English outposts. In the north-east Andrew Murray, son of Sir Andrew Murray of Petty, one of those knights who had been taken at the rout of Dunbar, also raised the flag of freedom. Initially these outbreaks were not co-ordinated but by August Wallace was strong enough to take on the English garrison of Glasgow, commanded by the redoubtable Bishop Bek. After extended skirmishing the English came off worst and the Prince Bishop was obliged to retire behind the walls of Bothwell Castle.

The English were to be expelled from Scotland, driven from their offices and benefices. Few who did not reach the shelter of the occupying garrisons were to leave alive. In the words of the English chronicler: 'They [the Scots] took old men, priests and women of the English nation (whom they had specially kept alive for the purpose) to bridges over the rivers; and when they had tied their hands or feet together so that they could not swim, they threw them or pushed them into the water, laughing and jeering as they struggled and went under.'[32]

Warenne was obliged to begin a muster of troops to confront the swelling tide of revolt. By late summer Wallace and Murray had joined forces at Stirling and it was to be there that the inevitable confrontation took place. The Scottish forces, devoid of magnate support, were under the joint command of both guerrilla captains. Though their partnership was not destined to be a long one it appears to have been entirely amicable.

In the first week of September the English, led by Warenne but with the increasing intermeddling of the obese treasurer, Cressingham, reached the town to find the patriots strongly posted to the north of the Forth. It is likely that the Scots had deployed a mile or so north-east of the wooden bridge spanning the river; this stood perhaps fifty yards upstream from the later sixteenth-century structure. The bulk of their forces were drawn up on lower south-facing slopes of the Abbey Craig which dominated the crossing point. From the high ground a timber causeway ran down to the bridge, the flatlands about being waterlogged meadow pasture, while a loop in the river covered the Scottish left. The position was a very strong one, ideal for defence. The bridge was narrow and would permit no more than two mounted men at arms to ride abreast. The wet ground beyond was entirely unsuitable for cavalry or heavy infantry.

It is not possible to estimate with any semblance of accuracy the number of patriots Wallace and Murray commanded or even how many English they were facing. The Scots might have been three to four thousand strong, their opponents perhaps twice that number. Muttering about cost savings Cressingham had sent a detachment back! When writing earlier to Edward, the Treasurer had intimated that he had collected a force of three hundred horse and ten thousand foot, though the latter is very likely an exaggeration.[33] On past performance there was every reason to suspect that the patriots would not fight; the magnates, these men's feudal superiors, had crumbled easily enough in the confrontation at Irvine, they lacked heavy cavalry and had few men at arms.

The only Scots nobles present were Lennox and the Steward who offered to act as intermediaries. Wallace's father was a tenant of the Steward who was therefore William's feudal lord. Quite what game, if any, Lennox and the Steward were playing is impossible to fathom but neither Wallace nor Murray was minded to compromise. It is no mean testament to the grit and determination of these two young men that they refused to be cowed by the presence of an English field army. Murray had witnessed the debacle at Dunbar, neither had ever commanded troops in pitched battle, the nobility had scarcely created an encouraging precedent.

Warenne's plan was a direct assault over the bridge spearheaded by mounted men at arms. Cressingham had apparently vetoed a suggestion that a flanking force be sent to cross by a known ford nearby, an eminently sensible notion but deemed unnecessary. The attack was due to take place early on the morning of 11th September but the earl overslept whilst his army milled about uselessly, so there could be no question of achieving surprise. Conflicting orders were given and a commanded party of mounted and dismounted men at arms was dispatched over the bridge. Presumably it was hoped that this manoeuvre would either tempt the Scots into abandoning their strong position and attacking or, being overawed, they would flee.

Undaunted, Wallace and Murray, with impeccable timing, launched their men in a downhill rush as the first English tried to deploy on the causeway. The lightly armed Scots swarmed over the men at arms, overwhelming the first wave who were cut or dragged from the saddle, while the foot, struggling in the morass, were hacked down in droves. Only the less encumbered Welsh spearmen, abandoning their weapons, escaped by swimming the river. Sir Marmaduke Tweng, a noted paladin, with a few resolute knights, kept their formation and fought clear to reach the relative safety of the bridge.

The press of men now trying to cross to succour their doomed comrades may have sufficed to bring down the wooden structure or the patriots might already have carried out some sabotage, but the wooden bridge collapsed beneath the great weight of armoured men and horses. Those already on the north bank were, for the most part, slaughtered. Cressingham, the hated tax gatherer, never lived to make the final audit, his gross carcass flayed by the vengeful patriots. Warenne seems to have lost his nerve completely, falling back upon Berwick with almost indecent haste, leaving Tweng to hold Stirling castle.

The unthinkable had occurred – the English had been roundly defeated in open field by a rabble of armed peasants and outlaws. Whilst total casualties were almost certainly not high, perhaps five hundred English and a few score of Scots, an army of mounted knights and men at arms had been thrashed and chased off the field. In a morning English authority in Scotland had collapsed.

Edward had seriously misjudged the extent of the Scots capitulation. Insofar as the Community of the Realm was concerned, his domination of the magnates was unchallenged, the brief flurry of revolt that ended in humiliation at Irvine showed he was on firmer ground with the nobility. The notion of a popular rising led by sons of the minor gentry is unlikely to have featured in his calculations.

Uppermost in his mind during the spring and summer of 1297 were the difficulties he faced in Gascony. Here two brigades were operating and these had had no reinforcement since being dispatched in the preceding January. One of the commanders had since died and the survivor, the Earl of Lincoln, was now hard pressed. Pushed onto the defensive he had been worsted at Bellegarde at the start of 1297. Anxious to relieve this pressure Edward signed an accord with Guy of Flanders for mutual support but was desperately short of cash from which to fund additional troops.

The cost burden of the king's wars had severely squeezed the exchequer and increases in taxation were resented. In February 1296 Pope Boniface had issued a bull entitled 'Clericis Laicos' which purported to prohibit the crown from taxing ecclesiastical revenues. This produced such howls of protest from impecunious monarchs that it had to be withdrawn, but the spirit of the edict was kept alive in England by the Archbishop of Canterbury, Robert Winchelsea. Edward ruthlessly countered the prelate's intransigence by outlawing the entire clergy who were then obliged to purchase a return to the umbrella of state protection, the consideration being equal to the amount of tax otherwise due. Such bullying cowed several of the leading clergy but not the archbishop, who remained boldly defiant.

The senior clergy were not alone in expressing their resentment of the king's autocratic style. Secular opposition was led by Roger Bigod, Earl of Norfolk, and the Earl of Hereford, Humphrey Bohun. Hereford, hereditary Earl Marshal and Constable, refused to serve abroad, despite threats from the king that his life would be forfeit. The earls knew this belligerence to be mere bluster as the king could not and almost certainly did not intend to make good on these threats. At the Salisbury Parliament in late February the rift widened to include Norfolk. The king's position was increasingly untenable – he could not seek to prosecute foreign adventures and quell disturbances in Scotland whilst at war with both barons and bishops. In the end he was obliged to temporise, to seek an accommodation and be reconciled with his archbishop whilst promising the magnates that service overseas would be a matter of contract rather than obligation.

For Edward the disaster at Stirling, whilst a humiliation, was not without benefit. The shock wave convinced both clergy and laity of the need for recompense from these upstart rebels. When Parliament met early in 1298 at Bury St Edmunds, Edward was voted a twelfth from the shires and an eighth from the towns. The clergy, asked for a fifth, vacillated.

In Scotland Wallace had not been idle. One of the casualties of Stirling was Murray himself who suffered wounds which were to prove fatal before the year was out. His injuries were such that he was unable to play any real part in the governance of the country in the wake of the English collapse. Wallace's strategy was now to capitalise upon victory and carry the war into northern England. On 18th October the Scots descended upon Northumberland. This raid was an extension of the guerrilla tactics Wallace had previously employed; he did not seek a further general engagement or attempt to reduce strongholds. This was a war of frightfulness, of robbery, massacre and despoilation.

The raid was well timed. The first stirrings of panic after the English defeat had subsided and the Scots achieved near total surprise. This was

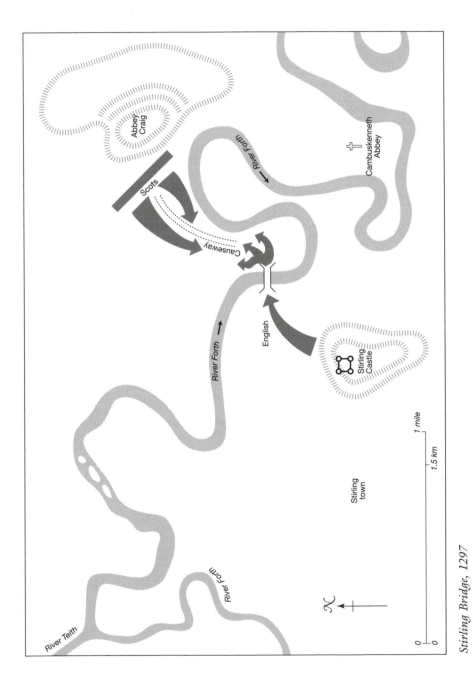

Stirling Bridge, 1297

not an army on the march with unfurled banners, knightly trappings and the cumbersome tail of baggage, carts and camp followers but a lean and hungry pack, each man mounted on a sturdy garron, carrying everything he would need, fast moving, able to live off the land, strong enough to discourage any sporadic local opposition, fleet enough to avoid organised pursuit. These tactics, the hallmark of the successful guerrilla fighter, were totally effective. Terror, like a rampant virus, spread throughout the marches; 'the service of God totally ceased in all the monasteries and churches between Newcastle and Carlisle, for all the canons, monks and priests fled before the face of the Scots, as did nearly all the people.'[34]

Tynedale was hard hit, as was Coquetdale, and Redesdale also suffered. The Priory at Hexham had not been totally abandoned; it is said that three of the canons had remained, possibly in hiding. When discovered by Scots they were jostled and abused as the raiders demanded the surrender of the abbey's valuables. The harassed clergy retorted that there was nothing left to steal. At this point, hearing the fracas, Wallace intervened to save the priests from further assaults and to request they celebrate mass, undoubtedly the most trying service they would ever conduct. When the worshippers trooped, in accordance with custom, to lay down their arms after the elevation of the host, the thieves returned and lifted the holy vessels and other ornaments. Shamefaced Wallace could only offer the canons a letter of protection. He suggested he would like to hang the culprits but admitted such elements of his army were hard to control.[35]

It was then Cumberland's turn to feel the heat of the Scots passage with empty byres, smouldering thatch and the corpses of the slain stiffening in the ruins of their pastures. Wallace did make a demonstration against Carlisle, his emissary a priest who boldly summoned the city to surrender: 'William the Conqueror whom I serve, commands you to give up this town and castle without bloodshed; then you may leave unharmed with all your goods.'[36] The citizens were not impressed. The Scots had no engines of war and though formidable in the field lacked the specialist skills and resources to crack so tough a nut as Carlisle. The bluff having failed, Wallace moved south of the city to beat up the settlements in and around the Inglewood Forest before swinging eastwards to fall upon Durham via Stainmoor.

At this point Cuthbert, perhaps the most potent of all northern saints, intervened to save the Palatinate from ruin. At Bowes a great storm arose, believed to be the manifestation of saintly wrath, and such was the violence of the tempest that the Scots were cowed and opted to withdraw. An alternative explanation lies in the fact that not only was it late in the season and the Scots already heavily laden with booty but scouts revealed that significant local forces were being mobilised in Durham. Wallace had no need to submit to the hazard of battle – the harrying of the north had been accomplished and besides, he needed to consolidate his position in Scotland.

Wallace, now dubbed as a knight, became sole Guardian. His task was not an easy one. He owed his position to the prestige of his victory at Stirling and all that he did was in the name of King John. This was not likely to appeal to the Bruce faction and Wallace was without a political faction of his own. From the start of the year he was keenly aware that the test of his office would come in the summer when the English invaded. To prepare for such a conflict required a major effort on a national scale – a field army had to be created and made ready to withstand Longshanks himself, the greatest commander of his age whose experience of warfare vastly exceeded that of Wallace and who, baronial and ecclesiastical dissent notwithstanding, had a far greater pool of resources.

The Guardian could never hope to match the English heavy cavalry – the magnates of Scotland with their retinues, even if all could be relied upon, were simply not enough, arms and armour were expensive and even French subsidies would not bridge the gap. To build a national army, mainly conscripts, Wallace would not shirk coercion, a major undertaking; that it was accomplished successfully speaks volumes. The backbone of the army would be infantry, spearmen for the most part, lightly armoured if at all, who would stand in dense columns or 'schiltroms' to withstand the charge of mounted chivalry. Magnificent as the triumph at Stirling had been, Wallace would be well aware that the incompetence of the English command, their lack of cohesion and contempt had all played a part in delivering his enemy to him. He could hope for no such boon in the coming campaign.

For his part Edward was equally thorough. The exchequer was moved to York and the matter of the coming invasion was discussed at a council meeting there in April. Those Scottish magnates who had failed to heed the king's summons to attend could now be attainted – this was a departure on previous practice and allowed for the redistribution of confiscated

lands, thus providing opportunities for enrichment which would tempt
hitherto reluctant English lords under the king's banner.

The muster was listed for Roxburgh on 25th June and the numbers
were impressive, perhaps as many as 3,000 cavalry, 10,900 Welsh foot and
14,800 from England.[37] It was one thing to get men on the payroll, quite
another to keep them there. Edwardian armies suffered very high levels
of desertion, wounds and disease accounted for more. Precise numbers are,
of course, impossible to provide, but in terms of suggesting how many
actually took part in the battle to come, it would not be unreasonable to
halve the totals for the English and Welsh foot. The king was also careful
to ensure the army was not without spiritual leadership – he uplifted the
banner of St John of Beverley and that of St Cuthbert.

By July the English army was lumbering through the Lothians, the fleet
keeping pace off the east coast. Bek had been detailed to capture Dirleton
and a couple of outposts but the Scots did not appear to offer battle.
Despite the habitual thoroughness of Edward's logistical planning, food
began to run short – a large army on the move is a hungry beast, needing
fresh meat and corn, small beer, ale and wine (the former was scarcely a
luxury as most water was unfit for drinking). At one point the fleet was
able to offload several tuns of wine. Strong drink and empty stomachs are
a bad mix and contributed to an unseemly fracas between the English and
the Welsh. By the third week of the month matters had become serious
and Edward, facing a will o' the wisp opponent, would have to start
thinking of retreat.

Two Scottish lords in his service, Gilbert Umfraville[38] and Patrick Dunbar,
Earl of March, brought intelligence that they had espied the Scottish host
encamped less than fifteen miles away by Callendar Wood. The English
spent the short summer night bivouacked to the east of Linlithgow, confident that battle would be joined the following day. In the night Edward's
destrier broke free and trampled its master, severely bruising his ribs. A lesser
man might have taken this as an ill omen; the king, as one might suppose,
merely gritted his teeth.

Had Wallace decided to fight or had battle now been forced upon him?
The mere fact that he had marshalled his field army suggests he was intent
on giving battle or, possibly, he felt the English were on the point of
withdrawing and vulnerable to attack. Part of his difficulty must lie in the
fact that, having trained the host and brought it onto the field, there

would be a very real risk of steady attrition through desertion if he did not advance to contact. His prestige and his role as Guardian rested on his military prowess. A further victory in the field may therefore have been deemed essential to maintaining his status.

The ground was chosen with care, his forces deployed on the southern flank of the wood, their front crossed by the fast-flowing burn which at its confluence with another stream running downhill from Glen village created a marshy plain, difficult to detect but largely impassable to heavy cavalry. The foot, made up from the general levy of adult males aged between sixteen and sixty, were formed into four commanded brigades of perhaps fifteen hundred men each. These schiltroms bristled with a hedge of iron-tipped twelve-foot spears, front rank kneeling, second rank with staves levelled over the shoulders of the first. Each was encircled with a line of stakes, roped or chained together, creating a makeshift palisade.

The purpose of these defensive formations was to resist the English chivalry. Wallace did have horsemen but they were few. He also had a contingent of bowmen under Sir John Stewart whose function was to provide missile troops to shield the spearmen from the lethal volleys from Edward's English and Welsh archers. The Scottish horse were there to protect the missile troops deployed in the open between the schiltroms from being ridden down.

These dispositions were all sound but suffered from several telling flaws. The mounted arm, whatever may be said of their conduct during the battle, were at a significant numerical disadvantage. In the shock of impact, as the mounted charge thundered home, their survival was precarious. Without them, however, the bowmen were exposed – if the archers were routed then the schiltroms, who need not fear cavalry if they held firm, were, in turn, horribly vulnerable to the arrow storm.

The spears were protected to their front by the morass but this, in turn, would impede them if they tried to advance. The schiltrom, like the great Macedonian phalanx of Alexander the Great, was intended as an offensive as well as a defensive arm. Indeed, when faced by missile troops, the spearmen had to be able to advance swiftly to contact or be shot down where they stood. It may be that Wallace did not feel sufficiently confident in the training of his men to contemplate offensive manoeuvring.

Edward had entrusted the van, comprised of mounted knights, to his two erstwhile political opponents Norfolk and Hereford. The more compliant yet experienced Bek led the main body and the king commanded the rear. The two earls were not disposed to heed their monarch's advice which was to let the archers 'soften up' the Scottish foot before the heavy horse were committed. They would hear none of this and ordered the advance. Their first surprise was the morass, which the king may well have detected. This forced them to echelon to the left whilst, on the other flank, the Prince Bishop also had to move around the bog. The next difficulty they encountered was the stiffness of the resistance. The despised spearmen stood firm and the English knights flailed aimlessly, lapping around the edges, impeded by the palisade and the unwavering spear points.

Bishop Bek was in similar difficulties, his advance marred by a very public row with his second in command Ralph Bisset, who would have none of his superior's caution. Although these attacks could not budge the schiltroms, the weight of English horse served to unman the Scots knights who promptly turned tail and fled the field. Sir John Stewart and his gallant bowmen were slaughtered. Edward now took control, recalling the cavalry and advancing his archers and Gascon crossbowmen. These had a perfect target: though they had seen off the horse, the spearmen had no protection against missile troops and the arrow storm burst upon them.

Untried, largely untrained, mostly unarmoured and now unsupported, the schiltroms nonetheless held their ground, even as their casualties mounted, gaps appearing in the line as men fell and reserves were used up. By mere valour they stood firm but, judging the moment, Edward called a halt to the barrage and sent the cavalry back into the assault. The schiltroms, dreadfully thinned, could no longer maintain their unbroken line. The knights hacked and battered their way through the spears, slashing and trampling. Hundreds died: 'they fell like blossoms in an orchard when the fruit has ripened.'[39] It was defeat. Wallace and his immediate retainers were able to escape the stricken field; many, however, were less fortunate.

Edward had won, if not the war then certainly a great battle. His reputation as a commander of genius was enhanced, the shame of Stirling expunged in a welter of Scottish blood. It would be easy to blame the defeat on the Scottish knights who fled the field – their actions did them little credit and hastened the end – but it is unlikely that they could have turned the tide. Wallace was defeated by the tactical superiority of the

English. Edward's deployment of the various arms at his disposal was masterly – on the day he was the better general.

The Guardian's defeat was not a shameful one, not a debacle such as Dunbar. His untried militia had fought well and died hard, the schiltroms had succeeded in holding off heavy cavalry, a significant achievement, one which the English were to forget. The 'what might have beens' were probably not much considered in the rush of victory but the horse had little to celebrate. The spears had, in reality, been broken by missile troops. Had the schiltroms been able to move forward rapidly and attack, the outcome might have been very different. The Scots learnt from the defeat at Falkirk, the English did not.

The victory was followed by a march through Fife. There was no further organised resistance. As the king was a man of noted piety he spared St Andrews, though Perth was less fortunate. Still hamstrung by logistical difficulties the English headed south-west seeking a junction with a promised Irish fleet at Ayr. No ships appeared and the hungry soldiers tramped wearily down the length of Annandale where Edward accepted the capitulation of Lochmaben. By the end of the summer the army was at Carlisle.

A great battle had been won, the disaster at Stirling avenged and the upstart Wallace driven back into the hills. This did not imply that the war was necessarily over, however. The Guardian was neither dead nor taken and Edward himself was not free of political difficulties. His earlier opponents Norfolk and Hereford had agreed to serve only on the under-standing that the king would honour his earlier concessions – both men knew Edward of old and probably suspected that, in the flush of success, the king might be tempted to renege on his earlier undertakings.

The tension was exacerbated when, still at Carlisle, Edward granted the lordship of Arran to Thomas Bisset, an Irish peer from Antrim. Both magnates now left the army but the king was bent on further distributions of confiscated Scottish estates. He did refrain from granting lands in Annandale and Galloway so as to avoid further alienating Norfolk and Here-ford, but he still gave Caerlaverock to Clifford and the Steward's estates went to the Earl of Lincoln. A number of these dispositions were made more in expectation than in reality.[40]

After sustaining so great a defeat as Falkirk Wallace could not hope to remain in office as Guardian and he relinquished the post. As a commoner he could not fall back upon an established faction or affinity who might rally around. The nature of his relationship with Bruce is uncertain, as indeed is the latter's role, if any, in the battle. The defeat had robbed him and Scotland of a viable field army. This did not operate in any way to prevent Wallace resuming the life of a bandit cum guerrilla which he had pursued so successfully before. The immediate following of diehards who clung to him would not desert him now. The following year he left Scotland on a form of diplomatic mission to the continent, first attending the court of Philip IV and in 1300 perhaps journeying as far as Bergen for an audience with Haakon V.

Despite the earlier accord between France and Scotland relations had now cooled and Philip had come to an agreement with Edward in June 1299 at Montreuil sur Mer incorporating a proposed union between the widower Edward and Philip's sister Margaret. There is a suggestion therefore that the French king found the Scots emissary something of an embarrassment and even offered to detain Wallace in France.[41] If this proposal was made then perhaps the Scots got wind of it and wisely decamped beforehand. At this time there is no particular evidence to suggest that Edward bore Wallace any marked ill will – the furious vengeance he was to pursue seems to have arisen later.

In 1299 Longshanks was aware that the victory at Falkirk had not entirely crushed resistance and whilst the patriots might be cowed they were not yet submissive. His plans for a further campaign in that year were frustrated by politics in both England and France, leading up to his accord with Philip which would leave him free to pursue a more proactive role in 1300. Bruce and John Comyn of Badenoch had been appointed as joint guardians, a partnership that veered between covert and outright antagonism. Comyn was a Baliol partisan, as Wallace had been, whilst Bruce was considerably less enthusiastic, being far more concerned with his own advancement.

In August 1299 at a meeting in Peebles the hostility between these volatile lords erupted into violence, with blows exchanged and daggers drawn. The argument had been fuelled by a dispute over the legality of Wallace's departure for France. His brother Malcolm was present and clearly seems to have been aligned with Bruce, notwithstanding that the Steward was his feudal superior. Once tempers had cooled it was recognised that the continued partnership had no future and Bishop Lamberton of St Andrews was elected as Guardian, with Bruce and Comyn acting as deputies under his direction.

William Lamberton was a determined patriot, an ally of Wallace who, as Guardian, had lobbied for his elevation when the existing incumbent had died in 1297. Lamberton was also closely identified with Bishop Wishart of Glasgow. He leaned more towards Bruce than Comyn and indeed had grappled with Buchan in the course of the unseemly fracas at Peebles. At the time his sponsor Wallace was suffering disaster at Falkirk the Bishop of St Andrews was on a diplomatic mission to lobby support from the Pope. He was regarded as sufficiently dangerous to merit an unsuccessful attempt to intercept and capture him whilst on the return journey.

Patriot sentiment was therefore divided between those who wholeheartedly fought for King John and those who despaired of their king but accepted his role as a necessary figurehead. In one respect the eclipse of Wallace strengthened the patriot cause in that the nobility, who would not deign to serve under a commoner, would be more easy with guardians drawn from the magnate class and more likely to relinquish their allegiance to the King of England. In reality the English grip was truly effective only in the south-east, the Lothians and the Merse, with a powerful garrison stationed at Berwick – as many as one hundred men at arms, a thousand foot and a further hundred crossbowmen.[42]

Wallace's chevauchee in 1297 had shown the vulnerability of the English marches and Edward had been at pains to prevent a repeat. Successful captains such as Robert Clifford, William Latimer, Robert Hastangs, John of St John and Patrick Dunbar were appointed to key positions. The Scot, Dunbar, Earl of March, was given a commission to hold down his countrymen south of the Forth whilst Clifford held the English west march and Walter de Huntercombe the east. Nonetheless Caerlaverock fell to the patriots which left Lochmaben isolated. There was a skirmish between the two garrisons in which the Scots appear to have been worsted and an attempt to leaguer Lochmaben came to nothing.

Frustrated by being unable to control events Edward, rather rashly, determined upon a winter campaign in November 1299. Magnate support was lacking and the king's summons for a muster of 16,000 foot at Newcastle produced no more than 2,500, most of whom quickly deserted. The projected campaign proved farcical and failed to prevent the fall of Stirling, a major boost to the patriot cause.

As ever Edward was undeterred by failure and determined upon a full muster for a summer campaign in 1300. The records relating to the expedition have been well preserved and the summons sent out from Carlisle at the end of the year show that some forty knights and three hundred and sixty-six sergeants were called up for unpaid feudal service, these were augmented by some three score of gentlemen volunteers with their affinities, perhaps ten–twelve men per squad or 'lance'. The Royal Household contained over five hundred on retainer boosted by recruitment to perhaps eight hundred and fifty – all mounted.[43]

The army was marshalled into four divisions, the first under the Earl of Lincoln, the second Earl Warenne, next the king's brigade and lastly that under the nominal command of Edward of Caernarvon, then only sixteen years old. Actual command in the field was exercised by John of St John.[44] The foot contingents were raised by commissions of array from Nottinghamshire, Derby and the four northern counties. A total of 16,000 infantry was required but perhaps just more than half of that number actually mustered at Carlisle. No Welsh were recruited. The king could clearly recall the difficulties of the Falkirk campaign and his remarks concerning his Welsh subjects, heavy with irony, do support the view that he was not entirely devoid of humour: 'We have given them leave to remain at home, because of all the great work which they have done in our service in the past.'[45]

The foot battalions were divided into companies of one hundred men apiece divided into five squads of twenty, all on 2d a day. The company was commanded by a mounted sergeant. The infantry were often of dubious quality and even more uncertain temperament; desertion rates of fifty per cent were by no means uncommon. Their role was to support the heavy horse who comprised the flower of the army. These legendary archers, 'the men of the grey goose feather', had yet to emerge as specialist troops. Longshanks' armies were larger, less specialised and generally more unwieldy than those which would be employed by his grandson, Edward III. It was to be the hard-fought, bitter lessons of the Scottish wars that helped to hone the English military machine that was to perform such prodigies of battle in France from the middle of the fourteenth century.

This great array was fed by an enormous logistical effort. Thirty ships from the Cinque Ports responded to the feudal summons but their unpaid service was limited to a fortnight and thereafter the 1,106 men who crewed these vessels were to be retained on wages. A further squadron of fifteen lighter boats and a brace of galleys were chartered. Provisions from Ulster were carried in a further flotilla of eight Irish craft which plied the narrow sea to Carlisle. The link between England's westerly bastion and Northern Ireland was well established and the ports of Ulster were a major source of re-supply for the Carlisle garrison (the Irish vessels also conveyed 300 tuns of wine).[46]

The field army marched from Carlisle on 4th July, advancing by Annan to Ecclefechan, swinging westward to Lochmaben and Dumfries before approaching the red sandstone walls of Caerlaverock, held by a patriot garrison. For five days Edward's men at arms made repeated and totally futile assaults and each escalade was thrown back. This was mere knightly horseplay: the real work was done by the siege engines.

The great trebuchets hurled hundredweight boulders clear over the ramparts to smash down into the courtyard and buildings below, pulverising timber-framed structures and sending lethal slivers of stone flying like shrapnel. The sixty-odd defenders capitulated. No terms were offered and most were imprisoned – rebels did not figure in the chivalric code.

Capturing the castle of Caerlaverock, important as it was, amounted to a very poor return for such heavy expenditure, but the campaign was dogged by foul weather and the patriots cannily refused battle. Buchan, together with his kinsman Comyn of Badenoch, attempted to open negotiations for a truce when the royal army, wet, filthy and with the foot deserting in droves, tramped into Kirkcudbright. Their demands reflected a not inconsiderable level of confidence – they required the return of King John together with restitution of forfeited estates.

The talks stalled as the English infantry continued to melt away – fresh recruits, en route to Carlisle were deserting before they even saw the marches![47] The cavalry managed to win a skirmish against a Scots force led by Robert Keith the Marischal whose attempt to 'beat up' a foraging party by the banks of the River Cree was forestalled and he himself was taken captive.

After the negotiations foundered the Scots appeared in force and a further confrontation took place, with both armies facing each other over the Cree. The Comyns were joined by Ingram Umfraville. The stand-off continued for a while, with neither side taking the offensive. Ironically it was the despised and depleted English foot who began the action by advancing, presumably without orders. The horse were drawn in after and a general, if rather piecemeal, attack developed. The Scots fled like a summer haze, leaving their baggage and supplies, melting back into the sheltering hills and mosses. It was perhaps at this point the king missed his nimble-footed Welshmen who could have turned the precipitate withdrawal into a costly rout.

The Scots might have been embarrassed but they were undefeated and there was little more for Edward to do. As the fine rain continued to fall the army moved, on 16th August, to Wigton, but the campaign was effectively over. By the end of the month the king was back in Carlisle with little to show for his efforts.

If neither side could claim any substantive edge in the military stakes the Scots were enjoying some success on the diplomatic front. Their pleas to the Curia resulted, on 27th June 1299, in an admonition delivered by Boniface VIII – 'Scimus Fili' ('We know my son'). This rejection of Edward's claim flew in the face of an earlier recognition, though, due to the envoy's persuasive entreaties, it made reference to the guarantees provided within the Treaty of Birgham–Northampton.

The unwilling messenger was Archbishop Winchelsea who knew the weight of the king's wrath all too well, threatened with suspension from his see if he prevaricated. Having finally tracked Edward to the northern frontier the archbishop was kept waiting and faced the inevitable explosion when the king comprehended the full measure of papal disfavour.

Longshanks was never either more wily or more resolute than when facing a crisis. Age had robbed him of neither grit nor guile. The marches were a long way from Rome and matters might be favourably resolved before the intervention could bite. In the autumn of 1300, however, the political and military situation was far from promising. The Scots had lost a single major bastion and their army had been seen off with only the whisper of a fight. Equally, Edward's expensive campaign had entirely failed to cow the Scots, who were honing their skills as guerrilla fighters, learning to exploit English weaknesses without exposing their own. A further round of talks was held at Dumfries, but again these failed to reach any consensus. Philip IV had proposed a truce, to last until 21st May the following year; the king was glad to agree.

Putting the lull to good use Edward concentrated on mending his fences with the disaffected magnates. Although he procrastinated endlessly the king was eventually forced to give way and reaffirm both Magna Carta and the Charter of the Forest.[48] These had been hotly debated at a stormy Parliament in London at the start of the year and the later assembly at Lincoln was equally robust. Ever the pragmatist, Edward knew when it was time to compromise, however thin his sincerity.

As an immediate riposte to 'Scimus Fili' an embassy was dispatched to the Curia in November, led by the Earl of Lincoln and Hugh Despenser. The advertised purpose was to caretake the Anglo-French dispute but the matter of Scotland had been thoroughly researched and a detailed rebuttal of the patriot case prepared. This defence was approved by the Lincoln Parliament. On paper the weight of the English argument was impressive, reaching back into mythical antiquity as far distant as Brutus of Troy[49] and concluding with the matter of Baliol's sworn fealty. The intention behind the epistle was more to derail Scottish attempts to secure papal mediation than to overwhelm their case.

Let the advocates haggle in the corridors of the Vatican; Edward was resolved on a fresh campaign in 1301. Summonses were issued in late winter for a muster on 24th June. The assault would involve two columns, one from Berwick under the direct command of the king, the other from Carlisle under the nominal leadership of Caernarvon, guided by the experienced Lincoln. As in the previous season, recruitment of adequate numbers of foot proved problematic. Some 7,500 appeared at Berwick, rather more in the west from whence the main offensive was to be mounted, while from across the water the Justiciar, John Wogan, mustered an Irish brigade. The king's brigade marched westward from Berwick along the banks of the Tweed in mid-July, crossing at Coldstream before moving via Traquair to Peebles, whilst the prince advanced on Glasgow, probably through Nithsdale.[50]

Caernarvon was on Clydeside by 23rd August and the following month laid siege to Bothwell Castle. As ever the English were able to demonstrate first-rate engineering skills: a movable siege tower or belfry was erected *in situ*, the various sections having been disassembled and transported on carts. By 24th September the castle had fallen, followed soon after by Turnberry.

The king went into winter quarters at Linlithgow where he was joined by his son once the bulk of the army had retired to the border. Edward's great scheme for the winter was the construction of a bridge over the

Forth, 'the Scottish Sea'.[51] but the project seems to have been frustrated for want of cash resources: Had the project gone ahead, 'we would have achieved such a success against our enemies, that our business in these parts would have been brought to a satisfactory and honourable conclusion.'[52] Not only did the engineering vision evaporate for lack of funds but troops were again deserting in droves – the prospect of a winter campaign in Scotland failed to enthuse and the lateness of the season may also have prevented Edward from seeking to recover Stirling.

The king was doubtless seeking to keep at least the core of a field army in existence throughout the winter, realising that merely taking castles and then withdrawing to leave isolated garrisons would not lead to a permanent conquest. A scattering of castellans could not hold down a hostile countryside and there was scant prospect of winning hearts and minds once armies had plundered and scorched, with the populace then having to endure the continuing depredations of predatory soldiery from the outposts.

Any plans for a renewed offensive in the spring had to be postponed due to the difficulties the English ambassadors were encountering at the Curia. Thomas Delisle and Thomas Wale had found his Holiness polite, outwardly accommodating, but totally non-committal. Edward was by no means the only master of prevarication. In the meantime, their Scottish counterpart Baldred Bisset appeared to be doing rather better. He and his colleagues had submitted a counter history of relations between the two kingdoms with an equally Homeric royal lineage beginning with a Princess of Egypt.[53] Bisset was able to argue that the English were by no means in possession of the realm; John de Soules was now Guardian and whilst he avoided direct confrontation with the invader and won no battles, neither did he suffer any defeat. With no progress being made in Rome Edward was prepared to agree to a truce to endure from 21st January until November. Baliol had already, in the course of the previous summer, been released into the care of Philip IV and subsequently fades into genteel obscurity.

The negotiations with the French, who were also instrumental in brokering the Anglo-Scottish truce of 1302, had begun at Canterbury early in the preceding year. A powerful team of English negotiators comprised the earls of Surrey and Warwick, Aymer de Valence, John of St John and Hugh de Vere. The French had won the concession over custody of John Baliol though they could not extract any recognition that he was still King of Scots – that thorny question remained open. The talks continued across the Channel at Asnieres, where the lead negotiator on the English side appears to have been Walter Langdon, the Bishop of Coventry and Chester, a highly skilled diplomat who had held a series of important royal posts including those of Treasurer and Keeper of the Wardrobe.

If the French held Baliol and the Pope was undecided, Edward still had the loyalty of the Bruces; their claim could always be dusted down and re-glossed. Although there was no campaign on the border in that year there was action in Flanders, where the chivalry of France were severely checked by Flemish spears at Courtrai.[54] Faced with such a serious reverse on his own doorstep Philip could not afford continued enmity with England. In these changed circumstances support for the Scots became a burdensome luxury and was cynically put aside. Pope Boniface was also losing interest in the whole tangled business so the patriots suddenly found themselves cast adrift.

The Scots were sensitive to the shift in the weather vane and in 1303 sent a powerful embassy to Philip to try to bolster their position. The Guardian, Bishop Lamberton of St Andrews, Bishop Crambeth of Dunkeld, Buchan and the Steward hastened to Paris. The King of France remained distracted by the consequences of the debacle at Courtrai, his own difficulties with the Curia and pro-English disturbances which had arisen in Bordeaux. The final draft of the treaty with Edward was sealed in Paris on 20th May 1303.

In terms of strict protocol Philip had not abandoned the Scots; he held a power of attorney from Baliol to act on his behalf and on behalf of his country as he thought fit. Five days after the execution of the alliance the Scots ambassadors wrote to their countrymen advising them of the situation. John Comyn was acting Guardian during de Soules' absence; it was very bad news indeed and the pragmatists in the patriot ranks began inevitably to think of coming to terms with Longshanks. Lamberton wrote privately to Wallace, no doubt to urge him to continue the struggle.

Whilst the truce of 1302 held the English had been able to maintain garrisons, perhaps a thousand men all told[55] guarding the key bastions of Berwick, Roxburgh, Jedburgh, Edinburgh, Linlithgow, Dumfries and Lochmaben. Still short of money Edward could not hope to repeat his

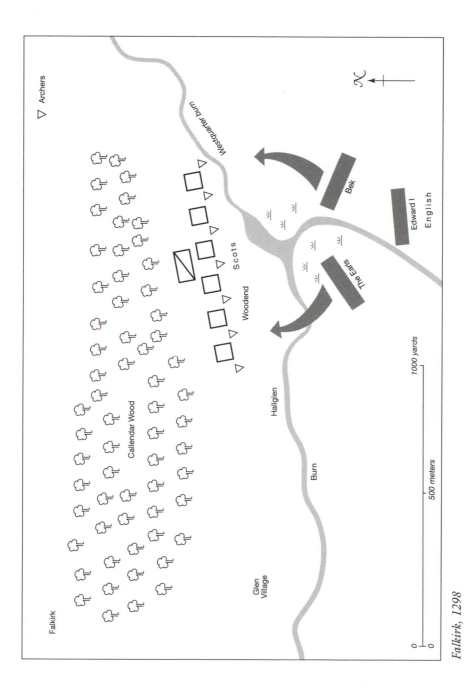

Falkirk, 1298

great programme of military architecture which had sealed the conquest of Wales. In the autumn of that year the patriots took the field led by John Comyn and Simon Fraser. Sallying out from Selkirk Forest they took the nearby tower and briefly encircled Linlithgow. Edward's Lieutenant in Scotland, John de Segrave, had been ordered to lead a reconnaisance which early in the year was to advance as far north as Kirkintilloch.

To counter the patriots a force was mustered at Wark under the army paymaster Ralph Manton, marching in search of the Scots in three disparate columns. Comyn and Fraser seized the moment and the initiative fell upon the battalion led by Segrave at Roslyn. In the fight the commander, his brother and sixteen other knights were captured, including Manton. Ralph Neville brought up his men to relieve the survivors. An order was given to put the prisoners to the sword but in the event only Manton was slain, apparently after trying to bargain for his life, offering the army's pay chest as a ransom. Fraser was not moved and killed the paymaster, 'cutting off his hands and his head'.[56]

These alarums were not permitted to distract the king from his intentions. The campaign of 1303 needed fewer troops than in previous years, perhaps 7,500 foot in total, and a correspondingly low turnout of mounted men at arms. Edward realised that the Scots would be likely to decline battle and that a large field army would merely consume additional resources to no advantage. He did get his bridge across the Forth: not the grand affair he might have envisaged but a series of pontoons, designed and built at King's Lynn and floated up the east coast.[57] Safely over the Scottish Sea the English laid siege to and took Brechin Castle.[58]

Continuing his fabian tactics the Guardian offered no serious resistance and Edward's advance proceeded unchallenged as far as the Moray Firth, setting the stamp of royal authority along the length of the north-east coast. In September the army turned south from Kinloss to Lochindorb and thence to Boat of Garten, following the banks of the Spey towards Kildrummy. By 5th November the king had established winter quarters in Dunfermline.

Whilst Edward was conducting his leisurely chevauchee north of the Forth, Aymer de Valence was active in the Lothians. Here the English power did not go unchallenged. Wallace had returned to Scotland and, along with Simon Fraser, was actively raiding the outposts, Segrave, Clifford and Latimer in fitful pursuit. In the west there was more action when the

Red Earl with a force of some 3,457 Irish kerns, carried in 173 ships,[59] mounted an amphibious attack on Bute aimed at securing Rothesay Castle, before striking at Clydeside and scrimmaging with patriot forces at Inverkip.

It is hard to gauge the effect, if any, on patriot morale of Wallace's return. Emerging from his old stamping grounds in Selkirk Forest he was still potent, but command appears to have been shared with Fraser and John Comyn. Annandale and Liddesdale were targeted, as was the English west march, the former undoubtably harried to chastise Bruce for his defection, though Fraser himself had only reverted to his patriot allegiance despite having taken part in the siege of Caerlaverock in 1300.

In January 1304 and still acting in concert Segrave, Clifford and Latimer led a commanded party out of Dunfermline seeking to beat up patriot forces south of the Forth. The raid was planned meticulously and in total secrecy. At Happenrew the English encountered both Wallace and Fraser, inflicting a sharp reverse and, though both leaders escaped the carnage, their position was greatly weakened. The increasingly isolated position of these diehard patriots was further marginalised when, at Strathord near Perth, the majority of the magnates submitted to Edward. They had accepted that without French support and without a second front in Gascony the king was free to concentrate his resources wholly against Scotland. The result of this was inevitable: Scotland would be conquered; Edward had already promised that the time was ripe, as he put it for 'an end to the business'.[60]

Only John Comyn refused unconditional surrender. As acting Guardian he demanded that all who submitted should be spared life and lands, that the laws of Scotland should be preserved as they had stood in the reign of Alexander III and not be varied or set aside without the consent of the Community of the Realm, a brave attempt to preserve the ideal of an independent kingdom. Edward had at least learned that savagery would achieve nothing and, with victory in his grasp, he could afford a show of magnanimity.

Those who submitted escaped without forfeit, those who had been dispossessed had an opportunity to buy back the lands they had lost, the tariff fixed by a sliding scale according to the perceived gravity of the buyer's intransigence. The Steward, Ingram Umfraville and de Soules were excluded from the general amnesty. They were not to be included in the king's peace until Wallace was hunted down. Thus the problem of the most constant patriot became a problem for the nobility of Scotland. De Soules, not deigning to submit, preferred exile in France. The guarantees Comyn required were not forthcoming although the king did advise he would give consideration to constitutional matters once Comyn had made his submission.

Edward had won – only the mopping up remained. True, Wallace and Fraser remained at large and the defenders of Stirling under William Oliphant still held out, but the king's authority was otherwise unchallenged. Leaving his winter quarters at Dunfermline, Longshanks summoned a Parliament at St Andrews which promptly outlawed these remaining patriots. Wallace was an outcast in his own country. The victor of Stirling Bridge, who with Andrew Murray had effectively re-invented the patriot cause, was not only abandoned but was to be hunted by his countrymen. Such were the bitter dregs of defeat.

The king could not claim fully to control Scotland whilst the garrison of Stirling Castle continued in defiance. The siege began in April. Oliphant's position was a delicate one – the Scots Parliament had disowned him but, in the course of parlay, he observed that his command had been conferred directly by de Soules and thus only the absent Guardian could order a capitulation. This was a neat argument and not without merit – as de Soules was in exile no early reply could be expected and the leaguer commenced in earnest.

Edward's master artillerist, Reginald the Engineer, had pulled together an impressive siege train, with engines brought in sections, two from Brechin and one from Aberdeen. Caernarvon was commanded to oversee the stripping of church roofs at Perth and Dunblane to provide sufficient lead for the counterweights needed to balance the massive trebuchets. A major logistical exercise was undertaken to tighten the net on Stirling's defenders; as well as carpenters, joiners and skilled labourers, arms, armour, crossbows and the components of Greek Fire, sulphur and saltpetre, were supplied from across the counties of England.[61]

Great engines such as 'Segrave', 'Forster' and 'Robinet' rained a constant barrage of missiles down upon the defenders. Open spaces within the enceinte became killing grounds as crashing boulders spat a blizzard of lethal shards. The defenders survived by crowding into caves and cellars burrowed into the living rock on which the fortress stands. Despite the weight of his years and the extent of his recent triumph, the king was everywhere, disdaining the riposte from the battered walls – a bolt pinned his surcoat to the saddle, he was thrown when his horse shied as a missile crashed to ground nearby.

The violence of the siege did not deter spectators. A grandstand was erected at a suitably prudent distance from the walls so that the queen and the ladies of the court might watch their paladins at work. After three months of intense bombardment and the fortress had still not fallen, the king sought to create a viable breach in the crumbling walls with the construction of a large battering ram but the idea failed.

More successful was the manufacture of a massive trebuchet, to be appropriately named 'Warwolf' – this great engine required a team of five master carpenters and fifty journeymen to assist. The building process was so laborious that the device was not ready to shoot until 20th July, by which time the garrison were already suing for terms. Not to be denied the spectacle of his creation in action Edward refused to allow a formal surrender until Warwolf had fulfilled its function. No terms were offered and Oliphant and his men must have feared the worst, but despite dramatic posturing, the king allowed himself to be persuaded towards leniency and their lives were spared. By the high summer of 1304 Edward had returned south to England, the 'business', as he had predicted, having been concluded.

Now there was only Wallace. It is not possible to say at which point Edward's resolve hardened into an implacable hatred; this was certainly not the case in the aftermath of Falkirk. Perhaps he recognised in the fugitive knight a will equal to his own and he perceived the unending threat such an iron resolve must represent. William Wallace was a brutal and vengeful man in an age of total war and all its attendant horrors. Alone of all the Scots patriot leaders he had never compromised. More resolute than Fraser, Comyn and certainly Bruce, he would remain defiant to the last. That end came in August 1305 when he was finally captured by John of Menteith near Glasgow.

He was taken to London and tried at Westminster Hall on the 23rd of that month. 'Trial' is perhaps something of a misnomer for the accused was permitted neither voice nor representation. As an outlaw he could not expect the benefit of due process and the verdict was never in doubt. At Smithfield 'he was hanged, as standard a punishment as drawing was for treason. He was cut down while still alive so that he might be spared none of the bestialities ahead. He was disembowelled and in all probability emasculated . . . his heart, liver, lungs and entrails were cast upon a fire.'[62]

In executing Wallace, Edward, in the longer term, created a martyr, one who even today remains a potent symbol of Scottish independence. In the short term, however, he was probably more successful. Wallace had been defeated, marginalised and finally abandoned. At the time his death, however heroic, did not suffice to reinvigorate the patriot cause. There was no sudden outpouring of national anger or defiance as a result; after all, it was the Scots Parliament which had pronounced the sentence of outlawry. Bruce's revolt the following year cannot be viewed as, in any sense, a continuation of the same struggle. Wallace had been steadfastly loyal to the cause of King John; Bruce was only ever interested in the advancement of King Robert.

In September 1305 the English Parliament debated the constitutional position of Scotland, nine of her peers meeting with a score of the king's councillors. John of Brittany was appointed as Lieutenant of the 'land' – the term 'realm' was carefully avoided and a series of administrative appointments were made. Most of the key bastions remained under English castellans; only Stirling and Dumbarton were given local commanders. There was to be a thorough overhaul of the Scottish legal system, with many of the more ancient and anachronistic processes deleted – in fairness to Edward this was probably overdue.

The king's proposals for the governance of Scotland were neither harsh nor arbitrary – there was consultation, even if the matter of sovereignty was closed to debate. Edward had learnt that a gentler hand was needed, the arrogance of the earlier settlement of 1296–7 was avoided. 'It was no small achievement for this elderly, conventional, conservative, unimaginative man that he had learnt anything at all.'[63]

In the end the Edwardian conquest failed, but not while Longshanks lived – it was his disinterested, self-obsessed son who was to fail. Whilst the old king remained active and in the field he seemed invincible. Indeed, he appeared to hold the magnates of Scotland in thrall – they appeared incapable of resisting him for any length of time:

Edward I failed in his Scottish wars. The task of conquering Scotland was an immense one, and failure is perhaps less surprising than the degree of success which the King achieved. His armies proved invincible

in large scale battles, as Falkirk showed, and his engineers had an
impressive record in siege warfare.[64]

That the durability of the conquest should prove so fragile derives from a number of factors. Edward had circled Wales with a ring of great concentric castles, Rhuddlann, Harlech, Conwy, Caernarfon and Beaumaris, even if the latter remained in its incomplete state due to a lack of funding. There was no more money to achieve a similar effect in Scotland so the king was obliged to rely on maintaining existing castles, supported by rather ad hoc outposts, invariably thrown up in timber and earth.

The isolated garrisons, when not supported by a mobile field army, were too dispersed to act in concert and provide mutual defence. Thus it was possible for the patriots to marshal their slender resources and concentrate upon reducing each in turn. The hungry garrisons, by preying on an already despoiled populace, provided a ready focus for discontent. The constant ravaging of the countryside by marauding English forces and the pernicious trend towards endemic warfare at local level discouraged any possibility of lasting accord or even grudging acceptance. The wild border hills, the fastnesses of Galloway, the west coast highlands and islands were ideal terrain for guerrilla forces and often impassable to regular troops, particularly heavy cavalry.

Edward relied heavily on the feudal summons, particularly for raising infantry, the quality of which was at best questionable whilst the vast logistical effort required to keep such large forces in the field consumed treasure at an extravagant rate. The need to fight a war on two fronts denied Edward, certainly until the treaty of 1303, the opportunity to concentrate his forces. The intermittent strife in Gascony meant yet more expense and the diversion of resources, whilst French cash and French arms supply boosted the patriots. It is significant that the cause collapsed when Philip IV withdrew his support.

By the end of 1305 it must have appeared to English and Scots alike that the business was indeed now at an end, with Scotland's future as a province of the Plantagenet empire confirmed. That the settlement, not even a year old, should be destroyed by the chain of events unleashed by a brutal murder in the hallowed precincts of Blackfriar's Kirk in Dumfries would have seemed inconceivable. Scotland's greatest paladin was about to take the stage.

Notes

1 Quoted in Prestwich, M., *Edward I*, London 1988 p. 475.
2 'Longshanks', i.e. 'long legs', a nickname derived from the king's height and horseman's physique.
3 Prestwich p. 386.
4 Ibid p. 469.
5 In law this declaration amounted to a 'tailzie' or as we would now refer to it an entail. In effect it was a statement of intent, not necessarily binding after the king's death.
6 Quoted in Fisher, A., *William Wallace*, Edinburgh 1986 p. 17.
7 'Custodes Pacis' – 'keepers of the peace' see Fisher p. 18.
8 Baliol (the surname derives from Bailleul) was an Anglo-Norman lord with estates in 17 counties of England and additional lands in Picardy. The castle at Barnard Castle in west Durham was built by Bernard Baliol, son of Guy, who was granted lands in Teesdale by William Rufus in 1093. Hugh de Baliol's son John, the competitor, married Devorguilla, the heiress of John of Galloway. John Baliol was a younger son whose brothers predeceased the father. He had no experience of government or even any involvement in affairs of state and does seem to have been temperamentally unsuited to the rigours of medieval Scottish kingship. David Earl of Huntingdon sired three daughters, one of whom was the mother of Bruce the Competitor. Despite the weight of his years Bruce was more worldly and outgoing than his rival Baliol and could claim his descent, through his mother, from William the Lion, see Traquair, P., *Freedom's Sword*, London 1990 pp. 30–1.
9 This was a 'nod' to the potential progeny of Yolande of Dreux, should she, as she hopefully alleged, be pregnant at the date of Alexander's death.
10 Caernarvon's grandfather Henry III of England was also the Maid's great-grandfather.
11 Anthony Bek, the Prince Bishop, cleric, soldier, diplomat and scoundrel, it was he who sold the Barony of Alnwick to the Percys in 1313 in his capacity as a trustee for the de Vesci heiress to whom he failed to account for the proceeds. His episcopal seat in east Durham at Seaton Holme has survived and now houses a leading local charity. It remains one of the oldest buildings to survive in County Durham.
12 Quoted in Prestwich p. 361.
13 Bek was granted the Liberty of Tynedale, formerly a fief of the Scottish crown, as compensation for pensions (perhaps better described as bribes) given to Norwegian delegates to facilitate the safe conclusion of the marriage negotiations. See Traquair p. 21.
14 Prestwich p. 362.
15 Ibid p. 364.
16 Quoted in Traquair p. 27.

17 Edward's credentials as an arbitrator were impressive. He had, *inter alia*, acted as a judge in a dispute over the inheritance of the throne of Sicily from 1286–1289. As a competitor in his own right his claim derived from his descent from Henry I of England who had married Matilda, a daughter of Malcolm II.

18 Edward was liable for a stiff penalty of £100,000 to be donated to the projected crusade if he tarried with the handover once a decision was made.

19 The precedent had been set by Malcolm IV of Scotland in the reign of Henry II of England, see Prestwich p. 372.

20 Quoted in Fisher p. 23.

21 Traquair p. 42.

22 The castellan of Wark on Tweed (from the old Anglo-Saxon 'Weorc' or fortification), Robert Ros, was one who clearly suffered from divided loyalties, though his conflict arose from matters of the heart rather than pure self-interest. The knight was hopelessly smitten with a Scots lady, Christine de Moubray. So blind was this passion that he was prepared to surrender the castle to the Scots. Unwisely he confided in his brother, William Ros of Kendal, who, taking fright at his sibling's folly, wrote to the king advising of Robert's traitorous intent. Edward detached a company to secure Wark but they were attacked at night by a Scottish force from Roxburgh led by Ros. In a confused skirmish the English disengaged without serious loss. Robert Ros was the principal loser insofar as, after this fracas, the lady wanted nothing more to do with him! See Traquair p. 43 and Prestwich p. 470.

23 Roughly translated this meant dig your way in and defend the town with a new ditch. The translation may have lost some of the scurrility of the original, see Traquair p. 46.

24 Quoted in Traquair p. 46; see also Prestwich p. 471.

25 Quoted in Traquair p. 49.

26 Quoted in Fisher p. 27.

27 'Have we nothing to do but win kingdoms for you?' See Fisher p. 30.

28 'Bon besoigne fait qy de merde se delivrer', see Fisher p. 30.

29 Quoted in Fisher p. 37.

30 See Fisher pp. 4–6.

31 The Clifford family were from Westmorland and, in 1282, Roger de Clifford served in Wales. He was killed in battle, contesting the passage of the Menai Straits, against Llewelyn of Wales. It was his son, another Roger, who first saw service with Edward in the Scottish campaign of 1296. He served as a banneret with a troop of fourteen lances, two knights and eleven men at arms. By the time of Falkirk he had risen to command a significantly larger force. He went on to serve Longshanks at the siege of Caerlaverock in 1300 and continued to serve, with distinction, under his son, acting for a time as warden of the English west march. He fought and fell at Bannockburn, see article by McGill, P., 'Military Service of the Cliffords during the Reigns of Edward I & II' in *Hobilar – the Journal of the Lance and Longbow Society* No. 18.

32 Quoted in Fisher p. 40.

33 Sadler, D.J., *Scottish Battles*, Edinburgh 1996 p. 41.

34 Quoted in Fisher p. 64.

35 The Gallowegians or 'Gallgael' were regarded as particularly ferocious. A chronicler describing their furious if ultimately futile charges against the English foot at the battle of Northallerton (The Standard) in 1138 observed: 'Many of them looking like hedgehogs with the shafts still sticking in their bodies.' Quoted in Oman, Sir C., *The Art of War in the Middle Ages*, Vol. 1 p. 393. Such men were notoriously difficult to discipline and David I appears to have suffered from the same problems as Wallace.

36 Quoted in Fisher p. 65.

37 Sadler p. 41.

38 The Umfravilles were lords of Redesdale and Prudhoe in Northumberland which predated their claim as earls of Angus. Members of the family fought on both sides and the Northumbrian Umfravilles were lions in the defence of Redesdale, much battered by the Scots. See Hedley, W. Percy, *Northumbrian Families*, 2 vols. Newcastle 1970.

39 Quoted in Sadler p. 44.

40 Prestwich p. 483.

41 Fisher p. 98.

42 Traquair p. 89.

43 Wages: a magnate was paid 8s. per day, a banneret 4s., a knight 2s., a sergeant or man at arms 1s. It is suggested that the cost of maintaining contracted troops could have been somewhat higher. Those who were contracted to perform the military obligations of the higher clergy were paid £100 to provide five knights each for forty days or around 10s. per man per day. See Prestwich p. 485.

44 Prestwich p. 484.

45 Quoted in Prestwich p. 486.

46 The supplies collected to feed the host included 7,000 quarters of wheat, 8,000 of oats, 4,300 malt, 1,000 of beans and peas and 1,000 quarters of wheat from Ireland. See Prestwich pp. 486–7.

47 Traquair p. 95.

48 The noble dissenters had wished to see additional clauses inserted into Magna Carta. As a result of negotiations these further provisions were, upon modification, enshrined in a separate document, *Confirmatio Cartarum*. See Prestwich pp. 427–30.

49 In Geoffrey of Monmouth's *History of the Kings of Britain*, completed in Latin *c*. 1136, Brutus of Troy was the first King of Britain, a descendant of Aeneas of Troy. On his death his kingdom was divided between the eldest son Locrinus, who ruled England, and the younger Alban, who was given what is now Scotland, but subject to the elder brother as overlord. Geoffrey's account, whilst highly colourful, was very popular with the Plantagenet kings and was largely responsible for the Arthurian cult which was flourishing at this time.

50 Prestwich p. 494.

51 Quoted in Prestwich p. 494.

52 Ibid p. 494.

53 The Scots' delegation, not to be outdone by Brutus of Troy, deduced a lineage for the independent kings of Scotland going back to a mystical princess of Egypt.

54 This significant battle took place on 11th July 1302, in the course of a Flemish revolt. A phalanx of Flemish pikes deployed behind a marsh-girt stream. Efforts by mounted men at arms to break their formation were firstly disordered by the wet ground, impeded by their own foot and then worsted when the phalanx advanced to contact before they could regain any cohesion. The French commander, Robert of Artois, with sixty-odd members of the nobility and perhaps as many as seven hundred knights and men at arms, perished on the field. See Chandler, D. (Ed.), *A Guide to the Battlefields of Europe*, Herts 1989 pp. 13–14.

55 Prestwich p. 497.

56 Traquair p. 111.

57 The cost was the not inconsiderable amount of £938. See Prestwich, p. 499.

58 The records indicate that quantities of sulphur were supplied to the besiegers which may suggest a very early use of gunpowder. See Prestwich p. 499.

59 Prestwich p. 499.

60 Traquair p. 112.

61 A 'petroleum-based incendiary liquid' invented and refined in the eastern Mediterranean, it had reached England by the late twelfth century, via France and the crusades. Gunpowder utilised a similar chemical mix but with the addition of saltpetre and was most probably developed in China in the eleventh century. See Nicole, D., *Medieval Warfare Source Book*, London 1999 pp. 294–5.

62 Fisher p. 128.

63 Prestwich p. 504.

64 Ibid p. 511.

Chapter 4

The Lion Triumphant

It was indeed a mighty undertaking that the king began, taking unbearable burdens upon his shoulders, for not only did he raise his hand against the mighty king of England and all his confederates and flatterers, but also devoted himself to a struggle against one and all in the kingdom of Scotland . . . like a drop of water reckoned against the waves of the sea.[1]

The rebellion of Robert Bruce, Earl of Carrick, which was to change the entire direction of the war with England and ultimately lead to the triumph of the patriot cause, a success so telling that the flame of nationhood could never thenceforth be extinguished, began with an act of murder. Worse, the killing was compounded with sacrilege as the victim's blood was spilt on consecrated ground. Quite why Bruce, on 10th February 1306, decided to stab to death John Comyn of Badenoch, 'the Red Comyn', in the Greyfriars' church in Dumfries has never been fully explained.

It cannot be that the killing was premeditated for only a fool would choose to slaughter his victim in church. There had always been bad blood between the two and this had erupted into violence before. It is possible that Bruce and Comyn had entered into a pact or band between them whereby Comyn would support Bruce as a candidate for the throne in return for the broad acres of his earldom, whereupon Comyn had promptly confessed the scheme to Edward.

A dramatic scene is conjured when Bruce alone, rather than with Comyn, is summoned to Parliament in London. The king shows the earl his half of the indenture and politely enquires if he recognises the seal. Bruce temporises, regrets he has forgotten his seal and requests a night's adjournment to consider the matter.

As he repairs to his lodgings a page of the Earl of Gloucester's household brings him the gift of a shilling and a pair of spurs – a broad hint to be on his way as speedily as he might. Using the coin to reward the messenger Bruce gallops north by forced stages to reach the temporary sanctuary of Lochmaben Castle. He arranges to meet Comyn in the Franciscan convent in the town, where the latter is accused of treachery. Harsh words and a blow struck in anger follow and the wounded man is bloodily dispatched by one of the earl's affinity.[2]

The affair is reported tersely in the English King's diatribe to Rome in condemnation of Bishop Lamberton of St Andrews: 'When Lamberton was made chief Guardian, Bruce rose against king Edward as a traitor, and murdered Sir John Comyn, lord of Badenoch, in the church of the Friars Minor of the town of Dumfries, by the high altar, because Sir John would not assent to the treason which Robert planned to perpetrate against the king of England, namely, to resume war against him and make himself king of Scotland.'[3]

Comyn's violent demise was not a beacon to rekindle the patriot cause; on the contrary it ensured a vendetta with his surviving kin. It need not detract from the achievement of Robert Bruce that his rebellion was sparked by a need for self-advancement rather than a loftier ideal of freedom from the English yoke. The move was daring to the point of foolhardiness. Bruce had received few tokens from Edward since his defection from the patriots four years earlier and he may have chafed at this. It is uncertain when his wife Isabel, a daughter of the Earl of Mar, had died but he had, in 1302, married his second consort, Elizabeth de Burgh, child of the Red Earl of Ulster, an advantageous match, though as yet without issue. At twenty-eight Bruce may have felt the time was ripe for him to raise his standard. Edward was nearly forty years his senior and would be unlikely to live for much longer.

It may also be that once his hot blood had cooled and he realised the consequences of leaving his enemy's blood so liberally splashed on consecrated stones Bruce had petitioned Edward for a pardon in the hope of staving off the inevitable retaliation. A bitter, internecine feud with the Comyns who were numerous, powerful and warlike can hardly have been an appealing prospect but the king was not minded to forgive and so Robert had no choice but to resort to arms.

In June 1304 Robert had entered into an agreement with Bishop Lamberton which may have been intended to keep the spirit of the patriot cause alive. The English supremacy was the triumph of Edward I, his relentless aggression and towering charisma had kept the Scottish lords in thrall. Bruce had obviously met Caernarvon and would have swiftly discerned that the son was altogether less formidable than the father.

At the outset the Bruce insurrection caught the English unawares. He moved to ensure control of certain key bastions in the west: Caerlaverock, Dumfries, Ayr and Dunaverty, Dalswinton and Tibbers soon fell to him. By the end of March, supported by the Bishop Wishart of Glasgow, Bruce was making plans for his coronation. A threadbare ceremony – much of the royal regalia and, of course, the Stone of Destiny, had been pilfered – was held at Scone on 25th March, the feast of the Annunciation. At the high mass, held two days later on Palm Sunday, the hereditary office of the heir to the Kingdom of Fife had to be performed by Isabel of Buchan. The new queen was scathing of her husband's pretensions: 'King of Summer', she labelled him.[4] The English found a nickname too, 'King Hobbe':

Now King Hobbe to the moors has gone,
To come to town he has no desire.[5]

The new king would indeed require all the support he could muster. Reaction in the realm to his elevation, and the spectre of English retaliation which it invoked, was lukewarm. There could be no immediate prospect of a rapprochement with the Comyns and their MacDouall allies despite the fact that Wishart had granted absolution for the murder of John of Badenoch. The bishop had already encouraged his protégé James Douglas to seek out the new king and proffer his sword. And a mighty blade this would be, despite the fact the Bruce, whilst in Edward's service, had harried Douglasdale, the young knight was keen to strike a blow at Clifford who was currently enjoying his family lands.[6]

With the west at least partially secure and the doorway to Ireland open, Bruce did not find himself without supporters. The earls of Athol, Menteith and Lennox attended the coronation and others such as Thomas Randolph, Gilbert Hay, Reginald Crawford, Robert Boyd, Neil Campbell and now the fiery Douglas rallied to his banner. From Selkirk Forest Simon Fraser sallied out to harass the English garrisons. The court progressed through the counties of the north-east, not a leisurely tour but a whirlwind advance. The king used flattery, cajolery and, when these failed, threats and intimidation to coerce the magnates and secure the vital supply line through the east coast ports. Robert's grip on power was, at best, tenuous. Comyn and MacDouall alike were baying for vengeance and others such as Patrick Dunbar and Malise of Strathearn found the odds too great to risk reverting to the patriot cause.

Retribution was not long delayed. In February Clifford and Percy took Tibbers and by the beginning of March had secured Dumfries.[7] On 5th April, Aymer de Valence, later to be Earl of Pembroke, was appointed to command in the east and began to build up his forces. By the middle of July he could deploy some 300 cavalry with a detachment of hobilers from the west march supported by 1,300 foot.[8] A fuller muster was ordered for Carlisle where Caernarvon was to lead.

The king was slowly and by now painfully making his way north, his physical condition deteriorating. The prince did not leave the west march until July but, by then, de Valence had routed the patriots in a bold attack at Methven near Perth. The Scots were caught totally unprepared on the evening of 19th June. So total was the defeat that the Scottish knights reversed their blazons to conceal their identities – no chivalry for a traitor.[9] King Robert, surprised and routed, fell back towards the west but suffered further reverses by Loch Tay and at Dail Righ (Dalry) near Tyndrum where he was assailed by the men of Lorn led by MacDouall.

The hunt was now on for the fugitive King of Scots, his slender forces scattered and demoralised. By the end of August his castle on Loch Doon had fallen and, far worse, the redoubtable Simon Fraser had been captured near Stirling. Bruce may have rested in the temporary haven of Dunaverty but, by September, this too was under siege. John Botecourt and John of Menteith brought engines from Carlisle by sea and battered their way past the crumbling walls, but Robert was already gone.

Worse was soon to follow. Having taken the surrender of Lochmaben, Caernarvon advanced to Perth and by September was before the walls of Kildrummy, held by Robert's brother Neil. The queen and the Princess Marjorie (Bruce's daughter by his first marriage) were within. Though they sought to flee to sanctuary at Tain, both were captured by the Earl of Ross. The women were delivered to Edward, and Neil Bruce, following his surrender, died a traitor's death at Berwick. The Earl of Atholl, Herbert de Morham, Thomas du Boys and Simon Fraser suffered a similar, dreadful fate in London, while Christopher Seton died at Dumfries.

Although Queen Elizabeth, as a daughter of the Red Earl, and Marjorie, on account of her tender years, were spared ill treatment, Robert's sister Mary, the countess of Buchan, was forced to live, exposed to the mob and the elements, in a specially constructed timber cage suspended from the walls of Roxburgh and Berwick. The ageing English king, aware of the inexorable advance of mortality, was savage in his haste to crush this wilful germ of patriotism.

After the fall of Kildrummy, Caernarvon's knights grew restive in the uncongenial Scottish autumn and twenty-two of them simply upped and left to tourney in France or seek other, more lively diversions. Such gross dereliction, all the more heinous because it went unpunished by the hedonistic prince, drew forth a mighty roar of royal wrath and dire conse-quences were promised for the offenders, although Edward allowed himself to be converted to leniency. By the turn of the year it was rumoured that Robert Bruce had sought refuge in Ireland, though he might expect short shrift from his father-in-law; more likely he was hiding on Islay.[10] Angus Og MacDonald was sympathetic; no friend of the MacDoualls, he had fight-ing men and fast-oared Hebridean galleys, so more men could be hired in from Ireland.

Nonetheless the season began badly, with Thomas and Alexander Bruce defeated and captured by Domnal MacDouall when they attempted a seaborne raid on Galloway, having landed from eighteen ships with Sir Reginald Crawford and Malcolm fitz Lengleys, the lord of Kintyre. The Gallowegians spared few; just a handful escaped. Fitz Lengleys was immedi-ately put to death, Thomas was taken to Carlisle, drawn through the streets and then killed. Alexander Bruce and Crawford were hanged and then beheaded,[11] the severed heads sent post haste to Caernarvon. Only one Bruce sibling, Edward, now survived.

In those early months of 1307 Robert the Bruce lived a precarious exist-ence, the partisan, hunted by his enemies, liable to be betrayed by those he might call friends. It is often assumed that support for the king began to snowball at this time, from a thin trickle to a swelling torrent, but this is almost certainly incorrect. He was a fugitive, constantly on the move if not on the run.

The MacDouall, John of Argyll, was relentless, using tracker dogs to beat the bracken, as though in pursuit of game. This was, nonetheless, a dangerous prey and for the patriots there were some successes. They came off best in a skirmish in Glentrool in April, even if the planned ambush failed in its prime objective. At Loudon Hill, on the tenth of the following month, Bruce bested de Valence, who was seen off with some, albeit minor, loss.

Edward I, failing in body if not in spirit, swiftly grew restive at the lack of decisive action. He was acutely aware he did not have time enough for a protracted guerrilla campaign. At the start of the year the sheriff of Cumbria had been instructed to gather a fleet for service on the west coast whilst the king summoned the last physical reserves dredged up by an iron will, determined to lead a summer offensive in person. But Longshanks had harried the Scots for the last time, dying at Burgh by Sands on 7th July.

With its guiding genius dead the English presence in Scotland faltered. The patriots were still few in number, short of arms and cash, but the initiative now passed to Bruce, who had learnt the rugged lessons of successful guerrilla warfare, who knew how to use the hostile terrain of Galloway and the wild uplands of Selkirk Forest to his advantage.

Even before Edward I was dead the mood amongst English commanders, perhaps particularly at the local level, was becoming increasingly pessimistic. Correspondence survives from May 1307, most probably written by the English castellan at Forfar, which appears to sum up the prevailing gloom:

> *I hear that Bruce never had the good will of his followers or of the people generally so much with him as now. It appears that God is with him, for he has destroyed king Edward's power both among English and Scots. The people believe Bruce will carry all before him, exhorted by false preachers from Bruce's army . . . May it please God to prolong King Edward's life, for men say openly that when he is gone the victory will go to Bruce. For those preachers have told the people that they have found a prophecy of Merlin, that after the death of 'le Roy Coveytous' the people of Scotland and the Welsh shall band together and have full lordship and live in peace together to the end of the world.[12]*

As his forces grew in numbers and his reputation swelled King Robert developed means of waging war that maximised his strengths – castles, when taken, were often not garrisoned but slighted, denying their use to the foe and avoiding the need for static garrisons. Frightfulness, the deliberate use of terror, was not scorned. Intimidation and blackmail went with the ruthless harrying of enemy lands, economic and social destruction, forcing the northern counties of England to repeatedly buy off the Scots. Filling the war chest by extortion, pitched battles were avoided, fabian tactics prevailed, the rugged terrain of the west provided ample refuge.

With his father at last gone Caernarvon, now Edward II, had pressing concerns other than Scotland. Besides, the war was Longshanks' obsession, not his. With the old king dead, the mainspring of the English effort was removed. In July the new king followed the body of the old as far as York before returning to Carlisle to resume the summer campaign. Edward now led an expedition, marching in three columns, into the western marches.

Bruce was temporarily contained in Carrick and Galloway, whilst the English proceeded to Dumfries where the king received the homage of those magnates who remained loyal. The advance continued through Nithsdale as far as Cumnock and Edward kept the field until late August, after which he retired to Carlisle. To all intents and purposes this was to be his last major effort for the next three years, during which the initiative lay wholly with Bruce and his supporters.

At the end of August de Valence was appointed as the king's lieutenant but was speedily replaced by Edward's cousin, John of Brittany. This has been viewed as a political shift, inspired by the counsels of the young king's boon companion Piers Gaveston. Edward's relationship with the Gascon knight had raised eyebrows during his father's lifetime but, free of the austere straitjacket of parental control, the king lavished honours and affection on his favourite. Whether the relationship between the two men was explicitly sexual is unclear but most contemporaries seem to have felt that it was and, as such, grossly repugnant.

Additional appointments of march officials or 'conservators' were also made for the counties of Cumberland, Westmorland and Northumberland. These measures were entirely defensive in nature. No new expeditions were planned, the garrisons in Scotland were left exposed, as indeed were the king's Scottish allies. Unfettered by English aggression Bruce could assume the offensive. In the autumn of 1307 the patriots broke out of the south-west, supported by the MacDonalds and MacRuairidhs. They advanced by way of the Great Glen to confront King Robert's enemies the Comyns. Catching his foes before they could muster against him, Bruce compelled their submission. His methods were by no means gentle and when Buchan fought back during the winter his lands were thoroughly ravaged, the 'herschip of Buchan'. The Earl of Ross spelt out the grim reality of his and Buchan's position in a letter to King Edward which was probably written in the last weeks of 1307:

> *Be it known that we heard of the coming of Robert Bruce towards the parts of Ross with a great power, so that we had no power against him, but nevertheless we caused our men to be called out and we were stationed for a fortnight with 3,000 men, at our own expense, on the borders of our earldom, and in two other earldoms, Sutherland and Caithness; and he would have destroyed them utterly if we had not made a truce with him, at the entreaty of good men, both clergy and others, until Whitsun next.*[13]

The few English garrisons were too scattered to offer much support and the Comyn was decisively defeated by King Robert at Inverurie in May 1308, even though the Bruce, dangerously ill over the winter, could barely stay upright in the saddle.

In the west Bruce's MacDonalds bottled up John of Argyll, sick and despondent, in Dunstaffnage. By March he was writing despairingly to Edward, partly to show how desperate the odds had become and partly to explain why it had been expedient to agree to a truce:

> *I was confined to my bed with illness, and have been for six months past, Bruce approached these parts by land and sea with 10,000 men they say, or 15,000. I have no more than 800 men, 500 in my own pay whom I keep continually to guard the borders of my territory. The barons of Argyll give me no aid. Yet Bruce asked for a truce, which I granted him for a short space.*[14]

Douglas too had been active over the winter, recovering his castle from Clifford's garrison, the celebrated mayhem of the 'Douglas Larder'.[15] This satisfying slaughter was followed by a thorough 'herschip' of Galloway in the company of Edward Bruce, Alexander Lindsay and Robert Boyd, causing many to flee in panic into the English west march. A skirmish was fought on 29th June 1308 against Donald MacCan, a further triumph for the patriots and in which Roland MacGachan, the 'Knight Roland', was killed.

By August, high summer in the highlands, King Robert was ready to settle with the MacDoualls, who, like all his native foes, were, without recourse to English support, forced onto the defensive. Still not fully recovered, John of Argyll directed operations from a galley anchored on Loch Awe.[16]

His kerns sought to contest the Pass of Brander, massing on the steep slopes of Ben Cruachan, from where they launched a storm of boulders onto the patriots toiling through the narrow confines. Douglas, however, swift footed and ever valiant, led a commando against the defenders, scrambling up the heather-clad slopes and putting the MacDoualls to flight. By autumn Dunstaffnage had fallen, John of Argyll was in full flight south and his father, Alexander, who surrendered with the garrison, bowed to the inevitable and offered his homage to Bruce.

By the latter part of 1308 the fortunes of the patriot cause were utterly transformed: the hunted had now become the hunters. From a few precarious toeholds Bruce had extended his sway over the western highlands, the Comyn lands in the north-east, Argyll and Galloway. Robert I was now king for all seasons. The main English garrisons still remained as it was mainly the lesser timbered fortifications that had fallen, but these increasingly isolated outposts were perennially under strength and under supplied, neglected by an indifferent throne wrapped up in domestic difficulties.

Edward II is one of England's least regarded medieval monarchs. Professor Prestwich finds he 'was one of the most unsuccessful kings ever to rule England. The domestic history of the reign is one of successive political failures punctuated by acts of horrific violence . . . Personal hatreds and jealousies were more important than constitutional principles, as was demonstrated in the final overthrow of the incompetent king by his queen, Isabella.'[17]

As prince he had formed his close relationship with Piers Gaveston which, regardless of any sexual connotations, was heartily disapproved of by his father, who had ordered the Gascon abroad. Isabella was a daughter of Philip IV of France, a woman of beauty, spirit and considerable courage, if also haughty, avaricious and ruthless. She was not of a temperament to be openly passed over in favour of the king's masculine intimates.[18] Professor Prestwich has divided the king's reign into three phases: that from his accession to 1311, the 'Gaveston Years'; then the intermediate period from the ordinances of 1311 to the triumph over the baronial opposition eleven years later; and the final span to his dethronement, the years of the Despensers.

The king undoubtably reacted, at least in part, to the austerity of his father's reign. He was hedonistic, indolent, bored by matters of state and much given to rustic pleasures such as ditching and thatching, 'lazy and incompetent'.[19] Physically he was tall and well proportioned, graceful in speech and manner, an accomplished horseman, but lacking in the single mindedness necessary to make a soldier.

The marriage to Queen Isabella was solemnised in Boulogne in January 1308 but by then Gaveston was already returned and installed as Earl of Cornwall whilst rumblings of discontent though still muted were already beginning to sound. A group of senior magnates, all men of proven loyalty in the days of Edward I, entered into a band or agreement pledging themselves to strive for the reform of 'things which have been done before this time contrary to his [the king's] honour and the rights of his crown, and the oppressions which have been done and are still being done to his people'.[20]

The clamour to be rid of Gaveston soon began to swell mightily and the king, his position weakened by the parlous state of the exchequer, was finally, in 1311, obliged to concede the appointment of a supervisory council of twenty-one 'Ordinancers' to co-ordinate necessary reforms. Throughout all this the English position in Scotland continued to decline – defeating and subjugating the Scots had been Edward I's obsession; his son was, at best, disinterested and became increasingly preoccupied with the baronial opposition.

In June 1308 he had gone through the motions of launching a campaign, issuing writs of military service and ordering a muster at Carlisle for 22nd August, though he easily allowed political developments in England to take precedence and the proposed army never materialised. Left to hold the line in Scotland south of the Forth were Robert Umfraville, Lord of Redesdale and Earl of Angus, Henry Beaumont and William Ros, with a troop of forty men at arms apiece. North of the river Alexander Abernethy, Edmund Hastings and John Fitzmarmaduke jointly held office with a force of one hundred and twenty men. In the south-west Buchan, John Mowbray and Ingram Umfraville held sway, again with forty men at arms for each.

Clifford had replaced John of Brittany as Lieutenant, his office alternating with John Segrave, and he had his own retinue comprising a hundred men at arms, sixty from his own affinity and a further forty knights drawn from the Household.

By the end of 1308 negotiations for a truce, at the prompting of France, were under way. In January 1309 Gloucester, with the mediation of two papal envoys, agreed a ceasefire to hold until the next All Saints (1st November). The agreement provided that both sides should withdraw to the lines they had held on the Feast of James the Apostle (25th July) in 1307. Needless to say King Robert had not the slightest intention of abandoning the extensive and hard-won gains he had amassed and the truce was, to all intents and purposes, an admission by Edward that he was in no position to resume the offensive.

Throughout 1309 the English remained largely on the defensive. Gloucester, who had succeeded Clifford, relieved a siege of Rutherglen castle, only to see the place fall to Edward Bruce later in the year. In July the Stamford Parliament resolved to renew a campaign that had been proposed for June then cancelled. A muster subsequently ordered for 29th September was deferred until October before being finally abandoned altogether.

Bruce had already held his first major Parliament, at St Andrews in March. His father-in-law, the Red Earl of Ulster, who had remained unshakeable in his allegiance to Edward, did mount an offensive, of the purely diplomatic sort, from Ireland intended to try to relieve the pressure on John of Argyll. The mission produced no tangible results but Ireland remained a major source of supply for the remaining English garrisons of the south-west.[21]

In November Edward's commissioners entered into negotiations for a proposed extension of the existing truce. At the end of the month Segrave was dispatched to Berwick, Clifford with the Earl of Hereford and John Cromwell posted to Carlisle, their brief to seek an extended truce until 14th January 1310. For his part Clifford was anxious to stretch this still further, till March at least or even into the early summer. Bowing to expediency the king had empowered the castellans of the most exposed garrisons, excluding only those in the south-west, to agree local arrangements into early June, till Whitsun (which fell on the 7th).

Bruce was never idle. During the truce he received the submission of both the Earl of Ross and the Steward, and he won over the Earl of Lennox

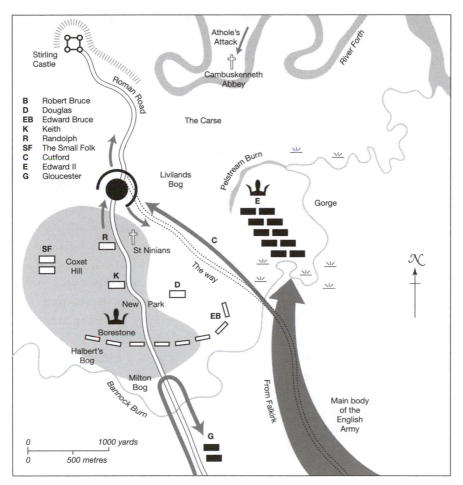

B   Robert Bruce
D   Douglas
EB   Edward Bruce
K   Keith
R   Randolph
SF   The Small Folk
C   Cutford
E   Edward II
G   Gloucester

Bannockburn 23rd June, 1314

who handed over the mighty fortress of Dumbarton as a token of his new allegiance. Since his capture in the shambles at Methven, Thomas Randolph had served England; taken now by the Scots he voiced a deep abhorrence of the unchivalric nature of guerrilla-style warfare. Bruce won him over, however. Created Earl of Moray in 1312, Randolph was to become one of the great captains of the age and a stalwart of the patriot cause.

In his dealings and ordinances Bruce referred to Alexander III as his predecessor, Baliol's kingship being effectively overreached. The Scots Parliament was more than willing to expunge the luckless King John. Bruce was accepted as satisfying the four pillars of legitimate succession: inheritance, virtue, election and conquest. The Scottish Church provided a resounding endorsement, known as 'The Declaration of the Clergy':

> ... *this people, being unable any longer to endure injuries so many and so great, and more bitter than death, which were being continually inflicted on their property and their persons for lack of a captain and faithful leader, agreed, by divine prompting, on Lord Bruce who is now king.*[22]

As an ally of the Scots, whilst Edward's father-in-law and also patron of Baliol, this put Philip IV in a somewhat delicate position. Publicly he continued to refer to Bruce as the Earl of Carrick whilst in private correspondence addressing him as King of Scots.[23] The campaign which Edward II now planned for the summer of 1310 was largely a device intended to frustrate the growing ranks of the opposition and to snatch the reins of government from the grasping hands of reformers. Philip was also pressing his reluctant son-in-law to journey to France and renew his homage for Gascony; even the rigours of campaigning in Scotland seemed preferable.

With the exchequer now removed to York, Edward and Gaveston might feel less threatened and, if the king had any doubt as to the seriousness of his affairs in Scotland, he received a sharp reminder in the form of a brutally frank letter written by four of his Scottish lords, Alexander Abernethy, Ingram Umfraville, Alexander and John of Argyll, addressed to Aymer de Valence, now, since 1308, Earl of Pembroke: 'We should lose both the land and those who still remain faithful to us by reason of our default and our laxity.'[24]

Edward's negligence was affecting northern England. Patriot success inevitably meant the northern counties were exposed. As far back as September 1307 'keepers of the peace' had been appointed to the English west march; in that November Gilbert Umfraville and William de Ros were given a similar role in Northumberland.[25] The ruthlessness of the patriot campaigns in Scotland had, by 1310, already swelled the marches with a desperate host of refugees. Dispossessed Gallowegians crowded their beasts into Inglewood Forest. Locals probably divined that worse was to come and in this they would have been entirely correct.

In England there was little enthusiasm for campaigning. Pembroke, Hereford,[26] Thomas of Lancaster and Arundel all pointedly failed to attend a briefing meeting at Northampton in August. Magnate support was limited to the earls of Gloucester, Warenne and, of course, the king's catamite, Cornwall. Undeterred, Edward ordered a muster at Tweedmouth where the host was put under the direction of Bartholomew Badlesmere and Nicholas Segrave acting, respectively, as Constable and Marshall. The Earl of Lincoln was left as regent.

The king commanded a host comprising some three hundred men at arms, fifty knights of the Household and perhaps three thousand foot, Welshmen in the main with a company of elite crossbowmen raised and equipped by the City of London and intended for service in the Berwick garrison. The outposts on the Tweed and through the Merse were stripped to provide additional manpower.

The delinquent earls had sent their basic feudal quota and the plan was for a combined assault, Edward in the east and the Red Earl from the west, leading a force out of Ireland to Ayr where they would act in concert with John of Argyll. De Burgh was to provide a force of five hundred men at arms, three hundred hobilers and two thousand foot.

Ships were ordered up from both the Irish ports and the west of England, but on 2nd August the Irish arm of the offensive was aborted. The declared reason for this cancellation was the difficulties caused by a poor harvest but this is less likely than the fact that the MacSweens, clients of Edward, had been driven out of Knapdale by Menteith. The king had granted the area to John MacSween in July, though his enjoyment was subject to him being able to expel Menteith. This feud over the local lordship was nothing new and had been festering for the best part of half a century. Patriot success in the west may have inspired fears of a possible attack on the Isle of Man and the Red Earl's knights were deployed to bolster Simon Montacute's garrison there.[27]

On 1st September the royal army forded the Tweed at Wark and carried out an initial sweep through Selkirk Forest. Meeting no opposition, the king turned west on the 21st to advance along the Clyde Valley as far as Renfrew. From here the army returned eastward, reaching Linlithgow by 23rd October. A week or so later King Edward was back in Berwick. The expedition, though it had failed to bring on a general engagement, had secured the vital garrisons south of the Forth and demonstrated that the English still had teeth. The king remained on the borders until June 1311, a convenient distance from his critics, whilst Gaveston was safely installed at Roxburgh, Warenne held Wark and Gloucester the Prince Bishop's castle at Norham.

Throughout the campaign of 1310 Bruce was too canny to accept the hazard of battle. He relied, as ever, on the guerrilla-style tactics which had served him so well to date, denying sustenance to the invader, hanging on his flanks and cutting up isolated detachments. Thus the campaign was by no means bloodless:

> *One day, when some English and Welsh, always ready for plunder, had gone out on a raid, accompanied for protection by many horsemen from the army, Bruce's men, who had been concealed in caves and in the woodlands, made a serious attack on our men. Our horsemen, seeing that they could not help the infantry, returned to the main force with a frightening uproar; and immediately leapt to arms and hastened with one accord to the help of those who had been left amongst the enemy; but assistance came too late to prevent the slaughter of our men . . . Before our knights arrived, up to 300 Welsh and English had been slaughtered, and the enemy returned to their caves. From such ambushes our men suffered heavy losses.*[28]

No sooner had the English departed than Bruce launched a retaliatory strike into the Merse. Edward led out the Berwick garrison to see him off and the Scots again fell back without engaging. One of the problems which confronted the English in 1310 arose from King Robert's policy of slighting the captured forts. This increased the isolation of the remaining garrisons in the larger holds and made the reoccupation of territory impossible without rebuilding, which was both time consuming and expensive. Longshanks had been able to maintain forty or so outposts and by 1310 Bruce had perhaps recovered a quarter of these.[29]

Edward now sought to consolidate the position by entering into a series of contracts or indentures with his nobles, appointing Robert Umfraville as his lieutenant in the far north, based at Perth, where Beaumont commanded the immediate garrison and with Percy and Pain Tiptoft in support. Umfraville could count on a couple of hundred men at arms plus the retinues of sympathetic Scottish lords.

Clifford was given the southern command based at Berwick, Roger Mortimer took over from Cornwall at Roxburgh, John Segrave became warden of Annandale and whilst Dungal MacDouall still clung on at Dumfries and Ingram Umfraville held Caerlaverock, the west was effectively ceded to the patriots.

In the meantime the regent Lincoln had died. His beneficiary Thomas of Lancaster[30] was to become the focus of baronial opposition, a man of limited ability, much taken with private feuds, lacking in charisma or serious political acumen, 'sulky, vindictive, self seeking and vicious'.[31] He was, nonetheless, by far the wealthiest of the barons, with vast estates in the north. The earl journeyed north to meet the king and do homage for his inheritance, but being very much of the reform party, he refused to cross the Tweed and, after some procrastination, the king met with the earl at Haggerston on the English side.

With the tide of opposition swelling alarmingly there is the suggestion that Edward was prepared to consider a permanent peace with Bruce in return, possibly, for military assistance against the dissenting magnates and a safe haven for Gaveston north of the border.

The reformers or 'Ordainers' were echoing the demands first aired in the constitutional crisis of 1297, but the opposition was now more broadly based. The rebels comprised a number of those peers who had opposed Edward I then but others, like Lincoln, had not been involved in the earlier crisis. The list of demands, not surprisingly, included the expulsion from the realm of Gaveston and a greater degree of control over the crown's finances.[32] The king's poor grasp of magnate politics and his abundant abuses of royal patronage had alienated many and thus deprived him of a solid affinity. The Ordainers' demands included not only the removal of Gaveston but a purge of the Household.

1311 was to be a difficult year. The king could not remain isolated in the north for ever, he was without troops and had not the means to pay the hire of more. He feared calling Parliament as this would be to play into the hands of the Ordainers. Casting about for expedients he attempted to levy a local tax from the marcher communities and, on 20th May, tried to organise a general muster without Parliamentary sanction. His attempts to raise mounted contingents from the magnates were no more successful. A muster was planned for 5th July, a still-born thing: the king conceded beforehand he had no choice but to square up to the opposition. Having reluctantly summoned a Parliament the court rode south from Berwick at the end of July, leaving Gaveston, hopefully out of harm's way, at Bamburgh.

At Westminster the king was obliged to submit the governance of his affairs to what was, in effect, a regency council. His finances were restructured and the services of his current Italian bankers, the Frescobaldi, dispensed with, although Edward soon had a new source of finance, provided by the Genoese Antonio Pessagno. Gaveston was, of course, banished.

Having learnt nothing from the wrack of his power the king procured his lover's return and by November Gaveston was restored to the realm. Facing new demands from the Ordainers for further expulsions from the Household Edward, having kept Christmas at Westminster with his paramour, determined on defiance and fled north. Civil war now appeared inevitable.

The situation deteriorated rapidly. The magnates were united in their opposition. Edward may have made further overtures to Bruce at this point[33] but found his own officers on the border holding the line, not only against the Scots but also against him. Having briefly rested at Newcastle the pair split up, with Gaveston sailing from the Tyne to the imagined safety of Scarborough Castle where he presently found himself besieged by superior baronial forces. With no hope of relief the Gascon surrendered on terms to Pembroke, one of the more moderate Ordainers.

The earl guaranteed his personal safety but matters were taken irrevocably out of his hands when the besiegers were themselves ambushed by the Earl of Warwick, frequently a victim of the favourite's waspish tongue.[34] Having learnt nothing the Gascon insisted on insulting his captors, who were most certainly not bound by any oaths regarding his continued well being. Presently he was handed over to a tribunal comprising the earls of Lancaster, Arundel and Hereford. Judgement was swift and Gaveston's final journey was to Lancaster's property at Blacklaw Hill where he was executed without further ceremony.

The patriots in Scotland had not failed to take advantage of these alarums in England. They now held the vital port of Aberdeen which served as a flourishing base for privateers, preying on enemy vessels in the North Sea. There were stirrings within the fastnesses of the border wastelands. Gloucester and Warenne mounted a sweep through Selkirk Forest before the former returned to England to take on the regency, vacant since Lincoln's death.

Bruce continued to consolidate his position in the north and west with a fleet of swift Hebridean galleys in his service. The much beleaguered John of Argyll had wintered at Berwick where he had spent the long winter nights pressing for relief in the west. These entreaties may have moved the king to summon a further attempt from Ireland early in 1311; John was to have command of three hundred men at arms, five hundred hobilers and no less than three thousand foot,[35] an impressive force to be conveyed in a fleet of sixty-two vessels raised both from Irish and English ports, which was to land at Ayr. The king advised that he was:

> *greatly desirous that the fleet which he had ordered to set sail for Scotland and the coast of Argyll, under the orders of his liege Sir John of Argyll, should be ready as soon as possible, seeing [that] it is one of the greatest movements of the Scottish war.*[36]

This last, bold assertion proved somewhat optimistic; the response, in terms of ships, was less than encouraging. The expedition was inevitably scaled down but seems to have met with some success, including actions at sea.[37] Of infinitely greater import was the Scottish reaction when Edward finally quit Berwick. Bruce launched two devastating chevauchees into northern England. Lanercost Chronicle states the relevant dates were 12th–20th August and 8th–23rd September. In the first of these raids:

> *. . . having collected a great army, he [Robert] entered England at Solway on the Thursday before the feast of the Assumption; and he burned all the land of the lord of Gilsland and the vils of Haltwhistle and a great part of Tynedale, and after eight days he returned to Scotland, taking with him a great booty of animals; nevertheless he had killed few men apart from those who wished to defend themselves by resistance.*[38]

The following month the pattern was repeated:

> *About the feast of the Nativity of the Blessed Virgin, Robert returned with an army into England, directing his march towards Northumberland, and passing by Harbottle and Holystone and Redesdale, he burnt the district about Corbridge, destroying everything; he also caused more men to be killed than on the former occasion. And so he turned into the valleys of the North and South Tyne, laying waste those parts which he had previously spared, and returned into Scotland after fifteen days; nor could the wardens whom the king of England had stationed on the marches oppose so great a force of Scots as he brought with him.*[39]

Despairing of any assistance from their king, now so thoroughly enmeshed in his squabble with the Ordainers, the Northumbrians bought local truces, to hold until Candlemas next year (2nd February). This handy blackmail funded a three-month siege of Dundee which fell to the patriots in April 1312. The raiding of Northern England was not merely blind revenge bent on destruction, it was a finely honed tactic of economic warfare.

The raids either wasted or impoverished the northern counties, in part thereby weakening their capacity to support a renewal of the war and also funding the patriot cause, paying for men, engines of war and material. There was little that King Edward could offer in response, his own border officials having turned against him, his magnates wholly bent on hunting down his detested favourite.

King Robert's war was a new type of conflict aimed at long-term damage to the economy of northern England rather than the winning of castles or battles in the field. His armies rode to war astride shaggy little garrons; these were not cavalry but mounted infantry, having the mobility of the former and the steadiness of the latter.

They travelled light, no lumbering baggage trains struggling through the miry roads, no great straggle of camp followers and whores stumbling behind. The raids were of short duration but well co-ordinated and clearly targeted, each man carrying his supply of meal in his pack and a flat stone for cooking under the saddle. Such swift-moving forces could confound and overawe any local opposition and then outwit or outrun any conventional forces mustered against them.

With northern magnates such as Clifford distracted by the hunt for Gaveston, Bruce struck again in that desperate summer of 1312:

> *When Robert Bruce heard of this discord in the south, having assembled a great army, he invaded England about the feast of the Assumption of the Blessed Virgin* [15th August] *and burned the towns of Hexham and Corbridge and the western parts and took booty and much spoil and prisoners, nor was there anyone who dared to resist. While he halted in peace and safety near Corbridge he sent part of his army as far as Durham, which arriving there suddenly on market day, carried off all that was found in the town, and gave a great part of it to the flames, cruelly killing all who opposed them, but scarcely attacking the castle and priory.*[40]

The Scottish chroniclers were naturally unsympathetic to the sufferings of the northern English, seeing this as just retribution for the woes inflicted on Scotland: 'The fruitless English nation which had unrighteously racked many a man, was now, by God's righteous judgement, made to undergo awful scourges; and, whereas it had once been victorious, now it sank vanquished and groaning.'[41] In the wake of Scottish raids and in the vacuum created by the breakdown of law and order, local disturbances fomented by indigenous banditti or 'schavaldores' flourished, a foretaste of the heyday of the 'steel bonnet' or reivers of the sixteenth century.

A pattern of life would gradually be created in the northern counties, particularly in the upland dales, where warfare, raiding and the blood feud or 'feid' became endemic. Even the buying of truces was no guarantee of peace; local incursions such as that which witnessed the razing of the vill at Norham early in 1312 still sparked, possibly, in this instance, as a retaliation against forays by the garrison.

In addition to the other benefits the continuance of the war in Northern England left Bruce unhindered in his efforts to reduce the remaining garrisons still holding out on Scottish soil. Though these were much diminished, the English presence was still formidable. With Dundee now recovered, Perth was the single major bastion north of the Forth; south of the divide the castles of Edinburgh, Stirling and Bothwell secured the Forth–Clyde isthmus, strengthened by outposts or peles[42] at Linlithgow and Livingston.

The Tweed was strongly held from Berwick along to Norham then Wark with the outlying fortresses of Roxburgh and Jedburgh in Teviotdale. In the west, though the English grip had been prised free over large areas, they still held on to castles at Lochmaben, Dumfries, and Caerlaverock with peles at Tibbers, Dalswinton, Buittle and the chain of forts in the English west march behind, Carlisle, Bewcastle and Harbottle.

The Scots were still lacking both the means and the experience to conduct full-scale sieges of major castles; therefore they were thrown back upon their ingenuity allied to boldness and cunning. On 6th June 1312 an attempt was made, by stealth, upon the walls of Berwick. Rope ladders fitted with grappling hooks were heaved over the parapet by a brace of sappers wielding a long pole. Only the providential barking of one of the dogs, clearly more alert that its master, gave the game away and roused the garrison in time to beat off the escalade.

A further consideration was that a protracted siege of a major citadel might tempt even the supine Edward into intervening in force. This was something Bruce wished to avoid at all costs. He did not seek direct confrontation – far better to nibble away at the crumbling ediface and rely on a swift seizure by *coup de main*.

Nonetheless, by January 1313 the siege of Perth was under way. With a fine irony the English castellan was that same William Oliphant who had so valiantly held Stirling against Longshanks nine years earlier. Though Bruce had already been bolstered by the defection to the patriot cause of the Earl of Athol, Oliphant defended Perth as resolutely as he had Stirling. As the place was not likely to fall to a direct assault, Bruce resorted to a Homeric ruse worthy of the creators of the Trojan Horse. He caused his engines to be dismantled, his trenches and works levelled, and departed with all of his men, only to return a few nights later and, under cover of darkness, wade the moat, secure a section of parapet sufficient to allow the storming party to open the gates and admit the host.

He then moved on to Dumfries, held by Dungal MacDouall, the killer of two of his brothers. That notwithstanding he permitted the garrison, in February 1313, to surrender on terms and depart. Both Caerlaverock and the pele at Buittle fell soon after. MacDouall withdrew into Rushen Castle on Man, soon to find himself once again besieged by the patriots. After five weeks this final bastion also capitulated and MacDouall was constrained to flee to Ireland. In the autumn the patriots seized Linlithgow.[43]

The northern counties of England had sought to buy a further immunity from August 1312 to hold until the following midsummer. Spring still brought an invasion scare; in the east the marchers were struggling to raise the requisite funds from their wasted lands. In April a desperate plea to the king for military assistance met with the curt and less than helpful reply that the Northumbrians must shift for themselves. All that Bruce had to do was amass sufficient forces for an attack and the demoralised marchers paid up without a blow being struck. This time they scraped together enough to pay for the truce to be extended until Michaelmas (29th September) 1314.

Due in part to the brilliance of their tactics and the ruthless energy with which they were employed, and in part to the feebleness of Edward II, the Scots had achieved a complete domination of the English marches, which lacked the means, the will and above all the leadership to respond effectively.

Matters were little improved in the west. As early as 1311 the inhabitants of the west march had struggled to meet the Scots' demands.

At Carlisle Andrew de Harcla was proving the kind of energetic warden who could be capable of resisting, but in 1313 the march suffered from fresh inroads as the Scots determined to administer a sharp reminder to the marchers:

> *On Tuesday after the octave of Easter* [16th April] *Edward de Brus, Robert's brother, invaded England by way of Carlisle, contrary to agreement, and remained there three days at the bishop's manor house, to wit, at Rose, and sent a strong detachment of his army to burn the southern and western districts during those three days. They burned many towns and two churches, taking men and women prisoners, and collected a great number of cattle in Inglewood Forest and elsewhere, driving them off with them on the Friday* [19th April]: *they killed few men except those who made determined resistance; but they made an attack on the city of Carlisle because of the knights and country people who were assembled there.*[44]

Taking prisoners, who were then held for ransom, was a useful means of both augmenting the raiders' income and concentrating people's minds on their obligations to pay.

By the late winter of 1313 Randolph, Earl of Moray, was before the walls of Edinburgh, the great citadel seeming invulnerable on its craggy summit. The place seemed safe from any assault but the resourceful earl had been approached by one William Francis, who was the son of a former keeper and, spurred on by a romantic attachment to a young lady of the town, had discovered a means of ascending the seemingly vertical cliffs.

Randolph, with a 'forlorn hope' thirty strong, guided by Francis, made the perilous ascent of the crag. The garrison were distracted by a sham attempt on the east gate whilst, with the aid of the invaluable rope ladders, Randolph's commando climbed the wall, swiftly silenced the sentry and proceeded to open the gates. The defenders were put to the sword and the great castle slighted.

On the feast of Shrove Tuesday Douglas made an equally daring attempt on Roxburgh. He and his men disguised themselves, clearly convincingly, as black cattle and approached the walls under cover of the herd. The ruse smacks of Hollywood fiction and yet it succeeded. The trusty rope ladders helped the Scots gain the parapet. A sentry who spotted the attackers was speedily dealt with '*stekit upwar with ane knyff*'.[45] The garrison were surprised and cut down to a man; the valiant castellan, a Gascon knight William de Fiennes, managed to hold out briefly in the keep but was mortally wounded and the place fell. Again the works were dismantled 'lest the English should ever hereafter be able to lord it over the land through holding the castles'.[46]

The war of outposts was an important element in the struggle, not only in terms of winning back that which had been lost but also in winning the confidence of the Scots themselves. Many of those who had declared loyalty to both Edwards had done so through fear or resignation. The patriot resurgence and the taking of the war into England won over many of the waverers: 'All those [Scots] who were with the English were merely feigning, either because it was the stronger party, or in order to save the lands they possessed in England; for their hearts were always with their own people, although their persons might not be so.'[47] The English garrisons were frequently their own worst enemies, despoiling and abusing the populace, extracting ransoms and generally presenting what might now be described as a 'negative impression'.

In England the death of Gaveston split the baronial opposition and at the same time removed the greatest obstacle to a 'rapprochement' with the king. By October 1313 an understanding of sorts had been arrived at. The Ordainers, in consideration for an apology over the killing, were received back into the king's grace. Earlier in the year, in May, Edward had attended his father-in-law in France to resolve his difficulties over homage for Gascony. This was particularly important as the king had negotiated a substantial advance from the papal coffers, secured on the ample revenues of the province.

Parliament, mollified by the truce, however shaky, with the Ordainers was still absorbed by the effects of Gaveston's fall; matters in the north came a very poor second. Nonetheless the members were minded to vote subsidies for the maintenance of the Berwick garrison and to establish a commission under Robert Umfraville to look into the state of affairs on the marches. Hostage taking was an area of singular concern. In November it was agreed that a major offensive should be launched the following spring and the host was to muster at Berwick on 10th June.

Adam Gordon, one of the king's loyal Scots, had made the journey south to present Edward with the dismal facts concerning the infamous conduct of his remaining garrisons. Gordon himself had been arrested and detained at Roxburgh on his way to the border. It is generally supposed that the threat to Stirling was the major factor influencing King Edward's decision to take the field in 1314. The castle is said to have been under siege by Edward Bruce from the summer of 1313 and that he had agreed with the castellan, Philip Moubray, that if the fortress were not relieved by midsummer's day the following year, 1314, it would be surrendered.

Had this been the case then King Robert would have been mightily put out for a major trial of arms was the very last eventuality he desired. A long and protracted siege sufficient to draw a large English army north flew in the face of his entire strategy to date. It does now seem, however, that the leaguer of Stirling did not begin until the spring of 1314. After the fall of Edinburgh and Roxburgh, Philip Moubray very likely did come south to press for the castle's relief and this added urgency to the planned offensive.

Perhaps a far more telling imperative was Bruce's proclamation in the Scots Parliament at Dundee in November 1313 that his enemies in Scotland had the space of twelve months within which they must offer their submission or suffer the irrevocable forfeiture of their estates. This ultimatum left Edward with no real alternative – if he failed to march then his adherents in Scotland would be forced into submission or be perpetually ruined. If the King of England refused to react to this threat then Scotland would indeed be lost and the fall of Stirling, however symbolic, relegated to a mere footnote.

The king's preparations were thorough. A steward of the Household, Edmund de Mauley, was appointed as castellan at Cockermouth and provided with rents to sustain his role. In the east the trusty and experienced Pembroke was made the king's lieutenant in Scotland with a primarily logistical responsibility. Antonio Pessagno, the capable Genoese banker, was placed in charge of the commissariat in England. Thomas of Lancaster and twenty-one other peers were summoned to appear at Newcastle by 1st June. By 27th March arrangements had been put in hand for the recruitment of those tradesmen vital to the army's continued success: masons, carpenters, joiners, smiths and farriers.

The numbers of foot summoned to appear were impressive; in addition to the baronial retinues, a further 10,000 northerners were to assemble at Berwick by 19th May. In the west John of Argyll became commodore of the naval squadron, whilst the Red Earl was commanded to bring 4,000

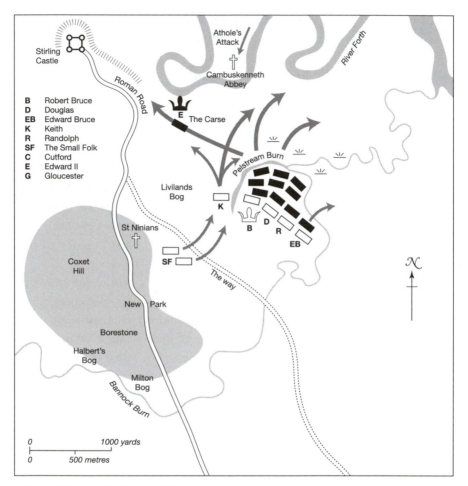

Bannockburn 24th June, 1314

men out of Ireland. Edward not only sent orders to twenty-seven Anglo-Irish magnates but wrote to nearly as many of the Gaelic chieftains, addressing each by name. The response was muted but the thoroughness of the attempt cannot be denied.

The final requirement was for no less than 22,140 English foot, although how many actually served can only be guessed at, certainly no more than half that total. Of the magnates both Lancaster and Warwick refused the summons, but Gloucester, Hereford and Pembroke duly appeared. The king might therefore have commanded some 2,000 heavy horse.

The Scots, inevitably, could not muster anywhere like these numbers and, as ever, they were notably deficient in the cavalry arm. Professor Barrow estimates the Scottish host at somewhere between 5,000–6,000 in total and this is very likely correct. The bulk of the Scots comprised relatively light infantry: 'Each was furnished with light armour, not easily penetrable by a sword. They had axes at their sides and carried spears in their hands. They advanced like a thick set hedge, and such a phalanx could not easily be broken.'[48]

When the English army finally mustered at Wark on 10th June it included a leavening of Scots still loyal to Edward, Comyns, MacDoualls and MacNabs. A vast and cumbersome train of two hundred carts was required to feed this monster. A logistical feat of no mean proportions, the marshalling and transport of the army and its great tail of supply wagons, livestock and followers was an epic in itself. It would be harder to imagine a greater contrast to the lean and hungry wraiths of Scots raiders who had so effectively terrorised the marches.

The army marched north from Wark, in a dazzling array, the hot spring sun glancing from plate and mail, a veritable forest of pennons heralding the pride of the English chivalry. Victory must have seemed assured. For all King Robert's successes the patriots had yet to win the field in a major fight. Edinburgh was attained and occupied without opposition. After a short halt to allow the fleet to attend for re-victualling the host, on 22nd June, advanced to Falkirk, site of the last fateful encounter. The next morning the old Roman Road echoed to the tramp of thousands of marching feet and the ring of iron-shod hooves as the English advanced upon Stirling. Moubray had undertaken to surrender in two days' time if the castle was not relieved.

The army of King Robert I presently held the high ground overlooking a wet and marshy plain known as the Carse of Balquhiderock. The road to the castle wound around the lower reaches, inside the area of woodland known as the New Park, the actual trackway passing between the Borestone and the Bannock Burn. The line occupied by the patriot forces was, on the right, protected by an untamed spread of forest and scrub; the left clung to the natural line of the escarpment running rearward to St Ninian's Kirk.[49]

Randolph commanded the first of four Scots divisions and this comprised the men of the north-east, from Moray, Ross, Inverness, Elgin, Nairn and Forres. Edward Bruce led the patriots of Buchan, Mar, Angus, the Mearns, Strathearn, Menteith and Lennox, his brigade livened by a torrent of wild Gallowegians. Walter the High Steward was, at least in name, the general of the third brigade, but as he was of tender years, his role was effectively filled by the redoubtable Douglas, followed by men from the border marches and Clydesdale. The last and most powerful division was under the king's direct command and beneath his proud banner mustered the Highlanders brought by Angus Og – his MacDonalds, Camerons, Campbells, Fraser, Gordon, MacKintosh, MacLean, MacGregor, Ross and Sinclair.

Bruce had some five hundred light horse under Keith who operated as a screen of skirmishers whilst the patriots laboured to improve their defences. The miry course of the Bannock Burn with its rash of feeders and tributaries was a sufficient barrier but this natural obstacle was augmented by lines of concealed pits and traps, sown with spikes or calthrops, intended for maiming horses, the precursor of the modern anti-personnel mine.

The king's brigade, which had been stationed by Torwood, had now been moved up to deploy along the line of trees crowding upon the New Park; his brother's command was drawn up on the rising ground to the left. To his left Randolph was positioned around St Ninian's, overlooking the Carse, whilst Douglas occupied the rearward by the Borestone. The reserve of camp followers and lightly armed kerns took up dead ground to the rear, Keith's hobilers ranged in front.[50]

Now the patriots were positioned to completely dominate the approaches to the castle. Edward, if he wished to dislodge them, would be obliged to execute a frontal assault over the most unfavourable ground. If he was to seek to outflank their position then he would be obliged to pick his way over the treacherous slime of the Carse. Neither was an inviting prospect.

A hasty council of war, convened as the English divined the strength of the patriots' dispositions, nevertheless resolved upon an immediate attack involving horse and foot combined whilst a commanded party of horse under Clifford and Beaumont attempted a flank march around the rim of the Carse to slip between the Scottish host and the castle. They would thus be placed to effect a technical relief of the fortress and equally handily deployed to deal death and ruin upon any stragglers if the patriots broke beneath the main assault.

As the English van moved to contact there occurred one of those encounters so beloved of balladeers. At this point King Robert, mounted on a humble palfrey, was trotting along the front of the Scottish line, showing himself to the men as befits so fine a commander. Sir Henry de Bohun then spurs forward, lance levelled, determined, if fortune should so favour him, to end the conflict with a single thrust. At the very last moment or fraction of a moment before impact the king turned his mount to avoid the lunge and, rising in the stirrups, dealt his adversary a fearful blow with his battleaxe, cleaving both helmet and skull. 'I have broken my good battleaxe,' was his only observation.[51]

The luckless de Bohun was not the only one to miscalculate for the whole advance was presently in difficulties, very serious difficulties, the adverse terrain, hidden obstacles and the massed spears of the waiting schiltroms combined to frustrate even the most ardent valour. Gloucester, attempting to reform, was ignominiously unhorsed and obliged to retire on foot, the attack faltered and stalled.

At first it appeared that Clifford and Beaumont might fare better and King Robert, ever watchful, was obliged to send Randolph a sharp order to engage forthwith. As the phalanx, its hedgehog points bristling, descended to cut the line of advance, the English knights swung around to meet the challenge. A fierce mêlée now developed, the horse lapping around the schiltrom, lances clashing with resolute spears, swords and maces hacking and slashing as the horsemen sought to break these impudent foot. They could make no headway. Sir Thomas Grey was unhorsed and taken, other saddles were emptied. As the English attack ran out of steam Randolph pushed his infantry on to complete the unthinkable, tenant farmers and tradesmen besting the pride of English chivalry.

So thoroughly had the English been chastened that Moray's weary men received a rapturous welcome from their comrades. Bruce too was impressed, to the extent he was prepared to dilute his customary caution and ask the men outright if they thought they could win the larger fight that lay in prospect:

I am full well assured that many an (English) heart shall waver that seemed erstwhile of mighty valour. And if the heart be dismayed, the body is not worth a mite. I trow therefore that a good ending shall follow this beginning. Nevertheless I say not this to you in order that ye shall follow my desire to fight; for with you will rest the whole matter. If you think it expedient that we fight, we shall fight; and if ye will that we depart, your desire will be fulfilled. I shall consent to do in either fashion right as ye shall decide. Therefore speak plainly your desire.[52]

By mid-afternoon the English were holding a second council of war, presumably somewhat less buoyant than its predecessor. It was clear that the present patriot line was inexpungable and that any further offensive action was doomed to failure. As the primary objective was the relief of Stirling, a victory in the field was not strictly necessary. King Edward ordered a more circumspect approach, avoiding the high ground and fording the middle reaches of the Bannock Burn. If the English considered they were unable to press their attack when the patriots were so strongly posted then, in all probability, they did not consider that they themselves might be attacked in turn.

The Carse, towards which the English now struggled, was, in the early fourteenth century, an expanse of low-lying agricultural land, traversed by the flow of the Bannock Burn, the Pelstream and a riot of small streams and drainage ditches, some of which were tidal. As the summer afternoon faded into evening the host stumbled over sodden fords and miry ditches, the press of men and horses jamming and slithering, chewing the wet ground into a quagmire. The supply wagons would be utterly defeated by the impossible terrain, which meant the army went hungry as spring shadows lengthened and light thickened. By nightfall the English host was crammed into a dirty, sodden enclave no more than half a mile square.[53]

The Scots too were in hurried council. Bruce was disinclined to fight again – the day's combat had achieved its objectives, Randolph and the ever valiant Douglas were all for moving onto the offensive. Bruce had remained steadfastly opposed to an attack – the risk was enormous: all that he had won by patience, skill and guile could be lost in an hour.

> *For Robert Bruce, knowing himself unequal to the strength of the King of England in strength or fortune, decided that it would be better to resist our King by secret warfare rather than dispute his right in open battle. Indeed I might be tempted to sing the praises of Sir Robert Bruce did not the guilt of homicide and the dark stain of treachery bid me keep silent.*[54]

It is said that Sir Alexander Seton who had just defected to the patriot cause convinced the king that the moment was right '. . . Now's the time!'[55] This enthusiastic admonition from one so newly arrived from the English camp finally swayed the cautious King Robert to hazard all. 'It greatly pleased his [Bruce's] heart and he was persuaded that men of such mind, if they set their strength to it, must indeed be right hard to vanquish'.[56]

At this time of year the northern nights are usually both short and mild. Sunrise on Monday 24th June, the feast of St John the Baptist, would be around 3.34 a.m. Gulping down a mess of oats (those who had the stomach, doubtless fortified with a dram), the Scots had, by 2.00 a.m., heard mass. Half an hour later dawn's pale outriders were visible in the sky and the schiltroms were on the move, the four brigades advancing in echelon.[57] Edward Bruce took the van on the right, followed by Randolph and then Douglas. The king's strong brigade formed the rear, with Keith's horse in reserve.

Posterity had cause that day to be indebted to Bernard, the Abbot of Arbroath, who took down the text of the king's speech to the host:

> *My lords, my people, accustomed to enjoy that full freedom for which in times gone by the Kings of Scotland have fought many a battle. For eight years or more I have struggled with much labour for my right to the Kingdom and for honourable liberty. I have lost brothers, friends and kinsmen. Your own kinsmen have been made captive, and bishops and priests are locked in prison. Our country's nobility has poured forth its blood in war. These barons you can see before you, clad in mail, are bent upon destroying me and obliterating my kingdom, nay, our whole nation. They do not believe we can survive. They glory in their warhorses and equipment. For us, the name of the Lord must be our hope of victory in battle . . . if you heartily repent of your sins you will be victorious, under God's command.*[58]

Each schiltrom was deployed in eight files with 188 spears in each, the men removing one or both of their leather-soled shoes to ensure a firmer grip on the sodden earth. A final reserve, the 'small folk', were moved forward to the line of the ridge so that they might be engaged to exploit any opportunity as it arose.

Their quarry had cumulatively spent an unhappy evening, unfed and crammed into the narrow ground; few would have enjoyed repose. One of

Edward's remaining Scottish allies, the titular Earl of Atholl, had mounted a spoiling raid to 'beat up' the patriot detachment stationed at Cambuskenneth Abbey. This had been a success – Sir John Airth and his slender force had been massacred.

Edward II could not at first believe the patriots were attacking. His forces, if deployed at a disadvantage, still enjoyed numerical superiority, especially in cavalry. Though the English were hemmed in, their position was by no means hopeless – to their right they were protected by the Bannock Burn itself; though the front on which they must fight was severely constricted, the previous day's deployment had not been made in expectation of an attack. The idea of attacking in echelon not only indicated the high level of discipline and cohesion within the Scots army but was also perfectly suited to the nature of the battlefield, each division crashing home to maximum effect, striking the English line as a series of hammer blows.

As skirmishers bickered in the no-man's land between opposing forces, the English knights rode out to engage the Scottish van, as if the débâcle of the preceding afternoon had never taken place. Gloucester, stung by the king's careless accusation of faintheartedness, rode full tilt at the mass of Scottish spears, his impetuous, quixotic gallantry soon costing him his life. Soon the early morning air was alive with the crash of spears, the screams of dying men and horses.

Great clouds of dust and steam would obscure the struggling mass so that a man, his vision already clouded by the red mist of battle, would struggle to see even that which was directly before him. Lances glanced from spear shafts, keen-edged blades hacked at the points, some horsemen, frustrated in their attempts to get to grips with the impenetrable hedge, hurled axes, maces, swords and daggers. All to no avail, the line could not be breached – as Randolph's brigade drew level the English knights were driven back through their own skirmishers.

As the schiltroms smashed, one after the other, into the waiting lines of English foot, a desperate mêlée ensued. The ranks on both sides were packed so tightly the dead and wounded scarcely had room to fall – once on the ground an injured man could likely measure his remaining span in seconds. English bills and Scottish spears lunged and parried, bit and thrust, the churned earth soon puddled in gore, spilt blood and entrails drenching the fighters.

One feature of the crowded field which was greatly to the Scots advantage was that the English and Welsh archers could not be properly deployed to rake the schiltroms. One body did manage to work their way around the Scottish left and begin shooting into the tightly packed ranks. Unshielded by their own scattered and winded chivalry the archers were, in turn, ridden down and scattered by a timely charge from Keith's light horse.

'Push, push, push . . .'[59] the Scots commanders urged as the fight continued, neither side having the advantage. For an hour or more the hosts remained locked, the dead and dying carpeting the mire. In the nature of medieval combat it would not be possible for the men to fight continuously for such a length of time. Wielding bill or spear, particularly, as with the English, on an empty belly, is exhausting. It would inevitably be the case that, along the line, the leading files would draw back from time to time, to regain their breath and summon up the energy to continue.

On the Scottish left, Douglas, his ranks denuded by the arrow storm, was hard pressed, but the English were in no better case. The rot, as ever, starts in the rear, those in the line lack the facility of retreat. Edward, though he had failed to exercise any recognisable form of generalship, did not shirk his knightly duty, fighting valiantly in the press until his Household, divining the day was lost, virtually dragged him from the stricken field.

For the English, disaster loomed.

The renowned paladin, Sir Giles Argentan, having seen the monarch safely on his way towards the castle, spurred back into the press to meet a hero's end. The defection of the royal standard was almost the final straw – the timely intervention of the 'small folk' sweeping down from the higher ground, bent on plunder and revenge, effectively ended the fight; the English foot dissolved in rout.

Hundreds of the fleeing men, exhausted, many injured, weighed down with harness, died in the thrashing waters of the Forth. More drowned or were trampled under in the Pelstream and Bannock Burn. The whole of the Carse became a giant butcher's yard, the narrow passage of the Bannock Burn before the confluence was choked with dead and dying, men and horses piled in great shuddering, moaning piles, 'Bannock Burn betwixt the braes of horses and men so charged was that upon drowned horses and men, man might pass dry over it'.[60]

How many died can only be guessed at but the casualties on the English side would certainly be numbered in thousands. Over one hundred knights, together with all their harness, horses and baggage, were taken – the triumphant Scots would pick the field clean. Bruce had perhaps lost several hundred.

Edward II refused the temptation to seek refuge in Stirling but fled south, half a thousand knights guarding his person. This was, in the circumstances, the only viable course of action and Edward, who might be censored for poor leadership, cannot be criticised for taking such swift steps to avoid capture. As serious as the defeat was, the loss of the king would have compounded the disaster tenfold. Moubray bowed to the inevitable and surrendered the castle.

Whilst Bannockburn did not end the war, it changed, beyond recognition, the nature of the conflict. From June 1314 for nearly two decades the Scottish commanders, particularly Edward Bruce, Douglas and Randolph, would carry on the war in northern England and Ireland, and the dwellers in the English marches would taste the full meaning of defeat.

'Maidens of England, sore may you mourn.'[61]

Notes

1 Quoted in Traquair, P., *Freedom's Sword*, London 1990 p. 150.
2 Barrow, G.W.S., *Robert Bruce*, London 1965 p. 198.
3 Quoted in Barrow p. 199.
4 McNamee, C., *Wars of the Bruces*, East Lothian 1997 p. 29.
5 Ibid p. 32.
6 James Douglas was a cousin of the Steward – his father William had been an uncompromising patriot who had commanded the Berwick garrison in the bloodbath of 1296. Though he surrendered at Irvine, the elder Douglas refused to hand over his son as a hostage. In consequence he was incarcerated, firstly at Berwick and later in the Tower, where he died (Barbour certainly suspected foul play). Bishop Lamberton met the younger Douglas in Paris where he was a student. It was here he learnt of the forfeiture of his family estates. Lamberton petitioned King Edward on his protégé's behalf but was rebuffed. See Reese, P., *Bannockburn*, Edinburgh 2000 pp. 86–7.
7 McNamee p. 31.
8 Prestwich, M., *Edward I*, London 1988 p. 506.
9 Ibid p. 507.

10 McNamee p. 36.

11 Ibid p. 38.

12 Ibid p. 41.

13 Quoted in Traquair pp. 152–3.

14 Traquair p. 152.

15 Ibid pp. 154–5.

16 Ibid p. 154.

17 Prestwich, M., *The Three Edwards*, London 1980 p. 79.

18 The coronation took place a month after the royal marriage. Gaveston took a leading role, walking before the new monarch bearing the crown and the sword of state. The French representatives, particularly Charles of Valois, were deeply offended by the obvious precedence given to the low-born Gascon. See Prestwich, *Three Edwards*, p. 81.

19 Prestwich, *Three Edwards*, p. 81.

20 Ibid p. 83.

21 McNamee p. 46.

22 Traquair p. 164.

23 Ibid p. 164.

24 Ibid p. 164.

25 McNamee p. 46.

26 Henry Bohun, Earl of Hereford, was the hereditary constable. He was later killed fighting against Edward II at Boroughbridge in 1322.

27 McNamee p. 48.

28 Quoted in Traquair p. 166.

29 McNamee p. 50.

30 Thomas of Lancaster was Lincoln's son-in-law. The older man's death confirmed Lancaster status as by far the wealthiest of the magnates.

31 Prestwich, *Three Edwards*, p. 84.

32 Ibid p. 84.

33 Bruce is said to have sent this pithy response: 'How shall the king of England keep faith with me when he does not observe the sworn promises made to his own liegemen?' – quoted in Traquair p. 168.

34 Gaveston had a waspish tongue and coined uncomplimentary nicknames for most of the magnates. This unfortunate brand of wit combined with his undoubted and frequently humiliating excellence in the lists contributed to the universal detestation.

35 McNamee p. 52.

36 Quoted ibid p. 52.

37 Ibid p. 52.

38 Quoted ibid p. 53.

39 Ibid p. 53.

40 Ibid p. 56.

41 Quoted in Traquair p. 168.

42 A 'pele' could best be described as a timber and earth bastion likely comprising a tower on an elevated site surrounded by a pallisade. These forts were constructed to provide links in the chain of greater castles.

43 An enterprising husbandsman, Matthew Binnock, jammed a haywain beneath the descending portcullis. The eight chosen men hidden within the load took and held the gate long enough for the assault party to come up. The garrison paid for their negligence with their blood and the works were slighted.

44 Quoted in McNamee p. 57.

45 Quoted in Traquair p. 175.

46 Ibid p. 175.

47 Quoted in McNamee p. 60.

48 Ibid p. 62.

49 Sadler, D.J., *Scottish Battles*, Edinburgh 1996 p. 48.

50 Christison, General Sir Peter, *Bannockburn*, Edinburgh 1960 p. 17.

51 Ibid p. 17.

52 Reese p. 142.

53 Christison p. 19.

54 Quoted in Reese p. 41.

55 Ibid p. 41.

56 Ibid p. 75.

57 Christison p. 22.

58 Quoted in Reese p. 146.

59 Sadler p. 52.

60 Quoted ibid p. 52.

61 Quoted in Prestwich, *Three Edwards*, p. 81.

Chapter 5

The Longest Stick

Richard and Robert began to tax the goods of the said men [of Northumberland] *in the seventh year* [of Edward II], *and they sat at Morpeth in the said county; and suddenly there arrived Stephen Segrave and many others with him and they told them that the lord king was retreating from Stirling with his army and was coming towards England, and on this they were terrified. They fled, and, like others of the county, stayed in the enclosed towns and castles and forts. And immediately afterwards, before the 1st August, there came Edward Bruce and Thomas Randolph leading the Scottish army . . .*[1]

If the defeat at Bannockburn was a disaster for English arms it was a particular catastrophe for the northern counties, now fully exposed to the wrath of the victorious Scots. The battle, hugely important as it was, did not end the war. It ended the period when Bruce felt constrained to rely mainly upon stealth and skirmish. It permitted him and his able captains to pursue a more aggressive strategy, taking the war far beyond the borders of Scotland, to the marches and as far south as Lancashire, into the waters of the North Sea and over the narrow passage to Ireland. From 1314 to the Treaty of Northampton fourteen years later the military initiative lay almost entirely with the Scots.

The objective of the subsequent Scottish campaigns was, above all, to wring recognition from Edward II of Bruce's sovereignty. Lesser but still important objectives were the recapture of Berwick and, if possible, of Carlisle, with the cost of the campaigns, as in earlier years, being funded by *danegeld* prised from the northern counties. The impact on these beleaguered northern shires was profound. The existing social order virtually collapsed, and the agrarian economy was ruined partly by the effects of war but exacerbated by climatic change and adverse weather conditions which resulted in years of famine and murrain.

The social order which had obtained in the previous century could not, for the most part, endure and as the century progressed, power and wealth in the north became concentrated in fewer and fewer hands, the 'new men' of the age whose tenure was largely military, paid servants of the king empowered to raise and maintain local forces for the defence of the marches. In these bitter years the marches went through a period of impotence when the Scots were able to roam virtually at will until a culture of local self-reliance based upon bespoke local forces, hobilers and mounted archers, led by experienced captains, came to prevail. The names of Percy, Neville, Umfraville, Dacre, de Lucy and Clifford would be synonymous with power in the north.

His dismal failure against the Scots was to haunt Edward II in the years that followed. His father had succeeded in diverting the opposition by glittering triumphs in the field. The spoils of war are mighty persuasive but Edward now had only the reverse, the bitter dregs of defeat. Victory in battle was the yardstick by which medieval kings might expect to be measured and he had spectacularly flunked the test.

Leadership of the opposition now focused on Thomas of Lancaster; Gloucester was dead and Aymer de Valence, Earl of Pembroke, was discredited through his role in the débâcle. Besides his availability and enormous wealth, Lancaster had little to recommend him. A man of modest abilities he was frequently diverted by personal jealousy and petty spite. He was never likely to prove the fount of either great ideas or inspired leadership. His initial aim, scarcely radical, was to secure the king's adherence to the ordinances of 1311. In September 1314 the king was obliged to stand by, impotent, as his administration was purged, household officials were sacked and a number of the sheriffs dismissed. The Lincoln Parliament of 1316 confirmed Thomas of Lancaster's role of chief councillor.[2] His appointees were by no means mere partisans. Merit was a clear denominator but half-hearted plans for a further Scottish campaign came to nothing. Edward never left the south and Lancaster proceeded no further north than Newcastle.

Although Edward II is justly viewed as an incompetent, he was by no means a fool. He understood the workings of government, politics and patronage, though he allowed his blind adoration of favourites to dazzle his common sense. In August 1316 he had sought to introduce new means of raising forces which would effectively remove the need to seek parliamentary sanction; summonses were directed at all £50 land-owners and the magnates were simply asked to provide such retinue as they were able for unwaged service. The response, however, was muted in the extreme.

The years from 1316–18 marked a brief flowering of amity between king and earl, their relationship consolidated by the Treaty of Leake. Edward was attempting to create an affinity by advancing certain younger lords such as Hugh Audley, Roger Damory and William Montague. Two of this new coterie of favourites scored handsomely when they were married to a brace of Gloucester's heiresses, thus each securing a slice of the late earl's great fortune.

Lancaster was being increasingly marginalised. He lacked political acuity and at this time was diverted by a private feud with Earl Warenne. The Leake agreement in 1318 provided for an advisory bench of seventeen councillors who were to deliberate all matters not otherwise requiring the assent of Parliament. The new favourites were distanced from the court whilst the earl and others received full pardon for all matters past. Leake was a triumph for the moderate reformers, of whom Pembroke was certainly the most influential. Lancaster certainly did not control the new panel; he had the right only to nominate a single banneret as member.

This *entente* was destined to be short lived for amongst the king's new favourites was the younger Despenser, who was to be another Gaveston. Whilst the Gascon had been annoying, the Despensers, father and son, were alarming. Clever, manipulative, ruthless and avaricious, Despenser was to abuse the royal patronage to build up a vast estate. The main area of his ambitions lay in South Wales where he looked for a greater share of the Gloucester inheritance and his impatient greed brought him swiftly into conflict with the marcher lords, including Clifford, Hereford and Roger Mortimer.[3] For Lancaster this should have been a heaven-sent opportunity to weld links between the marcher lords and his own northern affinity, but he lacked the wit or the resolution. Even the other favourites Audley and Damory found themselves fighting to hang onto their gains.

The marchers were not slow to assert their right and in 1321 they drove the upstart Despenser from South Wales by force of arms. Caught offguard the king was obliged, in August, to agree to his favourite's exile. It might seem that Edward had learnt nothing from the Gaveston years, but, he had come to appreciate the value of patience. His surrender in the summer was a mere device intended to lull his enemies into a false sense of security. Cannily he had marked the cracks in the opposition and selected, as his first target, Bartholemew Badlesmere,[4] an individual already renowned for duplicity and cordially detested by Lancaster, who would certainly not raise a hand to help, too blinded by his own conceit to realise that the lesser man's downfall presaged his own.

After a cunningly manufactured *casus belli* Badlesmere's castle in Kent was besieged and taken.[5] Having effortlessly sailed over this first hurdle the king then squared up to the marcher lords. Harrying the despised favourite was one thing but their collective nerve failed when confronted by the royal banner. Again Lancaster remained aloof, as though none of this concerned him. His turn was next. Isolated by his own hubris the earl soon found himself confronting a royal army. With the opportunity for concerted action gone, Lancaster had few friends left to call upon. The forces he could muster, however were still formidable and the two hosts scrimmaged around Burton on Trent before the Lancastrians began to retreat north, almost certainly to seek sanctuary in Scotland.

In this they had not reckoned with Andrew de Harcla. Well advised by his own spies and raising a force of marchers from Cumberland and Westmorland, he executed a forced march to cut off the rebel's retreat at Boroughbridge. On 16th March Lancaster and Hereford found the bridge and crossing held against them. The tactics of this relatively small encounter are extremely interesting in that this was, as Sir Charles Oman points out: 'The first conscious attempt on the English side to use dismounted men at arms combined with archers may be Andrew Harcla's petty victory over the Lancastrian rebels at Boroughbridge in 1322 when we are told that he dismounted all his cavalry "in the Scottish fashion" to assist his archers to hold a bridge and a ford.'[6]

In terms of scale the action may indeed have been a small one but de Harcla did win a signal victory. Hereford with Clifford assailed the bridge head on whilst Lancaster attempted the ford. Both attacks were seen off with loss. Hereford, in attempting to rally his followers recoiling from the fight on the bridge, was mortally wounded by an ungentlemanly thrust from below and with his demise the heart went out of the Lancastrians. Foiled in their attempt to move north, the earl's army evaporated during the course of the late winter night. The next day it was de Harcla who followed up his advantage and advanced. Lancaster was forced to surrender. His subsequent condemnation and execution came as no surprise.

Edward's triumph was complete. He had isolated and mopped up all of the political opposition – executed with Lancaster at Pontefract were Clifford, Mowbray and a score of lesser fry, while perhaps a hundred others were quietly done to death or forced into exile. At York the Ordinances were finally annulled. The Despensers now came into their own, father and son competing in ruthless rapacity. Both were universally loathed: 'For the brutal and greedy father had in the past wronged many; and promoted the excommunication of many: As a justice of the forest he had accused many from poaching from royal hunting grounds, many of these he vilely disinherited, some he forced into exile, from many he extorted unjust sums of money; and collected a thousand librates[7] of land by means of threats. ... By a general judgement he justly lost what he had accumulated from the losses of others.'[8]

King Robert I might now appear secure in his hold over Scotland (John Baliol had finally died in genteel exile in 1313), but he was aware that without formal recognition by the crown of England his victories could still be reversed. After the defeat at Bannockburn Edward II had spent a fortnight at Newcastle, from where he sought to call up Henry of Lancaster (the earl's brother) and other magnates to restore his shattered army. He then fell back upon York where Pembroke was appointed as captain of all royal forces north of the Trent. The earl was given wide powers, but in practical terms there was little he could hope to achieve.

By then the Scottish army was already ranging through the marches virtually at will. Northumberland was wasted as far south as the Tyne and the raiders crossed at Newburn to enter the Palatinate, compelling the terrified citizenry to buy a further truce. In the west de Harcla was able to organise some resistance and clashed with the Scots at Reycross on or around 4th August.[9] In November he struck back at Dumfries but these were isolated beacons in a sea of passivity. Already starved by earlier incursions the Northumbrians had neither the resources nor the will to resist. For many the only remaining option was permanent flight and these savage years witnessed a diaspora particularly from the hard-hit upland dales.

Durham, richer, more populous and further from the wild border, fared marginally better, being able to purchase truces. The years after Bannockburn witnessed a dramatic increase in long-distance Scottish raids, the flying columns moving through the northern counties effectively unopposed, extorting cash and ransoms, destroying crops and lifting livestock. Nothing was beneath the raiders' consideration – books, vestments, bed linen, pots and pans, iron, always scarce in Scotland, was much prized.[10] In tandem with this policy of extended chevauchees was the pressure exerted on the two key bastions of Berwick and Carlisle and the additional gambit of Edward Bruce's campaigns in Ireland.

Though the Scots were to enjoy an unchallenged military supremacy in the north which endured up until the peace of 1328, their efforts against Carlisle were doomed to failure. Berwick fell in 1318, but in the same year Edward Bruce suffered disaster at Faughart in Ireland.

A raid which extended as far south as Furness in Lancashire in 1316 was counted as a great success because it yielded a substantial haul of the precious iron. The policy of 'frightfulness', of deliberate and thorough destruction, was so completely pursued that in addition to burning crops and cutting down fruit trees even the rabbit warrens at Bamburgh were systematically dug up.[11]

The form of hobiler warfare which Bruce had developed was ideally suited to the role. The raids tended to follow similar patterns, a wide U-shaped swathe cutting first through the English east march, down through Northumberland into Durham before swinging westwards along the river valleys and over the Pennines into the west. The wilder ground here suited an army which would by now be replete with loot and facilitated a less risky route home through Westmorland and Cumberland.

On the march the army might be split into several marching columns. Randolph and Douglas were King Robert's most indefatigable captains. Fortified places were generally avoided, as was any general engagement; this was war fought for politics and economy, not for glory. The Hainault chronicler Jean de Bel has left a vivid description of the Scots as they appeared in the field, dating from the time of the Weardale campaign of 1327:

. . . one and all are on horseback, except for the camp followers
('le ribaudaille') who are on foot, that is to say the knights and squires
are mounted on great runcies, and the other folk of the country are all
on little hackneys. And they do not bring wheeled vehicles, because of the
various mountains through which they pass in this country.[12]

It was obvious that after the fall of Stirling, Berwick would be the Scots'
next major objective and in anticipation of an attack the town's defences
were overhauled in both July and December 1314. The walls and wooden
palisades were pointed and repaired, timber outworks including a barbican
were added, the whole entailing an expenditure of some £270.[13] The
mood of the garrison was fragile, verging on paranoia.[14] Conditions were
exacerbated by poor harvests and deteriorating weather, the spectre of
famine adding to the townspeople's fears.

As Bruce had earlier threatened, all those who had held cross-border
estates lost their lands (this included Bruce himself who had forfeited
manors in Cleveland). The Umfravilles were now no longer earls of Angus
or Baliols lords of Galloway; Dirleton, previously held by the Vaux family
from Gilsland, was also sequestered. The Umfravilles were lords of Redesdale
and proved energetic in its defence, but the neighbouring upland valley of
Tynedale, an ancient liberty, administered by the King of England since
1296, had previously been enfeoffed to the Scottish crown and, faced with
the pressure of constant inroads, the inhabitants now tended to revert:

At this time the people of North Tynedale, deserting the king of
England and his faith, gave themselves up completely to the king of
Scotland. They treated their neighbours the Northumbrians inhumanely,
carrying off their goods and taking them away as captives. The women
too went riding in warlike manner, stealing the goods which their men
did not care about, such as shorn wool and linen and carried them
off.[15]

The creation of a caste of professional march warriors charged with local
defence did not always bode well for the inhabitants. The folk of Bamburgh
complained that, having purchased an expensive truce from the Scots under
Randolph, they found the castellan demanding an equal fee, plus he was
happy to charge them for storage of their goods within the castle walls![16]

When Parliament met at York following the king's withdrawal from Newcastle, the question of ransoms was naturally high in the order of business. Bruce may have made overtures for a permanent peace; if so, they were rebuffed. Edward was perhaps less shaken by the disaster at Bannockburn than might be imagined. True, his army had been roundly thrashed, but the overall balance of power in terms of military resources still lay with England, even though Edward's difficulties with his magnates implied that these would be uncommonly difficult to harness. The Earl of Hereford was the Scots' most valuable prize, one of the greatest English magnates and the king's brother-in-law. His release was negotiated in exchange for the ladies of Bruce's family, Bishop Wishart and Donald, Earl of Mar.[17] King Robert also courteously returned the royal seal which had been overlooked in the rout.

Bruce now held a parliament at Cambuskenneth where the lands of those who had fallen in arms against the crown were escheated. Others who were willing to submit, including Patrick Dunbar, the Earl of March and Ingram Umfraville, were permitted to swear the oath of allegiance. John Comyn, Earl of Buchan, the king's inveterate foe, had died in 1308 with no male issue. One of his co-heiresses had married Henry Beaumont who thus gained a claim to the earldom, even though the lands were sequestered by the crown. Beaumont and others who were similarly deprived, the 'disinherited', would return to haunt the kingdom in the years after King Robert's death.

Death was a subject much on the king's mind during the early months of 1315. Apart from his daughter Marjorie, now married to the Steward[18], the king had no legitimate male heir. For a monarch whose throne had been so precarious since 1306 and who was still at war with England, this was a matter of the utmost gravity. The council which met in April to consider the situation determined that Edward Bruce would be heir apparent, the throne entailed in his favour until a male heir was born. Should he predecease and a minor be left as king on Robert's death (as proved to be the case), then Randolph should stand as Guardian.

The English did succeed in recapturing the Isle of Man in February; otherwise the military initiative lay completely with the Scots. Although he failed in his bid to take Carlisle, Bruce was able to grant lands in Cumberland to his adherents and this must be taken to imply a degree of control. In the reign of David I the Scots had envisaged a pale that stretched as far south as the Tees in the east and perhaps to Morecambe bay in the west. Bruce could hope to make that a reality.

On 20th January 1315 the truce which the burgesses of Durham had purchased from Randolph was due to expire. At this time the king's lieutenant north of the Trent was John de Eure and it may have been he who facilitated crisis talks at York where the leading clergy and magnates met to consider the defence of the northern frontier. The delegates resolved upon the appointment of four northern lords as captains of the marches with power to raise local forces. An appeal for assistance was dispatched to King Edward but met with no effective response. It was suggested that the locally raised militias could be funded by a form of local tax – this in an area already denuded of wealth by the Scottish inroads. Whilst the debate continued, the Scots harried the length of Tynedale almost to the gates of Newcastle.

In June it was the turn of the Palatinate:

In the year [1312] *Sir Robert Bruce came into the Bishopric of Durham with a great army and so secretly had he come that he found people sleeping soundly in their beds. He sent Sir James Douglas to the district of Hartlepool with many armed men while he himself remained in the vill of Chester* [le Street]. *Sir James despoiled the said town and he lead back as captives many burgesses and many women. Having collected much booty from the whole countryside they all returned to their own country.*[19]

Hartlepool was most likely targeted because it was a handy naval base for operations against Scottish privateers and perhaps because the residents had refused to recognise Bruce as their lord, the manor having previously been in his ownership.

In spite of the thoroughness with which Durham was 'taken up', this raid was a mere diversion. Carlisle remained the prime objective. As a response to the attack on Durham, Pembroke was, on 5th July, appointed to command the northern shires and together with Bartholemew Badlesmere began to concentrate a contract army at York. By this time the Scots were before the beleaguered walls of Carlisle, though confounded by de Harcla's and the inhabitants' spirited defence. By the time Pembroke was approaching the city the Scots had withdrawn and the earl joined with the castellan in the pursuit. By 21st August Pembroke was back in Newcastle from where he planned an attack on the Merse in September – in the event he did not advance beyond Berwick and, with his tenure of office now expired, he handed over his lieutenancy to Henry Beaumont.

In the late summer King Edward was making what appeared to have been genuine efforts to base himself in the north for a major 'push' against the Scots in the autumn, acting on the advice of his most seasoned councillors of the calibre of Warenne and Hereford. These good intentions foundered on the grim realities of the king's previous failures and his lack of resources (Pembroke's contract army had consumed most of the parliamentary subsidies), the weakened state of the northern shires exacerbated by the effects of famine.

The Irish intervention which began in May 1315 and ended with the death of Edward Bruce in October 1318 eased the pressure on northern England. For the Scots it was a major logistical exercise to fight on two fronts simultaneously and the periods of intense activity over the Irish Sea afforded corresponding relief to the marchers.

> *The Earl of Carrick, Sir Edward*
> *Who was braver than a leopard*
> *Thought that Scotland was too small*
> *For himself and his brother both*
> *And therefore to one and all announced*
> *That he of Ireland would be king.*[20]

The presence of Edward Bruce in Ireland was 'to leave its mark on the country for generations'.[21] The bitter and destructive campaigns waged by the Scots ultimately achieved nothing other than to pile more death and destruction on a land already ravaged by famine and feud. The objectives of this intervention may have comprised the following: the opening up of a second front in the Irish Sea would put further pressure on the English and could result in the western seaboard becoming a Scottish 'lake'. Carlisle, that vital fortress, the gateway to the west, could be dramatically weakened and isolated if its supply route from Ireland was severed.

The taking of Man by John of Argyll in February 1315 and the suspicion that a major attack from Ireland might be launched that summer could imply the descent upon Ireland was, at least in part, a pre-emptive strike. The Scots' capability was bolstered by a substantial army shipment from Flanders which docked on 18th February.

More cynically, Edward Bruce was removed from affairs in Scotland – his volatile personality could be channelled into the Irish adventure, thus reducing the risk of civil strife at home. The chronicler Fordun makes some telling observations on the character and temperament of the king's younger sibling: 'The cause of this [Irish] war was this. Edward was a very mettle-some and high spirited man, and would not dwell together with his brother in peace unless he had half the kingdom for himself, and for this reason war was stirred up in Ireland.'[22]

There is also the romantic notion of Bruce's appeal to notions of pan-Celtic brotherhood, a rising of the Gael against the tyranny of the Anglo-Saxon. Whilst such an approach might have a propagandist value, it was scarcely sustainable. Bruce, like most Scottish magnates, was Anglo-Norman, the Red Earl was his father-in-law. Nonetheless, the king was sup-ported by the clans of the north-west and the manifesto he issued makes a strong claim to a common cause with the native Irish:

> *Since each Christian man is obliged to assist his neighbour in every difficulty, so also should those who proceed from a common root, who share the same race, ancestors, and country of origin. On that account we have now and for a long time been overwhelmed by sympathy with you in your servitude and oppression. Affronted by the vexations of the English, we are bound to attend to your plight, and with the help of the Most High, to expel from the borders of your land with all force the unnatural and barbaric servitude imposed by the English, so that, as from earliest times, the Albanic and British people having expelled their enemies, should become one in perpetuity.*[23]

Edward Bruce could command a force of 5,000–6,000 picked veterans, a formidable instrument of war. The expedition was ferried in a fleet of swift Hebridean galleys and undoubtably included a number of 'galloglas'[24] from the Isles. Randolph, John Soules and Philip Moubray all accompan-ied the army, whose first objective was mighty Carrickfergus castle, under siege by 22nd July. About the same time as Bruce was investing Carlisle, Domnall O'Neill, the king of Tyrone, offered Edward Bruce the vacant title of High King. The Scots failed before the walls of Carlisle and made little initial headway against Carrickfergus which resisted stoutly. Their lack of expertise in siege warfare was a major handicap and one which went some way to seriously offset their prowess in the field.

The first Anglo-Irish army sent against him, drawn mainly from Connacht, was cleverly confounded when Bruce nimbly played off some of the
various contending factions. These divisions were to plague the native Irish
for years to come but the Red Earl, leading the Anglo-Irish, was scattered
at Connor in Antrim. Bruce then marched south to defeat Roger Mortimer
in battle at Kells in Meath. Wherever the armies marched, wholesale
despoilation followed: 'Theft, famine and destruction of men occurred
throughout Ireland for the space of three years and a half, and people used
actually to eat one another throughout Ireland.'[25]

In 1316 the Scots Irish secured another victory near Athy in Kildare
and, at Dundalk, Edward was enthroned as High King. To consolidate his
brother's successes King Robert brought a second force over early the next
year, mainly comprising more galloglas from the Western Isles. By 1317
the brothers' army was able to make a demonstration against Dublin,
the seat of English lordship, marching as far south as Limerick before
retreating north. These chevauchees not only spread devastation through a
starving and divided land but sowed a whole plague of local feuds in their
wake. The O'Donnells beat up Sligo whilst the O'Moores, O'Tooles,
O'Byrnes and O'Hanlons fought it out in Leinster. In southern Ulster
the local warlord, Felim O'Connor, king of Connacht, turned against the
Anglo Normans but was crushed by William de Burgh and Richard de
Bermingham at Athenry in August 1316.[26]

By 1318 Edward Bruce's campaign was rapidly running out of steam,
the land exhausted by the ceaseless strife and wholesale destruction that
followed the Scots–Irish like a pestilence. With perhaps no more than
2,000 men, supported by the de Lacys, enemies of Roger Mortimer, Bruce
again marched south. Richard de Clare the Lord Lieutenant of Ireland,
with a vastly superior force, confronted him at Faughart, just north of
Dundalk. Though his captains urged caution in the face of such odds
Bruce would not countenance withdrawal. Like a punch-drunk fighter who
doesn't see it's time to quit the ring, Bruce attacked. The Scots fought
hard and well but the end was never really in doubt and Edward Bruce fell
amongst the wrack of his army.

Berwick upon Tweed was the other crucible of war. The Scots had
established an effective naval blockade which sealed off the harbour. With
the port out of action, supplies had to be diverted to Newcastle and
then carried overland. In the cold January of 1316 the Scots mounted a

combined attack from land and sea under the cover of the winter's night. A providential moon broke through the clouds at the critical moment and gave the game away, and the assault was beaten off.

On 14th February the Gascon knight Raymond de Caillen led a sortie, contrary to the express orders of Maurice Berkeley, the castellan. The raiders were intercepted by the indefatigable Douglas at Skaithmuir near Coldstream and a sharp action ensued. The enthusiastic de Caillen fell by Douglas' hand; a score of men at arms and three times as many foot were also killed. A second commanded party under Robert Neville who sallied out to relieve the first were also cut up and Neville too was slain.[27]

For the demoralised garrison the situation soon became critical. Relationships with the townspeople were strained to breaking point, desertion was rife and starvation imminent. A truce of sorts was negotiated to hold until Whitsun but the Scots would not relinquish the pressure on the beleaguered town. With the concord between King Edward and the Earl of Lancaster now enjoying its brief flowering, plans were made for a full feudal muster, the numbers available to be augmented by a demand on the vills that each should supply and victual one soldier for a period of sixty days. These plans were frustrated by an outbreak of fresh disturbances in Wales.

In June King Robert mustered his own forces around Duns. On the 24th of that month the Scots struck through the wasted manors of Tynedale and down into Durham. The gentry of North Yorkshire, sheltering behind Richmond's formidable ramparts, were quick to buy a truce so the raiders moved westward by Swaledale to Furness where they lifted a quantity of iron. Any effective riposte was frustrated by an unhelpful row which erupted between King Edward and Thomas of Lancaster. The latter retired to his own strength at Pontefract, leaving the king to salvage what he could from any hopes of a campaign. A muster was planned at Newcastle for 6th October but fresh discord broke out over a disputed succession when the Prince Bishop died. Henry Beaumont was pushing for his own brother Louis to follow the late Bishop Kellawe – so bitter was the wrangling that the matter was decided only by papal intervention.

The autumn campaign therefore never took place. Instead truce negotiations were entered into. By now King Robert, together with Randolph, was enmeshed in his brother's Irish adventure, leaving Douglas and the

Steward as Guardians. With Scots' attentions thus divided it was possible to negotiate a ceasefire to hold until the following summer. Over the winter, matters in the north were left in the hands of the Earl of Arundel who was able to supplement the garrison outposts with a mobile field force, raised under contract and including nearly five hundred hobilers.[28]

Arundel proposed to keep his men's ardour sharp with a series of punitive raids, the first of which was aimed at beating up the area of Jedwood Forest. The raiders crossed over the high neck of Carter Bar. So thorough were the preparations that Douglas, in residence at his manor of Lintilee, was initially caught off guard. Never one to shirk a fight the Douglas mustered such men as he had available and struck at the English van under Thomas de Richmond, killing the knight and besting his men. Returning to Lintilee the Guardian discovered a company of English foragers making free at his table. These unbidden guests were soon dealt with and Arundel, perturbed by his losses, withdrew.

Undeterred by this reverse the resilient earl next planned a naval expedition against Fife. A squadron of five ships sailed from the Humber carrying men at arms who, on making landfall on the banks of the Forth, frightened off a local militia led by the sheriff, then proceeded to loot and burn at will. The timorous official, in full flight, ran into a commanded party led by the Bishop of Dunkeld. The prelate was made of much sterner stuff and turned the locals around to join in his attack. The English were again seen off with loss.

Events outside the British Isles now began to have an increasing influence, for in that year Pope John XXII was elected with a manifesto for a new crusade. Brokering a peace between England and Scotland was therefore very much on his agenda. He was prepared to exert pressure on Edward but also renewed Bruce's excommunication. This was no trivial matter. King Robert was a pious man in an age of religion – to be cut off from the body of Christ was an anathema and something he would naturally strive to overcome. In practical terms, however, the king was not to be diverted from his objective of taking Berwick. A lasting truce would render this unattainable and he therefore resorted to prevarication.

In the summer a brace of cardinals arrived in England. In the autumn they journeyed north, their diplomatic mission coinciding with the proposed consecration of Louis Beaumont, now secure in his appointment. The combined party comprising the two papal envoys and both Beaumont brothers was ambushed by a renegade knight Gilbert de Middleton[29] and his company of schalvadores and all were taken prisoner. The cardinals were robbed and manhandled but soon released whilst the Beaumonts were held for ransom at Mitford castle near Morpeth. This incident may be viewed as a simple act of brigandage, exemplifying the breakdown of law and order in the north. Alternatively subsequent writers have been tempted to see Lancaster's hand in the affair (he opposed the appointment of Louis Beaumont), and possibly also that of Robert Bruce, he being anxious to keep the cardinals from intermeddling in Scotland. The Bishop-elect and his brother were released in October. Middleton soon faced the gallows for his crimes, though he kept silent as to any encouragement he might have had in the affair.

If Bruce had somehow intended to frustrate the cardinals' mission then he was largely successful; when members of their entourage did finally locate the King of Scotland they would not address him as such. Bruce, as ever, was courteous but insistent: he would have his rank acknowledged. As for their suggestions of mediation he vacillated, intimating that the matter would have to be debated before a full council, which might not be expected to assemble before Michaelmas (29th September). The king was determined to bring Berwick under his sway before listening to terms. Again, however, the Scots could make no impression on the walls and by the end of November the siege had been abandoned.

The terms of the papal truce were pronounced by the cardinals in London; a public announcement in Scotland proved more problematic. The friar who was dispatched to complete the task had a difficult journey, being denied safe conduct and robbed. The cardinals had no option but to reiterate the sentence of excommunication against the king and place the realm under an interdict.

Dire as this was, the state of English politics denied Edward any opportunity to exploit the papal ban. Relations with Lancaster had sunk to a new low and the constant wrangling between the king and the greatest of his magnates undermined plans for a campaign. Just how close the earl had become to the Scots at this point is open to question; clearly the divide was immensely beneficial to Bruce. As the king sought to arrange a muster at York for early September, Lancaster mustered his own retainers at Pontefract and even went so far as to break down the bridges leading northward from the city. For all his belligerence the earl lacked the stomach for a full-scale rebellion and the papal envoys whom he'd escorted to York were able to broker an accord, however shaky, with the king.

If Edward had hoped that pressure from the Curia would compel Bruce to the negotiating table then he had, not for the first time, gravely underestimated his opponent. King Robert would have Berwick. In 1317 the defence of the town had been entrusted to the burgesses, largely as a cost-cutting exercise and one which might effect a reduction in the tensions between the garrison and the civil populace. By the spring of 1318 Wark, Harbottle and Berwick were all under siege.

On 2nd April Douglas led a surprise attack on the town walls by the Cow Port. It is said the Scots were assisted by one of the citizens, Peter or Sym of Spalding,[30] who was a relation of the Steward and it was he who facilitated the escalade. The Scots gained the walls and a fierce fight ensued as members of the garrison contested the ramparts and narrow streets. At length the survivors were bottled up in the castle, commanded by Roger Horsley, which continued to hold out until 11th June when finally compelled, through hunger, to capitulate. By that time both Wark and Harbottle had also surrendered. As might be expected, the English traders in Berwick were subjected to robbery, abuse and summary ejection from the town, though there was no wholesale slaughter.

From now on Bruce tended to allow offensive operations to be conducted by his captains Randolph and Douglas: both were formidable and vastly experienced. By distancing himself from a direct involvement in raids the king could deflect papal criticism and blame attacks on over-zealous subordinates. He did not, however, distance himself from Berwick. The capture of the town and castle was a major coup, marking as it did a return to the status quo of 1296. It provided the Scots with a major and secure base on the border, a vital seaport and a further boost to soaring morale. In the early months of 1319 the king was active in supervising the strengthening of the defences whilst also organising a spoiling raid against the partially finished works at Dunstanburgh.

If the loss of the Tweed frontier were not sufficient, Mitford was sold out to the Scots by a traitor and, with their rear now secure, Randolph and Douglas launched a great chevauchee down the east coast, sweeping through Northumberland and west Durham as far as Barnard Castle and the Tees. It is possible that this destructive sweep through Durham was intended to instruct the new Bishop Louis Beaumont in the wisdom of buying truces.

Beaumont was of a more aggressive temperament than his predecessor and the Scots perhaps reckoned that a mite more terror was required.[31] The raiders then made for Ripon by way of Richmond, a commanded party 'took up' Wensleydale before meting out similar treatment to Hartlepool. Both columns then marched south, converging on Knaresborough.

It is unlikely that the town was selected at random. The garrison had, in the wake of Middleton's rising, turned against the king and royal forces laid siege to the place from October 1317 to the following January. It is highly probable that the Scots might have expected a 'friendly' garrison. In this they would have been disappointed, but the town was thoroughly taken up and razed before the Scots marched westward to cross the Pennines via Airedale, Ribblesdale and Wharfedale prior to turning north, replete with loot.

It was the fall of Berwick which drove Edward to seek a further accommodation with Lancaster and which then led directly to the accord of Leake. Harvests had improved and the loss, desperate as this might be, was compensated in part by the news of Edward Bruce's defeat and death in Ireland and the recapture of Carrickfergus Castle. In 1319 therefore the king determined on a major campaign to recover Berwick. A muster of 24,296 foot was proposed, though barely a third of this ambitious total actually served.[32] Lancaster contributed half a thousand and Edward was able to call upon perhaps 1,400 horse, victualled by a fleet of seventy-seven ships. Harcla's marchers were employed to hold the remaining border garrisons. The recapture of Berwick would obviously help to restore local morale, it would re-establish the defensive line on the Tweed and perhaps draw the Scots out to fight.

Once the walls were invested and the engines in place an amphibious assault was launched under the cover of an artillery bombardment, but King Robert's refurbished defences stood the test. The number of engines was increased to boost the effect of the artillery and fresh attacks launched. There was desperate and sustained fighting along the landward flank of the walls and the outworks changed hands several times, but still the defences held.

Despite the potency of the threat to Berwick, Bruce was reluctant to accept the hazard of battle and sought to relieve pressure on the garrison by once again launching Douglas and Randolph against the eastern counties. By 3rd September the Scots had pushed into North Yorkshire. It has been suggested that they were seeking to capture Queen Isabella, then at York. This does seem a mite fanciful but several of the chronicles agree that this was the Scots' objective; '... indeed if the Queen had at that time been captured I believe Scotland would have bought peace for herself.'[33]

It was said that a spy in York betrayed the plan to Archbishop Melton and also offered to reveal the location of the Scottish camp. The queen was packed off to safety in Nottingham and the archbishop, perhaps recalling the glorious episode of the battle of the Standard at Northallerton in 1138, prepared to lead local forces against the raiders. As the majority of able-bodied men liable to muster had already marched to the siege of Berwick, Melton pulled together a scratch force of what remained. This motley assembly advanced upon the Scots, who were encamped at Myton some three miles east of Boroughbridge on the banks of the Swale, near its confluence with the Ouse.

It is highly unlikely the Scots could be taken by surprise and they deployed in schiltrom formation, setting fire to nearby haystacks to confuse the attackers. As the archbishop's force stumbled forward the raiders bellowed out their fearsome war cries and tramped towards them. It was enough: the citizens bolted, allowing the Scots to mount up for the pursuit. The 'Chapter of Myton', so called because so many ecclesiastics fell in the rout, was a complete disaster. The mayor of York was amongst the dead and many prisoners were taken, several of them members of the Royal Household, including the notary Andrew Tang.[34]

Having decimated the archbishop's rag-tag army the Scots advanced to Castleford before, in their by now habitual manner, swinging westward through Airedale and Wharfedale. The raiders seem to have split into two marching columns and entered Lancashire by differing routes, some moving through Lonsdale others along the Greta Valley. At 'Gratirhals' this second party was ambushed: 'In returning homewards through western parts of England, they were set upon by a throng of Englishmen at Gratirhals, a very narrow pass. But the Scots prevailed and the English were scattered, and many were killed, including Sir Henry Fitzhugh, and they returned with great rejoicing to their own country taking many knights and squires with them.'[35]

Henry Fitzhugh held Bowes Castle from John of Brittany as Earl of Richmond and whilst there are two rivers of this name the Greta in this context most likely refers to that which flows into the Tees.[36]

News of the disaster at Myton brought confusion to the siege lines around Berwick. The southern barons were all for ignoring the defeat and maintaining the pressure, the northerners favoured abandoning the siege, fearful of further Scottish inroads. Lancaster decided the day by withdrawing, which effectively brought the leaguer to an end. The English had barely been ten days before the walls, from 8th–18th September. The earl's indecent haste to abandon the siege lines inevitably raised fresh doubts as to his loyalties. The king withdrew the remainder of his forces to York to consider how best to protect the marches. Whilst these deliberations continued, Randolph and Douglas struck again.

On All Saints Day (1st November) the Scots crossed into the middle march over Gilsland Waste. In a dozen days of mayhem they penetrated as far south as Brough on Stainmore, garnering a haul of beasts and ransoms as they took up Cumberland on the return journey.

Despite their string of successes and the retention of Berwick, the Scots were as much in need of a respite as were the battered English. Edward had exhausted his treasury with nothing but fresh humiliations to show and Bruce, having secured Berwick, needed time to mend his relations with the papacy. On 12th October safe conducts were issued to a dozen Scottish negotiators to attend at Newcastle where, on 22nd December, the terms of a two-year cessation were agreed. Not unsurprisingly in the circumstance, the terms favoured the Scots. Harbottle was returned but only on condition that the defences would be slighted and custody given back to the Scots if a permanent peace could not be agreed on the expiry of the current truce.

Negotiations with Rome were more difficult. The king's failure to recognise the papal truce was viewed as a most serious dereliction. Bruce together with his bishops were summoned to the Curia to explain themselves. They did not attend but letters were sent by the king, the leading clergy and the nobility. The submission offered by the magnates contained a precise summary of reasons why the Scots should be free of English rule. It was clear, concise, yet heavy with heartfelt emotion. It became known as the Declaration of Arbroath and the simple grandeur of the language has rung down through the ages:

For so long as a hundred of us remain alive, we will never in any way
be bowed beneath the yoke of English domination; for it is not for glory,

riches or honour that we fight, but for freedom alone, that which no man of worth yields up, save with his life.[37]

The passionate eloquence of this correspondence produced the desired effect. His Holiness was minded to refrain from further interdict against the Scots and urge both sides towards mediation. Notwithstanding the spirit of unity underlying the Declaration of Arbroath, within a few months of its submission a handful of the signatories were plotting King Robert's downfall. These were William Soules, Edward Moubray, David Brechin, Patrick Graham and Eustace Maxwell. Bruce was to be supplanted by Edward Baliol, the son of Toom Tabard.

After the death of Edward Bruce the king had drawn up a fresh entail or tailzie in favour of his son-in-law, the Steward, but without a male heir he remained vulnerable. At the 'Black' Parliament held at Scone in August 1320, the conspirators were exposed. Several of the ringleaders suffered the full ghastly fate of the traitor, a barbarity rarely practised in Scotland. Maxwell was cleared of complicity but Soules and his aunt, who was also implicated, received a sentence of life imprisonment. Moubray had already died, but in a grotesque parody his corpse was disinterred and condemned. Ingram Umfraville was tainted with suspicion but wisely absented himself from the realm – he never returned.

The truce which held from November 1319 until January 1322 served the interests of both sides. It empowered Bruce to rebuild his forces after the losses sustained in Ireland whilst it also permitted Edward II to deal with the baronial opposition. Negotiations were conducted at Bamburgh; John of Brittany appeared for the English side as Pembroke was detained in France with the support of Bartholemew Badlesmere and the bishops of Worcester and Carlisle. William Soules, as yet free of the stain of treachery, and Alexander Seton deputised for Bruce. The debate ranged over the historic issues, the English harking back to Baliol's homage. Nothing was finalised, though there was the suggestion of an extended truce to endure for twenty-six years.

When matters with Lancaster 'hotted up' in the early part of 1322 the Scots struck, almost certainly in support of the rebels. It is alleged treasonable correspondence confirming the collusion was discovered on Hereford's corpse after the fight at Boroughbridge, though there has to be a question of whether this was genuine.[38] Durham was targeted from the

15th–30th January; so savage was the taking up that the episode earned the epithet of 'the Burning of the Bishopric'.[39] It may be that this was intended to proclaim Scots' support for the rebels whilst chastising Louis Beaumont for his defiance. Whilst Bruce ravaged the area of south Durham around Darlington, Douglas paid another visit to Hartlepool and the Steward terrorised Richmondshire.

In order to march against Lancaster Harcla had been constrained to negotiate a local truce in the west. Having won the battle against the rebels he met Edward II at Gloucester with a request that the king take action on the marches. Edward advised that this would not be feasible until after Michaelmas, though Harcla was greeted with the title of Earl of Carlisle in recognition of his good service against the late rebels.

A muster at Newcastle was proposed for 13th June, soon deferred until 24th July. The numbers the king intended to raise were, at least on paper, impressive.[40] Recruits were drawn from east and west, from Wales and Ireland. The largest contingent was to assemble at Newcastle, with a lesser muster at Carlisle and substantial detachments from Ulster. This was to be a conventional campaign of heavy and light horse with a host of foot and archers, victualled at least in part by the fleet. Edward had not learnt the lessons of hobiler warfare. The Scots would be bound to adopt fabian tactics, wasting the land before the invaders and avoiding battle, the great host made vulnerable by the sheer weight of its logistical 'tail'.

With the lighter and infinitely more mobile forces under his command Bruce struck first, crossing into the English west march in mid-June, the raiders adopting their customary two-column formation, the first led by the king in person, the other by the well-tried partnership of Randolph and Douglas:

> *Robert de Brus invaded England with an army by way of Carlisle in the week before the Nativity of St John the Baptist* [around 17th June] *and burnt the bishop's manor at Rose, and Allerdale and plundered the monastery of Holm Cultram, notwithstanding that his father's body was buried there; and thence proceeded to lay waste and plunder Copeland, and so on beyond the sands of Duddon to Furness.*[41]

Lancaster was razed by the king's column. When the second detachment came up the army went on to destroy Preston[42] before retracing their route back to Scotland. By 24th July the raiders were safe home, unmolested by English forces, despite having lingered for five days in the vicinity of Carlisle, vigorously applying spear and torch.

It was not until 12th August that Edward's host marched into the Merse. By the 19th Musselburgh had been left in flames but the army was already beset by supply problems. The previous year's harvest had been insufficient and extra supplies of grain had to be imported by sea from Gascony, the lumbering, fat-bellied cogs at the mercy of Scots and Flemish privateers.

Two days later the English marched into Leith. Still the Scots would not commit to battle, but hunger, demoralisation and dysentry thinned the ranks just as effectively. A commanded party which descended on Melrose was intercepted and seen off by Douglas and, by 2nd September, the English army was withdrawn south of the border. All in all the campaign had been a very expensive fiasco.

The army was a hugely expensive beast to feed and maintain. Edward, having spent all available monies, had no choice but to disband his forces, retaining only the knights of the Household, including the younger Despenser. The king found time to vent his frustrations on the castellans of the major east march holds, Bamburgh, Warkworth, Alnwick, and Dunstanburgh, lambasting each for the poor state of their works and the inertia of the garrisons. Scapegoating the individual officers was a shoddy attempt to shift the blame for the parlous state of the region's defences. Conventional garrisons behind castle walls were no answer to hobiler warfare; the whole thrust of Bruce's strategy was to avoid attacking fixed defensive positions.

Even Louis Beaumont, the Bishop of Durham, did not escape censure, being rebuked for neglecting Norham. The Prince Bishop's northerly bastion was, in the event, soon put to the test for, by 17th September, the Scots appeared before the walls.[43] This was, however, nothing more than a feint, intended, in all probability, to draw such royal forces as the king commanded into north Northumberland. The main blow fell, once again, in the west. On 30th September Bruce led his army back over the Solway at Bowness and the Scots spent a further five days taking up the lands around Carlisle, doubtless accounting for what little they'd missed in July.

The redoubtable Harcla was, unusually, caught offguard – he had disbanded his western army and the speed of the Scots' attack left him no time to regroup: he was constrained to fall back into Lancashire where he sought to raise fresh forces. The west was spared further wasting, however, for King Robert's objective was not mere plunder but to capture the person of Edward II. A bold plan, but carefully conceived and cunningly executed. The Scots now reversed their habitual pattern and came on eastwards over the Pennines. The clearly excellent spy network which Bruce maintained had informed him of the English king's whereabouts and the paucity of forces under his command.

Edward II was heading south from Barnard Castle when, on 2nd October, he learnt of this fresh incursion. Orders were immediately sent to Harcla and numerous other northern magnates to join a muster of North Yorkshire levies at a moorland location, known as 'Blakehoumoor' near Byland. The rather optimistic intention was that the barons would raise a conscription of all able-bodied males between sixteen and sixty. The king was much angered when Harcla failed to appear. Whether this was due to intentional tardiness or, as was quite likely, the difficulties the earl experienced in recruiting, he did however, succeed in finding recruits in Lancashire: 'This he did, having taken command of the county of Lancaster so that he had 30,000 men ready for battle; and since the Scots were in the eastern march, he brought his forces by western parts to reach the king.'[44]

Whilst he waited for the magnates to come in, the king established his headquarters at Byland Abbey where, on 12th October, he received the unwelcome news that the Scots were across the Pennines. In the immediate vicinity he had only Pembroke, Richmond (John of Brittany) and John de Birmingham with their retinues. The royal forces fell back towards Rievaulx with a view to mustering on Blakehoumoor. Randolph's division were already at Northallerton and Edward faced the very real prospect of being caught between the earl and King Robert who was marching to cut off his retreat.

Blakehoumoor has been identified as Scawton Moor, an area of high ground overlooking Sutton Bank and Roulston Scar.[45] Edward sent a most urgent summons to Pembroke, Richmond and Beaumont 'to attend with all possible power'.[46] Randolph was by now barely fifteen miles distant at Malton whilst Bruce's brigade were storming through the Vale of York. The English, completely outgeneralled, took up the best position they could along the summit of the ridge. The ground favoured the defenders in that the direct access to the higher ground was through a narrow approach.

Randolph and Douglas led the van against the pass which was hotly contended whilst the king sent his nimble Gallowegians to outflank the defenders on the ridge. Richmond, his meagre forces drawn up by Coxwold and Old Bylande, held on for as long as possible, allowing his king, 'being ever chicken hearted and luckless in war',[47] time to make good his escape before he and the other survivors, including the French knight Henry de Sully, surrendered to the Scots.[48] The field thus yielded a fine crop of prisoners (Richmond and Robert I were longstanding enemies and the earl was not ransomed for two years) and an even finer haul of loot: for the second time all of King Edward's baggage and papers fell into the King of Scots' hands.

This was to be Bruce's last battlefield command and though he had won another sparkling victory and further humiliated Edward II, the raid failed in its main objective which was to capture the English king. As a result the war was to drag on for several more weary years. Edward was chased to the gates of Bridlington from there, more sedately, he was able to progress to York. Here, belatedly, he was joined by Harcla who suffered the full range of royal fury for his laggardly advance.

Having thoroughly beaten up the East Riding, the Scots, loaded with prisoners and spoil, recrossed the border early in November:

> And syne with presoneris and catell
> Riches and mony fayr jowell
> To Scotland tuk thai hame thar way
> Bath blyth and glaid joyfull and gay . . .
> That thai the king off Ingland
> Discumfyt in his awne countre.[49]

Notes

1 Quoted in McNamee, C., *Wars of the Bruces*, East Lothian 1997 p. 72.

2 Prestwich, M., *The Three Edwards*, London 1980 p. 86.

3 The Mortimers were powerful marcher lords. The grandfather of Roger Mortimer had been a steadfast adherent of Henry III in the course of the Barons War, had assisted Longshanks in his escape from de Montfort's custody and had fought with distinction in the ensuing campaign and battle of Evesham. His division sealed off de Montfort's escape route over the Avon and it was said that Mortimer was responsible for the death of Despenser, a de Montfort partisan in the fight. In Edward II's reign the Despensers seem to have reserved a particu-

lar hatred for the Mortimers. See Mortimer, I., *The Greatest Traitor*, London 2003 pp. 7–8.

4 Prestwich p. 54.

5 The instrument of the king's vengeance was Queen Isabella – when Badlesmere's wife denied the haughty young queen a night's lodgings at Leeds Castle. See Mortimer pp. 111–13.

6 Oman, Sir Charles, *The Art of War in the Middle Ages*, London 1924 Vol. 2 p. 101.

7 A measurement of land holding.

8 Mortimer p. 107.

9 McNamee p. 72.

10 Ibid p. 75.

11 Ibid p. 76.

12 Quoted in McNamee p. 76.

13 Traquair, P., *Freedom's Sword*, London 1990 p. 199.

14 Two young boys who had gone to play outside the walls lost a songbook and when this could not be found both were accused of 'trafficking' with the Scots. A subsequent enquiry did however clear the two accused, one aged eleven and the other nine! See Traquair p. 199.

15 Quoted in Traquair p. 200.

16 Traquair p. 201.

17 Ibid p. 201.

18 The son born to Marjorie and the Steward would, after decades of waiting, ascend the throne as Robert II, the first of the Stewart kings. Robert I did not produce a male heir, the future David II, until 1324.

19 Quoted in McNamee p. 79.

20 Quoted in McNamee p. 166.

21 Quoted in Hayes-McCoy, G.A., *Irish Battles*, Belfast 1969 p. 39.

22 Barbour, quoted in McNamee p. 194.

23 Quoted in McNamee p. 192.

24 A galloglas was a West Highland or Hebridean mercenary who served the Irish kings or chieftains. In the fifteenth century the galloglas devolved into a distinct military elite who carried their own distinctive weapons and wore particular garb. See Marsden, J., *Galloglas*, East Linton 2003.

25 Quoted in McNamee p. 192.

26 Hayes-McCoy p. 40.

27 Traquair pp. 210–11.

28 Traquair p. 213.

29 The Middletons, a Norman family, proved resilient. They were able around 1350 to recover the Manor of Belsay by marrying the daughter of Sir John Strivelyn to whom the lands had been granted after Sir Gilbert's fall. It was he who began the construction of Belsay Castle which remains as one of the finest Northumbrian Hall Towers. The Middleton family remain at Belsay to this day.

30 McNamee p. 85.

31 Ibid p. 88.

32 Traquair p. 220.

33 Quoted in McNamee p. 91.

34 McNamee p. 94.

35 Quoted in McNamee p. 95.

36 McNamee p. 95.

37 Quoted in Traquair p. 224.

38 McNamee p. 96.

39 Ibid p. 96.

40 28,500 were to muster at Newcastle, 11,000 at Carlisle, from Ireland were expected 300 men at arms and 7,000 mixed foot and hobilers. A further 10,000 were levied from Wales. In June a further muster of an additional 10,000 foot, at the king's remuneration, were also demanded. These wildly ambitious numbers were significantly watered down by the York Parliament but the king was determined to draw forces from the southern counties. Whilst the loyalties of these might be less prone to division, their level of training, discipline and equipment was much poorer than that of their northern contemporaries. See Traquair p. 228.

41 Quoted in McNamee p. 98.

42 There was at least some attempt at resistance: in a skirmish on Hornsby Moor two Scots were captured. See McNamee p. 98.

43 It was from the course of this siege that the story of Marmion emerges, to be subsequently immortalised by Scott. The Lincolnshire knight is offered a superb new helmet by the lady he fervently admires if he will prove himself at the siege of Norham, 'the most dangerous place in England'. Compelled by chivalry Marmion joins the garrison and launches a quixotic single-handed sally against the Scots. Eventually unhorsed, he is rescued from capture by his comrades who utilise the diversion to mount a sally in force and the Scots are discomfited.

44 Quoted in McNamee p. 100.

45 McNamee p. 101.

46 Ibid p. 101.

47 Quoted in McNamee p. 101.

48 Oman p. 100.

49 Quoted in Traquair p. 230.

Chapter 6

'Nothing but
their naked bodies'

*We are bound to him for the maintaining of our freedom both by his
rights and merits, as to him by whom salvation has been wrought unto
our people, and by him, come what may, we mean to stand. Yet if he
should give up what he has begun, seeking to make us or our kingdom
subject to the King of England or to the English, we would strive
at once to drive him out as our enemy and a subverter of his own
right and ours, and we would make some other man who was able to
defend us our king.*[1]

Following an exhumation of the body of Robert Bruce in 1996 the
physical features were cleverly reconstructed to show the king's face as
it might have looked in his prime.[2] In the visitor centre at Bannockburn
there is an image of how the ageing paladin may have looked towards the
end of his life, scarred by old wounds and disfigured by the ravages of the
disease which finally may have killed him.[3] It is impossible to say how
accurate such forensic sculpture may be but it is naturally tempting to
accept the image being offered as a lifelike representation. It is a wondrous
thing to look upon the face of Scotland's greatest king.

After the rout at Byland, Bruce might have finally expected Edward II
to accept the need for a permanent settlement, but no overtures were
immediately forthcoming. Though the military honours had all gone to
the Scots and their ability to dominate the north of England was virtually,
apart from Andrew Harcla in the north-west, unchallenged, they lacked the

means to compel the English king to come to the negotiating table. King Robert's strategic objectives at this point were twofold: firstly to force Edward to recognise his status as king of Scots and secondly, to abandon and renounce all claims of overlordship.

Certain writers have gone so far as to suggest that the victory at Bannockburn was a political error, leaving the English burning to avenge the humiliation.[4] However, without the victory, Bruce and his captains would have been unable to achieve the military hegemony that ensued and to reap such handsome rewards from their terrorising of the marches.

Despite the weight of such minor successes as Mytton and Byland, the war was effectively a stalemate. The English could not bring on a general engagement that might wipe away the stain but the Scots, however deep and hard they raided, however many byres they emptied, could not seriously damage the English nation or its vibrant economy as a whole. The north might tremble mightily but not even Randolph and Douglas could extend their reach south of the Trent where the overwhelming preponderance of wealth was located. Events on the marches were of only passing interest to southerners, who saw no good reason to treat with the foe whilst he remained unchastised.

Throughout the crucial years 1314–27 the Papacy exhibited strong pro-English bias. The Gascon Clement V was unashamedly partisan and John XXII who succeeded him in 1316 viewed the Scottish question as an annoying distraction from his principal aim of promoting a pan European crusade. This naturally required the two great powers, England and France, to observe at least a degree of cordiality.

In Hugh Despenser the Younger Edward II found the perfect replacement for the murdered Gaveston. Made chamberlain in 1318 Hugh was a different proposition from the Gascon. Able, shrewd and capable, he was also vicious, ruthless and avaricious to a degree unparalleled even in an age of relentless self-advancement. One of his most cherished and oft promoted objectives was to build up his holdings in South Wales and his rapacity swiftly alienated the powerful marcher lords Hereford, Clifford and his nemesis Roger Mortimer. He even succeeded in alarming other royal favourites Audley and Damory as he sought to grab further portions of the great Gloucester inheritance.

The disturbances that, in 1322, culminated in the fight at Boroughbridge broke out in the previous year when the marchers collectively turned on Despenser and chased him out of the principality. However, as Thomas of Lancaster could easily match the king's favourite in vindictiveness, the chance to form a united opposition was lost and the king, cannily biding his time, was able to pick off his enemies piecemeal. Although Edward acceded to the marcher lords' demand in August 1321 that the younger Hugh should be exiled, the favourite's sojourn abroad was shortlived.

Having mopped up the fragmented opposition, beginning with Badlesmere and finishing with Lancaster, cowing the marcher lords in between, the king's position seemed, by the summer of 1322, to be inexpungable. The redoubtable Earl of Pembroke died two years later,[5] thus removing the last advocate of moderation. Between 1322 and his fall in 1326 the younger Despenser obtained nearly forty landholdings and lived a lavish lifestyle funded from the public purse whilst his father, equally unscrupulous, was elevated to the earldom of Winchester.[6]

The royal coffers amply charged with the bounty from sequestered estates, the king's finances were infinitely improved. The younger Hugh's clerk, Robert Baldock, was raised to the office of chancellor, the king's half brother Thomas of Woodstock, Earl of Kent, with Arundel completed the inner circle. Any residual opposition or 'contrariants' were swiftly stamped upon.

For Hugh the younger vulnerable widows were a favoured target, Pembroke's countess being no exception. Though he was careful to remain within the bounds of the law, those bounds contained a strong element of elasticity. By 1324 Hugh had the colossal sum of £6,000 on deposit with the royal bankers, Bardi and Peruzzi.[7] Another means of cash generation was to bully others into admitting fictitious debts and oblige them to pay up. Despite such reprehensible conduct, the younger Hugh was a skilled and innovative administrator who overhauled the operation of both Household and Exchequer. These reforms were motivated by mercenary rather than reforming instincts and did nothing to improve the government's increasing unpopularity.

One of those who had particular cause to feel aggrieved was Queen Isabella, a woman of haughtiness and spirit who found herself virtually abandoned at Tynemouth during the abortive campaign of 1322. Ignored and humiliated by her husband who was clearly more at ease with his male favourites, she was further marginalised when further trouble in Gascony flared into the War of St Sardos in 1324.[8] As a member of the Capetian line she was treated with open hostility, her lands sequestered and her French staff sacked. Edward found employment for her as his envoy sent to her native land to negotiate terms with her brother Charles IV. One of the terms of the proposed accord and upon which the French king remained insistent was that Edward should attend in person to do homage for the Aquitaine.

The king was by no means eager to comply. The Despensers feared what fresh challenge might arise if he was out of the country for any period of time. As an alternative Isabella suggested Edward should confer the Dukedom of Aquitaine upon their son, Prince Edward, who could then be sent to perform the necessary obeisance. On the face of it this seemed like an ideal compromise but neither the king nor his paramour saw the trap ahead. Once in France the lad remained firmly under his mother's control and she was forming plans of an altogether different nature. Whilst on the continent Isabella had come into contact with an influential group of exiles, prominent amongst whom was Roger Mortimer, who had man-aged a daring escape from the Tower the year before.[9] The relationship between the marcher lord and the queen blossomed into a scandalous romance and their liaison became the catalyst for a swelling opposition in exile.[10]

Edward dispatched his confederate Walter Stapledon, now bishop of Exeter, to remonstrate with his erring consort and persuade her to return. In this he was unsuccessful. Isabella demanded the removal of the Despensers as a condition precedent to any reconciliation, almost certainly in the knowledge that her besotted husband would demur. Others who crossed, ostensibly as emissaries, did so solely to join the ranks of the disaffected. The Earl of Richmond and even Kent together with the bishops of Here-ford, Winchester and Norwich all now espoused the queen's cause.

Though unable to remain in France, the exiles found a base in Hainault. The count of Hainault's daughter Philippa was espoused to Prince Edward and here they were able to recruit a battalion of mercenaries, some seven hundred strong, under John of Hainault. Edward seemed blind to the threat that was looming over the Channel, neither he nor Despenser were fools and yet when the blow fell, in 1326, both were totally unprepared. In that September the queen and Mortimer landed in Suffolk and carried all before them.

The London mob showed its affiliation by murdering the king's creature Bishop Stapledon, whilst Edward and the Despensers, father and son, fled to Wales where they might hope to find friends. In the event very few allies came forward. The elder Hugh was bottled up in Bristol, in the defence of which he was assisted by the Earl of Mar who had become the king's friend and still found England more congenial. The earl was lucky to escape from the débâcle with his life.[11] Hugh Despenser was taken and executed.

Edward and the younger Hugh were closely pursued across Wales by Isabella and John of Hainault, fearing:

> ... that if the king could reach Ireland he might collect an army there and cross over into Scotland, and by the help of the Scots and Irish together he might attack England.[12]

The fugitives took ship from Chepstow but sailed no further than Glamorgan where they fell into the hands of Henry of Lancaster, surviving brother of Earl Thomas, and both were made captive. The king was sent to safe custody at Kenilworth, while Hugh met his inevitable death at Hereford. The court which speedily convicted him pronounced the awful sentence:

> Hugh, you have been judged a traitor since you have threatened all the good people of the realm, great and small, rich and poor, and by common consent you are also a thief. As a thief you will hang, and as a traitor you will be drawn and quartered, and your quarters will be sent throughout the realm. And because you prevailed upon our lord the king, and by common consent you returned to the court without warrant, you will be beheaded. And because you were always disloyal and procured discord between our lord the king and our very honourable lady the queen, and between other people of the realm, you will be disembowelled, and then your entrails will be burnt. Go to meet your fate, traitor, tyrant, renegade; go to receive your own justice, traitor, evil man, criminal![13]

For Isabella revenge was undoubtably sweet. In a swift campaign she, with her lover Mortimer, had overthrown Edward's despised regime and destroyed the unholy pairing of the Despensers, father and son.

For the north the rout at Byland had been but another chapter in an unending history of humiliation and suffering. Although Archibald Douglas, brother to James, was taken in a skirmish in November 1322, the following spring brought fresh alarms, first in March, then again in May. The only remedy was to prepare for mass evacuation – beasts from the west march were to be driven into safer pastures in Yorkshire, the population were to abandon the countryside and seek refuge behind castle walls. The king did order the northern magnates to be ready with all the forces they could muster but there was no attack that year.

If the Middleton rebellion can be viewed as more than mere banditry, as an expression of rage and frustration at the failure of the administration to curtail the Scots, the overtures which Andrew Harcla, now Earl of Carlisle, made to King Robert might be seen as a further expression of this swelling anger. It does seem remarkably foolhardy for a single, and newly created, magnate without royal sanction to open negotiations with the enemy. These talks which were held with Bruce at Lochmaben went beyond proposals for a renewed truce. What was discussed was the basis for a lasting settlement to be binding on both realms. It appears clear that the earl did not represent himself as having any authority for his initiative and it was his intention, once suitable terms had been agreed in outline, to 'sell' the idea to king and parliament.

Two versions of the draft treaty survive. The first or 'Copenhagen' version, which differs from the second, which may be Harcla's personal copy, is slightly amended to render its consumption by the English more palatable. Perhaps the main concession was that, henceforward, both kingdoms would be separate and self-governing, each ruled by its own free prince without obligation and retaining its own laws and customs. There can be little doubt that Bruce welcomed the approach. He was now 48, and while for the moment still strong but without a male heir, unlimited time was not a commodity he possessed.

Each would, in good faith, act in the best interests of the other; a dozen arbiters, half drawn from each kingdom would hammer out the fine detail. Bruce had privily agreed with the earl that if he invaded England Harcla's lands would be spared and the earl covenanted likewise should he lead men into Scotland. If Edward II should, within one year, accept these terms then Bruce, in recognition of the lasting accord, would under-take to pay compensation in the amount of 40,000 marks (£27,000) in ten equal annual tranches for the losses incurred by the north. Furthermore, he would endow a monastery in Scotland funded by an annuity of 500 marks to offer prayer for those killed in the war. Lastly Edward would have the right to choose a wife from amongst his own immediate kin as consort for any male heir born to Bruce (provided that the arbiters deemed this arrangement beneficial).[14]

Finally, and significantly, neither monarch should be obliged to make restitution or accept into his service those lords who had previously fought against him. On this Bruce was adamant – there was no place in Scotland for the 'disinherited'. This uncompromising stance was to prove a stumbling block throughout all future negotiations and even after the conclusion of the final peace, to remain a festering sore that would erupt to bring havoc to Scotland. This class of disappointed magnates included such powerful characters as Henry Percy, David Strathbogie, Thomas Wake and, most vociferously, the formidable Henry Beaumont.

Perhaps the most remarkable aspect of these discussions, concluded on 3rd January 1323, was that the detail of the Lochmaben Treaty bears so close a resemblance to the accord reached thereafter. Harcla's initiative could be viewed as pragmatic and indeed heroic. His main weakness at home was that as a 'new' man he had made a host of enemies in the course of his meteoric rise. Had he been Percy, Mortimer or Pembroke, matters might have gone differently. But the earl's conduct was turned into the basis of a charge of treason, one which numbers of his contemporaries were only too keen to believe. His rival Anthony de Lucy led the chorus of hate and procured the earl's arrest. He was tried before Geoffrey le Scrope, Chief Justice of the King's Bench. The trial could be perceived as a triumph of jealousy over policy. The king was not prepared to entertain private overtures and Harcla went to the gallows, stripped of earldom and knighthood.

The supreme irony was that very soon after Harcla's fall, serious negotiations between the two governments were entered into. Edward appointed Walter Stapledon, Bishop of Exeter, Hugh Despenser the younger and Robert Baldock. Randolph and Lamberton appeared for the Scots, along with the French knight Henry de Sully, he who had been captured earlier at Byland. A continuing bar to any lasting accord was Edward II's refusal to recognise Robert Bruce as King of Scots, whilst the latter insisted, understandably, on a full acceptance of his regality. This nearly undid the entire peace process. Bruce wrote animatedly to de Sully to remind him:

You ought to remember well enough, sir, how it was contained in our letters sent to the King of England and also how we charged you verbally, that we desired and desire always to negotiate with the King of England aforesaid in the form of a final peace between him and ourselves, saving always to us and to our heirs our kingdom free and quit . . . on this matter we have received letters of yours and transcripts of the king's letters saying that he has granted to the people of Scotland who are at war with him a truce; and this manner of speaking is very strange to us, for, in the other truces which have been made between him and us, we have been named the principal on one hand as he has on the other, though he would not style us king . . . And do not wonder therefore that we have not agreed to this truce . . . And we send you a copy of the king's letter, for we think you cannot have seen it. And if you have seen it, it seems to us that you have treated us too lightly.[15]

No lasting accord could be agreed but a truce for thirteen years was concluded at Bishopthorpe near York on 30th May. Eight days later the draft was ratified by King Robert sitting at Berwick. If the pernicious question of sovereignty was fudged, there was agreement that all occupied territories were to be returned (this would affect the Scots' presence as *de facto* rulers of Tynedale). No new works were to be constructed in the marches as far south as the Tyne on the English side and embracing the sheriffdoms of Berwick, Roxburgh and Dumfries. Castles like Dunstanburgh, already in the course of construction, could remain. The subjects of each realm were to have no trafficking between them and neither monarch should receive the enemies of the other. Lastly Edward II undertook to employ his best endeavours to assist in procuring the lifting of the excommunication and interdict (in fact he did precisely the reverse).

As a useful beginning the truce appears entirely fair and reasonable. In England, however, it was viewed as tantamount to surrender, especially amongst the 'disinherited'. Particularly vociferous was Henry Beaumont, a member of the king's council and not one afraid to speak his mind:

And when the king enjoined each of those present, singly, including Henry, to give their advice, the said Henry, with an excessive motion and irreverent mind, answered the king frequently that he would not counsel him in his behalf. The king moved by such an answer ordered him to leave his council, and Henry, in leaving the Council said, as he had said before, that it would please him more to be absent from the council than to be present.[16]

It is harder to assess the popularity of the extended truce in Scotland. It may be that the Scots favoured a continuation of the war, as many of the magnates and countless of their affinities had grown rich on the spoils. A report to Edward II suggested that peace was by no means the preferred option for most Scots; Bruce himself confessed in correspondence that he was having difficulties in restraining his followers. For the Scots, warfare was now equated with prosperity. Merchants from the low countries continued to defy the English blockade which implies the return was worth the risk.

When, on 1st March 1324, Queen Elizabeth finally greeted her husband with a healthy male child, the impetus to discover a pathway to a lasting accord received a significant boost. The position was complicated by the breakdown in Anglo-French relations following the accession of Charles IV and the squabble in Gascony which, the following autumn, sparked the War of St Sardos. Whereas Edward might have ventured the hope the Scots would offer military aid, the dispute over Aquitaine led the Scots to believe they could add to their demands.

Renewed discussions were opened in July 1324 but now the Scots demanded a 'perambulation' of the Anglo-Scottish march. Quite what was implied by this rather enigmatic statement is by no means clear but it might be that Bruce had some idea for a Scottish pale or at least a form of 'buffer' zone. Once again the negotiations foundered over English claims to overlordship. Matters were scarcely improved when Edward II brought Edward Baliol from genteel obscurity in Picardy to a place at the English court.

If this were not sufficient evidence of bad faith, an embassy was dispatched to the Curia, headed by the Bishop of Winchester, John Stratford, later to be Archbishop of Canterbury. His brief was not only to seek the continuance of the interdict but to increase its rigour. The English now demanded no Scot should be created a bishop of the Scottish church, 'for it is the prelates of Scotland who encourage the nobility, gentry and people in their evil acts'.[17] Despite any pro-English leanings, the Pope took the view this was a sanction too far. As no Englishman could enter Scotland and no Scot become a bishop then the people would be entirely deprived of their senior clergy, an unacceptable extreme. Nonetheless, it was conceded that when appointing any Scottish bishop the bull authorising the sovereign of the realm to hand over to the appointee the temporalities of his new see should be addressed only to Edward II.[18] A significant snub to King Robert.

The news from Rome was not all bad. Late in 1323 Randolph attended the Curia and pressed, with considerable eloquence, for his master to be recognised as King of Scots. The earl's golden words carried the day and on 13th January 1324 his Holiness wrote to Edward, in terms verging on the apologetic, explaining the reasons for his decision to recognise Bruce. With England and France once again on bad terms the Scots looked towards their old ally and a team of negotiators comprising Randolph, Master James Ben (Lamberton's successor to the bishopric of St Andrews), Masters Adam Murray and Walter of Twynholm, the new chancellor who followed Abbot Bernard, were dispatched accordingly.

In April 1326 the Scottish emissaries concluded the terms of what became the Treaty of Corbeil. The main provision of the agreement was a joint undertaking for military aid should hostilities break out with England. As the War of St Sardos had so recently flared this led to an expectation in England that the Scots might attack, regardless of the truce which then obtained. Hugh of Angouleme, the papal ambassador to the English court, was one who leaned to this view. Writing to his master the Pope as early as 22nd May 1324 he advised: 'He who acts as king of Scotland has held his solemn council in a certain castle called Berwick. Although what was discussed is not known, it is generally believed that if there should be war, which God avert, Bruce will come to Charles IV's aid by every means in his power'.[19]

The Treaty of Corbeil was the resurrection of the Franco-Scots treaty of 1295 and from the Scots' perspective may be viewed as opening a window onto the European stage. Conversely it bound them to a fickle and utterly selfish ally whose entreaties led to several disastrous offensives, Neville's Cross, 1346 and Flodden in 1513 being prime examples. One of the terms of the treaty was that any permanent settlement with England was automatically void in the event of an Anglo-French war and thus undermined any efforts to seek a full accord.

It is by no means easy to identify the extent to which what we would now define as patriotism played a role in this period. There was a growing feeling of nationalist sentiment, as distinct from purely local or regional affiliation, though whether service to the ideal of nationhood would be justification for rebellion against a feudal superior is questionable. Both Edward I and Edward II would clearly have held that it was not. There was recognition of the concept of a 'just' war, borne of a need to defend the homeland, but loyalty to one's superior was still the cement which knitted the structure of society. The idea, as Professor Barrow expresses it, of 'Scotland for the Scots' was not perhaps yet a recognisable currency. For the English therefore to formally relinquish any claim to suzerainty was fundamental. Only with a full quit claim could nationhood be assured; anything less was to raise the spectre of continued dominion.

The renewed *entente* with France led to heightened tension on the marches in 1326, sporadic raiding intensified and both de Lucy in the west and Percy in the east were on full alert. The Scots were not alone in violating the terms of the truce. In September a Flemish vessel, the *Pelarym*, was seized off Whitby and the crew together with the Scottish pilgrims on board were murdered – even the women were not spared.

By the end of the year Edward II was imprisoned, his favourites dead and his regime collapsed. Percy, Beaumont and the other disinherited lords had been swift to offer their swords to the exiles. Isabella and Mortimer wasted little time. A parliament was summoned and the old king's formal abdication was accepted on 20th January 1327. On 1st February the fourteen-year-old prince was crowned as Edward III. The Scots welcomed the young monarch with a night attack on Norham, a bold attempt to scale the walls. The commando was detected and beaten off, but the message was clear: new king, old war.

In England a regency council was appointed headed by Henry of Lancaster. At the outset Roger Mortimer was careful to stand aside and at least let the appearance of government reside in the hands of the council. The penal Acts of 1322 were, insofar as was possible, repealed, though there was no rush to resurrect the Ordinances. In his own way Mortimer was every inch as unscrupulous as Hugh Despenser, assuming his lordship of Denbigh whilst Isabella galloped through the dead man's vast reserves. Those who opposed Roger were removed or silenced. Thomas Wake, Lancaster's son-in-law and one of the principals of the Disinherited, lost his office as keeper of the Tower. Lancaster, his eyesight failing rapidly, was steadily marginalised, whilst in 1328 Mortimer created himself Earl of March, an entirely new honour. His hubris now running on overdrive he refused even to allow the king precedence, treating the young monarch as an equal.

For all of their avarice and repression, the regime of Isabella and Mortimer remained inherently unstable. They had no constitutional position and survived as long as they could exert control over the king. This young man, however, was an altogether different proposition to his father. Independent and strong willed, he soon found Mortimer's restraining hand firstly irksome and finally intolerable. One thing the regime could not afford to do was to renew the war with Scotland – peace became the main objective, with compromise the means. Money was also a problem – the treasure chest they had inherited from Edward II, the ill-gotten legacy of Arundel and the Despensers was soon spent.

For Bruce the triumph of the new regime offered an exciting opportunity though Mar, restored to the his earldom on his return to Scotland, continued to plot the release of the old king. On the marches Percy was instructed to ensure that the terms of the truce were upheld and that there should be no further provocation such as a repeat of the 'Pelarym' incident. The Abbot of Rievaulx, jointly with Ivo of Aldburgh, was empowered to facilitate further talks aimed at securing a lasting settlement. At a preliminary meeting convened, after some prevarication, at Tweedmouth the English confirmed their willingness to abide by the Bishopthorpe agreement, though matters did not progress beyond this. Bruce was prepared to add a degree of urgency by massing his forces on the border.

The marchers responded in kind. A muster was ordered for 18th May at Newcastle. Some weeks prior to that the threat was perceived as sufficiently imminent to warrant plans for an evacuation. By the beginning of June the negotiations were stalling. A final effort to hold talks at York foundered when the disgruntled Scots slipped away in the night, leaving some robust suggestions nailed to the door of their chambers. The English were prepared to talk but not to compromise – for the Scots this amounted to less than nothing.

The young king was eager for a fight, Isabella and Mortimer felt they needed to appear willing, but the campaign of 1327 was, from the cynical standpoint of the regime, mere window dressing. Continuance of the war was no longer a viable option; a show of strength was appropriate but not necessarily serious in intent. The sensibilities of the marcher lords were important to the regime's stability – the 'war' party of Beaumont, Wake,

Strathbogie and Percy should not be alienated, they had defected once already.

The forces assembled at York for the forthcoming campaign comprised both horse and foot, mounted men at arms, infantry following on. The invaluable John of Hainault supplied a seven hundred-strong brigade (he was still awaiting payment for his services the year before). The chronicler Jean le Bel served in the mercenary ranks and provides a participant's view of the action. Matters began badly. Isabella gave a banquet for the officers at York whilst outside the commons squabbled. Hainaulters disputed a game of dice with Lincolnshire archers, harsh words were swiftly followed by blows, the swords of the men at arms settled the argument but left a number of dead – this was scarcely an auspicious beginning.

On 1st July the army, sober and depleted, marched from York. If Roger Mortimer appeared distracted this would be because he had received disturbing news from the south: Edward, lately King of England, had escaped from captivity in Berkeley castle. Compared to this, Scots' depredations were a mere pinprick.[20] The English left the northern capital in a blaze of silken banners and burnished mail, the full panoply of chivalry, as though a decisive encounter was somehow preordained. The divisions advanced through Overton and Myton in Swaledale to Topcliffe where they halted to receive intelligence, then on via Northallerton and Darlington to Durham which was reached on 14th July.

By this time the Scots were already in the field, two columns, one entering through the west march and the other passing North Tynedale. As ever Douglas and Randolph, now seconded by Mar, James Stewart and the ransomed Archibald Douglas, were the generals.[21] The invasion occurred mid-June and by early July the western division had penetrated as far south as Appleby and Kirby Stephen. By the 12th Anthony de Lucy was writing to King Edward suggesting that the Scots were bent either upon besieging Carlisle or seeking battle in the east. Most likely the western force marched via Weardale to link up with their comrades who had spread fire throughout Northumberland and Durham. The Scots were not necessarily seeking battle but their offensive which might now be considered a 'pre-emptive strike' would be virtually certain to frustrate any attempt by the English to invade Scotland.

This has been perceived as a high-risk strategy, especially as King Robert was absent from the realm in Ulster, yet it must be conceded that the military hegemony the Scots had enjoyed since 1314 would certainly promote the value of offensive action. Not only this but the composition of the opposing forces (of which the Scots would be well aware) would clearly show that the English had not yet espoused the realities of hobiler warfare and that their traditional reliance on heavy cavalry would be a major weakness.

Jean le Bel records how the men watched the summer sky lit by the flames of burning villages, how the English army lumbered after the Scots pelting over the barren uplands of West Durham towards Blanchland in Northumberland. The hard-riding hobilers were a will o' the wisp opponent, sensed rather than seen, their path marked only by a great swathe of destruction. Breathless and frustrated the English drew rein at Blanchland and a hasty council of war was held, presumably at the local abbey le Bel refers to in less than flattering tones. With the struggling foot and baggage still spread out on the march it was decided to attempt a flanking move towards the banks of the Tyne, aimed at cutting off the raiders' retreat.

With only a loaf of bread tied to their saddles, a commanded party of mounted men at arms set off after the Scots. This was an effort to emulate the tactics of manoeuvre which constituted the essence of hobiler warfare. But these were still mailed knights on heavy horses and the thirty-five-mile dash to the river over trackless mire and peat hags took a toll on both men and mounts. By the evening of the 20th July the force reached the Tyne by Haydon Bridge and splashed across the brown waters. There was not a single Scotsman in sight; rain, however, there was in abundance, a steady, unrelenting downpour that soaked through rusting mail and sodden wool. The rain refused to ease off, the men were tired, hungry, demoralised and isolated. In the night the river rose and proved unfordable. There was no forage and each rider was obliged to spend a miserable night clinging to the horse's bridle.

The rain was without end. Without food, without forage and without any sight of the foe the party spent several wasted, miserable days by the swollen banks of the Tyne. It was not until the 31st, with the bulk of the army somewhere in the vicinity of East Allendale, that an enterprising squire, Thomas Rokeby,[22] stumbled on the Scots. The lad was captured but immediately released for the Scots had been equally ignorant of the whereabouts of the English. Having encamped the army at Blanchland Edward, the next day, 1st August, marched some nine miles towards the Wear where he finally found his enemies.

The Scots were and remained strongly posted, refusing to abandon the high ground and accept battle. After a further stalemate on the night of the 3rd Douglas silently broke camp, succeeded in crossing the river undetected and proceeded to occupy an equally strong position in Stanhope Park. The following evening, with that panache for which he was justly renowned, the Scot led a commando in a night attack on the English camp. The objective was not merely to 'beat up' enemy quarters but to capture the young king's person. Many casualties were inflicted and Edward's retainers fought a desperate mêlée around the royal pavilion – the king's chaplain was amongst the dead. At length the attack was beaten off and the English, badly shaken, were left to count the cost. On 5th August the camp was on full alert and the men stood to arms that night only to discover, to their considerable surprise, when they looked out next morning that the raiders had disappeared in the night, slipping away over the miry ground to put sufficient miles between them and any prospect of serious pursuit.

On entering the abandoned camp the chronicler was astonished to observe that:

> We found more 500 good, fat beasts, already dead, which the Scots had killed because they could not take them with them, and did not want to leave them alive for the English. We found more than 400 undressed-leather pots, hanging over the fire and full of meat to be roasted ... We found five poor prisoners whom the Scots had left in this wood, all naked, tied to trees in spite, two of them with broken ribs.[23]

This, from an eyewitness, was the stark, brutal, degrading and wasteful reality of hobiler warfare. That apart, the Weardale campaign of 1327 was effectively over. A costly, humiliating fiasco. It is said Edward III wept tears of frustration.[24] This was a harsh lesson in how wars were fought on the marches, but if the new king was nothing else, he was quick to learn. With the raiders vanished into the summer haze there was little left for the English army to do but withdraw to York from whence they had come.[25]

But the Scots were not done. Barely had the English retreated than King Robert fell upon north Northumberland. This was to be the ailing paladin's last campaign and he set his banners before defiant Norham whilst Randolph demonstrated against Alnwick and Warkworth. The king laid serious siege to the Queen of Border Fortresses. The county was thoroughly wasted, prompting the other marcher districts to barter for a truce. Dearly bought, this was to subsist until Whitsun (22nd May) the following year. Apart from Norhamshire the rest of the Palatinate was included, as was Richmond, most likely Cleveland, Cumberland, Westmorland and Allertonshire.

It has to be doubted that Bruce was bent on the permanent annexation of Northumberland; this must have been a case of a 'mite more terror'. Yet it is certain that he was granting lands in the north of the county to those of his affinity:

> *The landis of Northumbirland,*
> *That next Scotland thar was liand,*
> *In fe and heritage gaf he*
> *and thai payit for the selys fee.*[26]

Prior to leading this invasion King Robert had been occupied in Ulster. Notwithstanding the defeat and death of Edward Bruce in 1318 the Scots may have maintained at least a token military presence in Ireland certainly until 1322.[27] When the Red Earl died in 1326 his province was in a parlous state – the havoc of the war had yet to be repaired, much of the land remained untilled, the tenants fled or murdered. As de Burgh's son-in-law Bruce might have felt he had an interest in the succession; he could certainly have wished to exert or establish some influence in Ulster if for no other reason than to protect his own 'back door'. There is evidence to suggest his overtures may have been neither unwelcome nor unsolicited.

John Darcy, the Justiciar, was loyal to Edward II. Having made the crossing at Easter (12th April) the king entered into an indenture with the magnate Henry Mandeville dated 12th July. The substance of this agreement was a truce to hold for twelve months from 1st August. This was not a blackmail situation as might obtain on the marches but a civilised accord in consideration of which the Scots were to pay compensation for losses incurred in the course of a recent raid on Rathlin. A prudent measure on King Robert's part as he was securing the neutrality of the Irish peers, a substantial diplomatic coup, especially from a man who was seriously ill at the time, 'so feeble and weak that he will not last much longer from this time, with the help of God, because he cannot move anything except his tongue'.[28]

As Isabella and Mortimer had been able to exercise full control of England only from January 1327, they could feel confident of Ireland only when the pro-Edward II Justiciar, Darcy, fled in May. Uncertainty bred disquiet and disquiet led to fresh disturbances, with the Gaelic Irish scrimmaging with the Anglo Irish. It is possible to discern Bruce's hand in this fomenting the discord to put further pressure on the regime. From the Scots' perspective the fall of Edward II brought the prospect of a permanent peace that much closer – Bruce clearly had little time now remaining and it is reasonable to suppose he might employ every conceivable device to bring the English to the negotiating table.

Correspondence between King Robert and Darcy's pro-Mortimer successor, the Earl of Kildare, survives, suggesting that Bruce may have been canvassing support for a landing in Wales to open up a new front in the principality. Most likely this was a bluff, dust in the eyes to increase the pressure. In any event the Irish spurned the overture as the king must have anticipated. If his objective was merely to neutralise Ireland as a source of armed support then the mission was successful. Bruce returned to Scotland in August, ready for his final grand chevauchee into Northumberland.

The fiasco of the Weardale campaign and the English regime's mounting debts made peace a priority, even though the king and the majority of the magnates, particularly the Disinherited, were against the idea. Nonetheless on 9th October Henry Percy, together with an experienced advocate, William of Denum, were instructed to open the negotiations. Bruce was not hard to find, his army still concentrated before Norham's battered walls. Having received the commissioners cordially enough the king drafted a series of six conditions precedent, all of which would have to be satisfied before any lasting accord could be achieved. These could be briefly summarised as follows. The Bruce, his heirs and successors should hold Scotland free and entire with no concept of overlordship; the young Prince David would be offered King Edward's sister, Joan of the Tower, as consort. There was to be no cross-border estate (nothing here for the Disinherited) and both countries would provide undertakings of mutual military aid, saving only, on the Scottish side, their current obligations to France. The very considerable sum of £20,000 would be paid by Scotland to England as compensation for damage done to the north during the war.[29] Edward III would, for his part, undertake to use best endeavours to secure the release from excommunication and interdict.

When the envoys reported to the king, then at Nottingham, it was agreed that matters could be progressed. The two key conditions of the marriage settlement and compensation were agreed in principal at the outset. The two contentious areas remained, those of sovereignty and cross-border holdings. Edward III, in correspondence, was still using the language of a magnanimous conqueror rather than the leader of a nation which had been completely outfought.

The talks which were subsequently held at Newcastle through November and December proved fruitful. The question of overlordship was conceded, the quitclaim to include the return of all historic records and papers, a clear and final admission of full independence. Other less difficult matters such as the drawing of borders and Scottish tenure of Man were likewise resolved. The clear irony is that the accord which was being hammered out bore a distinct resemblance to Harcla's draft of 1323.

One key element was lacking – consensus on cross-border estates. This was to prove the thorn which returned to puncture all hopes of a lasting peace. The Disinherited, men of the calibre and temperament of Beaumont and Strathbogie, were simply not going to fade away. But on this point Bruce was adamant: those who swore fealty to the King of England should never enjoy holdings in Scotland. Despite the very considerable progress that had been made and continued to be made, this pernicious question was not at any time resolved in the negotiations or in the final draft of the proposed treaty.

However, matters progressed over the winter and in February 1328 Scottish envoys journeyed to York where Parliament was sitting. On 1st March the king issued a series of letters patent bearing the royal seal, endorsed by both Council and Parliament, which, after over thirty years of bloody, unrelenting conflict, spelt out the terms for a lasting peace:

> *Whereas we and some of our predecessors, kings of England, have*
> *attempted to gain rights of rule, lordship or superiority over the kingdom*
> *of Scotland, and terrible hardships have long afflicted the realms of*
> *England and Scotland through the wars fought on this account; and*
> *bearing in mind the bloodshed, slaughter, atrocities, destruction of*
> *churches, and numerous evils from which the inhabitants of both realms*
> *have suffered over and over again because of these wars; and having*
> *regard also to the good things in which both realms might abound to*

their mutual advantage if joined in the stability of permanent peace,
and thus more effectually made secure, within and beyond their borders,
against the harmful attempts of violent men to rebel or make war; we
will and concede for us and all our heirs and successors, by the common
counsel, assent and consent of the prelates, magnates, earls and barons
and communities of our realm in our parliament that the kingdom of
Scotland shall remain for ever separate in all respects from the kingdom
of England, in its entirety, free and in peace, without any kind of
subjection, servitude, claim or demand, with its rightful boundaries as
they were held and preserved in the time of Alexander of good memory
king of Scotland last deceased, to the magnificent prince, the lord
Robert, by God's grace illustrious king of Scots, our ally and very dear
friend, and to his heirs and successors.[30]

This was everything Bruce had striven for. John Baliol was effectively expunged from the record, Bruce's succession followed the death of Alexander III. It would seem that any hope Edward Baliol might have had of restitution was now stillborn, but the fact remains that within four years the son of 'Toom Tabard' would be *de facto* king of Scotland, for a while at least. The claims of the Disinherited must have seemed like a distant mirage in the face of such a momentous admission. It was twenty-two long, hard years since Robert Bruce had taken the Scottish crown but here was a full, formal, apparently unanimous and clear admission of his right to the throne, free in perpetuity from interference. All documents and records purporting to justify claims to suzerainty were to be nullified or repealed.

As further recognition of Scotland's inalienable claim to full nationhood the treaty was to be sealed in Edinburgh. A powerful delegation was to attend headed by Henry Burghersh, bishop of Lincoln and skilled diplomat, William Ayermin, the Bishop of Norwich, Sir Geoffrey le Scrope,[31] Henry Percy with William de la Zouche of Ashby. It was not without significance that both of these last were affected by the loss of their cross border estates. The embassy reached the Scottish capital on 10th March and had been given full power and discretion to conclude the final negotiations.

King Robert was again laid low with his illness and the conference was held 'in a chamber within the precincts of the monastery of Holyrood in Edinburgh where the lord king was lying'.[32] A week of talks was sufficient for the final, complete draft to be agreed on 17th March. The Scots were present in some force: for the clergy, John Lindsay of Glasgow, William Sinclair of Dunkeld, John of Plimour (Moray), Maurice of Dunblane, Roger of Ross and Simon Wedale of Galloway. The lay magnates comprised Duncan of Fife, Patrick Dunbar Earl of March, Murdoch of Menteith, Hugh of Ross and the anglophile Donald of Mar. In attendance the chancellor Abbot Bernard of Arbroath, Gilbert Hay, the Constable with the Marischal, Robert Keith, Andrew Murray of Petty and Bothwell, the Pantler and son of Wallace's old comrade in arms together with others who had fought in the grim struggle.

The bones of the treaty were as set out in a series of five deeds, all of which bore the date 17th March. The principal terms were defined in two indentures, one in Latin, the other in French. In a couple of notarial instruments Bruce confirmed his undertaking in respect of the compensation monies, lastly the king's letters patent regarding the marriage settlement. The two realms were thus agreed, and the principal clauses of the agreement dealt with the original six points Bruce had specified the preceding autumn.

Edward III renounced any and all claims to English overlordship, this to bind his successors in perpetuity. All of the papers relating to 'the great Cause' were to be returned. There was talk of sending back the pilfered regalia and even the Stone of Destiny, but an angry mob prevented the stone's removal.

The marriage between Prince David and Princess Joan was to be solemnised as soon as both parties attained an appropriate age. If this did not take place by Michaelmas (29th September) 1338 then Bruce would face a huge indemnity of £100,000. This was a colossal penalty but by the end of September in that year both children would have been of age for several months (Prince David would be fourteen in March). In consideration of the marriage contract King Robert would, prior to the following Ascension Day (12th May), endow the bride with lands producing at least £2,000 of income per annum. Should Joan die before the marriage took place then Edward could introduce another bride of the blood royal. Conversely if David predeceased then the marriage of Joan or another of equal station could proceed to the next Scottish male heir (at this time Robert the Steward, Bruce's daughter Marjorie's son, later Robert II).

The matter of the Disinherited was not resolved. Neither side, however, wished to delay the enactment of a final peace. But this open wound would eat like a cancer into the fabric of the accord. It is likely that Edward and the English administration felt that the Scottish attitude would soften with time and persistence.

Mutual military aid was assured saving the Scots alliance with France as provided by the treaty of Corbeil; if the Scots were drawn into hostilities through their obligations then the English, the present agreement notwithstanding, could respond in kind. There were a number of new assurances from both sides, aimed at creating a stable peace: should any party in Ireland engage in warfare against England then the Scots would refrain from offering assistance. Likewise if the Scots faced rebellion on the western seaboard or from the Hebrides the English would remain aloof.

The agreed compensation in the amount of £20,000 would be paid over by means of three annual instalments to be made at Tweedmouth. Lastly the English king and his advisors would take a proactive stance in assisting in negotiations with the Curia. In this Edward proved as good as his word: both excommunication and interdict were lifted by a papal bull issued in October 1328. The final treaty was ratified by the English parliament at Northampton on 4th May.

The royal marriage was formally contracted at Berwick on 12th July, the queen having brought her young daughter north in June. Neither king was present. Edward might have agreed to terms but for England this was the 'Shameful Peace' brought about by Mortimer's desperation rather than through any collective act of the national will and to the chagrin of the young king. It is possible that Isabella used the occasion to canvas support amongst the magnates for some understanding over the Disinherited; it may be that some of the peers were less inflexible than the ailing king.

The Treaty of Northampton ended the war between England and Scotland; it did not heal the widening rift in the English polity. The débâcle of the Weardale adventure and the hurried nature of the peace negotiations, topped by the bitter gall of abandonment of suzerainty, broadened the gulf between the king and the Earl of March, as Roger Mortimer was now styled. The regime was increasingly tyrannical, opposition was ruthlessly suppressed as the queen grew greedier, and Mortimer's arrogance swelled. It was said she was carrying his child. His offhand treatment of the sovereign suggested ambitions well beyond an earldom. In the course of the autumn a swelling tide of resentment spilled into positive action. Lancaster, Wake and others, including John Stratford the influential and able Bishop of Winchester, refused to attend Parliament. The perceived betrayal of the Disinherited had spawned a ready-made opposition. Their demands were that the king should 'live off his own', that is he should support himself from the revenues of the royal estates rather than requiring additional fiscal support from others. This was intended to curb Isabella and Mortimer's extravagance. It was conceded the king should be offered sufficient funds to engage in warfare when circumstances demanded but that he should, at all times, accept the advice of the Council. These resentments were not, of course, being expressed directly at the king but were aimed at the regime.

And the regime struck back. Lancaster was failing physically, losing his eyesight and insufficiently robust to stand up to Mortimer's bullying. The earl succeeded in detaching both of the king's uncles, Kent and Norfolk (precious little good this betrayal brought to the former who was subsequently arrested for treason and after a sham trial, executed). The Earl of March was now a virtual dictator, universally detested but too strong for shaking. He remained determined to relegate the king to a nominal role, the royal household stuffed with spies, and he seems to have gone so far as to try to drive a wedge between Edward and his young consort Philippa of Hainault.[33]

Edward III was not of a compliant disposition. Already he was building up an affinity of like-minded, and strong-minded, young men – Richard de Bury, William de Montague and Robert Ufford. If he needed a further incentive to seek Mortimer's removal from power this arrived on 15th June 1330 with the birth of a son, Prince Edward of Woodstock, the future 'Black Prince' of legend.[34] Parliament was summoned to meet at Nottingham in October amidst a cloud of rumours and uncertainty. It was felt by some that the earl was planning to seize the throne.

The grim fortress of Nottingham Castle was bristling with his hired spears. The castle stands upon a mighty crag but the rock is honeycombed with caves and passages. Beyond the walls, on the evening of 19th October, Sir William Montague waited with a picked commando of two dozen men at arms. A local, William Eland, with the connivance of the castellan, guided the party through a subterranean tunnel that lead into the heart of the private apartments. At the top of the stairs leading from the passage stood a stout postern, kept locked and bolted. Earlier in the evening the king had asked to be excused from the great hall on the grounds, supported by his compliant physician, that he was feeling unwell. No sooner had the court retired than Edward slipped from his chamber to unbolt the postern. Once admitted the conspirators made straight for their quarry. A steward of the Household, Hugh Turpington, coming across the raiders, shouted the alarm and drew his sword. He was speedily dealt with and his master seized, despite the wailing of the queen.

Roger Mortimer, master of the sham trial, now attended his own. Taken to London he was judged on the 26th of November – in keeping with his own practice he was denied the right to speak, the verdict and the traitor's death which followed a foregone conclusion. Edward III had come into his own. His mother was sent into comfortable retirement at Castle Rising in Norfolk.

In the preceding year, on 7th June, King Robert I had died in the new house he had built at Cardross in his 55th year. The exact nature of the illness which brought about his death has not been identified. Jean le Bel describes his condition as 'La grosse maladie' – leprosy[35] – though this has never been proven. There does seem to have been a reluctance on the part of Scottish writers to describe the king's disease in detail. His dying wish was that his heart be removed and borne to the Holy Land, to symbolise the great crusade he had not lived to undertake. Such a mission was not an easy one and demanded a warrior of renown equal to the task. Inevitably the choice fell on James Douglas who, bearing his precious burden and en route to his own quixotic end,[36] sailed from Montrose for Flanders early in 1330. Randolph was appointed as regent.

The first Scottish War of Independence had been a savage, bitter and bloody trial, bringing death, maiming, impoverishment and suffering to untold thousands. If any single man involved had earned the distinction of greatness it was Robert Bruce. It was he, admittedly for personal reasons, who had revived the moribund patriot cause in 1306. It was he who, with the persistence of genius, had succoured and nurtured the uncertain flame of freedom from those desperate days of skulking in the heather to the triumph of Bannockburn. For a further fourteen years he had fought unceasingly to bring about recognition of national independence. He established a degree of military superiority which the Scots were never to enjoy again. Of course he was not alone – he was served by men of distinction such as Lamberton, Randolph and Douglas; others who had gone before, Wishart, Wallace and Murray, had all done their part.

The Treaty of Northampton and the abandonment of English claims to sovereignty remain Bruce's cardinal achievement and despite the fact that Scotland's nationhood would within a few years of the king's death again be under threat, the fact of that success could never be fully undone. From time to time the flame would indeed flicker, but it would never finally go out.

Notes

1 Quoted in Traquair, P., *Freedom's Sword*, London 1990 p. 254.
2 The forensic sculpture was undertaken by Newcastle Dental Hospital.
3 This disease may have been paralytic leprosy, though no clear diagnosis has emerged.
4 Barrow, G.W.S., *Robert Bruce*, London 1965 p. 333.
5 It was said that the earl had in fact been murdered 'suddenly on a privy seat', quoted in Prestwich, M., *The Three Edwards*, London 1980 p. 94.
6 Prestwich p. 94.
7 Ibid p. 94.
8 The conflict began when one of the French king's vassals set out the construction of a new bastide at St Sardos in the Agenais. This activity was demonstrably in breach of the terms of the earlier treaty and Convocation of Paris. The local Gascons showed their displeasure by falling upon and levelling the offending works. In retaliation Charles IV ordered the seizure of the English bastide of Monpezat. The outraged Gascons once again mustered and saw off the attackers, capturing their leader in the process, whom they proceeded to hold to ransom. Edward II, fearing the matter should escalate, was at pains to placate Charles, ordering the captive's release and offering to pay compensation for the damage wrought by his over-enthusiastic subjects. This offer was refused and the king confiscated the duchy. See Neillands, R., *The Hundred Years War*, London 1990 p. 30.
9 On 1st August 1323, the feast of St Peter, the patron of the Tower celebrated in the usual, vinous way within the fortress. Whilst ensuring his comrades imbibed with gusto, the deputy lieutenant Gerard d'Alspaye stayed sober. Once the drink had taken effect he repaired to Mortimer's cell and began to lever out the masonry. Both Roger and his fellow prisoner Richard de Monmouth were at length set free. This was, however, merely the start of their adventure. Having passed through the kitchens where the cook had already been suborned, they scrambled up the wide chimney shaft to emerge onto the roof. Already

provided with rope ladders, they were then able to descend into the outer ward. Further use of the rope ladders helped them clear the curtain wall. Now, at the riverbank they were met by two accomplices with a skiff who rowed them safely across to Greenwich. Here one of Mortimer's men was waiting with fresh horses and the escapees galloped off into the night. When the alarm was raised Despenser's first thoughts were that they must make either directly for Dover or perhaps for Wales. Mortimer had double guessed his opponent for he now made for Porchester where another small boat ferried him to the Isle of Wight where he took ship for the safety of Normandy. See Mortimer, I., *The Greatest Traitor*, London 2003 pp. 130–2.

10 Isabella's flagrant adultery was all the more shocking because of her previously expressed abhorrence. It was she who had discovered and exposed the infidelities of her sisters-in-law who had cuckolded their royal husbands. The women and their lovers suffered dreadfully.

11 Mar remained an anglophile and continued to plot for the restoration of Edward II. On the death of Randolph he was appointed regent and subsequently led an army to destruction at Dupplin Moor in 1332. It was said he was stung into mounting an attack by accusations of treachery, based on his previous connection to the English court. He died in the battle.

12 Quoted in Mortimer p. 162.

13 Ibid p. 162.

14 Barrow pp. 351–2.

15 Quoted in Traquair p. 234.

16 Quoted in McNamee, C., *Wars of the Bruces*, East Lothian 1997 p. 237.

17 Quoted in Barrow p. 354.

18 Barrow p. 354.

19 Quoted in Barrow pp. 355–6.

20 The fate of Edward II remains something of a mystery. The chronicler Geoffrey le Baker, writing some thirty years after the event, conjures the highly lurid scene when the deposed king is horribly done to death by having a red-hot plumber's iron thrust through the anus. However, this version of events has been challenged due to the testimony of a Genoese cleric Manuel Fieschi who claimed to have heard the former king's confession some years after his supposed death. The alleged king's version of events was that he had succeeded in escaping from Berkeley Castle after killing a porter whose corpse was interred as a handy substitute. Having got clear of his former prison Edward made his way firstly to Ireland and then to France where he had been received by the Pope at Avignon. From the papal court he had journeyed to Cologne and from there to Italy, where he became a hermit. Whether this is true or not is open to continued speculation, though it is certainly possible Edward III believed his father had survived. Having disposed of Mortimer, the alleged murderers were never brought to justice. See Mortimer pp. 244–66 and Prestwich p. 99.

21 Barrow p. 357.

22 Rokeby went on to have a distinguished career and commanded a wing of the English forces at Neville's Cross in 1346.

23 Quoted in Traquair p. 245.

24 Barrow p. 359.

25 The final account submitted by John of Hainault came to the staggering total of £41,304. He claimed for the loss of horses left behind in England the sum of £21,482 though the animals in question raised only some £920 on resale. At the time of the Weardale fiasco the Hainaulters were still awaiting settlement of their bill for supporting the previous year's coup. So impecunious was the regime that Isabella had to pawn the crown jewels to meet the cost of the first instalment.

26 Quoted in Barrow (notes) p. 360.

27 McNamee p. 242.

28 Quoted in McNamee p. 243.

29 It was thought that this sum was considerable as it was represented nothing more than the profits reaped from the raiding of north of England.

30 Quoted in Barrow p. 363.

31 This was the same Scrope, chief justice of the King's Bench, who had presided over Harcla's trial and condemnation. It is not recorded whether the learned judge saw any irony in his present role.

32 Quoted in Barrow p. 364.

33 Prestwich p. 113.

34 The title of 'Black Prince' is not recorded as being in use prior to 1569.

35 Quoted in Barrow p. 444.

36 Douglas carried both a safe conduct and recommendation to Alfonso XI of Castile and Leon from Edward III. The Spaniard was engaged in a war with the Moors of Granada who had recently been reinforced from Morocco. The redoubtable Scot was persuaded (presumably without any great difficulty) to accept command of a division of the king's army which engaged at Tebas de Ardales on 25th March 1330. Legend relates that when the local forces were falling back Douglas, with a small band of Scots, disdaining flight, charged into the midst of the horde and they were at length overpowered and slain, the bodies being later recovered and found surrounded by piles of Moorish dead. With Douglas died Sir William Sinclair, Robert and Walter Logan. See Barrow pp. 445–6.

Chapter 7

The Disinherited

Blood axeth blood as guerdom dew
And vengeance for vengeance is a just reward
For look what measure we to other award
Take heed ye princes by examples past
Blood will have blood, either first or last.[1]

E dward III was a welcome contrast to his father and his reign was to witness some of the most famous of famous victories. Names that have rung with jingoistic echo ever since, Crécy, Auberoche, Neville's Cross, Poitiers and Najera: 'This king Edward was forsooth of a passing goodness, and full gracious among all the worthy men of the world.'[2] Professor Prestwich provides a balanced view of the man, his achievement and his failings: 'The views of historians have been ambivalent; many find it hard to give full credit to a man whose greatest achievements lay in aggressive warfare inspired by an opportunistic personal ambition.'[3]

Prestwich goes on to find that Edward III was less focused on his goals than his grandfather and that his apparent good relations with the contemporary polity were due more to appeasement than ability. This may be unfair. Edward inherited a situation with Scotland that had been driven by his mother and her paramour's compelling desire for a settlement, an accord that had left at least one by no means insignificant group amongst the magnates totally dissatisfied – the 'Disinherited'.

The rather vague undertakings in relation to compensation for those nobles deprived of their cross-border holdings had come nowhere near meeting the expectation of many of those lords whose Scottish estates were now forfeit and granted to others of the patriot party. The fierce Henry Beaumont, an experienced fighter – 'an arrogant man with a haughty disposition'[4] – had married one of the nieces and heiresses to the estate of the late Earl of Buchan and had received the vacant title from Edward II in 1312.

Beaumont's son-in-law, a young man of even less compromising temperament, David Strathbogie, had aspirations toward the earldom of Athol and, through his mother, Joan Comyn, had inherited a claim to the estate of John Comyn of Badenoch. The equally redoubtable Umfravilles, lions of Redesdale, which had suffered dreadfully in the course of Scots raiding, had been earls of Angus since 1243 and Gilbert Umfraville was also Beaumont's great-nephew.

After the débâcle of Lancaster's attempted coup against Mortimer, Beaumont, together with the disgraced earl's son-in-law Thomas Wake, another of the class of the Disinherited, sought refuge in France. Edward, the son of John Baliol, was also living in quiet forgotten exile, a player without a game, the able son of a wholly discredited father. With Mortimer disposed of, Beaumont and Wake were returned to royal favour and the young king certainly pursued their claims by all diplomatic means. To no avail, the Scottish lords were either blind to the threat of these potent exiles or considered the danger to be minimal.

Languishing, irrelevant and largely forgotten, on his father's estates in Picardy was John Baliol's son Edward – at this point he was not viewed even as a contender:

> *Historians have treated Edward Baliol with even more contempt than they reserve for his father . . . 'Young and warlike, poor and ambitious, with few lands and great pretensions' he was a dangerous foe.*[5]

Edward III had been diligent in pursuing the cases of Beaumont and Wake by judicial and diplomatic means. Both had been active in his cause against Mortimer. The last tranche of the Scottish compensation fell due in 1331 and it became obvious that neither was to be offered anything. The realisation inevitably pushed both lords into the camp of the Disinherited and in the summer of that year Beaumont, the natural choice for leader, journeyed to France to make contact with Edward Baliol. In the autumn both men returned to England. The Disinherited were no longer a handful of embittered and largely impotent exiles, they were becoming a faction, well led, increasingly aggressive and now, with the addition of a viable pretender at their head, a flag to fight for.

Beaumont mortgaged his acres to raise cash, the Archbishop of York donated funds. The Treaty of Northampton might have bought peace with the Scots but it would not heal the wounds. The northern shires had no cause to love their neighbours in the opposing marches and an opportunity for potentially serious mayhem was not likely to be overlooked. The king, meanwhile was in a more delicate position, to openly support the opposition would be in flagrant breach of his treaty obligations. He was not yet ready for all-out war. Besides, the Disinherited were, at best, a forlorn hope, more likely to prove an irritation than be decisive.

With the redoubtable Randolph as regent the Scottish peers had some grounds for complacency. On the 23rd November 1331 the ageing paladin knighted the seven-year-old king who was crowned as David II on the following day. War was not yet inevitable. In the following spring Edward launched a further diplomatic offensive, this time concentrating on the case for Wake. Perhaps he realised that Beaumont was no longer interested in a judicial solution whilst Wake had not fully subscribed to the cause of the Disinherited. In any event these overtures were harshly rejected, 'let the ball roll'[6] the regent is said to have quipped. Randolph did not live to witness the folly of such flippancy, dying suddenly on 20th July. His replacement, Donald, Earl of Mar, elected at Perth on the 2nd August was a man of limited experience and less proven ability. Unlike his predecessor his was not a name to conjure with.

Whilst he had given strict orders to his officers on the marches to prevent any movement, of troops over the border and in May 1332 instructed the wardens to arrest anyone causing a disturbance, the king was happy to overlook the fitting out of a fleet of eighty-eight ships on Humberside. As a further precaution against Scottish retaliation Edward made Henry Percy his lieutenant on the border with authority to raise local forces if the need arose. If the Disinherited should fail, as seemed at this point likely, then the marches, as ever, would bear the brunt of retaliation.

In their finished fleet the adventurers set sail from Ravenspur on 31st July and on 6th August made landfall at Kinghorn. After a sharp skirmish Beaumont, leading the van, drove off local forces under the Earl of Fife, Alexander Seton and an illegitimate son of Robert I. After three days spent in unloading and securing the ships the Disinherited boldly marched four-teen miles inland to Dunfermline where they captured a patriot supply depot intact. By the 10th they were marching towards Loch Earn on the road to Perth. In terms of numbers Baliol commanded no more than say 1,500 men, of whom roughly two-thirds were archers.

This manoeuvre was interrupted when they found their further advance blocked by a superior force under Mar. The patriots were deployed on the far banks of the Earn and though numbers for both sides are uncertain they considerably outmatched the Disinherited. The regent certainly seems to have overestimated the force he was confronting and made no move during the rest of that hot summer day, 8th August, other than to put a strong contingent by the river crossing. If he was cautious there appears to have been no such constraints amongst the knights who were with him:

> *Cheerfully drinking wine, they expressed their contempt for the small numbers of the opposition side, singing songs and saying that . . . they would make ropes for themselves from the Englishmen's tails to tie them up on the following day.*[7]

Whether it was his intention simply to block any attempt to force the crucial bridge or whether he planned a more offensive move the next day is unknown, but Beaumont could not afford to tarry. Already outnumbered by Mar, a second patriot army, led by the Earl of Dunbar, was a mere eight miles distant at Auchterarder. During the short hours of darkness he and Baliol seized the initiative. Guided by a local sympathiser, Andrew Murray of Tullibardine, their men crossed by a little-known ford to storm the regent's camp, putting to flight or killing any who opposed them, though most of the slain were camp followers and squires. Though this was a sharp reverse for the patriots and must have led to some return to sobriety, Mar, by stationing the bulk of his men by the bridge, had, by good fortune, avoided immediate catastrophe.

There has been some question as to the regent's true loyalties, though his hesitation was probably due more to uncertainty than deceit. As the summer's day broke the earl sought a parlay with the invaders. Undismayed by the essential failure of the night attack Baliol had withdrawn from the wrecked camp, deploying on the slope behind, and was now drawn up in battle order. His position, straddling the high ground with a narrow glen in front, was a strong one. Dismounted knights and men at arms formed the main battle, with skirmish lines of archers extended on the flanks echeloned towards the centre, the whole line forming a kind of crescent. A mounted reserve of mercenary horsemen, no more than forty riders in all, were held in reserve.

The Bruce bastard hotly accused the regent of treachery when he sought to negotiate and this insult stung Mar into action, leading his host up the confines of the valley towards the enemy position on the ridge. The patriots were deployed in a strong central column of schiltroms, perhaps split into three divisions with a commanded brigade on each flank. The proud banners of no less than twelve earls blazoned above the advancing host: the regent himself, the earl of Fife, Randolph of Moray, Murdoch of Menteith John Campbell, the Scottish Earl of Athol (David Strathbogie fought with the Disinherited) and Alexander Bruce of Carrick.

At the first shock the powerful central division crashed into the ranks of the Disinherited and by sheer weight of numbers pushed them back. The fight became a gigantic scrum. The English knight Ralph Stafford yelled out an order: 'Ye English! Turn your shoulders instead of your breasts to the pikes',[8] giving more force to the push; though they lacked numbers the gradient was in the defenders' favour. As the flanking columns hurried on they were met by a storm of arrows from Beaumont's archers and, shot down in droves, recoiled onto their own main body. The press became so thick that many died of heatstroke or suffocation and the living had scarcely room to lift their weapons: 'In a short space they were thrust so close that they were crushed to death by one another, so that more fell by suffocation than the sword.'[9]

The attack halted, faltered and broke, the survivors streaming down the bloody slope already thick with their own dead. Leading the reserve and all who could mount, Beaumont, leaping into the saddle, swept after the fugitives, hacking and stabbing at the mob in relentless pursuit. When the slaughter was finally done, Donald, Earl of Mar, the earls of Menteith and Moray, Robert Bruce the bastard lord of Liddesdale, Alexander Fraser, the High Chamberlain, eighteen lesser nobles, nearly sixty knights and perhaps 2,000 of the rank and file lay together in death.

The carnage in the centre of the field was truly dreadful. The pile of Scottish dead was said to be 'greater in height from the earth towards the sky than one whole spear length'.[10] For their part the Disinherited reported only thirty-odd knights and men at arms, including John Gordon and Reginald de la Beche, slain. Not one archer is said to have died. Baliol appeared to have won himself a kingdom and Dupplin Moor, as the battle came to be called, became a model for later English victories at Halidon Hill and Neville's Cross. (Baliol himself and Gilbert d'Umfraville fought again at Halidon Hill.) The lesson was plain: lumbering spearmen would always be vulnerable to longbowmen and should not seek to engage unsupported – a lesson that went unheeded.

Baliol had won a resounding victory but not yet a kingdom. Perth soon fell to the invaders but the second patriot army, yet unblooded, began a half-hearted leaguer. Battle on land was followed by battle at sea, with a sharp naval fight on 24th August over the dark waters of the Tay. Baliol's success sparked defections from the patriot cause; in the south-west Maxwell and MacDouall erupted out of Galloway, spreading flames across the lands of Dunbar's officers. Consequently John Randolph, Andrew Murray and Archibald Douglas were detached to try to stem the tide. With their ranks first dramatically thinned and now sundered, the patriots faltered and Baliol seized the moment to have himself crowned at Scone on 24th September.[11]

His position remained precarious. Fife had submitted and was left to hold Perth whilst the new king hurried towards the western marches to bolster his supporters there and recover his family's traditional power base in the area. The rest of the Disinherited lords now fanned out across the realm to claim their separate prizes. In doing so they exposed the fundamental weakness of their cause. They were not truly a faction united by common purpose and allegiance but a disparate group of adventurers who, having achieved signal success, lacked the cohesion to exploit their advantage.

The patriots drew breath and rallied, Andrew Murray, son of the posthumous victor of Stirling, was now named Guardian. By 7th October Perth was once more under their control and Murray was hot on Baliol's heels. His ardour led to ignominious capture in a skirmish over the Tweed crossing at Kelso and he was sent south into England where he was to languish for the next two years. From Roxburgh where he was based in November Baliol spelt out the real cost to Scotland of his ascendency, homage to Edward III as overlord and the ceding of an English 'Pale' on the marches comprising some 2,000 'librates' of land.[12] Baliol offered to marry Princess Joan if the marriage to the young David II did not proceed.

This then was the price, the loss of all that the preceding generation had fought, bled and starved to achieve.

If the Disinherited has been surprised with the swiftness and scope of their achievement, this success caught their patron, Edward III, somewhat unprepared. The English Parliament met at York early in December when Beaumont and Strathbogie found themselves arguing with envoys of the patriot cause. Nothing was decided and matters were held over until after the Christmas festivities. In Scotland Edward Baliol did not enjoy a pleasant advent season. Archibald Douglas, younger brother of Sir James 'The Good', was now appointed Guardian whilst Murray was out of action. He did not waste time. As on 16th December Baliol prepared to hold Christmas court at Annan, he was surprised by a well-executed dawn assault. Numerous of his adherents, including his own brother, were killed in the raid and Baliol was forced into precipitous and humiliating flight. In the words of a contemporary chronicler 'with one leg in a boot and the other bare'.[13]

This sudden disintegration seriously undermined Baliol's position. In a morning he had gone from being a crowned king to a landless usurper. English members of Parliament would find little to attract them in so flimsy a cause. If Baliol was to be restored, this could be achieved only by military intervention on a substantial scale – Parliament would not be inclined to undertake too large a commitment. In the early part of January with both realms held fast in the frozen grip of a medieval winter, Edward III moved his court to York where it was to reside for the next five years. On 30th January the northern levies were summoned,[14] in the spring the king would take the field on behalf of his vassal. It would appear unlikely that Edward intended a full-scale conquest of Scotland after the manner of his illustrious grandfather; he rather intended to neutralise the Scots by the instalment of a pliant puppet ruler which would leave the English king free to concentrate upon matters in France.

Short-lived as it had been, Baliol's incumbency had given him a taste for power and he remained game for another try. It was he who opened the campaigning season of 1333 with a chevauchee through the marches, moving westward through Teviotdale and along the banks of the Tweed, slighting the tower at Oxnam as an opener to the siege of Berwick. Such moves can hardly have surprised the patriots and both town and castle were stoutly garrisoned, Dunbar in the former and Alexander Seton holding the latter. By March, however, Baliol had completed a ditch and pallisade around the defences and had succeeded in cutting off the water supply. Meanwhile Strathbogie was scouring the Merse for provisions. If the town was prepared, the surrounding areas clearly were not. There appears to have been no attempt at any kind of 'scorched earth' policy to deny sustenance to the invaders – Haddington was surprised and taken on market day!

By the middle of the month matters were hotting up. Archibald Douglas sought to relieve pressure upon Berwick by launching spoiling raids into the English west march and north Northumberland. On 22nd March the Scots descended on the west over the wild sweep of Gilsland waste. Anthony de Lucy, Harcla's successor, immediately struck back, harrying twelve miles into Dumfriesshire. In the process the English encountered and defeated a sally from the garrison of Lochmaben at Dornoch. In the fracas William Douglas, due to win fame and a degree of notoriety as 'The Knight of Liddesdale', was taken, whilst his comrades Humphrey Boys and Humphrey Jardine were both slain. The Scottish inroads achieved nothing and played to Edward's propaganda by providing justification for war. Until now the king had been striving to maintain the delicate fiction that these alarums in Scotland were none of his doing, and were merely the work of internal rivals.

In April King Edward marched north. By the 8th he was at Durham and had reached Tweedmouth opposite Berwick, by 9th May. The formidable Scots privateer John Crabb had defected to the English and now led a squadron of three vessels, *Gracedieu*, *Jonete* and *Nicholas*, which were transporting the royal artillery from York.[15] The encirclement of Berwick was complete, with perhaps as many as 12,000–13,000 soldiers in Edward's besieging army. On 27th June a combined land and naval assault was launched. Bundles of faggots coated with tar which were intended to be used against ships attacking the seaward defences started a serious fire in the town and it is possible that it was in the course of this action that the keeper's son William Seton lost his life.

In order that they might combat the flames threatening to engulf the entire town the Scots begged a truce. This was granted as a preliminary to a formal surrender but when the scorched defenders remained defiant further assaults followed. None was successful but the Scots were glad to negotiate another cessation this time with the provision that, if not relieved within fifteen days, the garrison would yield. Hostages were handed over to promote good faith, including Seton's younger boy Thomas.

As the action dragged on into the heat of July the English particularly began to suffer from desertion as men, wearied by the danger and discomfort, looked longingly towards their homes. On the 11th Douglas slipped over the Tweed at Yair Ford and advanced rapidly along the south bank as far as Tweedmouth. From there, when the tide was low, he sent a company, led by William Keith, over the shifting sands and into the town. Keith took over the baton of command from Seton; technically the place had been relieved. Next day Douglas drew up in battle order on Sunnyside Hill, perhaps more for show than effect, then marched off into north Northumberland to launch a feint against Bamburgh (where Queen Philippa was in residence), seeking to divert Edward and failing completely. Bamburgh's massive walls, high on their dolerite outcrop, could laugh at any attempt at siege.

This partial relief was followed by an ugly incident. The Scots within pressed for the release of the hostages averring that the town was now relieved. Edward countered by pointing out that this was not in fact so — the relieving force had arrived from the English side of the Tweed and not from the north as had been specified. When the garrison demurred young Thomas Seton was hanged (some sources claim that his elder brother William had also been a hostage and was killed at the same time). A dreadful prospect for their father watching from the battered ramparts:

> *They kennt the tread o' their gallant bairns,*
> *As they cam forth to die*
> *William he mounted the ladder fyrst,*
> *And threw himself frae the tree.*
>
> *Thomas he was his mithers pride,*
> *And he looked sae bauldly on:*
> *Then kissed his brothers lyefless hands,*
> *When he found the breath was gane.*
>
> *He leaped from off the bitter tree,*
> *And flouchtered in the wynd.*
> *Twa bonny flowers to wither thus,*
> *Nd a' for yae mans mind.*[16]

The king was not done. He warned that two hostages a day would suffer a similar fate unless the Scots capitulated. The defenders hastened to enter into a new accord and, for the avoidance of doubt, this was evidenced by two separate indentures sealed by both Dunbar as castellan and Keith as keeper of the town. The terms agreed were that the new truce would hold until sunrise on 20th July. There were three specific means whereby relief could be deemed effective: a Scottish force crossed the Tweed by Berwick, or the relief force won a pitched battle against the besiegers, or a commanded party of two hundred men at arms could punch through the lines by either land or sea and enter the town with no greater loss than thirty of their number. The hour of decision approached.

Keith was permitted to pass through the trenches and seek out Douglas who was blundering somewhat aimlessly around Northumberland. The meeting took place near Morpeth and the keeper spelt out the terms, saying quite bluntly that either Douglas marched to the relief of the town or it would be handed over in accordance with the terms of the indenture.

Marshalling his battalions Douglas led the way north. On the 18th the Scots re-crossed the Tweed and made camp at Duns Park. The following morning they marched the dozen or so miles to the summit of the evilly named Witches Knowe. By midday they reached the top of the rise. Before them, some two miles distant, on the opposing slopes of Halidon Hill, awaited the English.

Having left no more than half a thousand men to deter a sally by the hungry defenders, the English had withdrawn from the trenches to deploy on the south-facing slope of Halidon. This eminence rises 600 feet above sea level[17] an ideal defensive site, the summit crowned by trees, a morass at the base. Edward formed his knights and men at arms into three divisions, or battles, all on foot and drawn up in line, with each battle flanked by contingents of archers.

The right was commanded by the Earl Marshal, Thomas, Earl of Norfolk. The earl was the king's half uncle and he had Beaumont and Edward III's younger brother, John of Eltham. The wings of that division were commanded by Strathbogie on the right and Umfraville on the left.[18] The king led the centre and Baliol took the left. The English army, thinned by death, disease and desertion, probably numbered no more than 8,000 soldiers.

Douglas may have had the more numerous host, perhaps 1200 knights and men at arms with some 13,500 spearmen formed into four dense schiltros. The separate brigades were commanded first, by John, Earl of Moray; the second nominally under the boy king but in reality commanded by Sir James Stewart; the third by Douglas with the Earl of Carrick; and the last by Hugh, Earl of Ross.

The intervening ground between the two opposing forces sloped gently from the Scots' initial position atop Witches Knowe down to the shallow valley bottom and then rose up the slopes of Halidon to the English defensive line by the crest. Although now much drained the lower reaches were, in the fourteenth century, extremely wet and marshy. The present farm at Bogend commemorates the vanished morass.

It would be a very sanguine individual on the English side who did not suffer a sharp intake of breath as the swelling mass of the Scottish host tramped into view, the densely packed steel-fanged ranks of the schiltroms with the myriad proud banners fluttering above. The noise would echo like the angry tide, swelling to a crescendo of thousands of marching feet as the columns swept down the intervening slope, a great roar of defiance bellowing in each man's throat. The sight must have been awe inspiring, knee trembling, but Douglas had overlooked the lessons of Dupplin Moor. Here, it was true, his men could deploy over more open ground, there was no single massing in the centre, the columns were spaced for mutual support and such tactics had prevailed at Bannockburn.

The Scots still had a great deal of ground to cover before attacking uphill against a well-posted enemy. Worse, they had not reconnoitred the ground, had not taken into account the treacherous morass into which the well-ordered ranks now stumbled. Maintaining the momentum of the advance, keeping the tightly packed hedgehog of bristling points together was of the essence; loss of speed, of cohesion could prove fatal. And then there were the arrows.

Calmly, methodically, volley after volley was loosed into the packed files, men dropping by the score, the tussocks soon slippery with blood. After the dreadful toil of that fatal climb the Scots never really came to grips, their momentum and valour spent. As the schiltroms wavered, Edward gave the order to mount and the English knights swooped like falcons, lance and mace replacing clothyard shaft. The rot, as is habitually the case, started from the back. The grooms and varlets holding the horses came to the conclusion the day was lost as the English mounted and promptly sought refuge in flight, thus denying their comrades any hope of salvation. The rout continued for five corpse-strewn miles.

Exactly how many Scots died in the battle of Halidon Hill cannot be accurately assessed but their loss was undoubtably severe. Besides Douglas himself a handspan of earls fell: Hugh, Earl of Ross, Malcolm of Lennox, Alexander Bruce of Carrick, Kenneth of Sutherland, John Campbell of Athol. Scores of knights and some hundreds of men at arms lay with the piles of spearmen, three scions of the House of Fraser fell and scarcely a noble family escaped without some loss. This was far worse than Dupplin Moor, though similar tactics, on a grander scale, had triumphed. The densely packed ranks of the schiltrom could not, over open ground, hope to prevail against sustained archery. The mass of lumbering men provided the perfect target. They were defeated as much as anything by the distance they had to cover with no protection from the relentless flail of arrows.

A single archer, however proficient, cannot determine the course of a battle, a knight's armour afforded considerable protection, but the effect of great bodies of archers loosing regular sustained volleys with each bowman perhaps shooting a dozen arrows per minute, was devastating. With the archers' positioned so as to loose in an overlapping spread of arrows the effect could be likened to that of machine guns on the western front during the First World War, a perfect killing ground.

Well might the English balladeer exult:

Scottes out of Berwick and out of Aberdeen
At the Burn of Bannock ye were far too keen.
King Edward has avenged it now,
and fully too I ween.[19]

With the calamity that had befallen the Scots army there was no point in further resistance and the defenders of Berwick opened their gates. For Edward, the stain of his father's débâcle at Bannockburn, the humiliations of Mytton and Byland, the frustration of the Weardale campaign and the shame of Northampton were expunged in an hour. In his joy of victory and in the magnitude of the Scottish defeat the king came to the understandable but erroneous conclusion that the war was won. He did not pursue his gains beyond the walls of Berwick, leaving Henry Percy as governor and Baliol to mop up in Scotland.

In part this course was dictated by financial constraints. Parliament had been wary over committing resources for the campaign and the king's exchequer had been obliged to bolster the war chest by means of hefty borrowings. The king had creditors and they were getting impatient. Victory on the borders, however dazzling, brought few pecuniary rewards. There were hardly any worthwhile ransoms, income from conquered territories or quantities of loot to assist in balancing the books. Though Baliol was now in command and with success at his back, he lacked the means to hammer home the fact of conquest whilst the patriots were still reeling.

Without the cash or the manpower to extend his sway north of the Forth Baliol set about establishing control of the marches. At his Parliament held in Perth in October he felt sufficiently in command to reverse all of Robert I's grants of land and restore all of the Disinherited to their lost estates. By doing so he immediately created a further class of dispossessed and thereby ensured that war would continue. The Earl of Dunbar was one who came over to the Baliol camp, presuming the patriot cause defunct. Thus he was able to reconstruct his castle which had been slighted in the course of the campaign.

Whilst the new or restored king was holding court he was obliged to receive envoys from his overlord, Percy, Beaumont and Ralph Neville, come to remind him of his obligations under the terms of the Roxburgh Accord. Edward was not about to let his vassal forget to whom he owed both throne and allegiance. Baliol was slow to respond and Edward found it expedient to ensure he had his own faction amongst the former Disinherited, including such powerful figures as Beaumont, Strathbogie and now Dunbar.

Under pressure Baliol was obliged to confirm the terms of the earlier agreement at the York Parliament in February 1334. A conference between the two monarchs was arranged to be held at Durham in June and on the 12th the Treaty of Newcastle was sealed. The terms were entirely dictated by Edward III: the town and county of Berwick were ceded to England, as were Roxburgh, Edinburgh, Haddington, Linlithgow, Peebles, Dumfries, the Forest of Selkirk, Jedburgh and Hawick. A week later at the Blackfriars in Newcastle Edward Baliol performed homage to Edward III of England for the kingdom of Scotland or at least what was left of it.[20] The English Pale in southern Scotland was now a reality, the marcher castles stuffed with English garrisons.

Edward III had ample grounds for feeling very pleased with himself and he had learnt from his grandfather's mistake in seeming too heavy handed with his present vassal's father. He might well consider that if Baliol was left to rule largely without interference then his people might come to accept him. By the same token he had, however, emasculated Baliol by relieving him of control of some of the wealthiest areas of his kingdom, thus denying him access to resources which would be necessary to win and hold the restless country beyond the Forth. Edward was always, at this time, obliged to keep one eye fixed on the Channel. Prior to the 1333 campaign there were rumours of French attacks on the south coast and a supply fleet had in fact been commissioned and set sail only to be blown hopelessly off course by contrary winds.

For some years Philip of Valois, King Philip VI, had cherished the ideal of leading a crusade against the infidel and in July 1332 he formally took the cross. Edward III was able to influence the King of France by suggesting he was prepared to join him in this venture. Needless to say these bland assurances carried no depth; Edward merely wished to neutralise Philip whilst he dealt, unhindered, with the Scots. Having resolved the Scottish question Edward would then deal with the pernicious matter of the Aquitaine.

After the disaster at Halidon the clamour from the Scots became very loud indeed, imploring Philip to honour his obligations under the terms of the Treaty of Corbeil. At the very least he felt constrained to offer young David and his queen a secure refuge in France. In the spring of 1334, David II took up residence in the Chateau Gaillard, Coeur de Lion's great fortress on the Seine, once the very symbol of Angevin power in France. With the young king in his care Philip could scarcely now exclude his ally from any negotiations with the English, nor could he be seen to recognise Baliol as king.

Despite the extent of the victory in 1333 Edward III and Edward Baliol did not control Scotland. Murray, having been ransomed, was now once more active as a guerrilla leader after the style of his father whilst Randolph and Robert the Steward, both very young men, were made joint Guardians. It was becoming increasingly obvious that Baliol could not hope to contain the patriots without continual English support. The summer campaign of 1334, whilst appearing to bring superficial success, could not fully mask the fact that the patriot cause was far from dead. Strathbogie was enjoying the Steward's estates in the south-west but an amphibious raid by the former holder, launched down Loch Fyne, ignited the habitual instability in the region. The English occupation also created fresh resentments and Duncan MacDouall reverted to the Bruce camp, giving them control of Wigtonshire.[21]

Baliol also succeeded in alienating both Beaumont and Strathbogie who were themselves locked in a disputed probate. Such fissiparous tendencies in the Baliol camp allowed the patriots to recover lost ground. Beaumont was besieged in his castle at Dundarg and obliged to surrender. Strathbogie, harassed by Randolph, bought a measure of security by deserting his former allegiance. At the same time Percy fell into dispute with Edward Bohun over their joint claim to lordship of Annandale. Settling with the choleric Percy proved expensive – he was awarded an annual stipend of 500 marks per annum from the Berwick customs revenue together with custody of the place, an office which carried a salary of £100 a year in peacetime and double that in war.[22] Bohun therefore gained Annandale and Lochmaben but, of course, he had still to hold them. Baliol's position was fast deteriorating as the patriots steadily reovered.

In the course of the next three years the cost of the war, for war it was, continued to mount. The nature of the expenditure had shifted from the expense of fielding armies to the steady drain of maintaining regular garrisons. In the wake of the victory at Halidon Hill Parliament had been more amenable to granting subsidies but the escalating costs continued to put pressure on the royal finances. Of the troops involved some were drawn from the Household, others raised partly through indenture, from the retinues and affinities of the northern magnates, shire levies and Welsh archers, recruited as mercenaries.

The increasing use of mounted archers and hobilers provided much greater mobility and Edward raised a field army of around 4,000 for his short autumn campaign of 1334, using Roxburgh as his base. On 28th December the king led a sweep through Ettrick Forest, essentially a show of strength to impress the troublesome natives. With no concessions to the grim winter landscapes Baliol, assisted by the earls of Warwick and Oxford, together with their retinues and the marchers under Anthony de Lucy, struck towards Peebles where Randolph was thought to be based. He was not, but the raiders spread fire and sword with zealous savagery. By the end of January there was little left to burn and nothing worth stealing so the chevauchee ran out of steam. Service on the border attracted few recruits and those in arms tended to quit as soon as their contractual term expired. The liberal application of such 'frightfulness' achieved little beyond alienating the few who might be persuaded to lend support to Baliol, the usurper held shakily in power by English lances.

On 2nd February Edward retired from the front, leaving John of Eltham in command, ably seconded by both Percy and Neville. At Newcastle Edward was confronted by envoys from France, their message clear and hostile. From Easter to midsummer the king vacillated, toying with both the French and papal ambassadors. By 23rd June he was ready to take the field again, his ships posted on the west and eastern coasts. The army which mustered at Newcastle was substantial, 12,000–13,000 strong[23], easily as big as the force he'd raised for the campaign of 1333. Edward marched his division to Carlisle to strike at the west; the earls of Warwick, Cornwall, Lancaster, Hereford and Buchan accompanied him. Command in the east was left to Baliol who was supported by the earls of Surrey, Arundel, Oxford and Angus with Percy, Neville, Thomas Berkeley and William Latimer.

The patriots were distracted by internal squabbling and had no recourse other than to engage in destroying anything that might succour the invaders. The campaign witnessed a repeat of the terror inflicted by the winter sortie but on a considerably more widespread and utterly indiscriminate basis. The raiders:

> . . . *freely marched through all the land on this side of the Forth and beyond it, burning, laying waste, and carrying off spoil and booty. Some of them, especially the Welsh, spared neither the clergy nor their monasteries, plundering regulars and seculars impartially. Also the seamen of Newcastle burnt a great part of the town of Dundee, with the dormitory and schools of the Minorite Friars, carrying away their great bell; and they burnt one friar who had formerly been a knight, a man of wholly pure and holy life. The bell they exposed for sale at Newcastle, where it was bought by the Preaching Friars of Newcastle for ten marks, although one party had no right to sell it and the other no right to buy.*[24]

The forces converged at Glasgow and then advanced upon Perth which was occupied on 7th August. The Scots wisely refused battle, preferring fabian tactics and guerrilla-style action. An early victim was Edward's brother-in-law

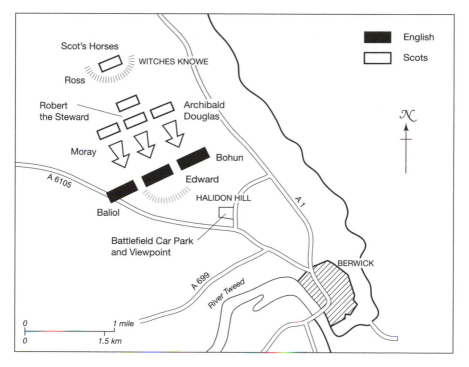

Halidon Hill, 1333

Count Guy of Namur, who had arrived at Berwick after Baliol had departed. Under his banner he had a handful of men at arms and perhaps a hundred archers. Undeterred he marched his company towards Edinburgh, only to be attacked near the Burgh Muir by a Scottish force under Randolph and Dunbar, soon reinforced by William Douglas. Namur conducted a skilful fighting withdrawal through the narrow streets of the capital and took refuge in the ruins of the castle which had been slighted previously. A desperate defence ensued, the English making a rampart of their dead horses. The odds, however, were unfortunate and the next day the count surrendered.[25]

Guy of Namur offered his sword to Randolph, who agreed a substantial ransom of £4,000 as well as extracting an oath that the count would refrain from further military activity against David II. This signal success was offset by the subsequent loss of Randolph who was, himself, captured by a sortie from the Roxburgh garrison. William Douglas escaped from the fight but his brother James was amongst the dead.

With Randolph a prisoner the Steward's resolve soon withered. Strathbogie had paved the way for his own capitulation which had then taken place on 18th August. The Scottish lords wavered and then began to seek terms; only the captive Randolph remained defiant. Edward remained in Perth for a month and it seemed as though the matter was decided. Baliol, Beaumont, Umfraville, Warwick, Lancaster and Neville laid siege to Dumbarton – a force from Ireland under John Darcy, the Justiciar had crossed into the west. By the end of September the field army was disbanding and Edward was back in Berwick, having given instructions for the rebuilding of Edinburgh Castle. The campaign, as brutal and militarily as indecisive as it had been, appeared to have achieved the objectives of bolstering Baliol's tottering position and of restoring the English Pale. The march counties were now to be reorganised and managed according to English precedent; only such diehards as Douglas, Murray and Dunbar remained in arms.

Strathbogie was now appointed as Baliol's lieutenant north of the Forth. His was not a disposition calculated to win 'hearts and minds' – choleric, ruthless and rapacious, he swiftly succeeded in alienating those who might otherwise have accepted his king. Notwithstanding the truce which was in place he laid siege to Murray's castle of Kildrummy, defended by his wife Christian Bruce. William Montagu, who was Edward's representative, granted Murray a release from the truce to raise the siege.

A picked battalion under Murray, Douglas and Dunbar made a determined forced march and, receiving local reinforcements, advanced through the dark November night to fall upon Strathbogie at Culbean and bring him, unexpectedly, to battle. Though surprised the earl was never one to refuse a fight and though the patriots barely mustered a thousand men it was their superior tactics which prevailed and Strathbogie, disdaining flight, died fighting. Culbean, though tactically little more than an extended skirmish, was an important and morale-boosting victory for the Bruce cause. The light of freedom, though dimmed, was not extinguished.

As the summer campaign had progressed Philip VI had been making increasingly threatening noises in support of his allies, suggesting he might send military aid if the determination of Scotland's kingship was not referred to independent papal arbitration. Edward detected mere bluster and replied that the matter of Scotland was now settled whilst putting the east coast ports on alert in the event of a French attack. In the event Philip's sole contribution was a single botched raid, soon dealt with.

Edward might also have understood that Pope Benedict XII was more concerned with relations between England and France and was anxious to avoid the Scottish question leading to war between these two 'super powers' of western Europe and the abandonment of the planned crusade. His Holiness took the pragmatic view that Edward would act as he saw fit and would almost certainly succeed in subjugating Scotland. He further perceived Philip's intermeddling as a barrier to a negotiated solution. Consequently, on 1st November, two papal ambassadors, the senior being Hugh d'Aimery, arrived at Newcastle. Edward was careful not to alienate the envoys whilst playing a practised game with the Scots, a series of short and inconclusive truces that, whilst appearing to favour the diplomatic option, left plenty of scope for more robust means.

On 26th January 1336 a Scots embassy comprising Murray, Douglas, Robert Lowther and William Keith arrived to join in the talks, and the bones of a draft treaty were swiftly hammered out. The bare draft was ready for parliamentary scrutiny by March. Edward kept substantial forces under arms in the marches lest anyone doubt his resolve to resort to force if the talks failed. The essence of the accord was that Scotland would recognise Edward Baliol as lawful king with the present David II as his heir presumptive (Baliol had no sons). When details of the agreement were relayed to him at Chateau Gaillard, David rejected the terms out of hand and the scheme began to wobble. Baliol's position was also slipping back into uncertainty to the extent he found it expedient to winter on Lindisfarne off the Northumbrian coast!

At the same time Benedict had grown dissatisfied with Philip as leader of the hoped-for crusade and withdrew the appointment. For Edward this was a setback – he could no longer dangle the carrot of English support for Philip's crusade. The King of France, humiliated and bitterly disappointed, needed no longer be distracted by visions of glory, needed no longer tread so lightly around papal envoys nor husband his ships for the crusade – he could now proceed to deal with the English. Throughout the spring and early summer of 1336 there were rumours of French raids but again these came to nothing.

Whilst appreciating the increased threat of French intervention Edward was not disposed to be conciliatory. Baliol, supported by Henry of Lancaster and a mobile force comprising some five hundred men at arms and as many hobilers, was able to retake Perth, lost over the winter to the patriots. A well-mounted amphibious assault carried the great coastal bastion of Dunottar, though the officer in charge, Thomas Rosslyn, lost his life in the fight.[26] The patriots suffered a further reverse when a daring sortie by John Stirling, the castellan of Edinburgh, leading a mere forty men at arms and twice as many archers, succeeded, mainly through bluff, in relieving the siege of Cupar.

In June Edward rode north leading his household knights, and by 12th July had reached Perth. His first move was to lead Lancaster's men in a lightening descent on Murray's siege works around Lochindorb Castle, stoutly held by Katherine Beaumont, Strathbogie's widow. Chivalrous as this might seem, and the speed of the advance very nearly caught the experienced Murray, the king's purpose was grimly tactical. The seizure of Dunottar had given the English a vital fortress on the east coast, the obvious and only viable objective of any French invasion. With typical ruthless efficiency Edward subdued the coastal towns, fire and sword his approved medium; Forres, Kinloss, Elgin and Aberdeen were reduced to ashes; by the end of the month the east coast of Scotland was a desert and the king returned to Perth.

In the south west the indefatigable de Lucy with John of Eltham was beating up Galloway,[27] whilst the equally determined Douglas 'hovered craftily on the skirts of the English army, inflicting upon it all the injury he could'.[28] De Lucy subsequently led his marchers, heavy with loot, back into Cumberland whilst Eltham marched north to join his brother at Perth. Again the campaign appeared to have been successful but fears over French intervention were growing daily and the need to strengthen the south coast defences took a further toll of the already over stretched royal finances. Additional parliamentary grants proved insufficient and Edward was obliged to extend his already extensive borrowing. The 'crusade' chests in the great cathedrals proved too tempting and were plundered. After hurrying south to look to the security of the eastern ports, the king returned to Scotland in the autumn to oversee the rebuilding of slighted castles including Bothwell before journeying south again in December.

The worsening diplomatic situation with France, the unresolved question of the Aquitaine and Edward's dynastic ambitions contributed to the steady slide towards war. For the whole of the next century, England, France and at least in part Scotland were to be locked into a series of campaigns which collectively came to be known as the Hundred Years War

– *La Guerre de Cent Ans.* The war with France was to have a very considerable impact on Anglo-Scottish relations and even though in the summer of 1336 it must have seemed that Edward III had effectively subdued patriot resistance, his attempts at control were to be frustrated by the same factors that ultimately defeated Longshanks: the effects of geography, escalating costs, sustained guerrilla activity and French intervention. Able and energetic as he was, Edward could not successfully prosecute war on two fronts.

The steady deterioration of his relationship with Philip VI and the need to divert increasing resources to secure the Channel ports against French attacks and then, latterly, to mount expeditions into France, inevitably diverted Edward from his aims in Scotland. By the close of 1336 he might have concluded that the patriots were subdued and yet this was far from being the case. Although the Scots had declined battle this was no evidence of faintheartedness; rather the sound application of tried strategy, guerrilla activity had been kept alive through the activities of Murray, Douglas and Dunbar. Baliol was increasingly exposed as a mere puppet whose position crumbled as soon as proactive English support was withdrawn, the price of that support robbed him of resources and totally undermined his position.

In 1152 Henry Plantagenet, who on the death of King Stephen two years later was to become King of England, married Eleanor of Aquitaine, who had divorced from the King of France. This famous and stormy union brought Henry the great prize of Aquitaine. As King of England he controlled Normandy and having relieved his younger brother Geoffrey of Maine and Anjou, intermeddled in Brittany. Geoffrey became Count of Lower Brittany and he together with Count Conan of Upper Brittany did homage to his all-powerful sibling. On his death Henry's Angevin possessions in France were greater in extent than the lands held by the king, although he was obliged to do homage to the French King for the Aquitaine. His rebellious son Richard I 'Lionheart' (1189–1199) managed to hold onto virtually all of his French acres but his successor King John (1199–1216) did not. Defeated at Bouvines in 1214, John's dismal reign saw the loss of most of his father's lands.

John's failure against Philip Augustus meant that his own son Henry III (1216–1272) was only able to retain a narrow coastal strip in Gascony, although the English continued to control Bordeaux and Bayonne and for these he was obliged to do homage. Edward I gained the County of Ponthieu on his marriage to Eleanor of Castile and a settlement of sorts was agreed by the terms of the Treaty of Paris in 1259. Louis IX of France was anxious to commit himself to a crusade and felt the need to achieve a lasting understanding with his brother-in-law Henry III. Under the provisions of the agreement the Aquitaine was restored to the English king in return for a formal quitclaim whereby the English abandoned any pretensions towards Normandy, Maine or Anjou. On paper this looked to be definitive but the treaty, concluded in haste, left many outstanding matters unresolved including the exact borders of the duchy itself. This in consequence led to a volatile frontier controlled by the construction of fortified hilltop towns or *bastides* the unsteady peace enlivened by occasional raiding. Edward I had a less than cordial relationship with Philip IV. A dispute which broke out in 1293 spurred the French king to confiscate the duchy the year after, an act that was supported by force of arms in 1294–5 and 1296. It was only papal intervention which restored Edward's position in 1297.

Edward II then fell foul of Charles IV when local trouble escalated into the War of Saint Sardos. The English king, largely to avoid having to do direct homage to his French counterpart, had nominated his son to be both Duke of Aquitaine and Count of Ponthieu. The death of Charles IV in 1328 proved a watershed – he was the last of the line of Hugh Capet whose descendants had ruled France since 996. The crown passed to Philip of Valois who ascended as Philip VI. It was arguable that Edward III had at least as good if not better a claim as a grandson of Philip IV. He derived his claim from his mother, sister to the dead king, but Philip, already the head of the regency council, moved swiftly and surely to secure the throne and Edward was in no position to intervene.

Philip began boldly and well. He firstly campaigned against the Flemings who had so humbled the French chivalry at Courtrai in 1302. This time there was no mistake and the Flemings were cut to pieces at Cassel in July 1328. Swelled by victory Philip summoned Edward to do homage for Aquitaine on pain of confiscation. Gritting his teeth the young King of England had little alternative and swore the oath on the 1st January 1329. This might have been an end to the tension but the terms of the oath were by no. means unequivocal. Philip was confident that Edward had undertaken full liege homage under the usual terms of which he could be summoned to France for military service to the crown. This was reminiscent of the relationship between Longshanks and John Baliol. Edward III, however, was not 'Toom Tabard'.

As the relationship with Philip continued to deteriorate Edward's concerns regarding French intentions were such that he did not mount a major campaign in Scotland during 1337. In May Philip confiscated the Aquitaine though Benedict persuaded him to reconsider. In October matters took their final turn – Edward formally withdrew his oath of allegiance, revoking the earlier undertaking given at Amiens. Papal intervention foundered and the king made it clear he was done with talking when Hugh Burgersh, Bishop of Lincoln, arrived in Paris on All Saints Day and threw Edward's defiance in Philip's face.

The war with France very probably proved Scotland's salvation, Bower certainly considered this to be the case: '. . . yet a fortunate thing for Scotland, for if the aforesaid king [Edward] had continued his war in Scotland, he would (as far as human judgement is concerned) have occupied it wholly and without difficulty.'[29] The chronicler may or may not be correct but there has to be a strong presumption that if Edward had been able, as he had in previous years, to devote the whole of his resources to establishing his authority in Scotland then, viewing the situation as it stood at the end of the 1336 campaign, he might have succeeded.

With the English king now diverted the patriots could step up their tried and familiar guerrilla tactics and begin to claw back the lands and castles held by the English. This type of warfare, undistinguished by set-piece battles, was both brutal and unrelenting, *guerre guerroyante*. Scorched earth became the standard tactic, terror rather than persuasion. The patriots wasted huge tracts of their own country to drive the waverers back into the Bruce camp and to deny sustenance to the invader. Famine and pestilence followed after. A description of the state of Tayside in 1339 shows the whole area was:

> . . . *to such a degree laid waste that there was almost no inhabited house left, but wild beasts and deer coming down from the mountains were often hunted around the town. So great then was the dearth and lack of provisions that the common folk were starving everywhere; and eating grass like sheep; they were found dead in pits. Nearby there lurked in a ruined building a certain peasant called Christy Cleke with his fierce woman; they lay in wait for women, children and young people, and after strangling them like a wolf, lived on their flesh.*[30]

For the ordinary inhabitants of Scotland this was a dreadful time. For the majority it probably mattered little who sat on the throne; David II was an exile in France, unknown and untried yet they were required to suffer what must have seemed endless hardship for his cause. It is very easy at the safe remove of six centuries and more to be seduced by the romantic panoply of chivalry, yet this was but a gloss, a veneer of nobility grafted onto the squalid and savage face of total war. For the villager or townsman of the day the tramp of armies was to be dreaded be they patriot or invader.

Once Edward had departed Baliol's authority disappeared like a scattering of leaves in the autumn wind. He became virtually a fugitive in his own realm as the patriots systematically began to win back the English-held castles, usually undermanned, poorly supplied and increasingly isolated in a hostile or barren landscape. Without a mobile strike force in the field there was no check on the patriot's ability to concentrate their strength against a series of objectives. They had developed their abilities as engineers and artillerymen employing a massive engine known as *Bourstar* or 'buster'.[31] Castles once recaptured were not held but following Robert I's policy slighted and rendered ineffective.

Edward did send Warwick north whilst dispatching his main army to Gascony. The earl, even with a stiffening of levies from the northern shires, was never able to muster more than say 3,500 men and was unable to prevent Murray laying siege to Stirling in May. This must have raised uncomfortable echoes of Bannockburn though Edward's response, racing north to raise the siege, was infinitely more effective than his father's.

As the patriots grew bolder and the Pale shrank by degrees, the northern shires of England braced themselves for the inevitable storm. The situation in the 1330s was considerably different from that which had obtained during the earlier years of the century. Provincial assemblies had been established and the English marches were now militarised zones able to recruit hobilers[32] and mounted archers. The appointment of men like de Lucy, Percy and Neville, magnates who had grown rich on the spoils and stipends of war, provided leadership and their retinues the basis of a standing army.[33] From the king's perspective this allowed him to draw unhindered upon the manpower of the southern shires to campaign in France whilst the north could, quite literally, fend for itself.

It was as well the marchers were ready for in the summer of 1337 the Bishop of Carlisle together with Wake and Clifford mounted a chevauchee into the Scottish west march, linking up with Warwick and his mobile force. De Lucy harried Galloway. In retaliation Murray descended on Coquetdale but was stoutly resisted by Umfraville. In October the Scots struck the English west march, but Percy and Neville saw them off after only three days. By the end of the year Murray was before Edinburgh's repaired walls. To lift the siege the Bishop of Carlisle again marched from the west whilst Baliol with de Lucy sortied from Berwick. This time the Scots refused to back down and Murray fought the relieving forces in an extended and confused skirmish at Crichton – neither was able to claim victory.

When Warwick's commission expired in November he was replaced by William Montagu, now created Earl of Salisbury, assisted by Arundel and Hugh Audley, the Earl of Gloucester. The demands of war on two fronts created ample opportunities for ambitious captains, the need to rely on good officers implied that able men must rise. For twenty-two weeks beginning on 13th January 1338 the English sat before the refurbished walls of Dunbar where the countess, the celebrated 'Black' Agnes, Randolph's sister, remained defiant. Despite Montagu's best efforts and the presence of a blockading squadron of Genoese galleys, the besiegers could make no headway.

At one point Montagu was obliged to desist from his operations to relieve Edinburgh where the governor, the energetic John Stirling, had now led a sortie too many and been captured by Douglas. The Scots issued dire threats as to what would happen to him if the rest of the garrison did not strike their colours. The bluff failed and Montagu raised the siege. He next brought Randolph before his sister's ramparts at Dunbar and threatened a similar grisly fate, more bluster and the countess was not moved – Randolph returned to safe captivity and Montagu was glad to agree the terms of a truce. Apart from his lack of success before Dunbar neither he nor Beaumont who was with him wished to be left behind when Edward's army departed for France where the pickings promised to be a good deal richer.[34]

The patriot cause suffered a major loss when Murray died suddenly in the spring of 1338. His uncompromising stance had kept the flame alive but his policies had resulted in wholesale devastation. The Steward, who now enjoyed a second term as Guardian, was considerably less energetic and a truce was to prevail until Michaelmas the following year. The English

Pale, though much assailed still held; Edinburgh, Stirling, Berwick, Roxburgh, Jedburgh, Lochmaben, Cupar and Perth remained under Edward's
control. It was the latter of these which formed the patriot's first objective
and was besieged in June 1339. Baliol had already quit the realm as his position tottered and though he joined a relief force the place fell before help
could arrive.

Cupar was next. The castellan, Baliol's chamberlain William Bullock,
clearly sniffed the wind change and promptly swapped sides. Baliol did,
however, succeed in lifting the siege of Stirling. The Steward was not the
most zealous of guardians and Douglas was out of action as a result of an
injury sustained after he'd taken a crossbow bolt in the thigh at Perth.

Edward was by now fully occupied with his proposed campaigning in
France. The great worth of the English wool trade could be used as a lever
to exert pressure on Louis of Nevers in Flanders; by offering concessions to
Brabant Edward could forge an alliance with Jean III. He already possessed
an ally in Hainault through his marriage connection. By building up a
series of alliances in the north Edward could seek to establish a springboard
for attacking Philip through the low countries whilst having an open door
in the south at Bordeaux. The Hainaulter Sir Walter Manny, destined to
be one of the king's most effective captains, scored the first hit when he
saw off a French squadron seeking to intercept the Bishop of Lincoln on
his return to England.

In spite of this intense diplomatic activity, facilitated by lavish subsidies,
Edward's early campaigns of 1338 and 1339 achieved little of substance. The
allies proved less than reliable and Philip cannily avoided offering the opportunity for a decisive encounter. On the 26th June 1340 Edward and the
English fleet engaged a superior Franco-Castilian-Genoese force at Sluys and
won a major victory. The land campaign which followed failed to capitalise
on this success and fizzled out as before. A truce was negotiated at Esplechin
near Tournai to hold from September 1340 to the following June.

These three years of war had cost the exchequer dearly and the gains
were very thin indeed. In addition to the subsidies there were the costs
of maintaining the fleet and of keeping an army victualled in the field.
To entice men into the ranks the king had, for a time, offered double
wages. The bill for subsidies in 1338 reached a staggering £276,000 and
the Wardrobe accounts for the years 1338–40 indicate an expenditure of
over £200,000. By the time of the truce the king owed some £500,000 in

1. Model armour in the European style, late 13th century
A11/130 © The Board of Trustees of the Armouries

2. Swords, European, 12th–13th century
DA4/605 © The Board of Trustees of the Armouries

3. Great helm, English, about 1370
DA12/226 © The Board of Trustees of the Armouries

4. Model armour in the Italian style, about 1390
Di2001/347 © The Board of Trustees of the Armouries

5. Bascinet, Italian, about 1390
A6/453 © The Board of Trustees of the Armouries

6. Mail shirt (Haubergeon) and aventail (neck/shoulders), German, mid-14th century
DA4855/201 © The Board of Trustees of the Armouries

7. Armour, German, late 15th century
DA11/247 © *The Board of Trustees of the Armouries*

8. Hand-and-a-half swords, European, 15th–16th century
DA4408/16 © *The Board of Trustees of the Armouries*

9. Armour, Italian, about 1510–20
DA6790/8 © *The Board of Trustees of the Armouries*

10. Matchlock gun, German, about 1510
A4/475 © *The Board of Trustees of the Armouries*

11. Bill, English, early 16th century
DA4/573 © *The Board of Trustees of the Armouries*

12. Basket-hilted sword, English, about 1510
A14/756 © *The Board of Trustees of the Armouries*

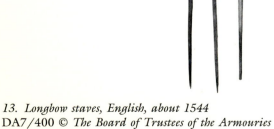

13. Longbow staves, English, about 1544
DA7/400 © *The Board of Trustees of the Armouries*

14. Jack of plate, English, 1558
A4855/283 © The Board of Trustees of the Armouries

15. Armour, English, about 1590
A8/796 © The Board of Trustees of the Armouries

16. Morion, English or Flemish, about 1590
DA4855/411 © *The Board of Trustees of the Armouries*

17. Burgonet, Austrian, about 1600
A5423/66 © *The Board of Trustees of the Armouries*

total.[35] It was the scale of this indebtedness which ignited the constitutional crisis of 1340–1. Edward's need for increased financial aid from parliament was met by a demand for concessions that sparked a right royal tantrum and the decimation of the administration with ministers being sacked in the autumn of 1340.[36]

Towards the end of the year, Randolph finally secured his liberty, being exchanged for Montagu who had been captured in France. His return marked a significant boost to the patriot campaign. His castle at Lochmaben was in the hands of William Bohun. The summer campaign opened with a raid on Annandale before Randolph was formally appointed to clear the west march of the surviving garrisons. Douglas received a commission to attend to the middle march and Alexander Ramsey the east. Before the walls of Edinburgh William Bullock, who had so recently abandoned his allegiance to Baliol, proved his worth by seizing the castle in a brilliant *coup de main* on 16th April.[37]

The fall of Edinburgh was a clear confirmation that the patriots were in the ascendant and that it was safe for David II to end his exile. Relations between the Steward and Randolph had not been mellowed by the latter's years as a prisoner. The young king was now seventeen, old enough to begin his personal rule. He and his queen made landfall at Inverbervie on 2nd June. David II was determined to show that he was his father's son and the tempo of the war began to quicken once again. Scottish raids now began to penetrate Northumberland, Randolph's banner being raised aloft as far south as Heddon on the Wall in Tynedale.

The challenge was sufficiently serious to draw Edward north. What he found can hardly have pleased him. The Christmas he spent at Melrose can scarcely have been a cheerful one, with the Scots under Douglas constantly on the prowl, snapping up supply convoys and harassing patrols. Edward cannot have been sorry to negotiate a series of truces, the first of which came into effect in December, and then slip back to London, leaving the highly capable Henry of Grosmont, Earl of Derby, in charge of his affairs on the marches. Having no war to prosecute Derby had to be content with the nearest alternative, a series of Anglo-Scottish tournaments. These proved to be extremely robust affairs, one of which, in January 1342, cost the lives of two English and two Scottish knights!

Derby had stood down his troops in February but the spring witnessed a series of lightning Scottish raids – the war was now being fought on English soil. Baliol's star was sinking rapidly, though he enjoyed a renaissance in the south-west. After MacDouall had deserted him in 1334 he had relied on Eustace Maxwell at Caerlaverock but he too had bowed to the inevitable and thrown in his lot with the patriots. Now when the usurper's fortunes appeared at their lowest ebb and his cause surely lost they reverted to their former allegiance, bringing another local magnate, Michael M'Ghee, over with them. This respite allowed Baliol to consolidate a base in Galloway and construct a redoubt on the island of Heston. This did not prevent David II from awarding fiefs in the south-west to those who remained loyal, including Malcolm Fleming who was granted the earldom of Wigton.

In April 1342, Stirling fell after half a year's siege and, in a well-executed raid, Ramsey secured Roxburgh on 30th March. Now only Berwick, Jedburgh and Lochmaben remained in English hands. As a reward for his bold *coup de main* Ramsey was made castellan at Roxburgh. This did not sit well with the choleric Douglas who did not scruple to kidnap the unfortunate Ramsey from Hawick Church and had him incarcerated in the dungeon of grim-visaged Hermitage where he was simply allowed to starve to death.[38]

Edward's affairs were scarcely proceeding any more favourably in France. In January 1343 he agreed a truce of three years' duration with Philip which was, at least on paper, to last until September 1346. On the Anglo-Scottish border, however, it was business as usual, with raid following raid and counter raid. In 1345 MacDouall swapped sides yet again, thus rendering Baliol's final bastion untenable, Heston was duly surrendered but the English still had teeth as the turncoat promptly discovered. A well-planned amphibious assault conducted by Thomas de Lucy and William de Dyfford recovered Heston and captured MacDouall. Baliol thus continued to skulk in Galloway though his cause had demonstrably run out of steam.

Despite the dazzling victories at Dupplin Moor and Halidon Hill, the long, bloody years of Baliol's posturing and Edward's intervention had achieved little. As professor Prestwich observes: '. . . from the English point of view, however, the opportunities presented by war in Scotland were an inadequate inducement for men to fight with the consistent determination required for victory.'[39]

Whilst matters in Scotland and France had reached their present position in the early 1340s, certain events had been taking place in Brittany which were to have a significant impact on the conflict. A contender for the dukedom was Jean de Montfort, who also held the earldom of Richmond. His rival was Jeanne de Penthievre who was married to King Philip's nephew Charles of Blois. De Montfort exerted his claim by force and seized the duchy. Although he seemed to be the stronger candidate Jean was aware he lacked King Philip's support and that Blois could expect royal aid. To shore up his position Jean de Montfort offered his allegiance to Edward in return for military aid.[40] Here was manna from heaven.

Before Edward could intervene, de Montfort was snared in his castle at Nantes and taken prisoner. His wife, another Jeanne, took up the gauntlet on behalf of her captive husband. In the early months of 1342 Sir Walter Manny a Hainaulter who came over with Queen Philippa, led an expedition to Brittany in support of Jeanne de Montfort who was besieged in Hennebont. The spirited countess was duly delivered and jointly with Manny began to win ground in western Brittany. In August William Bohun, Earl of Northampton, crossed with a second expeditionary force. Vannes was taken, though it was soon lost and, more significantly, Blois received a very bloody nose at Morlaix.[41] The Breton countryside was now witness to a savage little war of skirmish and ambuscade. In October the king came over in person, bringing fresh reinforcements who again took Vannes and laid siege to Rennes. Philip had mobilised a French army to raise the siege when papal envoys managed to successfully negotiate the truce agreed in January 1343, known as the Treaty of Malestroit. The cessation had little real effect in Brittany where the war of attrition continued. By May 1345 the English were in almost total control of the duchy.

Notes

1 Quoted in Neillands, R., *The Hundred Years War*, London 1990 p. 68.
2 Prestwich, M., *The Three Edwards*, London 1980 p. 214.
3 Ibid p. 214.
4 Quoted in Traquair, P., *Freedom's Sword*, London 1998 p. 257.
5 Ibid p. 260.
6 Lynch, M., *Scotland: A New History*, London 1991 p. 129.
7 It was a common jibe amongst the Scots that the English had tails.
8 Oman, Sir Charles, *The Art of War in the Middle Ages*, vol. 2 London 1924 p. 104.
9 Ibid p. 105.
10 Ibid p. 105.

11 Baliol and his faction remained sufficiently insecure to the extent that the guests remained in full harness when they consumed the coronation feast! See Traquair p. 263.

12 A 'librate' was a parcel of land assessed at £1.00 per annum in value.

13 Traquair p. 265.

14 Ibid p. 266.

15 Ibid p. 267.

16 Quoted in Sadler, D.J., *Battle for Northumbria*, Newcastle upon Tyne 1988 p. 59.

17 The present A6105 skirts the flank of Halidon Hill which is located some three miles north west of Berwick upon Tweed. Although the intervening valley is now drained, Bogend farm remains and the lie of the land as it stood in 1333 is clearly discernible.

18 Oman p. 106.

19 Ibid p. 107.

20 The remains of Blackfriars can still be seen in Newcastle, located behind one of the better preserved sections of the medieval walls on the western fringe of the city centre. Blackfriars is now a centre for arts and crafts adjoining the city's bustling Chinatown.

21 Traquair p. 275.

22 Ibid p. 277.

23 Ibid p. 279.

24 Quoted in Traquair p. 280.

25 In the course of the fight one of Namur's riders skewered a Scottish man at arms, Richard Shaw, at the same moment as being transfixed by the Scotsman's lance. When the dead body was stripped the corpse proved to be female! (See Brown, C., *The Second Scottish War of Independence*, Gloucs. 2000 p. 60.)

26 Traquair p. 285.

27 Ibid p. 286.

28 'ad pugnandum potentes' see Robson, R., *The Rise and Fall of the English Highland Clans*, Edinburgh 1989 p. 34.

29 Quoted in Traquair p. 288 (after Bower).

30 Ibid p. 289.

31 Ibid p. 291.

32 It may have been Andrew Harcla who introduced among the English the use of light cavalry/lancers known as hobelars or hobilars. Most likely they already existed as indigenous light horse and as such may be the ancestors of the 'Steel Bonnets' of the sixteenth century. They were able to fight either as mounted skirmishers or as infantry. Their local knowledge and sturdy garrons meant they could cover ground as quickly as any Scottish raider. The fiasco of the Weardale campaign of 1327 clearly indicated the weakness of heavy cavalry when confronted and confounded by fast-moving light cavalry who refused to engage

head on. The hobilar wore a simple iron helmet and a mail shirt or jack and roide with sword and lance.

33 As early in 1316 Anthony de Lucy had garrisoned Staworth Pele in South Tynedale with a complement of 15 men at arms and 40 hobilers. The English Highland clans who had returned to war-ravaged Tynedale and Weardale after the exodus caused by Scottish raids after Bannockburn were ideal recruits. The 'riding' clans later to be celebrated in border balladry – Charltons, Dodds, Milburns and Robsons from Tynedale, Halls and Reeds from Redesdale, their numbers swelled by those who had moved into the area on the basis of military tenure, Forsters, Fletchers and Hedleys (see Robson p. 35).

34 Beaumont in fact ended his career in France, dying there in 1340.

35 Edward had recourse to various sources of taxation-based revenue; he directly taxed the laity which, in 1337, raised £114,000 and also taxed the clergy which netted some £57,000 in that same year (see Prestwich p. 216).

36 Another ingenious means of driving up royal revenues was to sell franchises to wool speculators, an early example of 'futures' trading with potentially enormous gains, with the franchisees paying a lump sum in advance to secure future income (see Prestwich p. 216).

37 Bullock's coup was worthy of any Hollywood blockbuster. He disguised himself and a squad of chosen men as merchants on a day when the garrison were expecting resupply from Inchkeith. The raiders cut down the guards, jammed the portcullis with props and summoned Douglas men who were in cover beyond the walls (see Traquair p. 294).

38 The callous murder of Ramsey sparked a vendetta that simmered until 1353 when retribution finally caught up with the 'Knight of Liddesdale'.

39 Prestwich p. 78.

40 Jean de Montfort already held an English earldom and he relied on the precedent of Henry II with his brother and Count Conan.

41 The battle took place on 29th September. The Earl of Northampton and Robert of Artois with a small body of English archers and men at arms were confronted by a superior force of French mounted knights and men at arms under Charles of Blois. The English all dismounted, took up a defensive position with both flanks secured by woodland, and constructed basic defences including pits to cover their front. The cavalry assault, though ferocious and sustained, made little headway and was finally seen off with loss. Oman points out that the contemporary chroniclers make no mention of the use of archers on the field, though a deployment *en herce* may be presumed with the archers on the flanks and pouring volleys of shafts into the tightly packed ranks of the mounted chivalry. Though not a large-scale affair, Morlaix was the first instance of these tactics, to be fully proven at Crécy, on the continent.

Chapter 8

Neville's Cross

No warring gonnes were then at use,
Men thought of no such thing,
For Englyshmen in fight did use,
The gallant grey goose wing.[1]

In July 1346 the residents of the Normandy coast were treated to the impressive if ominous spectacle of an English army disembarking at St Vaast. A great heaving, sweating, cursing panoply of men and horses, humble palfreys and jittery, prancing destriers, splashing through the surf. The crowded sails had brought some 15,000 men under the personal command of the king, accompanied by his eldest son, Edward of Woodstock. Grooms struggled to get the beasts ashore and harassed marshals were swiftly swamped in piles of gear and an endless stack of provisions. The peaceful Cotentin became transformed into a sprawling camp of war. If the local populace had foregone the spectacle and sought refuge in flight they would have chosen wisely.

It was, however, not Edward's immediate intention to wage war in Normandy. He was proposing to march swiftly inland towards the distant Aquitaine to join forces with the dynamic Henry of Lancaster. In the event he was seduced by the counsels of a renegade Norman knight, Geoffrey de Harcourt, who argued that the land about was unprepared and offered a swift and easy conquest. On 26th July the English appeared before the ancient walls of Caen. The keeper, Raoul, Count of Eu, Constable of

France, despite the hopeless odds, put up a stiff fight and the place was taken only after a costly escalade.

With this vital bastion secured the invaders advanced to Lisieux where, on 1st August, Edward received overtures of peace. These were summarily rejected and the chevauchee continued. By attacking in Normandy the English had caught King Philip unawares, though he was not slow to begin gathering substantial forces for a muster at Paris. As they continued their hitherto unopposed march inland beneath the clear hot skies of summer the army must have marvelled at the richness of the land and the lack of organised resistance. But resistance there was, sporadic at first but growing as the Seine bridges were slighted one after the other and bands of skirmishers began to nibble at the invader's flanks.

On the 13th August the bridge at Poissy, whilst damaged, could be repaired and the carpenters and engineers performed prodigies of labour to establish a viable crossing. Within two days the whole of the army was over and marching northward towards the chalk downlands of the valley of the Somme, the next great river barrier. A day after the English had passed the Seine King Philip led the van of his army out from Paris. By the 21st, after gruelling marches of seventeen hot, weary miles each day, Edward reached the Somme.

Here he was confronted by the same difficulties as before. French partisans had broken down all of the bridges over the wide, sluggish river. The northern banks were well defended and efforts to force a passage met with rebuff. A local guide, whose desire to earn English gold easily overcame any lingering patriotism, revealed the existence of the tidal ford of the 'White Stain' or 'Blanche Taque'. Again the far bank was seen to be bristling with over 3,000 defenders under the Sieur du Foy, but on the 24th the English van, under Sir Hugh Despenser, waded into the retreating waters of the ford. Covered by a deluge of arrows, they stormed the banks, driving the French back towards Abbeville whilst the remainder of the tired English crossed without further opposition. Edward could now legitimately consider himself to be on home ground – the county of Ponthieu had formed a portion of his grandfather's dowry, though successive French kings had regularly confiscated the land to bring their English vassals to heel. By now King Philip had reached Abbeville where he would be greeted by the news of the loss of the ford at Blanchetaque. He might have fretted that the chance to force a decisive encounter had passed; in this he would have been mistaken.

Edward did not intend to skulk back towards the Channel to the safety of his ships. He knew the worth of his army and he chose his position well. On Saturday 26th August the English deployed along the long crest of the ridge that runs between the villages of Crécy and Wadicourt. With both flanks secure and a gentle slope to the fore, the falling ground just enough to tempt a foe into attacking without being steep enough to make him think twice. The 16-year-old Prince Edward, newly knighted as the army came ashore, was given command of the van on the right, advised by a stiffening of such experienced captains as the earls of Warwick and Oxford with the redoubtable Sir John Chandos. Northampton took the left wing by Wadicourt and the king held the centre, setting up his command post in a windmill which provided him with a panorama of the battle about to unfold.

War to the medieval mind was no game of hazard but a trial before God, with divine will as the final arbiter. In his public pronouncements Edward was swift to stress that the almighty guided his strategy '. . . by his righteous judgement and of his lawful power . . . out of respect for our right and according to our deserts'.[2] Before the battle he harangued the soldiery to remind them of the justice of their cause. War might be bloody, brutal and remorseless but it was fought according to God's will and the French had only themselves to blame for the suffering God had obliged Edward to inflict.[3]

Despite this reliance on providence Edward had never neglected the mechanics of war. He chose his officers well and with care. Whilst most senior commanders were drawn from the ranks of the established nobility, the 'new' men of the age, captains such as Thomas Dagworth, Walter Bentley, Robert Knollys, Chandos, Sir Walter Manny from Hainault and the Gascon Captal de Buch, all achieved advancement though merit. The mundane aspects of logistics and victualling were never overlooked. Edward's armies were smaller, leaner and far more professional than those larger hosts commanded by his grandfather.

The office of Marshal who, with the Constable, was responsible for matters of supply, billeting and the fixing out outposts, was hereditary, though from 1338 the holder was in fact female, Margaret, the daughter of Thomas of Brotherton. Therefore in the field the function was exercised firstly by the Earl of Salisbury and, after his death, Warwick who nonetheless held the post 'at the King's pleasure only'.[4]

As English armies campaigned in such diverse locations as the Anglo-Scottish border, Normandy, Brittany, Aquitaine and Spain, matters of supply became all important.

> *Much more was done than in the past to provide weapons. In 1341 the government ordered the collection of seven thousand, seven hundred bows and a hundred and thirty thousand sheaves of arrows. The Tower of London was developed into a great central arsenal. So great was the demand in 1356, that critical year for the war, that supplies became hard to find; the chamberlain of Chester was told that no arrows could be found in all England, as the King had taken them all for his use. The Black Prince therefore ordered the arrest of all the Fletchers in Cheshire, and forced them to work for him.[5]*

As well as being well led these English armies were well equipped. The chronicler Jean le Bel, writing of the earlier campaigns of 1339, commented unfavourably on the shabby armour of the English many still wearing the outmoded 'great helm' of the previous century and flowing surcoats.[6] The fourteenth century saw the use of plate armours become universal with the surcoat now replaced by the tight fitting jupon, and the bascinet with its distinctive 'pig face' visor become the model for knightly headgear:

> *The armies that went to France were undoubtably well equipped. Accounts show that ample quantities of horseshoes, bows, bowstrings, arrows and other military requirements were provided, while axes, sickles, hand mills and portable ovens ensured that the soldiers could live off the land. In 1359 there were even light leather boats carried in the baggage train, so that the monotonous diet of the army could be supplemented by fishing.[7]*

The contract system spurred the growth of specialist companies of archers, usually a hundred men divided into squads of twenty, each troop having, in addition to the officers, its own chaplain, standard bearer, surgeon and (in the case of the Welsh), an interpreter. Contract armies were often employed when the king himself could not be present on the campaign. The army that was to fight at Crécy had been organised through the household department of the wardrobe in the traditional manner. The growth in the employment of contract armies both in France and on the borders arose from the fact that many of these were not led by the king but by his appointees so the household would not assume its customary function.[8]

The lessons learned by the English in their war with the Scots proved an excellent education which paid handsome dividends in France. The harrow formation that had won the day at Halidon Hill was to serve throughout. Dismounted men at arms in the centre with each brigade flanked by bodies of archers whose shooting created overlapping volleys that rained death and confusion on their less prepared foes, hustling men at arms onto the bills of the waiting foot. The Scottish wars provided other lessons, instruction in the value of 'frightfulness' – 'The English had learned more from the Scottish War than the art of fighting battles. They had discovered the efficacy of the plundering raid, the total war of the Middle Ages, with destruction of villages and crops, ransoming and slaying of the civilian population.'[9]

As he surveyed the valley before him King Edward had perhaps 10,000–12,000 men under his command. His scouts would already have informed him that King Philip had certainly twice perhaps three times that number but his army was much more a feudal host, a polyglot concentration of companies not just from the widespread regions of France but from Germany, Bohemia, Genoa, Flanders, Hainault and Savoy.

As the English deployed, these mixed brigades toiled the twelve miles to Crécy, soaked by a violent storm at around 4.00 p.m., units hopelessly mixed with orders bellowed in a dozen tongues and dialects. The host lumbered into view, a great horde of men and horses spilling like a flood over the landscape, the marshals strove frantically to impose some degree of order. Eventually the army was formed into eight divisions or battles with the van led by the ageing and blind King John of Bohemia.

The only regular formation comprised a battalion of Genoese cross-bowmen who began the fight when they advanced, in good order, towards the English. The evening sun shone full in the mercenaries faces as they loosed their quarrels. The short deadly bolts either fell short or studded harmlessly into shields. The crossbow was a formidable weapon and the Genoese were professionals – with a great shout the English loosed in reply, the clothyard storm ripped into the Italians, men began to drop, the crossbow could never match this rate of shooting and the surviving Genoese began to fall back.

Disdaining such faintheartedness the waiting men at arms surged into the attack, riding down those stumbling survivors who impeded them. Up the wet hillside, soon churned into a mire, into the relentless hail of arrows that transfixed men and horses, destriers thrashed in the mud, their great hooves striking out. Men shuddered and died singly and in piles, the attack slowed to a crawl, any semblance of order lost and still the arrows kept coming.

The van recoiled onto the main body following, men strained and cursed merely to keep their footing, the great numbers proving a curse rather than a blessing. With a great jarring crash the two lines collided. In spite of their losses the French struck hard. For a while it seemed that the prince's battle must fold beneath the dreadful weight of the onslaught but the king coolly held his reserves in check, sensing that the line would hold. Packed together in dense masses of mixed horse and foot, the French attacks lacked cohesion and momentum. The fighting was fierce and bloody with casualties on both sides but the hacking bills and those terrible arrows did fearful execution. The French fell back over the corpse-strewn ground.

But the fight was not yet over. Between around six in the evening until midnight the French mounted charge after charge, seeking by mere valour to win the field, and each time their losses mounted. King Philip had long since lost control of his army which fought on like a punch-drunk bruiser, battered, bloody but unwilling to concede defeat, lashing out blindly against his opponent. Half a million arrows had been loosed, something in the order of 10,000 French and allies had fallen, including the blind King of Bohemia with a great swathe of nobility, many more were taken. The English had lost perhaps 500 dead.

It was a perfect victory. The pride of French chivalry had been humbled, who would now dare say God did not favour Edward's cause? After collecting the spoils the English marched on towards Calais. Given the magnitude of his triumph Edward might have been justified in expecting the city to open its gates. It did not. The siege was to continue for eleven grim months until the 4th August 1347 and tie down the bulk of English forces before the walls. King Philip's eldest son, John Duke of Normandy, who had been seeking to counter Henry of Lancaster in Gascony, marched his forces northward to shore up the king's battered army, leaving Aquitaine at the mercy of the English. By the end of October and before he retired into winter quarters Lancaster had made significant gains, including Poitiers.

Even before the disaster at Crécy King Philip had written to David II begging him to intervene. The King of Scots needed little prompting; the need to succour his ally, the desire to win glory on the field and the suspicion that England was stripped bare of fighting men with '. . . only priests, friars, clerks, craftsmen and tradesmen remaining', fed his resolve to strike.[10] By the 6th October the king had mustered a substantial army with contingents from throughout the realm, at a muster or *wapinschaw* at Perth, perhaps as many as 12,000 men were gathered, equipped with fresh arms from France.

> *For you shall read that my great grandfather*
> *Never went with his forces into France*
> *But that the Scot on his unfurnish'd kingdom*
> *came pouring, like the tide into a breach,*
> *With ample and brim fullness of his force;*
> *Galling the gleaned land with hot essays,*
> *Girding with grievous siege castles and towns;*
> *That England being empty of defence,*
> *Hath shook and trembled at the ill neighbourhood.*[11]

The campaign began on a sour note when the Earl of Ross felt constrained to withdraw after being implicated in the assassination of a rival, Ranald MacRuaridh.[12] As the army moved towards the west the king took time to lay siege to an English-held tower at Castleton, situated at the junction of the Esk and Liddel Water. After three days spent in preliminaries and filling the moat with rubble and fascines, a general assault carried the defences.

This relatively unimportant hold had been assailed previously by Douglas and Randolph together but the attempt had been abandoned when the two captains quarrelled. The keeper, renegade King Walter Selby, was summarily executed.[13] Douglas now maintained that the king had done sufficient to meet his obligations to his ally and no further military action was required. Such blatant self-interest could scarcely prevail and the army crossed into the English west march, its path marked by empty byres and burning thatch – even Lanercost Priory was torched.

Despite the fact that Carlisle was desperately unprepared for any kind of attack,[14] the Scots turned east and continued their depredations down the length of Tynedale. The Priory at Hexham suffered the same fate as Lanercost though King David gave orders to spare Corbridge, Durham and Darlington. This decision was due to tactical rather than humanitarian considerations – he needed these settlements as supply points. After spending three days wasting the shire the king moved southward from Hexham towards Ebchester and Durham. By 16th October the host was encamped at Bear Park within sight of the towers and spires of Durham. In keeping with traditional practice it was agreed the city and the Prince Bishop's mesnie lands around would be spared in return for a consideration of £1,000. The monks were given two days to collect the cash. As they waited the Scots 'made them great mirth'.[15]

In his bold assumption that the English marches had been left largely undefended the king was mistaken and here the normally acute Scottish intelligence appears to have failed him. As the Scots were sweeping through Tynedale the northerners were mustering. Though the prince Bishop was in France with King Edward John Fosser, the Benedictine Prior remained to oversee the defence of Durham and, in the process, left an invaluable account of the battle to follow. The good prior also experienced a powerful nocturnal visitation from St Cuthbert who bade him convey the saint's sacred banner to a field of battle before Durham. It is also said that the King of Scots, whilst still in Northumberland, had a dream wherein the saint warned him to repent of his savagery and spare the people of Durham or face the consequences of saintly wrath.

The wider spiritual needs of the gathering army were provided for by William Zouche, Archbishop of York, whilst such battle-hardened knights as Ralph, Lord Neville, Sir Henry Percy, Sir Thomas Rokeby, Gilbert Umfraville, the ever resilient Edward Baliol, accompanied by the titular Earl of Angus, took command.

Inevitably the number of fighters who mustered at Richmond in mid-October is uncertain, though it is likely they were far fewer than their Scottish opponents. Professor Prestwich suggests that there were perhaps a thousand men at arms from the baronial retinues, perhaps three times that drawn from the Yorkshire Dales and another thousand from Lancashire. Baliol commanded no more than one hundred horse.[16] On 14th October the English marched, via the present line of the A66, a wild and windswept highway, to Barnard Castle, tramping behind the corporeal cloth of St Cuthbert, a relic of great potency.[17]

After a day there they continued, on the 16th, to advance to Bishop Auckland and then, in the autumn darkness, they pushed on to Merrington past Ferry on the Hill towards Sunderland Bridge. On the march Percy commanded the van with Umfraville and Neville; John de Moubray, Rokeby and a Northumbrian knight John de Coupland had the centre whilst the archbishop brought up the rear. If the Scots' intelligence was faulty, that of the marchers was very much the opposite: they knew where the enemy lay and were resolved, despite the poor odds, to offer battle.

Dawn on 17th October brought a thick autumnal mist that blanketed out the hills and folds – both sides were advancing on a collision course without being aware. As the English groped their way forward they stumbled into a commanded body of Scots, perhaps half a thousand strong, under Douglas, who blundered into Rokeby's division. A confused mêlée ensued with the astonished Scots suffering loss as they pelted back towards the sanctuary of their camp.

In spite of this sharp reverse and clear evidence the marchers were about and in force, King David remained effortlessly complacent. 'There are no men in England but wretched monks, lewd priests, swineherds, cobblers and skinners. They dare not face me: I am safe enough.' Under the continuing illusion he was facing a mere handful of prickers the king ordered his breakfast to be made ready and the silken tassels on his standard to be embellished whilst he prepared to shoo the impertinent attackers away.[18] He made no effort to strengthen his camp or to consider a more propitious choice of ground.

From the walls of Durham looking west the ground rises quite steeply by a couple of hundred feet to crest an irregular north–south ridge formation which is broadened in places by a series of bluffs or promontories. The land is uneven and undulating with patches of dead ground and unexpected folds. Its average width does not exceed 500 yards and therefore offers poor potential for a deployment in force, even less for a stately and steady advance in column. To the east towards Durham the ground falls quite markedly and to the west it descends into the twisting valley of the little River Browney.[19] Immediately to the east of this tributary stood Arbour House and eastward again from the hillock on which the farm stands there lies a sharp and unexpected little ravine which would further constrict the already narrow front of an advancing army. A major weakness of the Scots' battle plan must be that the area had not been fully scouted and its pitfalls revealed.

Beyond this ravine still moving eastward the crown of Crossgate Moor is relatively clear before the ground, once again falls away towards the mire of the Flass bog in the depression of Flass vale. As they advanced to contact, the English clearly enjoyed the inestimable advantage of knowing the country and drew up on the southern rim of the ridge where the terrain offered a front of perhaps 1,000 yards with a gentle decline before. The left of the English line was thus anchored in the curve of the Browney by Quarry House, the right on the edge of a spur jutting over the bluffs. Such a deployment would allow a massing of between 10–15 men per linear yard. For defensive purposes the position was ideal. Baliol's mounted reserve was stationed in dead ground to the right rear.[20]

In front of the English position, lying on the eastern flank of the ridge, stands a bronze age barrow known as the Maiden's Bower, in the fight this undoubtably lay behind the Scottish lines. One of the enduring images of Neville's Cross is the procession of clergy from the cathedral to the vantage of the barrow, the muted robes of the monks interspersed with the glowing copes of the episcopal party, the sacred shroud of the saint borne aloft on a lance tip. Despite the obvious partisan stance of these ecclesiastics they went unmolested by the Scots, 'a great number and multitude of Scots running and passing by them with intent to have spoiled them yet they had no power'.[21] It has been suggested that the monks were able to signal back to their brethren in the cathedral tower giving note of Scots dispositions though this is unlikely as any observer in the tower would immediately command a superior view of the field.

The importance of the lessons the English had learnt from their earlier encounters with the Scots has already been noted and had paid a valuable dividend at Morlaix, Crécy and Auberoche. 'Edward III and his commanders won their victories in France by the application and development of tactics learned in the Scottish wars. The army would normally be divided into three battalions of dismounted men at arms, with archers placed on the flanks at an angle . . .'[22] It should not be forgotten that one of the most important lessons had been the need for mobility, thus when we speak of the English 'marching' we really mean riding, each man on the back of his sturdy little garron.

Accounts relating to the famous or infamous 'White Company', a brigade of mercenaries under the formidable martial talent of Sir John Hawkwood fighting in Italy in the following decades, describe the soldiery being formed into sub units or 'lances', each of three men. One of these was a groom or varlet whose function was to hold the mounts at the rear and bring them forward for pursuit (or flight); the remaining two, the men at arms, fought as a team, one covering the other. Those northerners who fought at Neville's Cross were certainly less organised and trained than the professional foot of the White Company. There was a likely preponderance of billmen over archers and, though the clothyard shaft would play its part, the fight was to be very much an infantryman's battle, with the billmen bearing the brunt.

King David appears to have had no doubts that an easy victory was his for the taking. He enjoyed superiority of numbers though the odds were probably less steep than the chronicler suggest. Bower gives the king some 20,000 men but such a host would be almost impossible to marshal in so confined a space. The Scots deployed in three brigades, each containing three schiltroms. If each battalion comprised one thousand spearmen, say three thousand per column with the king's division the strongest, then the army likely comprised some 10,000 men, still twice the potency of the English. From their initial position the Scots commanders could see that their enemies were posted on the crest of the ridge but the incline was by no means severe. They prepared for battle.

Douglas led the van on the right, the king commanded in the centre and gave the left to his nephew, Robert the High Steward.[23] To cope with the confined ground and to add weight to his attack the king advanced his divisions in echelon, a tactic that his father had used to such deadly effect thirty-odd years before at Bannockburn. The crucial differences were that in the earlier fight the English had been so dreadfully constricted by the unfavourable ground that they had been unable to effectively deploy their missile troops and the attack had enjoyed a measure if not of total surprise then certainly unexpectedness. On this day it was the English who had chosen to fight, not as invaders but in defence of kin and property. The sacred banner of St Cuthbert that had guided an earlier army to victory at Northallerton in 1138 now flew above them. They were ready.

The Archbishop, William de Norwell, Bishop of Carlisle and Rokeby took the left, Lord Neville the centre and Percy the right. As Rokeby's bowmen stepped forward to deliver their opening volleys, John Graham, Earl of Menteith, begged leave of King David to lead a mounted charge against them (a further echo of Bannockburn). The request was denied but the headstrong earl charged anyway, losing men and horses to the deadly clothyard shafts. He himself had his mount killed beneath him, leading to a rather undignified scramble back to the safety of the tramping spearmen.

On the Scottish left Douglas was almost immediately in difficulties when his men blundered into the ravine east of Arbour House. The steep decline concealed a patchwork of dykes and hedges that further disordered the struggling files. For the longbowmen, then, a perfect target. Bowstrings thrummed in the crisp autumn air, the fog now vanished as the sun rose. Scots began to fall, the arrows taking a savage toll. Despite their mounting losses the Scots strove to close contact. Those not already mired in the ravine inevitably began to edge to the left, colliding with the main battle in the centre, slowing both. Still the arrows came. More Scots fell till the two flanks met with a mighty crash of spears, lunging points, hacking bills, a slashing, thrusting frenzy. For all their furious valour the Scots could make no headway, their onslaught diluted by the difficult terrain, their numbers thinned by the arrow storm.

In the centre the king's division, advancing over less tangled ground, came swiftly to contact, the dead falling amongst the serried ranks as the archers lashed the schiltroms. Charging home with superb elan the Scots pushed their opponents back, weight of numbers beginning to tell almost immediately. Likewise the Steward's division achieved some initial success, driving the English left almost at right angles to the beleaguered centre. This, in the event, proved of assistance to the hard-pressed marchers for it permitted Baliol to launch his horsemen in a series of well-co-ordinated charges that blunted the attack.

Though few in number the unexpected arrival of cavalry threw the Scots on that wing into consternation. This was the very moment of crisis when the outcome of the day hung in the balance. Had the Steward single-mindedly committed his considerable reserves where the archbishop had none, the tide might yet have turned. Weight of numbers would have told in the fierce mêlée and a mere hundred horse could not have kept the schiltroms at bay indefinitely.

King David's nephew was neither particularly experienced nor dynamic. His subsequent indecision was construed by some of his contemporaries, not least his uncle, as tantamount to deliberate treachery. At best he was faint hearted, for instead of advancing, throwing every man he could into the fray, he hesitated and then withdrew, leaving the English mauled but intact. Given the narrow confines of the ridge he might well have taken the view that massing more men in column would achieve nothing and he may have intended to withdraw and regroup. Whatever the reasoning, the decision was flawed and the outcome ultimately fatal.

Sensing their moment had come the English commanders moved onto the offensive. The fight still raged fiercely in the centre so Neville shored up his line with Baliol's remaining cavalry. Rokeby advanced against the Steward's wing now pulling back in some disorder and Percy fell upon Douglas' struggling battalions. The Scottish right wing was the first to fold, the survivors streaming pell mell over the broken ground of the ravine, leaving the enclosures piled with writhing mounds of dead and wounded. The Steward's withdrawal was hammered into a rout and the flanks of the English army, like the jaws of a massive trap, closed about the king's division in the centre.

The battle had now raged for perhaps an hour and a half. It had as long again to continue, a vicious, exhausting slogging match; the Scots in the centre were by no means yet ready to concede defeat and contested every foot of ground. King David had already suffered two arrow wounds[24] but held on grimly as his men fell about him. Finally, as the long-awaited Yorkshire contingent under Lord Lucas straggled onto the field, the Scots were overwhelmed and broke, fleeing back over Crossgate Moor. The king was able to rally a hardcore of seasoned fighters for a final stand astride the current line of the A167 on Crossgate Moor before being carried along in the final rout. He briefly sought shelter under the span of Aldin Grange Bridge where he was taken prisoner by John de Coupland, though not before he had knocked out a couple of his opponent's teeth.[25]

Despite the magnitude of the disaster the Scots seem to have been able to withdraw in some order, isolated pockets turning on their pursuers with a flurry of sharp actions erupting over the moor, including a substantive rearguard fight on Findon Hill. Beside the king a clutch of earls – Duncan of Fife, Menteith, William of Sutherland, Malcolm of Wigton, Douglas and a posse of other knights – were taken. Randolph, the Earl of Strathearn and William Keith, the Earl Marischal, were all killed. The Lanercost Chronicle was swift to applaud the ruin of the Scots, this enthusiasm doubtless fuelled by the wanton destruction of the Priory:

About the third hour, on a field hard by Durham, the English host came upon the Scots, led by the earl of Angus in the front line, a man of noble

*stock and valiant, ever ready to do battle for his country. The Bishop
ordered that no man should spare a Scot and he himself rode against
them with such a staff* [mace] *that without confession he absolved
many Scots of all future trouble in this world. Then amid the blare
of trumpets, the clash of sword on shield, the hurtling of arrows, you
might hear the wailing of the wounded. Arms were broken, heads
shattered, many lay dead upon the field. Before the hour of vespers
the battle was over and those Scots who had not fallen, fled. David
who called himself King of Scotland, was taken and sent in chains to
the Tower.*[26]

The number of dead is difficult to assess. The Scots would have suffered
heavily, from the arrow storm, in the mêlée and above all in the rout.
Many of the stragglers would have been picked off by vengeful locals as
they struggled towards the sanctuary of the border. It is therefore likely
that several thousand fell whilst English casualties would probably be in the
hundreds. In recognition of his outstanding leadership Ralph Neville
was awarded the unique distinction of the right to burial in the cathedral,
the first layman to be so honoured.[27]

*She hath been then more fear'd than harmed my liege;
For hear her but exampled by herself:
When all her chivalry hath been in France,
And she a mourning widow of her nobles,
She hath herself not only well defended,
But taken, and impounded as a stray,
The king of Scots; whom she did send to France,
To fill King Edward's fame with prisoner kings . . .*[28]

King David's grand chevauchee had achieved nothing and ended in disaster. His capture effectively neutralised his country as France's ally. He had
failed to demonstrate any of his father's genius for war. The northerners
had been better led, they had chosen their ground well, made effective use
of their small mounted reserve and deployed so as to maximise the killing
power of the longbow. There was, however, one difficulty remaining. In
English eyes David was not king of Scotland but a valueless usurper –
Edward Baliol was the true king and he, despite the weight of his advancing
years, was game to try once more.

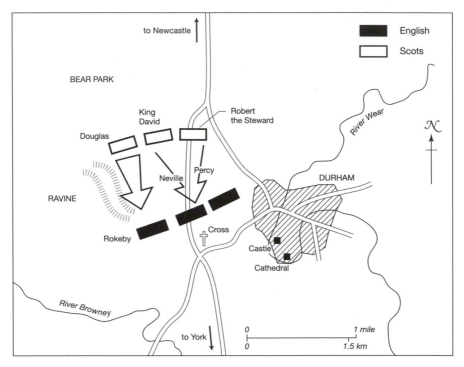

Neville's Cross, 1346

As the siege of Calais monopolised English resources through the long months of 1347 King Edward had little practical support to offer his vassal, despite the stunning victories of Crécy and Neville's Cross. Calais had not capitulated and the French, though beaten, were not cowed. The forces therefore available to support Edward Baliol were slender. Percy and Neville were each contracted to supply 180 men at arms and the same number of archers for service in Scotland. With King David captive and Randolph dead the guardianship devolved onto Robert the Steward, the man who had least to gain by the king's release. The new Guardian found himself beleaguered by internal strife and the Baliol threat.

In May 1347 the Disinherited marched out of Carlisle with a total complement of a little over 3,000, a small force soon eroded by detachments detailed for garrison duty in captured castles. Despite this paucity of numbers Baliol was able to extend his sway over virtually the whole of the Scottish border lands, the sheriffdoms of Berwick, Roxburgh, Peebles, Dumfries with the forests of Jedburgh, Selkirk and Ettrick. Though he was also able to re-establish his grip on his ancestral holdings in Galloway and occupy Maxwell's proud seat at Caerlaverock he lacked the means to push beyond the strategic barrier of the Forth. The Steward despite his inactivity was able to retain both Edinburgh and Stirling.

Baliol's success was to repeat the chimera of his earlier conquests; he had neither the muscle nor the affinity to maintain a grip on power. The Scots might be defeated but they were not ready for serfdom. Too much blood had been spilt in the fight for independence to let the throne pass to England's creature. The Steward was thus able, for a consideration of £9,000, to buy a truce to hold until 9th September.[29]

> *This half-hearted invasion was Baliol's last attempt to secure Scotland. Baliol's failure to take any of those strategic strongholds except those along the border meant he was unable to hold the countryside.*[30]

Baliol was perhaps glad to be bought off so he could seek to consolidate his position, though that of the Steward was scarcely more encouraging. Many of the leading Scottish nobles were captive and Edward, cannily, was in no hurry to accept ransoms. The defeated were of more use as impotent captives than as war leaders on their own marches. The earls of Menteith and Fife who had previously sworn allegiance to England were both tried for treason and the former suffered the full horror of a traitor's death. Fife was luckier – kinship to Edward saved his life.

In France English arms continued to enjoy success. After the fall of Calais the terms of an eight-year truce were agreed. On 12th October a stunning victory won by Sir John Dagworth when he broke the siege of La Roche Derrien in Brittany yielded an additional bonus with the capture of Charles of Blois, the Valois candidate for the dukedom. Edward now held the King of Scots, the Constable of France and the titular duke of Brittany.[31]

An attempt to recover the Calais Pale was beaten off in 1349 and the following year, on 29th August, witnessed a further fleet action off Winchelsea. The Castillian Carlos de la Cerda, a confederate of Charles of Blois leading a largely Spanish squadron, was soundly defeated and half his vessels taken. A year later Philip VI, borne down by the weight of his defeats, finally succumbed to be succeeded by his son, John of Normandy, 'Jean le Bel'.[32] The new king's attempt to mount a campaign in Aquitaine in 1351 was frustrated by Sir John Beauchamp and the chance capture of the important French outpost at Guines further strengthened the Pale.

With the key bastion of Calais finally secure and his armies triumphant Edward need be in no hurry to sell the King of Scotland back to the Scots. The Steward was scarcely pressing in his overtures and David was left to shift for himself. Since February 1347 he had been lodged in the Tower and in the following year he was able to secure an emissary from the Scottish Assembly to treat with his captor.

Edward felt he could afford to be greedy and a further appeal directly to Pope Clement VI in 1350 did little to improve upon the terms being demanded. In return for his freedom David II would be obliged to swear homage to the throne of England, to hand over key fortresses as security for his good vassalage. Further to perform knight service against his erstwhile allies the French upon demand, to restore the Disinherited to all of their former lands and, perhaps the most bitter pill of all, to accept Edward or one of his sons as his successor should he die childless.

Such terms were clearly unacceptable. David would immediately realise his countrymen would consider this far too high a price for his personal freedom. In the spring and summer of 1350 the negotiations continued. Two separate but related embassies left Scotland to treat firstly with the English marcher lords and, through them, with the crown. Sir William Douglas, having proved a useful and skilled negotiator, was released from captivity to carry the English demands to the Assembly.

The revised terms included the repayment of a ransom of £40,000 – the Scottish castles currently in English hands would be returned once the deposit was paid over. John of Gaunt, the king's younger son, was to be nominated as David's heir (the king was, of course, still a young man so there was every possibility he would father a son). The Disinherited were still to be restored though this condition begins to sound hollow, more a matter of form than substance. Baliol would be aware that negotiations were in progress and must have been equally aware that he was being relegated to the margins.

The Steward, who like Baliol saw nothing of benefit in these proposals, made overtures to the French court, pointing out the risks to France if Scotland fell under English domination. At the same time, however, Baliol was also appealing to Paris for recognition of his claims. King John sought to neutralise him by promising the return of his family lands in France if he came to terms with King David.[33] Douglas, who appears to have adopted the role of 'honest broker' between the two powers, returned to the English court in the following spring bringing a draft of the Scots' reply. Matters were sufficiently cordial for a conference to be arranged to take place at Hexham on 24th April. Although the requisite safe conducts were granted to the Scots due to attend, these never arrived – the Steward found means to delay them and effectively destroy the accord.[34]

Determined not to be sabotaged by his nephew David called a Parliament to assemble at Dundee with the authority to set aside the Steward's prevarication. By August an impressive Scots delegation comprising four bishops, four earls and four knights was in conference at Newcastle. After a month of tough talking the two parties had each refined their position. The Scots wanted the whole of the English Pale to be returned forthwith, a waiver of ransom and a truce to endure for 1,000 years (this was a compromise on sovereignty, a form of concession that fell short of a full submission). For their part the English were still insisting on military service, restoration of the Disinherited (but with adequate compensation for the current landowners) and the recognition of John of Gaunt as heir presumptive. In November the captive king was given leave to return home and present the terms to the Scottish polity in person. When Parliament met in February 1352 the assembly was prepared to accept a hefty ransom but refused any suggestion of submission. Matters reached such a pitch that disturbances between the royal affinity led by Douglas and the rival faction supporting the Steward threatened to raise the spectre of civil war. To his credit David was not prepared to buy his freedom by shedding the blood of his countrymen – he bowed to the will of the majority and returned to custody.[35]

Another who had enjoyed a brief taste of freedom was Charles of Blois whom Edward proposed to release in consideration of an oath of fealty. This would have resulted in the paradox of the English sponsoring both claimants to the dukedom. However, Jeanne de Penthievre, Charles' strong-minded wife, thought the terms too high and packed her husband back off into captivity. After Dagworth had been killed in an ambush his command devolved onto the equally energetic knight Sir Thomas Bentley, who in August 1352 met a superior French army under Marshal de Vesle, which had occupied Rennes and was pushing into Brittany at Mauron, and won a further signal victory.[36]

Whilst the French were reeling from this fresh catastrophe Edward instigated peace talks which convened at Guines in April 1354. The terms were uncompromising: the Aquitaine was to be held in fee simple by the English crown without homage, together with Poitou, Touraine, Anjou Maine and Normandy. Had the draft treaty been ratified then the king would have presided over a continental empire as large as the Angevin inheritance of Henry II. The fatal error was to permit a delay until the autumn when it was proposed the concord should be ratified by the Pope at Avignon. In the interim King John and his nobles recovered their collective nerve and they threw out the draft. By the following June a resumption of the war had become inevitable.

One of the provisions of the abortive Treaty of Guines was that the French would renounce their Scottish alliance. Clearly this would have dramatically weakened King David's negotiating position. In July 1354 the basis of an Anglo-Scottish agreement was hammered out at Berwick: a ransom of 90,000 marks was to be paid in equal annual instalments spread over a nine-year term, with a truce of equal duration. Cannily the Scots continued to prevaricate whilst they waited to see whether the Guines accord was finally ratified. When talks failed they withdrew from the negotiations. As the storm clouds gathered the following spring the French sent a force of sixty men at arms under Garancieres with a significant cash incentive[37] to assist the Scots in their decision to resort once again to arms.

Edward riposted by ordering a major muster at Newcastle in the summer, the threat of which was sufficient to persuade the new Earl of Douglas to seek a temporary truce. There was a climate of enmity within the ranks of the Scottish nobility. Douglas was on poor terms with Patrick Dunbar, the Earl of March and had, earlier, offered the Earl of Northampton *carte blanche* to waste his enemy's lands. Never one to brook such a slight March struck at Norham and executed a textbook ambush of the forces who pursued him.[38]

The Scottish Earl of March was in the field once more in November when, on the first of the month and in the company of Garancieres and Thomas Stewart, he led a bold amphibious descent on Berwick. Having secured the harbour in the course of a daring night attack, the Scots succeeded in driving the defenders into the refuge of the castle from whence all efforts to dislodge them failed. Sir John Coupland, who had continued his inexorable rise since his fortuitous capture of the Scottish king, attempted a relief but was beaten off. Edward was greeted with the news of this reverse on his return from Calais, by which time the French paladins had undertaken the reverse journey and promptly marched north. Such was the terror of his name that the citizenry would recall with horror the treatment meted out to their forbears by the king's grandfather and immediately hastened to submit.

For his French campaign of 1355 Edward proposed a series of linked offensives springing from Picardy, Normandy and Aquitaine, though in the event hostilities did not commence in earnest until the following spring. The formidable Henry of Lancaster landed in Normandy but King John forced him to retire into Brittany. Edward, Prince of Wales, had taken the field in late July and, having crossed the Dordogne on 4th August sought a juncture with Lancaster, unaware that the French were now between the two English forces and in very considerable strength. By September the prince, his small army replete with booty and beasts, was falling back towards Bordeaux. On the 9th King John entered Blois and in the following week closed in on Edward, with some outpost skirmishing flaring around Poitiers.

As the French had interposed themselves between the English and their base the prince was obliged to seek favourable ground upon which to receive them. As the two sides parlayed on Sunday 18th September the English were deploying along a ridge some nine miles south-west of Poitiers, using the time spent in negotiations to fortify their lines. Matters were serious. The French, perhaps as many as 30,000 strong, had seized the strategic initiative. The prince commanded at best say a fifth of those numbers, his army comprising English archers and Gascon men at arms in roughly equal proportions.[39]

King John had grounds for savouring his advantage and the terms he sought were harsh, including the prince's submission. In the circumstances there was only one option – to fight. Though the odds were steep the English army comprised mainly tried veterans led by experienced captains such as Warwick, who took the van, the prince the centre with Chandos and Sir James Audley, Salisbury and Suffolk holding the rear. That swashbuckling Gascon, the Captal de Buch, led a mounted reserve.

As the glittering array of the French army swelled over the opposite ridge and began to crowd the ground between, many of the Anglo-Gascons must have quailed at the sight, the air alive with the tramp of thousands of marching steel shod feet, the forest of banners fluttering proudly in the late summer morning. Sensing the shiver run through the ranks the prince, surrounded by the comforting sight of his battle-hardened commanders, paused to address the army:

> *Now, Sirs, though we are but a small company, let us not be afraid, for victory falls not to multitudes but where God will send it. If the day be ours we shall be honoured, and if we die, we die in a good quarrel and the King, my father, and others, will avenge us. Therefore be of good heart and do your duty this day.*[40]

Douglas was present amongst King John's army with a strong contingent of his countrymen; like the French, the Scots had earlier defeats to avenge. On the earl's advice King John bade all of his men dismount and split them into eight battles or brigades whilst a commanded party of three hundred picked cavalry under a brace of marshals Clermont and D'Audrehem were advanced to test the defenders' mettle. The broken ground and the skilful use of existing features hid the English dispositions from this probing attack. Clermont and Chandos had traded abuse as the French skirmished earlier. Both, as it transpired, claimed a certain heraldic device and the marshal objected to sharing his colours with a commoner.

The horse came on in good order, well in check, a dense column of the very pride of French chivalry. It was around 8 a.m. on Monday 19th September. As the French cantered up the rising ground the English archers, partly concealed behind a thick hedge that stretched over the swell of the ridge, let fly, bringing men and horses crashing to the ground. Clermont and many of those who followed him were killed and the attack stalled.

As the surviving horsemen fell back in disorder the Dauphin Charles led the van forward, perhaps two thousand men, tramping up the slope already strewn with French dead. Again the bowmen stepped forward and shot into the tightly packed ranks. Despite mounting losses the attackers struggled up the hill to come to contact, a fierce sprawling mêlée around the hedge. The fight raged fiercely for half an hour till the French broke and dissolved in rout, pelting back towards the safety of their own lines, their panic, swift as contagion, spreading to Orleans division. Despite these losses the king's division was still intact and its complement of eight thousand was sufficient to overwhelm the exhausted English, tired, bloody and virtually out of arrows. The battle hung in the balance.

It was now, in the moment of crisis, that the experience of the English commanders told. Chandos urged the prince not to sit on the defensive but to seize the moment and order a general advance. This was a bold move and a risky one – the English would be abandoning their defensive position that had served them so well and staking all on the chance of the mêlée. Leaving a screen of archers, scarcely more than a skirmish line to hold the ridge, the prince gave the order to mount, to sweep down upon the mass of the French, an iridescent, steel-tipped avalanche.

A savage contest erupted as the English broke from the shelter of the hedge and smashed into their astonished ranks. As the French attack was halted the archers closed in on the flanks, loosing into the tightly packed ranks. Men fell dead in droves but more took their places. Froissart records the scene:

> *The King's battalion advanced in good order, and gave many hard blows against the English. The King himself with the Lord Philippe* [his fourth son] *attacked the earls of Warwick and Salisbury, who rode with the Captal de Buch, the Lord Pommiers and others. Here too fought the Duke of Athens, Constable of France, the Duke of Bourbon, with many good knights from the Bourbonnois and Picardy, with men of Poitou and the Lords of Pons and Parthenay, and many more. The Lord Douglas of Scotland was in the King's company and fought there valiantly till he saw all was lost. Then he saved himself as fast as he could, for he dreaded capture by the English. Here, in the forefront of the English, fought Sir James Audley, with his four squires. He was severely wounded but maintained the fight and the advance as long as he could. As for King Jean, he proved himself a good knight, aye . . . had a fourth of his people fought so well as the King, the day would have been his.*[41]

True to the code of his chivalric order the French King fought with Homeric valour, his young son by his side. Mere valour could not alone suffice, however. A flank attack by the English mounted reserve under the Captal de Buch finally decided the issue and the French were utterly defeated, the survivors put to ignominious rout. Apart from the several thousand dead, stiffening in the September sun, the King of France, his son, seventeen lords, thirteen counts, five viscounts and over one hundred knights banneret were 'in the bag' along with a vast haul of booty and the glory of a famous victory.

As the King of France lost his liberty, a former King of Scotland was about to give up on his claim. As his son campaigned in Aquitaine Edward III had crossed the border to chastise the Scots for failing to ratify the Treaty of Berwick. On 20th January of that year he was at Roxburgh when he had an extraordinary interview with Edward Baliol. The king had supported his vassal since the heady days of Dupplin Moor nearly a quarter of a century earlier. By now Baliol was utterly worn out and disheartened.

No mean soldier, he had still failed to hang on to almost any of the gains he'd made after Neville's Cross; even his ancestral lands in Galloway were now lost. It was time to throw in the towel and he was prepared to assign his claim to the Scottish throne to Edward for a consideration of 5,000 marks. This he received and a generous annuity of 2,000 marks. The paladin of the Disinherited disappears into obscurity, dying at Doncaster in 1364.

Edward's chevauchee through the Lothians was so frightful and so thorough in its destructiveness that it became known as the 'Burnt Candlemas'. Brutal as the lesson may have been it may well have convinced Robert the Steward of the need to resume negotiations. In the late winter of 1357 the Steward presided over a council at Perth where it was agreed that the Bishop of St Andrews should lead a delegation to London. By May the parties had hammered out the working draft of an agreement. This was then polished in the course of a further sitting at Berwick in late September. By the 25th King David was there on licence and on 3rd October the treaty was sealed.

A ransom of 100,000 marks was to be paid by means of ten equal annual instalments backed by a truce of even duration. Both Baliol and John of the Isles were recognised as allies of the English Crown and thus inviolate. A total of nine hostages, drawn from the first rank of the nobility and including the Steward and attending on a three-man rota, were to be available, though in fact none was ever actually demanded. On 5th October David II ratified the treaty and gained his full liberty.

Although the king was restored, the realm would groan under the weight of the ransom. From Edward's perspective the mere fact of the obligation effectively neutralised Scotland and left him free to pursue his ambitions in France. The magnitude of the English victory at Poitiers and the loss of her king spurred a wave of popular unrest in France with local disturbances, rural unrest by frustrated rustics or 'Jacquerie' leading to virtual anarchy and bloodletting. France too was to be burdened with a hefty ransom. As a result of papal intervention a two-year truce was agreed and in May 1357 the captive King of France arrived in London from Bordeaux. Such an important prisoner created quite a stir whilst the serious business of bargaining continued. A draft Treaty of London was negotiated in January 1358 followed by a further concord in March the next year.

The Dauphin Charles, whose regency had got off to such a shaky start, had begun to mature into the role of government. He rejected the initial terms and risked Edward's wrath. This was not slow in coming. In November 1359 the king led a further campaign in France, advancing from Calais, storming through Picardy to threaten Rheims. Charles kept his nerve and cannily refused to be drawn. He rejected any notion of battle and relied instead on a guerrilla-style campaign, harassing supply lines and 'beating up' isolated detachments. Edward was accompanied by two of his sons, the Black Prince and John of Gaunt (now wed to Henry of Lancaster's daughter Blanche, heiress to the great wealth of the Duchy).

On 13th April 1360 the English army, encamped to the south of Paris, was struck by a sudden storm of cataclysmic proportions. The violent weather lashed the English host like the wrath of God; thunder and lightning echoed through the heavens, men and animals were literally struck down dead. Somewhat shaken by the biblical fury of this inclemency Edward withdrew and dispatched his eldest son to open negotiations. This was followed by a further embassy under Lancaster who met with the French delegates led by the Bishop of Beauvais. The final result was the Treaty of Brétigny.

Not unsurprisingly the agreement favoured the English. King John's ransom was the staggering sum of three million gold ecus and Edward was confirmed in his conquests. The Aquitaine was ceded outright and its boundaries extended to include Poitou, Saintonge and the Limousin, Quercy and Agenais, a vast swathe of land, fertile and abundant. To the English negotiators it must have seemed like a major political coup crowning two decades of successful military activity, but in fact the victory was illusory.

That year saw the very height of England's fortunes in France – over the next twenty years most would be lost. Edward III would eventually decline into a peevish old age, losing that great and irresistible mastery of affairs, prone to the dictates of capricious mistresses. His eldest son would win a further great if ultimately empty victory in 1366 at Najera before dying before his father and leaving a minor as heir. The French, led by the Breton knight Bertrand du Guesclin, the 'hog in armour', would steadily claw back so much of what had been lost.

France's ally David II of Scotland had ample cause to rue his ill-judged intervention which had led to military disaster, humiliation, the loss of good government, internal dissent and a crippling financial burden. For two years the realm was simply unable to fund the cost of the instalments and the king came south again to try to negotiate easier terms. He was prepared to offer limited restitution to the rump of the Disinherited and to recognise Edward or one of his sons as heir presumptive in the event he died childless – on condition the two nations would remain as separate states. David has been viewed as both weak and unpatriotic but in reality he had little choice – there were too few cards in the deck to negotiate on equal terms.

In any event the Scottish Parliament, meeting in March 1364, rejected the terms. Over a year later the Assembly offered a ransom of £100,000, payable in tranches of £4,000 per annum. In 1369 the king again sought to renegotiate. At this point matters in France had deteriorated considerably from the triumph of 1360 and Edward was disposed to be reasonable. David had already paid off £44,000 and the debt was now consolidated as 56,000 marks at 4,000 marks a year.

All told David II has not enjoyed a good press. He is frequently portrayed as a feckless monarch ruled by voracious sexual appetites.[42] This pejorative view is perhaps unfair. Many of the reforms he instigated were to form the basis for the energetic rule of the later Stewart kings and the fact that he was able to accept the rejection of certain of his proposals by Parliament indicates a good working relationship based on pragmatism and the ability to compromise. It has been said that '. . . for the Scots the legacy of the long war was the emergence of a coherent political community held together by common interests, a loose alliance with France and a freshly renewed national identity'.[43]

His return marked an end to the slack abuses of the Steward, though the rift was never truly healed and the perceived defection on the field of Neville's Cross continued to fester. The rise in customs duties during the 1360s did, at least in part, offset the otherwise intolerable burden of the ransom payments. The king had learned he needed to consult with the community and to accept their wishes even if these were contrary to his own.[44]

His relationship with the nobility was never an easy one. Even though he raised the Steward, March and Douglas to earldoms in 1357, all three opposed him six years later – possibly their resentment over the degree of influence the Drummonds were exercising over the throne prompted their rebellion. Queen Joan died in August 1362 and the king turned to Margaret Drummond, the widow of Sir John Logie. By 1369 they were estranged and David remained childless. Despite his having taken up arms against him the king felt obliged both to pardon the Steward and confirm his right of succession. By 1371 David was 46, still childless and had his sights on Agnes Dunbar. It was, or so it seemed, by no means too late for an heir. However, in that year the king died suddenly and Robert the Steward, eight years his senior, at last came into his own, the first of the Stewart kings of Scotland.

Notes

1 Contemporary ballad, *c.* 1350 quoted in Neillands, R., *The Hundred Years War*, London 1990 p. 93.
2 Quoted in Prestwich, M., *The Three Edwards*, London 1980 p. 188.
3 Ibid p. 189.
4 Ibid p. 190.
5 Ibid p. 192.
6 Ibid p. 191.
7 Ibid p. 195.
8 Ibid p. 194.
9 Ibid p. 197.
10 Traquair, P., *Freedom's Sword*, London 1998 p. 297.
11 *Henry V* (I:III).
12 Traquair p. 297.
13 Ibid p. 297.
14 Ibid p. 297.
15 The garrison in fact is reported as having comprised no more than eight men at arms and seven hobilars with, on 29th September rations for three weeks at most, see Traquair p. 297.
16 Burne, A.H., *More Battlefields of England*, London 1952 p. 116.
17 Traquair p. 297.
18 Ibid p. 297.
19 Burne p. 118.
20 Ibid p. 120.
21 A commemorative cross was later erected on the top of the Maiden's Bower and the Benedictines would pause there for prayer as they journeyed to and

from Beaurepaire. The sacred corporax cloth of St Cuthbert which Prior Fosser had been inspired to utilise as a banner was destroyed, with so many other relics in the course of the reformation. The legend is that the cloth came into the possession of a man named Whittingham whose French wife, an ardent Huguenot, promptly cast it into the fire to demonstrate her fine contempt for such popish baubles.

22 Prestwich p. 197.

23 Burne p. 120 – the field is now much obscured by subsequent building. The line of the present railway neatly cuts across the English line, whilst the A167 bisects Crossgate Moor north to south. Baliol probably took station around what is now the junction between Crossgate Peth and the A167. Much of the combat would have been fought in and around the grounds of Durham Johnson School (which, fittingly, was the scene of a symposium on the battle held in October 1996). There is a current battlefield trail accompanied by a useful leaflet available through tourist information offices.

24 One of the arrowheads had to be extracted by a barber surgeon brought from York whilst the wounded king was temporarily incarcerated at Bamburgh. The chronicler Froissart recalls that the king still suffered headaches some twenty years later, caused by a fragment lodged in the skull – see Traquair p. 299.

25 Sir John de Coupland, who before Neville's Cross had held only relatively minor posts, profited extensively from his good fortune of being the one to capture the Scottish king. He was raised to the rank of banneret and awarded a pension of £500, a very substantial annuity in addition to a full indemnity for all previous murders and felonies. Coupland's success launched him as one of the 'new' men of the border. Latterly he was elevated to the sheriffdoms of Northumberland and Roxburgh, became constable of the castle there and keeper of Berwick. Like the Percys he proved ruthlessly adept at acquiring lands, an excess of avarice over scruple that earned him the enmity of numerous of his neighbours. His methods finally outraged the 'older' families to such an extent that a gang of them ambushed Coupland and did him to death on Bolton Moor on 20th December 1363 (see Lomas, R., *County of Conflict*, East Lothian 1996 p. 54).

26 Extract from *The Lanercost Chronicle* quoted in Neillands p. 107.

27 The original cross, now known as Neville's Cross, was one of several that ringed Durham and predates the battle. It was destroyed in 1589 by 'some lewd and contemptuous wicked persons' (quoted in Burne p. 126). The socket survived and was used as the base for a later milestone. Later vandalism in the form of twentieth-century road widening saw the base moved some distance to its present location on the north side of Crossgate Peth, just east of the junction with the A167.

28 *Henry V* (I:III).

29 Traquair p. 301.

30 Ibid p. 301.

31 The captives were treated in accordance with the chivalric code to which Edward was so devoted. There was a strong element of pragmatism in this insofar as, depending on the fluctuating and uncertain tides of war, the captor might one day become the captive. All three important prisoners took part in revels and tournaments, the Constable with such unbounded enthusiasm that, on his return, his enemies were successful in having him arraigned for treason, condemned and executed. On St George's day 1348 the king established the Order of the Garter with a great ceremony at Windsor. Edward the Black Prince was a founding member, as were Walter Manny, Chandos and the Gascon Captal de Buch.

32 The king had a fascination with chivalry that verged on the quixotic. To compete with the English Garter knights he created The Order of the Star whose members were sworn never to quit the field whilst the day was un-decided. That the French took this pledge seriously was evidenced on the field of Mauron where some ninety members of the order fell.

33 Traquair p. 304.

34 Douglas had committed himself to a pro-English stance and subsequently held Hermitage Castle in Liddesdale for Edward. However, his godson, also named William, returned from France to recover the lands the older Sir William had fraudulently occupied. In August 1353 the feud culminated in the death of the elder Douglas in Ettrick Forest and the disenfranchised godson reclaimed both his inheritance and his allegiance, thus returning Hermitage to Scotland – see Traquair p. 304.

35 Traquair p. 304.

36 This period also witnessed the famous set-piece skirmish known as 'The Battle of the Thirty' when rival garrisons, the English under Sir Richard Bambro from Ploermel and the French led by Robert de Beaumanoir of Josselin, staged a lethal duel between thirty paladins from each side. Bambro had such doughty fighters as Knollys and Sir Hugh Calveley but the bulk of his contingent was made up of German mercenaries. The fight raged for the best part of the day, a mass gladiatorial spectacle watched by a large and no doubt appreciative crowd: 'They fought with the short swords of Bordeaux, with lances and daggers and axes and gave each other marvellous great blows, and did right noble deeds of arms; there has not been such deeds these hundred years past and thus they fought together until the English were worsted and those who lived taken into Josselin as prisoners.' Bambro and eight of his side perished, the French lost four dead. Despite the fact that the fight was in violation of the truce and served no conceivable military objective the survivors were universally regarded as true paladins of chivalry (see Neillands p. 118).

37 The actual sum was 40,000 gold moutons, Traquair p. 305.

38 One of those taken was Thomas Gray of Heton who, whilst captive in Edinburgh until 1357, used the time to commence his chronicle *Scalacronica*. Another prisoner was less fortunate. His captor sold him on to one of the

French knights who promptly executed his purchase in revenge for the death of his father at the hands of the English in France.

39 Neillands p. 127.
40 Ibid p. 126.
41 Ibid p. 130.
42 One of David's mistresses, Katherine Mortimer, was done to death in a scene worthy of Webster or Ford at their most inventive on the lonely road to Soutra in 1360. Her assassin, possibly a past admirer but certainly no stranger, engaged the unfortunate young woman in conversation and, as she leant towards him from the saddle, stabbed her to the heart and she tumbled lifeless onto the track. Suspicion inevitably pointed towards the Steward, jealous at Katherine's influence over the king.
43 Lynch, M., *Scotland: A New History*, London 1991 p. 133.
44 Ibid p. 136.

Chapter 9

Landscape of War

They were kneeling in a small box-shaped pit sunk into the stone floor, huddled together in fear, their arms and hands entwined in support. Normally the hole would have been used to store grain and covered with the wooden trapdoor that now lay upright on its hinges behind their backs. It would have been the ideal place to hide. Close the lid and the pit would be nearly invisible. There would have been just enough room for three people to lie beneath it. What gave them away? I wondered. A cough? A sob?

Two of the women were in their twenties, the third was an old lady. Someone had shot her in the mouth and her shattered dentures cascaded with her own teeth down her front like mashed melon pips. One girl had been shot repeatedly in the chest. It was difficult to tell if the other had had her throat cut or been shot; a great gash of blood crescented her neck. The expression on their faces had survived the damage. It was so clear. A time valve that opened directly onto those last moments. So you saw what they saw. I hope beyond hope that I never see it again.[1]

This the reality of war. Though the account refers to a modern conflict in the Balkans, the horror would have been repeated times without number during the three hundred years of border conflict. We have, to a degree, come to accept the sanitised version of 'high-tech' war suggested by the use of 'smart' weapons and camera footage that shows the clinical and apparently bloodless removal of enemy targets. But the true, merciless features of war are never far behind, savage and degrading. The medieval or Tudor inhabitants of, say, Corbridge or Jedburgh would have no difficulty in recognising the scene Anthony Loyd so graphically describes.

> [Malcolm] *commanded them no longer to spare any of the English nation, but either to slay them all or to drive them away under the yoke of perpetual slavery . . . Old men and women were either beheaded by swords or stuck with spears like pigs destined for the table . . . babes were tossed high in the air and caught on the spikes of spears . . . Malcolm watched all these things without pity; merely ordering his slave drivers to make haste.*[2]

Thus a twelfth-century chronicler describes the savagery of Malcolm Canmore's raid of 1070. Even allowing for an element of propagandist embellishment the story repeats the echo of wanton slaughter. Behind each glorious battle and chivalric deed this murderous reaction lurks. The English were swift to taste this bitter reality when Wallace rode south in the wake of his victory at Stirling Bridge. Bruce, having achieved the ascendency, began to repeat the pattern after 1311. He first struck from the west carrying fire and sword through Tynedale via Harbottle and Redesmouth. The following year he wasted North Northumberland.

> *Scotland was hammered into nationhood by the Wars of Independence, but the anvil of its forging was the border countryside. And the borders has never recovered from that historical curse.*[3]

Terror was an instrument of policy then as now and for Bruce 'frightfulness' paid dividends. In 1312 he was offered £2,000 to secure a respite and the promise of 'free transit and access whenever he wished to ride further into England'.[4] The City of Durham created an internal tax mechanism to raise revenue to buy off the rapacious Scots in the triumphant years after Bannockburn. In 1327 the Monastery of Blanchland petitioned the crown for relief, intimating that the Scots had destroyed forty acres of wheat and rye, one hundred acres each of oats and hay with the further loss of five hundred sheep to the value of 20 marks. Supplies were dispatched from the crown depot at Newcastle.[5]

We have further evidence of the destructiveness of these cross-border raids from the archives of the Bishopric of Durham. The see held a number of estates in north Northumberland (the area known as 'North Durham' existed on county maps till the mid-nineteenth century). The churches of Norham and Holy Island enjoyed income from thirty-one townships, twelve in Norham and nineteen within the bounds of the extended parish of Holy Island. The rents were collected in part by the local clergy and in part by the cathedral treasury officer or bursar through his agent the Proctor of Norham. Until the fateful summer of 1314 the Proctor could expect to pull in £400–£420, but in that year of Bannockburn the income dipped to £280 and declined disastrously in the years that followed, a mere £9 in 1318–19 and struggling to hit double figures in other years.[6]

The impact of the continuing nature of the war was also felt by the gentry. Estates which had been profitable declined in value to almost nil. They were obliged to extend the defences of their sometimes hitherto undefended manor houses and to incur the considerable cost of providing war horses, arms and armour, with the potentially crippling incidental risk of ransom. To add insult to these very real injuries the crown not infrequently compounded the loss through a tardy exchequer.

In 1320, the lord of Ellingham, Robert de Clifford, a martial name, petitioned for an annuity of £62 to offset the losses he had incurred in the service of the crown. These included, *inter alia*, the sum of £100 paid as a ransom after he was taken at Bannockburn, the consequential loss of horse and armour to the value of 100 marks, together with his expenses whilst serving with the garrison at Berwick and compounded with a loss of income from his manors which he assessed as £100. His case was not unique and many knights simply gave up the unequal struggle. John of Rothbury craved retirement to a monastery alleging destitution as a result of his involvement.[7]

Others, perhaps even more desperate, resorted to banditry, the most celebrated being Sir Gilbert de Middleton. On 13th August 1317 as previously recorded he, with a gang of desperadoes ambushed and kidnapped Louis Beaumont, the newly elected prince Bishop.[8] The erring knight and his brother soon paid for their lawlessness with their lives but their acts of brigandage could be viewed as an extreme expression of a wider protest against the impotence of the crown in the face of sustained Scottish attacks.

Bruce and his able lieutenants had learnt that blackmail was a far more effective weapon than the torch. The warfare they now waged was economic, impoverishing the north of England whilst restocking their own damaged economy. One of those who had participated in the capture of de Middleton was John de Fawdon, who was rewarded by the grant of an annuity. Some years later he was obliged to petition for the arrears, his loss exacerbated by the cost of ransoms, having twice been captured by the Scots and having had his property damaged on no less than three occasions.[9]

The Treaty of Northampton brought some relief and it is perhaps remarkable how swiftly wasted manors recovered. The Proctor of Norham saw his revenue rise from a low of £22 in 1327–8 to a healthier £220 in only three years.[10] Though the English border counties suffered in the periods of Scots ascendancy, the marchers were always enthusiastic participants in the wars. Quite when the pattern of riding names and cross-border raiding that was to mature into the anarchy of the 'Steel Bonnets' first arose may be unclear but the upland English families of Tynedale and Redesdale[11] were providing men at arms by the beginning of the fourteenth century. In 1306 a brigade of longbow men, three hundred strong in three commanded companies, were raised for service in Galloway under Sir Geoffrey de Mowbray who was engaged in hot pursuit of the fugitive King of Scots.[12]

It was inevitable that local cross-border 'arrangements' were frequently entered into without the knowledge or authority of national governments; such an arrangement was to cost Sir Andrew de Harclay his position and his life. In areas like Tynedale with an historic link to the Scottish crown a pattern of active collaboration appears, a case of 'if you can't beat 'em, join 'em!' This notwithstanding the Northumbrian highlands were savagely mauled and progressively depopulated during these terrible years, 'From the miseries that now engulfed the highland area for years to come, the collaboration with the enemy of a section of her population brought no more relief to Tynedale than the red banner of the Umfravilles to Redesdale, for all its golden cinquefoil and orle of crosses.'[13]

In 1315 the newly appointed keeper of Tynedale, Sir Anthony Lucy, found that the Scots had stolen all of the draught animals and wasted crops; even the fruit trees of Tarset had all been cut down.[14] The effects of this comprehensive wasting meant that the area failed to benefit from years of plenty whilst the effects of years of want were exacerbated. An inventory of Comyn–Talbot manors in the valley, carried out in 1325, graphically illustrates the extent of the devastation:

Walwick and Tarset manors destroyed; hopes at Tarset, Emmel,
Carriteth, Kielder and Thorneyburn reduced in annual value from
sums as high as £26 13s. 4d. down through 13s. 4d. to nil; acre values
down from twelve through four pence to nil; only one of fourteen 20 acre
bondages in Charlton and ten of thirty-eight acres of demesne near
Tarset still farmed.[15]

The situation in the English west march was rendered somewhat less desperate by the active resistance inspired and led by Harcla who had been active in the years before Bannockburn holding a series of march appointments. Carlisle was, for Bruce, an early and important objective. Its capture would expose the whole of Cumberland and Westmorland to Scottish domination. When the blow fell in 1315 Harcla had only a tiny garrison with which to resist a siege: four knights, fifty men at arms, fifteen esquires, one hundred and fifty bowmen and a handful of hobelers plus such local militia as the townspeople could furnish to man the long circuit of the walls. The Lanercost Chronicle provides an illuminating view of the leaguer which carries the immediacy of an eyewitness account:

On every day of the siege they assaulted one of the three gates of the city,
sometimes all three at once; but never without loss, because there were
discharged upon them from the walls such dense volleys of darts and
arrows, likewise stones, that they asked one another if stones bred and
multiplied within the walls. Now on the fifth day of the siege they set up
a machine for casting stones, next to the church of Holy Trinity, where
their king stationed himself, and they cast great stones continually
against the wall, but they did little or no injury to those within, except
that they killed one man. But there were seven or eight similar machines
within the city, besides other engines of war which are called 'Springalds'
for discharging long darts, and staves with sockets for casting stones,
which caused great fear and damage to those outside. Meanwhile,
however, the Scots set up a certain great berefrai like a great tower,
which was considerably higher than the city walls. On perceiving this the
carpenters of the city erected upon a tower of the wall against which that
engine must come if it had ever reached the wall, a wooden tower loftier
than the other, because, when it was being drawn on wheels over the wet
and swampy ground, having stuck there through its overweight, it could
neither be taken any further nor do any harm. Moreover the Scots had

many long ladders, which they brought with them for scaling the walls in different places simultaneously; also a sow for mining the town wall, had they been able; but neither sow nor ladders availed them aught. Also they made great numbers of fascines of corn and herbage to fill in the moat outside the wall on the east side, so they might pass over dry shod. Also they made long bridges of logs running on wheels, such as being strongly and swiftly drawn with rope might reach across the width of the moat. But during all the time the Scots were on the ground neither fascines sufficed to fill the moat, nor those wooden bridges to cross the ditch, but sank to the depths by their own weight.[16]

The season was uncommon wet and whilst this augered dreadfully for a diminished harvest the incessant rain compounded the besiegers' difficulties and the defenders won the day. The strength of the Scots lay in their speed and ferocity, lightning raids by mounted infantry who could carry all of their provisions and strike virtually at will with superior force. The technical difficulties of siege operations against a determined defence exposed their weaknesses – they simply lacked the engineering skills to overcome city walls. The account shows a woeful lack of engines and an inability to overcome the problems of crossing dry and wet ditches, mounting mining operations and establishing what might now be termed 'fire supremacy' over the garrison.

Harcla's finest hour was to occur in Yorkshire when forces he commanded confronted rebels led by Thomas of Lancaster at Boroughbridge. Drawing up his infantry in columns akin to the Scots' schiltrom and doggedly pushing back every attempt to contest the river passage, he won a signal victory. For his achievement he was made Earl of Carlisle, though within a year he was himself disgraced and executed, succeeded to his warden by his rival Sir Anthony Lucy who clung tenaciously to power throughout the alarums of 1327 and 1330, remaining in office until his death in 1343.

The remorseless fury of man in the early fourteenth century was matched by the tribulations caused through climatic changes. The preceding century had been a time of plenty. Evidences of cultivation would show that husbandry, the growing of cereal crops and particularly oats, had been feasible at altitudes of as great as 1,200 feet, far higher than would be viable at present. Traces of terracing of hillsides are visible in the Cheviots and Lammermuirs, perhaps most noticeably in Coquetdale where abundant examples survive. The early 1300s then appear to have been colder and wetter, more akin to that which we experience today, a climatic shift that led to the abandonment of the higher pastures.

It is impossible to provide an accurate figure for the number of inhabitants of the border counties of both realms in 1300. Scotland may have had a total population of around one million and, by referring to later but pre-industrialisation census information, it is possible to construct estimates. Roxburghshire was perhaps the most populated county with perhaps 27,000 souls, Berwickshire (excluding the garrison town) might have had 19,000 inhabitants, Peebleshire some 7,000 and Selkirkshire, dominated by the large swathe of Ettrick Forest no more than 3,000.[17]

In England there is no Domesday evidence, only that to be gleaned from the census of 1377. From this, and allowing for a projection of mortality levels occasioned by famine and then contagion, we might deduce a total population of the northern counties of perhaps 70,000. Famine, occasioned by bad harvests, struck in 1315, 1316 and 1317 and a considerable level of mortality resulted, perhaps as high as 15 per cent of the total population.[18]

Worse was to follow. In the autumn of 1347, a year after Neville's Cross, Genoese cogs docking in Messina in Sicily brought a lethal cargo. The dead and dying sailors aboard had contracted a form of plague to become known as the Black Death. The ships had come from the Crimea and the contagion which had swept unchecked through Asia now entered Europe:

The diseased sailors showed strange black swellings about the size of an egg or an apple in the armpits and groin. The swellings oozed blood and pus and were followed by spreading boils and black blotches on the skin from internal bleeding. The sick suffered severe pain and died quickly within five days of the first symptoms. As the disease spread, other symptoms of continuous fever and spitting of blood appeared instead of the swelling or buboes. The victims coughed and sweated heavily and died even more quickly, within three days or less sometimes in 24 hours. In both types everything that issued from the body – breath, sweat, blood from the buboes and lungs, bloody urine and blood blackened excrement – smelled foul.[19]

The plague in fact had three variants, each more deadly than the last. In the bubonic form the infection is transmitted to humans by the fleas from infected rats and attacks the lymphatic glands. The incidence of mortality is high, occurring within two to five days, but not inevitable. The infection occurs mainly in warmer weather and is not, in the human context, contagious. The pneumonic form is more pernicious. It strikes at the lungs, is invariably fatal, unaffected by seasonality and highly contagious. The third and rarest variant, the septicaemic, kills within hours.[20]

When the plague raced through England in 1348–9 it might have killed almost half the extant population, though actual mortality levels fluctuated widely from 20 per cent in some areas to as high as 80 per cent in others. There is some evidence from death rates in townships in County Durham to suggest that as many as half the inhabitants succumbed. In the more isolated rural communities in the border dales it is likely that fewer, in percentage terms, may have died. For a while Scotland seemed safe, to the extent that the disease was dismissively referred to there as 'the foul English pestilence'.[21]

A trifle premature as it transpired for, with befitting irony, the plague crossed the Tweed in 1349 when it erupted amongst the members of a raiding party mustering to strike towards the weakened English marches at Caddonlea by Galashiels. Thereafter the whole of the border suffered along with both realms. Again we cannot but guess at the total number of deaths but it may be supposed that some 30 per cent of the population perished. Suffering amongst humans was matched by animal pestilence, murrain devastated both cattle and sheep in the course of recurrent outbreaks in 1361, 1379, 1392, 1401–3, 1430–2, 1439 and 1455.[22]

If the century was a lean time for farmers it was to present ample opportunities for masons and those others in the construction trades. The uncertainty and continual vicissitudes of war spurred a boom in defensive architecture such as had not been witnessed since the days of Hadrian. In 1200 Northumberland had contained eleven large castles including Bamburgh, Alnwick, Mitford, Harbottle, Morpeth, Prudhoe, Wark and Warkworth (the impressive and distinctive keep was added around 1400). These comprised the royal garrisons and larger baronial holds and had been sufficient in number and strength to meet the threat of earlier centuries. But now, and especially in the face of Scots supremacy after Bannockburn, they were simply not enough. In terms of combating the hit-and-run guerrilla tactics at which the Scots excelled, they were ineffective. These raiders came to pillage and to terrorise rather than to conquer, to overawe rather than to confront, to overwhelm scratch defences and retreat as swiftly as the ebb tide in the face of superior forces.

A major fortress such as Bamburgh could be expected to withstand a 'siege royal', that is when the king or a large army under royal direction launched a sustained assault employing the full besieger's arsenal of stone-throwing engines, mining and escalade. A second degree of attack would be that instigated by a senior baron with comparable if lesser resources and the third level was a minor leaguer or 'insult' by local or skirmishing forces.

The main change evident in the course of the thirteenth century was that wood was replaced by stone as the preferred medium of construction. In the fourteenth century, as hostilities intensified, existing castles were strengthened by additional works, most often in the form of an outer gateway or barbican, such as that which was built at Alnwick between 1310–15. In 1313 Thomas of Lancaster began the construction of Dunstanburgh on a dolerite outcrop by Craster on the Northumberland coast. After Robert Bruce had recaptured Berwick in 1318 it was possible that the fortress of Earl Thomas could have been developed into a commercial harbour. His execution in 1322 meant that the castle reverted to the crown, though when Berwick was again retaken nine years later, its putative role as a potential North Sea port declined. It remained a formidable hold and the works were extended at the end of the century by the addition of the covered approach and barbican.

Strong castles, rectangular in plan and comprising curtain walls around a courtyard with towers in each corner, were built in the 1330s and 1340s at Chillingham, Ford and Ogle. Lesser but well-constructed towers appeared at Langley and Haughton, each of three to four storeys, buttressed by projecting towers with the great hall on the first floor over a barrel-vaulted basement. Raby and Lumley castles went up in the 1380s and 1390s. In the early years of the century the regulation of castle building continued to be controlled through the issuing of the 'licence to crenellate'. This was a military form of planning consent requiring the royal seal of approval and instigated as a means of preventing random castle building by contentious magnates. After Neville's Cross, however, these controls were relaxed in the north and landowners were openly encouraged to construct or extend their defensible works.

The impressive rectangular tower of Hexham Gaol dates from 1330–2, Belsay and Chipchase, near Humshaugh were built mid-century along with

Bothal (1343), and Greystoke in Cumbria dates from 1353. Both Belsay and Chipchase remain as excellent examples despite subsequent rebuilding. Identical masons marks may be observed at both. As he prepared to invade France in 1415 Henry V commissioned a survey of the defences of Northumberland and the list shows that seventy-five towers had been erected in the course of the preceding half century or so. Many of these were the result not of new building but of the militarisation of existing manor or hall houses, eloquent testimony to the dangers of the times.

Perhaps the best preserved monument and one which admirably illustrates the fourteenth-century transition from domestic hall to fortified outpost is Aydon Hall or Castle which lies a mile and a half north of Corbridge and a half mile or so west of the present village of the same name. The original early medieval hall occupies an elevated position above the plunging, timber-clad banks of the Cor Burn which sweeps around on two sides. Licence to crenellate was issued to the castellan Sir Robert de Reymes in 1305, though the surviving hall range dates from a good twenty to thirty years earlier (the property, in largely unchanged form, was still a working farm until the 1960s). Sir Robert, a veteran of the wars,[23] squared off the inner bailey or courtyard with a defensible parapet. There was no keep, a feature or lack thereof which Pevsner considers to be 'of outstanding architectural importance'.[24]

These defences proved insufficient as the century wore on and the place changed hand several times. By the mid-1300s a much more extensive and heavily fortified outer ward was constructed. This runs north from the east flank of the hall, following the steep decline, then north-west to an apex finished with a strong half round tower, then south-west past another tower and the main gate. There is ample evidence that the walls would, in time of attack, be surmounted by timber galleries to provide extra protection for the defenders.

Grim-visaged Hermitage, the sentinel of Liddesdale, was in existence during the Wars of Independence and was for a time the residence of the renowned Sir William Douglas, 'the Knight of Liddesdale'. It was his widow who remarried into the west march Dacres who held the place till the late 1350s. It was they who constructed the oblong central core of what remains today, two long sections of curtain with a small courtyard area. It is said Hermitage thus 'reflects the style of some fourteenth century north English fortified manor houses'.[25] by 1400, however, having reverted to Scots ownership, the fortifications were strengthened by the addition of the corner towers.[26]

In the Scottish west march Caerlaverock had, towards the latter part of the preceding century, been moved from its original foundation to its present, much larger site. The place was extensively re-fortified by the Maxwells after 1373. The castle had changed hands a number of times during the Edwardian era, most memorably in the course of the siege of 1300. Thus the tide of fortification swelled over both sides of the border as a militarised society came into being, a society for whom war swiftly became the norm rather than the exception, where a trial of arms became the accepted means of settling any dispute. This pernicious trend was granted significant emphasis by the growth in importance of a landowning class whose primary function was to wage war, one whose acres, swollen by the profits of discord, bred keen broadswords and for whom peace was not something to be by any means desired.

'To ambitious men of action the blast of war resounds with opportunities.'[27] William de Percy was a Norman knight of Norse descent who crossed to England in the wake of the conquest in the affinity of Hugh d'Avranches. The family settled in Yorkshire following the Conqueror's 'harrying' of the north, an extensive and detailed exercise in brutality that had wasted vast tracts of the county. Yorkshire estates therefore were no plums but uncertain fiefs for young men of grit and ambition. The Percy clan extended its acres by judicious marriage and good service. A Percy fought against the Scots beneath the banner of the saints at Northallerton in 1138.

At the start of the fourteenth century the Percys held no lands in Northumberland. Henry Percy I (like royalty the Henrys are numbered sequentially) served in the Wars of Independence and on 19th November 1309 purchased the barony of Alnwick from Anthony Bek the Prince Bishop. Bek had also served with some distinction and like Percy was worldly and acquisitive. The sale may well have been a fraudulent one as the Bishop was acting in his capacity as trustee of William de Vesci, the previous owner who had died, without legitimate male issue, in 1297.

Henry I died in 1314. His grandson Henry III (died 1368) added to the family holdings in the county. In 1327 he contracted to serve on the border for a hefty annual retainer of 500 marks but, cannily, he exchanged the fee for the acquisition of the barony of Warkworth, an extensive and valuable tenure which included the manors of Rothbury, Corbridge and

Newburn. Warkworth was in the gift of the crown, having reverted on the death, without issue, of Sir John Clavering in 1332. Some three years later he was further rewarded by the transfer of the barony of Beanley – this had come into the crown lands after its surrender by the Earl of Dunbar.

Thus in two generations the Percys had become the leading magnates in Northumberland. The loss of cross-border estates which was the inevitable consequence of the Wars of Independence and the need for a defensible frontier created opportunities for those who were prepared to take on the military obligations of a frontiersman; those who, like the Percys, were quick to profit from the parlous state of other landowners who had wearied of the expense and uncertainty of the wars.

The Percy hegemony on the eastern border reached its apogee during the long career of Henry IV (died 1408), the first earl and father of Hotspur (who would have become Henry V had his father not outlived him). In his heyday, the years from his elevation to the earldom in 1377 to the family's disastrous rebellion against the king in 1403, the Percy was a local titan, one who played a major role in national politics and whose support proved important to the usurper Bolingbroke in the crisis of 1399.

The earl secured several highly advantageous marriages. In 1373 he purchased the wardship of the late Earl of Athol's two eligible daughters whom he then married to his younger sons. Both boys predeceased their father who then inherited the extensive estates their widows had brought, including the barony of Mitford. Seven years after this ruthlessly successful marriage brokering the earl himself married again, this time to Maud, widow of Gilbert de Umfraville, who had also died without issue. Prior to the Umfraville's decease Percy had bought half the manor of Prudhoe and he now gained the remainder. His new wife was also a substantial heiress in her own right and the earl now found himself lord of Langley and Cockermouth baronies, the latter an extensive and wealthy holding in Cumberland.[28]

The Douglases had risen to fame during the Wars of Independence – it was inevitable that so powerful and aggressive a marcher family should, from time to time, clash with the Percys when the obligations of their respective offices and the rapacity of their natures should collide. Whether there was ever a Douglas–Percy feud as has so many times been canvassed is highly doubtful. There was personal animosity over contested lands in the Jedforest but such disputes were by no means uncommon and each supplied the leadership for their respective nations on the fields of Otterburn (1388) and Homildon (1402). Thereafter, however, both Henry Percy 'Hotspur' and Archibald Douglas, victor and vanquished, fought together against Henry IV of England at Shrewsbury (1403).

The dozen years from 1357 to the resumption of the French War of Edward III in 1369 were relatively tranquil. Large tracts of the Scottish border remained in English hands, a buffer zone or Pale that was the legacy of the earlier victories. These comprised Annandale in the west, parts of Roxburghshire and Berwickshire in the centre and east. There is some suggestion that the marcher lords might have maintained some garrisons in Liddesdale to keep a corridor between Annandale and Teviotdale open. As mentioned, the Dacres were in possession of Hermitage Castle at this time, though it may have been recaptured by the Earl of Douglas in 1358.[29] Berwick remained a major English bastion; local disturbances, petty raids and forays occurred, undoubtably on a regular basis, but there were no major cross-border incursions nor do the magnates of either realm appear to have been active.

This queasy calm would pass for the nearest to a settled peace. Over the next decade resurgent Scots aggression would raise the tempo to that of an 'undeclared war'.[30] Limited military operations undertaken by magnates which could be written off or disclaimed by the central government, which, in the case of the administration of David II's successor Robert II, almost certainly condoned or connived at such attacks. In the later years of King David, however, Scotland was still burdened by the cost of his ransom whilst the French had been obliged to accept the humiliating terms of the Treaty of Brétigny, the high water mark of Edward's achievement. The very last thing a king of Scotland wished would be to provoke his southern neighbour at a time when the whole might of England could be summoned for a riposte.

Henry Percy IV certainly held the Jedforest area in 1369 and the English grip in Roxburghshire and Berwickshire was anchored on the key castles of Roxburgh and Jedburgh. Possession of Berwick enabled the garrison to dominate the Merse and the key line of the Tweed itself was secured by Norham and Wark. Notwithstanding this impressive concept of defence in depth, with the Pale acting as a buffer against renewed Scottish attacks, it was inevitable that Scots military activity would begin to focus on the recovery of these lost lands. As the 1370s progressed it is possible to detect an almost 'Maginot Line' attitude amongst the English wardens as the military initiative passed indisputably to the Scots, with the bitter memory of past defeats fading and as a new generation of able and aggressive commanders sought to win their spurs.

Perhaps the most distinguished of these was George Dunbar who was probably behind the seizure, ostensibly by the octogenerian Patrick Dunbar Earl of March, of lands in Berwickshire held by the English knight Sir Edward Letham on his death in February 1368. Admittedly this was not a military action in the strict sense and, in the west, the English lords of Annandale were already sharing their rents with their Scottish neighbours, but it was to prove the thin end of the wedge. The totality of the Pale was never fixed in the sense of defined boundaries and graduated through levels of control to varying and diminishing degrees of influence. From 1369, however, the renewal of the French wars provided the catalyst for the steady encroachment and reoccupation of the English-dominated areas.

From the resumption of hostilities with France to the death of Edward III and the minority of Richard II, the war in France went badly. The heady days of Crécy, Auberoche and Poitiers consigned to the past whilst under the leadership of the wily Breton knight Bertrand du Guesclin the French steadily ate into the earlier, extensive English gains. Edward, the Black Prince, vigorous paladin of the earlier wars, was mortally sick and his last great victory at Najera in Spain proved to be an empty one as the attempt to deny the French a Castilian alliance ultimately failed. It is evident that the Scots were active in support of their allies as a number of Scots were taken, along with du Guesclin, in the rout at Najera.[31]

When the venerable Earl of March died and George Dunbar succeeded to the title he immediately began to exert pressure in the Mearse, forcing, the Berwick garrison onto the defensive. At the same time an indenture dated March 1371 and entered into between the Earl of Hereford as Lord of Annandale and his appointed keeper of Lochmaben, Walter Stapleton, provides that the latter shall keep the castle fully prepared and victualled, able to withstand a siege of six months during which time the earl would attend to his relief. Such an agreement, expressed in these terms, would tend to indicate that a sustained attack by the Scots was clearly within the contemplation of the parties at the time.

If so then a likely candidate to lead such renewed aggression would have been the formidable Archibald Douglas 'the Grim', an experienced, tough-minded diplomat and soldier who had suffered capture at Poitiers. Appointed as west march warden in 1364 he had served David II with loyalty and zeal. No friend to the English and keen to profit from recovered lands, Douglas was the ideal captain. The terms of the treaty agreed between Edward III and David II in June 1369 reflected the relative uncertainty of the English position: the truce was to endure until 2nd February 1384, a term of fourteen years, the rents from both Annandale and Roxburghshire were to be shared. More telling still, the capital residue of the ransom was slashed from 84,000 to 56,000 marks and the annual instalments reduced by 2,000 marks, a hefty adjustment very much in the Scots' favour.

David himself remained on good terms with his erstwhile captor and did not directly renew the French alliance on the resumption of hostilities. This attitude of reasonableness was undoubtably at odds with the swelling belligerence of the younger knights and magnates who seized on the war to pounce upon the English-held lands of the Pale.

Robert II was perhaps an unlikely candidate for the role of conqueror. He had waited long and generally patiently for the crown. His military record was undistinguished at best, marred by his questionable actions at Neville's Cross. In his youth he cut an attractive figure as described by the chronicler John of Fordun – 'tall and robust, modest, liberal, gay and courteous; and for the innate sweetness of his disposition generally loved by true-hearted Scotsmen'.[32] In later life Andrew Wyntoun speaks of him in similar terms . . . 'a tenderer heart might no man have'.[33]

'Niceness' is not necessarily a quality sought in successful commanders. Edward I was not a nice man, nor was Robert Bruce. It could, however, be said that Robert II has had a rather poor press and unfairly so. In the course of his reign he avoided any full-scale conflict with England and his negotiators continually did well on the diplomatic front. At the same time he profited from English failures in France to reduce the salients of the Pale. His subjects maintained a policy of constant and co-ordinated aggression, wresting the military initiative back from the English. The king was, for a while at least, able to convincingly blame Scottish inroads on his unruly marchers whilst making protestations of amity.

Shortly before his coronation the new king was beset by the 'Douglas Demonstration', an assertion of the family's feudal rights and perhaps an expression of frustration at the lack of a proactive policy under David II.

The rump of the nobility rallied to the king and Earl Douglas was obliged to retreat. Despite this unpleasantness Archibald 'the Grim' remained in royal favour and was dispatched to France to negotiate terms for a renewed alliance assisted by his kinsman James Douglas of Dalkeith.

On 30th June 1371 terms for a defensive alliance were agreed with Charles V. These were essentially moderate – both realms would support each other in the face of renewed English force and neither would conclude terms without mutual concurrence. Nonetheless the Scots were not obliged to break the terms of the subsisting truce with England. However, the draft of a second and far more aggressive accord was prepared whereby the French undertook to underwrite the outstanding balance of David II's ransom and supply military aid. Even though the second treaty remained as merely an expression of intent, the fact that such terms were discussed would serve to indicate a heightened level of Franco-Scots collusion and to serve notice that the Scots would be pursuing operations, even on a limited scale, on the border.

The first two years of the new king's reign did not, however, witness an upsurge in violence. The Scots remained wisely cautious whilst the English strove to maintain good relations. As the war in France continued to go badly England could ill afford to open a second front against Scotland, besides which with the establishment of the Pale, Edward had no strategic objectives remaining on the border other than maintenance of the peace. As an example of reasonableness it fell to Percy as warden to meet the cost of a fine of £100 levied by a warden court against Sir Hugh Dacre when the latter defaulted (this was a considerable sum and the disgruntled warden spared no efforts to recover his outlay, ordering the arrest of Dacre and threatening to levy distraint against his lands and chattels).[34]

Judging the moment, King Robert now chose to be awkward over the ransom payments, raising the contentious though seemingly trivial matter of the form of receipts for payment or 'quittances' insisting the King of Scots should be recognised as a free prince free of any claims of overlordship.

Although an uneasy calm prevailed, by 1372 the English garrisons were being strengthened and placed on alert. Sporadic raids continued and there is a suggestion of Scots' naval activity on the west coast, with a further hint that the English administration might have flirted with the Lord of the Isles, perhaps seeking to recruit his galleys as a mercenary squadron. French successes multiplied; the Welsh rebel Own Lawgoch profited from the Franco-Castilian naval co-operation to launch an impudent raid on Guernsey.

The following year the simmering Douglas–Percy confrontation over possession of the Jedforest erupted into open hostilities and the English crown was quick to appoint a neutral commission comprised rather pointedly of non-marchers to decide the matter. Percy himself was not directly embroiled as he was serving in France under John of Gaunt. The employment of outsiders as arbitrators tends to support the view that the administration saw the marchers as being as much a cause of conflict as the solution to it. This suspicion, by no means unjustified, lent credence to Robert II's repeated assertions that he was the victim of unruly local magnates who insisted on taking the law into their own hands without royal sanction.

In spite of the obvious diplomatic game being played, there was an essential dichotomy for both realms in dealing with their respective marchers – in time of war, martial tendencies were both appropriate and necessary, success would be rewarded with captured estates. Peace, for the marchers, had become an abstract concept with little to recommend it. That England now required good relations with her northern neighbour as befitted the expediency of the 'bigger picture' might not necessarily appeal to local gentry anxious not only to retain their holdings in the Pale but to sustain the salient to protect the marches from the inevitable exposure that elimination of the English outposts would entail.

The Earl of Dunbar remained foremost amongst those Scottish lords seeking to wrest back control of the lost lands. By the end of 1373 Berwick was increasingly isolated in the east and the earl was nibbling at the flanks of both Annandale (the Scottish claim to lordship here had devolved onto him) and Teviotdale. Although the king remained aloof, apparently disapprovingly, from these attacks he was quick to parcel out those estates being recovered, often to diverse members of the lesser nobility or gentry, thus ensuring these men acquired a stake in maintaining the re-conquest.

John, Earl of Carrick, the king's oldest son and designated heir, led what amounted to an unofficial war cabinet in which March and Douglas were both prominent. The rumbling ulcer of the Jedforest was skilfully played down to avoid a pretext for serious hostilities. Percy had meanwhile secured further advancement when, in December, he was given the west march wardenship in addition to his current appointment in the east.

If the crown was satisfied, the English marchers were not. Nor were they under any illusions as to their neighbour's longer-term objectives. Percy's eldest son, yet another Henry, soon to be known as 'Hotspur', undertook rebuilding at Berwick between 1372 and 1375. At the same time work was going on at Lochmaben and Gaunt was building at Dunstanborough.[35] From 1374 the Scots began to increase the pressure. The following year they were ruthlessly active in the west whilst King Robert continued to publicly deplore such apparent lawlessness. In the same year Edward III was moved to grant redress to the see of Durham for the Prince Bishop's lands in north Northumberland being 'for the great part near the march of Scotland and in Scotland, and are almost entirely laid waste by the King's enemies, the Scots'.[36]

1376 proved no less violent. March finally drove the remaining English garrisons from Annandale and, to all intents and purposes, thereby eliminated the salient, but his activities and those of his fellow marchers were curtailed by the negotiation of an Anglo-French truce at Bruges which was to hold until the following summer. Although this was, in reality, little more than both sides drawing apart to draw breath before further resorting to arms, the Scots were careful to avoid any escalation which could have prompted major retaliation.

In the course of the lull the English crown did mount an offensive on the diplomatic front and this met with some success, rents being once again collected from Annandale. Cannily the Scots avoided any serious provocation; the upsurge in violence was again laid at the door of the conveniently unruly marchers but the recovered lands were not surrendered. At the same time further building work was being carried out at Scottish castles, most noticeably on the great mount of Edinburgh.

The English were not really in a position to adopt an overtly aggressive stance. Negotiations with the French were stalling despite the intervention of the papal nuncios who were prepared to offer Edward III lands 'elsewhere' in consideration for his abandoning his continuing claims in France. Such proposals might have caused stirrings of alarm in Scotland but the French, as Edward's health declined and his masterly control began to slip, saw little need for compromise. Throughout this period there was substantial cross-border trade, commerce could still flourish in the uncertain climate, indeed English producers were keen to export wool through the Scottish east-coast ports as customs duties were less. Scottish mercenaries, despite the alliance with France, continued to serve under English colours. Sir John Swinton, leading a company of three hundred spears, followed Gaunt in the chevauchee of 1373.[37]

On 10th August 1377 the Earl of March launched a surprise attack on the English-held township of Roxburgh. Ostensibly the raid was in retaliation for the killing of one of his followers on the preceding year's market day. The huddled houses were put to the torch and the hapless citizens to the sword under the very nose of Sir Thomas Percy, the castellan. It had not been a good year, the war in France continued to go badly, a predatory Franco-Castilian fleet cruised the Channel and terrorised the south coast of England.

Edward III finally died on 21st June, leaving ten-year-old Richard, son of the Black Prince, as his heir. The descent on Roxburgh was not simply a casual atrocity but a deliberate raising of the stakes. The death of the old king and the uncertainties of a regency council, together with French successes, prompted the adoption of a more confrontational strategy.

Percy, now Earl of Northumberland, countered with an incursion against the Merse but the Scots won a hard-fought skirmish at Carham and Sir John Gordon succeeded in capturing the keeper of the Berwick garrison, Sir Thomas Musgrave. Co-ordinated attacks in the west were launched by Sir John Johnston and the English were altogether on the defensive. Northumberland, never one to miss out on an opportunity, was petitioning at the end of the year that his remuneration should be paid on a wartime rather than a peacetime rate – so great were these disturbances.[38]

By way of rubbing salt into England's wounds Robert II chose this moment to oust the monks of Durham from their base at Coldingham and replace them with Scottish clerics from Dunfermline. This decision may well have been made on tactical considerations; it was said the Durham cell was a 'listening post' in the English cross-border intelligence network and was even used as a supply base for raids.[39]

Whilst continuing to rehearse the well-tried diplomatic arguments that these incursions were solely the work of unruly marchers the Scottish crown made no effort to check this aggression, which continued throughout the following season. An English retaliatory strike into the Scottish west march was sharply rebuffed and the Scots marchers descended on Tynedale.[40] Though the Scots certainly had the best of the skirmishing their marches also suffered as the tempo of violence increased. In June

1378 the two sides met to discuss terms. The mood of the Scots may be gauged from the appointment of March and Douglas as lead negotiators. Hard bargaining won them an important concession – hitherto the English had been wont to impound Scottish trading vessels as a reprisal for attacks on land but it was conceded that this remedy, effectively legalised piracy, could not be resorted to.

The Mercers, father and son, had been victims of this policy, being captured and held at Scarborough in 1376 or 1377. Thomas, the younger, upon his release joined forces with the French and Castilian corsairs to ravage the east coast of England. Both Thomas and his father John were clients of Douglas and it may be possible to detect the earl's hand in this seaborne onslaught Not surprisingly Scarborough was one port which received Thomas' most particular attention. An English privateer, John Philipot, was commissioned to fit out a squadron and confront the allied pirates. In this he was entirely successful. Mercer, along with fifteen prizes, was soon captive.[41]

On 25th November, whilst Northumberland was distracted with fire fighting along the whole of the frontier, a company of Scottish freebooters, no more than half a hundred, pure opportunists as it would appear, succeeded in a sudden, surprise attack on Berwick Castle. They killed the keeper, Sir Robert Boynton, and held out until the next month when the warden descended with a sizeable force. Ironically the incident was almost as much of an embarrassment to March who offered to assist in the recovery, so blatant a challenge threatened the insidious subtlety of his strategy. It was at the siege and storming of the castle that Henry Percy, only fourteen, is said to have earned the sobriquet 'Hotspur'. The raiders refused all quarter and all but one fell in the final escalade.

The Dunfermline monks were swift to make grants of land to both March and Sir John Swinton, giving these tough fighters a clear stake in the retention of Coldingham. Matters calmed somewhat in 1379 as there was talk of Richard II seeking a Scottish bride, although in line with muddled English policy of the day there were also hopes of a French marriage. The talks foundered as the English were demanding, reasonably, resumption of the ransom payments which had been stopped and, less reasonably, recognition of Richard's overlordship.

Gaunt had been appointed, in February of that year, as Lieutenant of the Marches and in his habitual way preferred a conciliatory stance. He was, in the event, distracted by his own ambitions for the throne of Castile which he had acquired by right of his current wife. There were some minor alarums but the English were again beset by a further outbreak of plague. At by the end of the season Scots' raiders carried the pestilence as unintended booty, a reiver's curse, back to ravage their own marches.

1380 began badly with a major and again unsuccessful English expedition under the Duke of Buckingham blundering into France. The alleged seizure of a Scottish merchantman by the mariners of Newcastle and Hull furnished Douglas with the excuse to mount a major sweep through Cumberland, sacking Penrith on the day of the town's annual fair and carrying off booty, beasts and ransoms. In spite of this harrying Gaunt refused to countenance a full-scale retaliation as Northumberland would have preferred. This amount of reasonableness smacked of timidity and March descended on Glendale. On 29th June the earl encountered Ralph, Baron Greystoke in a sharp skirmish at Horse Rigg. Again the English were worsted with Greystoke and over a hundred of his riders taken prisoner.[42]

Stung by Greystoke's humiliation Gaunt did unleash a sizeable force against the marcher lords: his forces included an impressive 14 bannerets, 162 knights, 1,492 squires and 1,670 archers, incurring the considerable cost of £5,000.[43] Despite this impressive array and the consequential burden on an already overstretched exchequer the army achieved little beyond wasting the Scottish west march and torching Dumfries. Gaunt's raid did, however, force King Robert to the negotiating table and whilst the best assurance he could wrest from the Scots was an extension of the peace to 30th November 1381 King Robert did, at least in part, return Coldingham to Durham.

In the diplomatic game as well as the military campaign the Scots maintained the ascendancy to the extent that March and the other Scottish lords were able to augment their incomes with thriving blackmail rackets. A petition from this time informs that the inhabitants of Redesdale, Wark and Berwick had recourse to buying off the Scots.[44] Combining military operations with economic warfare of this nature added to the effective-ness of the Scottish effort. As lands were lost, rents declined, blackmail impoverished the local economy whilst more and more had to be spent on defensive works. The passage of armed forces of either nationality boded ill for local inhabitants – Gaunt's army of 1380 is said to have caused as much loss in England as it wrought damage in Scotland.

Matters were not helped by the fact that relations between the Duke and the Earl of Northumberland were at this time somewhat less than cordial. Percy was afforded an opportunity to score points when the Peasants' Revolt of 1381 broke out in the south of England the following year. Gaunt was a prime target for the rebels, who burnt down his magnificent palace of the Savoy. Caught totally wrong footed the duke appears to have suffered a loss of nerve, even though he was still in the north, some considerable distance from the troubles. Seeking temporary refuge in one of Northumberland's castles he was astonished to discover that he was to be denied admittance. 'How cometh this to pass,' he is said to have expostulated, 'is there in Northumberland a greater sovereign than I am?'[45]

In June the Duke had, once again, been in negotiations with the Earl of Carrick at Ayton in the Scottish east march when he had conceded a postponement of further payments until the expiry of the truce in 1384. Now, abandoned by Northumberland, he fled over the border to seek sanctuary in the households of both Carrick and Douglas. Once fear of the rebels had abated and the rebellion suppressed, Gaunt returned to power, his eminence undiminished. He wasted no time in confronting Percy, harsh words passed between the two at a council meeting in October, followed two weeks later by a virtual brawl in the drink-fuelled atmosphere of the feasting hall. Further unseemly exchanges passed between the two magnates at a subsequent meeting to the extent the king felt obliged to intervene and ordered a formal reconciliation.

For Gaunt, still smarting from the humiliation of his forced flight into Scotland, more was needed. In December he engineered the earl's removal from his plum appointments of captain of Berwick and east march warden. Percy's rival Lord Neville now enjoyed both offices whilst Northumberland was offered the paltry prize of wardenship of the newly created middle march. The following March he received partial recompense when he was reinstated as warden the east, the middle march appointment being suspended, but to act jointly with Neville. For Percy this was a further insult but Gaunt hadn't finished. When he himself was given the Lieutenancy in May 1382 he again sacked Percy from the joint wardenship of both east and west, recreating a lesser appointment in the revived middle march.

The Scots marcher lords had resisted the urge to profit by the anarchy of the Peasant's Revolt; wisely they had chosen to shelter Gaunt in his hour of need. For this the duke was clearly in their debt and such kindly forbearance must have boded well at the negotiating table. Although the disturbances had not spread to engulf the north, the rebellion dented the crown's already strained finances and removed the prospect of any expeditions to France. The Scots, cannily biding their time, did not want to unleash further overt hostilities whilst England, however impoverished, was not actively engaged against the French. Furthermore Charles V had died in 1380 and his successor Charles VI remained a minor. The Scots could therefore not be totally confident of French support – dealing with a regency council was a different matter from negotiating with the sovereign.

In the spring of 1383, nonetheless, a fresh incursion into the Low Countries was planned in support of Pope Clement VII. The papal schism had created rivals for the throne of St Peter and the French candidate, sitting at Avignon, was Urban VI. The raid met with no more success than its immediate predecessors. The Scots, on the other hand, did reach an accord with the administration of Charles VI on the 15th June whereby the French would, the following year, fund military activity on the border in the sum of 40,000 gold francs with the guarantee of an expeditionary force of 1,000 men at arms together with additional armaments and materiel.

With this assurance the Scots struck at Wark in the same month, storming the castle and obliging Gaunt to seek terms, but Carrick would agree to nothing more than a cessation until the expiry of the fourteen-year truce the following February. The duke was given some hope that the Scots were prepared to discuss a lasting peace but their representatives failed to attend the October session of the English Parliament as agreed and meanwhile the depredations continued. By the end of the year widespread devastation had been caused: Embleton barony, Hepburn, East Ditchburn and Newton-by-the-Sea are all reported as being laid waste.[46]

Faced with the reality of Scottish duplicity Parliament in England began to tire of further conciliation. Demands were made that the outstanding arrears on the ransom payments should be made good, full compensation for the recent violations of the truce was to be made, failing which the Scots would face the renewal of the claim for English sovereignty backed by force of arms. As 1384 dawned, both sides were preparing for all-out hostilities. What the Scots had perhaps failed to anticipate was the Anglo-French accord agreed on 26th January. Thus when the truce expired Robert II would likely find himself facing the full weight of English wrath without the succour of his allies.

Notes

1 Loyd, A., *My War Gone By I Miss It So*, London 1999 pp. 152–3.
2 Rose, A., *Kings in the North*, London 2002 p. 56.
3 Moffat, A., *The Borders*, Selkirk 2002 p. 211.
4 Robson, R., *The Rise and Fall of the English Highland Clans*, Edinburgh 1989 p. 23.
5 Lomas, R., *County of Conflict: Northumberland from the Conquest to the Civil War*, E. Lothian 1996 p. 41.
6 Ibid pp. 41–2.
7 Ibid p. 43.
8 Mitford Castle stands as an impossibly romantic ruin, glowering over the present village just west of Morpeth. The Middletons regained the manor of Belsay in the mid-fourteenth century when a Middleton married the daughter of Sir John Strivelyn who had begun the construction of Belsay Castle. Having regained the estate the family retains ownership to this day.
9 Lomas p. 44.
10 Ibid p. 44.
11 The 'Liberties' of Tynedale and Redesdale were the wildest and most troublesome tracts of the English middle march – 'Redesdale and Tynedale . . . The only alleagiance the warriors of these wild regions was loyalty towards their own clans' (Trevelyan, G.M., *English Social History*). The Lordship of Redesdale was granted by William I in 1075 to his kinsman Sir Robert de Umfraville 'Robin with the Beard', and retained by his descendants until 1436. Tynedale was handed to Malcolm IV of Scotland by Henry II of England in 1157 as, in effect, compensation for the Scots abandoning their claim to the whole of Northumberland. The lordship was forfeited after the defeat and capture of William the Lion at Alnwick in 1174. Later Alexander II did homage to King John for the Liberty. Possession was confirmed by Henry III as a clause of the Treaty of York in 1237 and extended by a further grant of estates in Cumberland in 1242. See Robson pp. 4–7.
12 Robson p. 22; these archers may have taken part in Bruce's defeat at Methven in the same year.
13 Robson p. 26.
14 Ibid p. 27.
15 Ibid pp. 27–8.
16 Quoted in Moffat pp. 214–15.
17 Moffat p. 197.
18 Lomas p. 71.
19 Tuchman, B., *A Distant Mirror*, New York 1978 pp. 92–3.
20 Lomas p. 69.
21 Moffat p. 219.
22 Ibid p. 220.

23 The effigy of Robert de Reymes, much restored in the nineteenth century, is now to be seen in Bolam Church in mid-Northumberland. The image of the knight gives a good impression of the arms and armour of the time of the Wars of Independence.

24 Pevsner, Sir N., 'Northumberland' in the *Buildings of England* series, London 1992 edn. p. 149.

25 MacIvor, I., *A Fortified Frontier*, Gloucs. 2000 p. 50.

26 Ibid p. 51.

27 Rose p. 46.

28 Lomas pp. 54–5.

29 MacDonald, A.J., *Border Bloodshed*, E. Lothian 2000 p. 14.

30 Ibid p. 9.

31 Ibid p. 21.

32 Bingham, C., *The Stewart Kingdom of Scotland 1371–1603*, p. 25.

33 Ibid p. 25.

34 MacDonald p. 29.

35 Ibid p. 37.

36 Ibid p. 38.

37 Ibid p. 44.

38 Ibid p. 49.

39 Ibid p. 47.

40 Ibid p. 53.

41 Ibid p. 54.

42 Ibid p. 61.

43 Rose p. 329.

44 MacDonald p. 65.

45 Rose p. 330.

46 MacDonald p. 73.

Chapter 10

Chevy Chase

It fell about the Lammas tide,
When the muir men win their hay,
The doughty Douglas bound him to ride
Into England to drive a prey.[1]

T he battle of Otterburn has achieved a fame which considerably exceeds
its historical significance and is often and wrongly cited as resulting
from the supposed Douglas–Percy vendetta. The primary and much quoted
source for the events of the battle and its preamble is the Flemish chronicler
Jean Froissart who wrote his substantial account only a year or so after the
fight and certainly interviewed some of those who took part. His account is
lively and well written but he does tend towards the 'tabloid' style and
does not trouble overly with detail. A frightful name dropper, he is concerned with chivalric deeds and probably gives the 2nd Earl of Douglas a
somewhat larger role than may be warranted. Both March, the most subtle
and seasoned of campaigners, and Moray were present and the boldness
of the Scottish tactics suggests the influence of March.

On the Scottish side both Fordun and Wyntoun provide accounts of
the battle, though neither is as contemporary as Froissart and substantially
agrees with his version. The English accounts of Walsingham, Higden and
Hardyng tend, not unsurprisingly, to gloss over the extent of the defeat.
The celebrated border ballads which largely account for the lasting fame
of the encounter are more literary than historical and cannot, therefore,
be relied upon.[2]

If the Anglo-French truce of 1384 had wrongfooted the Scots then this was scant comfort to the northern shires which, at the beginning of the year, were bracing themselves for the onslaught. The crisis was sufficient to demand the return of Northumberland who now added the title of Admiral of the Northern Fleet to his offices in command of a squadron of ships with a complement of 800 sailors and marines.[3]

Despite having taken defensive measures themselves and put their major holds on alert, the Scots marcher lords were poised to strike. As early as February Archibald the Grim, Lord of Galloway, in concert with the earls of Douglas and March, swooped upon Lochmaben castle which, it appears, capitulated without a fight. So sudden was the collapse that accusations of treason were levelled against the keeper Thomas Featherstonehaugh. The fall of Lochmaben meant the loss of Annandale and the final elimination of the western flank of the English Pale. Small wonder that a scapegoat was needed.

Whether the castellan was bribed or whether he simply lacked the manpower and resources to resist must remain conjecture, but Douglas swept through Teviotdale, driving the English outposts before him till all that remained were the twin bastions of Jedburgh and Roxburgh. From the Scots' perspective a very satisfactory start to the year and the total lack of any effective response was no doubt heartening. Northumberland's strategy, such as it was, relied mainly on the defensive, the initiative had passed entirely to the Scots with their wily and aggressive marchers.

It seems likely that Richard II shared this perception for in April he commissioned Gaunt along with two of his other uncles, the earls of Buckingham and Cambridge, to mount a chevauchee into the Lothians, a two-week spate of widespread destruction that wasted large tracts of the east coast and likely saw a number of townships including Haddington go up in flames. As damaging as such retaliation was, the Scots cannily avoided the hazard of battle and resorted to a scorched-earth policy: all livestock and movables were taken to safety and the invaders starved of any sustenance from the blasted landscapes.

Inevitably the English, with so large a host, suffered problems of supply and victualling and were obliged to withdraw. A foraging party put ashore at South Queensferry was cut up by the locals under Sir William Cunningham and Sir Thomas Erskine.[4] As was ever the case with English forces drawn mainly from the affinities of the leaders, as much havoc was raised south of the border as north. Gaunt, who was no doubt mindful of the shelter previously afforded to him by the men whose lands he'd been ravaging and preoccupied by his ambitions in Spain, was probably glad to retire to Durham, where he handed his commission to Percy on 23rd April.

Poor communications with their allies had left the Scots isolated but a company of French adventurers joined in a raid into Northumberland in June whilst an amphibious English force sacked Dumfries. On 7th July both sides agreed to an indenture, sealed at Ayton, which brought the Scots into the Anglo-French accord, although this was effective only until 1st October. Robert II had fallen back on the weary rhetoric of helplessness, that the conflict was instigated by unruly marchers. In part this was true for the king found himself increasingly marginalised as the war faction became more clamorous. In November the Earl of Carrick was appointed Lieutenant of the Kingdom, regent for all intent and purposes, supported by the aggression of the Douglas faction. Earl William had died and was succeeded by his fiery son James as the 2nd earl.

The campaign of 1384 had yielded significant gains though these had been won at the not inconsiderable cost of the devastation of the Lothians. Nonetheless the English response had been unimpressive and must have been perceived as offering further opportunities, especially if operations the following year would be able to benefit from direct French intervention. The situation was made more complex by the virtual elimination of the English Pale; the northern counties were now more exposed than they had been for several decades. If sufficient force of arms could be brought to bear then it might now be the Scots who could resurrect the Pale of the twelfth century and extend the Lion's sway to the Tyne.

For England the cost of maintaining the northern frontier was substantial. In August Northumberland had been paid the very considerable sum of £8,666 13s. 4d. for maintaining the defence of Berwick, Roxburgh and Carlisle plus a further emolument of £4,000 for forty-two days' active campaigning.[5] To this outlay must be added the wages of the other postholders and the property costs of defensive works. The earl was not afforded the time for self-congratulation, however, for in December a party of Scots successfully assaulted Berwick Castle, whether by a skilful *coup de main* or corruption is open, as ever in border affairs, to debate. This was more than an embarrassment for Percy whose enemies were quick to apply censure and he was obliged, to save his position, to buy back the castle for a ransom of 2,000 marks; Gaunt, their feud still simmering, opposed his reinstatement.[6]

As the autumn of 1384 dragged into the winter of the following year King Richard's administration was clearly aware of the danger posed by a continued Franco-Scottish *entente* and diplomatic efforts were begun to separate the allies. As early as the preceding November Carrick and his council had been planning just such a joint offensive, the French in Scotland to be led by Jean de Vienne whilst the redoubtable Oliver de Clisson mounted an amphibious assault on the south coast. Despite these growing tensions Archibald the Grim still found it expedient to conclude a local truce with Percy on 15th March which was to hold until 1st July. This should not be viewed as implying a split in the Scottish leadership, the Lord of Galloway was scarcely a dove, but such an understanding does serve to indicate the measure of autonomy which the wardens enjoyed and which the demands of their role necessitated.[7]

The force which de Vienne led over the Channel in May was substantial, 1,350 men at arms and 300 crossbowmen. Having successfully avoided English naval patrols the French made landfall on the east coast, but it was not until early July that the dispositions for the coming campaign were agreed upon. The French appear to have entertained notions of laying waste the whole of the English border and their objectives seem to have been based on a total lack of understanding of the nature of marcher conflict. It may therefore be suggested that an element of disharmony was evident between the allies from the outset and that relations deteriorated rapidly on the march.

On 23rd July the allies crossed into the English east march and swiftly 'took up' the castles at Cornhill, Wark and Ford, slighting the works in each case. Even before the attack commenced the English had been mustering at Newcastle. A very substantial force, 12,000–14,000 men,[8] was preparing to follow the sacred banner of St Cuthbert. This was a royal army to be led by the king in person, Richard anxious to win his spurs, and one which had been raised by the archaic means of the feudal levy, perhaps a comment on the crown's inability to pay wages. Most of the magnates were present including Gaunt who brought the largest company together with both Northumberland and Hotspur.

In the face of so mighty a host the Franco-Scots swiftly retreated and on 6th August the English crossed onto Scottish soil. Six days later

Edinburgh was in flames after the invaders had laid waste the Scottish middle march and burnt the abbeys of Dryburgh and Melrose. The justification for this desecration was provided by the running sore of the papal schism with England and Scotland, each maintaining an opposing allegiance to the rival candidates.

The Scots wisely relied on their habitual fabian tactics, denying the means of supply and avoiding pitched battle. This pragmatic approach to warfare was at odds with the chivalric notions of their allies who were frustrated by the refusal to fight. As ever this policy was the correct one. The English encountered logistical problems, the king quarrelled publicly with his uncle (which must have given the Percys some comfort) and by the 19th of the month the expedition was back in Newcastle. This should by no means imply the Scots had escaped without loss: their own punitive raid had been seen off and large tracts of the country wasted, the capital and other towns reduced to ashes. The vaunted French alliance had failed to produce any tangible gains and was soon to dissolve in acrimony.

Despite the cracks in the relationship the allies could still muster for a joint retaliation against the west in late August or early September, causing alarums in Carlisle and spreading fire down the Eden valley before moving into the middle marches prior to an attack on Roxburgh. It was now that the final wrangles destroyed the already fragile accord. De Vienne apparently had the notion that Roxburgh should be taken in the name of Charles VI rather than that of Robert II. This idea was not unnaturally repugnant to the Scots who now determined they had had quite enough of French assistance. Their guests' lack of understanding, their casual rapacity in seizing their victuals from the people of the country coupled with their open disdain for the poverty and squalor of the realm had failed to endear them and the joint venture proved a total failure.

Having rid themselves of their troublesome allies the Scots still had energy for further campaigning before a truce, brokered in September, came into effect on 24th October. The king's younger son Robert Earl of Fife, with the Earl of Douglas and the Lord of Galloway, led a further raid into the west march, wasting the lands around Cockermouth, whilst Hexham and the east march also suffered. These incursions provided scope for younger knights to show their mettle: Archibald the Grim's bastard William Douglas of Nithsdale fought with distinction around Carlisle whilst Hotspur showed his worth in the east.

The war of 1385 had, to all intents and purposes, ended in stalemate. The Franco-Scots alliance had achieved nothing of worth and the experiment of close co-operation was not repeated. Conversely the English invasion, costly and destructive, had failed either to bring the enemy to battle or to overawe. On a local level both sets of marchers had suffered much and won little. With the buffer zones now gone, the northern counties of England would sorely feel their loss. Richard II's lumbering host had done almost as much damage in England as it had in Scotland and the marchers may well have considered the price of royal intervention too costly by far. Southern England had been spared the spectre of a French landing which failed to materialise, though the prospect was the cause of widespread alarm.

The Scots having tested the worth of their continental ally and found this wanting would be less concerned in future about co-ordinating their actions with those of the French. From now on their policy would be more open to pure expediency, attacking when the opportunities seemed ripe for local success. The disappointments of the year had achieved that which English diplomacy had failed to do – they had driven a clear wedge between the French and the Scots. Conversely, the Scots would not now be inhibited by the implications of their strategy on the situation on the continent.

It must also be considered, especially in relation to the Anglo-Scottish borders, that military actions were never as clear cut as a summary of the historical events might suggest. The constant climate of strife was catalyst for a host of local disturbances, petty raids and feuds, the details of which are scarcely recorded, if at all. Nonetheless this climate of chaos would burden local inhabitants with an equal quantum of misery as the larger but rarer baronial or national operations.

The following years, 1386 and 1387, did not witness any large-scale campaigning, a truce was agreed to run from 28th June 1386 to 31st May the following year. John of Gaunt was distracted by his adventure in Castile and whilst there were constant alarums in the south of England over a feared French descent, none occurred, whilst English naval activity in the Channel met with some success.

In both kingdoms there was a measure of unrest. The reign of Richard II had failed to fulfil the glorious heritage of the young king's father and grandfather. Apart from failure in France there was growing unease amongst the peerage who had come to resent the royal favourite Robert de Vere,

Earl of Oxford. Though none could doubt the value of his illustrious lineage the earl was impecunious to a degree, a handicap that excessive royal patronage had done much to repair. De Vere had become the king's lieutenant in Ireland in 1386 but the following year he had been worsted and forced into exile after a brush with a group of disaffected nobles at Radcot Bridge. This faction, the Lords Appellant as they became known, comprised the Duke of Gloucester with the earls of Arundel, Warwick, Nottingham and Henry Bolingbroke, the Earl of Derby, John of Gaunt's eldest son and heir.

The Lords Appellant, by frightening off Oxford, edged the king into a position whereby he was forced to either accept their reforms which would inevitably entail a ruthless purge of his favourites or be deposed. Richard had no choice but to comply, though the bitter gall of his submission would fester and the 'Merciless' Parliament that convened in January 1388 censured a host of his followers, though only a few were executed. Northumberland remained carefully aloof from this turbulence, though he could not fail to note that the Nevilles had incurred the enmity of the rebellious peers. On 12th April Hotspur was appointed as east march warden and captain of Berwick when Sir Ralph Neville was summarily dismissed. To add to the family's difficulties John, Lord Neville of Raby, was seriously ill at this point and died in October.

The dissident peers were no more friendly to France and on 10th June Arundel led an expedition across the Channel. This was clearly useful to the Scots who now began to plan their own campaign for the summer. The offensive was to consist of a three-pronged assault. William Douglas of Nithsdale and Sir Robert Stewart of Durisdeer led a diversionary force against the English administration in Ireland which successfully rebuffed a local force from Dundalk, burnt the town of Carlingford and raided the Isle of Man before returning to Galloway.

The central and main thrust was to be launched by Fife and Archibald the Grim against the west march whilst March, Moray and Douglas made a further demonstration in the east. Fife's chevauchee carried fire and sword down the Eden valley, ravaged the lands around Carlisle and torched Appleby in Westmorland.

The force which the three earls commanded has been estimated at 6,600, including grooms and a handful of camp followers,[9] and assembled in late July or early August at Jedburgh. There is some difficulty with dates as the Scottish sources insist the battle of Otterburn was fought on 5th August whilst the English prefer the 19th, St Oswin's Eve. The invaders advance command post was established around Southdean Kirk near Bonchester Bridge.[10] Froissart claims an English spy had infiltrated the councils of the leadership and this is by no means impossible – espionage was rife and good intelligence vital to both sides. The spy was discomfited when, having gleaned the Scottish plans, he found, on trying to make good his escape, that in accordance with prevalent local custom, his horse had been stolen. Attempting to withdraw on foot aroused suspicions; those dressed and spurred after the manner of a gentleman did not normally proceed as would a commoner. Arrested and put to the question, doubtless without much finesse, the agent was made to reveal all.

The Scots swept through Northumberland, their passage, as ever marked by burning thatch, and shocked and stumbling refugees. Passing like a whirlwind through the northern shire they entered Durham, spreading the flames of invasion to the city walls. The narrow, noisome lanes were crammed with the dispossessed, the summer sky aglow with the light of burning thatch and byre. Northumberland caught totally off guard by the speed of the Scots' descent remained immured behind the thick walls of Alnwick whilst he despatched Hotspur and his brother Ralph to Newcastle to raise the country and townspeople so that the invaders might not return home unchallenged.

The earl had clearly been taken in by the deception, believing the expedition to be far stronger than it was. Whilst Northumberland remained inert at Alnwick, Hotspur wasted no time in assembling a body of knights to form the nucleus of an army. In addition to his brother Ralph he was joined by Sir Matthew Redman, the captain of Berwick, Sir Robert Ogle, Sir Thomas Grey, Sir Thomas Holton, Sir John Felton, Sir John Lilleburn, Sir Thomas Abingdon, the Baron of Hilton, Sir John Coppledike and the Seneschal of York, Sir Ralph Lumley.[11] Having wasted the land between Tyne and Wear the Scots came to the gates of Newcastle where there was some skirmishing around the 'barriers' (timber outworks beyond the barbican). Froissart relates that Douglas and Hotspur met across snarling lances and that the Scot had the better of the encounter, making off with Percy's pennon.[12]

Much has been made of this incident as the motivation for the pursuit of the Scots army and the battle which followed and, whilst the idea has a chivalric appeal, it should not be considered as anything other than anecdotal. Hotspur's decision to follow the retreating invaders and bring them to battle was the proper response of a march official. At this juncture the English still seem to have been under the misapprehension they were facing the full might of the Scots army and it was probably not until the next day as the host moved off northwards that English scouts or 'prickers', shadowing the retreat, brought Percy an account of their true numbers.

Sir Adomar of Athol commanding the scratch garrison of Ponteland Tower was surprised, his enceinte taken by storm and himself made captive. The victorious raiders then moved on to Otterburn Castle some thirty English miles north of Newcastle. Redesdale was Umfraville country and this fortalice proved a tougher nut altogether.[13] Lacking in siege engines the Scots' attempts at an escalade were rebuffed. Froissart gives an account of the council which followed the unsuccessful attack. The more cautious were for a continued and swift withdrawal but Douglas wished to stand fast and allow Percy the opportunity to recover his lost guidon in a further trial of arms.[14]

This version must be treated with some caution. For the Scots to offer battle when they had achieved the whole of their strategic objectives makes no sense at all; consistently they preferred guerrilla-style operations, avoiding the hazard of a general engagement. Froissart makes it clear that the plan was not to withdraw fully but to lead off to the west, presumably via Teviotdale and Liddesdale, to join with Fife in the ravaging of Cumbria. Northumberland had been completely out-generalled and left impotent at Alnwick and it has to be assumed that, at this point, the Scots were not aware that Hotspur was in pursuit. It is more likely that the army remained by Otterburn to allow both men and horses to rest and recuperate before further gruelling marches westwards.

The Percy brothers had not been idle. On the 19th of August (English version) they led their followers, perhaps as many as 8,000 strong, 'after dinner' (say sometime past noon) on the road to Otterburn following in the wake of the invaders. As they were able to cover the entire distance to Otterburn before nightfall, arriving at dusk, say, at that time of year around 9 p.m. it is reasonable to suppose (following Colonel Burne) that the force was mounted probably on ponies or garrons, the host trotting through the dusty heat of that distant summer's afternoon. Having covered the distance and with the Scots' camp in view, Hotspur determined upon an immediate assault.

Northumberland's eldest son has been recently described as a 'clumsy' general but this may be unduly pejorative. He had, by his bold and sudden approach, achieved the element of surprise, every commander's trump. Against this his men were much fatigued from the forced march. By attacking at dusk and fighting in the semi-darkness of the summer's evening he was sacrificing the tactical superiority of the longbow and adding the considerable hazard of night operations. It must, however, be remembered that bringing the Scots to battle was any English warden's prime objective. Percy enjoyed numerical superiority and at least some of his officers, particularly Umfraville, had sound local knowledge; most of the others were battle tried and mettlesome.

If he delayed till morning it was highly improbable the earls would be so obliging as to attend upon his convenience. More likely they would slip away under the cover of night and put as many miles as possible between themselves and their pursuers. Quite simply this was Hotspur's best chance of bringing on a decisive encounter. He took it and he lost, but the decision, in the circumstances, was probably the right one.

It is likely the Scots had made their camp in the narrow neck of the valley, perhaps a mile north of Otterburn. The gap between the hills on either flank is no more than 1,000 yards across and the river about 20–5 yards width, we know the season was hot and dry so the water would be brown and sluggish but still a substantial obstacle. It is safe to assume firstly that all of the fighting occurred to the north and secondly that the English advanced along the line of the then roadway which conformed to the current line of the later turnpike (now the A696). The terrain remains remarkably unchanged save that the now cultivated slopes to the north of the Rede were heavily forested.

Colonel Burne places the Scottish camp astride the pass at its narrowest neck somewhat to the east of the two ancient earthworks that command each flank. He is entirely correct in dismissing both of these as likely locations; neither could possibly hold such a complement, not to mention horses, baggage, accumulated loot and impedimenta. Froissart states that the Scots made rough cabins out of branches and turf, a notion Burne dismisses, and in this perhaps he is wrong. As the sun beat fiercely on those

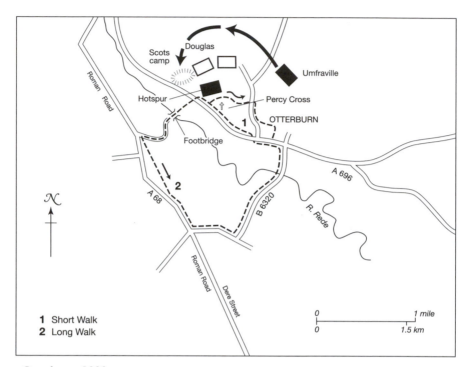

Otterburn, 1388

cloudless August days it is possible the Scots sought shelter from the sun
rather than wind or rain and we might well take the Fleming at his word.

Half a thousand yards to the east of the camp a slight ridge runs at right
angles to the slope and down towards the river, forming a natural defensive
line 500 yards in length. In all probability a scattering of vedettes clustered
on this ridge sounded the call to arms as the English came in sight, the
Percy banner and those of the other knights gaudy in the clear, still light.

Froissart goes on to tell that Douglas had planned for this contingency
and devised a strategy to hold any assault along the line of the ridge whilst
a commanded party prepared a flank attack from dead ground to the
north.

> *His host he parted had in 3,*
> *As leader ware and try'd,*
> *And soon his spearmen on their foes*
> *Bare down on every side.*

Throughout the English Archery,
They dealt full many a wound;
But still our valiant Englishmen
All firmly kept their ground.[15]

Whilst the chronicler awards Douglas the lead role in the Scottish tactics we may be tempted to discern the more experienced and wily hand of George Dunbar. Despite Froissart's assertions it would be folly indeed for a commander to commit himself to leading a flank attack of this nature when he had able subordinates about him. More likely March gave Douglas and his affinity the task which certainly demanded strong nerves, initiative and valour.

The two armies collided in the gloaming. We have no real idea of the English dispositions, though we may assume that the order of battle comprised the van, perhaps under Ralph Percy with Hotspur leading in the centre. The rear was possibly under Umfraville who was also detailed to make a flank attack to secure the rear of the Scots' position and frustrate a fighting retreat. The English would be divided into companies of billmen, all dismounted led by knights with the archers serving as footmen. The Scots were likely to be formed into their customary schiltroms, stiffened by dismounted men at arms, contact first occurring when the English crested the shallow ridge, a shivering clash of staves in the gathering dusk. The combat was fierce and hot, as Froissart recalls:

Of all the battles and encounterings that I have made mention of heretofore in this history, great or small, this battle that I treat of now was one of the sorest and best foughten without cowardice or faint hearts.[16]

As night fell the fitful moon scudding behind clouds lit a scene of fearful carnage. Medieval combat was, at best, close, bloody, exhausting and disorientating. The dry ground would give off vast clouds of choking dust, steam of sweat engulfed the fighting men. Those in full harness with 'pig face' visors down could see but little in the heat of day but in that darkened haze, their vision further dimmed, not telling friend from foe, straining for the glint of flashing steel or thrusting point. The maimed and wounded thrashed on the bloodied turf, many dispatched by the simple expedient of thrusting a thin-bladed dagger[17] through the eyes slit of the visor directly through the face into the brain, the shuddering corpses stripped as they fell.

What of the flanking movements? It might be supposed that Umfraville moving north and west might collide with Douglas advancing to the north and east. It is clear that no such encounter took place. We have no exact account of the English flank attack, Froissart had no detailed knowledge of the terrain and was relying on survivors' accounts which might themselves conflict:

> *It is not an easy task to describe a battle. Springs and motions escape the eye, and most officers are necessarily taken up with what is immediately near themselves; so that it is next to impossible for one to observe the whole: add to this, the confusion, the noise, the concern that the people are in, whilst in the heat of action.*[18]

It could be surmised that Hotspur had detached Umfraville and his battalion some time prior to the advance to contact and that they proceeded for a little way north via the line of the road now leading north out of the village towards the present Otterburn Hall. They then veered west below the wooded crest of the higher ridge before coming down past where the old quarries now lie to take the Scots camp by surprise:[19] 'Suddenly the Englishmen came on them and entered into the lodgings weening it had been the masters' lodgings, and therein were but varlets and servants.'[20]

The marchers slew or scattered the grooms and servants left behind in the camp and must surely have paused to avail themselves of all that lay within, 'liberating' many of the spoils. Quite what happened to the attackers once they had ransacked the camp and finished kicking the corpses is harder to ascertain. Colonel Burne decides that having 'beaten up' the Scots' camp Umfraville's force were led by the sound of the battle on the shallow ridge to the east to retrace their steps and rejoin the flank of their comrades now hotly engaged.[21] This may be a rather optimistic assessment. If Umfraville's force was comprised either in whole or in part of local dalesmen then it would be more likely they simply dispersed with the loot they had accumulated.

The actions of Douglas and his affinity are easier to follow. Again, as Burne correctly asserts, if we accept that the main fight was raging along the crest of the rise then it would be possible for a body of troops to move towards the exposed flank of the English position, having circumvented the higher ground to the rear and left flank of the camp, and then erupt, like a thunderbolt, from the lee of the dead ground.

The attack certainly achieved surprise and discomfited the English who, with the benefit of superior numbers, had been gradually pushing the Scots down the reverse slope. Despite the shock of Douglas' men charging from the shadows, the line held. Both Hotspur and Ralph rushed to shore up the flank and the clamour of the fight swelled to a new crescendo. Froissart relates that the Douglas banner was at risk of capture – saved by the valour of Sir Patrick Hepburn and his son of the same name.[22] Froissart goes on to remind us that he had previously been a guest of the earl's father at Dalkeith and met Douglas as a boy. The 2nd earl is very much the hero of his tale and his beserker charge against the English at the height of the fray as Hotspur's men press hard has a Homeric ring. Even if we accept a certain element of licence it is difficult not to be stirred:

> ... then the earl of Douglas, who was of great heart and high of enterprise, seeing his men recule [withdraw] back, then to recover the place and shew knightly valour he took his axe in both his hands, and entered so into the press that he made himself way in such wise, that none durst approach near him, and he was so well armed that he bare well off such strokes as he received. Thus he went ever forward like a hardy Hector, willing alone to conquer the field and to discomfit his enemies: but at least he was encountered with three spears [probably bills] all at once, the one strake him on the shoulder, the other on the breast and the stroke glinted down to his belly, and the third strake him in the thigh, and sore hurt with all three strokes, so that he was borne perforce to the earth and after that he could not be again relieved.[23]

The wounded earl was struck on the head with an axe as he fell and sustained another wound to the thigh. The fearsome combination of these injuries swiftly proved fatal. Had the battle been fought in daylight the death of Douglas could have proved disastrous to the Scots' cause, but in the shadow of night, only the earl's retainers were aware he had fallen. The English failed to perceive such a signal success or the Scots to comprehend their loss. The fight continued, with the hero's corpse stoutly defended by his retainers including his chaplain, William of North Berwick who, armed with an axe like his fallen master, performed such prodigies of valour he was afterwards made archdeacon of Aberdeen.[24]

Exhaustion and hunger began to tell on the English. Slowly they were pushed back, Douglas' surviving retainers maintaining the pressure on the flank and the line beginning to crumble. Hotspur swapped strokes with a Scottish knight named Montgomery (Douglas and Percy never fought hand to hand as the ballad suggests):

The Percy and the Douglas mette;
That ether of other was fayne;
They struck together,
With swords of fyne Cologne [German manufacture]

Till the bloode from ther helmets ranne,
As the mist doth in the rayne
Yelde thou to me sayd the Douglas
Our ells thou schalt be slayne.[25]

Hotspur was taken, as was his brother Ralph, the blood from his numerous hurts running freely from his greaves, together with Sir Ralph Lumley and a number of other knights and, after a chase and a stiff combat, Sir Matthew Redman submitted to Sir James Lindsay. Hotspur had had his battle but it was the Scots who won the day, the remnants of the English army dissolving into the dark. Without question Froissart is correct when he describes the encounter as being hard fought and he is also undoubtably right in finding that the exhaustion of the English consequent on their fatiguing march was a prime factor in the defeat.

As the piles of bloodied flesh moaned and writhed, pallid and shocking in the silvered light of the fitful moon, it would be time to assess the butcher's bill. It seems likely that the Scots suffered few casualties; besides Douglas, his standard bearer Sir John Hart and Sir John Towers, there were hardly any fatalities of note. Though the English had many taken, none of the senior officers was killed, though the rank and file were unlikely to have been so fortunate, having no commercial value.[26] Froissart gives the unlikely number of English dead as 1,840 with 1,040 taken prisoner. He claims the Scots lost no more than 100 dead but with some 200 taken, mainly, as it would appear, in the course of the English withdrawal, which implies this was no rout.[27]

The following day as the triumphant Scots held their ground a further English force came up. This was under the command of the Bishop of

Durham and may have been 10,000 strong,[28] which may not be so improbable as it sounds if the Prince Bishop's division had succeeded in rounding up numbers of the stragglers stumbling back towards Newcastle. The Scots, full of their victory, easily frightened off these new opponents. According to Froissart, the terrifying din of their war horns was sufficient to unnerve the English.[29]

Having secured another and bloodless win the Scots, bearing Douglas' corpse, marched towards Melrose where the earl was duly entombed amongst his forebears and then the army, replete with prisoners and loot, dispersed.

It is often remarked that Otterburn was a battle without consequences – a pointless exercise in gratuitous bloodletting to satisfy the vaunting hubris of Douglas and Percy. This is not the case. The effects of the battle were felt keenly by the English administration. Hitherto policy had determined that it was the function of the marcher lords to seek out and engage with the enemy. The trick had been to corner the invaders rather than to defeat them. Once battle was under way the result was not presumed to be in contention. Otterburn rather upset this theory. An inferior force of Scots, taken largely by surprise, had outfought a larger English army, an army which was neither badly led nor lacking in motivation. Crucially the attackers had been denied the tactical use of the longbow which had served them so well in the past, at Dupplin Moor, Halidon Hill and Neville's Cross.

Trepidation was balanced by outrage and the king proposed a major retaliation which, due to the lateness of the season, had to be postponed. Hotspur, far from being censured, was the hero of the hour and part of his ransom was met from the public purse with private donors, including the Prior of Durham, chipping in.

The scale of the victory raised Scottish morale to a new zenith and signifies the high water mark of the preceding two decades. Perversely it focused the minds of the English king and council on the problems of the north and may have inspired a new resolve to seek a final, military resolution to the Scottish problem such as had not featured since the heady days of the 1330s. It may also have acted as a further stimulus to Anglo-French negotiations. Even before the border campaign of 1388 both sides were tiring of the continental war. The Scots' victory which, had it occurred in say 1346, would have been a major boost to their allies was now of no value. The failure of earlier co-operation had led to a lack of any common purpose; events on the Anglo-Scottish border were no longer a major concern of Charles VI.

Another loser, what might now be termed 'collateral damage', was the Earl of Carrick. Douglas had been a pillar of his faction but, on his death, the title went to the Lord of Galloway, Archibald the Grim, who was created 3rd Earl. He now threw his not inconsiderable weight behind the king's younger son, the Earl of Fife, whose influence eclipsed that of his brother and he became Guardian after a bloodless shift of power in December 1388.

By the autumn of that year the grip of the Lords Appellant had begun to slacken and Richard II was able to flex some constitutional muscle. Neville was reinstated as, in October, the Scots launched an unsuccessful assault on Berwick. This was swiftly followed by a retaliatory thrust against the Merse. Immediately after the turn of the year Cumbria was harried once again. The English planned a major spring offensive to be led not by Northumberland but by the Earl of Nottingham, no admirer of the Percys and supported by Neville in the east, Beaumont and Clifford in the west. The Scots, under Fife's energetic leadership, struck first, wasting a great swathe of Northumberland to the banks of the Tyne. Although Nottingham's army bore the spiritual shield of St Cuthbert's banner his reaction was sluggish, only those doughty fighters Sir Matthew Redman and Sir Robert Ogle actually advanced to contact, cutting up the invaders' rearguard.[30]

In spite of these alarums there was no grand strategy for the invasion of Scotland in 1389, but on the diplomatic front, moves were afoot to finally fracture the continental alliance which had withered since 1385. An Anglo-French truce was concluded on 18th June to hold until the 16th August 1390. By then Robert II, whose caution and prevarication had in fact served his country rather well, was dead. The old king died on 19th April 1390 and was succeeded by John Earl of Carrick. The name John still possessed such an unfortunate resonance in the memories of his countrymen that the new monarch swiftly changed it, ascending the throne as Robert III.

In England John of Gaunt had returned from his quixotic foray to Castile to find the administration a seething labyrinth of hostile factions. In his absence he had been persuaded to heal the breach with Northumberland and showed favour to the newly released Hotspur who was indentured into the king's service for an annual retainer of £100 and, in June 1390, made warden of the west march.

Despite his escape from the clutches of his dissident nobility the troubles of Richard II were by no means over and those of Robert III were merely beginning. For the marchers it rather looked like business as usual.

There can be little doubt that the enduring fame of the battle of Otterburn is due to both Froissart and the balladry which followed. The Homeric quality of the fight and Douglas' glorious death are the stuff of legend and have ensured the encounter ranks alongside Agincourt as one of the most famous of medieval battles:

> *I never heard the old song of Piercy and Douglas, that I found not my heart more moved than with a trumpet; and yet it is sung by some blind crowder with no rougher voice than rude stile; which being so evil apparelled in the dust and cobweb of that uncivil age, what would it work trimmed with the gorgeous eloquence of Pindar.*[31]

Notes

1 'Ballad of the Battle of Otterbourne', see Scott, Sir Walter, *Minstrelsy of the Scottish Border*, London 1892 pp. 164–73.

2 Burne, A.H., *More Battlefields of England*, London 1952 p. 131.

3 MacDonald, A.J., *Border Bloodshed*, East Lothian 2000 p. 75.

4 Ibid p. 79.

5 Ibid pp. 84–5.

6 Ibid p. 85.

7 Ibid p. 86.

8 Ibid p. 89.

9 White, R., *Battle of Otterburn*, 1857, quoted in Burne p. 130.

10 Sadler, D.J., *Battle for Northumbria*, Newcastle upon Tyne 1988 p. 78. The ruin of Southdean Kirk still stands by the roadside near Bonchester Bridge (NT 632092) with a plaque commemorating the events of 1388.

11 *Chronicles of Froissart* transl. Berners, ed. Macaulay London 1924 p. 371.

12 Froissart p. 371.

13 Ibid p. 371.

14 Ibid p. 371.

15 Scott 'Battle of Otterbourne'. The field today is marked by Percy's Cross which was placed in its present position in 1777, the year the turnpike road was constructed. The original 'battle stone' which is said to have marked the place where Douglas fell was situated some 150 yards east. As the road was

completed the Duke of Northumberland offered to underwrite the erection of a more substantial memorial. However, the owner of the land, a Mr Ellison, feared the duke might be seeking through this gesture to seek title to the site and therefore built the monument at his own expense. The monument which has now been turned into a 'picnic site' does provide, looking west, an excellent view of the field with the ridge along which the main combat took place only a few yards away and one is able to ignore the ubiquitous wooden tables and benches that represent the late twentieth-century contribution.

16 Froissart p. 374.
17 A nasty if effective means of disposing of an armoured opponent once he was down, the 'rondel' or 'ballock' knives were coming into vogue at this time.
18 Black, J., *Culloden and the '45*, New York 1990 p. 165 (after Lord George Murray).
19 Froissart p. 373.
20 Ibid p. 373.
21 Burne p. 138.
22 Froissart p. 373.
23 Ibid p. 374.
24 Ibid p. 375.
25 Scott, 'Battle of Otterbourne'.
26 Froissart p. 380.
27 Ibid p. 380. In the nineteenth century when construction work was being carried out at nearby Elsdon Church it is said that a mass of bones were discovered beneath the flagstones in the nave. The remains were identified as being mainly those of young adult males and it is presumed this was the last resting place for many of the English dead. Mr Charles Wesencraft has advanced an intriguing theory that the battle did not take place on the site traditionally identified but by Battle Hill, just south of Elsdon village.
28 Ibid p. 379.
29 Ibid p. 379.
30 MacDonald p. 114.
31 The words of Sir Philip Sydney, beau sabreur of the late Elizabethan age, whose own death on the field of Zutphen was easily worthy of a Hotspur or Douglas, quoted in Sadler p. 83.

Chapter 11

'At Holmedon met'

On Holyrood Day the gallant Hotspur there,
Young Harry Percy, and brave Archibald,
That ever valiant and approved Scot
At Holmedon met.[1]

Travelling northwards from Wooler along the present A697 with the Glen flowing to the east, bisecting the alluvial flatlands the west is suddenly crowded with the outriders of the Cheviot range. These hunched, steep-sided hills, deployed like a primeval bodyguard around the bare sweep of the central massif, glower over the fertile reaches of Millfield plain below. Until the seventeenth century much of the land was unreclaimed bog, whose quaking entrails resisted any attempt by the plough. Nearest of the hills to Wooler is now called Humbleton. Previously it was known as Homildon and in its shadow was fought one of the most dramatic of the border battles.

One of the principal sources for the violent events of 14th September 1402 is the Scottish chronicler Bower, writing some decades after and without the immediate benefit of eyewitness testimony. He has the Scots deployed actually on the slopes of Homildon, with the English archers scrambling up Harehope Hill to the north to loose the arrow storm. A casual glance at the Ordnance Survey map, supported by a perambulation of the ground, will show that this is patently impossible. The tussocky sides of both hills are far too steep for armoured men to deploy and then give battle and neither summit could accommodate the numbers present. The distance from the small plateau atop each is well out of bowshot.[2]

Robert III of Scotland has not generally enjoyed a better press than his father, physically handicapped and increasingly dominated by his able younger brother the Earl of Fife and Menteith, latterly Duke of Albany. He was further marginalised by the internecine bickering between Albany and his mercurial eldest son, David, Earl of Carrick, later Duke of Rothesay. Furthermore his reign was characterised by lawlessness and near anarchy in parts of the realm, particularly in the north-east where his younger, illegitimate brother Alexander Stewart, known better by the savage epithet of the 'Wolf of Badenoch', abused his office to harry and terrorise.

The new king was also faced with a far less favourable international situation. Both England and France had grown weary of war so the fertile soil of the 1370s was turning barren, the developing *entente* between the relative superpowers enabling the English to concentrate energies and resources against their troublesome northern neighbour. The military initiative which had lain firmly in the hands of aggressive Scots commanders such as March, Moray and the Douglases now began to pass back to the English, themselves led by a new and full-blooded generation: Hotspur, his brother Ralph, Umfraville, Clifford and Neville.

As ever local raids proliferated, whatever the notional truce between the sovereign states. The borderers were relied upon in time of war to supply light horse and skirmishers. In the upland dales society had passed from the mainly agrarian, with the odd foray to a militarised culture based on loot and lifted livestock. It was simply not possible to turn the tap of aggression on or off as the expediencies of diplomacy dictated. Business as usual meant sword and lance, peace was economically unsound. Berwick appears, once again, to have been seized by a *coup de main* in 1390, though soon recovered, and Albany was able to renew the terms of the French alliance on 30th March 1391.[3] Even if England and France were not at war it was in Scotland's interests to remain close to France so that her ally might not be tempted to see her independence as merely another piece on the board. At the same time, the Earl of March, perhaps an odd choice for diplomatic discussion, was negotiating for the return of the Coldingham Cell to Durham, clearly a conciliatory move and the Prince Bishop recovered his outpost in the early months of 1392.[4]

In spite of this there is evidence that the English were slow in providing redress for breaches of the truce and that Umfraville was active on the marches. At the same time the English were again preying on Scottish shipping, a highly satisfying form of economic warfare whilst, at the higher diplomatic level, Richard II was actively seeking to have the Scots excluded from any Anglo-French accord. By way of further provocation the English marchers were insisting that truce days be held at locations within the former Pale, a clear statement that these lost lands were not forgotten.

For Scots this was plainly unacceptable. The whole impetus of war and diplomacy for the last two decades had revolved around the recovery and consolidation of these lost territories – for them the border was now fixed and immutable. Territorial claims were reinforced by renewed demands for the balance still owing of David II's ransom but so long as the Scots could rely on French support, England could not afford to contemplate full military action, however tempting the prospect. For Richard II, starved of glory, the reconquest of the Pale demanded the French be prised free of their alliance.

Deprived of opportunities to display their prowess on the field, the chivalry of England and Scotland had recourse to private combats, duels of chivalry, highly formalised but savage, sanguinary and frequently *à l'outrance*. The origin of such encounters is lost in the mists of time but is undoubtably as old as the concept of knighthood itself; as far back as 858 Charles the Bald met his brother Louis of Germany to settle their mutual grievances by a trial of arms. The duel of chivalry reached England in the twelfth century[5] and Edward III, that paladin of knightly valour had challenged Philip of France in 1340. The gauntlet was again thrown down by Richard II forty-odd years later when he offered to meet Charles VI. Neither of these royal bouts took place but Richard was enamoured of the concept and the duel of chivalry flourished in his reign.[6]

Such encounters, always beloved of the crowd, were fought out in the lists according to a strict set of rules, with a panel of judges and heralds appointed to ensure fair play. Nonetheless much blood was spilt and the loser could look forward to the *coup de grâce* being administered by the obligatory dagger thrust through the visor. In March 1390 the king provided a safe conduct for John Dunbar, Earl of Moray, to enter England to seek satisfaction of the Earl of Nottingham. The pair met on 28th May when Moray sustained wounds which soon proved fatal.[7]

In the same year a celebrated duel between Sir David Lindsay and John, Lord Welles was fought amidst the full pomp of the tourney on Old London Bridge before what would now be termed a 'capacity' crowd. The

King and Queen of England attended, as did many of the nobility. The quarrel between these two paladins had arisen at a banquet in Edinburgh. Welles was acting as an English ambassador and offered to settle the question of whether the English or the Scots were the more valiant in battle by fighting any knight who wished to pursue the point. Sir David picked up the gavel. Most chivalric duels were fought on horseback in a similar manner to the tourney.

At the first course both men shattered their lances, no advantage either way, although the Scot maintained his seat so well that some in the crowd loudly opined he was strapped to the saddle. The indignant knight promptly dismounted, knelt to the royal pair and then vaulted back into the saddle, no mean feat in full harness. At the second course lances were again splintered without advantage, but at the third Welles was dismounted and hurt. At this point the helpless knight might have been disposed to measure his life in seconds but the Scot chose to be merciful and indeed aided the prostrate rider until he was assisted from the field. Such chivalrous conduct won the enthusiastic approbation of the crowd, commons and gentry alike, and the victor was much feted despite being a Scot.[8]

A further encounter was proposed between the redoubtable Sir William Douglas of Nithsdale and Sir Thomas Clifford. Both of these were active marchers and the Englishman had a claim to lands in the Scottish west march which had been granted to Douglas after the elimination of the Pale. The duel was never fought, at least not in England, for both knights departed on crusade, to the dank forests of East Prussia to fight the baltic heathen under the banners of the Teutonic Knights. Inevitably the mettlesome pair met and chose to settle their differences, resulting in the death of Douglas.[9] This attrition was damaging to Scotland which was thus deprived of two seasoned commanders, Douglas and Moray, for absolutely no gain.

Not all Scots came to England lusting for the blood of their personal enemies. Some chose to enlist and fight under English colours; John Lindsay was given safe conduct to travel to Calais and join the garrison there, at that point commanded by Nottingham.[10] Others served Charles VI – peace had little to offer those who sought advancement under arms.

Despite the best efforts of Richard II and his negotiators it proved impossible to sever the Franco-Scots alliance and thus place the northern kingdom effectively at the mercy of its larger neighbour. In 1392–3 diplomatic moves were initiated towards a more lasting settlement but these foundered in the face of renewed English demands for resumption of ransom payments and the reoccupation of the Pale. There was talk of a marriage alliance but this too was mere froth and by 1394 the king was diverted by the first of his campaigns in Ireland. The Scots took advantage of these operations to gear up their harrying and whilst Neville defended the west march with vigour, Northumberland was criticised for lack of activity in the east.

Early in the year a commanded party of Scots under Sir William Inglis descended on Jedburgh Castle in a classic night attack, taking the defenders completely by surprise. The castellan, Sir Thomas Strother, soon regained the fortress but the enmity between the two officers sparked yet another duel, presided over by both Northumberland and Douglas. Strother was killed and the victor was rewarded with the Barony of Manor in Peebleshire. This might be seen as evidence of royal collusion or at least tacit approval of the raid.[11] The Irish campaign of 1394–5 clearly worried the administration of Robert III, all the more so as the English king achieved a fair measure of success, securing the submission of a number of the Irish chieftains. Activity along the border then appears to have been increased in the hope that this might oblige the king to desist from harrying the Irish and return. The English retaliated in what was by now the custom and preyed on Scottish shipping.

Richard II appeared to have won back full control of his kingdom and sovereignty from the Lords Appellant. Triumphant arms in Ireland were matched by a diplomatic coup when a twenty-eight-year truce was agreed with France in March 1396. The accord was sealed by a dynastic union between the widowed king and Isabella, the teenage daughter of Charles VI. Richard had gone so far as to press his new father-in-law not only to recognise his claim to overlordship of Scotland but to promise aid if his claims were resisted. Charles was not moved to abandon his allies completely but the peace marked a diplomatic defeat for Robert III.

Despite this reverse the Scots were not overawed and refused to enter into any accord for a period in excess of twelve months. Neither country had any appetite for serious hostilities. Gaunt met with Rothesay early in 1398 and concluded the terms of an indenture on 16th March.

This accord not only confirmed the status of the current truce but set down mechanisms for dealing with breaches, with the promise of more detailed talks the next year aimed at securing a more permanent settlement. The Scots Council was minded to accept the reality of the Anglo-French accord, though in May 1399 the truce was still extended for only a further twelve months. It is likely at this time that the Scots were aware of rumblings of discord in England and that Richard II's position, which had seemed inexpugnable after the successful conclusion of the Irish expedition, was about to crumble.

Even though relations appeared to be improving there were still regular alarums on the marches. At the warden's day on 26th October 1398 Adam Gordon, together with his affinity William Bard and Adam French, were summoned to appear at the next truce day following on pain of a swingeing £3,000 fine to answer allegations arising out of a raid into Glendale. Archibald, the Master of Douglas and shortly to be 4th earl, struck at Roxburgh where, it was claimed, he had caused some £2,000 worth of damage.[12]

The King of England had nursed his wrath against those lords who had first opposed then humiliated him. His recovery had been swift and complete; his triumph in Ireland had gone some way towards creating a military reputation. Richard was a brittle and unstable character, capable of spectacular rages. His relations with the nobility were indifferent at best and his popularity was not improved by the devious expedients he employed to shore up his frequently parlous finances:

> There are the unpleasant facts of forced loans, crooked pardons, blank charters and the grim joke of 'le plesaunce' and the crowning act of folly which in confiscating the Lancastrian Estates cost him his throne and his life.[13]

Richard's increasing tyranny was driven by his need to raise cash. The war in France had been ruinously expensive, the cost of maintaining the border defences was a constant drain and campaigns in Ireland, whilst adding lustre, did not produce a financial return to match the outlay, no vast haul of pilfered lands and ransoms.

By 1398 he had eliminated or sidelined all of the Lords Appellant – Henry of Derby, Earl of Hereford, old Gaunt's son and heir, would soon be in temporary exile, sentenced to six years' banishment after his feud with the Earl of Norfolk. Harsh as this sentence had been it did not entail a loss of estates for it was customary to have the exile's lands administered on trust by attorneys until his return and reinstatement. Besides, when his father died Hereford was heir to the vast Lancastrian patrimony, an inheritance that would place him on par with the king. Richard's fear of Hereford ran deep. No friend to the throne, capable and determined, his enmity would drastically weaken the royal prerogative. Hereford was banished in October 1398; the following February Gaunt died.

Richard's difficulties were exacerbated by events in Ireland where local warlord, Art MacMurrough, threw off his earlier allegiance and made war on the viceroy Roger Mortimer, the English Earl of March who was defeated and killed in battle at Kells in Carlow. The king determined to revenge Mortimer's death by mounting a fresh expedition against the rebels. An expedition to Ireland, however necessary and however successful the outcome, was not something to stir the blood. The place was impoverished, dirty, trackless and permanently wet. Little glory could be expected against a guerrilla foe who would seldom oblige by offering battle and where death came as a sudden arrow or a dirk thrust in the night. Besides, the king could simply not afford so large and costly an undertaking. Richard, with the perverse obstinacy of a weak man, was determined to have his war and Gaunt's death opened a window of opportunity in terms of finance.

If Hereford's attorney were reversed, if his banishment were to be extended for life and his conduct deemed treasonable, then the whole of his estates would be forfeit to the crown. At a stroke the king would have neutralised a major threat and ended his impoverishment. In order for Hereford to be declared a traitor Richard had to resort to some dubious means, including forging parliamentary rolls. Such conduct, blatantly illegal, 'sent a thrill of fear through every man of property in the land'[14] and provided a clear focus for the swelling tide of unrest. A more ruthless man than Richard would have ensured his rival met with an early death but by depriving Hereford of all that was rightfully his the king turned an Appellant into a mortal foe and gave his opposition a natural leader: 'he frightened all men though he struck down few.'[15]

On 29th May Richard's armada sailed for Ireland and months of fruitless campaigning against an enemy who remained both elusive and potent, denying battle but cutting up supply columns and stragglers whilst the army, thinned by disease, stumbled round the inhospitable landscape. In late June, Hereford, proclaiming himself Henry of Lancaster and, with his supporters crammed into three vessels, weighed anchor at Vannes in Brittany, making landfall at Ravenspur on 4th July. Whilst careful to broadcast only the fiction that he sought nothing more than the restoration of his rightful inheritance, Lancaster swiftly occupied the castles of Pickering, Knaresborough and Pontefract. At that moment everything hung in the balance. The king was far away in Ireland but, as yet, no men of property had declared for the rebel cause. Then he received offers of support from both Northumberland and Hotspur, effectively winning him the north. Neville was quick to follow. With the Percys in his camp Lancaster's position was dramatically improved. The march south quickly became a triumphal progress as royal support simply melted away. Richard had left his surviving uncle the Duke of York as regent who, with such forces as remained to him, confronted the Lancastrians on 27th July as they approached Bristol. There was no battle. As his army crumbled York accepted the inevitable though, to save face, he made a show of conceding that his nephew had no intentions beyond recovering that which was rightfully his.

It was probably in the middle of the month that Richard, still in Ireland, learnt of the invasion. His position was serious. The rebels were galloping through the realm whilst his own forces were scattered in the trackless wastes. With such troops as he could quickly muster the king was able to reach Milford Haven by 25th July. He was just in time to witness the defection of York, and his remaining adherents, sensing the hopelessness of their position now chose the moment to desert. With the Lancastrians in force at Bristol Richard made a dash for North Wales where he could count on a handful of strong castles and some measure of local support. The king was undoubtably in serious difficulties but did not consider himself beaten.

The rebels, though they enjoyed vastly superior numbers, were by no means secure. Richard was still king and remained undefeated in the field. It fell to Northumberland to lead a team of negotiators sent by Lancaster to treat with the king behind the massive walls of Conway Castle. The terms expounded by the earl were reasonable. Richard would remain on the throne though Lancaster would recover his lands in full and the king would accept the good advices of the peers. This was a return to the days of the Lords Appellant. Richard accepted almost certainly on the basis that he was not bound by terms extracted under duress. Lancaster had arrived at the same conclusion and arranged, with or without Northumberland's connivance, that the king's modest entourage was ambushed and taken prisoner. Richard's rule was effectively over.

Kidnapping the person of the king did not end the reign. Richard was the lord's anointed and so sacred a bond could not be easily untied by mortal hand. Lancaster was determined to try. His objective was clearly to take the throne, though the mechanics produced a major constitutional crisis. The 'Deposition' Parliament met on 30th September. By 13th October Lancaster was crowned Henry IV. Richard was persuaded to abdicate his throne and assume the role of a private gentleman. He was a guest, though doubtless by no means willing, at the great banquet which marked the end of the session, when he was described as 'Sir Richard of Bordeaux, a simple knight'.[16] There was no question of his being set at liberty and although his actual fate is unclear he died, possibly as a result of starvation, whilst a prisoner in Lancaster's castle at Pontefract.

It might be expected that the Scots would be swift to capitalise on such disarray but the Scottish polity was scarcely in any better shape. In January 1399 Rothesay had been created Lieutenant of the Kingdom but the struggle between the unstable duke and his formidable uncle, Albany, continued until the former's rather sudden death in 1402. In the autumn, whilst the spectre of the plague again raised its head on the English side, the Scottish marchers cut free, scoring a signal triumph with the taking up of Wark Castle whilst the keeper, Gray of Heton, was embroiled in the debates of the Deposition Parliament.[17] It seems there may also have been a skirmish in Coquetdale when Umfraville saw off a body of raiders with some loss. Robert III continued, rather pointedly, to refer to Henry IV as Duke of Lancaster, a slight that would rankle with any usurper.

The Lancastrian coup sent ripples of unrest through the Anglo-French concord and the Scots were emboldened to step up the incidence of inroads. The English responded with increasing levels of privateering. It is unlikely that the Scots were contemplating any large-scale offensive – even though matters were uncertain in England, it did not detract from the fact that the *entente* with France was holding and the convoluted politics of the competing factions within the Scottish polity seriously inhibited any concerted action. Besides, the border was far from defenceless – Hotspur, his brother, Neville, Clifford and Umfraville were ready and more than willing.

In the following year the Scots suffered a major setback when the Earl of March defected to the English. The loss of so active and experienced a captain cannot be overstated. For a generation George Dunbar had been the most energetic and consistently successful Scottish commander. The breach was occasioned by an act of near criminal folly and hubris on the part of Rothesay who, having agreed to wed a daughter of the earl's, then expressed a preference for a Douglas bride. The insult was compounded by the duke's refusal to return the dowry portion which March had already advanced. On 18th February the disaffected earl, who had failed to receive redress from the impotent king, wrote to Henry IV and by July had transferred his loyalty to England.[18] This must have been bitter gall for so steadfast a veteran, most of whose wide lands now fell into the rapacious hands of the Douglases.

When the ageing 3rd Earl died some time around Christmas 1400 Archibald, Master of Douglas, inherited the title and estates. The sequestration of the Dunbar lands made him the most powerful magnate in southern Scotland, at this time firmly wedded to the Rothesay faction. Quite possibly the Dunbar acres were the price of that support; if so the Duke made a poor bargain. The 4th Earl of Douglas became known as the 'tineman' or loser; he was an enthusiastic campaigner as constant as he was unsuccessful. No army he led ever achieved victory. Disaster at Homildon was compounded by defeat at Shrewsbury, a record of failure he maintained until his last catastrophe and death on the field of Verneuil in 1424.

Despite the Douglas' best efforts March had retained control of the three key bastions of Lochmaben, Cockburnspath and Fast Castle, off the Berwickshire coast. Together these, added to the English footholds at Jedburgh and Roxburgh, could unlock the lost territories of the Pale and give the English back control of great swathes of southern Scotland. For Henry IV here was a heaven-sent opportunity to chalk up a major victory, to achieve that which had constantly eluded his deposed rival. Having entered into negotiations with the Lord of the Isles to potentially open up a second front or at least create a significant nuisance, Henry, having revived the claim to overlordship, planned to lead an army into Scotland. This represented an enormous gamble. The Lancastrian had inherited an empty treasury, there was unrest in Wales and his supporters, not least the Percys, were expecting their due rewards.

The royal army is said to have numbered some 13,000 men,[19] a very substantial force indeed, hugely expensive and supported by the fleet which cruised off the east coast providing victuals for the land army and seizing on targets of opportunity amongst Scottish shipping. In the event this grand expedition, like so many of its predecessors, failed to yield any significant results. The vast unwieldy army advanced through the marches applying fire and sword but failing either to bring the Scots to battle or win any significant castles. As ever the Scots relied on fabian tactics and a scorched-earth policy which soon exhausted the invaders' provisions. Henry's army remained on Scottish soil for no more than a couple of weeks in the latter part of August[20] before returning southward. In all probability the inhabitants of Northumberland would be as glad to see the back of the royal troops as the Scots.

English privateers may have enjoyed more success. There is evidence of a number of amphibious raids up the length of the east coast: prizes and loot made such expeditions attractive. The English certainly did not have it all their own way – the Scots scored a signal triumph over an Anglo-Irish squadron at Strangford.[21]

The split in the Scottish Council prevented the formulation of a cohesive policy such as had obtained in the previous reign. Activity on the border was more local and unco-ordinated. The rise of a proactive generation of English marchers and the apparent lack of good intelligence meant the Scottish response was far less effective than in the previous decades. Both Bamburgh and Redesdale were targeted but the ever vigilant Umfraville trounced the raiders invading his glen and captured their captain, Sir Richard Rutherford. The Scots did entertain hopes of a distraction in Wales where the legendary patriot Owen Glendower had raised the banner of revolt. Initially these disturbances amounted to very little and a truce was agreed to run from 9th November, though at first this was to subsist for no more than a mere six weeks; later the term was extended to a year, expiring on 11th November 1401.[22]

If Rothesay was too stupid to comprehend the scale of his blunder in alienating Dunbar he was about to receive some sharp reminders. In February 1401 Dunbar, the Scottish Earl of March, and Hotspur led a raid against East Lothian though they were chased back to the border by Douglas, now the principal general of Scots.[23] The earlier truce had not been sealed by the king of either realm; Henry IV was still unsure of his throne and the council of Robert III remained paralysed by the feud between Albany and Rothesay. A further truce, ratified by both governments, was negotiated by Douglas and Northumberland in September to hold for twelve months from when the current accord expired in November. Whether Douglas, perpetually itching for a fight, was serious in these negotiations has to be doubted. Rothesay's star was fast waning and the troubles in Wales had flared once more. Douglas undoubtably saw this and the English administration's ongoing difficulties in Ireland as the climate of opportunity.

In spite of the agreement to maintain the truce the unresolved matters of the English Pale and the overdue ransom payments hung like black clouds over any hopes of a lasting peace. With the earl of March officially recognised as an ally of England, his remaining holds in Scotland stayed inviolate, tempting bridgeheads in both east and west. Rothesay, to consolidate his crumbling position, preferred a conciliatory approach. This did not sit well with Douglas, hitherto his most powerful supporter. When the earl switched his affinity to the Albany camp, the duke's grip on power was effectively broken. Albany therefore favoured war, not because he saw this as best policy but because it was the inevitable price for the support of the hawks under Douglas. The peace negotiations ended unsatisfactorily on 23rd October and notwithstanding the extension of the truce Douglas was harrying Bamburgh within the month. From November onwards the English border officials were paid at 'war' rates – a telling comment on the perceived worth of the truce.[24]

In the spring of 1402 the Lancastrians suffered a blow on the Welsh marches when Sir Edmund Mortimer was defeated and captured by Glendower. Worse, he then defected to the rebel camp, opening a yawning gap in the English defences. Henry IV was thus obliged to concentrate his meagre resources in prosecuting the war in Wales. At the same time the hawkish Earl of Crawford was on a diplomatic mission to France where he managed to sway the aggressive faction of the powerful Duc d'Orleans. Crawford, in recompense for his support of Albany, was granted command of a joint Franco-Scottish naval expedition which was being prepared for operations in the Channel. Within the year he had secured the important sinecure of Admiral of Scotland.[25]

Rothesay was diminished but not yet extinguished, so the Albany affinity had to tread carefully in the early months of the year. In February

Douglas wrote disingenuously to Henry complaining of alleged breaches of the truce by Northumberland and his sons. The king replied in placatory if non-committal terms, negotiations were promised but never took place. By then Rothesay was dead, in circumstances best described as mysterious, and Albany's position was inexpungable. On 23rd May Henry ordered a general muster of levies from all the northern shires, though in the event these had to be diverted to Wales.[26]

In the late spring and early summer both sides sent out raiding parties. March was working closely with the Percys, a formidable partnership of former adversaries, but Douglas was by no means idle. Thomas Haliburton, the lord of Dirleton, beat up the lands around Bamburgh whilst Patrick Hepburn of Hailes led a more substantial force deeper into the east march. The raiders were tracked over the border by March, ambushed and severely cut up at Nisbet Hill in the Merse. Hepburn together with 'the flower of the youth of Lothian' fell in the fight.[27] John and William Cockburn, Robert Lauder, John and Thomas Haliburton, leader of the earlier chevauchee, were all taken.[28]

Douglas had, however, planned his major stroke for the late summer and the English border was on standby in August. The army which crossed the border was certainly a large one, perhaps as many as 10,000–12,000 men.[29] Led by Douglas it included many of the leading Scottish magnates. This was no mere raiding force but a national army. The earl was accompanied by Albany's son Murdoch, his fellow earls of Moray, Angus and Orkney, lords Montgomery and Erskine, with those redoubtable captains Adam Gordon and Sir John Swinton. Mustering at Bamburgh under the joint command of March and the Percys the English forces comprised contingents stripped from every corner of the marches as well as Cheshire bowmen whom Hotspur had recruited for service against the Welsh rebels; Percy was joined by Ralph, Baron Greystoke, Sir Henry Fitzhugh, Sir Ralph Eure, William lord Hilton and Umfraville together with the keepers of both Roxburgh and Dunstanburgh. Lincolnshire levies mixed with the Welsh marchers and apprentices from Newcastle.[30]

The Scots had every reason to feel confident – theirs was the most powerful force to have crossed the Tweed in a generation. Despite the reverse at Nisbet Hill the military initiative had largely been theirs of the past two decades. Otterburn had proved they could win a general engagement and the bulk of English forces were isolated in Wales. However,

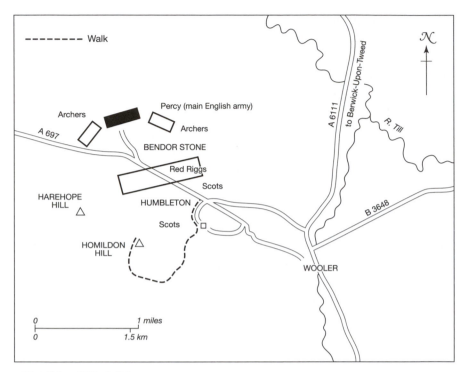

Homildon Hill, 1402

several factors had changed, not least of which was the defection of the Earl of March, the principal architect of earlier Scottish successes including the fight at Otterburn. His watchers added to the march wardens' own intelligence network had given ample warning of the attack and the decision to fight had clearly been made from the outset. It would be easy to see the cool, experienced counsels of the exiled Scottish peer directing the English effort and, after all, he had a significant score to settle with Douglas who now occupied the bulk of his former lands.

In that distant, hot September the Scottish host raged unchecked in north Northumberland, amassing such beasts and booty as the locals were unable to spirit away. Returning, strung out on the march, bleating ewes and stumbling cattle lifting great clouds of dust, the host passed Wooler when scouts brought sudden and unwelcome tidings: an English force, arrayed for battle, blocked their northward route on Millfield Plain.

It would seem likely from the ground that the English had deployed facing south along Glendale with the narrowing valley to the rear. Their left, therefore, would rest on the lower slopes of Harehope whilst their right was anchored by the wet ground by the river itself. The Battle of Bendor Stone which is said to mark the site possibly stands in what would have been the left centre of the line. Whether the marchers were arrayed in the traditional three battles is unclear; perhaps they were drawn up in the harrow formation, with blocks of archers interspersed between companies of dismounted men at arms.

It may be that the archers were massed on the flanks to fully enfilade the Scottish position. The chronicle description of the English bowmen advancing into the defile or valley between Harehope and Homildon hills would suggest that there was such a concentration. Northumberland was in overall command though there can be little doubt that the fight was directed by March. As a Scot he would know only too well how horribly effective the longbow could be directed at inert masses of spearmen. We have no note of numbers but it may be assumed that the English army was considerably smaller.

Douglas, even if not the sharpest of commanders, would have immediately comprehended his peril. The English had effectively severed his line of withdrawal and he faced the terror of all Scots' generals, the arrow storm, with little or no space for manoeuvre. Consequently it is likely he deployed his forces in the traditional manner, dense-packed schiltroms of bristling spears supported by dismounted knights and men at arms. His only hope was that the English would attack and that his superior numbers would hold the line.

It would be easy to forgive George Dunbar if he relished this moment – all his past hurts at the hands of Douglas and the Rothesay faction would be paraded in his mind as he prepared to destroy his fellow countrymen. The archers were advanced, probably initially in front of the billmen, then as opportunity offered deployed towards the flanks. Ridpath, following Bower, records that the Scots were 'posted on the hill of Holmedon the English seized a hill over against it placing their archers in the interjacent valley between these eminences'.[31] They had a perfect target, favoured by the terrain, wind and weather. None of those present on the Scottish side would have been old enough to remember the earlier defeats at Halidon Hill or Neville's Cross. This was to be a cruel baptism.

The archers shot methodically, up to fifteen aimed flights a minute, the shafts whistling in great feathered clouds to punch though plate and mail.

The lightly armed spearmen with rusted mail, jack or gambeson had scant protection. Men died, not quickly but thrashing in wild agony, pierced by a welter of shafts which, like lethal rain, continued to pour. The screams of the wounded and dying, the shuddering of maimed limbs carried through the ranks. It is a natural reaction for men under such punishment to seek to edge away from the source of their pain and the schiltroms probably began to shuffle inwards from the flanks, bunching up. The archers, unopposed, merely continued their advance, the deadly volleys never slackening, blood pooling on the dusty ground.

In blind red clouds the sun arose,
Which saw that fatal day,
Where breathless on the green hill side,
Fu mony a braw Scot lay.

For sair the English bowmen gall'd
The van that ungeared stood,
Nae thirsty shafts 'een reached the earth
Unstained in Scottish blood.[32]

It is said that Hotspur wished to capitalise on the archers' initial success by launching his men at arms but March counselled delay: let the archers do the work of knights, as long as the Scots stood motionless the work of slaughter could continue. No army could sustain such punishment indefinitely and at some point the Scots attempted to charge and come to contact with their tormentors. This advance may have been led by Douglas and Murdoch. A poor general he may have been but the 4th Earl was certainly no poltroon.

It is also possible that Gordon and Swinton, by no means the best of friends, led this attack. Equally their action might have been later, an attempt to stem the rout. In any event the attack was stillborn. The arrow storm beat too hard, the rain of death incessant and the line began to waver, foundered and then broke as the English finally advanced. The rest was mere butchery. Some seven hundred are said to have fallen on the field, with half a thousand more drowned or held under in the stampede to cross the Till and seek safety in flight.

It is most likely that the charge led by Swinton and Gordon was a final attempt to beat off the English foot. These two valiant knights were reconciled just before the end and the chroniclers give Swinton a fine speech as the two paladins, determined to try the last attempt to rally:

> *Oh my brave countrymen what fascination has seized you that you stand to be shot at like deer instead of displaying your ancient courage and meeting your enemies hand to hand. Let those who will follow me that we may gain the victory or die!*[33]

The butchers' bill included both Swinton and Gordon, Sir John Livingstone of Callendar, Alexander Ramsay of Dalhousie 'and about eighty other knights'.[34] Douglas, who had sustained a handspan of wounds including the loss of an eye, was captured along with Murdoch, Moray, Angus, Orkney, Montgomery, Erskine, Stewart of Innernethy, Sir Patrick Graham, Sir Robert Logan and Sir Adam Forster. The battle was a triumph for the English marchers and a disaster of some magnitude for the Scots. The military supremacy of a generation was wiped out in an afternoon and, with crowning irony, by the very hand of its principal architect. For the English, however, Hotspur was the man of the hour:

> *In faith it is a conquest for a prince to boast of.*[35]

Amongst the haul of prisoners were two knights of Teviotdale, Sir Walter Stewart of Forest and Thomas Ker. In the days of the Pale both of these had sworn allegiance to the Percys but a march jury acquitted both of treason. For Hotspur, however, this was not enough. He would have the blood of each and with a fine contempt for judicial process had both men executed. The motive for this seems to have amounted to nothing more than personal malice.[36]

The defeat naturally damaged Albany's regime, though to what extent it is hard to determine. He was the sponsor of the war policy even if Douglas was its principal exponent. No doubt the duke fell back on the trusted expedient of laying all the blame on incompetent subordinates, not difficult when the officer in question was a badly wounded prisoner. In any event Robert III was not likely to intervene and Albany, having rid himself of his troublesome nephew, had no serious challengers.

For Henry IV the victory opened up bright prospects for the reoccupation of the Pale. The Scots were utterly defeated, March held those vital castles, the time seemed ripe. The king therefore ordered that the noble captives were not to be immediately ransomed but held as prisoners of war. This must have discomfited the hopeful captors, disappointed of cash prizes, and this act is sometimes viewed as both high-handed and a deliberate affront to the Percys. Quite likely it was nothing of the kind. To hold the Scottish military leaders close was an obvious move when contemplating an invasion. Both Northumberland and Hotspur would have seen the glittering prospects opened up by their victory and would be as keen as Henry to capitalise on their success.

That which undid the potential consequences of Homildon was the Percy rebellion of the following year, an ill-starred enterprise that brought the whole edifice of the earl's power crashing down.

Lack of ransoms was just one of the grievances afflicting Hotspur and his father. The earl was claiming unpaid arrears of salaries and expenses, outstanding since 1399, amounting to the colossal sum of £20,000[37] and whilst this was likely an exaggeration the debt was considerable. The fact of the matter was that the king simply could not pay. His overstretched Treasury was empty: the debts of the Irish campaign he had inherited, the crippling burden of the cost of defending the northern frontier and now the fresh burden of the war in Wales had stripped the Exchequer bare. On 2nd March 1403 Northumberland was given the whole of southern Scotland, the vast single fief of the entire Pale. Obviously the English did not possess these lands, nor was there money with which to fund an expedition – the grant was an empty gesture, the best the impoverished monarch could offer.

This was too much. Northumberland had presumably hoped for great things after his sponsorship of Henry in those uncertain days after his landing at Ravenspur. The earl saw himself as a senior statesman, a kingmaker. He had lost sight of the fact that kings do not necessarily warm to kingmakers – a man who breaks his oath to one king may develop the habit. Percy would at least have expected total control of the north yet the king continued to offer advancement to the detested Nevilles.

Hotspur had been given high office in Wales, becoming chief justice of Chester, North Wales and Flintshire, keeper of the lordship of Denbigh and gaining several key castles. At Easter 1401 he had recovered the vital bastion of Conway after Glendower had stormed the place in a surprise attack and he had followed this with a sharp, punitive campaign against the rebels. Two years later he was still owed wages and costs.[38] The turncoat Mortimer, now wedded to Glendower's daughter, was also related to the Percys and there was clearly a plot afoot in the spring of 1403. Northumberland wrote to the king in June begging funds to prosecute operations north of the border. The king declined to send cash, largely because he had none to send, but replied that he would lead an army north to join with the earl in invading Scotland.

By 13th July the royal army had advanced as far as Nottingham when Henry received the disturbing intelligence that the Percys were in revolt. Northumberland was marshalling a hostile force in the north whilst Hotspur was recruiting in Cheshire where he was joined by the Earl of Worcester who arranged to 'liberate' the meagre funds Henry had intended to dispatch to his son Prince Harry, campaigning against the Welsh rebels further south. This was bad news indeed. Worse was to come for it appeared that Glendower was proposing to march north and link up with Hotspur – a most formidable coalition.

The Percy manifesto now being proclaimed accused the Lancastrian king of being both usurper and perjurer. They averred that, at Doncaster in 1399, he had sworn a solemn oath that he sought only the return of his rightful inheritance, a promise he had obviously failed to keep. There was more. They claimed Henry had deliberately starved Richard to death and that the English Earl of March was the rightful king. Caught totally unprepared the king's first instinct was to fall back on London and marshal greater forces. He was dissuaded from this course by none other than the exiled Scottish Earl of March who was in the royal service. George Dunbar proved as powerful an advocate for the ruin of the Percys as he had been for the destruction of Douglas. His inveterate enemy, the captive 4th Earl, having recovered from the wounds he had sustained at Homildon, had now made common cause with his captor – the prospect of remaining incarcerated at the king's pleasure clearly did not appeal.

March proposed that the royal army march north and west to deal with Hotspur before he could be reinforced either by his father from the north or the Welsh rebels from the south. On 11th July Percy had reached Chester where he was joined by Worcester. By the 16th Henry had advanced to Lichfield where he summoned the local levies. The designated juncture between Hotspur and Glendower was to take place at Shrewsbury, the chief crossing place on the upper Severn. Three days later the royal army had moved on to Stafford. Prince Harry (Shakespeare's Prince Hal, later King Henry V) was already at Shrewsbury, having returned from punitive raiding in Wales. It was doubly vital for the king to win the race to the town if the prince's smaller force was not to be crushed between the advancing rebel armies.

The following day the king's army marched (or more likely rode) the full thirty-two miles to Shrewsbury, a substantial feat on bad roads, choked with the dust of midsummer. The race was won but by the narrowest of margins for Hotspur came up the same day. Finding the town occupied and the royal army strongly posted must have given the rebels a most unpleasant surprise for it was they who were now isolated, cut off by the great river from their friends to the south and west. Seeking an alternative crossing place Hotspur dragged his tired men to the village of Berwick three miles to the north-west.

There is a story, probably apocryphal, that Percy had been warned by the inevitable soothsayer that he would die before Berwick. If true then here was a fine irony. His situation was verging on desperate.[39] His raw troops were untried, new to their officers without the cohesion that a long campaign engenders. They faced a superior foe without any immediate prospect of relief. Glendower was in fact nowhere near, still lingering in Carmarthenshire. He was to blame flooding and other natural disasters for his failure to engage. His faintheartedness was fatal to both Percy's cause and his own.

Hotspur knew he could not rest at Berwick – the river was at his back and the royal vanguard was already testing his scouts. To retreat was equally risky – his scratch army would most likely disintegrate under any sustained pressure and it was an awfully long way that they had come. In the circumstance he made the only decision that was open to him, to select favourable ground and make a stand. The terrain was largely even and unpromising. However, a single ridge, a mile or so north-east of his present position, by the hamlet of Harlescott, offered the best prospects. Shakespeare has rather coloured our view of Hotspur, casting him as a young man of fiery temperament and rash honour. His disposition was bold certainly and he could be petty, thuggish and cruel, but he was, at this time, a man of thirty-nine, well into middle age by the standard of the day, and an extremely experienced and, by and large, successful commander.

The position ran east to west and the rebels deployed along the crest of the ridge, a frontage of some 800 yards. The royal army, hot on their heels, drew up out of bowshot, perhaps 300 yards to their front.[40] The royal army, swelled by the shire levies, was significantly larger, a force of 12,000–14,000; the rebels had perhaps 8,000 or 9,000 at the most.[41] This day, the 21st July 1403, would witness a military phenomenon of dire import. At Homildon missile troops alone had won the day; here on the shallow ridge by Shrewsbury, both sides, for the first time in English history, would employ the longbow. The battle-winning weapon that had decimated the chivalry of France, Scotland and Spain would be drawn in aid of civil strife – 'the sory bataille of Schrovesbury between Englysshemen and Englysshemen'.[42]

As was customary on such occasions there was an attempt to negotiate a settlement, with the Abbot of Shrewsbury acting as intermediary. His efforts, however, were in vain and after a lull of a couple of hours the slaughter began in deadly earnest. The royal army was deployed in two divisions or battles. The king commanded the larger of these on the right whilst the sixteen-year-old Prince of Wales led the left. Both sides advanced their archers and a murderous missile duel ensued. Victory in an archers' battle depended on a number of factors but the side which shot fastest, sent the greater weight of arrows into the air would likely gain the advantage. Casualties on both sides could be heavy. In this fight Hotspur's Cheshire bowmen swiftly gained the upper hand, their sustained volleys thudding into the ranks of the king's men. With the dead and dying carpeting the ground, the royal archers faltered and then fell back.

With a great roar, 'Esperance, Esperance Percy', Hotspur sent his infantry charging down the shallow slope, hoping to capitalise on the discomfit of the royal bowmen to rout the king's division. With a thunderous clash the two sides collided, the fury of the assault pushing the royalists back a good score yards and more. But the line held and the mêlée became general. It is said that Hotspur and Douglas jointly led a commanded party of thirty of their best and most valiant knights towards the royal standard, killed the usurper and the day was won.[43] The tactic is reminiscent of the final charge of Duke William's two dozen knights over the bloody ground of Senlac Hill to cut down the last of the Saxon kings. Harold, however, did not have George Dunbar to advise him. The cunning renegade had provided a number of 'lookalikes' dressed in the royal livery, men who were either extraordinarily brave or particularly dim witted. Percy and Douglas hacked down several of these shadow warriors but failed to menace the king.

As the fight raged Prince Hal committed his division which appears to have escaped the archery duel with rather less damage and which rolled back the right flank of the outnumbered rebels. The prince was struck a glancing blow to the face by an arrow. Hotspur was less fortunate. When he raised his pig-face visor to gain a clearer view of the attack enveloping his right, a shaft pierced his eye, penetrated the brain and he was killed instantly. With his death the rebel cause expired. The survivors dissolved in rout, their scramble over the corpse-strewn ridge, harried by the royal army, mounted now for the pursuit, three long and savage miles, field and ditch, track and mire.[44] Douglas, once again wounded (this time he had lost a testicle), was again captured.[45] Worcester, also wounded, was unceremoniously executed on the field.

Hotspur's corpse was recovered from the field, 'and there beyond them all lay the bravest, rashest, staunchest knight in England'.[46] At first inclined to respect his fallen adversary the king ordered the body taken the sixteen miles to Whitchurch for interment. He soon relented of this noble sentiment, however, and had the cadaver exhumed and placed on public display in Shrewsbury market place, propped upright between two mill-stones so that all could see this famous paladin of chivalry had died a traitor. Thereafter the body was salted, the head struck off and impaled above Micklegate Bar in York, the torso hacked into quarters to be displayed at London, Bristol, Chester and Newcastle.

> *For worms brave Percy; Fare thee well great heart! –*
> *Ill weaved ambition, how much thou art shrunk!*
> *When that this body did contain a spirit,*
> *A kingdom for it was too small a bound![47]*

The disaster at Shrewsbury marked the end of the Percy rebellion. The Earl of Northumberland remained at large in the north, enthusiastically harried by Neville, now Earl of Westmorland and obliged to submit. Penitent, humbled, desolate and defeated he threw himself on the king's mercy at York on 11th August, greeted by the awful spectacle of his eldest son's severed head. In a few short weeks the mightiest of over-mighty subjects had been reduced from 'King of the North' to a landless felon, shorn of offices and acres. Westmorland became warden of the middle march whilst the vast spread of Percy estates were to be held on trust by Lord Say.

The east march and Berwick were handed to the king's younger son, Prince John. Despite the weight of Northumberland's offence Henry was inclined to mercy. The disgraced earl was tried in February 1404 by his peers and, whilst freely admitting partial guilt, still managed to shuffle the bulk of the blame onto Hotspur. Parental grief could not be allowed to interfere with expediency.

He was convicted of complicity rather than the capital crime of treason and suffered a swingeing fine which though painful was a good deal less worrying than the exquisite agony of a traitor's death. Upon his taking a fresh oath of loyalty, the king magnanimously returned both manors and sinecures, accompanied by a formal reconciliation with Westmorland and March. Sir William Clifford, castellan of Berwick, had refused to surrender his office until Henry undertook to permit Hotspur's son to inherit his dead father's estates – these being subject to attainder. By November 1404 Northumberland had recovered the keeping of both Berwick and Jedburgh. In the circumstances he had, in material terms, escaped lightly, very lightly.

But the wound still festered. The dreadful sight of his son's butchered remains above Micklegate Bar stuck deep, no show of amity could bury so profound a loss. By the time winter was on the wane the earl was in treasonable correspondence with Glendower and Mortimer, both still undefeated in the field. On 28th February 1405 the allies entered into what was described as a 'Tripartite Indenture' – a fantastical pact whereby they agreed to divide England and Wales between them once they had accomplished the mere trifle of unseating the king.

In the spring the Welsh rebels took the field whilst Northumberland sought to stir up trouble in the north. His attempt was stillborn. Those who heeded his call were corralled by the vigilant Westmorland then tricked and disarmed by a ruse at Shipham Moor. Storming north with righteous fury and a powerful siege train the king reduced the Northumbrian castles by mere threat and harried the ageing traitor over the border. Like Gaunt before him Northumberland, accompanied only by his remaining confederate Lord Bardolph, sought sanctuary amongst his erstwhile foes, particularly Sir David Fleming who was also the designated guardian of his grandson, Hotspur's heir.

Any hope of safety north of the border proved wholly illusory. The renegades would be useful currency in Albany's bid to find ransoms for

Douglas and his own son Murdoch. Forewarned of the regent's intentions by their host, the pair fled southwards to join Glendower – Fleming himself was subsequently slain in a brush with the Douglases. The earl's next journey was to France to solicit aid for the Welsh rebels. In this he was successful insofar as an expedition was mustered, but once again the French found their Celtic allies skulking in rain-shrouded mountains uncongenial and soon tired of the game.

Undeterred, Northumberland, who had been attainted in absentia, sought to seduce the Flemings, but the canny burghers were not disposed towards such quixotic ventures and declined. By early 1407 he was back in Scotland trying to stir up trouble on the borders where, although there was some unrest, the former magic of the Percy name was wearing thin. By now grasping at straws Northumberland and Bardolph were persuaded by intelligence emanating from Yorkshire that the climate, in that merciless winter of 1407–8, was ripe for insurrection. The author of this intimation was a Percy adherent of long standing, Sir Thomas Rokeby, the Sheriff of Yorkshire, a man upon whose word the earl might be expected to rely. In doing so, however, he was placing himself within the jaws of a trap. Rokeby intended to betray his former patron and reap the rewards that were bound to accrue.

Like a patient angler casting his lures in the certain knowledge that the fish awaits the hook he drew the rebel peers towards their final ruin. His clever conjuring and the web of their own desperation proved irresistible. In December Northumberland and Bardolph were rowed over the icy waters of the Tweed, the very frontier the earl had made a career of holding. They took passage down the east coast, the cold, wild breakers of the North Sea and the keening of the east wind their principal companions. By the end of the first week they had made landfall at Seamer. The perfidious sheriff had undertaken to arrange a muster at Tadcaster. That dreadful cold and bleak January Northumberland spent in recruiting, calling upon former retainers and clients around Thirsk. This was the traditional Percy heartland – Topcliffe and surrounding manors had been theirs since after the Norman Conquest.

It was not until the middle of the following month that the dreadful truth of Rokeby's intentions was revealed. Far from summoning a muster of rebels the sheriff had deployed his available forces in a carefully laid ambush by Knaresborough. Determined to try the last, the ragtag army battled through the bitter snows to skirt the Lancastrians and struggle through to Wetherby. From here the road led straight to Tadcaster, a strategic gateway on the longer route south. The very next day, however, 19th February, the hounds closed in. Some two miles south-west of Tadcaster, on the frozen ground of Bramham Moor, the old fox turned for the last time. The issue was never really in doubt, though the confused, untidy skirmish echoed through the afternoon. Unhorsed, slashed and hacked to bloody ruin the 1st Earl of Northumberland gasped out his life in the reddened slush whilst his last command dissolved around him. Lord Bardolph fared no better. The king in the north was king no more.

Notes

1 *Henry IV Part 1* (I:I).
2 The steep conical hill is in fact crowned with an iron age settlement, already ancient when the armies clashed below in 1402.
3 MacDonald, A.J., *Border Bloodshed*, East Lothian 2000 p. 75.
4 Ibid p. 119.
5 Baldick, R., *The Duel*, London 1965 p. 28.
6 Ibid p. 29.
7 MacDonald p. 121.
8 Baldick p. 29.
9 MacDonald p. 122.
10 Ibid p. 121.
11 Ibid p. 125.
12 Ibid p. 132.
13 Hutchinson, H.F., *The Hollow Crown*, London 1961 p. 202: 'Le Pleasaunce' the king's pleasure, commonly had to be bought. In 1399 the seventeen counties which had supported the Lords Appellant were censored as traitors and were obliged to pay a fine of £1,000 per shire to compensate for such behaviour.
14 Hutchinson p. 208.
15 Ibid p. 208.
16 Ibid p. 230.
17 MacDonald p. 134.
18 Ibid p. 137.
19 Ibid p. 139.
20 Ibid p. 140.
21 Ibid p. 141.
22 Ibid p. 143.
23 Ibid p. 144.
24 Ibid p. 147.

25 Ibid p. 147.
26 Ibid p. 152.
27 Ridpath, Rev. G., *Border History*, Berwick 1858 edn. p. 371.
28 Ibid p. 371.
29 Ibid p. 371.
30 Ibid p. 371.
31 Ibid p. 371.
32 Quoted in Sadler, D.J., *Battle for Northumbria*, Newcastle upon Tyne 1988 p. 87.
33 Ibid p. 86.
34 Ridpath p. 371.
35 *Henry IV Part 1* (1:1).
36 Sadler p. 87.
37 Rose, A., *Kings in the North*, London 2002 p. 354.
38 Rose p. 356.
39 Burne, A.H., *The Battlefields of England*, London 1950 p. 66.
40 Ibid p. 66.
41 Ibid p. 66.
42 Brenan, G., *History of the House of Percy*, London 1898 (2 vols.) Vol. 1 p. 79.
43 Burne p. 68.
44 Ibid p. 68.
45 Ibid p. 68.
46 Brenan vol. 1 p. 82.
47 *Henry IV Part 1* (V:IV).

Chapter 12

Sausages without Mustard

*The realm of England was out of all good governance, as it had been
many days before, for the king was simple and lead by covetous counsel
and owed more than he was worth. His debts increased daily but
payment was there none; all the possessions and lordships that pertained
to the crown the king had given away, some to lords and some to other
lesser persons, so that he had almost nothing left to own. And such
impositions as were put on the people, as taxes and taillages, all that
came from them was spent in vain, for he had no [great] household
nor maintained any wars.*[1]

The fifteenth century in England opened with the dramatic usurpation
of Henry Bolingbroke, who having deposed and likely murdered or
connived at the murder of Richard II, assumed the throne as Henry IV.
It was at one time fashionable to trace the origin of the internecine strife
which tore at the vitals of English polity for thirty years, later labelled as
the Wars of the Roses, to this single act and that God's judgement on the
English for unnatural regicide followed with fearful symmetry.

Latterly this view has been challenged with many modern historians
tracing the root of conflict no further back than the disturbances of the
1450s and the increasing weakness and corruption of Henry VI's inefficient
regime. For a period, between the battle of Towton in 1461 and the further,
less bloody but equally disastrous, Lancastrian defeat at Hexham in 1464,
the action of the wars shifted northward to Northumberland and the border.
Margaret of Anjou, Henry VI's desperate queen was prepared to trade the

two great northern bastions of Berwick and Carlisle as the price for Scottish intervention.

Prior to his final foray in 1408 the 1st Earl of Northumberland had 'skulked' in Scotland and even after his death there is evidence the wilder elements of his following from Redesdale and Tynedale did their best to keep his memory alive: 'the efforts of his adherents, aided by the scots of the Merse and the men of Tynedale, Redesdale and Hexhamshire to restore the Percies . . . kept the north in turmoil.'[2] The riding names from the upland valleys were happy to launch general attacks on anyone they felt to be antipathetic to the earl's cause, a convenient cause to sponsor extensive and largely indiscriminate brigandry. The first Parliament of Henry V in 1414 made angry reference to those 'large numbers of men from the Franchises of Tynedale, Redesdale and Hexhamshire' guilty of 'many murders, treasons, homicides and robberies and other crimes'.[3] The dalesmen were accused of consorting with the Scots to promote joint mayhem, and large-scale confiscation of property was proposed as a remedy but, as ever, pragmatism won the day, the middle march needed its free spirits with sword and lance when the border was threatened.

Bolingbroke's grasp on the sceptre remained shaky until his death in 1413. His successor, Shakespeare's Prince Hal, now Henry V, was ruthlessly determined to pursue his ambitions in France, a quest which consumed the meteor of his reign. The new king had earned his spurs in the Welsh wars against Glendower. His ruthless professionalism confounded the French. The campaign of 1415 became expensively and almost fatally bogged down in the foetid trenches around Harfleur where dysentery stalked the army and decimated the ranks. The year might have ended in ignominy with the half-starved survivors staggering ragged and emaciated into Calais but for the French determination to provoke an engagement. Agincourt, 'Crispin's Crispian', was the most famous of famous English victories, the longbow's finest and bloodiest hour. Henry's reputation as a commander of the first division was assured and his subsequent campaigns in Normandy produced significant gains.

These campaigns were both efficient and ruthless; the civil population suffered horribly. 'War without fire is like sausages without mustard', the king is said to have remarked.[4] Henry's own death, ironically from dysentery, robbed him of the final dazzling prize, the throne of France, so tantalisingly near, and left his kingdom with an infant for a king.

When leaving for France in 1415 Henry had taken steps to ensure the defence of the north, but on Magdalen Day (22nd July) a Scottish force said to be several thousand strong struck at Glendale. They were met by Ralph Neville, Earl of Westmorland and Robert Umfraville, 'Robin Mend the Market', both seasoned fighters. Beneath the hunched summit of Yeavering Bell, crowned by the tumbled ramparts of an iron age fort and within sight of the old royal palace of the same name, the Northumbrians trounced the invaders. Details are scarce and though Neville is credited with no greater force than 'seven score spearmen' and perhaps three hundred archers, the running fight left sixty-odd Scots breathless and several hundred taken – the pursuit spilling over the length of a dozen miles or more.[5]

Sir Gilbert, ninth Lord Umfraville, had already followed Henry V with distinction at Agincourt. His uncle Robert, the victor of Yeavering and a handful of other scrimmages, was illegitimate and succeeded to the title only after his equally valiant nephew was killed in the disaster at Bauge. 'Robin Mend the Market' died in 1436 to the balladeer's lament:

Of sapience and verray gentilnesse,
Of liberal herte and knightly governaunce,
Of hardiment, of trouthe, and grete gladnesse,
Of honest mirthe withouten greviaunce,
Of gentille bourdes [jests] *and knightly dalliance,*
He hath no make [equal]*, I dare right well avouwe,*
Now he is gone, I may nought gloss him nowe.[6]

For Northumberland the early decades of the fifteenth century were possibly less traumatic in terms of Scottish incursions than the fourteenth. Evidence from local, surviving records suggests that the eastern county sustained seven major inroads pre-1450, practically a state of calm compared with the preceding century. Moreover these attacks appear to have been more parochial rather than directed by any central policy. There is, after 1405, some suggestion of a gradual recovery of economic conditions in Northumberland after the ravages of the earlier period.[7] Several larger forays erupted south of the Tweed in the early 1420s when the Scots were fighting doggedly against the English in France, propping up the Dauphin's failing cause, often at significant cost to themselves. The last years of the reign of James I in 1436–7 saw discord flare once again with the Scottish king attempting sieges of both Berwick and Roxburgh.

In the early fifteenth century the northern kingdom had troubles enough of its own:

In those days there was no law in Scotland, but he who was stronger oppressed him who was weaker, and the whole kingdom was a den of thieves; murderers, herschips, and fireraising, and all other misdeeds remained unpunished; and justice, as if outlawed, lay in exile outwith the bounds of the kingdom.[8]

One of the more colourful incidents of misrule was the gladiatorial show which came to be called, somewhat grandly, the Battle of the Clans in 1396. The Crown incurred an expense of £14. 2s. 11d. in constructing a wooden arena on the Inch of Perth to allow sixty combatants, drawn in equal numbers from two feuding clans, to slog it out manfully. King Robert III was both Master of Ceremonies and, as it appears, a form of referee. It was he, rather unsportingly, who ended the slaughter by casting down the royal baton; by this time the threescore paladins who had begun the day had been whittled down to a mere dozen bloodied survivors. The feud continued unabated.

The later days of Robert III's reign had been marred by an unseemly power struggle between the king's brother, the Duke of Albany, and his eldest son the mercurial Duke of Rothesay. This headstrong prince had a particular knack of making enemies and alienating the few supporters he could muster. His three-year tenure as Lieutenant of the Kingdom was an unmitigated disaster but, unabashed by failure, he refused to resign and in 1401 the exasperated king was persuaded to order his arrest. He was subsequently imprisoned, and died, in Albany's Castle of Falkland the following year. His death may have been due to natural causes but many suspected foul play.

Though the ageing monarch seems to have exonerated his brother from complicity in Rothesay's death he was determined to play absolutely safe with his surviving younger son James, born in 1394. Four years after the demise of his heir the king, in declining health, determined to send James to France. The prince had the signal misfortune to be captured when his vessel was intercepted by English pirates. This was in flagrant breach of the subsisting truce. Such niceties aside, Henry IV would not let so useful a catch slip through his fingers. Though he became king on the death of his father in 1406 James had entered upon eighteen years of captivity in England, leaving the way clear for his uncle Albany to assume the regency.

The duke was an active and avaricious head of state, rapacious, vengeful and corrupt. Despite the weight of his advancing years, his grip remained firm till he died in 1420, by then in his eighties. Nonetheless, when Robert III finally breathed his last the Scots Parliament immediately recognised James as king but Albany remained in *de facto* control with the office of 'Governor'; he even had a fine seal struck. The duke had regal affectations if not ambition and was in no hurry to hand the sceptre on to the young king who remained impotent as a prisoner of the English court and he made no effort to free the king. His contemporaries said of the regent 'he semyt to be a mychty king'.[9]

James's captivity, whilst dreadfully frustrating and humiliating for a young man of spirit, was by no means uncomfortable, at least at the outset. His education as a prince was not neglected, and he was taught the knightly skills of jousting and swordplay, at which he excelled. Henry IV even boasted the young monarch received a far better education as a 'guest' in England than he would have in his native land.

Albany, meanwhile, had sufficient to keep him occupied without raising any trouble on the border. In the north-east Robert III had appointed Alexander, Earl of Buchan, his and Albany's illegitimate half brother as Justiciar for the northern lowlands. Notorious as the 'Wolf of Badenoch' this Alexander was a colourful character even in an age of lawlessness, one who so abused his office as a front for private mayhem he was outlawed. The highlight of his criminal career was the sacking of Elgin Cathedral in 1390.

His son Alexander, also a bastard, having followed in his father's footsteps as a freebooter, secured a quantum leap up the social ladder when he married the widowed Countess of Mar, ostensibly by force though the lady may not have been that unwilling. Shortly after Donald, Lord of the Isles, became embroiled in a dispute with Albany over the succession to the Earldom of Ross which he claimed by right of his wife. Albany disputed the claim, preferring, to no one's surprise, one of his sons to inherit. Donald was no mere highland brigand, but an educated and cultivated man who enjoyed diplomatic relations in his own right with the English court who treated with him as a free prince. He prepared to enforce his claim by force of arms, leading a highland host to descend upon Inverness and put it to the torch.

If he thought ten thousand brawny highlanders could totally overawe the northern lowlands he was mistaken. He was hotly opposed by Mar leading a scratch lowland army by Inverurie some fourteen miles northwest of Aberdeen on 24th July 1411. The battle was long and bloody. Many brave men fell on both sides, including the formidable chief of the MacLeans and a score of lowland knights, amongst them Sir Alexander Scrymgeour, the hereditary standard bearer of Scotland. In the blood dimmed twilight of the 'Reid Harlaw' it was Donald and his battered highlanders who slipped away, leaving the field to Mar.[10]

After the death of the ailing Henry IV Albany opened negotiations with his successor Henry V not, as might have been the case, to secure the release of the captive king, but rather to procure the release of his own son Murdoch who had been taken at the same time. In 1416 Murdoch was ransomed for a consideration of £10,000.

The new King of England treated his captive with a good deal less cordiality than his father whose dying wish had apparently been that James should be freed. From Henry's perspective a captive King of Scots was a sound insurance against interference in his French wars. In the event it secured nothing – in 1419 Albany's younger son, John, Earl of Buchan, led a force of some 6,000 Scots to fight in France.

Early in 1421 King Henry had returned to England leaving his brother the aggressive Duke of Clarence in command of operations across the Channel. In February the English under the duke and John, Earl of Salisbury, marched south from Paris to the Loire, almost to the gates of Orleans, before turning west to plunder Anjou. By Good Friday, on 21st March, an English force of perhaps 3,000 was resting near the small town of Bauge. Unknown to them a Franco-Scots army under Buchan and the Sieur de Lafayette, Constable of France, as many as 5,000 strong, was fast approaching, determined to bring on a general engagement with the invaders. A string of easy victories may have made the English complacent. The duke's archers were dispersed on foraging detail but they succeeded in capturing a Scottish knight who was brought before Clarence, then at dinner, blissfully unaware so potent an enemy force was at hand.

The duke then found himself in a dilemma. To fight on Easter Sunday was unthinkable but to wait for a further two days was utterly alien to his fiercely combative nature. Therefore he simply couldn't and indeed wouldn't wait; an immediate attack was ordered. Several of his senior knights, including the redoubtable Gilbert Umfraville, protested at the arrant folly of committing the troops: they had to battle against a foe of uncertain strength without reconnaissance and with half the men dispersed. The duke retorted angrily and insultingly, casting doubt on the courage of his knights, a demeaning and unjustified slur. Stung by his bile Umfraville and the others protested no more but led a mere 1,500 English into the township of Vieil Bauge.

Almost immediately they clashed with the Scots van seeking to secure both the town and the vital river crossing. An untidy mêlée erupted around the bridge, Scots and English hacking and hewing over the narrow confines. The Earl of Buchan, cannily refusing to let his main body be drawn into the scrum, deployed the rest of the army on open ground, along a ridge behind the town. Meanwhile Clarence, dismounting by the bridge, led a commanded party through the thigh-deep waters to outflank the Scots contesting the crossing. With more English joining in the Scots were discomfited and driven back through the streets in near rout.

Doggedly Clarence drove his tiny army in pursuit, not pausing to gauge the odds or dress the lines; the English blundered uphill towards the ridge held by the Franco-Scots. Timing the moment to perfection Buchan led a spirited charge downhill to crash into the disordered ranks with vastly superior numbers. The Duke of Clarence was unhorsed and killed, the English driven pell mell down the slope; many more joined their general in death including Umfraville and Lord Roos. The tiny force was decimated. The Scots had given the French that which had so long eluded them, a victory in the field.[11]

The defeat was a shock to the previously soaring morale of the English though Salisbury managed, skilfully, to lead the survivors of the expedition back into the secure haven of Normandy.

When Albany, replete with years and villainy, finally died in 1420 he was succeeded, both in his dukedom and his governorship by his son Murdoch. The new regent was a pale and ineffectual shadow of his father; his poor fiscal management and inability to collect customs dues on which the royal income depended made him the butt of his peers. Even the Earl of Douglas, formerly an ally of Albany, pillaged customs revenue without regard for his son. In December 1423 the king's release was, at long last, negotiated.

Freed from the chains of his confinement James returned to his kingdom determined to exert his will as sovereign and to remedy the ills which
had overtaken the nation during Albany's tenure.

A King such as Scotland had never yet had.[12]

As well as being fit, athletic and trained as a knight James was also
an accomplished scholar and linguist. He enjoyed some success as a poet,
his most famous work 'The King's Quair', being written in 1423 as a love
poem to Joan Beaufort with whom he'd fallen in love and who was
to become his queen. His earlier frustrations with Albany had led him to
flirt with the powerful Douglases and to write darkly to the regent:

*. . . that . . . we be nouch send to sek remede of our deliverans otherquare
in tyme to cum.*[13]

In 1414 there had, at long last, been an attempt to resolve the festering
sore of the papal schism. Three years later these efforts finally bore fruit
when Martin V was elected to the throne of St Peter. In Scotland Albany
remained doggedly loyal to the disenfranchised Benedict XIII but James,
straining against the bonds of his confinement and seeking to score
points, was quick to acknowledge Martin. Albany reluctantly followed
suit in 1419, supporting the new pope did not help the king spring free of
his shackles. As loyal sons of the Church both Albany and later James were
ruthless in their suppression of heretics, as was Henry V in England.

The captive king was forced to undergo the humiliation and shame of
being used as a pawn in Henry's French conquests. In 1420 he was brought
to the siege of Melun, like a tame bear, obliged to command the largely
Scots' garrison to surrender and, when they refused, forced to witness the
spectacle of them being hanged for their defiance. After the disaster at
Beauge the king was next taken to witness the siege of Meaux, being present when the city surrendered on 10th May 1422.

One can only speculate on the shame and turmoil such degradation
must have caused James, being forced, as a spectator, to applaud the ruin
of his countrymen and allies whilst he was held impotent, but Henry's
days, like his victories, were numbered. Even his iron will could not defy
nature and, racked with dysentery, he died on 31 August. On his deathbed
he is said to have bemoaned that: 'Wherever I go, I am bearded by Scots,
dead or alive'.[14]

Finally in, December 1423, under the terms of the Treaty of London, James was released in return for a ransom of 60,000 marks to be paid by means of six annual instalments. The term 'ransom' was not actually employed for unlike David II this King of Scots was never a prisoner of war, his capture being wholly illegal and in time of peace. The consideration was more delicately expressed as being a contribution towards the cost of the young man's education and maintenance at the English court. As, in fact, the Household accounts show these costs as never exceeding £700 per annum, the king's education appeared an excellent investment for the Exchequer. One of the terms of the accord which the English were anxious to see included, ordered the withdrawal of all Scots from the French service and no more to be sent. Whilst James agreed to no further reinforcements he would not recall those already serving; in all probability such a call would have gone unheeded.

In April 1423, the English regent, the late king's formidable brother John, Duke of Bedford, strengthened the Anglo-Burgundian alliance by a series of marriage ties, saddling himself, it was said, with a plain bride as part of the bargain. With the English bolstered by a Burgundian contingent the allied army mustered at Auxerre to counter a Franco-Scots force marching into Burgundy from Bourges. On 31st July the two armies collided at Cravant on the otherwise somnolent banks of the River Yonne.

The French, perhaps 10,000 strong, were deployed on the eastern bank opposed by less than half that number of English across the sluggish, brown tinged swell of water. The Yonne was perhaps fifty yards wide at this point and by no means deep; it remained, however, a formidable obstacle and neither side was willing to commit to an assault against a defended bank. The stand-off lasted perhaps three hours when Salisbury, leading the English, resolved to break the deadlock and ordered his men at arms into the water.

The attack, in the classic manner, was covered by archers, a 'creeping barrage' of shafts that kept the defenders' heads down and tumbled more than a few into the Yonne. As the infantry waded through the shallow waters a commanded party under Lord Willoughby mounted a fierce attack on the single bridge. This was hotly defended by a body of Scots but at length these were driven back; this reverse cracked French morale and they fled, leaving their Scots allies to stand firm and bear the brunt. The battle was a triumph for Salisbury and a disaster for the Dauphinists. Casualties, mainly incurred by the Scots, totalled perhaps as many as 3,000 with hundreds more as prisoners, including John Stewart.[15]

The following year Bedford decided to resume the offensive and chase the French out of the old Angevin provinces of Anjou and Maine. Undeterred by the reverse at Cravant the Dauphin managed to muster another French army, bolstered by a large Scots contingent sent in April and led by the Earl of Douglas. This was the same Archibald Douglas dubbed the 'tineman' after his débâcle at Homildon twenty-two years earlier. On his arrival he was immediately given command of the joint Franco-Scots army and created Duke of Touraine.

The Dauphinists crossed over the Loire into Normandy, their army numbering as many as 15,000. Bedford riposted by stripping the Norman garrisons and marching south from Rouen. He was joined by Salisbury, John Lord Talbot, a redoubtable warrior, Shakespeare's 'Bull Talbot', and a contingent of the Burgundians under John Lord de L'Isle Adam who, as Bedford believed he already had sufficient numbers to deal with Douglas, were dispatched into Picardy.

On 17th August 1424, in the heat of a baking summer's day, the two hosts met on open ground north of Verneuil. Bedford by now commanded a force of 10,000; the French were reinforced with Italian mercenary crossbowmen. As well as such fomidable captains as Salisbury and Talbot the English had other experienced knights, the earl of Suffolk and sir John Fastolf. Bedford deployed in the classic formation which had stood the English so well for the best part of a century – his dismounted centre astride the road archers on each flank. The bowmen sought, in their habitual manner, to strengthen their position against the horse by planting stakes in front of the lines, but this time the sun-scorched earth was as solid as concrete and the stakes could not be easily driven home. Facing them the French, under the Count of Aumale, were deployed in the centre and on the left with the Scots to the right, a screen of light horse and crossbows on either flank. Douglas was in overall command.

The English began the fight by advancing, around 4 p.m., when some of the fierce August heat had gone from the day. Not waiting to be attacked French cavalry charged the English archers on Bedford's right and the unthinkable occurred. With no stakes put before them and shaken by the fierce élan of the horse, they fell back and then routed. At this point, had the horse wheeled to fall upon the flank of Bedford's exposed centre, the day would have been won but instead they descended on the English baggage park. This was resolutely defended by a reserve of archers who left the attackers sprawling amongst the leaguered wagons.

The English men at arms in the centre were given a respite to order their lines and form a front to the exposed flank. With the position secured Bedford, swinging his great war axe, led the attack on the French main battle under Aumale, which, after a mêlée lasting an hour and a half, gave way. The Scots on the right were resolutely attacked by Salisbury and with equal resolve conceded no ground whatsoever. In this fight no quarter was asked or given, a bloody, gasping mêlée where men fought face-to-face, sweat and blood mingling, heat and wounds sapping strength and will.

The Lombard horse with mounted crossbowmen had also attacked the English camp and were just as sharply seen off, their contribution, such as it was, giving no succour to Douglas and the hard-pressed Scots, and permitting the English to lap around their flank. Bedford, reforming his division after returning from the pursuit of the beaten French, completed the encirclement. The end was not now in doubt though the Scots fought on, almost literally to the last man, perhaps as many as 6,000 were slain including Douglas, the Earl of Buchan, Lord James Douglas, the 'Tineman's' heir with fifty other Scottish knights. The disaster at Verneuil marked the end of direct Scots involvement in the war with France.[16]

The reverses over the Channel did not deter James. Free at last of the hated shackles of confinement, he threw himself, with all of his considerable powers, into the task of kingship. He was finally crowned on 2nd May 1424, some eighteen years after setting sail for France. The state of the nation had declined dramatically under Murdoch's incompetent rule. The royal finances had crumbled as the great magnates continued to plunder customs revenues at will. The king began the serious task of promoting legislation to restore law and order in his first Parliament at Perth.

He overhauled crown revenues and provided for the defence of the realm, regular local musters or 'wapinshaws' were to be held and, at the same time, he tried to encourage his subjects to emulate the English by practising archery. In this he was unsuccessful as the lures of golf and football remained stronger than that of the butts. In 1425 he finally had his reckoning with the House of Albany. Murdoch was arrested in May, and he with two of his sons and the Earl of Lennox were subsequently beheaded at Stirling. Taken with them was Sir Robert Graham of Kincardine who escaped the axe by absconding – his experience engendered an intense hatred of James, an obsession that was to bear bitter fruit.

Having exerted his will in the lowlands it was time to confront the ulcer of the highlands where the royal writ ran sketchily if at all. In 1428 the king summoned fifty clan chiefs to attend a council in Inverness. Without preamble he promptly incarcerated the lot to await his pleasure though, in the event, only three were executed: rough justice nonetheless. The fount of the 'highland problem' remained the Lordship of the Isles. Donald, he who was defeated at Harlaw, was dead and his son Alexander inherited the mantle of lordship. The young man was treated to gentle cautions, stiffened with a brief period of imprisonment, as an education in good behaviour.

This restrained coercion failed to achieve its purpose for he soon re-belled and, in the family tradition, sacked Inverness. James responded with vigour, marched on Lochaber and defeated Alexander on 23rd June 1429. The chastened MacDonald was forced into a degrading show of humility at Holyrood Abbey on 28th August as a reminder of his fall. His kinsman Donald Balloch took up the sword of Clan Donald and rebelled in turn. He outfought Mar, the victor of Harlaw, at Inverlochy in 1431. Again James marched west to stamp his authority on the troublesome glens. Faced with such a potent demonstration of kingly resolve Donald fled to Ireland.

Despite these successes the administration throughout the 1420s was beset by problems of finance, exacerbated by the need to pay off his ransom, James faced inevitable opposition over his plans for higher taxation. There was some comfort as customs dues began to flow once again now Murdoch's inept hand had been removed but these increases began to tail off again by the early 1430s.

Throughout his reign the king continued his work of legislative reform, basing his court at Perth, and in 1426 he created the Court of Session. His relations with his southern neighbour remained equable. Henry VI was the least warlike of kings of England and his marriage into the powerful Beaufort clan did no harm. The Beauforts were the issue of John of Gaunt's pre-nuptial and longstanding relationship with Katherine Swynford whom he did eventually marry. They were legitimised by Richard II though speci-fically excluded from any claim to the throne itself. In time the influence of the Beauforts, as Dukes of Somerset, grew and their pernicious influence over King Henry VI became as strong as it was corrosive.

James abided by the terms of the Treaty of London and cannily maintained a distance from the Dauphinists in France. In 1427 he sent an embassy to the English court proposing that the subsisting truce should be converted into a perpetual peace, but this promising initiative coincided with a vicious quarrel between the regent Gloucester and Queen Joan's uncle Cardinal Beaufort.

In same year Charles VII sent an embassy asking for more Scottish help and the new alliance to be cemented by marriage between the Dauphin Louis and James's eldest daughter Margaret. The King of France did not ask for a cash dowry which James would have struggled to provide but settled for the use of a brigade of 6,000 fighters, manpower and martial spirit being commodities he possessed in abundance. James signed a draft treaty at Perth which was subsequently ratified by Charles at Chinon in November 1428. The following year, against all expectation, saw the turn of the tide in France. The English were before the walls of Orleans; if the city fell the French crown could come tumbling after. The appearance of Joan of Arc and the deliverance of the defenders was little short of miraculous. For the English the defeat was ominous.

After the relief of Orleans James renewed the truce with England until 1431 the which, before its expiry, was extended until 1436. When the unhappy princess departed towards her loveless marriage the English once again, drawn by the inescapable lure of ransom, violated the truce by trying to capture her at sea but this time they failed and she was married at Tours in May 1436. Stung by these violations James raised his standard and laid siege to Berwick, though he achieved little.

On 30th September 1436 some two miles south of Wark and a mile-and-a-half west of Mindrum Hill at Piper Dene ('Pepperden'), Henry Percy 2nd Earl of Northumberland and Warden of the east march leading a raid, with a force of perhaps 4,000, was met by William Douglas, Earl of Angus, warden of the Scottish middle march supported by Adam Hepburn of Hailes, Alexander Ramsay of Dalhousie and Alexander Elphinstone. A fierce battle ensued and ended in the rout of the English who may have lost as many as 400 dead and 300 taken captive. Included amongst the slain were Clennel of Clennel, John Ogle and Sir Richard Percy. The Scots lost Elphinstone and two other knights; other accounts say the English had 1,500 taken but few killed.[17]

On the 1st August the king brought a large Scottish force before the formidable ramparts of Roxburgh. His artillery train was impressive: 'fine large guns, both cannons and mortars', commanded by Johannes Paule with other German gunners.[18] Roxburgh at this time was one of the strongest holds of the borders. Originally an iron age fort on a prominent elongated mound just west of the present town of Kelso, it was elevated to a tribal capital in the early Saxon era and certainly had a stone keep as early as 1134. Within the extensive enceinte were barracks, stables, kitchens, smithies and to address the more spiritual needs of the garrison, the Church of St John.

The place was commanded by Sir Ralph Grey with a complement of eighty men-at-arms, well provisioned and not overawed by the great show of ordnance before the walls. The castellan refused to yield and the siege began in earnest. Northumberland, no doubt smarting from his rebuff at Piper Dene, was in Durham with both the Prince Bishop and the Archbishop of York. Having heard of the Scots' attack on the 6th August he had, within four days, mustered a sufficient force to march to the relief of Roxburgh. The weary English covered the eighty miles in five days, taking the besiegers completely unawares, driving them from their trenches; if not a rout it was certainly a very hasty withdrawal.

This reverse, a humiliation if scarcely a defeat, marked the end of current hostilities. James appeared at the height of his powers an imposing man still young and vigorous if somewhat inclined to corpulence. His position on the throne appeared unassailable but if he had no direct challenger he did not lack for enemies. Chief amongst these was Sir Robert Graham, and the king, perhaps careless of his own security, played into the conspirators' hands. He held Christmas that year in the Dominican Friary at Perth which lay outside the walls and was certainly never intended for defence. On the night of 20th February 1437 Graham and his fellow assassins struck, breaking into the royal apartments. The king sought to escape by pulling up floorboards and jumping into the undercroft below his chamber but the murderers followed him down and he was brutally stabbed to death. The queen herself was wounded trying to save him.

If the conspirators thought their bloody night's work would bring them univeral approbation, they were fatally mistaken. Most were hunted to extinction within a very short time and the six-year-old heir was crowned as James II. Disfigured by a purple birthmark which covered half his face, we have a portrait from life of the young king, a likeness by the German knight Jorg von Ehingen – 'James of the Fiery Face'. This shows James attired in a stylish black doublet and hose with fashionable pointed shoes and a wide brimmed hat; his hand rests, somewhat uneasily perhaps, on the hilt of his dagger.

Archibald Douglas, the 5th earl, was appointed as Guardian. Unlike his energetic if doomed predecessor, the 'tineman', this earl was more given to sloth than martial fury. Their warlike tendency was normally an abiding characteristic of the clan, as Shakespeare approvingly relates:

> *. . . renowned Douglas whose high deeds,*
> *Whose hot incursions and great name in arms*
> *Holds from all soldiers chief majority*
> *And military title capital*
> *Through all the kingdoms that acknowledge Christ.*[19]

The minority was beset by the machinations of Sir William Crichton in alliance with Sir Alexander Livingstone of Callendar, a marriage of uneasy convenience which was allowed to prosper whilst the Guardian was consumed by lethargy. Queen Joan, who might have exerted some influence, weakened her position by remarrying rather unwisely. Her new consort was Sir James Stewart, 'The Black Knight of Lorne'.

Douglas died in the spring of 1439 and his heir, William, was a youth of sixteen. This young earl was of a different stamp, aware of his position as the greatest magnate in the land, arrogant and overbearing, amongst his many titles he retained that of 3rd Duke of Touraine. In November 1440 he and his younger brother were entertained as royal guests in the capital, whence they came accompanied by a great retinue. At the end of what came to be known as the 'Black Dinner' both of the youths were seized, most likely on Crichton's orders, and after the hasty parody of a trial were summarily executed in the castle courtyard. The plates were barely cold.

> *Edinburgh Castle, Toune and Towre,*
> *God grant thou sinke for sinne,*
> *And that even for the black dinoir*
> *Earl Douglas gat therein.*[20]

It might have been expected that this sudden and bloody deed would provoke an instant reprisal from the Douglas affinity but none came. The murdered earls' great uncle was 'James the Gross', brother of his grand-father the 4th earl. In the absence of a direct heir James the Gross became 7th earl. The lack of a blood feud suggests the new earl was perhaps not unhappy with his sudden elevation and either winked at the means or cheerfully acquiesced. Ageing and obese, he died in 1443 to be succeeded as 8th earl by his son William, another feisty teenager only eighteen years old. This William was more circumspect than his predecessor and insti-gated a policy aimed at capitalising on the divisions between Crichton and Livingstone whilst reuniting and extending his Douglas estates. This he achieved, in substantial measure, by marrying the 'Fair Maid of Galloway', the sister and heiress of the murdered 6th earl.

His was a talented and ambitious generation. His younger twin, James, became Bishop of Aberdeen; the next brother, Archibald, was created Earl of Moray; Hugh acquired the Earldom of Ormond and John, the young-est, inherited the lordship of Balveny. The rise of the Black Douglas in Scotland has been likened to the rise of York in England, each the greedy and 'overmighty' subject with an eye on the throne. In the case of Douglas this is probably a calumny too far: the earl was not opposed to the crown, indeed his line had fought and bled for kings of Scotland since Bruce's day.

The 8th earl more likely sought to be *primus inter pares* of the nobility, almost independent of if ultimately subservient to the state. His relentless ambition and the seemingly inexorable rise of his name was contested by the able and astute Bishop Kennedy. Douglas made a band with the bishop's hostile neighbour the choleric Earl of Crawford who attacked and wasted Kennedy's lands. The churchman riposted with the most potent weapon in his spiritual arsenal, excommunication. This was no small matter in the fifteenth century, and though he remained unrepent, Crawford was later killed in an affray. Doubtless men muttered this was God's judge-ment on the excommunicate. The Earl of Douglas had charm as well as ruthless ambition and the young king seems to have developed an affection for his powerful subject.

The economic and political links which the realm enjoyed had been much strengthened and increased by a series of advantageous marriages made by the daughters of James I. In 1448 James II was eighteen and in need of a suitable bride; at the same time Charles VII was earnestly trying to woo Burgundy away from an English alliance and was able to persuade the king to marry the Duke of Burgundy's niece, Marie of Gueldres.

In the previous year the current truce with England had expired and the spring of 1448 saw an upsurge in border conflict. In May the English attacked Dunbar; the Scots swiftly retaliated with a descent on Alnwick. In July the English rode north again, this time targeting Dumfries. Not to be outdone the Scots hit Warkworth. True to the fighting spirit of his ancestors Douglas was the mainspring and thus the hero of Scottish aggression.

On 23rd October the earl's brother Hugh, Earl of Ormond, defeated an English force at Sark near Lochmaben. The Earl of Northumberland, that same Percy who had been vanquished at Piper Dene but had so spectacularly raised the siege of Roxburgh, led a force some 4,000 strong through the English west march, splashing across the border near Gretna. His brother-in-law, Richard Neville, Earl of Salisbury, was, at that time, warden in the west and the passage of the Northumbrians through his fief was a gross breach of etiquette.

This may well have been intentional. The 2nd earl had worked assiduously to repair his family's fortunes in the wake of his father Hotspur's death as a traitor. The Nevilles had increased their own power at the expense of the Percys and the ensuing acrimony would, in a few years, spill over into violent unrest in Durham and North Yorkshire. The flames would be dampened but would re-ignite and form part of the larger conflagration that was to become the Wars of the Roses.

The Northumbrian force camped between the River Sark and Kirtle Water where Ormond found them. His numbers were more or less equal, his army split into three divisions in the usual way. Exploiting the element of surprise the Scots had gained, he launched mounted charges against the English archers deployed on both flanks. Discomfited, the bowmen dissolved in rout leaving the main ward, who had remained mounted, horribly exposed.

Northumberland was accompanied by his heir Lord Poynings who was captured struggling to facilitate the earl's escape. With their backs to the river the English had nowhere to run; over five hundred are said to have been drowned. Sir John Pennington, who commanded the English right wing, was also taken. The principal Scottish casualty was Sir Thomas Wallace of Craigie, 'to whose prowess the success of his countrymen was chiefly owing. For he received his death wounds in a vigorous attack on the left wing of the English army; wherein that wing was routed, and its leader

Magnus killed, on whose great courage and experience in war the English had placed their chief hopes'.[21]

A further truce was negotiated towards the end of 1449 and the following year Douglas was appointed to lead a Scots' embassy to the papal court, a signal honour but also one which had the useful effect of getting him out of the country. In the course of his travels Douglas attended the English court where he formed what could only be construed as a treasonable connection with Richard Duke of York. This was dangerous ground indeed, for the duke was estranged from the throne; Henry VI was in thrall to his queen and her Beaufort allies. York was seriously disaffected and perhaps, like Douglas, felt his services to the crown had, apart from costing him dear, brought him no recognition, whilst other and less able men controlled the king.

While Douglas was away he had left his lands in the care of his youngest sibling, Balveny. Whether he had permitted disturbances to arise or whether this was a mere pretext James quelled what he saw or preferred to see as unruly behaviour by levelling Douglas' holds and executing several adherents. John, Lord of the Isles and Earl of Ross, the son of that Alexander who had rebelled against James I, now raised the fiery cross and, in keeping with family policy, torched Inverness. James II dealt with these fissiparous highlanders as swiftly as his father had done.

Douglas, on his return from Rome, found his position in the country much weakened and had to undergo the added humiliation of being admonished before Parliament. The king soon learnt of his treasonable negotiations not only with York in England but with John of the Isles and Alexander Lindsay, the new Earl of Crawford. James summoned Douglas to explain himself at Stirling. The earl demanded a full safe conduct which was granted, though it did him precious little good.

One could excuse any scion of the House of Douglas being wary of dining with royalty but, on the 22nd February 1452, the earl supped with the king. At least the 8th earl was allowed to finish his dinner before James and he retired to the king's solar. Once there, however, the earl was confronted with his treachery, angry words followed and the king, his rage fuelled by excessive imbibing, drew his dagger and slashed the throat of his guest. Whether the king had intended to murder Douglas must be in question but, once the first blow was struck, the royal attendants rushed into the chamber and finished off the stricken earl with a barrage of strokes.

This time there was to be no blind acceptance of so base a deed. The murdered earl's twin, the Bishop of Aberdeen, now 9th earl, descended on Stirling with fire and sword that May. His ally Crawford came out in the north but was swiftly defeated by the Earl of Huntly near Brechin. The king now marched against Douglas who submitted at Dumfries. In the subsequent enquiry into the circumstances of the 8th earl's death, Parliament saw fit to exonerate the king, concluding, most understandingly, that Douglas had been 'guilty of his own death by refusing the King's gentle persuasion'.[22]

James was generous to the new earl; clearly he did not want to make lasting enemies of the whole name so he was prepared to allow the Douglas to marry his widowed sister-in-law. The earl was not to be so easily bought off and wasted no time in sending an embassy to make contact with York in England. That inveterate rebel Donald Balloch returned torch in hand and burnt Inverkip, but Crawford and the Lord of the Isles had had their fill of rebellion. Both craved forgiveness.

In England the enmity between York and Somerset reached its bloody finale in the streets of St Albans, ushering in a series of conflicts that would periodically engulf the realm for the next thirty-odd years. In the same year King James finally confronted the earl in the field at Arkinholm where the rebels were utterly routed. Douglas and Balveny escaped but Moray was slain in the fight, Ormond wounded, taken then executed. By a particular irony the royal forces were commanded by Douglas kin the 4th Earl of Angus, ushering in the rise of the Red Douglas as surely as the day saw the final eclipse of the Black.

The king now employed his formidable artillery to reduce the Douglas holds of Abercorn in West Lothian and Threave in Kirkcudbrightshire. Located on an island in the broad sweep of the Dee near Castle Douglas, Threave was an impressive fortress, built by Archibald the Grim in the fourteenth century. Some years prior to the disaster at Arkinholm, in 1447, the 8th earl had constructed an artillery work around the base of the central tower. Two lengths of wall had towers at either end to hold small pieces of ordnance, and the were 'battered' outward at the base to maximise deflection and studded with gun loops for the defenders' early 'gonnes' or crossbows.

The great tower with remains of the curtain still stand, battered and defaced but both imposing and uncompromising. Perhaps this sums up the very character of the Black Douglas.[23] In the siege of 1455 the castle does not appear to have been in any way structurally damaged; possibly the threat of the great guns was enough. The castellan was Sir John Fraser, who may even have been bribed to surrender.[24]

One of the great guns in the king's train was the legendary bombard known as 'Mons Meg' which was originally cast in Flanders and may have formed part of Marie of Gueldres' dowry. Artillery was by no means unknown in Scotland even as far back as the closing years of the previous century. We know Robert II possessed at least one small piece in 1384.[25] James I, in the last year of his reign and whilst sporadically at war with England, spent £590 on commissioning new ordnance.

The Burgundian alliance ushered in by the king's marriage to Marie of Gueldres gave James access to the burgeoning foundries of the low countries. This connection fuelled his already keen interest in the science of gunnery. The great guns were useful for far more than simply battering down castle walls. The mere fact they could do so rendered traditional medieval designs for defensive architecture largely obsolete. Guns quite literally spelt power – the power of princes, for such was the princely cost of casting, transporting and servicing heavy ordnance that usually only the crown could afford to buy. At a stroke the sovereign gained an immediate and overwhelming advantage over his nobility; no longer could they safely blare defiance from behind castle walls.

The Scots Parliament of 1456 enacted that, in time of war, certain of the nobility should provide what were defined as 'cartis of war' – effectively a mobile firing platform, each having two guns with two chambers apiece. This was early field as opposed to siege artillery intended to give the army's available firepower a significant boost. Although the longbow remained the favoured missile weapon of the English, the hand-held firearm, or 'gonne', was coming into increasing use. Slow, temperamental, prone to damp and misfire, not infrequently as dangerous to the firer, these early muskets had the inestimable advantage of being easy to use nor did they require the years of training and physical stamina needed to bend the great yew bow. The frightful noise and great clouds of sulphurous smoke added a diabolical dimension of their own.

It should be noted that James II generally enjoyed good relations with the bulk of the nobility; the internecine strife with the Douglases and their allies was the exception rather than the rule. The patrimony and thus the wealth of the crown greatly increased in the reigns of both James I and II with the acquisition of the earldoms of Carrick, Fife, Lennox, Mar, Strathearn, Moray and Buchan. After settling the feud with Douglas, the king threw himself into the business of government and law-giving, bringing that same restless energy which had so characterised his father. On the border the considerable independence of the march wardens was reduced and their plenipotentiary power to try cases of treason was curtailed. In 1458 a further Act was passed to enforce the practice of archery; this had proved unpopular in the previous reign and enjoyed no more success now. The English remained unchallenged at the butts.

After the disaster at Arkinholm, Douglas sought refuge with his ally York, now in the ascendant after the bloodletting in the streets of St Albans. James wrote a strongly worded letter of protest at the more than favourable treatment the renegade was enjoying. York, his own regal ambitions rampant, replied haughtily and added spice to the insults by resurrecting the English crown's claims to overlordship, the old gripe which, whilst it had remained dormant, had never completely submerged. This was too much to bear and, in 1456, James retaliated with fire and sword. In August he swept into North Northumberland, penetrating, in a six-day chevauchee, twenty miles south of the Tweed and, in the process, was said to have levelled seventeen villages.[26]

His venom, it has to be said, was directed more towards York than King Henry. Once that feeble monarch had succeeded in wresting the reins of power, albeit temporarily, back from his overmighty cousin, a truce was first proposed and then concluded in July 1457 to endure for two years. By 1459, however, the pot was once more firmly on the boil with a renewal of disturbances in which the hand of the exiled and irrevocably vindictive Douglas was clearly discernible. The following summer James took the field, ostensibly as ally of the now deposed Henry, held captive by the resurgent Yorkists after the rout at Northampton.

James's army included a force brought by the Lord of the Isles, a measure of the power and confidence of the crown. James, like his father, laid siege to the great prize of Roxburgh. His enthusiasm for his great guns led him to supervise the laying of each and when he ordered a cannonade to mark the arrival of his queen it was one of his own guns which burst; a fragment of iron smashed the king's thigh and he expired from the wound.

This Prince mair curieous nor became him or the maiestie of ane
King did stand neir hand by the gunneris quhen the artaillezerie was
dischargeand.[27]

Despite this grievous blow and the prospect of a further minority rule, the queen did not lose her head. She, quite rightly, ordered the siege to be continued and the garrison, commanded by York's brother Lord Fauconberg was, after a stiff resistance, obliged to yield. The works were afterward slighted and now only the overgrown mound remains, mute testimony to the effectiveness of the destruction.

He showed such valour against his enemies, and such clemency to those
who submitted themselves, that all estates were much afflicted for his loss.
And his death was the more lamented because it was sudden, and in the
flower of his youth too; after he had escaped so many dangers, and when
the expectation of his virtues was at the highest.[28]

This sudden and violent taking off of a young and aggressive King of Scotland, leaving a minor heir, might otherwise have been seen as a time of opportunity for the English, but south of the border there was strife enough for all without needing to strike a blow against the old enemy to the north.

Notes

1 Quoted in Bingham, C., *The Stewart Kingdom of Scotland 1371–1603*, London 1974 p. 30.
2 Robson, R., *The Rise and Fall of the English Highland Clans*, Edinburgh 1989 p. 58.
3 Ibid p. 58.
4 Sewars, D., *Henry V as Warlord*, London 1987 p. 124.
5 Sadler, D.J., *Battle for Northumbria*, Newcastle 1988 pp. 69–70.
6 Robson p. 53.
7 Lomas, R., *County of Conflict: Northumberland from the Conquest to the Civil War*, Edinburgh 1996 p. 56.
8 Quoted in Bingham p. 30.
9 Lomas p. 56.
10 Bingham p. 33.
11 Neillands, R., *The Hundred Years War*, London 1990 pp. 240–1.
12 Quoted in Bingham p. 36.
13 Ibid p. 38.
14 Ibid p. 42.

15 Neillands pp. 240–1.
16 Ibid pp. 242–3.
17 Sadler pp. 88–9.
18 Rose, A., *Kings in the North*, London 2002 p. 389.
19 *Henry IV Part 1* (III:II).
20 Quoted in Bingham p. 70.
21 Ridpath, Rev. G., *Border History*, Berwick 1858 edn. p. 281.
22 Quoted in Bingham p. 79.
23 Tabraham, C., *Scottish Castles and Fortifications*, Edinburgh 1986 p. 47.
24 MacIvor, I., *A Fortified Frontier*, England 2001 p. 52.
25 Quoted in Bingham p. 52.
26 Lomas p. 58.
27 Quoted in Bingham p. 87.
28 Ibid p. 87.

Chapter 13

War in the North

On the 24th August 1453, Thomas Percy, Lord Egremont, younger son of the Earl of Northumberland, lay in ambush by Heworth Moor, north-east of York. With him he had perhaps a thousand men-at-arms and archers; their intended quarry the bridal party attending Sir Thomas Neville and his new wife Maud Stanhope. The bride and groom were accompanied by Sir Thomas' parents, the Earl and Countess of Salisbury, his brother John, the future Lord Montagu and all now travelling north from Tattershall Castle in Lincolnshire where the marriage had been celebrated. Though the affair, on the surface, may appear as little more than a local and largely bloodless brawl, it also represented the first major, armed clash between the two pre-eminent northern magnates, who were also involved in the campaign to reform and ultimately remove the Lancastrian administration.[1]

Some writers have seen the Percy–Neville feud as the catalyst which led mere factionalism to degenerate into civil war. Since the heady years of the late fourteenth century, when the power of the Percys was unrivalled in the north, the Nevilles had risen to challenge and indeed eclipse that supremacy.[2] The almost princely independence of the Percys confirmed a quasi-regal status in the north, 'the dominant individual in northern society was Henry Percy fourth Earl of Northumberland'[3] – a view which thus persisted even after the end of the period known as the Wars of the Roses, and when the Nevilles were utterly crushed. This view is not without its critics who view the rebellions of the first earl and Hotspur, his son, as attempts to throw off the yoke of royal control, which both Richard II and Henry IV sought to exercise. The family failed to regain the level of autonomy they had enjoyed in the 1360s and 1370s and Hotspur's rebellion had ended in defeat and a traitor's death at Shrewsbury. By the time Hotspur's son, the second earl, was able to reverse his father's attainder, in 1416, the rising star of the Nevilles, had, at least in part, filled the void.[4]

Under the steady hand of Ralph, first Earl of Westmorland, the Nevilles had remained staunchly loyal to the House of Lancaster, and had steadily increased their estates and spheres of influence. The earl died in 1425 and his effigy in Staindrop Church, County Durham, shows him wearing the distinctive 'S' collar of a solid Lancastrian.[5] Having held the north for Henry IV when the Percys rebelled he cemented his relationship with the Crown by marrying Joan Beaufort, Salisbury's mother and, herself, a daughter of John of Gaunt; with the Beauforts, in the person of the rapacious Duke of Somerset, high in the Council of Henry VI, the Neville allegiance seemed secure.[6] The policy, begun by John of Gaunt, of buttressing the power of Neville as a counterweight to that of Percy, was continued by Henry VI and the expansion of the former's affinity was, not infrequently, at the expense of the latter.[7]

The prestige of the Nevilles was particularly evident in the Palatinate, where the influence of heir rivals was noticeably weaker. Salisbury and his brothers, William, Lord Fauconberg ('Little' Fauconberg, one of the paladins of the Yorkist cause in the years 1455–61), George Lord Latimer, Edward, Lord Abergavenny, and his son Sir Thomas are consistently named in commissions of the peace. At various times Fauconberg was seneschal, steward, justice of assize, justice of gaol delivery; Latimer was chamberlain and Thomas also held similar offices to his uncles including that of commissioner of array for the wards of Chester, Darlington, Easington and wapentake of Sadberge.[8]

Richard, Earl of Salisbury, inherited the bulk of the Earl of Westmorland's estates in Yorkshire, centred on the manors of Middleham and Sherriff Hutton. The scale of this inheritance, Salisbury being the son of Westmorland's second wife, sparked a deep division with the senior branch which retained the title and lands in the north-west. Undisturbed by this family rift Salisbury went on to steadily develop the scale of his holdings. His own eldest son, also Richard, added the dazzling Beauchamp inheritance and the earldom of Warwick to his titles and was to become a key figure in the political landscape, bringing the power of his name to its absolute zenith and ultimately to its utter ruin – 'Warwick the Kingmaker' as history has dubbed him. Always something of a swashbuckler, he '. . . had energy, dash and courage. A skilful propagandist, he had great success in rousing the common people to his cause and was well noted for his open handed generosity. Yet he was also self-interested and arrogant . . . acquisitive and unscrupulous to a degree . . . unusually ruthless in his treatment of defeated enemies'.[9]

The three ridings of Yorkshire were parcelled out, in terms of land ownership, between four of the greatest magnates in the realm, including the Crown, as Duchy of Lancaster, the Percys, Nevilles and the Duke of York, Salisbury's brother-in-law. The Percy holdings east of the Pennines were interspersed with those of Salisbury and York, though the latter showed but little interest in his northern estates.[10] Having taken from 1416 to 1440 for Northumberland to recover his father's lost inheritance in full, Salisbury, who had been created earl in 1429, had ample time to consolidate his hold on manors in Cleveland, Westmorland, Cumberland and the lordship of Raby.[11]

The bickering with the senior branch continued throughout this period and even the negotiated settlement of 1443 did not expunge the latter's grievances; Salisbury could not then count on the support of his cousins in any trial of strength with the Percys.[12] In the same year Salisbury was appointed as warden of the west march, an office which allowed him to further increase his affinity throughout Cumberland and Westmorland. By 1441, he may have had an annual income of some £3,000, perhaps £500 less than the Prince Bishop but probably a thousand a year more than Northumberland.[13]

The Percys, as noted, had long been active in border affairs; Hotspur's adventures at Otterburn (1388) and Homildon (1402) had proved the inspiration for some celebrated balladry and, in the family tradition, Northumberland's son Henry, Lord Poynings, was appointed as east march warden in 1440. Ten years after his own appointment Salisbury was reappointed in the west, this time jointly with Warwick. A significant privilege of the warden's office was the right to raise and maintain military forces, ostensibly for the defence of the border, but Lord Poynings' retinue, by virtue of his office could, in times of strife, be used to swell the affinities of his father and brothers.[14]

The Percys' long and active presence on the marches fuelled their and their affinity's arrogance. In January 1453 a band of Percy tenantry could feel confident in their boast that no sherriff or other officer of the crown could wield power within, specifically, the manor of Topcliffe or, more generally, on any Percy land. This posturing was encouraged by the thuggish conduct of Egremont who had threatened the life of the Sherriff of Cumberland, one Thomas de la Mare, a servant of Salisbury.[15] Created baron at the age of 25, in 1449, Egremont typified all the adverse traits of his line '. . . quarrelsome, violent and contemptous of all authority, he possessed all the worst characteristics of a Percy for which his grandfather is still a byword'.[16] Salisbury's sister, Eleanor, was married to Northumberland, but the ties of blood counted for little in a game with such high stakes; both leading families now had a mature but still rapacious patriarch, each with a brood of restless and potentially lawless younger sons, and no shortage of available manpower.[17]

The marriage of Maud Stanhope to Thomas Neville had finally driven the volatile Egremont, with or without the tacit consent of his father, to take up arms. The bride had been married before, to Robert, Lord Willoughby of Eresby, who had died the previous summer. She was also, and significantly, the niece and co-heiress of Ralph, Lord Cromwell, as acquisitive and choleric as any Percy or Neville. A stout Lancastrian he had been granted leases of two former Percy manors at Wressle and Burwell in Lincolnshire. Two years later, in February, 1440, he bought out the reversionary interest. Cromwell and Northumberland, smarting at the continued loss, particularly of Wressle, upon which much Percy wealth had previously been lavished, had already clashed in the courts; by broking the union of his widowed niece to a Neville he was clearly compounding the perceived injury.[18]

Tension had been mounting throughout the early summer of 1453. In June the king had summoned both Egremont and John Neville; by the end of that month the future Lord Montagu was planning to waylay his rival. On the 2nd July Henry VI dissolved Parliament to come north and confront his quarrelsome vassals. He proposed that Egremont and his affinity should make ready for service in Gascony where their martial ardour could no doubt be put to better use, but the scheme came to nothing. On 12th of that month the king established a commission of oyer and terminer, the membership of which included both earls, Viscount Beaumont and fourteen others.[19] The commission was reissued two weeks later but to little effect, Salisbury, who unlike Northumberland, was on the Council, undoubtably used his influence to pack the membership with allies who included Neville adherents such as Sir James Pickering, Sir Henry Fitzhugh, and Sir Henry le Scrope of Bolton.[20]

Despite the commission's credentials it proved inneffective amidst a rising tide of disorder and, by the end of the month, a new and less overtly partisan commission was set up under the leadership of a Northampton-shire knight and member of the Council, Sir William Lucy, supported by leading counsel. Immediately Sir William set to work summoning Ralph Neville, Sir John Conyers, Sir James Pickering, Sir Ralph Randolf, Sir Thomas Mountford, Richard Aske, Thomas Sewer, and John Alcombe. On 10th August nine Percy adherents were summoned together with Sir Ralph and Sir Richard Percy.[21]

York, as the economic capital of the north, was important to both factions who actively courted the citizenry. The city, as a mercantile centre, was suffering from the general recession of the 1450s, the loss of Gascony had seriously affected the all-important wine trade, the north sea was infested by pirates, relations with the Hanse were deteriorating and the final defeat in France heralded decades of economic uncertainty. Clearly recession and unemployment provided a further reservoir of manpower which could be drawn into the mire. Egremont had determined to spring his ambush on Friday 24th August. His aim can only have been to decim-ate the Nevilles; of the 710 persons named on indictments laid before the Duke of York the following summer some 94 per cent of the accused come from the gentry or yeomanry but slightly more than 15 per cent are citizens of York.[22]

Undeterred by their failure at Heworth (a fracas between the Percys and the bridal party of Thomas Neville and Maud Stanhope), Richard Percy and a band of unruly adherents embarked on a spree of vandalism, culminating with the kidnapping of Lawrence Catterall, the bailiff of Staincliff wapentake, who was dragged from his devotions in Gargrave church on 9th September and subsequently incarcerated first in Isel Castle and latterly at Cockermouth. Clearly he had somehow offended the Percys, though quite how is unrecorded.[23] On 25th September a brace of Percy retainers, John Catterall and Sir John Salvin, pillaged the dwelling of William Hebdon, the vicar of Aughton; the day before John Neville had plundered North-umberland's property at Catton.[24]

Apparently impotent in the face of the rapidly escalating violence the king, on 8th October, wrote plaintively to both Salisbury and Northumberland

entreating them to exercise some measure of control over their siblings –
by this time the king's mental health had seriously deteriorated though
the queen and court faction did their best to conceal the fact. It is unclear
as to the exact nature of his malady; some writers have suggested catatonic
schizophrenia, but the king's incapacity further weakened the government's
grip on law and order. By 17th October Egremont had assembled a
following of 50-odd, fully armed and harnessed, who gathered at Topcliffe.
A number of these, perhaps twenty, were from Northumberland or the city
of Newcastle.[25]

Heedless of royal admonition both sides were squaring up for a further
brawl and a confrontation appears to have occurred on 20th October at
Sandhutton; Salisbury and Warwick joined Sir John and Sir Thomas and
the Nevilles were supported by such old friends as Sir Henry Fitzhugh
and Sir Henry le Scrope, declaring their true colours. The Percys were
led by the earl and Lord Poynings, with Egremont and Richard. Whether
any serious blows were exchanged seems doubtful: there are no records
of casualties but any pretence by the senior magnates as to the rule of law
was clearly dispensed with. Battle lines had been drawn even if the fight
was not begun.

As the tempo of strife rose the king's grasp on reality declined and
it had, by now, become impossible to hide his condition. Matters were
complicated by the birth, on 13th October, of a son, the future Edward of
Lancaster, for this meant that York's hopes of the succession were dashed.
Increasingly vociferous the duke, as senior member of the peerage, was
demanding to be appointed as regent during the king's illness, demands
which the queen and Somerset were equally determined to resist. On 25th
October the Council met at York. Both Salisbury and Warwick were in
attendance, Northumberland and Poynings, markedly, were not. York had
married Salisbury's youngest sister, Cicely, the celebrated 'Rose of Raby',
and had spent his career to date as a diligent if undistinguished servant of
the crown. He had given good service in Normandy only to see his efforts
dissipated by the chronically inept Somerset. Moreover, most of his labours
had been conducted at his own, considerable expense. Effectively exiled to
Ireland he achieved considerable in that notoriously unruly province, '. . . a
somewhat austere, remote and unsympathetic figure, with little capacity or
inclination to seek and win support from his fellow noblemen or from the
wider public . . .'.[26]

He cordially detested Somerset and, two years earlier had, in exasperation, rebelled after the loss of Bordeaux and Gascony for which he, along with many others, blamed the king's favourite. Raising a substantial force he set out to march on London, confronting a royal army at Blackheath. Though many peers shared his contempt for Somerset few were, as yet, prepared to commit to such drastic action. Bloodshed was, however, avoided, largely through the mediation of Salisbury and Warwick. York recieved assurances that his detested rival would be removed from office but found himself confounded and humiliated by the king's vacillation and duplicity.

Henry's breakdown dramatically altered the balance of power and York, now with the full backing of his brother-in-law and nephew, secured the Protectorate. Despite his Beaufort blood Warwick had quarrelled with the equally rapacious Somerset, whose next journey was to the Tower. With the Nevilles now firmly aligned with York it became almost inevitable that the Percys should gravitate towards the queen's party despite its present eclipse. Thus the hitherto local rivalry between these two great houses was transferred to the national sphere and their enmity linked to that of Lancaster and York.

A number of writers have suggested that the tide of lawlessness was fuelled by the return of unemployed soldiery, redundant after the final defeat in France. Other commentators, including Ross,[27] have pointed out that the size of English armies in the hundred years war was never very large, no more than a few thousand. The martial temperament of the riding names served to provide a pool of available, totally mercenary and ruthlessly professional fighting men. A surviving indenture from 1452 and entered into by Salisbury and Walter Strickland, a Westmorland knight, provides, *inter alia*, that the latter will supply 74 billmen, 'horsed and harnessed' – 69 bowmen, likewise arrayed – 76 dismounted billmen and 71 foot archers, a by no means unimpressive total.[28]

In addition to his dispute with Percy the choleric Lord Cromwell had litigated against Henry Holand, Duke of Exeter, and the affair had become so heated that both parties, in July 1453, had been temporarily incarcerated. The marriage of his niece to Sir Thomas Neville gained Cromwell the friendship of Salisbury which, in turn, pushed Exeter towards Northumberland. When, on 27 March 1454, York was finally appointed as Protector and Salisbury, a mere five days later, was raised to the office of Chancellor, the Percys can scarcely have found occasion to rejoice. The new chancellor was swift to summon firstly Egremont and then Richard Percy to wait before him on pain of forfeiture and outlawry.[29] The Percys might laugh at the feeble strictures of their king but they would have little doubt that their arch rival was in absolute earnest.

York's appointment marked an era of firmer government, though the Nevilles were clearly, and as always, motivated by self-interest. Sensing the mood, Sir Thomas Neville of Brancepeth (not Salisbury's son but a younger brother of the Earl of Westmorland, and no friend to his cousins), took the opportunity to pillage the property of Sir John Salvin at Egton in Eskdale, with a company of two dozen men-at-arms and lifting £80 of gear.[30] By May the Protector was writing a strongly worded summons to Northumberland ordering him to appear before the Council on 12th June; Lord Poynings and Ralph Percy was summoned to appear ten days before. On 3rd April Exeter was sacked from his lucrative and prestigious office of Lord Admiral.

The Percys were not minded to follow the path of humility. On 6th May they extensively vandalised the new chancellor's town house in York and attacked one of his tenants, John Skipworth. Many of those involved had been 'out' at Heworth the year before; by the middle of May Egremont was mustering his affinity at Spofforth, and where, on 14th, he was joined by Exeter, rankling at his loss of office. The riot spilled into the streets of York, the armed mob spreading understandable alarm amongst the burgesses, and brutally assaulting the mayor and recorder. The wave of anarchy swept through the north riding whilst Exeter strove to raise more havoc in Lancashire and Cheshire. The Council did not remain inactive whilst these troubles erupted; Sir Thomas Stanley, the Duchy of Lancaster's receiver for the counties of Lancashire and Cheshire, ably assisted by Sir Thomas Harrington, drove Exeter from the north-west. By 19th May York, supported, no doubt, with enthusiasm by Cromwell, arrived in York; the rioters fled the city.

Exeter was one of the king's closest blood relatives, tracing his own line through John of Gaunt, and it may well be that he saw the chance, in an otherwise localised brawl, to win centre-stage by deposing York and assuming the Protectorate himself. On 21st May he returned to York with Egremont and his affinity, once again seeking to intimidate the much-abused mayor and spreading a pattern of random disorder throughout the whole county. Percy was even prepared to solicit aid from James II, the

Scots having violated the truce negotiated the previous year and the English herald dispatched to Edinburgh to register the Council's protest was kidnapped at Spofforth. The rebels, for the disturbances were now of sufficient seriousness and intent to justify the term, even schemed to lure the Protector into an ambush outside the city walls.

York, meanwhile, had summoned both ringleaders to appear on 25th June whilst he built up his forces. By the 15th he was ready to move, being joined by Warwick and Lord Greystoke. Seven days later the Protector's forces were further augmented by those of Lord Clifford, the Earl of Shrewsbury and Sir Henry Fitzhugh. Of the many who received summonses a number suffered forfeiture and a few were outlawed. Exeter, Egremont and Richard Percy all failed to appear.[31] The rising, however, had failed and Exeter crept back to London. By 8th July he was in custody and on 24th he was safely incarcerated in Pontefract Castle. York did not feel he was able to return to the capital so long as the Percys remained in arms.

The situation remained tense until well into the autumn when a further confrontation took place, in rather confused circumstances, at Stamford Bridge, a Neville manor some miles east of York. Whether any actual fighting occurred is doubtful, but the Percys were confounded by treachery when one of their own bailiffs, a Peter Lound, defected with 200 followers. The Neville faction, thus suddenly reinforced and led by Thomas and John, pounced on their discomfited enemies and captured both Egremont and Richard.

The prisoners were sent, probably via Middleham, to confinement in Newgate gaol. Arraigned in front of the Protector on 4th November both were given swingeing fines. Salisbury was to be compensated in the amount of 8,000 marks, and other members of the Neville clan awarded lesser amounts – the total amounted to 16,800 marks, an indebtedness the Percys could not, in the short term, hope to discharge and thus, as no doubt was intended, remained behind bars.[32] The Neville–York faction appeared triumphant but any rejoicing was short-lived for in December the king recovered his wits and was deemed able to resume the reins of government. On 7th February 1455, Somerset was released and restored to favour. Salisbury, his position clearly hopeless, resigned as chancellor on 7th March and Exeter regained his liberty less than a week later. By May the opposing factions were beyond any hope of compromise and clashed bloodily in the streets of St Albans; Somerset, Northumberland and Lord Clifford were all amongst the dead and the hapless king under the 'care' of the Yorkists.

Exeter was, by 21st June, back in confinement, this time in Wallingford. On 31st July York issued a general amnesty, though if he expected this to dampen the rancour of the surviving Lancastrians and particularly the successors of those who had fallen in the battle on 22nd May, he was hoping for a very great deal. The uncertain winter of 1455–6 may have witnessed further disturbances in the north, orchestrated by Egremont who, having escaped Newgate on 13th November, undeterred and embittered by his father's killing, would never willingly submit to the Nevilles. He seems to have occupied the coveted manor of Wressle, the spark that had led to that first confrontation on Heworth Moor (a prize that was finally granted to him in 1458).[33] By 14th January 1456, Exeter was also again at liberty though equally unrepentant. He, together with Shrewsbury and Henry Beaufort, now Duke of Somerset, was plotting to murder Warwick on 5th November.

The hapless king's futile but well-meaning efforts to reconcile his predatory nobles culminated in the, almost farcical, 'love-day' on 25th March 1458. Both sides entered bonds for damage done to the other and the accord also absolved their respective affinities. However, when hostilities were resumed the following year the old loyalties exerted their same pull. In June 1459, the queen, now firmly in control of her consort's affairs, summoned a meeting of the Council to be held at Coventry. York, Salisbury and Warwick were to be excluded. Salisbury, at this time, was at Middleham and his eldest son in London. York invited both to join him at his castle of Ludlow. As Salisbury hurried to comply a superior force of Lancastrians, under Lord Audley, sought to bar his path at Blore Heath, near Newcastle under Lyme, on 23rd September. The Yorkists acquitted themselves with skill and valour, many of the defeated Lancastrians, including their commander, being left dead upon the field.

Despite this victory the confrontation which followed at Ludford Bridge went badly for the Yorkists. The defection, with his following, of Andrew Trollope, a hardened veteran of the French wars, prompted a collective loss of nerve and the leaders took refuge in ignominious flight, abandoning their troops. York and his younger son, the Earl of Rutland, made for

Ireland, Warwick, Salisbury and Edward, Earl of March, the duke's eldest, to Calais where Warwick still held the captaincy. The 'Parliament of Devils', as it became known, attainted the Yorkist lords but the disaster at Ludford Bridge did not deter Warwick from maintaining a lively campaign at sea or from sailing to Ireland to confer with his uncle in March 1460.

A couple of months later, on 26th June, the Calais exiles landed at Sandwich to a rapturous welcome, the Kentishmen flocking to Warwick's banner. Having secured the capital they engaged the royal army at North-ampton on 10th July. The timely defection of Lord Grey of Ruthyn proved decisive and the unfortunate King Henry, once again, found himself the puppet of the Yorkists. Lord Egremont was amongst the Lancastrian dead.

In September York returned to the capital, making it plain that he came not as protector but as a claimant in his own right, a political blunder which alienated the majority of peers who were not yet ready for a change of monarch, however unsuitable the present incumbent. Warwick was unprepared for this change of stance, clearly both angered and alarmed. On 24th October Parliament passed an attempt at compromise, the Act of Accord, which secured Henry's throne but passed the succession to York.[34] Margaret of Anjou's reaction is not recorded but she would never acquiesce to legislation that disinherited her son. Anthony Goodman has pointed out that the Act rested on a largely untenable basis and the nature of the conflict was changed to a war of succession and '. . . what some contemporaries regarded as a war of the north against the south'.[35]

The Act quite simply went too far. The king's administration was corrupt, venal and inefficient, his queen and her dead favourite, Somerset, may have been detested, York, clearly had been ill-used and, equally clearly, had not set out to win the crown, but '. . . whatever the manifest defects of his administration, the King was regarded as a man set apart from other men by the solemn rites of his coronation; in particular the ceremony of unction (anointing with holy oil) made him a semi-divine being'.[36]

The queen was soon preparing to contest the settlement. Lord Poynings, now 3rd Earl of Northumberland, Clifford (whose father had also died at St Albans), Lord Neville (of the Westmorland branch) and Lord Greystoke attended a muster of, predominantly, northern peers either at Hull or Pontefract. Resentment of the Act swelled the ranks, the lateness of the season notwithstanding, and she may have been able to command as many as 15,000. Aware of the rising tide of opposition in the north, York, accompanied by Salisbury and Rutland, marched out of London early in December, his forces probably less than half of those likely to be arrayed against him.[37]

Having celebrated Christmas at his castle of Sandal, near Wakefield, York accepted the hazard of battle and deployed his men to face the Lancastrians, now commanded by Somerset, on 30th December. The decision was a rash one. His army was decimated, himself and Sir Thomas Neville slain upon the field, young Rutland cut down by vengeful Clifford and Salisbury taken after the fight, apparently by a servant of Andrew Trollope, whose cunning duplicity may have again played a part in the Yorkists' defeat. The captive earl was conveyed to Pontefract and the victors may have been inclined to spare his life, mindful of ransom, but, as some chroniclers argue, the common people of the area, having no love for him, dragged the earl from his quarters and struck off his head.

Flush with victory, the heads of their fallen foes barbarously impaled above Micklegate in York, the queen's army swept southward. By 16th February they were at Dunstable. Warwick, mustering troops from the south and east, advanced as far as St Albans and battle was joined on the 17th. Over-extended and with a lamentable failure of intelligence, Warwick was severely mauled, losing the royal pawn in the near rout. He subsequently blamed his failure on the defection of a Kentish captain named Lovelace, though this may have been nothing more than propaganda. Sir John Neville was taken but not deprived of life. Somerset was mindful of the fact that his own brother Edmund Beaufort was a prisoner of Warwick.

The Earl of March had been leading a Yorkist army on the Welsh Marches, seeking to block Margaret's Welsh adherents, and the eighteen-year-old earl won a resounding victory over the Welsh Lancastrians at Mortimer's Cross. The queen vacillated before London, the city hostile, its citizens in dread of the uncouth northerners, the 'boreales bobinantes' who, being unpaid, were ravaging the towns and manors of the south. On 4th March Edward, the English Earl of March, rode to Westminster. Under Warwick's expert tutelage, he finally threw off any pretence of fighting to rescue the king from evil counsellors and assumed the throne as King Edward IV.

Before Edward crossed the fateful Rubicon, the Lancastrians were already in retreat, the host lumbering northward, its passage marked by pillage and wholesale destruction. The queen may have felt that as her husband's cause still enjoyed the support of the majority of peers she could afford to abandon the attempt on London and seek to establish an impregnable defensive line in the north, behind the great natural barrier of the Aire, with York as the alternative seat of government. Neither Edward nor Warwick was blind to the enormous peril the undefeated Lancastrian field army presented; the issue could only be resolved by a decisive encounter.

Norfolk was dispatched to the eastern counties to recruit, Warwick to the midlands. On 11th March the redoubtable Fauconberg marched north from London with the van, Edward following soon after. With the royal family safe behind the walls of York Somerset had been making his dispositions. He had the veteran Trollope, Northumberland, Clifford, Exeter and Ralph Lord Dacre of Gilsland, his host, perhaps as many as 30,000 strong, was drawn up on the gentle plateau that swells between the villages of Towton and Saxton.

In the biting sleet of a bitter Palm Sunday, the biggest and bloodiest battle ever to be fought on British soil occurred at Towton. At the end the Lancastrians were routed, suffering terrible loss '. . . King Edward told me that in all the battles he had won, as soon as he had gained victory, he mounted his horse and shouted to his men that they must spare the common soldiers and kill the lords of which none or few escaped'.[38] The flower of northern chivalry including Northumberland, Dacre and Clifford, who had been struck down by an arrow in the skirmish at Dintingdale the day before, perished. The magnitude of the disaster should have sounded the final knell for the House of Lancaster but the war in the north and particularly in Northumberland was to drag on for a further three years.

The Act of Attainder, passed by Edward IV's victorious Parliament, attainted all of the northern lords who had fallen in the battle, Northumberland, Lords Clifford, Neville and Dacre; many others from the northern counties also featured: Sir Humphrey Dacre, Sir Thomas Findern, Sir John Heron, Sir Henry Bellingham, Sir Robert Whittingham, Sir Ralph Randolf, Robert Bellingham of Westmorland, Thomas Stanley, John Smothing, Robert Bolling, Robert Hatecale, Richard Everingham, Richard Cokerell (these last five from York), Roger Wharton from Westmorland and Rauf Chernok from Lancashire. Of all of these attainted, a significant number, including Bellingham, his brother, Randolf and Stanley had been implicated in the disturbances of the early 1450s – though Stanley had previously been of the Neville faction.[39]

A number of the border fortresses were to be significant in the conflict of 1461–4 but none more so than the three large castles of Alnwick, Bamburgh and Dunstanburgh. Of these the first was a hold of the Percys and much improved by them over several generations.[40] The site enclosed an area of some seven acres, in plan something of an elongated triangle with a large shell keep on the levelled motte, separating the east and west baileys. The Percy castellans had, over time, added a range of seven semi-circular towers, studding the old keep and also adding a further rash of towers to the main curtain. The enceinte was latterly strengthened by the addition of a substantial gatehouse and barbican. The fortifications which confronted the Yorkist besiegers in the mid-fifteenth century had stood thus for over a century, a constant bastion against the Scots.[41]

Bamburgh occupies a spur of the whin sill rising 150 feet from the coastal plain, even bigger than Alnwick, encompassing a site of eight acres or so along a narrow ridge running east to west. A strongpoint since the iron age, the fortress enclosed three baileys, east, west and the inner ward, with a massive twelfth-century keep located between the east and inner baileys. At this time there were fortified gateways at both the eastern and western extremities.[42]

Begun by Thomas, Earl of Lancaster, Dunstanburgh also commands a dolerite outcrop. The castle was much rebuilt by John of Gaunt whilst warden of the marches during the 1380s. On the north the cliff falls sheer so no man-made defences were needed; nature also provided strength to the north and west so that substantive works were only required on the southern flank. The inner ward dates from John of Gaunt's time as does the 80-feet high gatehouse keep which originally was also provided with an outwork or barbican. The weakness of this arrangement was apparent to the original builders, who then devised a more ingenious covered entrance to the west. An attacker, even if he took the gatehouse, would be obliged to turn through 90 degrees to attack the bailey.[43]

After receiving the doleful tidings of defeat Queen Margaret fled northward into Scotland, accompanied by her beleaguered husband and young son, Edward of Lancaster. The lords who had survived the carnage on the field and Bloody Meadow, Somerset, Exeter, Roos and Sir John Fortescue, soon joined her.

There is a general perception that the northern shire of England was solidly Lancastrian in sentiment, following the lead of the powerful Percy dynasty, who '. . . have the hearts of the north and always have had'.[44] The rivalry between the Percys and the Nevilles has already been discussed, and though the power of the latter prevented the former from enjoying a hegemony in the north, the power and prestiges of the Percy name remained largely unchallenged in Northumberland. At the turn of the fourteenth century the family held no lands in the county; by the end they were preeminent.

On 22nd April, some three weeks after Towton, King Edward progressed northward to Newcastle and it was there, on 1st May, he watched the execution of Sir James Butler, the fugitive Earl of Wiltshire, whose happy knack of slipping out of tight spots had finally failed him. With him was John Neville, Lord Montagu who had previously been held captive in York. He had apparently been spared the fate of the other Yorkist lords taken at Wakefield, when he had himself been captured at 2nd St Albans, as his brother Warwick had Somerset's brother Edmund prisoner at Calais. Having thus set his seal on the north Edward hurried south, content to leave matters in the north in the capable hands of the Nevilles.

Bates casts an interesting light on the activities of the defeated Lancastrian court; he contends that Margaret was unable to flee directly to Scotland as she needed an official safe conduct to cross the troubled border. Bates asserts, clearly incorrectly, that she was besieged at Newcastle by Yorkist forces under the king's command. Slipping through the net he next has her fleeing to Wark where she was again trapped by a Yorkist detachment under Sir John Conyers and Lord Ogyll, the former destined for notoriety in his guise as 'Robin of Redesdale'. A scratch force of loyal Lancastrian gentry rallies to the queen's cause and raises the siege, allowing the fugitives to slip across the border unmolested.[45]

With the death of James II of Scotland before the walls of Roxburgh on 3rd August 1460, his heir, now James III, was only eight, and the land was ruled by a regency council which quickly divided into two factions, the 'old' lords led by Bishop Kennedy of St Andrews, and the 'young' who supported Mary of Guelders. Queen Margaret, for her part, was desperate for allies and was prepared to squander the hard-won strength of the borderland in the bidding. On 25th April, Berwick, the key to the eastern marches, was surrendered and she was also willing to trade Carlisle in the west. The Cumbrians proved unwilling to accept the queen's summons and grimly barred their gates.

A Scots–Lancastrian force was dispatched to leaguer the city and the Yorkists perceived the threat sufficiently potent for Edward to bring the date of his coronation forward to 28th June in order that he might be free to march north. In the event this did not become necessary as the resourceful Montagu, mustering local forces, soon dispersed the besiegers. Margaret demonstrated a real lack of understanding of her Northumbrian subjects and adherents when she ceded Berwick; by the time the city was finally retaken by Richard of Gloucester in 1482 it had changed hands no less than fourteen times, and a vast outlay in blood and treasure expended to maintain its position as an outpost of England.[46]

There were further alarums. The French were said to be about to descend on the Channel Islands led by Margaret of Anjou's indefatigable champion, Pierre de Breze. With the death, on 22nd July, of Charles VII, the likelihood of French interference diminished. The new sovereign had little time for his dead father's paladin and de Breze was stripped of his offices and disgraced. In England the spark of rebellion flared briefly in East Anglia and, more seriously, in Wales, where the Lancastrians continued to hold several key castles. By the autumn the Welsh rebels were defeated in the field and their strongholds systematically reduced. By the end of the year only Harlech was still holding out.

Pierre de Breze remains one of the most quixotic figures of the age, never faltering in his support for Queen Margaret. He had earlier commanded a French fleet sent against Warwick in the Channel. Despite the shabby treatment he received from Louis XI he remained loyal, dying gloriously on the field on Montlhery.[47]

Warwick had an equally loyal Burgundian ally in the Seigneur de la Barde who, after having fallen under the spell of the earl's powerful charisma, led a commanded party of handgunners, sent by his master, Duke Philip, to bolster the Yorkist ranks after the disaster at Wakefield.[48]

In the north the Lancastrians tried briefly once again, raiding as far south as Brancepeth near Durham led by Lords Dacre, Roos and Richemont Gray, with poor King Henry trailing along. If their lordships had hoped that the sight of the royal personage might inspire the local populace to rise in his favour, then they were swiftly dissillusioned. True to his new allegiance the Prince Bishop, Lawrence Booth, hitherto a staunch Lancastrian but won over by the young king's easy charm, mustered the county levies and swiftly saw the invaders off. 'The problem here [the north] was a complicated one, Henry VI and his supporters were sheltered and aided by the Scots, and, to a lesser extent, by the French. The region itself was remote, difficult of access, and dominated by the great fortresses.'[49]

In July Warwick was made warden of both east and west marches, ably assisted by his brother Montagu, and the Nevilles jointly continued mopping up operations until September, when Alnwick Castle surrendered and was garrisoned by 100 of the warden's men-at-arms. Early in October Dunstanburgh also capitulated, the surrender terms negotiated by the castellan, Sir Ralph Percy. It might have seemed that the Yorkist triumph was complete, but as long as the Lancastrians had a base in Scotland, the border was unlikely to remain tranquil.

Edward, motivated by the commendable, but not infrequently misplaced, ideal of reconciliation had been prepared to overlook Ralph Percy's previously staunch affiliation and had permitted him to remain as captain of Dunstanburgh, an error of judgement which bore bitter fruit when he opened the gates to his former comrades. Sir William Tailboys, leading a Lancastrian raid from over the border, easily retook Alnwick. At the same time, Lord Dacre, sweeping into the west march, captured Naworth.[50]

Both Edward and Warwick perceived that diplomatic overtures to the Scots, aimed at depriving the Lancastrians of their foothold in the northern kingdom, was the only certain means of establishing firm control of the English marches. Warwick held preliminary talks with Mary of Guelders in April 1462, followed by a further meeting in July, but the Scottish council, already divided, seemed determined to sit on the fence and wait upon events. In March the Lancastrian envoys Somerset and Lord Hungerford returned from an abortive mission to the French court. Undeterred and as resolute as ever, Queen Margaret borrowed £290 from the regent, Marie of Gueldres, and in April sailed from Kirkcudbright to France. In her desperation she was prepared to trade Calais as she had Berwick.[51]

Whilst Warwick sought an accommodation with Mary his forces in Northumberland went on to the offensive. By July Montagu had accepted Dacre's surrender and regained Naworth, a vital bastion of the west. In the east Tailboys handed the keys of Alnwick to the Yorkist triumvirate of Lord Hastings, Sir John Howard, and Sir Ralph Grey. Bamburgh fell to Sir William Tunstall. There is some mention of military operations, possibly a further attempt at a leaguer at Carlisle, though, more likely, no more than raid and counterraid, the habitual pattern of strife on the border.

'... The support and sympathy of the local population worked against what was regarded as a hostile government and enabled even small forces of active rebels to defy it for months on end.'[52]

Worcester is, in fact, the only chronicler who details the surrender of Alnwick. An entry in the Paston letters (the contemporary correspondence of the family of Sir John Paston of Norfolk) places Lord Hastings at Carlisle with Warwick in July, though this would not in any way have prevented him from accepting the surrender of Alnwick. Equally there is no reason to doubt Tailboys as castellan: he remained a staunch Lancastrian until greed intervened as he subsequently embezzled funds placed under his control.[53]

The Paston letters also place Sir William Tunstall at Bamburgh in the autumn of 1462. His brother, Sir Richard, belonged to the opposite camp and had been at the castle in the summer. The fall of these great border holds and the lack of any real material support from either France or Scotland would appear to have sounded the death knell for King Henry's faltering cause, but Queen Margaret was to prove, not for the first time, that she was a force to be reckoned with.

On 25th October she made landfall, possibly, as Worcester asserts, at Bamburgh; the expedition was led by the faithful de Breze and comprised some two thousand French men-at-arms. The invaders promptly marched on Alnwick, which, being poorly supplied, surrendered without a fight. Hungerford and the younger de Breze were left to command. Bamburgh, which capitulated soon after, was entrusted to Somerset. In a neat reversal of fortune the Yorkist Sir William Tunstall was taken by his Lancastrian brother, Sir Richard. Dunstanburgh also changed hands again. Despite these notable successes few local adherents rushed to join the queen's banner – it remains uncertain, as no private papers have survived, whether her objectives were to foment a popular rising in Northumberland or merely to establish a viable bridgehead for a larger Franco-Scots invasion.[54]

What is certain is that, having captured and garrisoned the three key bastions, she, with the bulk of her expeditionary forces, immediately took ship, presumably intending to make for Scotland. At this point, however, the forces of nature intervened and a vicious storm arose; some ships were lost, and though the queen and de Breze succeeded in making landfall in Scotland, much of her cash and valuables had to be jettisoned. Of these fresh French troops some 400 disembarked at Bamburgh, presumably in the hope of joining the garrison, but, baulked by the Yorkist presence, they withdrew, apparently in good order, after firing their ships, to Holy Island. Here the invaders scattered the few defenders but were soon assailed by a determined force under the Bastard of Ogyll and 'one Maners, a squire'. Under pressure the French sought refuge in the priory from where the survivors swiftly sought terms.[55]

Though clearly taken by surprise at Queen Margaret's return, Warwick, showing his customary energy, marched north on 30th October, followed by the king on 3rd November. By the 16th the royal division had entered Durham, where Edward succumbed to a debilitating bout of measles which kept him immured for the rest of the year.[56]

Meanwhile, the earl assumed control of the siege operations which he personally directed from Warkworth, leaving the Duke of Norfolk in command of the army's main supply base at Newcastle. Day-to-day responsibility for the leaguer of Alnwick was vested in the Earl of Kent and Lord Sealys, the Earl of Worcester and Sir Ralph Grey lay before the walls of Dunstanburgh whilst Lords Montagu and Ogyll were stationed at Bamburgh. Warwick rode around the siege lines every day and the forces which he was said to command vastly outnumbered the beleaguered defenders who, at Bamburgh, were led by Somerset and the turncoat Sir Ralph Percy and, behind the walls of Dunstanburgh, by Sir Richard Tunstall and Thomas Fyndern. John Paston records that William Hasildene, Matilda Walsh and John Carter acted as purveyors for the besiegers of Bamburgh and the king's own pavilions were erected by William Hill, a servant of the Master of the Tents. He goes on to suggest that Warwick commanded a force of some 10,000, whilst Somerset could barely muster 300 defenders.[57]

Thorough as these siege preparations had been it would appear that the mere show of strength was sufficient to overawe the defenders; there was no bombardment, the ordnance, including both siege and field pieces, remained stockpiled with Norfolk in Newcastle. The lighter guns were intended for use in the field against the Scots should they seek to intervene or mount a relief, but there was an expressed reluctance to use the heavier pieces against the walls of the Northumbrian fortresses.

The Yorkists did not wish to be responsible for slighting any of the border holds, whose prime function, beyond mere internecine strife was, and would remain, to resist the Scots. Besides, there was little pleasure to be had from campaigning through a Northumbrian winter, '. . . Tough, hardy and used to discomfort as they were, medieval soldiers had a deep distaste for winter campaigning . . . Henry V had forced his armies to maintain winter sieges in northern France, but no one had yet attempted them in the even bleaker conditions of Northumbria in December'.[58]

On Christmas Eve the Lancastrian lords negotiated the surrender of both Bamburgh and Dunstanburgh. The terms were scarcely unfavourable. For the abandonment of their allegiance to Henry VI both Somerset and Percy were to be restored to their titles and estates. For their part both swore fealty to Edward IV. Given that no escalade had been attempted and that neither garrison was yet suffering any great privation, no naval blockade having been enforced, these defections appear difficult to reconcile. It may be that Somerset was jealous of the overall command entrusted to de Breze or that both he and Percy had despaired of relief. King Edward seemed perfectly willing to accept the integrity of his new subjects, despite Somerset's pivotal role in the Lancastrian war effort, his slaughter of the king's father, brother, uncle and cousin, and despite Sir Ralph Percy's fickle allegiance.[59]

In the meantime the garrison at Alnwick remained defiant, they had cause for comfort for valiant de Breze was on the march with a predominantly Scots relieving force. Warwick appears to have been seized with that fatal indecision which sometimes beset him in moments of crisis, and recoiled. The mere speed of his withdrawal led to an equal consternation amongst the Scots who swiftly came to suspect that they were to be drawn into a trap. As a consequence the campaign swiftly degenerated into a near farce, the invaders, with the bulk of the defenders, slunk back to Scotland without a blow being struck and the Yorkists resumed their abandoned lines.[60]

The depleted garrison wasted little time in coming to terms and Warwick appointed Sir John Astley to command, with Sir Ralph Grey as his deputy, an office bitterly resented by the latter who felt the senior post should have been his – a disappointment that was to bear bitter fruit.[61]

The position at the end of 1462 appeared to have reverted to the Yorkist supremacy seen in the summer, but Edward and Warwick's grip was flimsier than the tactical position would suggest. Percy remained a Lancastrian at heart and Grey continued to smart over his lack of preferment. In the spring of the following year Sir Ralph opened the gates of Bamburgh and Grey handed over not only the keys of Alnwick but also the person of his despised rival '. . . And within three or four months after that false knight and traitor, Sir Ralph Grey, by false treason took the said Sir John Astley, prisoner, and delivered him to Queen Margaret, and then delivered the castle to the Lord Hungerford and unto the Frenchmen accompanied with him.'[62] Having recovered their foothold in Northumberland and for so little effort the Lancastrians laid siege to the great border fortress of Norham, a hold of the Prince Bishop and a great prize for their Scots allies whose many previous attempts hand met with rebuff.

Undoubtedly frustrated by the loss of Alnwick, Bamburgh and Dunstanburgh, which Sir Ralph Percy had also gifted, Warwick moved swiftly to raise the siege of Norham, scattering Queen Margaret and her borderers in a lightning descent. So swift and so decisive was the Yorkist riposte that both the queen and hapless King Henry were nearly taken. The Lancastrian forces garrisoning the castles remained supine though they could clearly have harassed Warwick's supply lines. In spite of this success the Yorkists made no attempt to recover their earlier losses, preferring to resume the diplomatic rather than the military offensive. Enthusiasm for the Lancastrian cause was clearly waning in Scotland. Berwick, that jewel of border fastnesses, had been recovered but the Scots had been repulsed, with almost contemptuous ease, from the stout walls of Carlisle and now Norham. Henry VI, perhaps sensing the mood, transferred his truncated household to either Bamburgh or Alnwick.[63]

Edward had obtained a grant of tax monies from Parliament, to be expended on raising forces for a campaign against the Scots, but no attack was ever launched. The Nevilles, supported by the Archbishop of York, had capitalised on their earlier success with a sweeping raid north of the border, carrying fire and sword into the Lothians.

Bates places Queen Margaret, her son and de Breze in the environs of Hexham and has the Lancastrian forces advancing from the direction of the town to attack 'Rel' or Ryal on the banks of the Devil's Water on 3rd April 1463. On being confronted by Montagu's Yorkists the mainly Franco-Scots force scatters and the queen is taken but seizes the chance to escape when her captors begin quarrelling over the spoils. With only the young prince and a single esquire she flees into Dipton Wood, losing her sole protector. Confronted by a local outlaw, intent upon robbery or worse, she so overawes the wretch with her regal presence and cool courage that he gives her and Prince Edward sanctuary in his cave. So intense was the rapport that she felt able to leave the boy in the reformed outlaw's care whilst she sought out her consort to the north.[64]

The cave has been subsequently identified as that below the crags on the left bank of the West Dipton Burn, some three miles south of Linnels Bridge, now called the Queen's Cave. It is not possible to ascertain how it came to be known as such, though the whole tale smacks of nineteenth-century romanticism.[65]

Tempting as it may be to conjecture a skirmish in 1463, none of the chronicles corroborates; we know that Margaret and de Breze were present at the siege of Norham and that their forces were surprised and scattered by Montagu, though Bates mentions this as a separate instance. The queen with King Henry and the Prince were obliged to shelter in a cave for five days with 'only a single herring between them'. Clearly the facts of the two incidents appear remarkably similar and it therefore seems likely that, if such dramatic events did occur, then the location was Norham and not Dipton. As neither the queen nor de Breze was present at the battle the following year the story cannot date from then.[66]

After the débâcle at Norham, and having satisfied herself as to the viability of Bamburgh's defences, Queen Margaret with Edward of Lancaster and the faithful de Breze took ship for Flanders to throw herself on the mercy of Philip of Burgundy, a paragon of chivalry, and his son, the Count of Charolais, better remembered as Charles the Bold, as mercurial as his father was prudent, and, for the moment at least, no friend to the house of York. Touched by the queen's plight and moved by her considerable presence, the Burgundians made amicable noises. The Count of Charolais wrote letters of encouragement to Henry at Bamburgh, conveyed by one John Brown and a servant of Exeter called William Baker. No practical assistance, however, was forthcoming.

Gregory[67] recounts that the Lancastrians sailed immediately for Sluys and that Warwick pursued her almost to the gates of Bamburgh. With her as she sailed on 30th July were Exeter, Fortescue and the surviving Frenchmen. The party filled four 'balynggarys' (or ballingers, large double-ended, oared vessels, often deployed against pirates in the Channel). Gregory further relates that a French drummer refused the evacuation and awaited Warwick's arrival, whereupon he demanded, vociferously, to be allowed to enter the earl's service. Doubtless impressed by a fellow adventurer he granted the request and the renegade remained in his household for a number of years.[68]

Unmolested by Warwick or Montagu, King Henry maintained the façade of dominion over his shrunken domain. In December 1463 he issued letters of protection to William Burgh, constable of Prudhoe, seeking to consolidate his party's grip on Tynedale. Early in the new year he granted a charter to the burgesses of Edinburgh. The French ambassador to the court at Bamburgh was a Pierre Cousinot who Henry entreated to carry confirmation of his wishes to Queen Margaret. These comprised, *inter alia*, a tripartite alliance between Henry, the Count of Charolais and the mettlesome Duke of Brittany; a plea to friends amongst the great lords of France that they would strive to distance Louis from Edward IV; a further plea to the Burgundians to send ordnance and provisions; a request to Margaret's father for more guns and for gunners to serve them; an instruction to the queen to canvass the Duke of Brittany, aided by Cousinot, to provide logistical support for a diversion in Wales to be led by the Earl of Pembroke; and lastly, a request for funds, always in short supply.[69]

Shortage of cash was a constant threat to the Lancastrians, deprived of Parliamentary grants and the revenues from attainted estates. There was little scope for aggressive action, even if King Henry had the ability or the inclination, and the year ended in an uneasy stalemate.

Notes

1 Griffiths, R.A., 'Local Rivalries and National Politics: The Percies, the Nevilles and the Duke of Exeter, 1452–1455' *Speculum* Vol. XLIII 1968 p. 589.
2 Pollard, A., 'Percies, Nevilles and the Wars of the Roses' *History Today* Sept. 1992 p. 42.
3 James, M.E., *The Murder at Cocklodge on 28th April, 1489* Durham University Journal LVII 1965 p. 80.
4 Weiss, H., 'A Power in the North? The Percies in the Fifteenth Century' *The Historical Journal* 19.2 1965 pp. 501–509.
5 Pollard *History Today* p. 42.
6 Ross, C., *The Wars of the Roses* London 1976 p. 31.
7 Weiss *Historical Journal* p. 503.
8 Ibid p. 504.
9 Ross p. 31.
10 Griffiths *Speculum* p. 589.
11 Ibid p. 590.

12 Ibid p. 591.

13 Ibid p. 593.

14 Ibid p. 591.

15 Ibid p. 592.

16 Ibid p. 591.

17 Ibid p. 592.

18 Ibid p. 594.

19 Ibid p. 594.

20 Ibid p. 595.

21 Ibid p. 595.

22 Ibid pp. 598–9.

23 Ibid 602.

24 Ibid p. 603.

25 Ibid p. 604.

26 Ross p. 28.

27 Ibid pp. 38–9.

28 Wise, T., *The Wars of the Roses*, London 1983 p. 29.

29 Griffiths *Speculum* p. 609.

30 Ibid p. 610.

31 Ibid p. 620.

32 Ibid p. 622.

33 Ibid p. 626.

34 Ross p. 47.

35 Goodman, A., *The Wars of the Roses*, London 1981 p. 41.

36 Ross pp. 33–4.

37 Gillingham, J., *The Wars of the Roses*, London 1975 p. 119.

38 De Commynes, P., *Memoirs for the Reign of Louis XI 1461–1463*, transl. M. Jones 1972 p. 187.

39 Rot. Parl. 1st Edward IV 1461 Vol. v fo. 477–8.

40 Pevsner, N. and I., Richmond, *The Buildings of England: Northumberland*, 2nd ed. London 1992 pp. 135–6.

41 Long, B., *Castles of Northumberland*, Newcastle upon Tyne 1967 p. 67.

42 Pevsner and Richmond pp. 155–6.

43 Ibid pp. 258–9.

44 Charlesworth, D., 'Northumberland in the early Years of Edward IV' in *Archaeologia Acliana* 4th Series 1953 p. 70.

45 Bates, C.J., *History of Northumberland*, London 1895 p. 195.

46 Lomas, *Northumberland – County of Conflict*, East Linton 1996 pp. 45–50.

47 Kendall, R.M., *Warwick the Kingmaker*, New York 1957 p. 86.

48 Ibid pp. 202–3.

49 Ross p. 56.

50 Gillingham pp. 140–1.

51 Scottish Exchequer Rolls, vii, Ramsay ii p. 290.

52 Gillingham p. 141.

53 Ross p. 60.

54 William of Worcester 'Annales Rerum Anglicarum' in *Liber Niger Scaccarii* (Ed.) J. Hearne 2 vols. Oxford, 1728 p. 470.

55 Ibid p. 480.

56 *Northumberland County History* Vol. I p. 44.

57 Worcester p. 480.

58 Ross pp. 62–3.

59 William Gregory's 'Chronicle of London' in *Historical Collections of a Citizen of London in the Fifteenth Century* (Ed.) J. Gairdner Camden Soc. New Series, XVII 1876, p. 219.

60 Ibid p. 219.

61 Ibid p. 220.

62 Ibid p. 221.

63 'The Year Book de Termino Paschae 4 Edward IV' in Priory of Hexham Surtees Society I 1864 p. cviii gives Alnwick as the location but Northumberland County History Vol. I p. 46 gives Bamburgh.

64 Bates pp. 198–9 gives Chastellain as his authority as he states that he heard the account from the queen herself though his version is somewhat circumstantial – Chastellain G., 'Chroniques des derniers Ducs de Bourgoyne' in *Pantheon Litteraire* iv pp. 230–2.

65 Tomlinson, W.W., *Comprehensive Guide to Northumberland*, Newcastle upon Tyne 1863 pp. 112–13.

66 Bates p. 199.

67 Gregory p. 222.

68 Ibid p. 222.

69 *Northumberland County History* Vol. I p. 46.

Chapter 14

Hedgeley Moor and Hexham

Henry Beaufort, Duke of Somerset, his brother-in-law Sir Henry Lewis and Sir Nicholas Latimer had all been attainted in 1461 and all three were amongst the prisoners when Dunstanburgh surrendered on 27th December 1462. In the circumstances they were, together with Sir Ralph Percy, treated with extreme leniency; their submissions secured a pardon and the return of their confiscated estates. Percy was confirmed as castellan of both Dunstanburgh and Bamburgh and on 17th March the following year received a commission to take the submission of other rebels.

Somerset fared even better; he fought with some apparent distinction against his former comrades immured in Alnwick and was fêted by King Edward. He hunted with his former mortal enemy, even acted as a knight of the bedchamber, nor was he denied compensation: cash grants were made and an annuity of 1,000 marks per annum was confirmed and honoured. Tournaments were held in his honour and Edward intervened to save him from what amounted to a lynch mob in Northampton.[1]

Why then did Somerset defect and resume his former allegiance?

He could, presumably, have accepted a safe conduct and withdrawn north of the border as other members of the Dunstanburgh garrison did. There is a suggestion that he'd made overtures to Warwick earlier in 1462. On 10th March 1463, his attainder was reversed yet, by 1st December he, like Sir Ralph Percy, had returned to Lancastrian colours.

Hicks asserts that this betrayal was not a refusal to accept what any intelligent man would have inescapably seen as inevitable but a triumph of conscience; quite simply, the commitment to the House of Lancaster, however hopeless the cause, ran too deep.[2] He was not alone: both Latimer and Lewis later rebelled in 1469–71; Sir Henry Bellingham and Sir Humphrey Neville also turned. Ross regards Edward's policy of clemency as naïve and culpable, a political blunder.[3]

This may be too harsh. Edward had won the crown by the sword, his following amongst the peerage was limited, and to survive he desperately needed to broaden the base of his support. To achieve this he had to win over former Lancastrians; killing was not, as recent history had proved, an effective remedy. The blood spilt at St Albans in 1455 had left a legacy of hate that had led to the carnage at Towton. Edward clearly judged that suborning his former enemies not only bought new friends but demoralised the remaining diehards and, by the end of 1462, he would have been justified in thinking that the embers of resistance were virtually stamped out.[4]

His contemporaries were equally censorious. Gregory, who was no friend to Somerset, observed that 'the savynge of hys lyffe at that tyme causyd mony mannys dethys son aftyr, as ye shalle heyre'.[5] Interestingly Hicks views Percy's defection as the more serious because of the power of his name in Northumberland, notwithstanding the fact that the king still held Somerset's brother and Percy's nephew as hostages.[6] We cannot ascertain exactly what motivated the turncoats, though conscience must have played a strong part for none can have been fooled by their chances of success; it may be they viewed their earlier submissions as no more than a necessary compromise with the *de facto* king, to buy time whilst they waited for an opportunity to revert to the service of their true king who, on any objective assessment was, at his best, but a pale shadow of the dynamic young Yorkist.[7]

Edward's policy of conciliation, a vital expedient, was at best a gamble and one which clearly failed, yet it was a gamble well worth the taking for had he been successful the embers of rebellion would have been truly expunged. As it was the Lancastrian cause in the north was to have one brief, final flowering.[8]

Early in 1464 sporadic unrest erupted throughout the kingdom, in fifteen counties from Kent to Cornwall and as far north as Leicestershire. The disruption was sufficiently serious for Edward to delay the state opening of Parliament. There is evidence in the chronicles that Somerset might have believed that King Henry had somehow raised fresh forces '. . . herynge y King

Henry was comynge into the lande with a newe strength . . .[9] Quite where these troops were coming from and how Henry proposed to pay them is not elaborated upon, but perhaps Somerset was prepared to believe that the Scots or the French were ready, once again, to intervene.

He can have had few illusions as to his fate should he fail. The clemency which he had enjoyed was a rare gift, especially for one as tainted as he and was not likely to be offered again.

Frustrated by his failure at Newcastle which, of itself would have made a considerable prize, being the Yorkists' main supply depot for previous campaigns in the north, and now securely held for Edward by Lord Scrope and some of the king's household, Somerset temporarily disappears from view. He was obliged to flee his lodgings in Durham, clad only in his nightshirt, and Gregory says that several of his affinity were taken together with his 'caskette and hys harneys'. Others of his following deserted from the Newcastle garrison: those recaptured were summarily beheaded.[10]

There is also some doubt as to King Henry's exact whereabouts. The Year Book claims he was at Alnwick, though this may not be entirely reliable for the same source places both Queen Margaret and de Breze with him when they were both unquestionably in Flanders.[11] The County History still locates the diminuitive court at Bamburgh, and it would appear much more likely that the Lancastrians should now be based in the north, given that Scottish support had cooled since the débâcle at Norham and the recapture, by Warwick, of the key bastion of Berwick.[12]

Somerset may have gone directly to his king or, quite possibly, he may have made for Tynedale, where a crop of castles, particularly Prudhoe, Hexham, Bywell and Langley remained loyal. At some stage, either in February or March, he was joined by his former comrades-in-arms, Sir Humphrey Neville of Brancepeth and Sir Ralph Percy, both with bodies of troops. With the duke now in command of the Lancastrian war effort a new dynamism is felt; the uneasy stalemate of the preceding autumn is galvanised by action. Somerset had need of haste: he must have been aware that the passage of time was increasingly detrimental to King Henry's flagging cause, deprived of aid from over the border and across the Channel.

The Scots were now keen to treat with the Yorkists and Montagu had been detailed to march north and ensure safe passage to York for the Scots' commissioners. These talks were initially scheduled to take place at Newcastle, commencing on 6th March, but the upsurge in Lancastrian aggression caused the start to be delayed until 20th April and the venue moved southward to less volatile ground. On 27th March Edward, announced his intention to come north and to arrange a suitable escort for the Scots' delegation waiting at Norham.[13]

The success of any such negotiations would be fatal to Lancastrian hopes, so Somerset was placed in a position where he was bound to take the field with all the forces that he could muster and chance all to frustrate the prospect of talks. Consequently he dispatched a commanded party of foot, 'four score spears and bows too',[14] under Humphrey Neville to attempt an ambush '. . . a little from Newcastle in a wood'.[15] Forewarned by scouts or spies, Montagu easily avoided the trap and chose a safer route to the city where he was reinforced by 'a great fellowship'.[16] Thus bolstered, he marched north, heading for Norham.

Somerset's only hope now rested upon a decisive encounter. Like a gambler determined to stake all on a single throw, by mustering every man he could command and stripping the garrison from Alnwick, he may have brought his strength up, as Gregory asserts, to 5,000 in all.[17] Even this seems a high figure notwithstanding the retainers of the Lancastrian lords, Hungerford and Roos, Percy, Bellingham and the turncoat Grey. Montagu's numbers are equally uncertain but it is likely that his army was the larger.

As the Yorkists marched north from Morpeth, the Lancastrians moved south. Both contingents were doubtless aware of each other's movements, both would be certain to employ the light border horse or 'prickers' as scouts, and such business was second nature to a local populace bred and hardened to war. Some nine miles north-west of Alnwick Montagu found Somerset drawn up in battle order blocking the road north.

The chronicles provide only scanty details of the battle which ensued but a careful examination of the ground, which is largely undisturbed save for the spread of cultivation, would indicate that the fight must have occurred on the higher ground, just north of where Percy's Cross now stands between Percy's Strip Wood and the site of 'Percy's Leap'. The ground is roughly level, slightly undulating, and rises towards the north. It is likely that the Yorkists first drew up where the wood now stretches; at this time the land was not under the plough but was an expanse of open moor.

Both sides would wish to secure any advantage which the ground offers and the Yorkists coming from the south would have had no opportunity to view the strength of their enemy until they had ascended the slight rise which swells from the location of the present memorial. The Lancastrians would not wish to have deployed to the south of the position suggested as this would have thrown away the advantage the contours of the field conferred.

Haigh[18] shows the Yorkists somewhat south of this position and indicates that the Lancastrians advanced to contact over the open ground. I think this unlikely: Yorkist morale was clearly the higher and Montagu is likely to have enjoyed superior strength. Besides, he was by nature an aggressive and confident commander. Frustratingly, the chronicles are silent on the details of the encounter and the initial deployment, and even the numbers involved cannot be estimated with any degree of confidence.[19] Somerset, though undeniably energetic, was prone to indecisiveness in moments of stress, a telling example being his failure to come to Lord Clifford's aid in the heat of the skirmish at Dintingdale, prior to the main battle at Towton.[20]

Almost certainly the fight began with the customary archery duel and Yorkist superiority was swiftly asserted. Before even striking a blow the whole of the Lancastrian left or rearward battle, commanded by Hungerford and Roos, dissolved in total rout, leaving the centre under Somerset, Bellingham and Grey, together with the right or vaward under Percy, horribly exposed. Morale was everything in medieval warfare and the Lancastrians showed a clear lack. Somerset had, after all, acted the turncoat before: the rank and file could be excused from thinking that he might do so again whilst they shed their blood in a hopeless cause.

Pausing only to bunch his files or columns into tighter order to conform to the enemy's shrunken line Montagu presumably led his men forward at the charge.[21]

The mêlée therefore probably took place in the vicinity of Percy's Leap, a short, savage and largely one-sided encounter. Somerset's centre, unnerved by the flight of their comrades, were not long in following, and if Somerset and his officers attempted a rally they were markedly unsuccessful. Percy, by now virtually surrounded, was left to bear the brunt. Though Sir Ralph appears to have fought valiantly, the outcome was never in doubt and he sustained his death wound attempting to break out of the ring.

An enigmatic legend lingers over his last moments. As his horse stumbled the twelve yards between the two outcrops he is said to have uttered: 'I have saved the bird in my bosom'. Quite what is meant by this is unclear

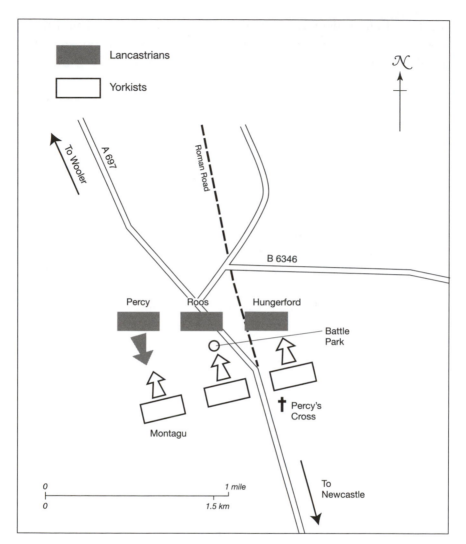

Hedgeley Moor, 1464

but it is taken to imply that he had remained true to his allegiance; quite which fealty cannot be entirely certain as he had changed sides on three occasions, though it may be presumed that he referred to his original loyalty to King Henry.

The Yorkist victory was complete, and though the chronicles give no note of casualties, cheaply bought. All of the Lancastrian officers, apart from Percy, and most of the rank and file escaped the field. Exactly how many fell cannot be ascertained; no grave pits have been excavated, but it is unlikely that the dead exceeded a few hundred on both sides.

Numbers may have been a factor but morale appears to be the dominant root of Yorkist superiority. Somerset was desperate and his men would know it. He had broken his oath to Edward as had Percy and Grey. Neither Hungerford nor Roos could be classed as fanatics; their conduct on the coming field at Hexham was to mirror that of Hedgeley, though neither would be so fortunate in their escape.

After the débâcle at Hedgeley Somerset appears to have withdrawn, in fairly good order, towards Tynedale. Montagu, burdened with the need to escort the Scots negotiators, was unable to mount a sustained pursuit. The surviving Lancastrian garrisons, no doubt much depleted, were left, for the moment, unmolested. The death of Percy was clearly a major blow and with the loss of so prominent a Northumbrian lord and, presumably, most, if not all of his affinity, King Henry's tenuous grip slipped further. Alnwick, Bamburgh and Dunstanburgh were not just important border fortresses: they constituted a viable bridgehead for friendly forces invading either south over the border or from across the Channel.[22]

With the Scots now in talks with the Yorkists, Somerset's desperate bid quashed and with the French also in negotiations at St Omer (since the preceding autumn), the Lancastrians were fast running out of allies. If Northumberland was no longer relevant as a bridgehead then Somerset had neither the men nor the materiel to sustain a campaign aimed simply at holding ground. For him to recognise this and retreat to a region which may have offered a further core of support made eminently good sense. Moreover, with the Scots swapping their sympathies, bargaining chips such as Berwick, or Norham, ceased to matter.[23]

Henry's prospects appeared brighter in the west for in March there were disturbances in Lancashire and in Chesire resistance flared brightly in Skipton in Craven, the seat of the Cliffords who'd shed much blood, including their own, in the cause of Lancaster.[24] None of these localised outbursts developed into a serious rising,[25] but the king clearly did not feel secure in the north and west. Though commissions of array were issued in Yorkshire and through the Midlands, no writs were sent to Northumberland, Cumberland, Westmorland, or, not unsurprisingly, to Lancashire or Cheshire.[26]

Shortage of money was a problem for both sides. Edward had received subsidies granted by Parliament from which to finance the war in the north, but the Lancastrian garrisons remained untroubled and, beyond the Nevilles' chevauchee after the relief of Norham, nothing of significance had been attempted against the Scots. In fact most of the money which had been wrung from Parliament together with a further grant from convocation had been swallowed up by existing commitments, most particularly the cost of maintaining the Calais garrison.[27]

For the first two years and more of his reign Edward had survived on loans and his indebtedness was now considerable. The need to raise taxes inevitably bred resentment, especially amongst the clergy. Armies and the fleet were hugely expensive and so far the taxpayers felt they had little to show for their contributions. The disaffection became so widespread and so vociferous that the king felt obliged to make a gesture of appeasement, and in November 1463 he remitted some £6,000 of the subsidy granted in the summer.[28]

Somerset depended upon such cash as he could, from time to time, raise or borrow and even that could disappear through defalcation. When captured hiding in a coal pit after the final defeat at Hexham, Lord Tailboys was weighted down with pilfered cash. 'He hadde moch mony with hym, bothe golde and sylvyr, that shulde hav gon unto King Harry; and yf it had come to Harry, lat kynge of Ingelonde, hyt wolde have causyd moche sore sorowe, for he had ordynyd harneys and ordenance i-nowe, but the men wolde not go one fote with hym tylle they had mony'.[29]

Henry appears to have taken up lodgings at Bywell Castle towards the end of April; after the coming fight the Yorkists found evidence of a hurried departure, the late king's helmet or 'bycoket' (a coroneted cap), '. . . richely garnysshed wt ij crownys, and his folowers trapped wt blew velvet'.[30] There was some suggestion that the Lancastrian ranks may have been augmented by, as one contemporary chronicler described, 'a great power out of Scotlade'.[31] In all probability this was no more than rumour though it is quite possible that Liddesdale or Teviotdale mosstroopers were enticed by the scent of plunder.

Bywell itself was not a large hold and possessed little strategic value, being nothing more than a large barmkin, or defensible enceinte, and a substantial gatehouse keep. It had formerly been a fief of the Baliol family, a name by no means unheard of during the earlier border wars.[32] It must remain questionable as to how much hold over Tynedale and Hexham the Lancastrians retained. They clearly held Bywell, Hexham, possibly Prudhoe and perhaps Langley and Aydon, though these garrisons were almost certainly stripped of men to swell the ranks before Hexham. Both Tynedale and Hexham were administered as 'Liberties' or 'Regalities' – effectively franchises where the crown sub-contracted the business of local government to others. In practice this led to a fair degree of autonomy.[33]

The Liberty of Tynedale covered a wide swathe of territory, 200,000 acres in all, encompassing the valleys of the North and South Tyne, and the Allen. In the thirteenth century the area was administered by the Scots and, like Hexham, had borne the brunt of many a foray and chevauchee since. Though by far the smaller, in terms of size, about 80,000 acres, Hexham comprised a fertile tract north of the Tyne and part of the higher and rougher ground around Allendale.[34] There is no evidence at this time that the flagging cause enjoyed widespread support; whilst many may have felt some degree of residual affiliation this did not extend to risking life and property.

With so many northern lords killed in the wars so far – two earls of Northumberland, Lord Egremont, Sir Ralph Percy, Old Lord Clifford and his vengeful son, Lord Dacre, and others of lesser rank – it is little wonder if local support was thinning. Even during the heyday of Queen Margaret, in 1459–60, she had been obliged to offer licence to despoil in lieu of wages. Somerset's shrunken domain can hardly have held out such an incentive.[35]

There is no indication of how long King Henry stayed at Bywell. In all probability he moved to Hexham and then fled further west. Certainly he was gone from the area before the battle and stories of the Yorkists taking Bywell immediately after his precipitate flight are fanciful. Somerset would never have left the king so exposed, nor, for that matter, could Montagu have afforded to ignore so valuable a prize on his approach. The mere fact that he left Bywell unmolested indicates that there was no royal presence. The castle at Hexham was both larger and, being further west, more secure. It is likely that, in the fifteenth century, the enceinte comprised the Moot Hall and the Gaol, both of which survive virtually intact, linked by a curtain wall, which has not.[36]

Montagu, by the end of the first week in May, had returned from York to Newcastle, and being aware, through scouts and informers, of Lancastrian activity in Tynedale, resolved to take the offensive. On this occasion he would not be hamstrung by diplomatic responsibilities and could devote the whole of his formidable energies to a decisive outcome. Thus, 'on xiii of May, my lorde Mountague toke his jornaye towards Hexham from Newcastelle'.[37] Advancing with his host along the north bank of the Tyne there can be little doubt that Hexham was his immediate objective, nor can there be much doubt that Somerset was aware of his peril.

Later writers, such as Hall and Grafton, maintain that Henry was on the field, though this is not supported by the more contemporary authors; Gregory states that the king fled northward to Scotland, though it seems far more likely that he headed west into Lancashire.[38] By the time he had crossed the Tyne, at either Bywell or Corbridge, Montagu was but a few miles from Hexham and only the Devil's Water stood between him and the town.

The stream follows a meandering course from the high ground of the 'Shire' towards the Tyne, in winter tumbling, foaming, between deeply cut banks, somnolent in summer. From Hexham the ground falls markedly toward Linnels Bridge, some two miles from the town, then rises steeply past Linnels in the direction of Slaley. The traditional site for the battle of Hexham, challenged by Dorothy Charlesworth, lies to the south of the present B6306 on low ground by the banks of the stream, as shown on the Ordnance Survey 1:25,000 map. The Year Book, perhaps the best contemporary source, describes the field as 'un lieu appelle Livels sur le ewe Devyls'.[39]

Worcester says a hill one mile from Hexham[40] Ramsay, who had clearly visited the site, or talked to someone who had, observes, tellingly, that [the site] 'is a nice sheltered camping ground . . . but a very bad battlefield'.[41] The Year Book, which also gives the date of the battle as 15th May, merely points to Linnels as the general area. Worcester refers to a hill which naturally supposes rising ground. Dorothy Charlesworth observes that the low ground does not really command any of the likely crossing places.[42]

It appears obvious to anyone studying the ground that the traditional site is a very unwise choice as a battleground. To the rear it is hemmed in by the water and to the front by sharply rising banks that totally inhibit any manoeuvre and make a gift of the high ground to any attacker coming from the east. Many later writers tend to take the sixteenth-century chroniclers at face value. Writing in 1995 Haigh shows Somerset holding the centre, deployed with his back to the river, Grey and Neville holding the left, Hungerford and Roos on the right.

It has been suggested that Somerset felt the barrier of the water to their rear might stiffen his men's lukewarm resolve and/or that he was taken by surprise at the speed and suddeness of the Yorkists' attack.[43] Neither of these arguments appears sound: few men are likely to be encouraged by a commander who chooses so weak a position, and it is hardly credible that Montagu's advance was undetected, given that the Lancastrians knew the terrain and undoubtably deployed scouts of their own.

Dorothy Charlesworth argues that whilst Somerset did, in all probability, camp on the low ground by the river on the evening of 14th May, he did not fight there but rather drew up his forces on the higher ground along the crest of Swallowship Hill. Had he not done so then Montagu, she contends, had little need to fight at all; he could have funnelled his men over the Devil's Water by the ford below Swallowship Wood, thus completely outflanking the Lancastrians without striking a blow. Once again the chronicles are of little help. Though all mention the battle none gives clear details: even Gregory provides no clear insight into the action though he does give the fullest tally of those captured and subsequently executed.[44]

If, however, as Dorothy Charlesworth supposes, the defenders occupied Swallowship Hill, no such manoeuvre would have been feasible. The crest commands all of the viable crossings with the river circling the base of the hill. As the ground, on both elevations, drops quite sharply towards the Devil's Water, it would be possible for Somerset to prop up flagging morale by refusing both flanks and forcing the Yorkists to attack in the centre.

I now submit that Grey and Neville did hold the left and Hungerford and Roos the right, but that the line curved in an arc to follow the contour. Those on the left dominated the ford below them and also that which lay to the north by Earls Bridge; from the right it was possible to cover Linnels and the southern ford by Newbiggin. This is, of course, mostly supposition based upon a reading of the many accounts and a careful study of the ground. Nonetheless, on a balance of probabilities, Charlesworth's view must be considered correct. This leads us dangerously close to Colonel Burne's idea of 'inherent military probability' but in the absence of any hard evidence this approach becomes, to a degree, inevitable.

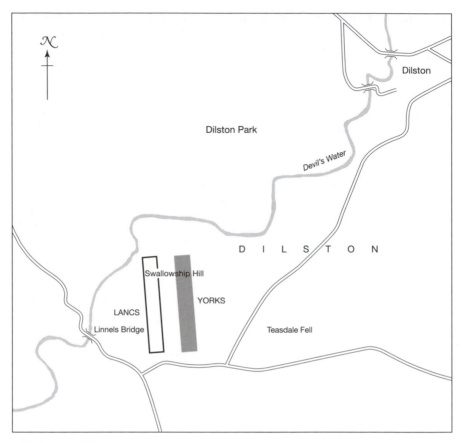

Hexham, 1464

It would be likely that Montagu also divided his forces into the traditional three 'battles' or divisions, he leading the centre, with the bulk of the shock troops. Though Montagu almost certainly had both more men and considerably higher morale, his divisional commanders were both former Lancastrians. Having seen first-hand, at second St Albans, how swiftly treachery can tip the balance, he cannot have felt entirely secure.

Lord Greystoke, who led on the left, had been on that very field of St Albans, under Queen Margaret's banner, whilst Lord Willoughby, on the right, had served with him. Neither had suffered the bloodbath at Towton, though Willoughby's father, Lord Welles, was among the many who failed to return. The son had submitted to Edward at Gloucester in September 1461, and had not wavered in his allegiance since.[45]

Whether the fight began with an archery contest, as was customary in battles of this period, is not recorded. What is certain is that any exchange of missiles was of brief duration, and that the Yorkists, led by Montagu in the centre, swiftly advanced to contact. The fighting was surely savage, but like Hedgeley Moor, superior Yorkist morale, undoubtably coupled with superior numbers, soon told. True to their past performance Hungerford and Roos were the first to give way, their broken ranks spilling down towards the river, choking the fords. More drowned than were cut down on the field. With his right gone Somerset struggled to alter his deployment but then his left dissolved in rout and his division crumbled around him. The battle was over, only the pursuit now remained.[46]

We have no note of casualties. Significantly, the chroniclers do not refer to any of rank being left upon the field: the noble blood which was shed was spilt by the headsman's axe in the rash of executions which followed. Doubtless there were dead piled on Swallowship Hill and more who drowned or were cut down as they sought to flee.

Worcester states that Montagu disposed ten thousand against Somerset's mere five hundred;[47] this cannot be right, as no general would give battle against such odds. Warkworth, on the other hand, says that the Lancastrian had 'gathered a great people in the north country'.[48] and that the Yorkists had no more than four thousand with which to oppose him. The position which Dorothy Charlesworth has the Lancastrians occupy spans a frontage of around a thousand yards. Allowing one yard for each fighting man and some space between divisions, a force of, say, four thousand would have been needed to give any weight to the deployment. It is unlikely that the Yorkists would have advanced with such confidence had their numbers not been at least equal to and, more likely, greater than, their enemy's.

Unlike the occasion of his earlier victory at Hedgeley, Montagu had no distractions and was able to harry the fleeing Lancastrians. Somerset was taken, along with Hungerford and Roos,[49] who were captured 'in a wood faste by'.[50] For Henry Beaufort, Duke of Somerset, there was to be no further clemency. Montagu, like his brother Warwick, did not share the king's concern for reconciliation; it was now time for retribution and the captive duke was dispatched the day after the battle in Hexham.[51] Hungerford and Roos were brought to Newcastle where they too faced the axe, 'behedid at Newcastle'.[52] Others, including Sir Philip Wentworth,

Sir Edmund Fitzhugh, John Bryce, Thomas Hunt and a border ruffian named 'Black Iaquys',[53] were also killed, either at Hexham or perhaps at Middleham, 'after some writers'.[54] At least one prisoner, Sir Thomas Husey, was executed at York.[55]

There could be no attempt to rally. The Lancastrian cause was ruined. With Somerset and most of the other rebel lords dead and King Henry skulking in the north-west, there was none left to lead. Humphrey Neville escaped the field, though, like Somerset, he had been attainted in 1461 and subsequently pardoned, therefore he could expect no mercy. Having previously succeeded in escaping from the Tower, he clearly had a flair for survival and, with Sir Ralph Grey, managed to rejoin the garrison at Bamburgh.[56]

Another who was less fortunate was the embezzling Lord Tailboys, whose stolen funds provided a welcome bonus for Montagu's weary following '. . . the sum was 3,000 merk. And the lord's meinie of Montagu were sore hurt and sick, and many of his men were slain before in the great journeys, but this money was departed among them, and was a very wholesome salve for them'. Tailboys' execution at Newcastle on 20th July marked the end of the killing.[57]

A mere fortnight after the battle, Montagu, before the king at York, and in the presence of his brothers, Warwick and George Neville, Bishop of Exeter, was created Earl of Northumberland, the high watermark of his house. Whilst at his northern capital Edward ratified the treaty with the Scots, concluded on 11th June and which secured peace for fifteen years.[58] Warwick had no desire to linger in the north but the king ordered him to remain and, jointly with the new Earl of Northumberland, recover the three key bastions of Alnwick, Dunstanburgh and Bamburgh, the only traces of Lancastrian resistance remaining.[59]

Before marching north King Edward had assembled his formidable siege train, 'the great ordnance of England',[60] the bombards 'Edward', 'Dijon', 'London', 'Newcastle' and 'Richard Bombartel'.[61] The relatively new science of gunnery had begun to outstrip the skill of the military engineer. Henry V had used his heavy guns to batter the walls of Harfleur in 1415, and the once formidable defences of Le Mans had been breached after a few days' bombardment.[62] It would appear that the term 'bombard' was applied to any large piece, there being, as yet, no standardisation of calibres.[63]

These monsters were fired from ground level, from behind a hinged timber shutter, rather like a larger version of the archers' mantlet and which provided some cover for the gunner and matrosses – whose calling was sufficiently hazardous even without the effects of enemy action. Most guns loaded at the breech, having a removable breech-block, shaped not unlike a beer mug. By the 1460s trunnions were coming into use and even the heaviest pieces were being furnished with serviceable if crude gun carriages. Elevation was achieved by the use of wedges.[64] One of the major difficulties facing any commander of the age seeking to avail himself of the power of artillery was that of transportation. The logistics of moving a siege train, especially over any distance and considering the generally appalling conditions of the northern roads, would constitute an administrative nightmare. Large teams of draught horses or oxen were needed, and a complement of pioneers would accompany the train, filling in the worst of the ruts and levelling gradients.[65]

The mere sight of the great guns appears to have fatally shaken any resolve the defenders of Alnwick may have retained after the débâcle at Hexham. On 23rd June the garrison surrendered on terms and Dunstanburgh capitulated the day after.[66] Bates, however, maintains that the latter fortress succumbed to an escalade and its captain, one John Gosse, of Somerset's household, was conveyed south to York and there executed 'with a hatchet'.[67] He goes on to assert that Dunstanburgh was the first castle to fall and that Warwick maintained the feast of St John the Baptist there.

He then expresses the view that King Henry was at Bamburgh all this while and escaped the net with the aid of Sir Henry Bellingham,[68] an opinion shared with the County History, which also names various others who assisted the late king in his flight: Sir Thomas Philip, William Lermouth, Thomas Elwyk of Bamburgh, John Retford of Lincolnshire, all described as 'gentlemen'; John Purcas of London, 'yeoman,' Philip Castelle of Pembroke, Archibald and Gilbert Ridley of Langley, Gawen Lampleugh of Warkworth, also a gentleman, John a Whynfell of Naworth, another yeoman, and Alexander Bellingham of Burneside in Westmorland.[69]

Bates also implies, as does the County History, that Sir Ralph Grey fled back to Bamburgh before the rout at the Devil's Water; this view may be based on a misunderstanding of an entry in Worcester's Chronicle '. . . Radulfus Gray fugit de Hexham ante bellum inceptum ad castrum Bamburghe, et post bellum de Hexham multi ex parte regis Henrici fugerunt in eodem castro'.[70] It is more likely that the writer is referring to Grey's flight immediately the battle began rather than before, and most of those who followed to Bamburgh will surely have been defectors from his division in the fight. Likewise, it may also be that those named as assisting Henry were present before rather than after the battle, though none of these names features amongst those taken and executed. Again, it is possible that some may have accompanied Henry in his flight or, along with others who fled at the first clash, sought safety behind Bamburgh's impressive walls.

On 25th June any illusions of security the defenders may have nurtured were rudely dispatched when the Yorkists, accompanied by their formidable train, arrived before the walls. The various accounts agree that Warwick sent his own Warwick herald and the King's Herald, Chester, to formally demand the castle's surrender.[71] If the garrison were to lay down their arms then they could expect quarter, but both Grey and Neville, too steeped in perfidy, were excluded from the general amnesty, 'as out of the King's grace without any redemption'.[72] Grey replied that he had 'clearly determined within himself to live or die in the castle'.[73]

The heralds responded to this continued defiance with a chilling rejoinder clearly aimed at the less resolute within: 'The King, our most dread sovereign lord, specially desires to have this jewel whole and unbroken by artillery, particularly because it stands so close to his ancient enemies the Scots, and if you are the cause that great guns have to be fired against its walls, then it will cost you your head, and for every shot that has to be fired another head, down to the humblest person within the place'.[74] This threat was nicely aimed at the Northumbrians who would not wish to provide any incentive for further Scottish inroads. Presumably the heralds did not see fit to mention the truce which the king had just ratified.

Thus began the only set-piece siege of the entire series of conflicts known as the Wars of the Roses,[75] and it was begun in deadly earnest; the great guns 'Newcastle' and 'London' blasted chunks of masonry from the walls and sent them crashing into the sea.[76] The smaller brass piece 'Dijon' fired rounds through Sir Ralph Grey's chamber – 'oftentimes'.[77] At this time the castle, which extended over a site of eight acres or so, comprised three wards or baileys, an east, a west and an inner with a massive central keep of Norman origin. There were two gatehouses on the elongated dolerite spur, at the eastern and western ends.[78] Grey seems to have established his headquarters in the first of these, clearly an exposed location, and bearing much of the attackers' fire. Perhaps he felt he needed to shore up the garrison's flagging morale but, in any event, one of the balls dislodged a masonry roof which fell in upon the defenders, injuring Sir Ralph and rendering him senseless.[79]

Neville, still the survivor, seized the moment of his ally's fall to open negotiations, bargaining for the lives of the garrison and successfully including himself. Only half sensible and needing to be tied to his horse, Grey was dragged to Doncaster to receive sentence from John Tiptoft, Earl of Worcester and Constable of England. One of the indictments was that he 'had withstood and made fences against the king's majesty, and his lieutenant, the worthy lord of Warwick, as appeareth by the strokes of the great guns in the king's walls of his castle of Bamburgh'.[80] The verdict was never in doubt. Worcester was no more merciful than Warwick, on whose orders he was himself to die, during the re-adeption of Henry VI in 1471, and Grey was executed on 10th July.[81] The war in the north was finally over, at least for the moment.

Notes

1 Hicks, M.A., 'Edward IV, The Duke of Somerset and Lancastrian Loyalism in the North', *Northern History* Vol. XX p. 24.
2 Ibid p. 25.
3 Ross, R., *Edward IV*, London 1974 pp. 51–2.
4 Hicks p. 31.
5 William Gregory's Chronicles of London in *Historical Collections of a Citizen of London in the Fifteenth Century* (Ed.) J. Gairdner Camden Soc. New Ser. XVII 1876 pp. 221–3.
6 Hicks p. 32.
7 Ibid p. 33.
8 Ibid p. 34.
9 Robert Fabyan, *The New Chronicles of England and France* (Ed.) H. Ellis London 1809 p. 683.
10 Gregory's Chronicle p. 223.
11 'Year Book de Termino Paschae' 4 Edward IV The Priory of Hexham Surtees Soc. 1 1864 p. cviii.
12 Gillingham, J., *The Wars of the Roses*, London 1981 p. 81.
13 Gregory's Chronicle p. 224.
14 Ibid p. 224.
15 Ibid p. 224.

16 Ibid p. 224.
17 Ibid p. 224.
18 Haigh, P., *The Military Campaigns of the Wars of the Roses*, London 1995 p. 81.
19 Gregory's Chronicle p. 224.
20 Boardman, A., *The Battle of Towton*, Gloucs. 1994 p. 75.
21 Haigh p. 80.
22 Gillingham p. 152.
23 Ross p. 56.
24 Ramsay, Sir J.H., *Lancaster and York*, Oxford 1892 Vol. II p. 302.
25 Paston Letters no. 52.
26 Ramsay Vol. II p. 302.
27 Ross p. 55.
28 Ibid p. 56.
29 Gregory's Chronicle p. 226.
30 Fabyan p. 654.
31 'Chronicles of London' (Ed.) C.L. Kingsford Oxford 1905 p. 178.
32 Long, B., *Castles of Northumberland*, Newcastle upon Tyne p. 76.
33 Lomas, R., *Northumberland – County of Conflict*, East Lothian 1996 p. 136.
34 Ibid pp. 154–5.
35 Boardman p. 38.
36 Charlesworth, D., 'The Battle of Hexham', *Archaeologia Aeliana* 4th Ser. Vol. XXX 1952 p. 62.
37 Gregory's Chronicle p. 64.
38 Ibid p. 323.
39 Charlesworth p. 63.
40 William Worcester 'Annales Rerum Anglicarum' in *Liber Niger Scaccarii* (Ed.) T. Hearne Oxford 1728 Vol. II p. 779.
41 Ramsay Vol. II p. 303.
42 Charlesworth p. 64.
43 Haigh p. 84.
44 Gregory's Chronicle p. 224.
45 Ramsay Vol. II p. 303 (note).
46 Ibid p. 303.
47 John Warkworth 'A Chronicle of the First Thirteen Years of the reign of Edward IV 1461–1474' (Ed.) J.O. Halliwell Camden Soc. Old Ser. X 1839 p. 4.
48 Ibid p. 5.
49 Bates, C.J., *History of Northumberland*, London 1895 p. 201.
50 Fabyan p. 654.
51 Bates p. 201.
52 'Chronicles of London' p. 178.
53 Actually 'Black Jack', a notorious border reiver whom Bates asserts was the same outlaw who had come to the aid of Margaret of Anjou after the alleged skirmish at Hexham the previous year, Bates p. 201.

54 Fabyan p. 654.

55 Chronicles of London p. 178.

56 Lander, J.R., *The Wars of the Roses*, London 1990 p. 103.

57 Gregory's Chronicle p. 219.

58 Haigh p. 87.

59 Ibid p. 87.

60 Ibid p. 83.

61 'Edward' is later listed in an inventory of 1475; the Master of the Ordnance, John Sturgeon, handed into store at Calais '. . . divers parcels of the King's ordnance and artillery including a bumbardell [bombard] called "The Edward" . . .' See Blackmore, H.L., *The Armouries of the Tower of London Ordnance*, HMSO 1976 p. 33.

62 Norman, A.V.B., and D., Pottinger, *English Weapons and Warfare 449–1660*, London 1966 p. 137.

63 A surviving example from this period, still on view in Edinburgh Castle, is the impressive 'Mons Meg' which may be considered not untypical of the heavy guns of this period. Cast in Flanders in around 1460, the barrel length is 13 feet 2 inches with a bore of $19^1/2$ inches – it could fire a stone ball weighing 549 lb and the shot is said to have carried for a distance of two miles. Its enormous weight necessitated the use of a crane to raise and lower on and off the carriage; Norman and Pottinger p. 140.

64 Rogers, Col. H.C.B., *Artillery Through the Ages*, London 1971 p. 19.

65 Norman and Pottinger p. 141.

66 Gillingham p. 153.

67 Bates p. 202.

68 Ibid p. 202.

69 *Northumberland County History* Vol. I p. 47.

70 William Worcester p. 280 (note).

71 Bates p. 202.

72 *Northumberland County History* Vol. I p. 48.

73 Ibid p. 48.

74 John Warkworth p. 4.

75 Gillingham p. 153.

76 *Northumberland County History* Vol. I p. 48.

77 Warkworth pp. 37–9.

78 Pevsner, N., *The Buildings of England – Northumberland*, London 1992 p. 136.

79 Warkworth pp. 37–9.

80 *Northumberland County History* Vol. I p. 49.

81 Haigh p. 88.

Chapter 15

'This Sunne of York'

James III of Scotland has been compared to Richard II of England and the likeness is scarcely complimentary. A noted patron of the arts and artists, James was a great builder but wholly unmilitary in his disposition. He was at best an indifferent horseman and had an unfortunate propensity for choosing and advancing unsuitable favourites. His reputation was blighted by the taint of sodomy. He was at least fortunate in that his widowed mother, Marie of Gueldres, was strong-minded and capable; the minority would not be disturbed by the depredations of over-mighty subjects such as the vanquished House of Douglas, and the young queen was to be ably advised by the redoubtable Bishop Kennedy.

Whilst the regent might be sympathetic to the woes of Margaret of Anjou, the Lancastrian party's fragile survival after the slaughter of Towton made her a high-risk proposition if not a downright liability. Bishop Kennedy naturally preferred the benign and feeble Henry to the young, aggressive and able Edward. The bloodless acquisition of Berwick was a considerable bonus but the continued poor showing of the Lancastrian remnant in Northumberland offered little further incentive.

Before the *entente* in 1464 Edward IV had sought to distract the Scots administration by fomenting trouble in the highlands. In this he had willing if uninspiring allies in Douglas and two other perennial traitors, the Lord of the Isles and Donald Balloch, who had returned to plague this reign as he had the last. Their accord, which was rather ludicrously styled the Treaty of Westminster – Ardtornish[1], provided that Douglas would be restored to all of his estates and the other two would partition the whole of the realm beyond the Forth, whilst all three would acknowledge Edward as their overlord.

In the event the Lord of the Isles, in keeping with family tradition, sacked Inverness whilst Douglas and his surviving brother Balvenie launched a chevauchee into the western march. This soon foundered with the loss of Balvenie who paid for his treason with his life. The highland jaunt, likewise, soon fizzled out and the Lord of the Isles submitted to the young king at the highland capital in 1464.

Edward's mischief-making had not been entirely a waste of time, for the queen came to perceive that the House of York was unlikely to be unseated and that it was necessary to think of coming to terms. 'It is credible to the intelligence of Marie of Gueldres that she seems to have been one of the first to see that Douglas and the Lord of the Isles might be neutralised if Scotland came to terms with Edward IV and abandoned what now seemed to be the lost cause of Lancaster.'[2]

In this regard Bishop Kennedy was particularly cautious. He had always favoured the pious fool over the licentious militarist and was reluctant to give offence to Louis XI who might yet send aid to bolster Henry's moribund cause. In 1463 the Queen died: she was barely thirty, her reputation, though less tarnished by unsuitable liaisons than that of Queen Joan Beaufort, did suffer latterly as a result of a possible affair with Adam Hepburn, the Master of Hailes. The disaster at Hexham and the decimation of the Lancastrian diehards which immediately followed persuaded Louis that Edward was now inexpungable and Kennedy followed suit. A truce with England to last until 1479 was agreed before the bishop followed the queen to the grave in May 1465.

By this time the king, at fourteen, was almost of age but fell under the influence or rather the control of the unscrupulous Lord Boyd of Kilmarnock who virtually kidnapped James in July 1466. Boyd assumed the office of Guardian and whilst his conduct was reprehensible his political instincts were sound. The marriage contract with Christian I of Denmark for the hand of his daughter Margaret was a singular coup which reaped unforeseen dividends when the cash-strapped father, unable to meet the full amount of the dowry, mortgaged his lands in Orkney and Shetland, the first step towards eventual annexation.

James used the occasion of his marriage, in the summer of 1469, as the opportunity to throw off the yoke of the guardian's faction though Boyd and most of his kindred escaped the axe by fleeing the realm.

In England there were serious rifts in the victorious Yorkist faction. Henry had been captured in 1465 and incarcerated in the Tower, no longer, at least for the moment, even a pawn in the devious game being played by the Earl of Warwick. Richard Neville was Edward's cousin, his mother a sister of the Earl of York, his wealth and prestige in the years after the victory at Hexham had soared. His brother John, Lord Montagu, was Earl of Northumberland and maintained a steadfast loyalty to the crown. Warwick enjoyed virtual plenipotentiary powers in the north, ruling with regal splendour from his great Yorkshire castles of Middleham and Sheriff Hutton.

The earl's standing as *primus inter pares* seemed assured. Edward's position was by no means wholly unassailable. Margaret of Anjou, with her young son and dead Somerset's vengeful brother, lurked in France. The king's affinity amongst the nobility was narrowly based; he seemed dependent upon the Nevilles and the continuing pervasive counsels of the Earl of Warwick.

If Warwick thought his young cousin was prepared to remain a mere cypher whilst the Nevilles governed the state then he was mistaken. Worse, he was humiliated by the king's sudden marriage to Elizabeth Woodville, a Lancastrian widow some years older, who brought a train of greedy kinsmen and dependants in her avaricious wake.

Dazzled by the cunning flattery of Louis XI, Warwick had been nego-tiating a French alliance in favour of the Burgundian cause preferred by the king whose sister was married to the mercurial Charles the Bold. Further disappointments lay in store when Edward blocked the marriages of the earl's two daughters to his younger brothers, George, Duke of Clarence 'false, perjured Clarence' and Richard, Duke of Gloucester, the future Richard III. Soon the Woodville brood were craving every eligible partner amongst the higher nobility; even octogenarian widows were not excluded provided they had lands and titles to offer.

Warwick, by no means alone amongst the peerage, viewed the meteoric rise of these greedy and ruthless parvenus with anger and alarm, seeing his own grasp on power fading. Never one to brook such perceived ingrati-tude with equanimity the earl bided his time, seducing the weak-willed Clarence to his cause whilst subtly fomenting discord in his northern marches. In the early months of 1469 a series of disturbances broke out in the north, particularly in Tynedale where a shadowy figure using the *nom de guerre* of 'Robin of Redesdale' emerged as instigator together with another of the same name, 'Robin of Holderness', in Yorkshire. There has been much speculation over the true identity of Robin of Redesdale, with Sir William Conyers of Marske in Swaledale being a prime candidate, an influential knight of Warwick's affinity whose brother John was Steward of the Lordship of Middleham.

It has, however, been suggested that the real Robin of Redesdale was Robert Tailboys, a descendant of the Umfravilles, the son-in-law of Heron of Chipchase and heir of that Lord Tailboys executed after Hexham.[3] The rising was claimed to be on behalf of the Percys, attainted since the third earl fell in the carnage at Towton. Both Tailboys, who'd previously employed the alias 'Rob o' Redesdale', and Heron were also under attainder so both had hurts to avenge. There was also a territorial link with Lincolnshire which subsequently proved such a fruitful recruiting ground for the rebels.

On 12th July Warwick's daughter Isabel was married to the Duke of Clarence in clear defiance of the king's wishes. Even as the wedding feast progressed the northern rebels were sweeping southward under Sir William Conyers' leadership. Edward, completely wrong-footed, was stranded at Nottingham whilst a loyal force under the Courtenay Earl of Devon and Sir William Herbert, Earl of Pembroke, advanced from the south-west to his relief. Herbert was a particular annoyance to Warwick, one of the king's most staunch supporters and one whose meteoric advancement was due to Edward's patronage.

The two hosts were set on a collision course. The king's muster was fatally hampered by the defection of Devon and his archers after a squabble over billeting arrangements in Banbury. Herbert was a doughty fighter but no diplomat and the fracas was to cost him dear. The encounter took place at Edgecote on 26th July when the loyalists were eventually overwhelmed by Conyers' northern rebels, reinforced, late in the day, by Warwick himself. Sir William fell in the fight but Pembroke and his brother, despite a valiant and stout-hearted resistance, were taken and summarily executed.

The king, rendered impotent by the destruction of his allies, found himself powerless in the hands of his former close allies Warwick, his brother George, Archbishop of Canterbury and, of course, his own brother Clarence. The Nevilles' triumph proved illusory for they found themselves unable to govern without the person of the king, who, biding his time, gradually eased free of the rebels' clutches and finally turned the tables on them completely.

Throughout these disturbances John Neville had remained loyal to Edward, disdaining his brother's treachery. However, in the following year, Edward prepared to reverse the Percy attainder and restore the title to the fourth earl. Montagu was to be compensated for the consequential loss of his northern estates by a grant of confiscated Courtenay estates in Devon, the hand of the king's daughter Elizabeth and the honorary title of Earl of Bedford. Henry Percy IV duly came into his own on 3rd March 1470.[4]

In the meantime the Earl of Warwick and his son-in-law had been fomenting fresh divisions in Lincolnshire, though this time the king refused to be caught unawares. Rather it was he who surprised the rebels, on 12th March, in the rout of Empingham – 'Losecote Field' as it became known. So great was the haste of the discouraged rebels to quit the field when the royal artillery played upon them that many cast off their livery to aid their flight, leaving the tell-tale evidence of their affinity behind them. Thwarted and fearful, Warwick and Clarence set sail for France, Isabel suffering an agonising delivery on board ship.

The Kingmaker was far from played out and now he set about creating his masterpiece – a rapprochement with Margaret of Anjou and the Lancastrian exiles. A seemingly impossible alliance between the case of Henry VI, still languishing in the Tower, and his erstwhile nemesis the House of Neville. Any other man would have failed, though he had an ally in Louis XI, whose intermeddling might well have proved decisive. Against all odds Warwick succeeded in establishing the basis of a working relationship with Margaret. His other daughter was to be wed to her young son Edward of Lancaster (thus effectively sidelining his other son-in-law Clarence who now became an obvious embarrassment).

The fruit of this extraordinary and by no means congenial union was the coup of 1470 whereby Edward with his remaining brother Gloucester was pushed into temporary exile in Burgundy whilst poor, confused and unwashed Henry became a spectator in his own 're-adoption'. Warwick's fragile grip on power began to unravel in the following spring when Edward and Richard returned, ostensibly so the king could reclaim his hereditary Dukedom of York.

In the mist-shrouded dawn of Barnet the Kingmaker was finally undone. Confusion and the fog conspired against him, with cries of treachery when the Lancastrian Oxford's men collided in the uncertain light with Montagu's division. John Neville, drawn inexorably at the end into the destructive web of his brother's scheming, fell trying to stem the rout. The earl was cut down in flight, and doomed Henry went back to the Tower.

No sooner had the dust of the battle settled than Margaret with her precious son appeared in the south-west, her army led by Somerset, obliging the king to set off on the hot pursuit that ended on the savage field of Tewkesbury. Gloucester covered himself with glory and burnished the military reputation he'd begun at Barnet. For Margaret of Anjou this was the final chapter; Somerset was dragged from sanctuary after the battle and executed, her son, upon whom all her hopes had rested, lay dead on the field.[5] Edward was king again and, with his heir slain, Henry VI now ceased to matter at all. He was quickly done to death in the Tower.

As ever fresh enmity between Lancaster and York bred disturbances on the border where the riding names were swift to espouse any cause that conferred licence to despoil. The civil strife in England might have provided ample opportunities for an aggressive King of Scots but James III was not cast in that mould. In outlook he was an avid anglophile, a trait which was scarcely likely to endear him to his nobility, their hostility honed by generations of strife. James in fact displayed an alarming lack of interest in things military; his passions lay in building and the arts and his reign saw a rash of construction projects. Such pacifist leanings, however, were out of step with the times: 'He delyttit mair in singing and playing wpoun instrumentis nor [than] he did in defence of the bordouris or the ministratioun of justice.'[6]

An incident occurred in 1473 when Bishop Kennedy's vessel the *St Salvator* was beached near Bamburgh and the Abbot of St Colm, a passenger, was taken hostage by opportunistic locals. This was a flagrant violation of the truce and a more warlike king could have found a ready pretext for war. Neither realm was keen to pick a fight, however; James had no interest in war with England and Edward had other plans, more particularly he was considering a renewed invasion of France. The victor of Mortimer's Cross, Towton, Empingham, Barnet and Tewkesbury, by far the greatest captain of his day, was about to re-ignite the Hundred Years War.

In the event the Edwardian expedition to France in 1475 won little glory although financially it was a resounding success. Louis XI, 'the Universal Spider', paid handsomely to avoid another Crispin's Day and the bargain was sealed by the Treaty of Picquigny. James had previously agreed with Edward to extend the existing truce for an unprecedented period of forty-five years.

The Lord of the Isles was again being troublesome, and after he had ignored a further summons to appear before Parliament a clutch of loyal earls, Athol, Crawford, Huntly and Argyll, were sent against him. The price of mercy was the resignation of the Earldom of Ross to the Crown and a general submission. In spite of these humiliations peace was denied the highlands, for the MacDonald's base-born son Angus Og kept the field and ensured that a climate of violence persisted.

The main problem facing the King of England and the King of Scotland at this time was that they both had younger brothers – headstrong, fiercely ambitious and disloyal.

Edward had to contend with the relentless plotting of Clarence whose return to the fold had been driven almost entirely by expediency after his father-in-law found him surplus to requirement. There was no love lost between the headstrong duke and the equally grasping Woodvilles. Clarence had also quarrelled with his sibling Gloucester who had scooped up Warwick's younger daughter Anne after the slaughter of Edward of Lancaster at Tewkesbury. Gloucester, who had served his brother with steadfast loyalty, had been rewarded with a dazzling array of high offices and now ruled Warwick's former fief in the north from Middleham.[7]

Few men have conspired more heartily to their own undoing than Clarence who finally fell irredeemably from grace and was executed in 1478. The earl had enjoyed, through his calculated largesse, some measure of popular support and blame for his demise was laid at the door of the queen and her unpleasant family. Whether Gloucester contrived his brother's end is a matter of speculation but he kept a neutral distance from the rapacious Woodvilles and this may have led them to underestimate him, an error of very considerable magnitude.

James III was likewise cursed with ambitious siblings and they rather than he had the nature and disposition to please a warlike nobility. Unlike Edward IV the King of Scots did not have the reassurance of so formidable a military achievement: 'The character of James III has been the subject or more dispute among historians than those of other Scottish monarchs. Between those who would paint him in the gaudy and sinister colours of an Edward II, and those who regard him as the wronged victim of a wild age, one may well hesitate.'[8]

Whatever James's preferred sexual orientation, his propensity for choosing low-born but comely favourites upon whom he lavished attention and largesse contrasted markedly with the conduct of his two brothers the Duke of Albany and Earl of Mar, whose martial athleticism and horsemanship corresponded with the knightly image expected of royalty. Of Albany it was said that he: 'lowit nothing so weill as abill men and good horse and maid gret cost and expenssis thairon; for he was wondrous liberall in all thingis pertening to his honour.'⁹

Like Clarence, Albany understood the value of manly show but appears to have heartily abused his office as warden of all three marches to enter into treasonable dialogue with the English. The exact details are scanty but in 1479, the year after Clarence's fall, both Albany and Mar were incarcerated. Albany had abused his position as warden to the extent of fomenting disturbances on a truce day as a result of which several Englishmen were killed and others taken captive. He was duly indicted for, 'the tresonable . . . iolacioun . . . of the trewis . . . be slauchteris and hereschippis tresonably committit contrar to the kingis hienes and to the comoun goud of his realme the said Alexander being wardain in the sammyn boundis'.¹⁰

There is some suggestion that the younger earl was suspected of dabbling in necromancy and the black arts. If so his diabolical leanings did him no good for he died in gaol, most probably of natural causes though some suspicion inevitably fell on the person of the king or at least those coterie of favourites who surrounded him.

Whatever the truth of his brother's demise, Albany did not intend to share the same fate. The following spring the duke received a gift of two casks of wine from sundry of his friends in France. One did indeed contain liquor but the other hid a coil of rope. He then invited his gaoler and three attendants to sup with him and partake of his liberality; they drank often and deep, the duke playing the affable host and ensuring their cups remained full. When the quartet of guards were reeling Albany and his manservant suddenly drew their daggers and fell upon them in a furious and bloody assault.

In a matter of moments all were dead, their bodies heaped unceremoniously on the fire whose lurid flames had lit the dreadful carnage. The murderous pair, drenched in gore, were able to make their escape even though, in the first instance, the rope proved too short and the accomplice broke his leg. He was carried to safety by his master who was presently on his way to France and sanctuary.

Although Louis was prepared to greet the duke with all due deference and make much of him, to the extent of arranging an advantageous match, he was not minded to sponsor any attempt on the throne of Scotland. In England, however, Albany found a more amenable ally in Edward who could clearly see advantage in a pliant and dependent King of Scots, an echo of Edward III and Baliol.

If the scheming of his maverick brother was not sufficient James was also beset by economic difficulties – unchecked inflation had seriously eroded the value of currency and the king had not been able to deliver a solution. His architect, Robert Cochrane, probably the most influential and heartily disliked of the royal favourites, decided to try his hand at economics by experimenting with the issue of copper farthings. 'Cochrane's Plaks', as the new coinage was derisively labelled, merely served to exacerbate the problem and fuel resentment against the preening minister whose incompetence was matched only by his mountainous conceit.

In 1480 Louis, in fear of renewed English aggression in alliance with Burgundy, made further overtures of amity to Scotland, one aspect of which was to be a rapprochement between the king and his erring brother. At first James preferred to tread the middle line and proposed a concord with Edward, offering his sister for the hand of Anthony Woodville, Earl Rivers, Edward's influential brother-in-law and regnant 'star' of the lists.

The English response was antagonistic in the extreme, laced with a series of impossible demands; James's eldest son to be educated in England, the surrender of Berwick, the reinstatement of that evergreen traitor Douglas and, if these were not enough, a formal recognition of English overlordship. It would not require a Machiavelli to detect the hand of Albany in this gross insult, and if the intention was to provoke hostilities then success was virtually guaranteed.

For once James girded himself for war. He renewed the French alliance and sent Edward an ultimatum in return, demanding he desist from further aid to Burgundy. In the summer the Earl of Angus descended on Northumberland, on 5th August his raiders torched Bamburgh and there was naval activity off the North Sea coast. The escalation of hostilities was forestalled by the Papal Nuncio who was canvassing the rulers of Europe for a crusade against the Turk and who was active in brokering a cessation.[11] James, at best a half-hearted warrior, was pleased to accept a truce but the pernicious influence of Albany remained, like a lurking cancer, in England.

The defence of northern England rested with Richard, Duke of Gloucester who, in addition to his appointments as Constable of England and Lord Admiral, had acquired his father-in-law's castles of Middleham and Sheriff Hutton. Gloucester, later Richard III, Shakespeare's 'Crookback Dick', remains one of the most enigmatic figures in English history and one who still commands a following of fervent admirers and equally determined detractors.

His reputation as a loyal and able servant of the king was untarnished in Edward's lifetime and it was not until the usurpation of 1483 that a more sinister aspect emerges. From 1471 until Edward's death he maintained a discreet distance from court and the grasping Woodvilles. His popularity in the north was considerable, especially in Yorkshire where he was venerated by the citizens of York itself. The Italian Dominic Mancini, an observer of affairs in England, noted that, after the fall of Clarence:

He came very rarely to court. He kept himself within his own lands and set out to acquire the loyalty of his people through favours and justice. The good reputation of his private life and public activities powerfully attracted the esteem of strangers. Such was his renown in warfare, that whenever a difficult and dangerous policy had to be undertaken, it would be entrusted to his direction and his generalship. By these arts Richard acquired the favour of the people, and avoided the jealousy of the queen, from who he lived far separated.[12]

Subsequent writers have disagreed over the effectiveness of Richard's policy in the north. His hagiographer Paul Murray Kendall believes his administration was the best and most impartial the region had seen. Less partisan authors have cast doubt on this, certainly as Professor Pollard suggests 'he had for long wished to mount a war against Scotland'.[13] Central to his success was to be the nature of his relationship with Henry Percy, Fourth Earl of Northumberland. This could never be an easy one; Percy would find it had to forget his family's earlier domination or the fact that his father and grandfather had died fighting for the House of Lancaster and he himself had spent his childhood as a virtual prisoner, his titles attainted whilst the hated Nevilles held his lands in thrall.

Richard went to considerable lengths to cultivate the earl, entering into a compact with him before the Council in 1473 and strengthening the working relationship with a formal indenture a year later. On the surface the pair worked well together and Richard exercised his authority with considerable diplomacy. Percy, for his part, had learned the value of discretion and was determined to avoid the hubristic rashness of his predecessors. On the marches both men did good and diligent service, the Duke from his base at Carlisle in the west and Percy from his family heartlands in Northumberland to the east.

Carlisle was the Crown's great bastion in the west, the red sandstone fortress that had defied every attempt by the Scots and which had avoided the fate of Berwick in 1461 by its spirited defiance and Montagu's timely relief, as described at the time in the Paston correspondence:

> *And howbeit, blessed be God, that he* [King Edward] *hath now good tidings, that Lord Montague hath broken the siege and slain of Scots 6,000 . . .*[14]

The city had maintained its importance since the late roman era and was the chief county town and the assizes for Cumberland, 'one of the chief keys and fortresses to the defence of this our realm'.[15] The population throughout this period was probably never more than, say, 1,500 but despite prohibitions there was a brisk trade with the Scots and Carlisle was a focal point for pilgrims on their way to the shrines of St Ninian at Whithorn and St Kintigern at Glasgow. Gloucester himself was linked to the veneration of both Ninian and that great Northumbrian saint, Cuthbert.

From the Crown's perspective Carlisle was of particular significance because it was a royal rather than a baronial castle, '. . . it [Carlisle] was of fundamental importance to the defence of the English west march against the Scots. This last function was vital, for it was this which more than anything else engaged the interests of the crown. The effectiveness of royal power was greater in some parts of the north of England than in others. But it was certainly real in much of Cumberland.'[16]

The king was the greatest lord in Cumberland. In addition to the fortress and city of Carlisle the crown held extensive estates in the great forest of Inglewood. In practice this authority was invariably delegated and no King of England actually set foot in the city from 1335 to 1617 (Gloucester's time in the west was prior to his accession as Richard III). The problem facing the central administration at Westminster was that of distance: the northern frontier with Scotland was simply a long way away.

Many southerners, including some contemporary chroniclers, viewed the north as a foreign country peopled by savages: the 'boreales bobinantes' or 'roaring northerners' whose unchecked depredations amongst the richer lands in the south during Margaret of Anjou's advance in 1461 had left bitter memories. The Crowland Chronicler for one had little doubt that the marchers were more trouble than they were worth, 'the north, whence all evil spreads'.[17]

The office of march warden had not infrequently been delegated to the Nevilles, assisted by the lesser noble families, Dacre, Harrington and Greystoke. Although the wardenship entitled the holder to draw down crown revenue, the costs associated with the office were considerable and the wardens frequently found themselves out of pocket. Despite a long association with the house of Neville the city remained neutral in the struggles of 1470–1. Traditionally the senior, western branch of the family, the earls of Westmorland, had been at odds with Salisbury and his sons. Edward was in fact able to send a message to the citizens in 1470 'for the reducing of the castle of our said city to our obeissance out of the possession of our rebels and enemies'[18] thus exhorting the loyal burgesses to seize the castle from Warwick's affinity, a mission they appear to have performed without demur.

Gloucester was therefore representing the tradition of royal control over the city and the west march as a whole. He was, however, personally proactive and it may be assumed, though it remains unknown, that he took pains to cultivate the magistrates as he appears to have done so successfully at York.[19]

Whether Gloucester ever won the heart and mind of the fourth Earl of Northumberland is another matter. Northumberland's lacklustre performance at Bosworth where he has been castigated for his failure to support the king with the division under his command may be evidence of his disaffection. This possibly arose from the significant erosion of the earl's power after the establishment of the Council of the North in July 1484 or, equally possibly, mere incompetence. What is certain is that in the 1470s and early 1480s the partnership of duke and earl certainly appeared, at least on the surface, to be both binding and effective.

On 12th May 1480 King Edward appointed his brother as Lieutenant General in the North. There were signs that the years of constant debauchery were taking their toll and the baton of high command now passed to Gloucester. With typical energy and efficiency the duke put the English borders on high alert, strengthening and victualling garrisons, though his measures fell short of issuing commissions of array which would have been required to support a major offensive. After the destruction of Bamburgh he retaliated, in September, with a chevauchee across the Scottish west march but returned in time to avert a squabble between the citizens of York and the Earl of Northumberland, the burghers stung by the Percy's arrogance and his heavy-handed efforts to bring the magistrates under his control.

The King's Council had determined upon a major effort against the Scots the following spring and this time the army was to be led by the king in person. Gloucester, meanwhile, used winter months to repair the walls of Carlisle and further strengthen other key bastions.[20] He also spent time in recruiting, having first carried out a census of able-bodied marchers deemed fit to serve. Money, as always, was a difficulty. Some funds were raised by individual grants or benevolences but a contract army, serving under indenture, needed to be paid. Inevitably this meant the imposition of taxes, never popular. The duke negotiated an exemption for the City of York in recognition of the sterling service already undertaken by its suitably grateful inhabitants.

The campaigning season opened with naval operations under the competent direction of Lord Howard who, in what might later be termed a 'cutting out' expedition, took eight large vessels off the Forth, sent a host of lesser craft to the bottom and still found time to despoil and torch Blackness. The war at sea was also prosecuted in the west; payment was made for '300 men at arms retained by the King to serve him against the Scots by sea on the west side of Scotland'.[21] The western squadron seems to have been based at Chester where it could afford protection to the fat-bellied cogs carrying wine from Bordeaux whilst still being able to harry Galloway and the Clyde.

This royal piracy may have displeased the powerful magnate family of the Stanleys who, apart from the fact Lord Stanley was Henry Tudor's step-father, had monopolised seaborne raids against the Scots for some time. They retained the lordship of Man until 1505. In 1457 they had led a descent on Kirkcudbright and, for the campaign of 1482, were able to field some 3,000 soldiers. Whilst Gloucester was warden, however, their role was limited to that of providing support; the duke remained very much in overall charge of operations.

In spite of this encouraging beginning the great land offensive of 1481 remained a still-born thing. The king's iron constitution was finally giving up the unequal fight and he lacked the robustness and probably the will to take the field. Local command therefore stayed with Gloucester who maintained a policy of aggressive patrolling and small-scale raids. There was one alarum in September when it seemed the Scots were threatening a major incursion. Richard had already returned to York, the campaigning season being all but over but, in concert with Northumberland, he reacted swiftly, ordering local musters to form the nucleus of an army with which to confront an invasion. In the event, none materialised.[22]

Gloucester used the lull to establish his siege lines around Berwick, the recovery of which appears to have been his prime objective. Although it was now October he intended to use the winter months to establish a full blockade of town and castle. English naval superiority would allow him to seal off the seaward flank and deny the defenders revictualling. Having conferred with the king who had travelled no further north than Nottingham, it was clear the next season's campaign would be commanded by the duke with the reduction of Berwick a paramount concern.

The winter of 1481 was one of the worst on record. The harvests failed and hunger fuelled the climate of unease that persisted throughout England. The quality of medieval kingship resonated throughout the realm like a finally tuned instrument – when the monarch's touch faltered, discord arose. King Edward, probably failing visibly in mind and body, was losing control of his kingdom, his court now the preserve of the detested Woodvilles whose ruthless rapacity angered nobles and commoners alike. The shortage of supplies severely tested Gloucester's logistical mastery but he pressed ahead and the lustre of his name proved a sure talisman for raising recruits. As ever the doting citizens of York responded heartily to their hero's call:

> For as much as the said Duke at all times have been benevolent, good and gracious lord to his city, it was thought . . . that it were spedeful and also thankful to his said grace to send unto him a certain people, well and defensibly arrayed.[23]

The duke, having mustered his army, took the field in the spring, raiding deep into the west and securing Dumfries. In June he journeyed southward to confer with the ailing king and his guest, the exiled Earl of Albany.

In terms of promoting dissent within Scotland a more perfect candidate would have been difficult to find. It is highly unlikely that so seasoned a campaigner as Edward, well aware as he was of the nature of disappointed younger brothers, ever viewed the Duke of Albany as anything more than an available tool for destabilising Scotland. The precedent of the wholly cynical relationship between Edward III and Edward Baliol is an apt one.

On 10th June 1482 Albany, styling himself 'Alexander of Scotland by the Gift of the King of England', and Edward agreed terms at Fotheringay Castle. In return for English arms winning him the throne the duke would accept Edward as his feudal superior, abandon the French alliance and make no further treaties without Edward's prior approval. He would divorce his French consort and marry the Princess Cecilia, sister of Edward IV. Furthermore, as the immediate compensation for the expense of the forthcoming campaign, he would, on its successful conclusion, surrender the key bastions of Berwick, Lochmaben, Eskdale and Annandale, thus resurrecting an English Pale in the borders.

It has to be doubted whether either party to this agreement believed its terms would ever be implemented. Albany was shrewd enough to realise that if word of the extent of his perfidy reached the nobility of Scotland then none would countenance his accession on such utterly degrading conditions.

By July Gloucester was on the move. His host is said to have numbered 20,000,[24] though this is undoubtably an exaggeration; half that total might be more appropriate. The army advanced to the siege lines around Berwick and the investiture of the town began in earnest.

James III was clearly aware that the day of reckoning was near; a couple of months earlier, in March, he had addressed Parliament in the following stirring manner:

> *Gif sa be that the King of England will nocht apply him to the pece but continew in his weir, our Soverane Lord takis witness of God that it is again[st] his will, and that he sal nocht be the causer nor occasion of effusion of Christen bluid, but in his richteous querel and defens; and sal, God willing, defend the realme in honour and freedome, as his nobil progenitouris has done in tymis bygane.*[25]

In anticipation of an English invasion James mustered his host on the Burgh Muir at Edinburgh and marched south toward the border by way of Lauderdale. The army was impressive in numbers and included a powerful artillery train. All was not well, however; the king had foolishly and as it transpired disastrously included his pack of toadies on his staff. The insufferable Cochrane was made master of the great guns in the unlikely expectation his appreciation of the new science exceeded his talents as an economist.

The dark mutterings from amongst the assembled lords were orchestrated by Angus, himself the son-in-law of the king's disgraced former guardian Lord Boyd. He was abetted by the earls of Huntly, Buchan, Crawford and Lennox with Lord Gray. It was Gray who is credited with invoking the old fable that it would be a good thing to 'bell the cat'. That Angus was prepared to take on the role earned him the sobriquet 'Archibald Bell the Cat'.

The resentment of the earls spilled into savage confrontation at Lauder. Cochrane's bombast when confronted not only cost him his life but doomed the rest. Without ceremony and to the impotent anguish of the king, all those who bore the taint of favouritism and sodomy were hanged from the parapet of Lauder Bridge. Only Ramsay, the youngest, was spared as he clung desperately to the king. As the opening moves in the campaign these events could hardly be deemed auspicious.

Gloucester was not prepared to wait at Berwick for the Scots to attack. Leaving Lord Stanley with sufficient soldiers to man the siege lines, he drew of the bulk of his host and marched into the Lothians, hoping to provoke a confrontation. Angus and the Scottish lords, their king a helpless captive, fell back, their ardour for slaughter clearly sated by the massacre. Gloucester harried them towards Haddington and, by the end of the month, had occupied Edinburgh. This was no random raid and the duke kept his followers in check: after all, he was presenting Albany as a saviour rather than as a mere English puppet. Having secured the city he prepared to engage the Scots army still mired in apparent impotence at Haddington.

The caution of the Scottish lords denied Gloucester his battle. On 2nd August they sent emissaries to negotiate a truce. For Angus and his faction to continue the war was pointless; with the king as prisoner and Albany on the loose they seemed to have no stomach for a fight. This may be viewed as evidence of faintheartedness on Angus's part but the earl had many times demonstrated he was no poltroon. On the contrary, the avoidance of battle may be viewed as a reliance on the well-tried fabian tactic of husbanding military resources and concentrating on guerrilla-style operations which had always proved so much more successful. The Scots may have accepted that Berwick could not be relieved but the town had been lost and won before. Gloucester could plainly not afford to keep so large a force in the field for any length of time so a trial of strength would have been a wholly unjustified gamble.

The terms they offered included a renewal of the marriage alliance between Prince James and the Princess Cecilia. Gloucester was negotiating for a return of the dowry already paid and a free hand to prosecute the siege of Berwick. The Edinburgh magistrates, understandably anxious to be free of their English guests, offered to pay back the dowry monies themselves by instalments. Albany acted as the honest broker and the duke, satisfied he had secured Scottish acquiescence, returned to the siege.

By the summer of 1482 Berwick had changed hands fourteen times since Longshanks took the place in 1296. Since the sack and ruin which followed, the town had become a frontier fortress, a 'bastide' of great strength. The medieval walls were originally constructed by Edward I as part of his rebuilding; when the town fell to the Scots, Robert I strengthened the defences yet further. The castle itself, though much added to in the Edwardian era, the curtain studded with stout towers, dated from 1160 and lay outside the north-west angle of the walls with a moat spanned by a timber causeway.[26]

By the time Richard returned Stanley had secured the town and only the castle continued to hold out. The rout of the Scots army meant that, with no hope of relief, its fall was only a matter of time. On 12th August Gloucester knighted a group of those who had served him well in the campaign and felt sufficiently secure to dismiss a large portion of his forces. There was a half-hearted attempt by a Scottish force to approach but this was easily shooed away. On the 14th the garrison capitulated. Berwick was once again in the hands of the English where it has remained since.

From the English perspective Gloucester's campaign might be viewed as a brilliant success, a triumph of logistics and generalship: Berwick recovered, the Scots humiliated and Albany the viper fully restored to the bosom of the body politic. Nonetheless, it could be argued that the campaign, which had been hugely expensive, had in fact achieved but little and the Crowland Chronicle records with typical sourness: 'This trifling gain, or perhaps more accurately loss (for the maintenance of Berwick costs 10,000 marks a year) diminished the substance of the King and the Kingdom by more than £100,000 at the time. King Edward was grieved at the frivilous expenditure of so much money although the capture of Berwick alleviated his grief for a time.'[27]

This view may be overly censorious and more likely reflects the chronicler's contempt for all things northern. For the marchers the recovery of Berwick was a signal success and for Edward too. His reign had begun twenty-one years previously when Margaret of Anjou had gambled this precious asset away, and now the Yorkists had wiped out the stain of her Lancastrian perfidy. The king's joy at the winning of Berwick may well have been diminished by the cost of the operation and the lack of any other visible gain.

It has to be doubted whether either Edward or Gloucester ever entertained any real hopes of Albany's lasting success, though for a while the duke's star appeared in the ascendant. His brother the king was now a helpless captive in Edinburgh Castle having seen his authority destroyed, his courtiers butchered, his army shamed, a vital bastion lost and his capital occupied by the enemy. But, having rid the monarch of his detested paramours, the nobility seemed undecided; their reaction had been swift and violent but not directed against the person of the king. Their aim was to remove the upstarts and teach James to respect his barons. This done, they knew not what to do next.

The king benefited from a sudden wave of popular support, orchestrated by Albany who, all the while, was secretly at pains to reassure Gloucester he remained true to the Fotheringay accord. Posing as the voice of conciliation the duke negotiated the terms of his brother's release which, of course, included the restoration of his own estates and titles. In return he swore an oath of loyalty to the king. It is unlikely that James believed a word of it but, for the moment, he needed his sibling's support, however galling the prospect. For a while amity prevailed; the king was circumspect in his relations with the nobility, easing himself back into the seat of power without giving cause for further unrest.

The brothers shared both bed and board. Albany restored to his office of Lieutenant of the Kingdom. For a wiser and less greedy man this might have been enough, but early in 1483 he dispatched Angus and Gray, both of whom were probably privy to the realities of the Fotheringay pact, on a mission to England to meet with Edward, now much enfeebled, and that seasoned conspirator the exiled Earl of Douglas.

On 14th March James again dismissed his brother from his offices – doubtless he was fully aware of the shallowness of his loyalty. Albany once again fled to England, though not before he'd opened the gates of Dunbar Castle to admit an English garrison.

The English Parliament which opened in 1483, the final year of King Edward's reign, made an extensive grant of land to the Duke of Gloucester. His position as warden of the west march was made hereditary and with this went the governorship of Carlisle, of Bewcastle and the Nicholforest, together with the shrievality of Cumberland. These holdings amounted to virtually all the royal estates in the county. There was more: the duke was licensed to create a buffer state, effectively a palatinate in the south-west of Scotland. He would hold Liddesdale, Eskdale, Annandale, Wauchopedale and Clydesdale, funded by a cash subsidy of 10,000 marks.

The holdings in Cumberland were of course already in being; the lands in Scotland remained to be conquered. This grant surely reflects the terms of the pernicious Treaty of Fotheringay but were, in reality, beyond Albany's gift. Under the original terms of the accord the rebel duke was to make over all of these lands to Edward who now assigned his rights to his brother. Richard would have to win this border kingdom for himself and the cost would be far greater than 10,000 marks.

The grant however refers to the duke having 'subdued great part of the west borders of Scotland adjoining to England, by the space of 30 miles and more . . .'[28] thus strongly implying that this great English Pale was already, at least in part, in being. Had this vast design come to full fruition Richard would have been the greatest northern magnate since the Conquest. The sweep of his territories would invite comparison with the ancient kingdom of Northumbria. He was already identified with the cults of Cuthbert and Ninian: could he now become another Siward the Dane whose huscarls unmade the King of Scotland in the eleventh century?

If 1483 began on a propitious note for Gloucester his fortunes were suddenly about to change in the most dramatic manner. In April Edward IV developed pneumonia and died on the 9th of that month. On the 13th or 14th the duke, still maintaining his office in the north, received word, probably from Lord Hastings, the late king's partner in depravity and no friend of the queen, that his brother was dead and the Woodvilles were about to seize power. Earl Rivers already had the young heir in his care and was summoned to bring the prince to London for his coronation as Edward

V. At this point Richard, the loyal and valiant brother, begins his transformation into the wicked uncle of legend.

In a brilliantly staged coup, aided by his allies Buckingham and to a lesser extent Hastings, he totally outmanoeuvred the queen's party, seized the person of the young king at Stony Stratford, and captured Rivers who was later executed. In this he maintained his general popularity: few would weep for any of the Woodvilles.

Quite when Richard, egged on by the Duke of Buckingham, decided to seize not only the prince and later his younger brother the Duke of York but also the crown, is uncertain. Hastings, who may have divined his former ally's intent, also went suddenly to the block and the boys were lodged in the Tower. Their fate remains one of the enduring mysteries of English medieval history though there is probably little room for doubt that they were subsequently murdered, most probably either on the orders of their uncle or with his connivance.

The two short years of Richard's reign were crammed with a fury of legislative and diplomatic activity, though the affairs of the border were by no means forgotten. The nature of Anglo-Scottish affairs in the Yorkist period appears, at least on the surface, unchanged from the generations of discord than had gone before. On at least one level this is true: the marchers of both countries had grown used to war, indeed for many it was a more natural state of affairs than peace, 'Till honour ennymis is our haile entent'.[29] The war with France which had been a corollary to so much strife was no longer a factor; despite Edward's chevauchee across the Channel in 1475, the Hundred Years War was over. On one hand this implied the Scots could no longer be drawn into military action in support of their ally but, on the other, it did mean the English Crown could now concentrate all its resources to prosecuting a war with Scotland.

Until the capture of Berwick in 1482 the English Pale which Edward III had sought to create in the borders had been totally eroded with the final fall of Roxburgh in 1460 and the handing over of Berwick the following year. James III was distinctly unmilitary and strove to avoid renewed conflict. The horror at Lauder had also shown he did not enjoy the support of the nobility with whom his relations were at best strained.

Once Richard became king he had no need to carve out a semi-independent principality in south-western Scotland. James III might, had he been more aggressive, sought advantage from the new king's insecurity but as ever James, notwithstanding the fact that the English had two garrisons firmly planted on what he would consider Scottish soil, preferred to make peaceful overtures. His request for a truce lasting eight months met with continued prevarication and, finally, an undertaking for two months only. Richard meanwhile had encountered and decisively quashed his former confederate Buckingham's effort at rebellion which for a while at least created an air of security for his regime.

The Duke of Brittany had been prepared to assist the Welshman Henry Tudor in his efforts to join his slender forces with those of Buckingham, and Brittany provided refuge for the survivors who escaped from the débâcle. Richard felt inclined to chastise the Bretons and a savage little naval war was soon escalating to include both France and Scotland as targets for English skippers hungry for prizes. Early in 1484 Richard was clearly contemplating a renewal of land-based operations. On 18th February he wrote to the magnates advising that:

> *by the advice of the lords spiritual and temporal . . . we be fully*
> *determined, by God's grace, to address us in person with host royal*
> *toward the party of our enemies and rebels of Scotland, at the beginning*
> *of this next summer . . . We charge you that . . . you dispose you to serve*
> *us personally in the said voyage, accompanied and apparelled for the*
> *war, according to your degree.*[30]

Fearing invasion and with the need to commence operations for the recovery of Dunbar, James prepared to raise forces of his own and the castle was invested in March. The difficulty for the besiegers was that, as long as the English maintained naval supremacy the garrison could be victualled from the sea. In anticipation of a siege Richard had earlier ordered the works to be strengthened and the leaguer by the Scots made scant progress.

Louis XI had died in the preceding year and his successor Charles VIII was a minor. The regency council, fearing English aggression, hastened to dispatch emissaries to Scotland seeking to renew the 'auld alliance'. In the circumstances James was happy to do so. At the same time Richard was preparing to step up the naval campaign; in March or perhaps April he commissioned four men of war 'to doo service of werre upon the see in the north parties'.[31] When in correspondence with the Holy See the king makes reference to 'this most serious war which we are waging with the very cruel and fierce people of the Scots'.[32]

In April, however, Richard suffered a devastating blow when his only son, Edward of Middleham, died. The lad's death was not only a great sorrow but the death of his hopes for a dynasty. Whether it was solely as a result of this grievous loss or coupled with an increasing insecurity as the exiles' clamour increased, the king's policy towards Scotland became considerably more relaxed. Plans for a land invasion were scrapped and a truce was agreed to endure until October. With the threat of an invasion growing daily more certain, Richard would need his northerners to be free of entanglement on the marches.

For the moment, however, the war at sea continued, and the fleet appears to have scored a signal success against the Scots off Scarborough in early July. Their losses at sea compounded by frustration on land, the siege of Dunbar having been abandoned, were sufficient to persuade the Scots to prefer negotiation and peace talks were underway in Nottingham by 7th September. Richard plainly had no further use for the exiled Duke of Albany. Realising he could no longer expect English support, the inveterate traitor made one final quixotic attempt, on 22nd July 1484, when a force of desperadoes which he commanded jointly with Douglas descended on the Scottish west march, attacking Lochmaben.

This was a final miscalculation. It was the town's annual fair and the streets were thronged. After a running fight the invaders were seen off in ignominious rout. Albany escaped once again but Douglas's luck had finally run out and he was taken. The Crowland Chronicler recorded the event, 'in that same summer . . . they inflicted no less destruction upon us, for the Scottish fugitives, Lord James Douglas and many others . . . besides many Englishmen . . . fell into their hands'.[33]

The fracas at Lochmaben, however, was not a defeat of an English army as such but the final desperate throw of two totally discredited gamblers who had little left to lose. As Richard had already sent intimations of peace to James it seems unlikely he sponsored or even encouraged the raid.

Given that the captured Douglas had no right to expect clemency this inveterate renegade managed to keep his head, being sentenced, with a fine irony, to spend the rest of his days as a monk in the Abbey of Lindores. Albany's quixotic career had another year to run. He returned to France in the hope of finding fresh enthusiasm for his plotting but his time was past. The duke was killed accidentally whilst a spectator at a tournament – one of the contestants' lances snapped on impact and he was struck by a splinter.

It was perhaps typical of the personal dynamism Richard's administration that he undertook the negotiations at Nottingham personally. The terms of the truce which were hammered out over the conference table to continue in effect for three years and the new accord was to be cemented by a match between Prince James of Scotland and Anne de la Pole, Richard's niece and sister of his designated heir the Earl of Lincoln. The return of Dunbar and Berwick remained contentious and unresolved; whilst he might negotiate on the former the king would never surrender the latter.

An element of the treaty was the level of royal control of the marches which was to be extended to the detriment of the wardens, whose role and authority was severely curtailed. Any warden who was considered to have waged or fomented war in time of truce was to be condemned as a traitor (this perhaps reflects a comment on Albany's tortuous scheming of 1479). Richard proposed that breaches of the truce, such as would inevitably occur, should be dealt with by twice yearly meetings between nominated delegates from the royal council of each realm.

The Council of the North which the king had established effectively took over the function of the warden's courts. Whether this was an assault on the Percy hegemony in the east is unclear. The king remained, nominally, west march warden though Dacre, his deputy, acted as proxy. The Earl of Northumberland continued as warden of the middle and east marches and as captain of Berwick. His commission, which ran out on 8th December 1484, does not appear to have been renewed. This potential emasculation of the Percy might explain his apparent indifference on the field of battle.

At first glance the contest on that famous day appeared an uneven one. Tudor was untried, his army outnumbered, the king was a proven general with superior force. The two hosts collided on 22nd August 1485 at Bosworth, one of the most momentous battles in English history. In the cloying dust and steam the last Plantagenet, having chanced all on a charge of his household knights, was hacked to death fighting in the press of his enemies. Whatever crimes he may have committed, and the debate continues to this day, his end was a brave one.

Henry Tudor, now Henry VII, was at the outset no more secure on his throne than the usurper he had defeated. The Wars of the Roses did not properly end until the final Yorkist Pretender, the Earl of Lincoln, was killed at the battle of Stoke in 1487. Henry, like James, was not of an outwardly martial disposition and though Scotland had renewed the historic understanding with the new King of France, James also sought accommodation with England. As a negotiator James enjoyed some success: Dunbar was recovered and there was some hope, through sustained diplomatic pressure, of securing the return of Berwick. For a time the town's status remained in suspension, the English enjoyed possession but not necessarily full proprietorship. A further meeting between the two rulers was listed for July 1488, later postponed until July. This was to prove too late for James III.

If the king had learned some degree of circumspection from the wholesale taking off of his coven of favourites he could not resist showering favour on the sole survivor, John Ramsay, now Earl of Bothwell, whose desperate embrace of the king's person had saved him from the rope at Lauder '. . . He was . . . so great a favourite with the King that nearly all the affairs of the Scottish Court were subject to his arbitration. Having been elevated but a short time before to the earldom of Bothwell by the King, he seemed to behave more extravagantly than the other nobles and great men'.[34]

The final act of the reign was precipitated by what should have been a minor squabble over the revenues of the Priory of Coldingham. The king, needing more cash to continue his ambitious plans for the chapel of Stirling Castle, appropriated the income thus alienating the Homes who had traditionally enjoyed the living. From this seemingly innocuous seed grew discord and open rebellion. Archibald 'Bell the Cat', the same Earl of Angus who had fomented the holocaust at Lauder, continued to lead the opposition which, from early in 1488, controlled the person of Prince James who became the unwitting figurehead of rebellion.

The king was a reluctant general at best and in May the forces who remained loyal had a brush with the insurgents at Blackness. The outcome of the skirmish was an accord between king and nobility, a 'Pacification' which saw power pass to what was, in effect, a regency council. The accord, such as it was, proved a still-born thing and both sides resorted to arms barely a month later.

The deciding confrontation occurred near Stirling Castle, a grotesque parody of the Bruce's great fight at Bannockburn. The fight of Sauchieburn, a brief, confused mêlée, saw the royal army, despite being the larger, worsted and the king injured and in flight. The hapless monarch, pausing for succour and the comfort of a priest, was mysteriously slain, undoubtably as a result of foul play. The first parliament of his son's reign rather succinctly summed up the mood of the nation on receiving this dolorous news:

James, King of Scotland, quhom God assolze, faider to oure Soverane Lord, happinit to be slane.[35]

Notes

1 Bingham, C., *The Stewart kings of Scotland 1371–1603*, London 1974 p. 92.
2 Ibid p. 92.
3 Robson, R., *The Rise and Fall of the English Highland Clans*, Edinburgh 1989 p. 62.
4 Gillingham, J., *Wars of the Roses*, London 1981 p. 160.
5 In *Henry VI Part III* Shakespeare has Richard murder Edward of Lancaster whilst the latter, having been captured with his mother, remains vociferously if unwisely defiant. The contemporary chronicles however assert that the young prince died on the field (far more likely).
6 Quoted in Bingham p. 100.
7 The extensive remains of the shell of Middleham Castle have become something of a shrine for Ricardians and the adjacent museum hosts a good display.
8 Quoted in Bingham p. 102.
9 Ibid p. 103.
10 Grant, A., 'Richard III in Scotland' in *The North of England in the Reign of Richard III*, (Ed.) Pollard Gloucs. 1996 p. 121.
11 The Ottoman Turks had captured Constantinople after the epic siege of 1453 when the last emperor of Byzantium died fighting in the storming. They had begun, thereafter, to encroach into Wallachia, despite resistance in 1461–2 from the spectacularly cruel Vlad Tepes and were threatening Belgrade.
12 Quoted in Murray Kendall, P., *Richard III*, New York 1955 p. 150.
13 Quoted in Grant, *The North of England in the Reign of Richard III*, p. 121.
14 Summerson, H., 'Carlisle and the English West march in the Late Middle Ages' in *The North of England in the Reign of Richard III* p. 89.
15 Ibid p. 90.
16 Ibid p. 91.
17 Ibid p. 90.
18 Ibid p. 96.
19 The 'Ballad of Bosworth Field' provides a list of Cumbrians who fought at Bosworth which includes Lord Dacre, his younger brother Sir Ralph, Lord Greystoke, Sir William Musgrave, Sir Alexander Heighmore, Sir Thomas Broughton, Sir Thomas Strickland, Sir John and Sir Robert Harrington, quoted in Summerson p. 103.
20 Ibid pp. 97–8.

21 Ibid p. 99.
22 Murray Kendall p. 153. There is no evidence of any major Scots incursion at this time and a subsequent fall-off in rents paid by Shoreswood, Tweedmouth, Fenham and Holy Island may be more likely attributed to damage caused by Gloucester's troops as they marched through north Northumberland (see Lomas, R., *County of Conflict, Northumberland from the Conquest to the Civil War*, Edinburgh 1996 p. 58).
23 Murray Kendall p. 154.
24 Ibid p. 168.
25 Quoted in Bingham p. 108.
26 The Castle of Berwick was extensively demolished in the nineteenth century to facilitate the development of the present railway line. However, the remains of a tower located in the south-east angle, the Constable Tower, together with a section of the original curtain wall, survive in Castle Vale Park and the grounds of the Abbeyfield Home. The White Wall, dating from 1297–1298 and descending from the south-west angle to the river bank, also remains, as does the Water Tower on the riverside, though this was rebuilt in the reign of Henry VIII. The medieval walls were generally more extensive than the magnificent Elizabethan ramparts which survive virtually intact, enclosing perhaps a third as large an area again to the north of the present perimeter (see Pevsner, Sir N., and I., Richmond, 'Northumberland' in *The Buildings of England*, London 1992 ed. pp. 174–5).
27 Quoted in Grant p. 122.
28 Quoted in Summerson p. 100.
29 Grant p. 116.
30 Ibid p. 131.
31 Ibid p. 132.
32 Ibid p. 132.
33 Ibid p. 135.
34 Quoted in Bingham p. 116.
35 Ibid p. 121.

Chapter 16

Flodden Field

Green Flodden! On thy blood stain'd head descend no rain nor vernal dew; but still, thou charnel of the dead, may whitening bones thy surface strew! Soon as I tread thy rush-clad vale, wild fancy fells the clasping mail; the rancour of a thousand years glows in my breast; again I burn to see banner'd pomp of war return, and mark, beneath the moon, the silverlight of spears!

But distant fleets each warrior ghost, with surly sounds that murmur far; such sounds were hear when Syria's host roll'd from the walls of proud Samar around my solitary head gleam the blue lightings of the dead; while murmur low the shadowy band- lament no more the warriors doom! Blood, blood, alone, should dew the hero's tomb, who falls mid circling to save his native land.

J. Leyden, 'Ode on visiting Flodden'

A new era dawning. The Welshman Henry Tudor had finally ended the long run of the Plantagenets when the Wars of the Roses reached their bloody finale in the slaughter on Bosworth Field. The Yorkist, Richard III, was slain and the House of Tudor stepped into the empty throne room. In spite of his success Henry can hardly have felt secure. Not only had his immediate predecessor come to such a sanguinary end but two out of three earlier monarchs had failed to emerge alive from the Tower. The general atmosphere of 'open season' that had attended the protracted course of the wars had not been confined to the barons and the lower orders. People were weary of the long feud, but the very nature of war itself was changing.

For years the formidable longbow had dominated every field upon which it had appeared and yet, though the 'cloth yard' shaft laid low many an armoured knight, the knights, as a class, had survived and continued to form the backbone of feudal armies.

Around 1249, however, an Englishman, one Friar Bacon, may by the mixture of sulphur, charcoal, and saltpetre, have produced gunpowder, of which he was able to say:

> *It is so terrifying that whole armies may be harmed or scattered by it.*[1]

The full arrival of gunpowder did not take place overnight, though by 1331 a German army was using cannon in Italy. These early cannon were scarcely sophisticated. Though smaller pieces were often cast in brass or bronze, the larger guns were fashioned from staves of wrought iron, laid side by side around a timber core and then welded together. Not only was the welding a somewhat uncertain art, but there were often weak spots in the wrought iron itself. Combined with this was a considerable variance in the relative strengths of different sources of powder.

The early gunner did not have an easy life, if for any of these reasons the gun burst on firing then he was undoubtedly a dead man. Perhaps one of the most famous persons to be slain in this fashion was James II of Scotland.

> *O, curs'd device! Base implement of death! Framed in the black Tartarean realms beneath! By Beelzebub's malicious art design'd to ruin the race of human kind.*[2]

It was the unfortunate James II who is credited with the commissioning of the mighty 'Mons Meg', with its thirteen-foot length and twenty-inch bore. The gun is said to have been made by one Molise McKim, the hereditary smith of Threave, and the name was derived from that of his nagging wife, whose verbosity he likened to the cannon's roar. An appealing fable, if highly unlikely as the piece was most likely cast in Flanders.

In general these larger, heavier pieces were restricted to siege warfare where, once in position, they could be used to batter the enemy's walls into oblivion. The main difficulty in the early cannon lay in transporting the unwieldy guns across difficult country; where, as on the border, this problem was acute, the effects of the cannon's development were considerably retarded. Nevertheless, the guns would still play their part at Flodden.

Though the longbow was beginning to suffer an eclipse, it still remained in widespread use. The real advantage of the early handgun was that it was very easy to operate, and did not require the constant practice at the butts. Simply a crude iron barrel lashed to a rough batten, or stock, the handgun was fired by lighting the touch hole, in a similar fashion to larger guns. Despite their rather 'do it yourself' appearance these early handguns could inflict fearful damage upon a group of advancing enemy. Thus the great foundation of the feudal host, the unarmoured, untrained peasant could, by a single stroke, demolish a substantial group of his social superiors. The finest armour, the surest mount, the keenest blade and the highest honour no longer sufficed.

> A chance bullet, coming nobody knows how or from whence, fired perchance by one that fled affrighte at the very flash of his villainous piece, may in a moment put a period to the vastest designs.[3]

Flodden has been described as the last great medieval battle. Those who fought and died did so in the manner of Bosworth or Stoke nearly thirty years before. However, the contest also witnessed the first full-scale artillery duel as a precursor to the mêlée and saw a bold, if ultimately, flawed attempt to introduce successful continental tactics into Scotland.

It was also the last serious attempt by a King of Scotland to intervene in England as an ally of France in a campaign which was both measured and innovative. Many of its objectives were achieved; large numbers of English troops were drawn north, the vital bastion of Norham, which had resisted many earlier attempts, was reduced, battle once joined seemed a better than even hazard even though the final roll of the dice produced catastrophe. Despite the magnitude of the defeat and the decimation of the upper echelons the battle produced few immediate consequences. No English counter-invasion was mounted; Surrey had fulfilled the terms of his appointment by seeing off the Scots and destroying their capacity for further military action in the short term. Henry was safe to pursue his war aims in France, which, in any event, accomplished little or nothing. Despite the loss of the sovereign and so many of his council, Scotland did not submit to England or descend into unbridled anarchy or factionalism. His infant son succeeded to the throne, the mechanisms of government continued to perform and this is perhaps the most fitting epitaph for James. Though writers ever since have tended to excoriate the king for his conduct of the campaign and his role in the battle, it was largely due to his tireless and successful efforts to overhaul government during the prior course of his reign that enabled the state to recover so swiftly from the blow.

James IV of Scotland, the man who organised and led this grand chevauchee into Northumberland, was one who appreciated to the full the value of artillery and shared in the interest the renaissance spirit showed in such inventions. Cannon were not the Scottish monarch's only interest, however; he was equally fascinated by ships; tournaments, where he could ride as straight and as hard as any; and clothes. He loved finery, music, and languages. He also tried surgery: he both held a patient and extracted a tooth.

Whilst he was not jousting or practising dentistry, James proved a keen administrator and genuine benefactor to his backward and generally impoverished people. He encouraged a little of the renaissance sun, that was burning so brightly in Italy to filter into his own dark glens. In 1493 he had finally broken the residual power of the Lords of the Isles and extended royal hegemony to the far Western Hebrides. For centuries the Lordship had fostered fissiparous tendencies amongst the highland clans. He reformed and stabilised the currency and his notion of a crusade was by no means fanciful; ever since the loss of Byzantium to the Ottomans in 1453 European rulers had pondered on the need to chastise the paynim hordes now spilling into the Balkans.

> *He of noble stature, neither tall nor short, and as handsome in complexion and shape as a man can be ... His knowledge of languages is wonderful! He is well read in the bible ... He is a good historian ... He never cuts his hair or beard it becomes him very well.*[4]

He inspired a genuine loyalty from his people that reached its tragic nadir on the bloody heath by Flodden Edge, where, ironically, the administrative and social élite he had done so much to foster perished with him.

It was James's great passion for all things military that sowed seeds of his own, and a great number of his subjects', destruction. His interest in artillery was intense and by 1508 the Scots were casting their own guns in Edinburgh under the direction of the king's master gunner, Robert

Borthwick. Acts were passed to encourage the practice of archery at the expense of more traditional pastimes, such as golf and football. Regular musters were encouraged and the basis of a professional army laid down.

In 1502 James was able to send a force of two thousand men to Denmark, and he reduced the dim vastness of the highlands and islands by swift campaigns to extend his authority over those parts. One of his greatest dreams was that of a great, unified, European crusade against the infidel. In spite of these aspirations James's first major encounter proved to be his last. Of his conduct in his only battle the chronicler Edward Hall gives a contemporary view:

> *O, what a noble and triumphant courage was this, for a king to fight in a battle as a mean soldier. But how so ever it happened, God gave the stroke, and he was no more regarded than a poor soldier, for all went one way.*[5]

This image of James as a quixotic and mercurial figure who rushed head-long to his doom and left his army leaderless when the fight was at its most desperate is one which has lingered and influenced many writers, from both sides of the border. Almost certainly it is unfair. James's conduct of the campaign was neither foolish nor ill-executed; he did in fact achieve considerable success insofar as his immediate strategic objectives were concerned. It is true he was defeated in the field but the issue was by no means certain at the outset; indeed it seemed at one point as though the English must be defeated by the radical tactics James had chosen to employ. His first choice of ground on Flodden Edge was sound, the position was virtually inexpungable, moreover he refused to be drawn by the chivalric taunting of his adversaries to commit his army to battle on less favourable ground.

One of the king's greatest passions was his navy. Until his accession Scotland had always lagged behind England in the race to command the seas. From the time of William the Conqueror the fleet had been employed to succour and victual English forces invading through the Lothians, a tactic repeated by Longshanks and Richard of Gloucester. The late fifteenth century ushered in what was to become the age of sail; the clumsy fat-bellied merchantmen of the medieval era were being transformed into sleek, purpose-built 'men o' war'.

Obviously the wild clansmen of the isles made ample use of their traditional galleys but James was determined to compete fully in the shipbuilding stakes. In the preceding century merchantmen were often pressed into service and converted to cumbersome warships with the addition of elevated fighting decks or 'castles' fore and aft which served as platforms for archers. Tactics tended to be restricted to grapple and board.

The advent of artillery saw light pieces being mounted in the castles which were extended in height to provide a more extensive gun platform with ordnance ranged between decks to enfillade boarders. Heavier guns were later mounted amidships to provide real ship killing potential. Private captains acted as seaborne mercenaries chartering the vessels, armament and crew to the crown; the risks might be great but equally so were the prizes. Robert I had seen the potential of a Scots navy but it was James who turned the dream into a potent reality.

Not content with an ambitious programme of shipbuilding, he engaged the services of a generation of able privateers, particularly Andrew Wood of Largs together with John Barton and his three formidable siblings Andrew, Robert and another John. Wood had begun his naval career under James III but by 1489 he owned two fighting ships, each of a respectable 300 tons, the *Flower* and the *Yellow Carvel.* In an engagement off Dunbar the pilot turned privateer outfought a small squadron of English raiders. Henry VIII was so enraged at the loss of his pirates that he gave his commission to a hardened sea dog, Stephen Bull, to exact a suitable revenge.

Bull's ships made to ambush Wood as he returned from a voyage to Flanders. Skulking in the lee of the Isle of May, the English moved to block the passage of the two Scottish vessels as they beat up the Forth. Undeterred, Wood ran out his guns and a savage action ensued, the great guns crashing over the ebb and suck of the tide. The unequal duel lasted all day, the ships fighting broadside-to-broadside, hull-to-hull; only darkness produced a lull and next day the battle began again with undimmed fury, a grand spectator sport for the awe-struck inhabitants who lined the shores to watch. Despite being unprepared and outgunned, Wood's seamanship and gunnery carried the day at last and the battered English struck their colours.

The Bartons were, if anything, even more colourful, with a penchant for piracy which led them into conflict with Portuguese and Dutch mariners; their feuds were sanguinary and pursued with savagery. Thomas Howard, Henry VIII's Lord Admiral, eldest son of the Earl of Surrey, with two ships encountered Andrew Barton in the Downs. The Scot also commanded two vessels, a pinnace named *Jenny Pirwen* and his larger flagship the *Lion*. Soon the Channel was echoing to the cannon's roar as the ships closed.

One of Barton's more potent weapons was a heavy weight which, swung on a beam, could be dropped through the decks of an enemy vessel. Well aware of the risk Howard had archers posted to snipe any crewman trying to release the device. When a brace of his sailors had fallen Barton dashed up the mast to unleash the weight, trusting in his armour, but a shaft pierced him through the vulnerable gap beneath the arm. His death signalled the end of the fight as the demoralised survivors capitulated.

Andrew Barton was James's most prized skipper, even something of a personal friend, and Howard was to evoke the memory of his defeat and death at his, the Lord Admiral's, hand, in the bitter war of words before the battle of Flodden.

The king's naval architects produced their finest creation in 1511 when the *Great Michael* was launched. In her day she was the most sophisticated warship afloat, 240 feet in length, 56 feet at the beam, her hull, crafted from imported Norwegian timber, near 10 feet thick in places. Her ordnance comprised 36 great guns and 300 lesser pieces, served by 120 gunners. The mighty vessel was crewed by 300 sailors and could carry a thousand marines. It was a particularly ironic postscript to the failure of the Flodden campaign that the dead king's proud young navy was sold off to France at a knock-down price, a dream that died with him.[6]

Long before the march to Flodden, James had quarrelled with the Tudors. As early as 1496 he had championed the dubious cause of the pretender, Perkin Warbeck, in his unlikely attempt upon the throne of Henry VII. By way of support James entered England and ravaged Northumberland, looting, killing and burning. The border holds of Tillmouth, Duddo, Shoreswood, Branxton, Howtell and Lantan were all destroyed. The next year he returned and planted his banners before the stout walls of Norham. The siege had barely lasted a week before the Earl of Surrey appeared and James withdrew.

Warbeck's price for Scottish aid was to have been the surrender of Berwick to the Scots. James proposed that possession of the town should be settled by a single combat between himself and Surrey. The earl, however, had more sense and contemptuously dispersed the Scottish forces. James's campaign had achieved little beyond the ruin of several towers and the cutting of a few throats. Henry VII, however, was distracted by an outbreak of discontent in the south-west and Surrey was instructed to agree terms for a truce, the provisions of which were set out in the Truce of Ayton, entered into on 30th September 1497.

Initially the accord was to endure for a period of seven years but the terms were ratified and enlarged by what came to be called 'The Treaty of Perpetual Peace' signed in 1502. By this agreement Princess Margaret, a daughter of Henry VII and sister of the future Henry VIII, was to marry James, something of a coup for the King of Scotland whose aggressive diplomacy seemed to have yielded significant rewards.

Surrey was a guest of honour at the wedding feast though it seems the earl had little time for his royal host. A veteran of Bosworth where his father Norfolk had died fighting for Richard III, he had nonetheless served the first two Tudors well and was, by now, a trusted if somewhat elderly retainer. By the time of the battle he would have exceeded his threescore years and ten and was much afflicted by gout. Like many peers before him he viewed campaigning on the border as a dismal chore. On being left behind to muster the north in 1513 he wrote of his opponent:

Sorry may I see him ere I die, that is the cause of my abiding behind, and if ever he and I meet, I shall do that in me lieth to make him as sorry if I can.[7]

It is one of the leading ironies of the campaigns in Northumberland and France in that fateful year that the only glory to accrue to English arms was won in the barren hills of northern England.

A further excuse to quarrel arose in 1508 when that notable reiver, the Bastard Heron, slew the Scottish warden, Sir Robert Ker, at a truce. The Scotsman's demise seems to have been mourned by few but the slaying of a warden was a serious matter and the affront to a national pride was still employed as an excuse for the war of 1513.

In that year, hungry for glory and having succeeded his father, Henry VIII was planning to mount an expedition into France in support of the Pope and the Emperor Maximillian. More important than the dignity of his allies was Henry's desire to impress upon the world that England was a first-rate power, totally elevated from the feudal mire of the Wars of the Roses. James, at this time, remained married to Henry's sister Margaret and this aggression placed him in a dichotomy. His relations with England had remained cordial if somewhat strained from time to time but he had also maintained close links with France. With these two old adversaries at peace no conflict of interest arose but with the two set to collide James could no longer sit on the fence.

Favouring the more traditional alliance with France and perhaps fearful of an increase in the power of England now firmly in the Imperialist camp since Henry's marriage to Catherine of Aragon, James attempted diplomacy, seeking to extract a guarantee of good behaviour from his brother-in-law. Needless to say this was not forthcoming.

More tempting to James were the convoys of weaponry and munitions arriving in Scottish ports from France. In May 1513 the French queen sent a 'secret' missive begging him to intercede, if only for her sake. Much has been made of this being generally perceived as more evidence of the king's folly that he would be swayed by an appeal to his chivalric instincts, but James was proceeding with considerable deliberation and the invitation was accompanied by a further and significant cash inducement of fourteen thousand crowns. As the month of June wore on, more and more French vessels were putting into Scottish harbours, bearing more cannon, handguns, pikes and a cadre of French officers.

Such obvious preparations were hard to hide and there was little doubt south of the border as to the nature of Scottish intentions. Undeterred, however, Henry, secure as ever in his own considerable arrogance, refused to surrender his designs on France. He did have sufficient sense not to strip the northern counties of able-bodied men, and also to entrust the defence of the realm to Surrey. Despite the weight of his years Surrey did not waste time in waiting for the Scots to actually invade. His job was to contain any incursion as near the border as he could; quite probably he envisaged a repeat of the largely bloodless campaign of 1497 or perhaps an assault on Berwick.

Though the forces he could command were scarcely awe-inspiring, the situation was far from being as bad as the ballad makes out.

There's none at home left in the land but jault head mouths and bursten freers, or ragged rustics without rules or priests prating for pudding strives of millners madder than their mules, or wanton clerks waking their wives. There's not a lord left in England, but all are gane beyond the sea, both knight and baron with his band, with ordinance or artillery.[8]

Surrey's preparations were begun before the end of June, though even by the middle of July the situation was still uncertain. Townspeople of the northern burghs began to make good their ancient walls awaiting, in all too familiar dread, the night skies as a blood-red flickering beacon of the invaders' path. On the 21st July the Earl of Surrey mustered such forces as he would take north at Lambeth. The most significant arm of this nucleus was the artillery train, less impressive on paper than its Scottish counterpart, comprising in the main light field guns, or 'falcons', and five four-pounders of 'serpentines'. The train was served by an experienced team of some four hundred gunners and drivers.

Meanwhile, north of the border, the pace was also hotting up as, on 24th July, James ordered a general muster of ships and men, stripping county and burgh to fill the ranks of his gathering host:

> *Each man made haste to mend his gear, . . . some made their battle axes bright . . . some from their bills did rub the rust . . . some made long pikes and lances light . . .*[9]

On the 25th the Scottish fleet sailed from Newhaven to succour the French, the largest and most formidable the nation had ever amassed. The two capital ships *Michael* and *Margaret* were joined by a host of lesser vessels. James had not succeeded in putting Scotland in the first rank of European powers, indeed he would not have expected to do so, but his country was now a player on the continental stage. The price, however, would be very high indeed.

There are inevitably many tales of evil portents at this time, of dire warnings of catastrophe, most of these are undoubtably apocryphal. It is said that whilst his brigades were drilling on the Burghmuir of Edinburgh and the king was at his devotions at Linlithgow, a seer approached and gave stark warning:

> *Thou wilt not fair well in thy journey nor none that passes with thee . . . meddle with no women nor use their counsel, nor let them touch thy body nor thou theirs, for and thou do it thou wilt be confounded and brought to shame.*[10]

Superstitious nonsense perhaps, for James was making most thorough preparations. His host was no mere feudal levy and nor was he unaware of the string of victories the English had scored against the Scots since Dupplin

Moor in 1332. In virtually every major encounter since the Scots had been worsted. Most of their successes had involved avoiding battle and relying on the guerrilla tactics at which they excelled. The longbow had exacted a high toll; lightly-armed Scottish spearmen were horribly vulnerable, all the more so if their advance, such as occurred at Halidon Hill or Homildon, ground to a halt, presenting the archers with a massed and static target.

Better protection was clearly important. James had set up a 'harness mill' at Stirling in 1496 to mass-produce basic or 'munition'-quality armours. His nobles had full armour in the Milanese style, and heavy wooden shields, pavises, similar to those carried on to the field by crossbowmen, were employed to shield the front ranks from the weight of the arrow storm.

The French were keen to see their allies adopt the tactics of the renowned Swiss Pikemen who now formed the mercenary core of major continental armies. These ideas were nothing new; as far back as 1471 the Scots Parliament had passed an ordinance abandoning the traditional spear for the longer 18-foot pike.

This weapon had its roots in classical antiquity; it was pike phalanxes, combined with the shock effect of cavalry, that had won Alexander his great victories over the Persians. The dense mass of bristling points acted as a virtual steamroller; the length of the shaft and the irresistible momentum of the advance smashing through enemy formations.

In the later fifteenth century the Swiss had reinvented the pike phalanx, dense columns of men, superbly disciplined, attacking in echelon and maintaining the discipline of the advance. They had employed these tactics against Charles the Bold at Grandson, Morat and finally at Nancy where the Burgundians were decimated and the duke killed. Since then the Swiss had turned their genius for battle into an export industry, fighting Europe's wars for wages, which if not paid promptly would result in an immediate defection. The Swiss were perfect mercenaries; they fought hard and well, furiously disciplined, utterly ruthless and with tremendous élan. Machiavelli was certainly impressed; he wrote:

> *The Swiss regiments at present are also based upon the model of the ancient phalanxes and follow their method both in closing up their order of battle and in relieving their ranks; when they engage they are placed on each other's flanks, not in a parallel line. They have no method of receiving the first rank, should it be thrown back into the second; in*

order to relieve each other, they place one regiment in the front and
another a little behind on the right, so if the first is hard pressed, the
second may advance to its assistance; a third is placed behind both these
and also on the right, at the distance of an harquebus shot. They have
adopted this disposition so that if the other two are driven back, the third
can advance to relieve them, and all have sufficient room either to
retreat or advance without falling foul of one another.[11]

The pike columns would thus advance from the right; the van or 'vorhut'
leading followed by the main body or 'gewaltschaufen' and finally the rear
'nachhut'. Speed and cohesion were crucial, engendered by constant drill
and ferocious discipline. The columns were co-ordinated with supporting
crossbowmen and/or arquebusiers as missile troops and their flanks protected by swordsmen wielding hefty double-handers. Though formidable,
the Swiss were not invincible; the columns were vulnerable to missiles and,
if checked, lost much of their effectiveness. As a weapon the pike was virtually useless in any kind of mêlée; if the column were halted the troops were
vulnerable, so sustained momentum was essential. The long dominance of
the Swiss Pikes came to an effective halt at the disastrous battle of Bicocca
in 1522 when the columns were halted and then mowed down *en masse* by
ordnance and musketry.[12]

The French party which disembarked at Dumbarton in late July or
early in August included a corps of forty captains under the Sieur D'Aussi,
dispatched to assist in training the raw Scottish levies in just these tactics.
No mean task; the Swiss spent years in training. They were highly
motivated – their wars were their trade, they had developed the full
co-ordination of the supporting arms, and they knew the weaknesses of the
puissant pike as well as its strengths. Details of the French shipment was
gleaned from documents captured after the battle:

To the western seaport of Dunbar the King of France sent to James IV,
King of Scots: First 25,000 gold crowns of full weight. Also forty
cartloads of powder. Two pieces of great ordnance called cannons.
Also a ship laden with 400 arquebuses and 600 hand culverins, with
their shot. Also a ship laden with bombards and other engines,
including 6,000 spears, 6,000 maces . . .[13]

Much of this arrived too late to be used in the coming campaign but the
real problem which afflicted the king and his instructors was one of time.

To thoroughly drill the Scots in pike tactics and to instil in them that *esprit de corps* and single-minded professionalism which so characterised the Swiss was clearly not possible. The host was comprised of contingents from all corners of the realm, conscripts from the lowland shires, dour borderers from the marches and wild clansmen from the highlands who fought under their own chiefs and in their own way. There was a distinct lack of trained support troops to succour the pikes once in action. James did use his better armoured knights and nobles to form the first ranks of the pike columns, their fine grade plate providing protection against arrows; even the rank and file might have munition-quality armour or half armour . . . 'no Scottish army had ever taken the field so well equipped with every appurtenance of war'.[14]

James has frequently been criticised for exposing himself by 'leading from the front' during the coming battle but this is to ignore, firstly, the range of disparate elements within the army and secondly, the importance attaching to kingship. The army needed the example of the king; it was the majesty of the sovereign and his willingness to share in the risks which made the army viable. Without James at its head his army was a toothless dragon. Besides, the Swiss tactics were such that once the attack was launched and the battalions advanced in echelon there was little a commander-in-chief could do to further influence the outcome, having made his dispositions and ordered the attack. The Swiss themselves seldom had a single overall commander; each division was led by a senior captain whose main responsibility was to ensure the ranks maintained their dressing and kept their momentum.

The Scottish herald, Lyon King At Arms, was commissioned to carry an ultimatum to Henry at Therouanne in Picardy, which the English were besieging. Delivered on the 11th August, the letter threatened dire consequences for the north of England if the siege, and the whole French escapade along with it, was not abandoned forthwith. James demanded of his brother-in-law that he:

> . . . *desist from further invasion and utter destruction of our brother and cousin the Most Christian King, to whom . . . we are bounden and obliged for mutual defence the one of the other, like as you and your confederates be obliged for mutual invasions certifying you we will take part in defence of our brother and cousin the Most Christian King. And we will do what thing we trust may cause you to desist from pursuit of him.*[15]

A further irony of the campaign was that the French attempted to lift the siege and their mounted force was sharply seen off by the English. This, little more than a mere skirmish and dubbed 'The Battle of the Spurs', was to be the nearest to a military triumph that Henry achieved.

By now Surrey was at Pontefract, where he established a council of war. A system of staging posts and warning beacons was established. Thus not only could news of any major incursion be relayed, but a rapid summons could be sent out to the shire levies. Throughout the campaign Surrey exuded an aura of calm capability whereas James, for all his zest, seems often over-confident and bombastic.

Some weeks before the main might of the Scottish host was ready to move, Lord Hume, with five thousand border lances, was already on the offensive, his hard-riding mosstroopers rampaging along the valley of the Till. Replete from this premature orgy of devastation, and doubtless encumbered by their loot, the Scots rode headlong into a well conceived ambush. Concealed in the tall broom of Milfield plain a thousand English longbowmen, under Sir William Bulmer of Brancepeth, waited in deadly earnest. No sooner were the Scots within the trap than the 'cloth yard' rain began to fall, transfixing the raiders in their saddles. As men thudded, writhing or still, into the dust the attack became a rout, the survivors pelting for the border, leaving half a thousand dead and as many prisoners. The English lost no more than sixty; with good cause the road the reivers took was known thereafter as 'the ill-rode'.[16]

Undeterred by this minor reverse, the bulk of the Scotts continued to assemble. In all the army is said to have amounted to nearly sixty thousand men but such a figure is clearly a wild exaggeration, a fair estimate of the numbers might be somewhat less than half that, say 25,000–30,000 for the campaign and, allowing for sickness and desertion, perhaps 18,000–20,000 on the field. James had also assembled a formidable artillery train, a mighty affair; teams of three dozen oxen were needed to pull each of the heavy siege guns or 'curtals', throwing a 60-lb shot, two 18-lb 'culverins', four 6-lb 'sakers' and six 'culverins moyenne'.

Despite the impressive array of guns, the gunners themselves were considerably diluted. Many of their number had been sent with the fleet, the gaps in the ranks being filled often with men of limited experience. This, alas, was a serious drawback, the full implications of which would only be realised later when the great guns were deployed in open field.

On 22nd August the Scottish army crossed the Tweed at Coldstream. Their crossing was unopposed, and the Scots were soon beneath the walls of Norham, no stranger to attack. James had last laid siege to this the 'Queen or Border Fortresses' in 1497.[17] The castellan John Anislow was confident the castle could hold. Surrey, anticipating that this was where the blow would fall, had written to provide assurance he would march to the garrison's relief.

The Scots' batteries were laid on Ladykirk Bank on the northern side of the Tweed and this time the weight of shot was far greater than anything the walls had been called upon to withstand before. Norham, with its great square keep, was essentially a Norman castle in design and the ancient masonry was soon cracking beneath the fury of the cannonade. Breaches were effected in the length of the curtain nearest the river and the western gatehouse was pulverised. With the breaches practicable, the infantry swarmed to the attack, scaling ladders to the fore. They were met by a hail of fire, arrows flicked over the meadow, the defenders strained and hacked at the masses of attackers determined to deny the Scots a foothold amongst the shattered stones. Three major assaults were launched and each flung back.

Legend, however, insists that the battle-scarred walls of Norham were able even to resist the battering of the guns until an English traitor, doubtless led astray by hopes of vast reward, slipped out of the castle and sought audience with James. This abject creature was able to instruct the Scots in how best to direct their fire, and it was his duplicity that brought about the castle's fall. Once success was guaranteed James repaid this informant with a rope around his neck. Again this tale is likely apocryphal for if the deserter advised, as it is said, that James should site a battery to the east of the castle then this flank was difficult and well covered by a ravine. The real problem for the defenders after five days of action was a shortage of powder and shot. With their ammunition virtually exhausted, further resistance became impossible and Anislow struck his colours on 29th August.

After the fall of Norham, James moved on along the east bank of the Till and dealt with Etal, and then Ford. This latter castle became James's headquarters and he made no further move till after the beginning of September. It has long been asserted that the reason for this dalliance was attributable to the charms of Lady Heron, who was all the more accessible since her unfortunate husband had been carted off to incarceration in Fast

Castle, a wild and forbidding coastal fortress. Heron had actually been surrendered a hostage after his half brother, the celebrated 'bastard', had slain the Scottish warden.

Whether James did proved susceptible is somewhat debatable. Sometime before the Scots arrived Lady Heron had begged assistance for the defence of her home from Surrey who had, in fact, offered to release several import-ant Scottish prisoners, including Lord Johnston and Alexander Hume, if Ford was spared. James appeared indifferent to this chance to redeem his subjects, preferring to storm Ford Castle, which was then pillaged and burnt in spite of a spirited resistance. The Scottish historian Pittscottie cast Lady Heron as a Mata Hari using her charms to lure the libidinous James into fatal dalliance; 'stinking adultery and fornication', was his uncompromising verdict.

There are no serious grounds for accusing James of tardiness or dereliction of duty at this time. He had already fulfilled his promise of aid to the French, substantive English forces were being mustered against him, men that might be otherwise deployed across the Channel. In order to achieve his strategic aims it was not necessary for the Scots to advance deeper into England; indeed, the closer to the border he remained then the further Surrey must proceed to engage him. The campaigning season was drawing to a close, and the weather was unseasonably wet and cold; the task facing the English grew harder by the day.

Inevitably, sated by this first orgy of looting, small groups and indivi-duals began to drift away. The highlanders, always fickle in their allegiance, and now short on provisions, also began to disappear. Coupled with this rash of desertions, an outbreak of plague further served to thin out the Scottish host, which might soon have lost nearly thirty per cent of its original manpower. Despite these losses which cannot have been unex-pected James still had a powerful army in the field, easily the equal of whatever Surrey might command.

Surrey was by now on the move. His riders carried news of a general muster in Newcastle, on 1st September, to all the counties of the north. Soon, the men of Lancashire, Cheshire, Yorkshire, Wensleydale and Swale-dale were on the move, filling the muddy roads and crumbled lanes. The quality of the recruits varied considerably. Surrey's eldest son, who was the Lord Admiral, marched north with one thousand two hundred well-drilled marines whose regular step and fashionable uniforms contrasted sadly with the bulk of the rough county levies, who trudged indifferently in their tangled columns.

All Lancashire, for the most part,
The lusty Stanley stout did lead,
A flock of Striplings strong of heart,
Brought up from babes with beef and bred.[18]

Sir Thomas Howard, the Lord Admiral, the same who had bested Andrew Barton in the engagement in the Downs, is described as a 'little, short, dark man' – he was nonetheless both capable and energetic. The command of the English army was to become a father and son partnership with the younger man filling the role of what would now be called a chief of staff. Bishop Ruthal found him to be '. . . . the very leader, conductor and setter on of our army'.[19]

On his way to the north Surrey delayed at Durham where he prayed at the shrine of St Cuthbert and took with him, to Newcastle, the saint's banner. Reviewing the forces he was to command, Surrey must indeed have felt the need for divine assistance. The city was teeming with over twenty thousand men, crammed behind her famous walls. Disheartened, disorganised, untrained and unfed, this motley host waited for leadership. Feeling unable to organise within the crowded confines of the town Surrey managed to drag his shambling army northward, to Bolton-in-Glendale, where he was at least able to carry out a proper review and arrange a command structure.

The only good news was the arrival of the admiral and his crack marines; for the rest the earl was beset by difficulties. He was faced by an enemy superior in numbers, arms and artillery and yet he must engage this enemy without delay, lacking the resources for a protracted campaign. Food was already short and all James had to do was to retire across the border and wait until hunger broke up the English forces; he would then be free to return and ravage the borders at will. Surrey himself felt that it would be folly now to give battle, but the younger men on his staff, the Admiral and Sir Edward Stanley, urged that an encounter was imperative and that somehow the Scots must be persuaded to fight.

Hoping to play upon his adversary's chivalric instincts Surrey resorted to a campaign of calculated insults aimed at his vanity. The dubious honour of conveying these taunts fell to the herald Rouge-Croix who, on 5th

September, was despatched to Ford where, it was believed, the Scots were still encamped. James, however, was not to be found at Ford. His new position was on the north-eastern slopes of Flodden Hill, from where he affirmed to the English herald he was more than willing to give battle but nonetheless detained Rouge-Croix (part of a herald's role was to glean everything he could of the enemy's strength and dispositions). A Scottish herald was sent back to Surrey to relate the king's intentions. Inevitably, this individual, Islay Herald, was detained by the English. Surrey's letter accused the Scottish king of entering England:

> *contrary to his oath and league, and unnaturally against all reason and conscience . . .*[20]

The Admiral also sent a personal letter to James adding further insults and reminding him of the unavenged defeat and death of Andrew Barton. Warming to his theme, Howard continued:

> *He nor none of his company should take no Scottish nobleman prisoner, nor any other, but they should die if they came into his danger, unless it were the King's own person, for he said he trusted to no other courtesy at the hands of the Scots.*[21]

Believing that the Scots must intend to fight on Milfield Plain, Surrey began the protracted task of heaving his cumbersome force on to the march. Apart from the hardcore of professionals from the fleet, the shire levies were as shabby and footsore as ever, though they now had an increasing hunger to contend with. Most of them, apart from Dacre's force of borderers, were a long way from home and marching toward an enemy of uncertain strength. The borderers themselves, astride their shaggy unkempt ponies, were hardly a comforting sight. Scarcely better groomed than their mounts, but armed to the teeth with lances, swords and axe, the borderers exuded an easy confidence and readiness for battle that must have amazed the raw recruits from quieter shires.

When the army was finally camped at Wooler, Surrey arranged to exchange Rouge-Croix for his Scottish counterpart, though the news that the herald brought can hardly have made their reunion a joyful one. The picture presented was one of unrelieved gloom for the English. The Scots were encamped in a strong position with considerable numbers, well fed, well armed and backed by their formidable artillery. The guns were dug

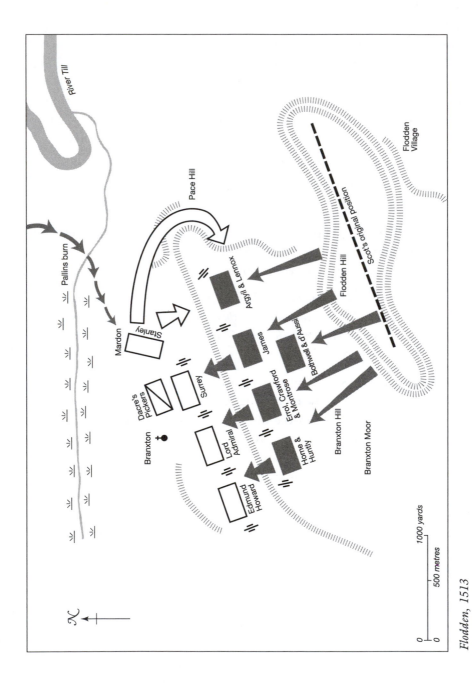

Flodden, 1513

into position covering the passage between the east end of Flodden hill and the line of the Till. This low-lying track of near morass was the only approach to the Scottish position, but any attempt to advance could be enfiladed by a devastating fire from the cannon above.

> *The King of Scots did lie with his army upon a high hill in the edge of Cheviot . . . and was enclosed in three parts, with three great mountains, so there was no passage nor entry unto him but one way where was laid marvellous and great ordnance of guns . . . as goodly guns as have been seen in any realm.*[22]

Such news could scarcely suffice to gladden the heart of even the most optimistic commander and, as Surrey and his despondent officers reviewed their situation in the rain at Wooler, there seemed little cause for optimism. As the men crouched wearily around their sodden bivouacs, depressed and enfeebled by cold, wet and hunger, rumours about the impregnable position and formidable strength of their enemy inevitably began to filter down. Morale, which had never been high, had reached its nadir.

The only immediate solution Surrey and his staff could think of was to intensify the campaign of abuse and draw James, through rage, down from his position of strength. Despite the best endeavours of the redoubtable Rouge-Croix who was dispatched with further taunts on the 8th September, James had more sense than to budge; he refused even to see the herald personally though his rage at the insults delivered may have been more simulated than real. James was in fact doing rather well; he was holding an English army in the sodden confines of Northumberland without incurring either losses or, as matters stood, significant hazard. To date his campaign had achieved all of his objectives; the border defences of England had been breached, her garrisons levelled and despoiled, large numbers of English troops now stood, virtually impotent, before his inexpungable position.

Surrey had committed himself to attacking the Scots by Friday 9th September and had desired the king to deploy his army on the level ground of Milfield Plain directly below Flodden Edge. This James refused to do – if the English sought battle then they must assault the slopes.

Legend relates that on the night of 7th September, as Surrey and his council sat in damp despair, the English camp was galvanised into sudden near-panic by the abrupt arrival of a squadron of unidentified horsemen.

Well mounted and heavily armed, they clattered into the midst of the encampment. Not apparently one to stand on formality, the leader of this stalwart band thrust his way, unannounced, into the council tent itself. Only when he stood before the earl himself did he deign to lift his visor. The countenance thus revealed was that of John Heron, he that had slain the Scottish warden, and harried the borders ever since. Despite his wild reputation and the price upon his head, Surrey was in no position to argue technicalities. Without further ado the erstwhile outlaw and his confederates, all men of similar stamp, were enrolled into the English army and attached to Dacre's command.

Legend further insists that it was Heron who suggested the decisive flanking march that so affected the outcome of the battle. Whether or not this is true is, and always will be, debatable. Nonetheless Heron certainly had the local knowledge and he was never one to be reticent about attacking the Scots. What is certain, however, is that the following morning the camp at Wooler was struck, the Till was forded and northward march on the western bank begun 'in cloggy mire and foule filthy waies.'[23]

This whole manoeuvre was conducted in full view of the Scottish host who, though doubtless amused at first by the ant-like scurrying of their foes below, must have become increasingly baffled, and then concerned. The English army marched steadily northward for eight miles past Doddington, where the ground rose to the heather clad moor and then finally out of sight altogether. A halt was made in the lee of Barmoor Wood some five miles to the east of Flodden Edge.

> *The rearward marched in array ever after*
> *as long as the light day lasted on the ground*
> *then the sun full soon shot under the clouds*
> *and it darkened full dimly and drew toward the night*
> *every man to his rest full readily him dressed*
> *beaten fires full fast, and fettled them to sleep*
> *besides Barmoor in a bank within a broad wood.*[24]

In fact the English had only proceeded as far as it was necessary to conceal their camp from the straining eyes of the Scots. The bulk of Watch Law rose between the two armies and effectively guaranteed concealment. As darkness fell the Admiral and some of his officers trekked to the summit of Watch Law to review the enemy position from this northward vantage.

It is likely that they were hoping to discern a viable means of mounting a flank attack but none presented itself; the only apparent alternative was to continue the northward march and come upon the Scots from the rear. The Scottish position would then lie to the south, atop and beyond Branxton Hill; though steep, the climb here was at least free from artillery bombardment. An English advance from the present northerly position might tempt the Scots into an attack, as they must either fight or submit to having their lines of communication and withdrawal irretrievably severed. The move was a bold one and fraught with hazard for if the Scots struck before the English could deploy, the army would fight with its back to a swollen river with hostile country beyond.

The scene in the Scottish camp was no less tense; if the invaders could not yet discern what was afoot they were aware that there was a risk their line of retreat might be cut off. The debate became heated and though few of those present survived the fight it appears there was opposition to the king's intention to lead the army personally in any encounter. Pittscottie credits his own grandfather, Lord Patrick Lindsay of the Byres, as being an outspoken critic of James's determination, likening the coming battle to a game of chance:

> So my lords, ye may understand by this you shall be called the merchant. and your king a 'rose nobill', and England a common hazarder that has nothing to jeopard but a bad halfpenny in comparison of our noble king and an auld crooked earl lying in a chariot.[25]

James probably realised better than his lords the value of his presence in the field. There was a wealth of precedent; Bruce had added lustre to his laurels by the defeat of de Bohun on the first day of Bannockburn, Henry V, Edward IV, Richard III and Henry VII of England had all led their armies in person. James's hastily raised and disparate army was unwieldy and untried, highlanders, lowlanders and borderers, schooled by French captains in the use of a Swiss weapon. If the men were to fight and fight well then they needed to be led; only the person of the sovereign had that potency, marching at their head and sharing the danger.

By first light on Friday the 9th, Surrey's army was on the move, bearing only their arms; pots, pans, tents and baggage were abandoned. As there was no food anyway this was no great sacrifice, and if defeat were to follow then there would be few returning. Surrey had run out of options and was chancing everything on this last gambit. Failure against such odds could only mean disaster. The English army that marched upon Branxton had to win through, or perish in the attempt. Again we can only guess at the numbers present in the English ranks; thinned by sickness and desertion like the Scots, Surrey had perhaps 13,000–15,000 men.

The army marched, or rather plodded, through Duddo, past the ancient ring of stones towards Twizel Bridge which the van reached probably around eleven. The rearward crossed roughly a mile up-river by the Mill-Ford. Once across they paused to restore their dressing and then moved off. The army advanced in two main divisions both with flanking brigades left and right. They were now moving south toward Branxton Hill, the ridge rising some 300 feet above a stream with a reverse slope up towards the highest point of Pipers Hill. Although quite steep the gradient up to the ridge was nowhere more than, say, 1 in 15. North of Pipers Hill (where the present monument stands), the ground falls away again, a drop of some 60 feet to the marshy dip of the Pallinsburn. This watercourse was a substantial obstacle with only two viable crossings, the more westerly at Branx Brig and the second to the east nearer the mouth at Sandyford.

This difficult terrain was not unexpected; local guides showed the way to the crossings with the Admiral leading the van over the more westerly ford and Surrey taking the rearward to the east. With him travelled the English guns, Branx Brig being unsuitable for the weight of the ordnance. At this point the English were advancing blind; the summit of Branxton Hill cannot be seen from the wetlands by the Pallinsburn. Anxious to discern any movement by the Scots, the Admiral hurried forward towards Pipers Hill from where the whole sweep of the ridge was plainly visible.

What he saw was alarming.

It is uncertain when the Scots first comprehended the English advance but at some point, perhaps around one in the afternoon, scouts would have reported the movement and James, together with his commanders, can have been left in little doubt as to what was intended. Their position, however, was far from critical. At present they were deployed facing south over Flodden Edge. A marked depression separated this position from the top of Branxton Hill; it was therefore necessary to turn the army about, march over the intervening neck of land, dragging the guns. This movement, once completed, would still leave the advancing English the unenviable task of charging uphill against superior numbers with more and heavier ordnance.

The day was by no means lost, neither was the situation critical. As they clambered up the tussocky slope Surrey's weary troops would be lashed by a storm of Scottish iron. If, upon reaching the bottom of the hill, the English either declined to attack or their attempt foundered, the Scots were in an ideal position to swoop down upon them with terrible momentum.

Forming up in the dip, out of sight of the English, the Scottish line comprised, on the left, Hume and Huntly's contingent, then the division of Errol, Crawford and Montrose. In the centre stood the king's division with the wild highlanders of Lennox and Argyle on the right. A fifth division commanded by D'Aussi and the Earl of Bothwell was left as a reserve. With the lowland divisions were those French captains who had landed at Dunbar and who had striven so hard to instil the tactics and élan of the Swiss. The Scots were thus deployed in conformity with Swiss precedent. Hume and Huntly would lead an echeloned attack, the clansmen with their great swords acting as flankers. Errol, Crawford and Montrose would swing into action next with the king's great division forming the rearguard. The highlanders under Argyle and Lennox would cover the exposed flank of the royal brigade.

Edward Hall quotes an eyewitness from the ranks of the English as he first beheld this great mass of serried pikes '. . . . four great battles all on foot with long spears like Moorish pikes'. Another account provides more detail of the Scots deployment:

> *The King of Scots army was divided into five battles, and every battle an arrow shot from the other, and all like furnished from the English army in great plumps, part of them quadrant, and some pike wise, and were on the top of the hill, being a quarter of a mile from the foot thereof.*[26]

As the massed ranks of the Scottish army were being pressed into formation James's gunners cursed, sweated and heaved to first dig free and then manhandle the unwieldy pieces to their new position. Again, at this same time, the rabble of camp followers began burning the heaped refuse created by the host. Thus the final manoeuvrings of both sides were obscured from the other by the huge and ominous pall of filthy smoke, emanating from the abandoned camp. There could hardly have been a more fitting omen. Whether the smoke cloud was a deliberate ploy to screen the army's manoeuvre or simply a happy accident is unclear.

Perched in massive concentration along the summit of Branxton Hill, the ranks of Scottish pikemen waited, like some giant hedgehog, their lines ablaze with proud surcoats and fluttering banners. The army must have seemed to fill the skyline in a great surge of menacing strength. Already the Admiral had come too far. His van had so far outstripped the rearguard and the cumbersome artillery that any sudden rush from the daunting host would surely sweep his slender forces back into the mire. Surrey was a mile and a half to his rear, the enemy less than half that in front. Messengers were dispatched to urge the earl to make all speed, stressing the danger of the Admiral's position. Around this time the Scottish gunners fired a handful of ranging shots, the balls splashing harmlessly in the bog (from where at least one was recovered in the nineteenth century). At length, as the rearguard hurried forward, the army began to deploy, the van leading off to the right.

It has been said that James should have attacked at this point but this does not allow for the nature of the Swiss tactics he was attempting to copy. The pike columns had to advance against the enemy when he was deployed so that the great momentum of the charge swept his forces from the field. This depended upon the enemy being within easy reach. Pike tactics did not lend themselves to extended operations. James was right to hold his forces in check till the moment arrived to deal a decisive blow.

By the time the English line was marshalled it was late afternoon, perhaps around four. Surrey had perceived the Scots were massing in four brigades and adjusted his line to suit; the original formation of six divisions was consolidated into three full brigades with Dacre leading a mounted reserve. The right was commanded by Edmund Howard, Surrey's third son: three thousand-odd raw levies, mostly from Lancashire and Cheshire, bolstered by a few Howard retainers and the hardcore of knights in their midst such as the doughty Bryan Tunstall. Next came the central division under the Admiral with Sir Marmaduke Constable's battalion attached, then Surrey to the left and Stanley in reserve.

The divisions of both the Admiral and his father had advanced to the lip of the decline that fell quite sharply to the stream at the base of Branxton Hill. This was to be of considerable importance. The Scots, in order to attack, would have to cross the miry waters and advance up the incline, thus losing most of the momentum of their sweep down the hillside.

The battle commenced with an exchange of fire, the great guns on both sides spitting roundshot. The Scots had the greater weight of metal but the English pieces under Nicholas Appleyard were lighter and easier to manoeuvre. This was significant and the guns generally had to be dragged back into position after each salvo; 'quick firers', guns mounted on sliding trails that soaked up the savage recoil, were not invented till the early twentieth century.

It has been said that the Scots ordnance suffered because the barrels could not be sufficiently depressed; this is untrue, the angle of the slope is not sufficient to prevent accurate fire. The heavier siege guns were cumbersome and slower to load. In counter battery fire, speed and accuracy are all important. The king's gunners were perhaps less experienced and the death of a captain would tell heavily. Although Borthwick survived, the gun crews seem to have suffered heavy loss and the first round went to the English.

John Leslie, a Scottish chronicler, wrote of the artillery engagement:

> *The English ordnance . . . shot fast and did great skaithe* [damage]
> *and slew his principal gunners; but the King's ordnance did small*
> *skaithe by reason of the height where they stood they shot over the English*
> *army.*[27]

Whilst we have already considered that the elevation requiring less than three degrees' depression would not discountenance the Scottish gunners, it could well be that the angle of fire did prevent the roundshot from 'bouncing' and thereafter striking down men and smashing guns. If the shot thudded harmlessly into the turf this could explain the failure of the Scots to inflict serious losses.

Having silenced the enemy guns Appleyard could turn his attention to the massed files of pikes, a gunner's dream, and shot was soon striking the serried ranks; roundshot is not aimed directly at the enemy ranks but is intended to strike the ground before and then bounce, smashing into the defenceless foot. It is not possible to say how many Scots were mangled by shot – in all probability the losses overall were not great. What was more devastating was the psychological effect of the bombardment upon raw troops, men who had never been fired upon before but were now expected to stand calmly amidst the crash of the great guns, the ear-splitting roar accompanied by foul, sulphurous clouds of smoke. They had to watch their comrades torn and ripped by shot that could sheer through a file of men like a knife through butter.

Clearly James could not allow his men to stand supine whilst flayed by the English artillery. His divisions were arrayed for attack and now was the moment. Hume and Huntly were the first to engage; their division was the 'vorhut' and they swept down upon the English like the wrath of God. On this flank the burn that flowed across the front of the Admiral and Surrey's divisions had levelled out so the attackers were not hindered by either a marshy decline or a slope beyond. Their attack could proceed as intended, the great mass of pikes moving like a bulldozer, their cohesion intact.

The daunting spectacle of several thousand borderers descending upon them in perfect formation, a bristling hedgehog of points, was altogether too much for Howard's raw levies. Stirrings of panic in the ranks, at first as gentle as the rippling waves fanned by a summer breeze, soon swelled to a cascade of fleeing men, scattering and stumbling in blind disorder. Those few who dared stand firm were swept away in the deluge, too few to even check the thousands pouring down upon the English right.

> *Then betide a check that Cheshire men fledden*
> *when the Scots and Cattericks seen our men scatter*
> *they had great joy of their joining and jollily came downward.*[28]

Christopher Savage, Mayor of Macclesfield, with most of his contingent fell either spitted on the levelled pikes or hewn by the Gordons wielding double-handers, the equals of the feared Swiss 'dopplansolders'. The Lancashire men were unsettled before the fight began, having been separated from Stanley's command, and disgruntled at not being permitted to fight, as was their custom, under his banner.

The plan was working. Next it was the turn of Errol, Crawford and Montrose, the 'gewaltschaufen', followed by the king's division, the 'nachhut'. James, true to his promise, prepared to personally lead the triumphant advance of his own central division. This has been seen as the ultimate act of folly, throwing all idea of generalship to the wind for the dream of personal glory, but the pike columns once committed could not be recalled and the supreme commander had little role to play once the order to charge had been given. James had perceived the initial success of

1. *James I*
PG682 *Scottish National Portrait Gallery (Artist unknown)*

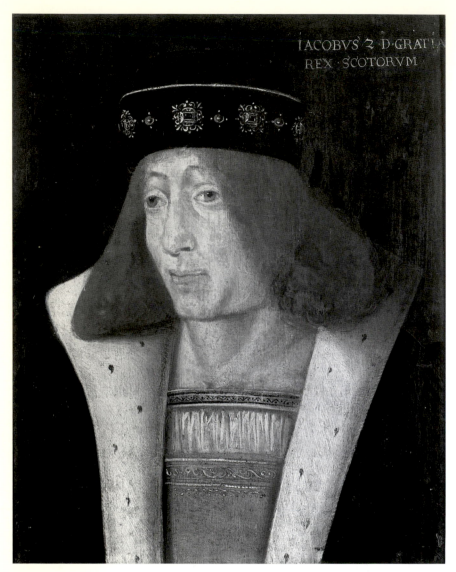

2. James II
PG683 *Scottish National Portrait Gallery (Artist unknown)*

IACOBVS 3 D GRATIA
REX·SOTORVM

3. *James III*
PG684 *Scottish National Portrait Gallery (Artist unknown)*

4. *James IV*
PG685 *Scottish National Portrait Gallery (Artist unknown)*

IACOBVS 5·D·GRA
REX SCOTORVM

5. *James V*
PG686 *Scottish National Portrait Gallery (Artist unknown)*

6. Mary, Queen of Scots
PG1073 *Scottish National Portrait Gallery (Artist unknown)*

7. Stirling Castle
A7456–19 © Crown copyright reproduced courtesy of Historic Scotland

8. Caerlaverock Castle
(Author's own)

Hume and Huntly. It was imperative that this should be followed up; for the Swiss tactics to lead to victory the juggernaut had to maintain momentum, the divisions following each other in a smooth echelon formation.

James led the largest division in the army, perhaps 20 ranks deep, each of 450 pikes. The men hastily removed their shoes to obtain a better grip of the wet grass. As they approached within bow shot the English archers let fly, the feared arrow storm of Crécy, Poitiers and Agincourt. Whilst some, perhaps many shafts, found their mark, the longbow could not stem the advance. The rain had dampened bowstrings, the wind deflected arrows, the plate of the nobles and the harness of the commons afforded protection, as did the great wooden pavises.

On the English right the situation was dire. One of the few who stood firm was the stalwart Bryan Tunstall who, hewing madly at the onrushing Scots, slew Sir Malcolm McKeen and several others before he was overpowered and slain.

But up to heaven with angels bright his golden ghost did flick'ring fly.[29]

Soon, Edmund Howard, supported by only a small band of retainers, found himself surrounded. Fighting desperately, hemmed in on all sides by their foe, the English fought with despairing courage, dropping one by one until Howard himself was the only survivor.

Such an important knight would inevitably bring a hefty ransom and was therefore worth considerably more alive. These economic considerations were ever uppermost in the minds of the borderers. Nevertheless, Howard continued to fight, striking down all who dared approach. It seemed that all was now up for the English on the right but Dacre's border horse moved swiftly to stem the rot. Though considerably inferior to the Scots in numbers, the English enjoyed the tremendous advantage of being both fresh and mounted. Well armed and born to fight, borderer fought borderer in deadly earnest.

At least the affray was more or less in deadly earnest. The underlying pragmatism that marked the borderers' code of survival did not rate international differences as weighty enough to necessitate a fight to the death. Therefore, after a brief but bloody clash, the two forces, as if by tacit agreement, drew apart and faced each other with sullen hostility. Neither Hume nor Dacre would ever admit to an 'arrangement'. Nonetheless the fight had been savage, three of Hume's family and four Gordon chieftains had fallen. Dacre had 160 men killed and wounded with several gentlemen captured.

In the chaos of the initial charge, the bastard Heron, with his own select troop of cut-throats, had hacked a bloody path through Hume's division to rescue the beleaguered Howard. Their mission accomplished, they cut an equally bloody swathe through the Scottish ranks to reach Surrey's division, slaying Sir Davy Hume and numerous of his troop *en route*.

The situation on the English right which had appeared disastrous had transformed, thanks to Dacre's intervention, into a stalemate. Though the Cheshire and Lancashire levies had been broken, Dacre's horse now solidly filled the vacuum. Hume and Huntly's division, in good order, retired some way back up the slope. In the Admiral's division the daunting sight of Errol, Crawford and Montrose together with the king's division sweeping down upon them *en masse* was enough to command the full attention of even the coolest warrior.

As the Scots descended the hill, the English longbowmen stepped forward and the familiar rain of death began to whistle down upon the advancing mass. The heavy wooden shields, or pavises, which could be raised by the holders as a protective screen and then discarded when the armies finally closed did good service, thus the arrow storm had less effect than in previous encounters. Though Scots did fall, the customary wholesale slaughter was avoided and the mighty rush of the advance remained unchecked.

> *The English shafts in volleys hail'd in headlong charge their horses assailed; front, flank and rear, their squadrons sweep to break the Scottish circle deep, that fought around their King but yet, though thick the shafts as snow, through charging knights like whirlwinds go, though bill-men ply the ghastly blow unbroken was the ring.*[30]

What King James had not planned for was the terrain, the sharp drop into the marshy bottom by the stream with the incline beyond and it was this which defeated his plan. The cohesion, impetus and impact needed to create the steamroller effect were lost. Men struggled and cursed, the unwieldy pikes dipping and dropping. The sustained onrush that had scattered Howard's division on the English right was lost in the centre. This momentum, this irresistible motion, was lost, and being lost could not be recovered. The charge was the very essence of Swiss tactics; there was no second line and no alternative plan, and failure meant defeat.

Once the two lines were finally engaged the serious business of killing commenced. Now the Scots began, too late, to discover how stiff and unwieldy a weapon their long pikes were. Though ideal for the smashing, grinding impact of the initial charge, in the cut and thrust of protracted hand-to-hand they were proving totally inferior to the bills borne by the English.

The English bill was a hybrid of the battlefield, born of a lethal union between an agricultural implement, the bill hook and the military spear. Originally the peasants' hook became mounted upon a long pole until, around 1300, the two weapons were fused to create a ghastly martial instrument sporting a blade, with a long spear-like head to the fore and a shorter narrow edge at the back. Far lighter and more versatile than the cumbersome pike, Surrey and the Admiral's men were able to lop off the heads of their enemies' weapons, then hack them down. Thoughts of hunger and fatigue were swept away in the rush of adrenaline as the English fought back savagely. Too outnumbered to consider giving quarter, they began to carve bloody gaps in the Scottish ranks.

This was no chivalric contest but rather a slogging, brutal killing, where the Scottish pike was running a very poor second. With methodical precision the Admiral's professional soldiers hacked, slashed and hewed, piling the Scottish dead in heaps. The charge of the king's division, somewhat less destroyed by the ground, still had sufficient killing punch to drive the English back almost a bow shot. But with terrible tenacity the billmen held their ground and slowed the Scottish advance.

The Scots of both divisions began to lose heart, to falter and then to run. At first a trickle, and then a torrent, they fled. In warfare involving large columns of men advancing the rot starts not at the front where usually there's nowhere to run and too great a press but at the back where men not fully engaged, morale crumbling, think of seeking safety in flight. Invariably the trickle swiftly builds to a stream and then a river and finally a spate.

Up to now the English had been desperately on the defensive against the might of the Scottish onslaught backed by their superior numbers. Now the field was already thickening with Scottish dead. Many had fled, leaving the remains of the earls' division and those with the king to face both Surrey and the Admiral. At last, the pendulum had swung to favour the English. The fear, hunger and despair that had haunted Surrey's army for so long was to be washed away in a torrent of Scottish blood. Many of the nobility had already succumbed to the slashing bills. The Scottish position had sunk from certain victory to equal contest and finally, to a desperate bid for survival.

The slaughter was to drag on for another two hours but even the arrival of Bothwell's reserve could not stem the tide of disaster. Indeed his men became more meat to the grinder, assailed in the flank by a spirited charge from Dacre's horse; the charge was beaten off but the doughty Cumbrian led his bruised horsemen against the left flank of the king's doomed column.

James, 'constrained to fight in a round compass', could sense the inevitability of defeat. His tactics, though sound, had failed him utterly. Gathering the survivors of his household to him he led them in a final, defiant charge against the banners of Surrey himself, falling with his retainers around him, scarcely a stone's throw from the earl's position. One legend at least claims that the doughty earl himself laid low the Scottish monarch in the final confrontation, though the reality is that the king, like his nobility, succumbed to the hacking bills.

However he finally met his end James died as he had led, like a valiant knight, the significance of his passing ignored in the frenzied carnage. Cut and slashed by bills, the king fell almost unnoticed as his men, now too occupied by the pressing problem of their own survival, fought despairingly in the gathering dusk.

The Scots died hard; accounts speak of the ferocity of the fight. The superlative armour of the Scottish knights afforded considerable protection but the flailing bills were relentless, smashing into plate, hacking them down, sharp points seeking gaps in the armour, daggers thrust through visors so there could be no mistake. It was the Swiss who had adopted the ruthless doctrine of 'no prisoners' but it was the English who excelled in practice on the field; none was spared in the agony of slaughter. The wet ground and the stream beyond were puddled with a thick ooze of gore, so much so that men removed their leather-soled boots to get a better grip.

Where was the Scottish right, the division of highlanders under Argyle and Lennox whose numbers, even yet, could stem the tide of defeat? The highlanders had problems of their own. Chief among these was the redoubtable Sir Edward Stanley who, rather than wait for the Scots to descend into the fray, had carried the fray to meet them. From his position on the extreme left of the English line Stanley could see that the eastern flank of the ridge, some 500 yards south of Mardon, was devoid of enemy presence. He had also perceived the potential of a re-entrant at the dip, the approach shielded from the view of those above.

He detached a commanded party to engage the clansmen from the front and to fix their attention whilst he led the mass of his battalion, divided into three companies, by this flanking route, his men also stripping off their shoes to facilitate the clamber. Below the lip of the ridge he reformed and dressed the ranks before bidding his archers loose. The effect on the highlanders, caught totally unawares, was immediate and dramatic.

The lightly armed and mainly unarmoured warriors dropped in scores and their discomfiture was completed when the English knights and men-at-arms crashed into their midst. The contest was short and sharp, the English fighting with a sustained ferocity that soon sapped the sagging morale of the stunned highlanders.

Both Argyle and Lennox, in the company of several notable chiefs, fell in a desperate attempt to rally their men. Their leaders dead, panic spread like wildfire amongst the highlanders and soon they were streaming downhill. Ironically, their flight must have taken them past the bodies of their king and his household. They probably never paused to look.

Stanley calmly led his victorious companies down the hill to complete the encirclement of the Scots still fighting in the centre. The slaughter went on into the twilight, ever decreasing bands of Scots vainly trying to parry the frenzied slashing of the English, now so drunk with bloodlust that even those too wounded to rise, or begging quarter, were not spared.

The only faint chance was the bloodied but still intact division of Hume and Huntly. The latter was anxious to advance but the former declined, too pragmatic to squander his force in such a vein endeavour. Hume saw his duty to the border as far outweighing his duty to the king. With his command, at least, intact Hume would have some chance of resisting the storm that would likely break once the Scots were defeated.

At last the darkness halted the massive slaughter. Dawn revealed a scene of hideous carnage. Surrey's army is said to have accounted for some ten thousand Scots though the tally was probably a good deal less, but included in the butchers' bill was the flower of their chivalry. One archbishop, one bishop, ten earls, nineteen barons and three hundred knights. It is said and probably did not lose in the telling that whole glens and towns were stripped of the cream of their manhood and joined their renaissance prince in a death more typical of a dark age hero.

The English gained a great haul of booty from the mass of Scottish slain and their abandoned camp. The pride of James's army, his great artillery train, fell into English hands. Henry VIII was quick to shower his victorious captains with honours. Surrey became Duke of Norfolk, the Admiral now being created Earl of Surrey. Sir Edward Stanley was made Lord Monteagle.

The host that had defeated the Scots had lost some one thousand seven hundred men in the battle, and of those that survived, only four thousand four hundred, under Dacre, remained in arms, to harry the Scottish marches.

On the morning after the battle a half-naked corpse was dragged from the macabre pile of Scottish dead. Taken to Berwick, this was formally recognised as the mortal remains of James IV of Scotland. The body was disembowelled, embalmed and then sent, first to Newcastle and then in a lead casket to London. Henry's Queen Catherine debated sending the grissly trophy to her husband in France but finally sent his bloody surcoat instead.

The remains proceeded through successive stages of degradation. At first housed in the monastery of Sheen, they were thrown into a lumber room when dissolution took place. Still later, workmen in the house cut off the head and used it for a macabre plaything. Thereafter it came into the possession of Lancelot Young, Elizabeth I's master glazier, who kept it on display at his home. Eventually it was buried in an anonymous grave.

The present, unassuming line of the B6352 runs westward along the base of Flodden Edge. The eye is instinctively drawn from the pleasant pasture land to the timber clad slope; the strength of the position is at once obvious, dominating Millfield Plain below. At West Flodden one may turn left to skirt the flank of the hill and traverse the saddle beyond that leads to Branxton Hill. The lowest point is crossed by the minor road that runs east to west through Branxtonmoor and Blinkbonny, now a pretty farmhouse in restrained, estate-style gothic. The road leads over the brow of the hill to dip toward Branxton. From the top, the formidable nature of the Scots' position is immediately evident.

You are now standing where the massed pikes of Crawford, Errol and Montrose's division deployed on the day of the battle, for many their first and last. As the cool wind whips over the brow of the hill it is not difficult to picture the vast phalanx of serried staves, the men shuffling nervous and uncertain, skeins of smoke from the burning rubbish eddying in the sharp breeze. A splatter of cold rain, followed by a tentative sun. Captains sweating in their harness as they strove to order the lines, men turning to empty their bladders, stale sweat, human waste and wet wool heavy in the air. To the east would have been the king's division with Bothwell and D'Aussi to your right rear in the dip. Beneath you the English, their brigades spreading out from the rise of Pipers Hill to your left, the Admiral's men standing just below the present monument with his brother's division to the west.

The air is split by the unearthly crack of the great guns, the labouring gunners and matrosses a frenzy of activity, each monster having to be laboriously hauled back into position after firing, the cloying stench of black powder and sulphurous smoke belching in the wind. The smack as English roundshot bounce murderously from the slope, here taking a man's head clean off, showering his comrades with a spray of bone and tissue, punching through a file of pikes, men dropping like mangled puppets.

As one descends the hill the line of the fatal burn can clearly be distinguished. Now under the plough the land is tamed and cultivated but the seriousness of the obstacle is plain, a fatal dip with a sharp ascent to the line occupied by the English. To the west the dip disappears, the contours rising to provide a far more level descent, the topography that facilitated the rout of Edmund Howard's brigade. At the base of the ridge the land swells to the left towards the monument atop Pipers Hill, beyond that Windy Law and the dip to the Pallinsburn, still very much in evidence though now largely drained, a far less potent obstacle than that which confronted the Admiral on the morning of the battle.

Flodden Field has, in fact, changed but little. The drain layer and the ploughman have dried the marshland and softened the landscape but it is by no means difficult to visualise the whole battlefield. Step down into the line of the dip and look toward the English position and you can see how so mundane a feature could lead to such a signal disaster and imagine the horror that resulted. The sodden grasses mired in blood, the line of the burn transfigured to a slaughterhouse, men falling in droves, hacked and maimed, crushed and trampled, their king, slashed by the frenzied bills, dying unheeded in the press. If it might be said that James failed as a king and general he certainly did not fail as a knight, nor did he desert those he led and they, true to their oath, fell around him.

Unbroken was the ring:
The stubborn spear-men still made good
Their dark, impenetrable wood
Each stepping where his comrade stood,
The instant that he fell.[31]

Notes

1 Quoted in Sadler, D.J., *Battle for Northumbria*, Newcastle 1988 p. 102.
2 Ibid p. 102.
3 Ibid p. 103.
4 Ibid p. 103.
5 Ibid p. 104.
6 Lynch, M., *Scotland: A New History*, London 1991 p. 160.
7 Hall, Edward, 'Kyng Henry VIII' quoted in Barr, N., *Flodden*, 2001 Gloucs. p. 60.
8 Quoted in Sadler p. 106.
9 Ibid p. 106.
10 Barr p. 61.
11 Machiavelli, *Art of War*, quoted Barr p. 39.
12 Oman, Sir C., *Art of War in the Sixteenth Century*, London 1937 Chapter 1 part VI.
13 Brewer 'Letters & Papers' quoted in Barr p. 46.
14 Burne, A.H., *Battlefields of England*, London 1950 p. 157.
15 Barr p. 11.
16 Sadler p. 107.
17 Norham Castle, one of the chain of fortresses securing the English east march along the line of the Tweed. Originally a 'motte and bailey' construction built by Bishop Ranulph Flambard in 1121 then rebuilt in stone in the reign of Henry II, following several Scottish captures in the earlier reign. The great square keep was built by Bishop Hugh Puisset and was raised to five storeys in 1423. The inner bailey is surrounded by its own moat which could be flooded; the outer curtain, the walls breached by the Scots' artillery, is mainly thirteenth-century work with towers added later. The west gate was refurbished in the fifteenth century when the barbican and drawbridge were added. See Long, B., *Castles of Northumberland*, Gateshead 1967 p. 142.
18 Quoted in Sadler p. 109.
19 Sadler p. 108.
20 Hall, Edward, 'Kyng Henry VIII' quoted in Barr p. 72.

21 Ibid p. 73.
22 Ibid p. 74.
23 Sadler p. 109.
24 Baird 'Scottish Feilde and Flodden Feilde' quoted in Barr p. 79.
25 Hall, Edward, 'Kyng Henry VIII' quoted in Barr p. 81.
26 James 'Articules of the Bataile' quoted in Barr p. 85.
27 Quoted in Sadler p. 110.
28 Baird 'Scottish Feilde and Flodden Feilde' quoted in Barr p. 102.
29 Quoted in Sadler p. 116.
30 Ibid p. 118.
31 After Scott, quoted in Barr p. 31.

Chapter 17

The Road to Solway Moss

His bearing was regal, his glance was eloquent
Of honour in war, skill in love's tournament;
Sweetness and strength together in his face
Showed Mars and Venus both had leant him grace,[1]

'Ye lied, ye lied, now, king,' he says,
Altho' a king and prince ye be!
For I've luved naething in my life,
I weel dare say it, but honesty –.[2]

In the cold grey dawn of a late autumn morning nearly thirty years after the disaster at Flodden another Scottish army was on the move, this time in the west. On 24th November 1542 a force some ten thousand strong began splashing over the chill waters of the Esk on to the low-lying plain of Solway Moss. In front of them was an English marcher force of, at best, one third of their numbers under the west march warden Sir Thomas Wharton. It would seem that the Scots were unstoppable, the warden's men were comprised almost entirely of border horse whilst the invaders were well found with horse, foot and guns. They were attacking on the orders of their sovereign James V though the king, stricken by an unspecified malady, had advanced no further than Lochmaben and the army had set off under the command of Lord Maxwell.

The king had inherited the throne at the age of only seventeen months when his father was killed. The French poet Pierre de Ronsard wrote the adulatory verse repeated above after he met James at the French court in 1536. De Ronsard was impressed by the young ruler's favourable air of reasonableness and strength. By no means all of his subjects, especially those drawn from the higher ranks of the nobility, would have shared this vision.

In 1513 Scotland faced the trial of yet another royal minority, all of the infant king's four predecessors had died violently and James IV's will had appointed the lad's mother Queen Margaret as Guardian. There was opposition to the queen's assuming the role of head of state. She was, after all, a sister of Henry VIII and anti-English feeling was, for obvious reasons, running rather high. If she were not to be a suitable regent then the most obvious candidate was Robert, Duke of Albany, the son of James III's mercurial brother by his French wife. The younger Albany had spent most of his life in France and knew little of the maelstrom of Scottish politics.

Margaret, as the royal widow, did not lack for allies. She was carrying the late king's second son[3] and possessed a powerful ally in Archibald, 6th Earl of Angus, the 'Red' Douglas. This earl had succeeded James III's nemesis Archibald 'Bell the Cat' after his elder brother fell at Flodden and headed a pro-English faction. A year after her husband's death Queen Margaret married Angus. The union was viewed by some as a victory of passion over politics though, in fact, it may have been quite the reverse and the queen was hoping to consolidate her position by cementing the Douglas alliance.

From the English perspective Flodden, whilst a notable victory, had been essentially a sideshow whilst the main war unfolded in France, though the battle was to be the only real glory attaching to English arms from the campaign of 1513. Surrey had been wholly on the defensive and his tired, wet and hungry army, burdened by a long train of wounded and weighed down with spoil, was in no fit state to mount an invasion even had the earl wished to do so. Dacre remained on the frontier with instructions to follow up the success with a series of raids. The Scottish west, Teviotdale and the Merse all felt the English presence. Sir Christopher Dacre of Gilsland, the warden's brother and an accomplished border fighter, led a foray that lifted some four thousand beasts, horses and a weight of gear. He was 'continewally birnying from the breke of daye to oone of the clok after noone'.[4]

The Scots, depleted as they might have been by the carnage at Flodden, were not slow to respond and torched five vills in the east. In the following spring Dacre continued the harrying and estimated his riders were lifting beasts at a ratio of 100:1 and destroying six habitations for every one razed by the Scots. He could report that the border dales 'lies all, and every one of them, waist now; noo corne sawne upon any of the said grounds'.[5] In the west his riders took up Annan and thirty-three vills, depredations the warden reported to Cardinal Wolsey with a palpable sense of achievement and expressing the hope that the good work might flourish and continue.[6] Despite this bullishness Dacre was too seasoned a campaigner to drift into complacency. Wark and Bewcastle were both repaired, whilst Maxwell struck back, raiding the Debatable Land and relieving the warden's tenants of some seven hundred stock.

If Queen Margaret perceived that the Douglas alliance would consolidate her position then she had miscalculated. By her marriage she forfeited her role as guardian to the infant prince and hastened the appointment of Albany as regent. The duke, happily for Scotland, was a man of an altogether different stamp from his perfidious father, and he possessed both strength and integrity. Arriving in May 1515, he was installed as regent on 10th July. A Francophile, he took up his appointment with some misgivings. Already marked for high office in his adopted country he faced immediate opposition from the Douglas faction and was obliged to besiege the queen at Stirling and remove both her sons by force of arms. The little king stayed in the castle under the tutelage of Lord Erskine whilst his mother sought refuge in England.

Dacre, anxious to discomfit the Francophiles, encouraged his royal guest to recover her sons by a *coup de main* engineered by Angus. When this failed both were obliged to retire south of the border[7] whilst Albany, championing the French interest, looked for ways to continue hostilities with England. Without considerable support, however, this was not going to be possible. Besides, most Scots lords felt they had bled enough and could summon up no enthusiasm for a fresh bout.

Albany was to act as regent from 1515–24 though his rule was interrupted by long periods spent out of the country attending to affairs in France. Two years into his appointment he negotiated the Treaty of Rouen whereby James V was contracted to marry the Princess Madeleine, third daughter of Francis I. Albany was as diligent as circumstances would allow; his long periods of absence immediately facilitated a breakdown in order. In 1516 he was obliged to deal with a rebellion from the Merse when Lord

Hume and his brother, having previously entered into treasonable correspondence with Henry, advanced their banners in revolt. Both paid with
their lives in the autumn of that year. Albany's policy on the border was to
try and strengthen royal control by relieving marchers of their appointments
as wardens and installing new men from outside, untainted by the interests
of kin and affinity. The Humes had, prior to their rebellion, already murdered one such appointee, the unfortunate Frenchman D'Arcy.[8] Meanwhile the Elliots, abetted by Fingerless Will Nixon and others, successfully
took up both Hexham and Haltwhistle.

In the autumn of 1518 Dacre moved against the more lawless elements
on the English side, targeting Redesdale where ten of the leading heidsmen
were arrested and escorted to incarceration with a full company as guard.
These proved insufficient when the party was set upon by a superior force of
dalesmen. In the resulting skirmish the bailiff of Morpeth and others were
killed, more made prisoner and the captives set at liberty. The Bishop of
Carlisle reported sourly to Wolsey that: 'There is more thefte and extorycyon
[blackmail] by English theffes than there is by all the Scottes of Scotland'.[9]

When Albany was safely occupied in France Queen Margaret felt able to
return. Her partnership with Angus had faltered and, in 1519, she was
casting about for the means to procure a divorce. Her brother, who at this
point had not experienced the need to divest himself of an unsuitable consort, refused to countenance the split and Margaret was obliged to petition
her erstwhile foe, the regent,[10] for assistance. The Douglas, his marital
difficulties aside, was feuding with the Earl of Arran, who represented the
pro-French party whilst Albany was away. The two sides clashed in a violent
scrimmage that spilled untidily over the streets of the capital in the spring
of 1520 with the Douglases gaining the upper hand.

The duke returned to his troublesome charge in 1521, banished Angus
to France and set about drumming up support for a resumption of hostilities against England. This was not forthcoming and Queen Margaret, glad
to see the back of her mettlesome spouse, was not prepared to lend her
support for a war against her brother. The regent appeared to be gathering
his forces in July 1522 and the queen promptly relayed details of his plans
to Dacre. Albany had meanwhile received scant co-operation from the
nobility and was obliged to accept the English warden's offer of a truce.
He had not despaired of instigating a border campaign and, in October
1522, crossed again to France with the message that any military activity

would be procured only with substantial assistance in terms of both men and materiel.

Henry was also prepared to make an offer to the Scots, a five-year truce with a marriage alliance, the hand of the Princess Mary. When these overtures were rejected the king, in his habitual manner, exploded in wrath and unleashed his marchers. A series of powerful raids were launched during the spring and summer of 1523 under the leadership of the elder Howard, now Duke of Norfolk, aided by his son Thomas, now elevated to the earldom of Surrey. They were assisted in the field by Dacre, Ralph Fenwick and William Heron. Tyne and Redesdale were turned loose against Teviotdale and the Merse. Dacre took up Kelso and the lands around. Albany, perhaps unused to the savagery of border conflict, complained bitterly about the scale of the destruction and was particularly horrified at the sacking of religious houses. Cardinal Wolsey, on the other hand, was able to observe that, by the end of summer '. . . there left neither house, fortress, village, tree, cattle, corn, or other succour for man'.[11]

In September Surrey, at the head of six thousand soldiers, led a strike against Jedburgh which, after a stiff fight, was taken and thoroughly slighted. Dacre was detached to deal with Ker of Ferniherst's castle nearby[12] where he found the Kers disposed to fight. As the English foot sweated to manoeuvre the guns into place the Scots launched a strong sally which was seen off only after the warden dismounted his eight hundred horse to fight in support. Having been subjected to a brisk bombardment the defenders eventually capitulated and the redoubtable Dand [Andrew] Ker made prisoner.

The Scots were not yet done, however, and mounted a raid on the English camp under the cover of darkness, penetrating the horse lines, stampeding and thieving their mounts. Several hundred horses were lost and Dacre, doubtless in search of a face saver, classified the incident as the devil's work, the evil one having been seen at least six times during the raid![13] Surrey gave a pretty accurate assessment of his subordinate: 'There is noo herdyer nor bettir knyght, but often time he doth not use the most sure order'.[14]

Despite the extent of these depredations and the flow of men and weapons from France the Scots could not be induced to mount a counter offensive. The best that could be managed, in the closing months of 1523, was a leaguer of Wark, commanded by Ferniherst seeking vengeance for the slighting of his own hold. The garrison was commanded by Sir William Lisle of Fenton and put up a spirited resistance. The Scots set up batteries on their side of the Tweed and were able to breach the walls of the lower bailey. A brigade, mainly French in composition, was launched across the river to attempt an amphibious assault. The attackers numbered some two thousand and were able to gain a lodgement in the outer works. Lisle then put in a counter attack which left numbers of the French dead and saw off the remainder. Many drowned in the scramble to regain the boats.[15] When the relief force arrived they counted some three hundred unburied dead, mainly French, around the battered walls.

In her ceaseless quest for power Margaret had now allied herself to the Arran faction and managed to wrest control of the king. Due to Albany's lobbying she finally got her divorce from Angus in 1525 and, the year after, married her third husband Henry Stewart who was created Lord Methven. In 1524 James attained his technical majority at twelve and was able to dispense with the regency. Though Albany was happy to retire his return to France provided a window for Angus who returned firstly to dominate the King's Council and then, in November 1525, he virtually kidnapped James and ruled as quasi-regent for the next three years.

To distract his royal charge, still immured at Stirling and whose education had been at best patchy, Angus was happy to provide endless amusement, hunting, hawking and, when he reached the age to be interested, women. As he grew towards maturity in these difficult circumstances James learnt the arts of secrecy; he was later to exhibit both charm and charisma, particularly to the commons, but suspected his nobles too much to develop the type of powerful affinity a monarch requires. In the meantime the Douglas clan enjoyed a monopoly of state appointments, running the country as their private fief. He did make appeals to both his mother and to Arran to prise him free of the Douglas grip but these produced no tangible results. With Margaret now wed to Methven Arran graduated more towards the Douglas camp.

Angus's brand of dictatorship was never calculated to make him popular and resentment at the manner he and his affinity were lining their own pockets found a champion in John Stewart, Earl of Lennox. Having failed to raise an army with which to liberate the king and oppose Douglas early in 1526, the earl tried again in high summer. Raising his banner at Stirling he swiftly formed a focus for the disaffected: Queen Margaret and her husband, James Beaton, Archbishop of St Andrews, the earls of Argyll, Moray, Cassilis and Glencairn, with a smattering of lesser gentry all joined his crusade.

Angus, his kin and the captive king were all in Edinburgh when the revolt flared. Never one to shirk a fight the Douglases marched out to confront Lennox. James was dragged along. When he sought means to temporise Sir George Douglas, Angus's brother, expostulated: 'Sir, rather than our enemies should take you from us, we will lay hold on your body; and, if it be rent in pieces, we will be sure to take our part of it'.[16] Faced with such brutal assurance the king could do little but acquiesce. Worse, he had to witness the rout of Lennox's force at Linlithgow and his subsequent murder. Angus appeared stronger than ever.

Amongst his appointments the earl was warden of both east and middle marches. Liddesdale was extremely active at this point, the names riding with the Tynedale men, the Charltons, Dodds, and Armstrongs in an unholy league: 'the Armstrangs and the theiffs of Ewysdaill were joined with the rebels of Tyndaill, and were comyn untoe theym and kepet all company togedders'.[17] Angus did make one major effort to check Liddesdale when he made a lightning descent on the valley and captured two of the wilder spirits, Simon Armstrong of Whithaugh, 'Sim the Laird', and his brother Davy 'the Lady' – the raid also netted four thousand beasts and saw most of the habitable places reduced to ashes.[18]

In 1525 the church made an attempt to mortify the reivers with a general form of excommunication. Gavin Dunbar, the Bishop of Glasgow, penned his epic 'Monition of Cursing', some fifteen hundred words of savage invective: 'I curse thaim gangand [going] and I curse thaim rydand [riding]; I curse thaim standand, and I curse thaim sittand; I curse thaim eatand, I curse thaim drinkand; I curse thaim walkand, I curse thaim sleepand; I curse thaim rysand, I curse thaim lyand, I curse thaim at hame, I curse thaim fra hame; I curse thaim within the house, I curse thaim without the house; I curse thair wiffis, thair barnis, and thair servandis participand with thaim in thair deides'.[19] This diatribe was read out from every pulpit in the diocese and throughout the marches. Not to be outdone the Bishop of Durham lambasted Tynedale in a similar vein. Neither had the slightest effect.

Two years after his initial raid Angus returned to Liddesdale to administer some more of the same medicine. Perhaps twenty from the riding names were killed out of hand, more were captured, and thirteen of these were dragged to a handy bridge and hanged from the parapet. The survivors were taken to Edinburgh as hostages. When their incarceration failed to secure any local improvement they, too, were executed.[20]

Matters in Tynedale were scarcely any easier. In the autumn of 1523, Sir Nicholas Ridley had entered into a dispute with Dacre and Fenwick over title to Plenmeller Common.[21] To give some teeth to his argument he dispatched his kinsman Will Ridley to raise the Tynedalers. Will found willing confederates in the Charltons of Hesleyside, Bellingham, Shitlington and the Bower, known collectively as 'the Hesleyside Band', Tom Charlton of Carriteth and one Percy Green, known only to be a notorious reiver.[22]

The band, with four hundred riders at their back, chased the keeper, Sir Ralph Fenwick, clear out of Tynedale and were joined by like-minded free spirits from Redesdale, Bewcastle and Gilsland. Through 1524 they terrorised at will and when Dacre pursued them they slipped over the border into Liddesdale where more eager recruits, perhaps six hundred in all, were ready and waiting. When Angus threatened, the outlaws moved on into the Threap. So widespread and persistent were their depredations that the Bishop of Carlisle, seeking to journey from Newcastle to his diocese, was obliged to conduct a sixty-mile detour![23]

Wolsey was outraged at the apparent ease with which the raiders were able to operate. Throughout the spring and summer of 1525 they plundered, seemingly at will, throughout Northumberland and Durham, riding in 'bushments', that is to say large bodies and with banners displayed – a blazon of open rebellion.[24] No garrison could be safely maintained in Tynedale and there seemed no hope of catching Ridley or his allies. However, in the autumn the raids died down and subsided. Will Ridley appears simply to vanish from history.[25]

The Ridley rebellion might be over but Tynedale was to remain unsettled and in no small part this was due to the efforts of Sir William Lisle who, since his stalwart defence of Wark, had drifted into banditry. He was a Percy vassal, sometimes Constable of Alnwick, and held the manor of East Woodburn in Redesdale.[26] Over the winter of 1523–4 he maintained a dispute with the Sheriff of Northumberland over the matter of some lifted beasts. Three years later, in August 1526, the Court of Star Chamber judged his crimes which included murder, robbery and sedition, sufficiently serious to imprison both he and his nephew Humphrey in Pontefract Castle, one of the strongest fortresses north of the Trent which already held a number of the Tynedale thieves.

The Lisles were later moved to Newcastle where they shared cells with a batch of Armstrong riders. Towards the end of June in 1527 the Lisles overpowered and slew their gaolers and they, together with the Liddesdale men, escaped from custody. In this they were abetted by a gang of forty odd reivers from the upland dales,[27] who brought swift horses to convey the escapees to the safety of Mangerton. As if this were not enough the Tynedale men incarcerated in Pontefract also slipped the leash.

Lisle now accepted the role of leader of a formidable outlaw confederacy, a 'wild ungracious man more given to cruelty than to any goodness. . . . captain of the thieves of both nations inhabiting the borders . . . the thieves and evil – disposed men both of Tynedale and Redesdale'.[28] As well as the Liddesdale men he could count upon Charltons, Hedleys, Ogles and Fenwicks, the entire, unholy alliance boosted by a network of spies and informers, including a fair number of females.[29] The band ravaged the whole of the South Tyne and Hexhamshire and forayed into Coquetdale, down the length of the Aln and as far south as Durham. The Sheriff, Sir Ralph Ellerker, with whom Lisle had previously tangled was a frequent victim.[30]

Lisle's liege lord was Henry Percy 5th Earl of Northumberland. Though he bore the illustrious name this Percy was more of a dilettante than a warrior, dubbed 'the Magnificent' by contemporaries on account of his ambitious building programmes around his residences.[31] His failure as warden led to the eclipse of the dynasty and men like Lisle no longer had the greatness of the Percys as both shield and restraint. At Christmas 1527, in recognition, as Ralph Robson asserts,[32] of the fact that only a Percy could maintain order, the 6th earl was appointed as east march warden.

The 6th earl was made of sterner stuff than his predecessor and swiftly set about the restoration of order. In January 1528, the career of Charlton of Shitlington was brought to a violent end. Both upland dales now submitted in short order. Fourteen rebels were hanged at Alnwick and a joint foray with Liddesdale intercepted and dispersed, with one of the Armstongs and one of the Dodds both being taken and subsequently executed. Liddesdale suddenly grew wary when Northumberland threatened a warden raid, possibly supported by Angus and, before the month was out, the revolt had collapsed and Lisle surrendered. For Sir William there could be no reprieve though, amazingly, Humphrey Lisle escaped the death penalty.

In the aftermath of the Lisle rebellion Dacre's son, Lord William, decided to impart a lesson of his own to Liddesdale and the Threap. He pulled together a force of perhaps two thousand riders and his principal targets were Johnnie [John] Armstrong of Gilnockie and 'Sim The Laird'. Dacre fell foul of the inevitable web of cross-border understandings and the Storeys betrayed his plans to the Armstrongs who successfully resisted the attack. Undeterred Lord William gathered ordnance and tried again, bombarding Gilnockie's hold at Hollows near Canonbie. Whilst he was thus occupied Johnnie took the opportunity to beat up Netherby and Gilsland. Even more humiliating, Ritchie [Richard] Graham whom Dacre had arrested and incarcerated in Carlisle on suspicion (almost certainly correct) of being in collusion with Liddesdale, escaped, raised his affinity, and joined the Armstrongs.[33]

Affronted, Dacre not only stepped up his campaign in the field but took the unprecedented step of banning the Liddesdale men from Carlisle market. It seems most anomalous that such notorious characters as Johnnie of Gilnockie and the other Armstrongs were accustomed to attend market days as though they were law-abiding minor gentry. Nonetheless, this level of intercourse was normal and Dacre's ruling appeared somehow petty and unsporting: 'I woll neithr suffer the said Armistranges to inhabit upon the Debateable grounde, nor yet suffer theim or any Scottisman of evill name or fame to com to Carlisle market'.[34]

In March 1528 he struck again at the Threap and levelled a tower belonging to Ill Will Armstrong but in May Liddesdale retaliated with Armstrongs and Irvines taking up eight vills and sixty houses on the English side. The day following this raid, whilst the thatch still smouldered and blood was still pooling on the dusty ground, a second foray followed the first, splashing over the Esk and Leven. Seventy beasts which had somehow escaped the attention of the previous night's visitors were rounded up and a further eight of the inhabitants cut down.[35]

The riposte was led by Christopher Dacre, Lord William's uncle, and the blow fell upon the Routledges, a relatively inoffensive name. Neutrality, however, was not an option and minding one's own business did not guarantee immunity. Liddesdale was now at war with the Dacres and planned accordingly. In the heat of August a body of Nixons and Crosers hit at Bewcastle and Thirlwell,[36] lifting stock and taking one of Dacre's tenants captive. The trod[37] was raised and the warden picked up the trail by Bewcastle.

The garrison had neither bestirred themselves when the raiders struck nor showed any enthusiasm for joining in the chase. This might have raised grounds for suspicion, allied to the fact the reivers were retiring by the same route they'd come but, big with vengeance, the warden's posse blundered on to within a mile of the line, straight into an ambush. The balmy summer night suddenly filled with the hiss of latches[38] and the clash of steel.

Armstrongs, Elliots and more Nixons rose like deadly wraiths from the heather and a desperate mêlée ensued. The English were unawares, unready and outnumbered. Between thirty and forty of Dacre's men were taken, more were killed and wounded and, of the captives, eleven were slain on the spot. This disaster spurred both sides to agree to a commission – the Scots conceded that the upland dale and the Threap were beyond their effective control. It was then proposed that the problem of Liddesdale be left not to the Scots but with the English and that it would then be 'open season' on the inhabitants. An echo of this, from the Armstrongs themselves, surfaced in December when 'Sim the Laird' met with North-umberland at Alnwick.

Sim reported that his kinsmen and their neighbours had nothing but contempt for royal authority. The dalesmen could mount three thousand riders, hardened reivers and moss troopers all and that there would only be order when England held sway. 'Sim the Laird' was not a leading mag-nate, not a Maxwell, Ker or Hume, but the Liddesdale men constituted a major power on the marches in their own collective right. An Armstrong, or an Elliot, Croser and Nixon belonged firstly to their name, then to Lid-desdale and at some remove to Scotland. The legacy of the centuries of war was this profound disaffection of the upland dales. Men who were expected to form the front line in time of war had no marketable skills in time of peace. For this they cannot be censured: both governments had conspired through their own enmity to create this particular monster and now it was out of control.

Although the Douglas had won the field at Linlithgow and crushed the visible opposition by force of arms, his political base continued to lack any depth. Arran soon withdrew his support and James came to detest the earl's pro-English stance as much as he loathed the Douglases. In 1528 the king managed a dramatic escape from Falkland and defied Angus from Stirling. The Douglas hegemony collapsed and the clan were swiftly bottled up behind the walls of Tantallon where they held out until November. The surrender terms allowed Angus and his kin to withdraw into England as pensioners of Henry VIII who was beginning now to think of divorcing Catherine of Aragon and had little interest in becoming embroiled in Scotland. A five-year truce was negotiated and Angus was to remain in exile south of the border.

Finally free of the Douglas oligarchy the king was able to turn his attention to the state of the realm. There was much to concern him. Both Highlands and border were unsettled and, having sought to reassert the royal writ north of the Great Glen, James was free to turn his attention southward. In 1529 and again the next year the king made strenuous efforts to establish order in the marches. He began quietly summoning a conference of the march wardens and leading lords to promote more effective policing. In November Liddesdale struck at Birkshawes. When the warden general's force, under Nicholas Ridley, attempted pursuit they ran into another ambush and were badly cut up. Of the score of prisoners at least four were subsequently done to death.[39]

In the spring of 1530 James decided to try again, this time with more effective sanctions. The magnates, Hume, Maxwell, Johnstone, Buccleuch, Patrick, Earl of Bothwell (the Keeper of Liddesdale), Douglas of Drumlanrig and Mark Ker were all summoned to Edinbugh and committed to a brief spell of incarceration to highlight the error of their ways. In a sweep through Teviotdale the king caught two notorious reivers, Adam Scott of Tushielaw – 'King of Thieves'[40] – and Cockburn of Henderland;[41] both were executed having been tried and convicted of treason, robbery and recet.[42]

In the summer James, with an army said to be ten thousand strong, confronted the problem of Liddesdale: 'The Kingis grace maid ane raid upoun the thieves and tuik of thame to the number of xxxii personis of the greitest of thame, nameit Armestrangis, Ellotis, Littilis, Irwenis, with utheris'.[43] The king had earned popularity with the commons for his many acts of charity and his habit of going about incognito amongst his people as 'the Gudeman of Ballengeich'.[44] This reservoir of goodwill did not extend to his more troublesome marchers. His approach to border justice was simple and direct: 'To put gude ordoure and reule apoun thame, and to stanche thiftis and rubberis committit be theiffis and tratouris'.[45] Liddesdale was not to see much of the Gudeman of Ballengeich.

One of the more colourful characters to fall foul of the king's justice on this occasion was that infamous bandit John Armstrong,[46] 'Black Jock' or 'Johnnie of Gilnockie', a brother of Thomas, the laird of Mangerton, and senior heidman of the name. Johnnie, as has been shown, was particularly active, commanding a significant following who spread fire, murder and black rent across the English west march. Something of a protégé of Maxwell[47], Johnnie may have been lured into the king's presence by assurances of clemency. If so he was to be disappointed.

Some accounts suggest that James was inclined to be merciful but the lavish attire of Armstrong and his confederates so outraged him that he decided the whole lot must hang. And swing they did. Gilnockie's end forms the substance of one of the most famous border ballads. All of the reiver's silver tongued pleading was of no avail: 'Efter this hunting the king hanged Jonnie Armstrange, quhilk monie Scottis man heavilie lamented, for he was ane doubit man, and als guid ane chieftaneas evir was upon the borderis . . . And albeit he was ane lous leivand yitt he never molested any Scottis man. But it is said, from the scottis border to Newcastle of England, there was not one of quhatsoevir estate bot payed to this John Armstrange ane tribut to be frie of his cumber, he was so doubtit in Ingland'.[48]

It may be that Gilnockie, when he rode to the truce at Carlenrig, was already a marked man. It is conceivable that Maxwell, a prisoner in Edinburgh, sought to buy the king's favour by sacrificing his creature;[49] it is also suggested that Johnnie was betrayed, for an unknown reason, by his brother. The outlaw's end may well have been in breach of either a specific assurance or the normal rules of the truce day. With him were hanged the whole of his affinity, several dozen of them, the spectacle no doubt intended to cow the Liddesdale names:

> *Here is ane cord baith grit and lang,*
> *Quhilk hangit Johne Armstrang,*
> *Of gude hemp soft and sound,*
> *Gude haly pepil, I stand ford,*
> *Whaevir beis hangit wi' this cord,*
> *Neidis never to be drowned!*[50]

Of the other thieves singled out for the king's justice most fared the same. One, Sandie Scott, enjoyed the distinction of burning, judged a fitting punishment for his crime of torching a house containing a mother and child who both perished.[51] Such draconian measures, whilst often effective, in the very short term seldom deterred the reivers past the end of summer.

Though the king might enjoy the confidence of the commons, his relationships with the nobility were considerably less cordial. His high-handed treatment of the magnates in 1530, however great the measure of his frustration, was ill-judged and smacked, certainly to the peers, of tyranny.

There was also the question of the royal marriage. Though James was contracted to marry the King of France's daughter Madeleine, the match was not solemnised until 1537. In 1525 the Imperialists won a great victory over the French at Pavia. Francis I, captured by his enemies and his position overall seriously weakened by the disaster, could not afford to upset Henry whom he needed as a potential ally. Relations between England and Scotland remained outwardly calm but a more permanent understanding was impossible due to the presence in the south of Angus, James's intractable opponent. Henry 'in supporting the infamous Douglases against their sovereign . . . in a manner forced James to fix a connection with France'.[52]

Though he did not yet possess a wife James did not lack for female company and he enjoyed a string of high-born mistresses of whom the favourite was Margaret Erskine (she bore him a son, James Stewart, Mary Queen of Scots' half brother, later Earl of Moray and future regent). Temporarily baulked in his quest for a French consort he looked at other suitable candidates and one whom he considered was Albany's niece and a papal ward, Catherine de Medici. Henry was immediately opposed to such a union as the inevitable result would be an increase in Albany's influence, essentially pro-French and, after the split, pro-papacy. Henry suggested that Catherine should wed Francis's younger son Henry, Duke of Orleans (the future Henry II).

The break with Rome provided James with additional bargaining power in Rome. Unlike Henry he never wavered in his allegiance. In 1532 he enacted measures to defend the rights of the established church in Scotland. Even at this early stage, there were some mutterings of discontent and the first stirrings of Lutheranism. In part these statutes were motivated by the earlier, well judged generosity of the Holy See, which, in the preceding year, had levied a tax on the Scottish clergy, the proceeds donated to the state, ostensibly for the defence of the realm. This 'Great Tax' provided a welcome boost to royal revenues and permitted the king to indulge his taste for extensive remodelling of royal residences in the Renaissance manner.

Such dissent as was brewing centred on St Andrews, an established base for intellectualism and, being an active port, an obvious point of entry for new and radical ideas. As early as 1528 Archbishop Beaton had felt obliged to condemn a relative, Patrick Hamilton, for heresy. More burnings were to follow and the flames served only to fan the swelling clamour for reform and to stimulate a wave of anti-clericalism.

Despite the general amity between England and Scotland the border was far from quiet. Throughout 1532, Ferniherst and Cesford were riding out of Teviotdale striking at the English east march. In November Northumberland, with fifteen hundred horse, conducted a retaliatory sweep through the Merse and Teviot. Branxholm was thoroughly slighted though neither of the Kers could be apprehended. No sooner had the raiders returned to England than Ferniherst returned the compliment, coming over the Cheviots to descend on Coquetdale. The trod caught up with him but the Kers hacked clear and withdrew unbeaten.

In 1534 the current truce was due to expire and both sides were anxious that amity should continue to prevail. Despite the earnestness of the negotiations it was business as usual along the frontier with Ralph Fenwick leading the Tynedale men against Teviot. Angus, too, was active in promoting discord whilst the Scotts were petitioning Dacre for aid in their feud with the Kers. Dacre himself was at odds with the Cliffords. In May 1536 the unholy alliance of Tynedale–Redesdale and Liddesdale fractured a rupture which promised fresh disturbances.

It was proposed that, on the final expiration of the current truce, a more durable accord be negotiated to endure for the lives of both monarchs and to subsist for a year after the demise of whichever of them should predecease. Henry, as part of the negotiation, offered the hand of his daughter Mary (notwithstanding the fact that he no longer regarded her as legitimate). James understandably demurred but did accept the Order of the Garter and was prepared to recognise the fact of Henry's divorce from Catherine of Aragon. Henry felt sufficiently encouraged to badger his nephew over potential reform of the Scottish Church and the benefits to be gained from at least a partial dissolution of the monasteries.

Francis I was sufficiently alarmed by these displays of goodwill to resurrect the Treaty of Rouen and promised James a French marriage. He remained reluctant to part with his delicate daughter Madeleine but offered a substitute in the form of Marie de Bourbon. At this point James was actively considering marrying his long-term mistress, Margaret Erskine, procuring her a divorce and seeking papal dispensation for a remarriage. Nonetheless, in September 1536, he travelled to France to inspect Marie de Bourbon. She was not to his liking, 'bossue et contrefaicte' (hunch-backed and misshapen).[53] Disappointed, he determined to press the King of France for the hand of his daughter.

At this time Francis was wracked with grief over the untimely death of his eldest son and heir and he took an immediate liking to the handsome young King of Scots. Finally, on 1st January 1537, James and Madeleine were married in Notre Dame. The child was extremely delicate though she revelled in her queenly status and her new husband received a very handsome dowry of 100,000 livres and the reimbursement of all his expenses. Francis's fears for his daughter's fragile constitution were well founded for she barely survived two months in the harsh northern climate and died on 7th July.

The fact of the French marriage may well have alarmed Henry but, in the autumn of 1536, he was confronted by a serious rising in England which appeared, at one point, to have the potential to topple his very throne. In the previous year the king had ordered a general survey of ecclesiastical wealth, the 'Valor Ecclesiasticus'. 1536 saw the enactment of the first anti-monastic legislation, the Act of Dissolution, whereby all those religious houses whose annual income was less than two hundred pounds were to be dismantled. In this Henry, normally so acute, has misread the mood of large parts of the country, especially in the poorer north:

Those who were enthusiastically behind the Henrician Reformation were probably a small minority. The majority, probably, were made up of that body of the largely indifferent . . . There undoubtedly emerged another kind, perhaps also a minority but maybe a larger one than the first, men of all sorts and conditions, who actively feared or disliked what was

*happening, even though they had not so far laid down their lives to
defeat it and might never actively have shown their opposition had not
others presented them with the opportunity to do so.*[54]

In October, firstly in Lincolnshire then, more dramatically, in Yorkshire
and the north-west, this discontent flared into open defiance. The Pilgrimage of Grace, as these disturbances became known, swelled out of popular
discontent which affected both commons and gentry, though, in many
instances, the latter required some coercion. By the 8th October the one-
eyed lawyer Robert Aske had emerged as the natural leader. He was joined
by several northern lords, including such influential figures as Thomas Darcy
and John Hussey. Pontefract was taken without a blow and the number
of Pilgrims swelled alarmingly.

Many members of the clergy and the threatened monasteries came
out with the rebels. This was essentially a clash of the old and the new but
exacerbated, particularly, in the west, by perceived social and economic ills.
All were, however, united in their determination to avoid further despoilation
of religious houses. The blame for the present ills was not laid at Henry's
door but rather upon the heads of his base-born and unpopular advisors,
principally Thomas Cromwell.

In early December the Pilgrims, guided by Aske, drafted their manifesto. This called for the removal of Cromwell and his cronies, condemned
the divorce and the breach with Rome, demanded a halt to further acts of
dissolution and begged for a parliament, a form of regional assembly to be
held in the north to properly consider the Pilgrims' grievances. Aske and
his fellow Pilgrims were neither radicals nor revolutionaries, they did not
seek to topple Henry, merely to persuade him. Aske's integrity cannot
be doubted, though he was fatally handicapped by a strong measure of
naïvety:

> *Aske was Henry's most loyal, as well as his most critical, subject, and
> it was his integrity, his simple confidence that Henry would hear their
> petition, his faith that the King would not break his word nor wreak
> bloody revenge which really defeated the Pilgrimage.*[55]

In Northumberland the Pilgrims were to find an unlikely ally in John
Heron of Chipchase, 'Little John'. The Tynedale and Redesdale men who
were to spearhead the pilgrimage in the north-east were not, to any discern-

ible degree, motivated by religious conviction. For the dalesmen any invitation to commit licensed, or unlicensed, mayhem was to be welcomed. As for Little John, his sympathies were driven by hatred of Thomas Cromwell. Heron had, for some years, nursed aspirations of gaining the inheritance of both Chipchase and Ford and it was Cromwell who, in 1535, made it perfectly plain he was to be disappointed.

Others who nursed grudges against Henry's much reviled minister were Sir Thomas[56] and Sir Ingram Percy[57]. The 6th earl was, by this time, a sick man[58] and entrusted the management of his wardenry to his able deputy, baron Ogle. Little John's son-in-law was Cuthbert Charlton, heidsman of the Bellingham sept[59] and, by the middle of October, the dalesmen were riding. The bailiff of Hexham, Reynold Carnaby, was absent when the rebel banners were first unfurled: he returned to find himself a target and was swiftly sent scurrying to the refuge of Chillingham Castle.

The monks of Hexham were persuaded to lend their support and thus a smattering of legitimacy to the rebels who summoned a muster at Chollerford for 16th October where a further attempt to capture the unfortunate Carnaby was agreed upon. By the close of the month the two disaffected Percys had come up from the family lands in Yorkshire and joined in a further council of war at Prudhoe, attended by Heron, Edward and Cuthbert Charlton, Geoffrey Robson and at least one of the Erringtons. Rumblings of discontent were already surfacing in Durham and the Percys proposed to use their influence in east Northumberland to raise the remaining gentry.

These were given an ultimatum: swear the oath of allegiance to the rebel cause within twenty days or face the unbridled storm from the upland dales.[60] This was no mean threat but the Percys' influence in the east march was, to a not inconsiderable degree, offset by that of Ogle who did a pretty fair job of keeping the gentry at home. Heron and the dalesmen, abetted now, almost inevitably by friends from Liddesdale, harried at will, laying waste an estimated sixty thousand acres, 'to the utter undoing of four or five hundred of Your Grace's true subjects, spoiled so sore that many were weary of their lives'.[61]

At the Doncaster assembly or 'Parliament' held by the Pilgrims in December, Northumberland was represented by John Hall of Otterburn for Redesdale, Edward and Cuthbert Charlton for Tynedale, together with Sir Thomas Percy. Overall the rebels appeared to be in a virtually inexpungable position. Whilst Henry blustered and vowed a fearful reckoning, his commanders on the ground, Thomas Howard, now Duke of Norfolk, and Suffolk, could only view the odds with alarm. Their scratch and unreliable levies looked set to bolt at the first push whilst the Pilgrims, well organised, drilled and ready, appeared formidable. It was some time before the king who, even in December, was upbraiding his officers for their perceived timidity, realised the extent and seriousness of the threat.

When Henry finally came to appreciate the full implications he swapped bluster for prevarication. Assurances were sent to the Pilgrims at York after the first Doncaster parlay and Norfolk was authorised to negotiate when the rebels presented him with their demands on 2nd December. These were reiterated at the second parlay on 6th December and included a general amnesty for all who had been 'out', and further assurances for an early northern assembly. When the duke conceded, the rebels, satisfied with their bargain, began to disperse.

Discontent had been singularly rife in the north-west where the rebel leaders had included the lawyer Robert Bowes[62] and Nicholas Musgrave.[63] The king's representative was Henry Clifford, the 1st Earl of Cumberland and an enemy of William Lord Dacre who, after experiencing the first rush of disturbances in Yorkshire, had retreated to Naworth to wait upon events.

The situation which confronted the Pilgrims of Cumberland and Westmorland differed from that facing the Yorkshire and Lincolnshire men in that the Cumbrians, in particular, were aware of the omnipresent risk from the Scottish marches. To turn their backs to the Solway and march south was to invite attack. The rebel manifesto issued by the northerners was very similar to that of the other Pilgrims, save that special notice was given that men should be ready to serve against the Scots should the need arise. Consequently it was resolved that Musgrave would lead a large contingent to Carlisle and thereby secure the city and the northern frontier. Lord Henry Clifford, the earl's nineteen-year-old son, had sought refuge in Carlisle Castle towards the end of October. One of the complaints laid at his father's door was that he had failed to take due precaution against the Scots, being too wrapped up in his feud with Dacre.

In addition to securing the frontier, the fall of Carlisle would send a powerful message throughout the whole of the English borderland whilst, at the same time, removing any threat from the garrison. On 30th October a large force, perhaps fifteen thousand strong, began mustering at Broadfield, just outside the walls on the Penrith road.[64] Carlisle was to be blockaded. Young Clifford now announced that he would maintain the defence of the city and entreated Dacre, their familial enmity notwithstanding, to join with him. Lord William could scarcely fail to respond and entered into an agreement with Clifford whereby he would support the city if Clifford would come to his aid should Naworth be attacked. In the event neither was to suffer any real prospect of an escalade and, as soon as calm returned after the Doncaster *entente*, Dacre returned to his Yorkshire estates whereupon many of his tenants promptly declared for the rebels.

The rather *ad hoc* leaguer of Carlisle continued throughout the autumn until the Pilgrims were advised of the outcome of the Doncaster negotiations which, at first, they were not disposed to believe. They were finally persuaded by the intervention of Lord William's doughty uncle Sir Christopher Dacre who, having procured a safe conduct, confronted the Pilgrims at their camp on the Broadfield. He prevailed upon them to return to their homes with the assurance that the garrison would take no punitive measures. Accordingly the rebels began to disperse and the wilder spirits amongst them took time to vent their collective spleen on one of the more unpopular Lakeland landowners, Peter Middleton of Castlerigg. He found himself besieged at his offshore manor on Lord's Island, just off the east shore of Derwentwater, a leaguer that was to continue until the defenders were relieved by Norfolk's advance in mid-February 1537.[65]

By Christmas, with Aske an overawed guest of his gracious sovereign, it would have seemed that the Pilgrimage of Grace was over and that had matters rested there the level of reprisal would have been mooted. The fragile harmony and thereby past assurances were shattered by fresh outbreaks early in the new year. The situation proved particularly unstable in the north-west where the Westmorland men resolved upon a second attempt on Carlisle.

Led by Musgrave and another rebel leader, Thomas Tebay, their numbers swelled by Pilgrims from Cumberland, Yorkshire and Lancashire, they had perhaps six thousand men and advanced against the walls arrayed in companies and with banners unfurled. Archers on the flanks loosed at the defenders lining the parapet. Christopher Dacre, canny border fighter that he was, suddenly appeared to their rear with half a thousand lances, mosstroopers all, whose lightning attack thoroughly disordered the rebel formations. As they wavered the garrison swept from the gates in a determined sally which completed the rout. Perhaps as many as five hundred of the Pilgrims fell in the fight and in the chase; another eight hundred were taken prisoner,[66] ample trade for Norfolk's gallows which were soon to be spread throughout the north-west, groaning with the weight of their many victims.

Although both Cumberland and Westmorland suffered dreadfully in the reprisals and most of the Pilgrims' leaders including Darcy and Aske also perished, the Northumbrians escaped lightly, very lightly indeed. Little John whose neck could have so easily have felt the weight of his boots was to be sent south for trial but, in the end, was merely bound over for a surety of two thousand marks.[67] The fact of the matter was that the dalesmen were needed. Natural leaders like Heron were an essential resource against the Scots and their more outrageous transgressions could, at least in some degree, be tolerated.

Henry had resolved to dispense with the services of his existing wardens and assume personal responsibility for the frontier. MacDonald Fraser thinks, almost certainly quite rightly, that the king had all the makings of a good warden: 'He was brave, tough, unscrupulous, clever, and altogether the kind of ruffian whom the reivers would have recognised as a man after their own hearts'.[68] He proposed to nominate three deputies to have day-to-day conduct of the marches; one of these was Sir William Eure and the other Thomas Wharton who, as MacDonald Fraser again correctly identifies, was to prove one of the most accomplished of all the English border officials.

These officers spent several trying months in 1537 attempting to procure the arrest of various fugitives who'd fled over the border after the collapse of the winter rebellion. James made all the right noises but nothing actually happened. The King of Scots was nonetheless anxious to avoid giving his uncle any pretext for armed intervention; he dutifully investigated the sources of a burst of seditious doggerel that incensed Henry and smugly reported to Norfolk that these insulting rhymes were clearly the work of English exiles! At the same time James was looking to shake up his own wardens. He had already tried giving several a further brief spell behind bars and now resorted to dismissing several officers. Maxwell, however, kept his job in the west and Dand Ker was appointed to the middle march; neither of these could be described as an exemplar of probity.

Having lost his first French wife in a matter of a few months James resolved to find a more robust substitute and his father-in-law was pleased to suggest the eligible widow, Marie de Guise, whose family were in the first rank of the nobility and would, over the course of the ensuing decades, come to exert great power in France and spearhead the Catholic faction during the Wars of Religion. This young woman was an altogether hardier specimen; tall, striking and highly intelligent.[69] To spice the attraction she was priced with a dowry of 150,000 livres and was awarded an honorary title as a Daughter of France.[70]

The king now had a wife who would bear him two sons, both of whom would die tragically in infancy and a daughter, the future Mary Queen of Scots. The couple were married by proxy in May 1538 and the new queen arrived in Scotland a month later. Marie de Guise was to prove a formidable and resourceful character, unswervingly loyal to the Church of Rome. An early protégé was the ageing Archbishop of St Andrews' nephew and successor, David Beaton: worldly, able and unscrupulous, neither celibate nor unduly pious, 'a renaissance politician in Holy Orders'.[71]

He gained a cardinal's hat in 1538 and was to become the king's leading counsellor. James himself was not blind to the failings of the unreformed church but also practised nepotism on an impressive scale; all of his illegitimate sons were made commendators[72] of the six richest abbeys and priories in the land, ensuring that the substantial incomes from each flowed into the royal coffers.

What James did not enjoy was the goodwill of the nobility. No sixteenth century king could rule without building up a powerful affinity amongst his magnates. James might be the 'Gudeman' to the commons but to the lords he was a cold, distant and autocratic figure, one to be tolerated rather than respected, to be endured rather than to be followed. As early as 1531, Bothwell, the former Keeper of Liddesdale, had promised Henry seven thousand armed supporters should he seek to seize the throne for himself.

At no time was James ever free of the dead hand of the Douglases. A malevolent potency in exile, Angus and his faction, though most had been heartily glad to see them go in 1528, had now upgraded to aggrieved status and were perceived as victims of royal oppression rather than as renegades. In 1537 Lady Glamis, Angus's sister and a woman of both beauty and spirit, was executed for allegedly plotting to poison the king;

her death at the stake caused widespread revulsion. By the time of his first marriage an observer noted that 'so sore a dread King and so ill beloved of his [noble] subjects was never in this land'.[73]

He also had the recurring problem of his mother; Margaret had now tired of her third husband and was seeking a divorce so she could remarry the second, Angus! Needless to say James remained adamantly opposed to the notion and the Queen Mother remained shackled to Methven till she died in 1541. Whether the king sincerely believed that Lady Glamis had tried to poison him cannot be ascertained but it is the case that, from 1537, James appears to have suffered from increasing ill health. The exact cause is unknown though he did suffer injuries as a result of an accident in the hunting field.

In the spring of 1540 Prince James was born, his brother Arthur early in the following year. The king's star appeared firmly in the ascendant; not only did he appear to have secured the dynasty, he had radically improved the state of the treasury, left bare in 1528 due to the reckless expenditure of the Queen Mother and her husband's extended pilfering. James now had substantive papal subsidies and two hefty cash dowries. His wealth enabled the king to indulge his passion for building, refurbishing Holyroodhouse, Falkland and Stirling as residences fit for a great renaissance prince.

In February 1540 Henry dispatched Sir Ralph Sadleir as ambassador to Scotland.[74] An able diplomat, Sadleir's job was to urge the reformation upon James and to work at undermining Beaton's influence, heavily pro-French. Despite the cardinal's influence and James's own loyalty to Rome, many of the nobility had already espoused the Protestant heresy.[75] The king remained deaf to any notion of dissolving the monasteries and in April 1541 his attention was diverted by overwhelming grief when both of his infant sons died, one almost immediately after the other. It is questionable whether James's fragile personality ever recovered from this terrible double blow and the tragedy occurred at a time when the international situation was in a singularly volatile phase.

Pope Paul III was trying to broker a tripartite holy league comprising the Empire, France and Scotland, the objective being the chastisement of heretic England and her excommunicate king. For Henry the prospect was nightmarish, his worst fears realised; England was safe from interference so long as France and the Empire remained at each other's throats; if they were to make common cause then Henry was horribly isolated. Vast sums were being spent on new and improved coastal defences, the great border fortresses being put into good repair, and additional works being undertaken at Berwick.

Sadleir came north again in August 1541 to propose that both kings should attend a summit at York. Henry did in fact make the journey, the most northerly excursion of his reign, and fretted at York for twelve days whilst James kept him waiting and finally failed to show. Such an insult was unthinkable and Henry's wrath overflowed. To make matters worst Liddesdale was riding again, the outlaws led by an English renegade Anton Armstrong, Bewcastle was thoroughly taken up and seven Fenwicks murdered. On his return to London Henry was greeted by the revelation of his teenage wife Catherine Howard's numerous infidelities. The king's consort was not to be forgiven and neither was James.

The borderers, as ever, were quick to gauge the prevailing mood. Wharton and Maxwell were already eyeing each other; the Scots warden was readying his allies in Liddesdale and occupying the Threap. Wharton proposed invading the latter to draw Liddesdale into a large-scale ambush. Tynedale and Redesdale were also to be let off the leash, though the upland dales had, since the split five years earlier, made up their differences with the Armstrongs and were wary of sparking new feuds. They were, however, perfectly amenable to taking up Teviotdale. The Liddesdale names had already visited Houghton Castle, scaling the walls with rope ladders, beating up the garrison and removing horses, plate and other gear. In November the king's commissioners were reporting that the frontier was disappointingly quiet except for the upland dales; 'who are so combeynede, confedderatide and knette in one that not for their officers or princes laws would they break their association'.[76]

All was not totally lost. The Kers were beating up Coquetdale and Elliots plundered William Carnaby's lands at Halton. Heron and the Fenwicks who'd suffered all too often from the attentions of Liddesdale torched a derelict property belonging to Heron and, armed with this pretext, set off to chastise the dalesmen. They rode fast and hard, so swiftly that the Tynedales had no chance to warn their allies and the raid destroyed thirteen Armstrong steadings and relieved them of an appreciable quantity of beasts.[77]

James did not want to hand his uncle a pretext for war. He had not wavered in his French alliance. Though the Pope's hoped-for crusade against the English heretics proved wholly illusory, neither Francis I nor Charles V could ever consider burying the hatchet and Henry had placed England firmly in the Imperial camp. Francis was too embroiled in enmity with Charles to send aid to James and it seemed inevitable that, if Scotland were invaded, she would fight alone. Wharton had devised a rather hare-brained scheme to kidnap the King of Scots whilst, in the summer of 1542, Robert Bowes, elevated to march warden despite his prominent role in the Pilgrimage of Grace and, accompanied by Angus, struck at Teviotdale, but was roundly thrashed at Hadden Rigg.

The rout at Hadden Rigg was a humiliation for Henry but, even on the day the battle was fought, 24th August, the decision to invade Scotland was ratified by the Council. Norfolk, despite the increasing weight of his years, was to command a muster of twenty thousand men at York for a grand chevauchee. Without Wolsey's brilliant logistical skills the muster was both slow and inefficient with a chronic shortage of beer.[78]

It was October before the host was marshalled on to the north road and the border was not reached until the 21st. James had the victors of Hadden Rigg as a vanguard and was mustering a national levy at Edinburgh. Norfolk swept through the middle march, torched Melrose and detached the Earl of Hertford with two thousand riders to harry Teviotdale. It was all depressingly familiar and, like so many English expeditions before, this one ran out of supplies and marched, footsore and hungry, back to Berwick within the week.

James fared little better. His alienation from the nobility, exacerbated by creeping heresy, meant he commanded little respect and the great national army refused to stir from Fala Muir, a stinging reverse for the king. Undeterred he strove, with some success, to raise a second army to be led by Maxwell, and planned a bold thrust in the west. And so it was that on that cold, grey morning of 24th November the host broke camp in the dank autumnal dawn and advanced from Langholm and Marston Kirk towards the Solway. The king, stricken by his recurring malady, remained at Lochmaben whilst Maxwell, remained in effective command. James had left secret orders with his favourite Oliver Sinclair that he should take over the leadership once the army crossed into England. Whether James had cause to doubt Maxwell is unclear but to propose a shift in command from one who was both a warden and a leading magnate to a relatively base-born and untried royal toady was rank folly.

In terms of intelligence James had completely humbugged Norfolk who remained in the eastern march convinced by false rumour that the attack would come there. Even Wharton with all of his finely honed instincts and web of informers was taken by surprise. He could muster barely three thousand lances and the Scots, horse, foot and guns, outnumbered him by three or four to one.

The sight of so many splashing over the cold waters of the Esk must have sent a shiver down the spine of every Englishman. Such a host must surely be unstoppable, a great coiling plague of men and ordnance struggling to maintain order on the barren waste of Solway Moss. Sinclair now advised Maxwell he was to be superseded. The warden's reply may only be guessed at, such a thing was unprecedented and contrary to all the usages of war. To all intents and purposes the Scottish army was now leaderless.

A lesser man than Wharton might have simply retired behind Carlisle's walls and prepared to sit out a siege but the warden was game for a fight, regardless of the unfortunate odds. He detached a mounted vanguard under Musgrave, his deputy, to harry the Scots. Wharton would fight a reiver's battle, avoiding the slog of the mêlée, nibbling at the flanks and exploiting any opportunities that arose. Musgrave's five hundred border horse swooped like hawks, struck, withdrew, reformed and struck again, their darting lances emptying saddles and staining the moss with bloodied puddles. Now like ravenous wolves they surged against the columns, the Scots like sheep, herding together.

Wharton discerned the makings of a miracle. The leaderless host shook and wavered. He committed the whole of his force to the attack and it was enough. The confused mass of Scots, deprived of leadership and purpose, broke, their morale dissipated in their officers' squabbles. As the warden observed: 'Our prickers . . . gatt them all in a shake all the waye'.[79] It was a rout; Scots surrendered by the score, sometimes to a single Englishman. Some gave themselves up to women from the fields. Their guns and gear, abandoned, strewed the plain; several hundred drowned in a panic-stricken dash into the boiling waters of the Esk. The shocked survivors regaining the Scottish side were promptly set upon by their own marchers and relieved of whatever kit they still possessed.

It was not Flodden. The loss of life was infinitely less but the humiliation a hundred times greater. Even a glorious defeat, however costly, reads better than a shameful rout. Maxwell was amongst the prisoners as were the earls of Cassill and Glencairn, Lords Fleming, Somervill, Olivaunt, Graye and the favourite Sinclair.[80]

For James this final, unthinkable blow was too much. In despair the sick man, deserted by his nobles, wandered aimlessly from palace to palace, from Lochmaben to Edinburgh, Tantallon and Linlithgow, where the queen was in the final stages of her third pregnancy. Arriving at Falkland in early December he retired to his chamber and awaited death. On the 8th he received the news that he now had a baby daughter. With no son to succeed him and the prospect of his infant child the prey of her great uncle, he turned his face, quite literally, to the wall and died on 14th December. John Knox, never one to succumb to the temptation of flattery, wrote his epitaph:

> *He was called by some a good poor man's king; of others he was termed a murderer of the nobility, and one that had decreed their whole destruction. Some praised him for the repressing of theft and oppression; others dispraised him for the defouling of men's wives and virgins . . . And yet none spoke altogether beside the truth; for . . . as the virtues could not be denied, so could not the vices by any craft be cloaked.*[81]

Notes

1 Quoted in Bingham, C., *The Stewart Kingdom of Scotland 1371–1603*, London 1974 p. 151.

2 Quoted in Bingham p. 152.

3 The queen's second son was Alexander, Duke of Ross, who died aged two.

4 Quoted in MacDonald Fraser, G., *The Steel Bonnets*, London 1971 p. 218.

5 Quoted in MacDonald Fraser p. 218.

6 MacDonald Fraser p. 219.

7 Margaret gave birth to a daughter, Lady Margaret Douglas, who became Lord Darnley's mother.

8 The unfortunate warden was pursued and viciously murdered by the Humes, his severed head tied to the saddle bow like a Celtic trophy.

9 Quoted in MacDonald Fraser p. 221.

10 Albany was extremely well connected – Pope Clement VIII was among his many relations.

11 Quoted in MacDonald Fraser p. 223.

12 The castle is located some two-and-a-half miles from Jedburgh on the right bank of the Jed. The tower is L-shaped, though the oldest sections date from

the end of the sixteenth century. Until quite recently it was used as a youth hostel. Refurbished by the Marquis of Lothian, it is open to the public.

13 MacDonald Fraser p. 219.
14 Quoted in MacDonald Fraser p. 221.
15 Bates, C.J., *History of Northumberland*, London 1985 p. 210.
16 Quoted in Bingham p. 163.
17 Quoted in MacDonald Fraser p. 225.
18 MacDonald Fraser p. 225.
19 The whole is reproduced in the Appendix to *The Steel Bonnets*.
20 MacDonald Fraser p. 229.
21 Plenmeller Common, adjacent to the South Tyne between Haydon Bridge and Haltwhistle.
22 Robson, R., *The Rise and Fall of the English Highland Clans*, Edinburgh 1989 p. 80.
23 Robson p. 80.
24 Ibid p. 80.
25 Ibid p. 80.
26 Ibid p. 82.
27 The rescue might possibly have been led by Johnnie Armstrong of Gilnockie.
28 Quoted in Robson p. 82.
29 Robson p. 82.
30 Ellerker was a leader of the Pilgrims though he probably joined under pressure. He was however, one of the emissaries sent to treat with the king in 1536.
31 The earl was responsible for the Lion Tower at Warkworth and the foundations of his proposed cruciform chapel, which he lacked the means to complete, may still be seen, see Bates p. 210.
32 Robson p. 83.
33 Graham had been taken to Carlisle impressively loaded with chains. Once within the walls these were removed and he was allowed to exercise at will. At the appropriate moment he managed an impressive leap through 'a privvy postern' and onto a horse brought by a confederate, see MacDonald Fraser pp. 230–1 (note).
34 Quoted in MacDonald Fraser p. 231.
35 MacDonald Fraser p. 232.
36 Thirlwell, i.e. 'Through the Wall', the castle, a medieval hall house astride the Irthing Gap, is built from Roman Stone and was itself quarried for stone to complete the farm adjacent. The site has been restored recently and opened to the public.
37 The 'Hot Trod' was a means of lawful pursuit whereby the posse could follow thieves across the border, proclaiming their lawful purpose by means of a lighted peat affixed to a lance head.
38 A latch is a form of crossbow carried by the border horse and particularly favoured by Scots' riders.

39 MacDonald Fraser p. 232.

40 Scott held a tower on a spur opposite the Rankleburn on the west flank of the Ettrick. Nearby was the 'hanging' tree from which he is said to have hanged his many victims and in which a deep groove was worn in the branch. It would not be unpleasing to think that he swung from the same but he was in fact executed in Edinburgh on 18th May 1529, see Borland, Rev. R., *Border Raids and Reivers*, Glasgow 1910 p. 186.

41 It is said that Henderson's end inspired the haunting ballad 'The Lament of the Border Widow' but this is untrue. He was not hanged from his own gate but taken to Edinburgh and executed, see Borland p. 183.

42 'Recet' was dealing in stolen goods.

43 Quoted in MacDonald Fraser p. 237.

44 Bingham p. 167.

45 Quoted in MacDonald Fraser p. 239.

46 Gilnockie Tower near Canonbie dates from the late sixteenth century, a classic border tower with pitched crowstepped gables and the 'long view'. It is not, however, the abode of Black Jock whose timber tower stood nearby at Hollows.

47 Towards the end of the century Cesford enjoyed a similar relationship with the murderous Geordie Bourne and took it very badly when Robert Carey captured Bourne and had him hanged for his many crimes.

48 Quoted in MacDonald Fraser p. 239.

49 Maxwell enjoyed the outlaw's confiscated lands but Johnnie was his tenant.

50 Quoted in Borland p. 181.

51 MacDonald Fraser p. 239.

52 Quoted in Bingham p. 173.

53 Ditto p. 173.

54 Quoted from Scarisbrick, J.J., *Henry VIII*, London 1968 p. 338.

55 Ditto p. 342.

56 Executed at Tyburn in June 1537.

57 Died in the Tower.

58 Died June 1537.

59 Robson p. 85.

60 Ibid p. 87.

61 Quoted in Robson p. 87.

62 Despite his prominent role in the rebellion he was exculpated and was serving as a member of the Council by 1539. He went on to enjoy a distinguished career as a border official.

63 Fate unknown, but the Musgraves served constantly as junior officers on the western march.

64 Moorhouse, G., *The Pilgrimage of Grace*, London 2002 p. 182.

65 Ibid pp. 183–4.

66 Ibid p. 310.

67 Robson p. 87.

68 Quoted from MacDonald Fraser p. 243.

69 Henry VIII also expressed an interest in the hand of Marie de Guise following the death of his third wife Jane Seymour. The lady felt constrained to demur, advising that the king might find her neck too slender!

70 Bingham p. 175.

71 Quoted in Bingham p. 178.

72 A commendator was a form of lay abbot in the pre-reformation Scottish church.

73 Quoted in Bingham p. 176.

74 Sir Ralph Sadleir was an experienced diplomat who served several Tudor monarchs and is said to have died the wealthiest commoner in England. He saw Mary Queen of Scots in her cradle and latterly was one of her gaolers, see Humphrey, D., *Our Man in Scotland*, London 1969.

75 By the end of James V's reign Beaton had compiled a 'blacklist' of three hundred and fifty peers tainted by the Protestant heresy, see Bingham p. 184.

76 Quoted in MacDonald Fraser p. 247.

77 MacDonald Fraser p. 248.

78 This was not a reflection on the army's desire for recreational consumption of alcohol. With the available water generally unfit, the men depended on 'small beer', a form of weak ale, as a staple beverage.

79 Sadler, D.J., *Scottish Battles*, Edinburgh 1996 p. 83.

80 MacDonald Fraser p. 253.

81 Quoted in Bingham p. 187.

Chapter 18

The Rough Wooing

Fair maiden Lilliard lies under this stane;
Little was her stature, but great was her fame;
Upon the English loons she laid many thumps,
And when her legs were cuttid off, she fought upon the stumps.[1]

Lilliard is part of the mythology of the battle of Ancrum Moor, a notable Scots triumph which revived morale at a time the marches were reeling under successive hammer blows. The last years of Henry VIII saw a sustained and savage policy of aggression intended to bring the Scottish polity to heel. The excesses of this time, 'The Rough Wooing', rivalled any of the horrors inflicted during the Edwardian wars whilst bringing about little or no political gain.

The princess Mary (the future Mary Queen of Scots) was barely a week old when her father so wearied of life. The king left no will and by dying intestate left no instructions as to the formation of a regency council. This oversight led to over half a year of unseemly wrangling as to who should have control of the reins of government.[2] The infant monarch was not to be crowned until September 1543 and spent much of her time within the secure confines of Stirling Castle.

James, 2nd Earl of Arran, was nearest to Mary in blood and heir presumptive. It seemed natural that he should be offered the regency but Mary of Guise, the dowager queen, seconded by Cardinal Beaton, formed the focus for a strongly pro-Catholic opposition. Arran himself appears to have leant more towards the Protestant reformers whose cause was beginning to emerge.[3] An attempted coup by the Queen Mother's party was scotched and Beaton incarcerated.

So great was the shock of Solway Moss that had Henry followed up his unexpected advantage by launching a full-scale invasion he might well have succeeded. But, for Henry, Scotland was never of prime importance. His eyes were generally fixed on the continent. So great was his ignorance of the northern kingdom that when he summoned the exiled Angus to court the earl was instructed to bring along such maps as he possessed![4] Henry's lack of knowledge of and disinterest in Scottish affairs were to hamstring all of his efforts to exert control. He failed to understand that the nobility were as much motivated by pure expediency as he, and he failed to appreciate that brute force would serve only to stiffen resistance – that breaking heads did not win hearts and minds.

His initial plan was to utilise the haul of prisoners to create a pro-English faction. The captives, some of whom were by no means unwilling, escaped the crushing burden of ransom if they swore to adhere to Henry's programme for the effective takeover of Scotland. They undertook, *inter alia*, to ensure the infant queen was conveyed to England so her upbringing might be under direct control of the crown and that they would facilitate the seizure and retention of certain key fortresses. Ten of the most trust-worthy or at least more amenable entered into a band or indenture whereby they would support Henry's claim to the Scottish throne if the young monarch died without issue.

With these assurances of amity the prisoners were conveyed to Berwick from where, upon the surrender of nominated pledges, they were released; virtually all were repatriated by the end of January 1543. Henry then be-came alarmed when he heard that Arran had plans to propose his own son as a consort for Mary; he sent instructions that the queen, the regent and the cardinal were all to be kidnapped and brought into England. Such extreme and generally impractical reactions came to typify Henry's policy. His lack of knowledge and naïve reliance on assurances promoted a reactive and insensitive policy, the twists and turns constantly betraying the king's inability to develop any real understanding.

Once Arran had safely corralled Beaton and clipped the dowager queen's wings, Henry felt more assured; on 10th February safe conducts were issued to Scots negotiators and, a mere ten days later, a three-month truce and the bones of an accord had been agreed. In March the king sent Sir

Ralph Sadleir as his ambassador to Edinburgh to provide Arran with assurances of support and, included in the 'package', was Henry's own manual or guide on how to engineer a swift transition from Rome to the reformed church, a step-by-step guide on the creation of a Protestant clergy. In terms of a more earthly reward for his compliance the regent could expect the princess Elizabeth as a replacement bride for his son.

Sadleir, who understood how matters stood only too clearly, advised that a strong pro-Catholic party, led by Cardinal Beaton and funded by French gold, was already gaining ground. The wily ambassador discerned three strands of political leanings: a strong Anglophile party under the influence of the reformers and Henry's suborned peers, a conservative Catholic party influenced by France, and a rump of opportunists ready to follow whoever held the advantage. Arran was cannily maintaining a foot in both main camps, recognising Beaton's influence and avoiding any clear rift with Rome.

In that spring the regent's half brother, John Hamilton, Abbot of Paisley, a noted zealot, had returned from France as had Matthew Stewart, the Earl of Lennox. The earl was closest in blood to the throne after Arran, something of a maverick who may have entertained hopes of marrying the dowager queen. At the same time Angus also returned after his fourteen years of exile; the doughty Douglas was an experienced bruiser who, himself, had been wed to the former dowager, Queen Margaret. Adding to the stew of politics the church was split, not only between conservatives and reformers but along more partisan lines; Beaton maintained an ongoing feud with Gavin Dunbar, the Archbishop of Glasgow.[5]

The first parliament of the queen's minority, convened in March, 1543, confirmed Arran in his office as Governor of the Realm. With his position thus strengthened the regent enacted several measures which appeared to favour the reforming party; William Tynedale's English translation of the New Testament was made freely available and proved extremely popular.[6] His promotion of Protestant teaching produced a conservative backlash which so alarmed the regent that, by the end of the year, he was furiously back-pedalling. Beaton was reinstated as chancellor and a series of repressive measures introduced.

Arran was thus forced, largely through his own weakness, to support a policy of enforced orthodoxy, spiced with the burning of heretics. Without state sponsorship the reformation was forced underground, driven by more localised considerations and increasingly influenced by the teachings of George Wishart.[7] In all of this Henry's moment had passed; with the queen influenced by her mother and the cardinal there arose the possibility that, were there any danger of her being removed to England, she might as easily find herself already in France.

Henry was growing impatient; he needed to be done with Scotland, to leave his will firmly stamped on the realm before turning to more important business on the continent. Here also matters were not proceeding entirely to his liking. The Emperor Charles was a difficult ally, easily as duplicitous as Henry himself though even he had some qualms about forming an alliance with a schismatic and heretic against a Catholic nation. Nonetheless, expediency eventually triumphed over conscience and the Anglo-Imperialist alliance was concluded on 2nd February. In June a final demand was sent to Paris as English troops were being ferried to Calais; a sharp engagement in the Channel on 6th June marked the beginning of overt hostilities.

On 1st July the Anglo-Scottish understanding was ratified with the signing of two treaties at Greenwich. These were at best half-hearted; the Scots were not obliged to abandon the French alliance and Mary, now betrothed to Henry's son by Jane Seymour, Prince Edward, would not come to England until she was ten. Despite the unsatisfactory terms Henry was pleased to find that his business in Scotland was now concluded; someone with greater insight and less hubris might have seen otherwise but, for the moment, Arran appeared compliant.

But a few days later, still in early July, Sadleir was reporting disquieting intelligence from the capital. Beaton, now in alliance with Lennox, was about to stage a coup, unseat the regent and open the doors to the French. In a furious panic Henry promised immediate military aid to shore up Arran's regime and instructed his emissary to neutralise the cardinal either through suborning or the assassin's knife; either remedy would suffice.

In the uncertain heat of that summer the spectre of civil war loomed. By the end of August Sadleir favoured the use of force; two days later Suffolk was commissioned to lead an expedition to buttress the regency. Early in September Sadleir reported the unsettling news that the two contending factions had reached an accord, the terms of which were unlikely to favour the English alliance. Henry's overweening arrogance and high-handedness had alarmed even the most enthusiastic anglophiles and on

11th December the Scots parliament annulled the Greenwich treaties in favour of a renewal of the French alliance. Henry was incandescent.

Having finally realised that Arran espoused no cause other than his own, the king turned to that proved renegade, Douglas, Earl of Angus, recently joined by Lennox. This revitalised anglophile faction was to facilitate a Protestant reformation, to secure the queen's person and keep her within their influence till she could be formally transferred to the protection of the English court, and to recognise Henry's interim role as 'protector' during Mary's infancy. Once the Lennox faction had achieved control of the government the king would dispatch an army to cement their grip. With this accomplished, Scotland would be prised free from any prospect of a future accord with France. Like most of Henry's designs for Scotland this one proved wildly simplistic and impossible to implement, but if sweetness and reason proved ineffective there was always brute force and the king was by no means unwilling.

On the borders Edward Seymour, Queen Jane's able brother, now Earl of Hertford, was poised for offensive action. The earl, with his younger, mercurial brother Thomas,[8] was chief amongst Henry's counsellors, a soldier of no mean ability, well schooled in the emerging tactics of renaissance warfare.

The face of battle was changing; broadsword and lance were giving way to pike and shot, and the longbow was about to enter honourable retirement though a final victory remained in store. From the cantons of Switzerland redoubtable pike columns had smashed the armies of Charles the Bold and gone on to dominate continental campaigns, serving both French and Imperialists until mown down by massed gunfire on the field of Bicocca in 1522.

English armies of the mid-sixteenth century included bodies of pikemen mixed with bills, archers and musketeers brigaded together as missile troops – 'the shot'. Cavalry, 'the horse', were divided into heavy, armoured shock squadrons akin to the French *gendarmes*, lesser armed lancers or *reiters*, with the hobiler retaining his traditional scouting and skirmishing role. Marchers from both sides of the line served Henry VII as border horse, something of an élite when they could be relied upon; often they were considered better suited to overseas service.[9]

The stylish, angular lines of gothic armours had been replaced with the fuller, more rounded shape of Flanders-made harness; the distinctive sallet-style helmet was being superseded by the swept brim of the morion for the foot and the open faced burgonet for the horse. Hand-and-a-half and double-handed swords were still much in evidence though the civilian fashion for the long, narrow-bladed rapier was gaining headway, fuelled by a lethal mania for duelling. Affairs of honour were no longer settled in the lists by combatants girded with full plate but by stylish, furious and often fatal encounters with rapier and left hand or *main gauche* daggers.

Whilst the army still marched in its traditional three divisions or 'battles', the beginnings of the regimental system were stirring. Captains commanded foot companies one hundred strong – these were increasingly brigaded to form stronger bodies of mixed pike and shot under a senior or 'grand' captain. On the continent tactical development was proceeding at a swifter pace: the French formed divisions (*legion*) of six battalions, each comprising a thousand. The famous Spanish equivalent or *tercio* was made up of a dozen or so companies, each with a complement of two hundred and forty.

As the army deployed in line of march, the columns, in the traditional way, massed one behind the other. The central block of each division was made up of pikes and bills with shot in front and to the rear. Archers followed on both flanks. The great guns were drawn, each by its team of oxen, parallel to the marching brigades whilst cavalry scouted and formed an enveloping screen of skirmishers. As far as can be ascertained it was Hertford (now Duke of Somerset) who, in 1547, first decreed that the foot should all wear red coats. The famous red was not formally adopted as the universal colour for infantry until the creation of the New Model Army nearly a century later.

The 'gonne' used by select companies of specialists in the fifteenth century was being replaced by the ubiquitous matchlock musket which would continue in service till the end of the seventeenth century and see action in battles from Pinkie to Killiecrankie. The mechanism, though crude, and horribly vulnerable to wind and rain, had the inestimable advantage of being robust, cheap to manufacture and requiring little training.

The musketeer might carry several made-up charges in a bandolier of wooden containers[10] – the charge was poured down the barrel, waded and rammed home with the ball and further wad coming next. A flask of fine powder was employed to prime the pan, and the ramrod or *scouring stick* was secured in loops beneath the barrel. When the trigger mechanism was pressed a lighted length of slow match, held in metal jaws, was lowered on to the pan, the cover sliding free as part of the effect. The weapon, God willing, then gave fire.

From mid-century the light horse might carry a short carbine (*arquebus*) and the more affluent or most adept looters could sport one of more pairs of horseman's pistols or *daggs*. The latter did not rely on the matchlock but utilised the more sophisticated and expensive wheelock mechanism. Here a serrated wheel, wound up like clockwork and by means of a spanner or key, was released by pressure on the trigger to revolve at great speed against a piece of pyrites held in steel jaws. The resultant shower of sparks ignited the priming powder and then the main charge.

Gunfire changed the sight and smell of battle. Great clouds of sulphur-ous fumes now enveloped the combatants after the first discharge; the monstrous crack of the great guns and explosive rattle of musketry con-founded the senses. The shot stood on the flanks of the pike block to protect their comrades from enfilading fire from the enemy's musketeers; when assailed by the horse the shot would shelter behind the staves, often joining in the mêlée with swords and clubbed muskets.

Whilst the art of war was undergoing such profound changes on the great battlefields of northern Italy, business on the Anglo-Scottish border went on very much as before. Henry's most active lieutenant was Wharton himself. The victor of Solway Moss was not the man to rest idly on his laurels; the climate of political uncertainty which prevailed in Scotland provided an array of opportunities. Wharton understood the border and the borderers; he was a hard man, inclined to be both ruthless and bloody, but in his capacity as an agent of the English crown the council would find little to complain of.

With so many of the gentry captive the warden thrust himself into the breach using his talents for flattery, intimidation and corruption to the full. English threats and English coin won over many of the most active riding names of the west and middle march. Wharton's overtures found willing listeners in Liddesdale. Gold won allies and it fanned the flames of local discord; the warden backed his allies in their feuds with neighbours, and he used internal discord and violence to disrupt any attempts to spon-sor a counter offensive.

Soon Wharton was able to boast, with a fair degree of veracity, that he'd turned Dumfriesshire into an extension of his own march. He ensured that the vendettas between the Armstrongs and Kers and Scotts were kept well alight. As well as warden raids or 'scathes'[11] the dalesmen were given full rein to lay into the Scottish marches. Early in 1543 the Redesdale men attacked Ancrum but were badly cut up by the hot trod; in March Liddesdale struck at the south Tyne but again the raiders were seen off with loss.[12]

There was nothing random in Wharton's policy; he was seeking to re-establish an English Pale in the west and middle marches. 'Taking assurance of the king of England' was a form of contractual undertaking whereby the marchers formally entered into the English service. They would receive regular wages, possibly even pension entitlement, with insurance against damage suffered and losses incurred in retaliation.[13] These were substantive bonuses for Armstrongs and Crosers who also received licence to 'spoil under Henry's wing'.[14]

In the autumn Wharton sent forays to harry Ker and Scott alike; the Storeys 'took up' Selkirk whilst the Cumbrians descended on Liddesdale to remind the recalcitrant of where their new loyalties now lay. Elliots, who had already judged which way the wind was blowing, shared in the spoil garnered from their neighbours. To demonstrate their commitment the Elliots beat up the villages around Jedburgh whilst Wharton attended to the torching of Bonjedworth. Through the long nights of the late autumn and winter the work of destruction went on. The warden understood the value of terror; he understood it was best dished out in penny packets to keep the fear alive so that none would know where the next blow might fall.[15]

With the turn of the year Wharton was looking towards Teviotdale, and planning to suborn the riding families there – Davidsons, Pringles, Taits, Youngs, Turnbulls, Rutherfords, together with the Scottish Robsons and Halls.[16] This formidable coalition could then be turned loose on the Kers whilst, further east in the Merse, Dixons, Trotters and Redpaths were to combine against the Humes.

When Hertford received his orders for the campaign of 1544 he was left in no doubt as to the extent of the king's displeasure with the Scots or the degree of ruthlessness expected. He was:

to put all to fire and sword, to burn Edinburgh town, and so to raze and deface it, when you have sacked it, and gotten what you can out of it, as that it may remain for ever a perpetual memory of the vengeance of God lighted upon it, for their falsehood and disloyalty. Do what you can out of hand, and without long tarrying, to beat down and overthrow the Castle, sack Holyrood-house, and as many towns and villages about Edinburgh as ye conveniently can; sack Leith and burn and subvert it, and all the rest, putting man, woman and child to fire and sword, without exception, where any resistance shall be made against you; and this done, pass over to the Fife land, and extend the extremities and destructions in all towns and villages whereunto you may reach conveniently, and not forgetting amongst all the rest so to spoil and turn upside down the Cardinal's town of St Andrews, as the upper stone may be the nether, and not one stick stand by another, sparing no creature alive within the same, specially such as in friendship and blood be allied to the Cardinal.[17]

This is probably be the longest single sentence ever construed in English and also one of the most chilling orders given in the language. Hertford was to visit such a swathe of destruction on the Lothians that even the worst of past horrors should be eclipsed. Hertford had sufficient wit and resolve to question the wisdom of the order, not, it has to be said, on humanitarian grounds, but more in terms of practicalities. He should rather, as he argued, concentrate on reducing and/or occupying key fortresses and Leith to secure the lowlands and deny the French any viable port as a base for counter-invasion. This reasoning was dismissed out of hand – it must be fire and sword alone. Henry had not formulated a policy as such; he merely wished to keep the Scots cowed whilst he was engaged in France.

Hertford had determined upon an amphibious operation supported by a swift moving column striking through the Merse. By 20th April vessels drawn from the ports of London, Ipswich, Kings Lynn and Hull had been assembled in the Tyne. Despite logistical difficulties the earl was keen to embark the army and, by 6th May, the fleet was off the Forth. William, Lord Eure had meanwhile led some three to five thousand border horse from Berwick to pound the Merse. Haddington was razed before the raiders rode the last fifty miles to rendezvous at the beach-head.

At the same time Eure's son, Sir Ralph, warden of the middle march, harried Teviotdale with a liberal application of torch and lance. Jedburgh was stormed and destroyed as was Kelso.[18] The marchers were joined by numerous of the Scottish riding names including Nixons, Crosers and even Olivers and Rutherfords from Teviotdale itself. The younger Eure was nothing if not thorough in his work:

The whole number of towns, towers, stedes, barnekins, parish churches, bastel-houses, seized, destroyed, and burnt, in all the Border country, was an hundred and ninety-two, Scots slain four hundred, prisoners taken eight hundred and sixteen, nolt [cattle] *ten thousand three hundred and eighty-six, sheep twelve thousand four hundred and ninety six, gayts* [goats] *two hundred, bolls of corn eight hundred and fifty, insight gear – an indefinite quantity.*[19]

Leith was taken virtually without resistance and the next day, united with Eure's column, Hertford descended on the capital, blasting the principal gate and proceeding to carry out his orders with gusto. Edinburgh suffered considerable damage before, sated with destruction, the raiders retired to their ships. Hertford left a lively account of the action, the great city burning amidst the lamentations of hapless civilians, the odd brave or foolhardy patriot sniping from the rooftops.

Savage as this assault had been it achieved nothing of consequence; resistance as ever was only hardened by wholesale wasting, the ineffectual Arran was replaced by Marie de Guise, and the anglophile party, not unsurprisingly, lost ground dramatically. Douglas reverted to his natural allegiance and was to do his country good service. Only Lennox, increasingly isolated, remained in Henry's pay. The earl had joined with Wharton in leading a diversionary raid in the west whilst Hertford and the Eures savaged the east and centre. Dumfries had been burnt and the area around extensively harried. The warden's role was sufficient to finally earn him a peerage.

Whilst his brother-in-law ravaged the Lothians, Henry had his eyes fixed firmly on France and on the campaign he was about to undertake jointly with his ally the emperor. It was intended that the allies striking from both east and west should converge for a triumphal march upon Paris. The king, despite his failing health, was determined to lead this grand chevauchee in person, a prospect that filled his councillors with alarm. It was obvious to all but Henry himself that the obese and ageing monarch was no longer sufficiently robust for the role of supreme commander and that field operations should be left to his Howard subordinates – Norfolk, who had fought so well many years past at Flodden, and Suffolk, his son.

The march on Paris proved a chimera. Without Wolsey's flair for logistics and attention to detail, the commissariat lumbered on in a perpetual state of near or actual collapse. Henry did not arrive at Calais until 14th July. Four days later, with Suffolk, he was before the walls of Boulogne whilst the elder Howard persisted in a fitful siege of Montreuil. This campaign would not boast a Crispin's day, there was never any serious prospect of a march on Paris,[20] Boulogne capitulated on 18th September and, by the end of the month, Henry had returned to England. The continental campaign had consumed both treasure and materiel at a stupendous rate but had achieved little of substance.

Meanwhile, the Emperor Charles, disgusted with the poor showing of his ally, had come to terms with the French at Crécy. Freed from the threat of invasion from the east the dauphin hurried northward to relieve Montreuil, sending Norfolk pelting towards Boulogne. It seemed as though Boulogne must be retaken but somehow the English clung to their gains whilst the field army scuttled back to the security of the Calais Pale.

Relations between the English, the French and Imperialists had always been fraught with mistrust and enlivened by duplicity. Henry had no cause to trust either Charles or Francis and had to live with the omnipresent spectre of a Catholic crusade against heretic England. Despite his isolation Henry was not inclined to compromise. Subsequent negotiations with the French, brokered with a nice irony by the emperor, dissolved in continued acrimony when the king insisted on the retention of Boulogne and an abandonment of the Scottish alliance.

Desperate for allies, Angus and Lennox had flirted dangerously with the clans of the western highlands and islands; the irrepressible Donald Dubh needed little encouragement and fanned the flames of disaffection. By the middle of 1545 the clansmen, who had, albeit briefly, reconstituted the old Council of the Isles, were treating with English emissaries. When Donald died from natural causes – a wonder in itself – in Ireland, the rising unravelled. Arran capitalised on this good fortune by turning on Lennox who was soon obliged to seek sanctuary in England.

As long as Angus was in Henry's pay Wharton would find no serious rival, but when the Douglas reverted to his Scottish allegiance the warden could no longer expect to have a monopoly of influence on the marches.

Having made his peace with the cardinal, Angus was appointed as lieutenant on the border; his arrival helped stiffen the residue of resistance in Teviotdale where Buccleuch, who had held on to Hawick, had struggled to keep the flame alive.

In February 1545 Angus was 'putting some stick about' amongst the riding names, bullying and cajoling. The earl might have lacked finesse but his blunt appeals could sway hearts and minds. Sir Ralph Eure was sufficiently alarmed to mount a chevauchee through Teviotdale, partly from the lust for conquest but also to remind his clients there who could wield the bigger stick. Henry had empowered the middle march warden to carve out as grand a swathe of territory as force of arms might secure and Eure, his name already a byword for ruthless savagery, was happy to comply.

His expedition comprised some three thousand lances; Angus could command barely a tenth of those numbers. In addition to his own marchers, led by his deputy Brian Laiton with a leavening of Northumbrian lairds, he commanded Scots from the middle march including Douglas of Bonjedworth[21] and a corps of mercenaries drawn from every corner of Europe – 'terrible people of the worst sort'.[22] Despite the odds Angus was itching to come to blows; on hearing of Eure's commission to annex Teviotdale the Douglas quipped that he'd witness the transfer of title himself 'with a sharp pen and in red ink'.[23]

Eure's riders swept through Teviotdale, his Scottish allies frequently at odds with the free lances. Melrose was torched and the Douglas tombs in the abbey there wantonly desecrated, an outrage that could only serve to stiffen Angus's resolve. The tower at Broomhouse with its elderly chatelaine was also razed; the rallying cry 'Remember Broomhouse' would echo the screams of many an Englishmen in the fight. The Douglas was now joined by Arran with further reinforcements led by the master of Rothes; the Leslies, Lindsays and Scotts under Buccleuch lessened the odds still further. Angus now had some twelve to fifteen hundred riders.

The English were by now encamped hard by the banks of the Teviot on Ancrum Moor, some five miles from Jedburgh. Angus had selected a shallow ridge as his first position overlooking the rim of the moor but he was persuaded, probably by the experienced counsel of Buccleuch, to withdraw and deploy in the dead ground behind, known as Penielheugh, the contours screening his line. The Scots prepared to fight on foot, sending their mounts to the rear and utilising their lances as spears. If the move was intended as a feint to draw the invaders out then it succeeded brilliantly. Laiton, leading the mounted van of the English, whooped over the rise to complete, as he anticipated, the rout. It was late afternoon on 27th February.

With the bright rays of the dying sun full in their faces the horse crashed into the levelled spears, muskets banged and quarrels flew, saddles were emptied, the wounded were trampled or dispatched as the Scots advanced, spitting men and mounts. The English van floundered and began to dissolve. The shot, posted on the flanks of the horse, could not stem the rot and the shaken survivors collided with the centre, commanded by Eure. 'Remember Broomhouse' – the marchers had many hurts to avenge, many empty byres, burnt vills, kin mired in their own gore. Douglas of Bonjedworth, together with the remainder of Eure's clients, collectively experienced a belated rush of patriotic sentiment and stripped off their tokens, swapping the cross of St George for the Saltire.

Some two hundred or so were killed including both Eure and Laiton, together with Lord Ogle and several captains,[24] with four times as many taken prisoner including many gentlemen of Northumberland. Those that escaped lost their harness, guns, arrows and all manner of gear, including, of course, the spoil. Arran was pleased to warmly embrace his old rival Douglas and, when being shown Eure's corpse, is said to have remarked: 'he was a fell, cruel man, and over-cruel, which many a man and fatherless bairn might rue ... [Angus] had done a good day's work for Scotland'.[25]

Ancrum Moor was not a major battle and did not effectively alter the balance of power but it proved a significant boost to Scots' morale and, equally important, encouraged their French allies. Francis was sufficiently impressed to dispatch three thousand foot and five hundred horse under Lorges de Montgomery to bolster the marchers, and the combined force launched raids from the Merse, beating up Wark and the adjoining vills.

In September Hertford repeated the lesson of the previous year. On the 7th of that month he marched from Berwick with Clifford, Earl of Cumberland, leading the van. Bowes commanded a thousand of the border horse whilst a further three thousand continental mercenaries served for pay. The Spaniards in the earl's service fell upon Kelso and laid waste town and abbey. Three days later Bowes took up Melrose whilst Hertford attended, once again, to battered Jedburgh. The harvest from plentiful Teviotdale was burnt. In all the raid destroyed seven religious houses, sixteen peles with two hundred and fifty vills.[26] Beyond that it served no purpose whatsoever.

1545 was a difficult year for the King of England; with the major continental powers at peace the French were free to effect the recovery of Boulogne and to intervene in Scotland. Fear of France meant Henry felt constrained to keep large bodies of men constantly under arms, not only on the border but along the vulnerable south coast. The campaigning of the previous year had cost some £650,000, a colossal sum; a further outlay of £560,000 would now be required to meet the demands of the stand-off with France.[27] In addition to Hertford on the borders, the king had a substantial complement with the fleet, what amounted to a standing army in the south, and the Calais and Boulogne garrisons.

From 1542 until his death in 1547 Henry spent some £2,000,000 on defence; the budget consumed all of the wealth of the monasteries and more. Now he was considering 'borrowing' plate from the reformed church to cover the deficit. Hertford, speaking as a good Protestant, approved: 'God's service, which consisteth not in jewels, plate or ornaments of gold and silver, cannot thereby be anything diminished, and those things better employed for the weal and defence of the realm'.[28]

On the marches 1546 witnessed a further rash of scathes and forays. In April Bowes,[29] with his deputy Roger Fenwick, beat up Teviotdale, replaying the raid he'd carried out under Hertford the previous summer. This time he did not escape unchallenged; a superior force of Scots marchers, riding from the Merse and beleaguered Teviotdale, attacked his column as it was about to recross the Tweed by Fairnington Crag. After some scrimmaging between prickers the two sides dismounted and Bowes deployed his archers on the flanks to cover a fighting withdrawal over the river. This was to be the longbow's last significant fight; over two hundred Scots were killed, as many captured, and the survivors put to flight; 'the archers so hailed them with sharp shot of arrows that the multitude was abashed and began to flee'.[30]

In the west it was also business as usual. Despite Wharton's energy and many successes the English were by no means universally successful, being worsted in at least one encounter in the field; both Caerlaverock and Lochmaben, vital bastions to control the Scottish west march, were lost. The warden held Robert Maxwell captive and determined to lay hands on Johnstone. Cunning as a fox, Wharton lured the laird from his strength at

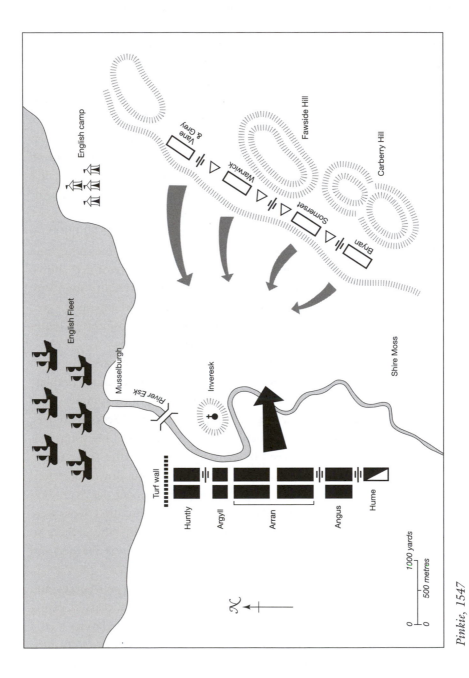

Pinkie, 1547

Lochwood by staging a raid on his brother's tower of Wamfray. The Johnstones were ambushed by a commanded party under the captain of Langholm. The marchers had anticipated such a move and were in sufficient numbers to best their attackers, taking a number, including the captain, prisoner. The warden, however, had also anticipated this outcome and had arranged a second ambush! This party, three hundred strong, under Wharton's son Henry, John Musgrave and Archie Armstrong of Mangerton[31] finally took Johnstone and freed the earlier captives after a hard-fought action.

With both the leading west march magnates in his grip Wharton was able to consolidate his hold on the west. With the Johnstones pacified and the Irvines keen to oblige, he could dispense justice from Carlisle clear almost to Clydeside and by the autumn he was able to observe that: 'the countrymen of Liddesdale and other parts stand in better order and obedience to the King than this twenty years before. They say themselves they were never in such order, for where great offenders have been, they may travel without trouble'.[32] In spite of this the west remained restless into 1547, with Arran himself taking a hand and recapturing Langholm. Wharton was sufficiently concerned to look to the state of Carlisle's defences.

Bowes, writing to the Council, described the pitiful state of the marches after the virtual holocaust of the preceding years; many had fled: 'save only women, children and impotent creatures, who, nevertheless by night times and upon holydays travail as they may to manure the ground and to sow corn . . . So wretchedlie can they live and induir the pain that no Englesheman can suffire the lyke'.[33] In the lull after the accord with France in 1546 both Bowes and Wharton had taken steps to put their own houses in order, curbing the lawlessness of their own marchers.

This was the classic dichotomy of border warfare – when hostilities flared the marchers were encouraged to don harness and harry at will, when a truce was agreed; they were expected to desist. That any denizen of Tynedale, Redesdale or Liddesdale should experience some difficulty in determining whether he was at peace or war is scarcely to be wondered at, especially if his fields were still smouldering and his byre empty. In May both wardens held assizes at Hexham 'to put down the English thieves . . . who steal cattle and put them into Scotland to make it appear as if done by the Scots; whereas the doers were really English or Scots of Liddesdale pretending to be English'.[34]

In the closing months of 1545 the Council had argued that, in the case of Boulogne, the game was scarcely worth the candle and the place should be handed back. Negotiations, once begun, proved tortuous; Henry was a master at this, and could match either of his European counterparts in bluff and duplicity. Earlier in the year, fearful of a Catholic crusade, he had entered into discussions with the German Protestants, currently at odds with their Catholic emperor. Their responses had proved lukewarm but, by September, fearful of the imperial wrath, it was they who were petitioning the king.

By the following spring the talks had achieved nothing and Hertford was dispatched to Calais with a sizeable force. This was little more than sabre-rattling and, by 24th April, the earl had resumed negotiations. These fresh overtures dragged on until June when it was finally agreed that the Scots should remain unmolested as long as they did not violate the truce. England was to retain hold of Boulogne for a term of eight years as security for a consideration of 2,000,000 crowns.

In May events in Scotland took a dramatic turn when a determined body of assassins, sixteen 'resolute' men[35] seeking to avenge Wishart's martyrdom, broke into Beaton's castle of St Andrews and murdered the cardinal. These diehard reformers, the 'Castilians', found themselves isolated and under siege. If short of support and materiel their spiritual needs were well served by John Knox who subsequently joined them. The leaguer dragged on for fourteen months with no relief from England. Whilst Arran maintained the landward blockade the French mercenary skipper Strozzi brought a fleet of galleys to seal off the seaward. In July 1547 the garrison accepted the inevitable and surrendered without terms. Those deemed to fit the status of gentlemen were incarcerated whilst the commons, including the vituperative Knox, were obliged to endure the galleys.

By the summer the emperor was hammering the German Protestants who, in desperation, appealed once again to Henry. The king dallied now with the notion of an Anglo-French and anti-imperialist alliance but neither of the prospective partners trusted the other sufficiently for so major an undertaking. Despite the accord Henry was determined to impose his will upon the Scots. As the year faded and the king's health declined, the ailing monarch was already preparing for a spring campaign. By late December his condition had worsened and it was obvious to both Hertford and Warwick, the two leading councillors, that the end was near. On 28th January 1547 Henry died; the timing of his death ensured the survival of that other ageing paladin Norfolk who was incarcerated in the Tower and awaiting his execution.

With the young prince crowned as Edward VI the government came under the control of his uncle, Edward Seymour, Earl of Hertford and now Duke of Somerset. The Lord Protector, as he was styled, continued the old king's policy towards Scotland; it was now more urgent than ever that Queen Mary be wed to King Edward. The sheer savagery of Henry's policy continued to haunt Somerset; the dowager queen was resolutely opposed to an English match in favour of her natural leaning towards France where her Guise relatives exercised considerable influence. As diplomatic efforts faltered, the duke, albeit reluctantly, came to the conclusion that only a military solution would suffice. By late summer preparations for a campaign were well under way.

For Wharton the accession of the young king had not affected his intention, despite the growing resistance, to maintain his influence in the west. To support the coming invasion he was liberal with guile and commerce to ensure the riding names stayed firmly in his pocket: 'The old laird of Mangerton, his son, and of the Liddesdales and others, once or twice a week are with me, and show themselves ever willing to serve the King's majesty . . . they are continually doing displeasure to the enemy'.[36]

Having left London on 22nd August, Somerset, with Warwick as his lieutenant, spent the remainder of the month marshalling his forces in and around Newcastle. At this time the city was still walled[37] and it is likely the men were encamped on what is now the Town Moor beyond the ramparts. The march north commenced on 1st September – the Lord Protector's army comprised some sixteen thousand foot, and perhaps four thousand cavalry.

Somerset's experience in and appreciation of the continental wars had convinced him of the need to bolster the mounted arm. The heavy horse were under Grey of Wilton, including five hundred drawn from the Boulogne garrison with two thousand demi-lances led by Sir Francis Bryan. Many of these were borderers. The mercenary captain, Pedro de Gamboa, commanded a couple of companies of mounted harquebusiers.[38] A contingent of Italians served under Malatesta and the army was stiffened by the Gentlemen Pensioners of the royal bodyguard.[39]

The foot comprised a mix of pikes interspersed with billmen and archers. Somerset had probably no more than six hundred English musketeers augmented by a few companies of continental mercenaries.[40] The artillery train was formidable, fifteen great guns, sixty odd field pieces, and a complement of fourteen hundred gunners, matrosses, drivers, sappers and labourers.

In Scotland, Arran was not blind to the potency of the threat Somerset's army posed and he had summoned a national levy to counter the threat. Certain of the nobility including the earls of Lennox (who had slunk back from exile in England prior to the 1547 campaign), Bothwell and Glencairn failed to appear but the force which mustered on the Borough Muir in Edinburgh was still some twenty-three thousand strong.[41] The missing earls were in treasonable correspondence with Somerset, though only a couple of score Liddesdale riders under Mangerton actually joined the English host.

As the host toiled up the north road, to Berwick and then on into the Merse, the advance was shadowed by the fleet under Lord Clinton. Four days out from Newcastle, sixteen or so miles into Scotland, and the army was nearing Cockburnspath. Here the Lammermuir Hills rush down to meet the sea, a dramatic swoop of high cliffs and hidden defiles. On such ground the Scots would have been safe from the great guns of the English ships and a bolder general might have been willing to risk a holding action, but Arran preferred caution.

The formidable defences of Tantallon were not tested; the English continued their march through East Linton to Longniddry. By 8th September they were crossing what are now the manicured fairways of Preston Grange Golf Course. Beyond these the land falls then sweeps upward again to form Fa'side and Carberry Hills. Somerset deployed his forces along the lower slopes facing north and giving the hostile garrison of the pele at Fa'side a prudent berth. To his front was arrayed the Scottish army, with perhaps half as many foot again, rank upon rank of serried pikes, their cavalry less formidable but with their position carefully chosen. If Arran was not a bold commander neither was he a foolish one, and his line was fronted by the wide stretch of the Esk as it bellied towards the sea. The steepness of the banks on the northern side conferred a further advantage.

Huntly, whose division included Argyll's three thousand-odd highland kerns, was posted on the extreme left of the line, that nearest the coast and most exposed to murderous flanking fire from the guns of the fleet, now riding just offshore. To shelter his clansmen from this hazard Huntly had thrown up earthen redoubts and artillery emplacements facing the sea. The regent himself planted his banners on Edmonstone Edge in the centre, whilst Angus took the right, his exposed flank shielded by Hume's fifteen hundred border horse with a morass beyond. The remainder of the Scottish guns which were neither numerous nor particularly well served were stationed on the flanks of the centre and right-hand divisions.

The only bridge lay inland from the small port of Musselburgh and was covered by Huntly whilst, moving west and inland, the river sweeps to the north in a great horseshoe bend; on the south side the ground rises to a knoll with Inveresk church now on the crest. Control of this high ground would have been prominent as Somerset and his officers held a council of war that evening. The Protector believed himself, correctly, to be tactically superior to the Scots with greater weight of heavy horse and ordnance.

Clinton's vantage allowed his topmast men a perfect view of the whole Scottish line, even if the redoubts balked his guns. The great numbers of foot and the strength of their position allowed only a frontal attack: a defended river crossing is not a prospect that is likely to appeal to any commander. Somerset's men would be under fire, obliged to splash through the waters of the Esk and then, their lines hopelessly disordered, storm up steep banks to engage a numerically superior enemy.

With his experienced eye it was obvious to Somerset that control of the knoll would be critical. If he could take and hold this eminence, dragging his heavy guns to the crest of the rise, then he could pulverise the Scottish line with a sustained cannonade, the necessary 'softening up' prior to launching a general assault. In this he appears to have been thinking of the outcome of the battle of Ravenna, where a strongly entrenched enemy, like the Scots and as deficient in cavalry, had been firstly subjected to an intense and concentrated barrage followed up by successive cavalry charges.[42]

On the morning of the 9th Hume's light horse splashed across the Esk to feint at the English line. This was mere sport, at best an attempt to cut up a few of their opposite number. Somerset refused to be drawn, turning down frequent requests from Grey to be permitted to engage. Finding themselves unopposed the borderers grew bolder, trading insults and abuse, an art in which the riding names excelled.

When Somerset finally gave way and allowed Grey to set upon them, they were both surprised and discomfited. A number were spitted on the English lances and more, including Hume, were taken. The survivors, doubtless much chastened, fled in considerable disorder. At a stroke Arran had virtually lost his cavalry arm; the shaken remnants could be of little tactical value.

The lack of an effective cavalry arm told against the Scots early the following morning, Sunday 10th September. By eight the English were moving forward, concentrating on securing the vital knoll. This movement, effectively a giant echelon to the right, throwing the weight of the army against the Scottish left and centre, left Somerset's flank exposed. Had Angus been possessed of an effective mounted arm he could conceivably have brought the Protector's plans to grief. Suddenly perceiving his peril Arran, who appears to have signally overlooked the potential of the higher ground opposite, ordered an advance.

There may be two reasons why he took this surprising decision. First, as mentioned, he realised that if the English guns could be safely placed on Inveresk hill the whole left flank of his army could be pounded at will. Possibly he mistook the nature of the English movement and thought the army, finding his own defensive position too strong, had decided upon a withdrawal and that this offered an opportunity for a decisive blow against their exposed flank.

As it was the English army was moving purposely forward, deployed in column of brigades with Lord Ogle's marchers acting as a screen. Behind came the mass of the foot battalions arrayed in the traditional three battles or divisions. Behind them the heavy horse in two brigades, the guns between the infantry formations.

As Huntly and Argyll's brigades moved smartly forward to the river crossing they lost the inestimable protection of their earthworks and were immediately exposed to enfilading fire from the ships which tore great gaps in the ranks of lightly armed highlanders. It is unlikely that the crashing roundshot inflicted high casualties – the clansmen moved fast and in open order but the psychological effect of the pounding cannot be overstated. To raw highlanders and islemen, none of whom lacked stomach for the fight and who would happily swap strokes with any who opposed them, the thunderous roar, the belching sulphurous fumes and the terrible effect of striking shot, shearing limbs and pulverising flesh, must have appeared as a vision of hell.

It was too much, they broke and the Scottish left began to unravel. Huntly was obliged to move his surviving battalions inland, pushing around the knoll to join with the centre. His files collided with those of the regent's brigades which had crossed the Esk west of Inveresk hill. Angus, somewhat belatedly, also advanced his division, which came up on the right of Arran's strong central column.

The Scots' deployment appears to have been further impeded by the need to bring up the guns which had to be dragged, seemingly by hand, in the wake of the pikes; in the event their artillery did not play a significant role in the fight.[43] The whole line now became a great bristling phalanx, a sight that impressed all who witnessed it. Surely such a great surge of serried points must prove invincible.

Somerset seems to have been momentarily wrong-footed. He had not expected to be attacked and was thus obliged to frantically slew the line around so he could concentrate his great weight of shot and musketry against this monster. The infantry brigades formed with pikes and bills in a strong central block, shot and bows on the flanks. To slow the seemingly inexorable advance of the Scottish pikes he committed his cavalry in a series of holding charges, using up the horse as the means to deny the Scots continued momentum. This was a costly expedient: Somerset's secretary Patten, an eyewitness, described the ensuing mêlée:

> [The Scots] *stood at defence, shoulders nigh together, the fore-rank stooping low before their fellows behind them holding their pikes in both hands, the one end of the pike against the right foot, the other against the enemy's breast, so nigh as place and space might suffer. So thick were they that a bare finger should as easily pierce through the bristles of a hedgehog as any man encounter the front of the pikes.*[44]

The Scots, despite the press, had advanced rapidly: had they been able to maintain this momentum then, in Swiss-fashion, they would have rolled over the English line. Cantering now towards them, over the stubble fields and hummocks, came the English cavalry. These were the tactics of Marignano,[45] the irresistible phalanx to be halted by a series of frontal charges. With a great, resounding crash, like the storm-tossed breakers rolling in upon the shore, the English horse collided with the immovable pikes. Pistol shot and the crack of arquebuses contended with the clash of blade on point, the screams and frenzied thrashing of dying men and horses.

Many of the English cavalry became casualties, Edward Shelley, the captain of the Boulogne company or 'Bulleners' as they were known, amongst them. Grey's horse were thrown back in disorder but Somerset now sent in the Gentlemen Pensioners and his border lances. These charged home against Arran's division with great élan but fared no better: piles of dead riders and their stricken mounts bled amongst the stubble.

With the advanced slowed, however, the pikes were exposed to the full weight of the English guns and shot which had been ably marshalled by Warwick whilst the horse bought time with their lives. They were mown down in droves: in some ways this was a repeat of Falkirk, Halidon Hill or Homildon with muskets replacing or certainly complementing longbows. As the great guns spat death from perhaps two hundred yards, the nimble shot and archers darted forward to shoot at point blank range whilst de Gamboa's mounted musketeers nibbled at the flanks.

With no means of continuing their advance and with no available cavalry to relieve the pressure, the Scots could only withdraw. Such a manoeuvre would have tested the most professional armies of the day. It clearly dismayed the regent who, exclaiming loudly that he was betrayed, leapt upon his horse and was last seen pelting in the general direction of Edinburgh. Virtually leaderless and without any prospect of continuing the fight on anything approaching even terms, the ranks shivered, as though a great wind had shaken them, then broke.

Angus's attempt to organise an orderly retreat foundered and the army disintegrated into a vast streaming torrent of beaten men, harried and speared by the surviving English horse, hungry for vengeance after their earlier mauling. Patten commentated that the ground vacated by the Scots resembled nothing so much as a wood yard so great was the number of abandoned staves![46]

The Douglas, as canny as ever, escaped the stricken field. The great stumbling bloodied mass of survivors were now pelting back towards Dalkeith. The pursuit was unrelenting and Grey's horse swooped: they struck and struck again like peregrines in the heat of the chase. It was said that as many as ten thousand Scots lay dead on the field and in the rout, and whilst this is undoubtably an exaggeration, loss of life on the losing side was high. The victors had lost perhaps two hundred and fifty, mainly from the horse, the foot had barely come to strokes. Though Shelley was the only noble fatality, many of the English cavaliers were injured, including Grey and de Gamboa.

As a tactical victory Pinkie was a triumph for Somerset but the political consequences were muted. The battle neither ended the war nor brought the Scots to their knees. It did facilitate the resurrection of an English Pale in the Lothians, with the English occupying key bastions including the old fortress of Roxburgh. In Teviotdale the Kers were brought over and Wharton, assisted by Lennox, was active in the west; Annan was sacked after a spirited resistance by the garrison. Somerset's proposals were a good deal less hubristic than his late master's; his approach showed a statesmanlike quality absent from Henry's bullying. What he envisaged was a true partnership of the united realms rather than the subjugation of the lesser. Edward and Mary's children would rule in the manner that in fact occurred after 1603.

This ambition, reasonable though it may now appear, was thwarted by the legacy of hate and mistrust which the harrying had engendered. In this his great victory hindered rather than facilitated any moves towards a lasting accord. Thus the war dragged on. The following April, the east coast towns of Musselburgh, Dalkeith and Dunbar were razed whilst Haddington was occupied. Lord Grey beat up Teviotdale and Liddesdale. The arrival of a French contingent six thousand strong under the Sieur d'Esse helped restore the balance; the English forts began to fall, including the windswept eyrie of Fast Castle, taken by a *coup de main* reminiscent of Randolph or Douglas.

The campaign of attrition was a savage business of outpost actions and skirmishes, fought with a brutal intensity as fierce and ruthless as any of the earlier wars: 'The Scots, paying back the ravages of years, were pitiless, and one hears of their buying English prisoners from the French in order to slaughter them'.[47] French gold was now as plentiful as English and cemented the return of many of the riding names to their allegiance, so much so that by midsummer 1548 Wharton was complaining to Somerset that: 'Many of the greatest thieves have had at one time in their purses both of his Majesty's and of the French king's . . . there are more riots and misdemeanours within these two months than in three or four years before'.[48]

The warden, as energetic as ever in the local maelstrom of marcher politics, had entered into an alliance with John Maxwell to confirm his grip on the key west march garrisons. Maxwell was at best an uneasy ally, like most of his contemporaries he played both sides in his own game. Wharton subsequently found it convenient to cast Maxwell in the role of turncoat when the warden was worsted in an extended skirmish with the Douglases when engaged in beating up Nithsdale.

In Teviotdale Ferniherst was retaken with French aid and the English grip began to be steadily prised free. Early in 1549 most of the surviving garrisons were pulled out; the medicine, however draconian, wasn't working. The young queen had been kept secure at Stirling throughout until she was moved first to Dumbarton and then, in July 1548, packed off to France to a royal marriage. This was cemented by the renewal of the Franco-Scots alliance, whereby the French undertook to maintain the independence of their ally. Arran's reward for brokering the arrangement was the substantial gift of the duchy of Chatelherault.

As proof of their intent the French underwrote the cost of constructing a new chain of forts at Eyemouth, Dunbar and Inchkeith.[49] The English policy had failed – with Mary safe across the Channel the Rough Wooing finally ran out of steam. Pinkie was Somerset's greatest triumph: throughout 1548 and 1549 he was distracted by internal disturbances in the south west and East Anglia and a growing split with his erstwhile deputy Warwick. The Protector finally lost his office and swiftly thereafter his head in October 1549.

Terms for a cessation were agreed between England and France the following year when Boulogne was returned. In 1551 Scotland was included in the peace, the terms of which included final agreement on the border line itself. On paper the Debatable land ceased to exist. Both sides had had enough of the war: the years of savagery had gained England nothing except a vast outlay of time and treasure. Scotland, too, needed a respite: the violence had severely damaged the economy.[50] Besides the killing of Wishart, the murder of Beaton and the defeat of the Castilians had not settled the religious question. The impetus for reform was becoming unstoppable and the young queen, now absent in France, would soon find herself the Catholic ruler of a Protestant state.

Notes

1 Quoted in Drummond Brown, R., *Brave Borderland*, London 1935 p. 187.
2 Lynch, M., *Scotland: A New History*, London 1991 p. 203.

3 Ibid p. 203.

4 Scarisbrick, J.J., *Henry VIII*, London 1968 p. 438.

5 When Beaton attempted to assert his authority by having his cross carried in procession into the nave of Glasgow Cathedral, his own clergy clashed with the representatives of the archbishop and a lively brawl ensued! See Lynch p. 204.

6 In mid 1543 an English observer noted approvingly that the inhabitants of Leith 'be noted all to be good [i.e. reformed] Christians', see Lynch p. 204.

7 Wishart's preaching tour lasted from 1544 until January 1546 when he was arrested and subsequently burnt as a heretic. His martyrdom was a *casus belli* to the reformers.

8 Thomas Seymour – 'a dangerous and lecherous man', see Scarisbrick p. 456. He married Henry's widow Catherine Parr, formerly Lady Latimer, and gained control of Princess Elizabeth whom he may have attempted to seduce. His conduct became so extreme that not even his brother could save him from the axe.

9 There was a perception amongst contemporary English observers that the Border Horse might do better on the continent where they were less influenced by private arrangements with their Scottish adversaries such as were found to obtain in relation to local service.

10 These wooden containers, typically twelve in number, were known as 'apostles' for obvious reasons and perhaps because the uncertainty in operating firearms of the period promoted a requirement for divine assistance!

11 A 'scathe' was a larger raid or warden 'rode' aimed at doing serious damage to standing crops, a form of economic warfare whilst the raid or foray was invariably aimed at lifting livestock purely for gain.

12 MacDonald Fraser, G., *The Steel Bonnets*, London 1971 p. 256.

13 Lynch p. 206.

14 MacDonald Fraser p. 256.

15 Ibid p. 256.

16 Ibid p. 257.

17 Quoted in Borland, R., *Border Raids and Reivers*, Glasgow 1910 p. 63.

18 Quoted in Borland p. 64. The younger Eure was the same who had held Scarborough Castle during the Pilgrimage of Grace. Hertford boasted that he had killed six hundred or so Scots in Leith for the loss of only seven of his own raiders, see Lynch p. 205.

19 Quoted in Borland p. 65.

20 Scarisbrick p. 448.

21 MacDonald Fraser p. 260.

22 Ibid p. 260 – the author may be doing these continentals a disservice. Serving as a mercenary for reward was by no means a disreputable calling in the mid-sixteenth century and certainly did not have the pejorative connotations it would today. Besides, it would be difficult to imagine any class of individual more savage, rapacious or untrustworthy than the Liddesdale men.

23 MacDonald Fraser p. 260.

24 Robson, R., *The Rise and Fall of the English Highland Clans*, Edinburgh 1989 p. 185.

25 Quoted in Robson p. 185.

26 Scarisbrick p. 469.

27 Ibid p. 453.

28 Ibid p. 454.

29 Despite his having been 'out' in the Pilgrimage of Grace, Bowes had not lacked for advancement and had now been ransomed after the débâcle at Haddon Rigg (see Chapter 21).

30 Quoted in Robson p. 191.

31 MacDonald Fraser p. 265.

32 Ibid p. 265.

33 Ibid p. 262.

34 Ibid p. 263.

35 Mackie, J.D., *A History of Scotland*, London 1964 p. 145.

36 MacDonald Fraser p. 264.

37 Newcastle retained its circuit of medieval walls until the civil war era and these were strong enough to provide resistance against the Scots army in autumn 1644, although the enceinte was breached in several places prior to the final, successful assault.

38 Oman, Sir C., *The Art of War in the Sixteenth Century*, London 1924 p. 359.

39 Ibid p. 359.

40 Ibid p. 359.

41 Ibid p. 359.

42 Ibid p. 363.

43 Ibid p. 363.

44 Quoted in Sadler, D.J., *Scottish Battles*, Edinburgh 1996 p. 88.

45 Oman p. 365.

46 Ibid p. 366.

47 MacDonald Fraser p. 275.

48 Quoted ibid p. 275.

49 It is estimated that between 1548 and 1550 the French invested the equivalent of £1 million in supporting Scotland. Initially they maintained a mobile field army six thousand strong and latterly, having constructed the garrison outposts, left some four hundred soldiers to man them. From Henry II's perspective this was never intended as mere altruism. He had an interest in maintaining Mary's position as a Catholic contender for the English crown and the presence of and dependence on so many French troops ensured Scotland remained within his sphere of influence. Clearly the king of France could expect no amity from the reformers should they take control of the government, see Lynch p. 207.

50 The Scots economy had been drastically affected to the extent that exports during the 1540s were running at only a seventh of the levels attained in the latter years of James V's reign. That notwithstanding, both government and

populace exhibited considerable degrees of resilience and there is no evidence to suggest that Scots society was ever minded to bend its collective knee to England. Later writers have tended to blame the English influence and quasi occupation for the spread of the reformation within the realm but this must remain questionable, see Lynch p. 207.

Chapter 19

The Two Queens

*Nothing is more remarkable than the light thrown on the social state
of Scotland at this time by the justiciary records. By far the larger part
of the criminals dealt with at the King's 'justice aires' were men of
good position, barons and landowners burgesses or provosts of burgh. The
humbler offenders were dealt with by the sheriff or at the baron's courts,
and do not appear but the following extracts from the records of the short
reign of James IV, in which the culprits are all landowners, or members
of their families, in Dumfriesshire or Galloway, illustrate the difficulty
of maintaining order when the upper classes were so unruly.[3]*

On the morning of 8th February, 1587, Mary Stewart, formerly Queen
of Scots, attended her final and most dramatic public function in the
great hall of Fotheringay Castle. She was then forty-four years of age and
had been a prisoner in England for nearly twenty of them. Her celebrated
auburn tresses had gone prematurely grey and she now wore a wig. That
morning she had taken some care with her appearance as befitted the solemn-
ity of the occasion. Dressed almost entirely in red, the blazon of Catholic
martyrdom, she prepared with dignity and courage to face the final test.

The day was fine and sunny which to Dr Fletcher, the rabidly Protestant Dean of Peterborough, represented a clear indication of the Almighty's heartfelt approbation. The hall held a near capacity crowd of some three hundred spectators, who like the doomed queen had to endure the good doctor's last-minute, unspeakably pedantic, attempts to divert Mary from her expressed faith. The dais upon which the headsman was to perform was, appropriately, draped in black, roughly twelve foot square and some two feet in height.

When, around 10 a.m., the denouement took place, the executioner bungled the job. Doubtless the crowd would have preferred a clean kill, a single clean and sweeping stroke instantly transporting his royal victim from this world to the next. However, the first blow missed the neck and drove into the back of the skull. Possibly this was not fatal and the head was only severed by the second stroke. Even then the butchery was not quite complete for the head still dangled by a stubborn sinew; this had to be cut by the expedient of using the axe blade as a saw. And then it was finally over. The queen was dead, her legend and the con-sequential major boost to the heritage industry of today was only just beginning.[4]

Since 13th May, 1568, that fateful day when the young queen, fleeing from the wrack of her cause at Langside, had crossed the Solway to throw herself uninvited on the mercy of her Protestant cousin, she had striven unceasingly as the prime architect of her own doom. For her son, James VI, who now sat on the throne of Scotland and presided over a realm firmly wedded to the Calvinist faith, her death could comfortably be des-cribed as convenient.

None of these dramatic events could have been foreseen in 1550 when peace, of a sort, came to the border in the wake of the Franco-Scots-English accord. Both sides recognised the need to take steps to bridle the more headstrong elements amongst their respective marchers. Now that the former Lord Protector's Pale had been abandoned, the line of former bastions had to be refurbished. Warwick, whose vaulting ambi-tion easily matched that of Somerset, was now elevated to the dukedom of Northumberland and made warden general on the borders with the re-doubtably pugnacious Wharton as his deputy.[5] The list of other leading officers comprised such experienced hands as Lord Eure, Sir Thomas Dacre, Sir Richard Musgrave and Lord Coniers.

Wharton had devised a comprehensive strategy for containment, boosting the regular garrisons with a network of local watches, patrols and beacons. This plan was given teeth by draconian sanctions against slackers though, as he of all people would be well aware, the web of cross border alliances and understandings would be extraordinarily difficult to unravel. In Scotland the situation was yet more difficult: in the west Lord Maxwell descended on the English Grahams more in pursuance of private murders than in any semblance of warden justice. He was repulsed by Dacre and a potent enmity now sprang up between them. Arran was seeking gainful employment in French armies for his troublesome marchers of Teviotdale and the Merse; Ker and Scott were at each other's throats.

John Maxwell became Scottish west march warden in 1552 after his brother finally found the flurry of vendettas his efforts had engendered too great a burden. Johnny himself despaired of his office after only a year and his successor, Douglas of Drumlanrig, lasted no longer.[6] In Northumberland the dalesmen were riding again and though the two national governments might be approaching some form of understanding. This amity had not percolated down to Tynedale, Redesdale or Liddesdale. It was noted in that year that the 'disunity among the inhabitants [of Northumberland] impairs the strength of the frontiers, for they will not help each other, and procure displeasure towards each other by the Scots. They refuse forage and victuals to the soldiers at reasonable prices, saying they had rather the Scots should have or burn it . . .'.[7]

One significant effect of Henry's savage efforts during the Rough Wooing had been to encourage the swelling influence of the French interest in the person of the dowager queen Marie de Guise Lorraine. This formidable lady, who had given to her daughter, the future queen of Scots, her height and regal carriage, had long been a rival of Arran's and had been 'out' in the war of 1548–9. She had inspired the troops before the walls of the fort at Inchkeith with a rousing address and, the following year, had engineered an extended visit to the French court by a body of influential Scottish nobles.

This attempt to win hearts and minds by a dazzling display of Renaissance splendour and the lining of purses was no more successful than earlier English overtures. Amongst those who enjoyed the King of France's hospitality were Lord James Stewart, the Commendator of St Andrews,[8] the earls Marischal, Huntly and Cassilis with Lords Maxwell and Fleming.[9] Arran, who had already been partly suborned with his French dukedom, was eased aside by Marie de Guise in 1554 when his 'tutory' or guardianship of the young queen was due, in the traditional way, to expire when the child attained her twelfth birthday.[10]

The new regent was a convinced Catholic but she was neither a fanatic nor heavy-handed; there was to be no return to the burnings of Beaton's day. The established church, headed by Archbishop Hamilton, was to hold a series of councils aimed at promoting reform from within in 1549, 1552 and 1559 but the Protestant reformers were steadily gaining ground. Since his release from the galleys in 1549 Knox had lived in England where he became, for a period, chaplain to the young king, Edward VI. He did not return to Scotland for another six years but when he did his influence was profound. Knox was not, like the earlier reformers, a disciple of Luther but preferred the greater rigours of Calvinism. His ideas took root, not just amongst the commons, but within the higher strata of the nobility, the genesis of a political faction who were later, and under the leadership of Lord James Stewart, to assume power as the 'Lords of the Congregation'.

The dowager queen was careful to promote a policy of tolerance and conciliation whilst she made genuine efforts to restore stability. The Parliament of 1555 sought to enact necessary legislative reforms, though the attempt to increase central government control over more local affairs prompted a backlash of craft riots in the burghs. It might be presumed that the death of Edward VI and the accession of his Catholic half sister Mary in 1553 would be bound to promote greater amity between the realms. However, this was not so. Mary Tudor married the Habsburg Philip of Spain whose imperialist connections were hostile to France. Four years later, in March 1557, the doting queen received a rare visit from her husband. This was not prompted by personal considerations of affection – Spain needed allies for the renewal of the war against Henry II. The besotted Mary bullied her reluctant council into a declaration of war in June.

In Scotland the regent was also coming under pressure to open hostilities with England but her nobles, like their English counterparts, now had little stomach for other men's wars. No major invasions took place and no full-scale battles were fought in this shadow war but the marches, as ever, bore the brunt of such fighting as occurred. Huntly was given the lieutenancy of the Scottish border, whilst in Northumberland Thomas Percy, son of the elder Sir Thomas and nephew of the last Percy earl, was restored to his title on 1st May 1556. Subsequently, on 9th August the following year he was appointed warden of the middle and east marches and also to the captaincy of Berwick.

Henri D'Oysel, the general of French forces in Scotland, provided provocation by recommissioning the fort at Eyemouth, a direct challenge to Berwick. The warden, aided by his younger and dynamic brother Henry, was not slow to pick up the gage. Huntly dispatched a body of riders, including the Lord James Stewart, to harry Glendale and menace Ford.[11] Henry Percy reacted with élan, raising the border horse and chasing the raiders clear of the Tweed. Striking into the Merse, Percy wasted sixteen vills. A mere eight days later the Scots were back, this time led by Huntly in person with D'Oysel in close support. The earl, his brother and Wharton mustered against them but their retaliation was this time less successful. D'Oysel's foot stood their ground and Percy was beaten off with the loss of a hundred of his riders.[12]

Determined to lend more support to her French allies, the regent had mustered a field army which she placed under Arran's command. Northumberland mustered his available forces at Lowick to counter any invasion. Having mustered at Kelso the Scots advanced towards the border but, once there, the lords declined to advance further. Despite the dowager queen's best entreaties her nobles would have none of it: this was not their war. In disgust D'Oysel determined not to abandon Marie and undertook to lead a commanded party, mostly his own soldiers and with their ordnance, against the walls of Wark.

Angrily the Scottish peers clamoured for his immediate recall and he was constrained to turn about and march again for Scotland. Inevitably the isolated column proved too tempting a target and was set upon by the marchers. D'Oysel put up a stiff fight and would have seen off his attackers had not the garrison of Wark under their officer, Captain Reed, launched a sally and tipped the balance, chasing the French back in disorder.[13]

Henry Percy followed up this success with a raid against Eyemouth. His force was attacked in the Merse by the Teviotdale Kers. The fight hung in the balance and it seemed the English must be worsted but Sir John Forster, despite wounds and having had at least one horse killed under him, fought like a second Achilles and inspired his countrymen to victory.[14]

In the summer of 1558 Henry Percy returned to hammer the Merse. He was accompanied by Sir George Bowes, the Marshall of the Berwick garrison, and some seven or eight hundred riders, together with two thousand foot. Duns and Langton were both thoroughly taken up and torched but, in the course of their withdrawal, the raiders were challenged by Scots hurrying from Kelso, several companies of foot and perhaps a couple of thousand horse.

The fight occurred by Swinton when a spirited charge by the Scottish foot discomfited their English adversaries, hampered by damp and spoiled powder. Reed and Sir Henry Lee strove to rally the foot whilst the horse charged the Scots riders who dissolved in rout. Now surrounded, the valiant foot continued to resist until they had sustained considerable losses in men killed or taken. Lord Keith, eldest son of the Earl Marischal, was amongst the haul of prisoners.[15]

The Scots struck back, crossing the Tweed with a mixed body of horse and foot. The mounted arm, perhaps a thousand strong, took up Glendale till attacked by the earl and his brother. The fight began at Grindon and spilled over the ground north of the Till as the raiders were driven back. The Scottish foot, not yet engaged, covered the disorderly retreat of the horse and maintained a fighting withdrawal to the Tweed. As they sought to re-cross the river they were assailed in the flank by several fresh foot companies detached from Berwick. The mounting odds notwithstanding, the Scottish foot formed into a protective pike column and the bristling steel-fanged hedge proved utterly impenetrable, even though harried for at least two miles into Scotland. Deprived of a victory Percy had to be content with burning Ednam.[16]

Undeterred, the Scots attacked again and this time the raiders were commanded by James Hepburn, 4th Earl of Bothwell, destined for later notoriety as Queen Mary's paramour. The earl dispatched his mounted arm to waste Fenton whilst keeping the foot in reserve at Haltwell-Sweir. Percy attacked him there, having driven in the horse. Met by regular volleys from the foot the English riders quailed and then broke. Over a hundred were captured.[17]

The impertinence of Eyemouth was compounded by a sconce[18] or pele at Edrington, held by a small garrison of sixteen Frenchmen. After a gallant defence the place was successfully stormed and an English outpost established on Halidon Hill. This vantage enabled the small complement to keep a watching eye over the broad plain of the Merse and offer protection to the haymakers working the fields below. In the summer's warmth the English grew casual, discarding their harness to indulge in sports and horseplay. A sally from Eyemouth thus succeeded in catching them totally unprepared and tumbled them pell mell from the hill. A relief from Berwick under Sir James Croft redressed the balance but only after a stiff fight with losses on both sides.[19]

Aside from the alarums on the borders Mary Tudor now had other concerns. The French had, in January 1558, laid siege to Calais, England's last great continental bastion, the only remnant of her French possessions. A proposal that the Scots should take the opportunity to leaguer Berwick fell on deaf ears. The subsequent loss of Calais was a disaster and Mary's stock, diminished by her rigid orthodoxy and regular burning of heretics, plummeted. When she finally died and was succeeded by her vivacious 25-year-old Protestant half sister Elizabeth, the Spanish alliance expired with her. The new queen had neither the will nor the resources to continue war with France and Scotland.

In Scotland there was no enthusiasm for the war and the regent's position was increasingly insecure. Her daughter had married the dauphin on 24th April 1558 and whilst her commissioners had been extremely careful to safeguard the reversionary rights of the throne to the Hamiltons (a leading Catholic family) should the young queen die without issue, her Guise relatives had procured her agreement to a secret accord that provided for quite the opposite. Mary had undertaken that, in the event of her predeceasing her husband and dying childless, then her crown would pass to her French husband. The couple were styled 'King and Queen of Scotland' an impolitic assertion which fuelled the rise of anti-French feeling.

By the late spring of 1559 Knox was back in Perth after a sojourn in Geneva. His return sparked a rash of religious disturbances and provided a focus for the Protestant opposition, the Lords of the Congregation, who now openly sought to oust the regent. Lord James Stewart appealed to England for aid. The lords had briefly considered throwing off their allegiance to Queen Mary and selecting one of their number, possibly Stewart, as an alternative, Protestant candidate, though he was rejected on the grounds of bastardy. The regent fought back, driving the rebels from Edinburgh. English help, horse, foot and guns, was needed.

This was a key moment, for the first time both realms appeared to have a common aim, albeit spurred on by necessity. But if the reformed religion was to survive in England and prosper in Scotland then both amity and consensus were required. Marie de Guise, though ailing, would not give up without a fight. Driven from the capital she and her French supporters fortified Leith and begged Henry II for relief.

The king was in a difficult position. He would naturally feel the tug of loyalty toward Marie de Guise but, equally, he had no desire to antagonise England and push Elizabeth back into the arms of Spain. Henry was faced with the threat of Calvinism in France which had grown steadily through the 1550s. The conclusion of peace with the Empire secured by the Treaty of Cateau-Cambresis freed him to deal with the heretics. His resentment of heresy, however, caused him to alienate Elizabeth by quartering the arms of England on the arms of Francis and Mary. As the Queen of Scots was a granddaughter of Margaret Tudor she could claim the throne as the legitimate Catholic contender. In the words of a contemporary doggerel:

The armies of Marie Quene Dolphines of France,
The nobillest lady in earth for till advance;
Of Scotland Quene, of Ingland also,
Of Ireland also God hath providit so.[20]

On 6th July 1559 Henry II was killed whilst taking part in a tournament and Francis became king.[21] In Scotland Marie de Guise was formally relegated when, in the autumn, the lords confirmed her deposition and reinstated her old rival Arran as head of the regency council. Though Elizabeth was loath to give support to a rebel faction, she privately dispatched Sadleir to Edinburgh with a war chest of £3,000 to fund their cause. At the same time the envoy was to enter into negotiations with the regent to procure peace, or what normally passed for quiet, on the border.

These discussions proved fruitful. Marie de Guise had no wish to provoke England and good work was done in relation to the conduct of truce days, exchanges of prisoners and assurances. So unsettled were the marches, however, that flare-ups became inevitable, Bothwell being a prime culprit. The regent herself was not above treading in the mire of marcher politics, she had connived with Dacre to attack Maxwell whose office she refused to recognise and to ensure the warden was too busy to lend support to the rebel lords. Dacre was only too happy to oblige. The lords soon got wind of this and protested, obliging Elizabeth to restrain her own warden.[22]

Sadleir, as experienced an observer of the state of the borders as any, was moved to observe at this time: 'It is more than xx years ago syns I had som understanding of this frontier, and yet dyd I never know it in such disorder; for now the office spoyleth the thefe without bringing forth his person to tryall by the aw; and the thefe robbeth the trewe man, and the trewe men take assurance of the theves that they shall not rob them, and give them yerely rent and tribute for the same'.[23] The ambassador laid the principal blame for this dolorous state at the feet of incompetent and corrupt officers and he selected both Dacre and Northumberland for particular criticism.

Robert Cecil, later Lord Burghley, the queen's most trusted advisor, was minded to heed this advice and replaced both wardens. Sadleir found himself in a caretaker role in the east march whilst Northumberland attended court. In November Norfolk was appointed as lieutenant north of the Trent with Grey of Wilton relieving Sadleir. At the same time a fleet under Winter was sent to cruise off the Forth to block any French intentions and so potent a reminder was sufficient to persuade both the Humes and Kers to lend their support to the rebel lords. Although both names remained true to the old religion, they found the French more objectionable at present than the English.[24]

On 27th February 1560 the rebels concluded an alliance with England, sealed as the Treaty of Berwick. Henry II's previous blunder in asserting his daughter-in-law's rights in England had convinced Elizabeth that the anathema of supporting rebels against her cousin's crown was the lesser evil. The treaty was a mutual defence pact and as the French failed to evacuate Leith an English army sat down before the walls at the end of March, the first time in such a long history of cross border incursions that a southern army appeared by invitation of the Scottish polity.

As Grey, supported by Hume and Ferniherst, had stripped the Berwick garrison to march against Leith, Sadleir again found himself in the caretaker role. Cecil came north to confer with his subordinate and gain first-hand intelligence on the state of the border. From Berwick he proceeded north to Edinburgh for further negotiations with Lord James.

Marie de Guise died on 11th June and her passing marked the final decline of French influence, even though she herself had been a paragon of moderation and most who had known her mourned. A second treaty was sealed at Edinburgh in July under the terms of which both French and English troops were to withdraw, Elizabeth's right was recognised and the arms of England were no longer to be quartered with those of France. The French refused to return either Calais or Boulogne and Mary refused to ratify the treaty.

Cecil, having now seen for himself the state of law and order in the marches, decided that firm action was needed. His proposals were prepared after detailed and lengthy consultation. He carefully considered past precedents and seasoned his findings with advice from experienced officers such as Grey and Wharton. One of his decisions was to considerably strengthen the defences of Berwick.[25] Lord James made similar efforts, summoning Maxwell to explain the dire situation which obtained in his march. Despite his indifferent record Maxwell kept his office as did Dacre. In the middle marches Ker of Cesford and Sir John Forster held sway, each as steeped in villainy as the other. Hume was confirmed in the east as was Grey.

The political solution in Scotland has rightly been described as conservative. Mary remained Queen of Scots and there was to be no overt interference from England. The religious consequences were considerably more profound. The reformers were now firmly in control and the Catholic church was disestablished by a parliament held the following month. The jurisdiction of the Pope was abolished, the mass was proscribed and Calvinist doctrine preferred as the basis for the new state religion.

The Treaty of Edinburgh represented a significant shift in Anglo-Scottish relations. The mutuality of faith, even if based on differing doctrines, led to a degree of understanding which would, only a few years previously, have seemed inconceivable. Despite this profound change the regime's position was far from secure. Mary, a Catholic, was still queen and the Lords of the Congregation remained as quasi-rebels. Elizabeth naturally did not lack for suitors: Arran proposed his son as a candidate and though his overtures were politely received there was little real prospect of a Scottish match. On 5th December 1560 Francis II of France died suddenly, leaving his young widow as a supernumerary at the French court. It seemed inevitable that Mary must return and take up her rightful position as Queen of Scots. The following spring the Lord James journeyed to France to prepare the ground for his half sister's assumption of power. Stewart was a consumate politician and stressed the need for moderation. Mary was clever enough to sense the merit in this and she cannily refused more extreme overtures from Huntly and the Catholic faction who wanted her to sanction a coup against the paladins of the new faith.

On the 19th August 1561, Mary Queen of Scots landed at Leith and took up residence at Holyrood House. Knox was outraged and poured out venom. Mary, a devout Catholic, dowager Queen of France, used to the splendour of a rich renaissance court, represented everything the vituperative preacher detested and he lost no time in making this plain. The Lord James, however, respected his half sister's right to worship in private as she chose whilst maintaining a conciliatory policy. The new religion was thus not threatened by the new queen who also benefited from the windfall of confiscated church revenues that boosted her already handsome income as dowager.

One of Mary's most recent biographers has suggested that Lord James, shortly to be advanced to the earldom of Moray, hated his half sister and coveted the throne. This seems unduly pejorative: he was already barred from the throne as illegitimate and, in these early years, his relationship with the young queen seemed both amicable and productive. His advices were sound and Mary made a good beginning by listening. She continued to reject Huntly's overtures and joined with Moray in suppressing the 'Cock of the North's' rebellion the following summer.

The earl, no mean commander, dispersed Huntly's rebels at Corrichie on 28th October 1562, and the rebel peer solved the problem of what to do with him by expiring, apparently of a stroke, shortly after he was taken. The Gordon hegemony in the north-east was broken and the spectre of a religious war, such as was beginning to erupt in France and which would tear the country apart for the next thirty years, diminished.

Mary, like Elizabeth, desired security on her borders. Maxwell and Dacre continued to scrimmage in the west whilst Teviotdale and Liddesdale were riding. Matters had improved in the east, to the extent that Grey, in June 1561, felt confident enough to relinquish his post and retire to the south where he died in December of the following year.

Lord James Stewart, before his elevation to the earldom, was instructed to proceed to Jedburgh and Dumfries to bring the wilder elements under control, a short, sharp shock treatment or 'dauntening'. Cesford and Ferniherst were bidden to assist in the work of apprehending thieves and promoting better liaison with their English counterparts. In that November

Lord James established his warden's court at Jedburgh and meted out justice: much of which, it has to be said, was of a summary and draconian nature, and known as 'Jeddart Justice'. Over a score of alleged malefactors were hanged and more sent to the capital and incarcerated. If there was insufficient rope to hand, men were flung into the Teviot and held under by lances.

The Lord James was too astute to believe that this form of uncompromising law enforcement could effect a lasting solution. He knew that only close and sustained co-operation between opposing wardens could achieve this. He would be well aware that the warden was often the major part of the malady rather than the remedy. He failed to curb Maxwell but did enter into constructive dialogue with Grey and Forster (it would almost certainly not have escaped his notice that Cesford and his opposite number were prime movers in the general discord). One of the proposals put forward was that the queens should meet in conference within the marches in 1562. For a multiplicity of reasons this summit failed to materialise. Mary was still refusing to ratify the Treaty of Edinburgh and Elizabeth found a variety of excuses (in all probability she did not want the Scottish queen to get an inkling of how parlous a state the English defence were in).[26]

Despite the failure of the summit Lord James still felt able to direct his powerful energies once more toward the marches. In the summer of 1562 he led an expedition against both Teviotdale and Liddesdale, supported by Hume, Cesford and three thousand horse. In July he made a lightning descent on Hawick where he arrested fifty-three wanted men. Though half a score were acquitted twice that number were condemned and drowned forthwith (due to the continued shortage of decent quality rope and suitably stout trees). A further half dozen were hanged from such standing timber as was available.[27]

In the autumn, Lord James, shortly to be Earl of Moray, was distracted by Huntly's abortive rebellion but returned to the border in November. This time he brought an adequate supply of rope. The following April Dacre was finally removed and replaced by Henry, Lord Scrope of Bolton who, despite not being a native Cumbrian, proved to be a highly efficient and energetic officer. On the east march there was an interregnum whilst a suitable replacement for Grey was sought and the vacancy was not filled until Francis Russell, 2nd earl of Bedford, was appointed at the end of the year.

Despite the continuing disorders there was a move towards closer working between the opposing wardenries. Men like Maxwell, Cesford, Hume and Forster were never going to put duty before expediency but the ancient enmities were being diluted by a broader notion of common purpose. The two stumbling blocks which remained at national level were the continued refusal of Mary to recognise the treaty and her insistence that Elizabeth should name her cousin as an heir.

In order to establish a platform for promoting this multinational approach to law enforcement, commissioners appointed from both realms met firstly at Carlisle on 11th September 1563 before proceeding to Dumfries where they remained in conference till the 23rd of that month. Both Scrope and Forster were included in the English delegation whilst Maxwell accompanied the Scots. The agenda was wide-ranging and many matters were debated, though it has to be said the conference was stronger on worthy intentions than resultant action. The marchers' instincts were honed to detect any intimation of instability in relations between the two realms which, once perceived, provided instant cause for fresh disturbances.

Once installed at Berwick by the end of March 1564 the new warden, Bedford, brought fresh impetus to the work of refortification and added his contribution to the swelling chorus of complaint against Cesford. The queen took steps to bring her mettlesome warden under control[28] Some uncertainty did arise over the vexed question of Mary's marriage. The young queen was a most eligible widow and certainly did not lack for suitors. She rejected Elizabeth's nominee, her own favourite Robert Dudley, Earl of Leicester and, in July 1565, she married Henry, Lord Darnley, Lennox's son. The queen has been heavily censured for what, as it transpired, was a most unsuitable match. Beneath his brash and handsome exterior Darnley was vicious, stupid and degenerate but at the time the union appeared ideal: Mary avoided the complications of marriage to a foreign suitor and united the two septs of the Stewart name. If policy was a factor in her decision Mary was undoubtably swayed by her consort's manly bearing; 'the lustiest and best proportionit lang man that sche had seen'.[29] She was to be sadly disappointed.

For a brief interlude the court flourished as a splendid renaissance showcase. Honours were showered liberally amid a dazzling round of masques and pageantry. Beneath the surface, however, the cracks were already visible. The Lennox ascendancy piqued both Arran and, more dangerously, Moray.

The threat of a Catholic revival alarmed Knox who needed little prompting to vilify the queen. In that summer the earls rebelled, but their adventure, dubbed 'The Chaseabout Raid', proved a still-born thing. The queen, supported by Bothwell, routed Moray and Arran with scarcely a shot being fired.

On 6th September the earl was at Dumfries begging for English arms to shore up his tottering enterprise. Elizabeth subscribed £1,000, Bedford found £500 more, and three foot companies were sent, though these could do little more than cover a hasty withdrawal. The queen, Bothwell and six thousand troops were closing in.[30] Moray found discretion the preferable option and bolted for the sanctuary of Carlisle from where he journeyed to London for a somewhat less than cordial interview with Elizabeth. Arran was permitted to retire quietly to his extensive estates in France. Maxwell, who had been quick to see which way the wind was blowing, kept his job and was left in charge of the borders jointly with Bothwell.

Much has been said and written concerning the character of James Hepburn, 4th Earl of Bothwell, and a good deal of it pejorative. Bedford had been complaining about his activities before the Chaseabout Raid, and the fragile near-tranquillity of the marches had been further upset by an outbreak of feuding. Maxwell was increasingly at odds with Johnstone, ushering in one of the bloodiest of all border vendettas, whilst the Elliots went to war against the Scotts. Bedford, charged with securing the frontier, felt sufficiently alarmed to requisition repairs to Carlisle, Bewcastle and other, lesser holds. Forster, ever the cunning fox, was quick to spot the potential in the Elliot–Scott feud and lent clandestine support to Martin Elliot of Braidlee.

Elliot did not require encouragement. Allied to the Crosers and Nixons with assorted desperadoes drawn from the Debatable Land, he led three hundred riders in a chevauchee through Buccleuch's territories in Teviotdale. Retaliation was swift and savage. The Scotts took up Liddesdale, emptying byres and leaving a fresh wailing of widows and orphans. Martin Elliot appealed first to Scrope, offering to hand over Hermitage as compensation for the hire of English lances. The warden demurred but Forster, as ever, was a deal less scrupulous, supporting the Elliot faction with cash and offering refuge on the English side when the Scotts pressed too hard, justifying such conduct with cynical detachment; 'the longer such conditions continue . . . the better quiet we shall be'.[31]

To bolster his ranks against Moray, Bothwell had tried to resolve the feud and add Elliot riders to his own. His efforts produced no visible result and in the summer Martin Elliot completely outfought the Scotts who were badly mauled in a classic border ambush. In the east, Bedford, wearying of Cesford's depredations, led a major warden raid into the Merse. His eight hundred horse beat up Chirnside and Edington, garnering hostages and loot whilst cutting down any who stood in their way.

On 9th March 1566, whilst the heavily pregnant queen was at supper in her private apartments, she was joined by the Italian secretary David Riccio. Presently a body of armed men, led by Ruthven and accompanied by Darnley, burst into the chamber with the express intention of murdering Riccio. The doomed man was dragged shrieking from the apartment, vainly attempting to cling to the skirts of the queen's gown, begging for mercy in a frantic mix of tongues: 'Justizia! Justizia, Madame! Save ma vie! Save ma vie!' No mercy was forthcoming and the Italian was lengthily and bloodily done to death. Darnley's dagger was left thrust into the corpse, a handy souvenir of the event and a tangible reminder of the consort's role in the affair.

It is not particularly clear why Riccio was deemed to merit such a savage taking off. He may have been suspected of being a papal agent and his death signalled, in fine dramatic form, a Protestant backlash. The lords certainly desired that Moray be pardoned and permitted to return. Arran feared the ruin of the Hamiltons with Lennox in the ascendant whilst the malleable Darnley may have been motivated by sexual jealousy, real or supposed. It may be supposed that Moray at least had an inkling of the plot, for he returned to Edinburgh the day after the murder.

However traumatised the queen may have been by this sanguinary event, she maintained a cautious and conciliatory approach, thereby dampening what could easily have been the spark that ignited a further civil war. She made an outward show of reconciliation with her husband. The conspirators received pardons and the royal heir, the future James VI, was born on 19th June.

Civil uncertainty furnished the well-honed antennae of the marchers with licence to plunder, and a state of renewed lawlessness developed in the summer of 1566. In the autumn, therefore, the queen announced her intention of proceeding to Jedburgh to dispense justice and supervise the restoration of order. The situation had deteriorated to the extent that: 'crewell murthere had becum commoun nocht onlie among thame that hes quarrell, bot kynnisfolk unnaturalie slayis utheris'.[32]

Darnley was supposed to accompany her in a show of royal togetherness but in the event did not. Mary was falling further under the influence of Bothwell and made a frantic dash to hermitage to tend her lover when he was grievously hurt in a scrimmage with one of the Elliots.[33] Possibly as a result of these exertions she became seriously ill herself and lay for three weeks in Jedburgh. Forster took a pejorative view of the queen's attempt at dispensing justice, declaring none was hanged though a number were fined. The chronicler Pitscottie took an even more cynical view: 'the puir men war hangit and the rich men war hangit by the purs'.[34]

In November Mary, having recovered her health, progressed through the Merse where, on Halidon Hill, she met with Forster. Her company included Bothwell, also recovered, Hume and Cesford with an escort of five hundred horse. Her run of misfortune continued for the warden's horse kicked out, striking the queen in the thigh and she was obliged to spend a further two days convalescing at Hume Castle.[35] As soon as the royal entourage returned to Edinburgh the troubles broke out afresh.

The infant prince was christened, according to the Catholic rite, amidst great pomp at Stirling on 17th December, the occasion marked by a glittering fête. Since the dreadful night of Riccio's murder the queen had striven, not without effect, to reconcile the old and reformed religions within her realm. She had established the role of the monarchy as the fount of tolerance and moderation and by the year's end she could properly claim to be the patron of both churches. At the same time she may have been plotting the death of her husband; Darnley had become repulsive to her and at best remained a liability.

The extent of Mary's complicity in the plot, prime responsibility for which was laid at Bothwell's door, continues to be a matter of speculation. On 10th February the following year the unwanted consort met his very loud end following an explosion at the house in Kirk o' Field where he lay ill. His death, however, was caused by strangulation. There has never been any unequivocal evidence to point the blame but Bothwell was universally regarded as the prime suspect. It has been suggested that Cecil, through his extensive network, was aware of the plot and lost no time in planting the idea that Bothwell had been encouraged or abetted by the queen. It has also recently been suggested that Cecil had a special hatred for Mary and was happy to seize on any opportunity to engineer her fall.

In this he had an indefatigable ally in the queen herself. After Darnley's murder the threads of her authority quickly began to unravel. The killing united all strands of the opposition; the dead consort became an emblem for all shades of opinion, a status he never enjoyed in life. The queen's fatal dalliance with the unstable Bothwell hastened her ruin. The earl was acquitted of the murder in a sham trial in April. Later in the month he 'abducted' the queen, using men he'd ostensibly raised for a warden raid against Liddesdale and, on 15th May, they were married, ironically in a Protestant service.

This was the paramount folly and led, inevitably, to a confrontation with the Protestant lords at Carberry Hill near Musselburgh on 15th June. It proved to be a bloodless battle. Mary's supporters wavered and she was forced to capitulate. For Bothwell this meant immediate exile and for the unhappy queen close confinement in Loch Leven Castle whilst Moray, now regent, worked out what was to be done with her.

The solution was obvious. The realm needed a Protestant ruler. Under relentless pressure and blatant intimidation from her gaoler, Lord Lindsay, Mary was coerced into abdicating in favour of her infant son who, on 29th July, at the age of thirteen months, was crowned James VI at Stirling, a bare six months after his baptism. His religious upbringing was to be strictly in accordance with Calvinist doctrine; the sermon at his coronation was give by Knox.

Instability was rife. Bothwell still had supporters on the marches and it required little tinder to ignite a conflagration. Moray was effective at winning over the border magnates and, in November, he staged a lightning descent on Hawick where he netted some thirty-four known desperadoes. Of these perhaps twenty received summary justice by water or rope; others were sent to Edinburgh for a sojourn behind bars and the remainder escaped with a stiff caution.[36]

This 'snatch' raid had the usual calming effect, albeit only temporary for, on 2nd May 1567, Mary made her dramatic escape from Loch Leven Castle and was escorted by Arran's relative, Lord Claude Hamilton, to Cadzow where her standard was once again raised. The regent was at Glasgow when he became acquainted with this alarming intelligence and acted with his customary resolution. He mustered such local forces as he had available, divining, quite rightly, that it would be best to meet the Marians in battle as soon as possible before resurgent support for her could begin to swell.

At this time Dumbarton was held by Lord Fleming, and Moray had no doubt that the seizure of this great bastion would be Hamilton's prime objective. Approaching from the west the Marians were intending to bypass Glasgow and avoid an encounter, swinging around the city through Langside, Crookston and Paisley.[37] In the course of the short campaign that was developing Moray was able to count on both Cesford and Hume, though Johnstone, Maxwell and Ferniherst fought for the queen.

The old village of Langside has long since been swallowed by the urban sprawl. In the sixteenth century it was a ribbon of rude cottages cresting a shallow ridge bisected by a sunken way lined with thick hedges, the inhabitants' gardens straggling down the southern flank of rise. Realising that possession of this quiet hamlet would be crucial, the regent dispatched a commanded body of horse led by Kirkcaldy of Grange to secure the place. It is said that each rider carried a musketeer as pillion! The foot were marshalled into two brigades, mixed pike and shot, with some wild highlanders interspersed, the van under Morton and the main body under Moray himself.

The flying column secured their objective, deploying in and around the hamlet. Their commander did not overlook the potential of the thick hedges lining the sunken way and posted musketeers on both sides. When the rest of the regent's army came up they were promptly moved into line of battle with the right occupying the crest of the ridge. The village formed the fulcrum with the no doubt startled inhabitants finding their humble dwellings converted into blockhouses. The centre and left stretched nearly as far as Path Head farm, keeping to the high ground near to what is now Queen's Park. The guns were unlimbered in front of the centre. It was altogether a very formidable position.

From Rutherglen, Mary's scratch army had advanced by Blackhouse and the Hanging Stone to what was then Clincart Hill (now Mount Florida). Here the high ground fell gently away before rising again toward Langside, a distance of some four hundred yards. The sight which greeted her scouts cannot have been encouraging and the strength of the regent's position would have been immediately and soberingly apparent. The queen had appointed Argyll as her field commander but was only with some difficulty persuaded to withdraw from personal danger to Cathcart Castle whilst the earl contemplated how best he might break through the regent's forces.

Both sides advanced their great guns for an opening duel of artillery. Great clouds of black and stinking smoke drifted over the vale, roundshot thumped into the hillsides; occasionally a man of horse would be struck down in a ghastly, shattered sprawl. That apart, neither side could gain any advantage and, to break the impasse, Argyll sent Hamilton forward with a commanded party of foot to essay a passage of the sunken road. The onus was on the Marians to advance; if the regent could hold firm and bar their passage then they would be obliged to withdraw. This would not suffice – to boost support for the queen's cause a victory was needed.

The narrow, sunken lane was a deathtrap. The musketeers poured volley after volley into Hamilton's men who reeled back in disorder, leaving their lifeless comrades choking the road. The gallant Hamilton reformed his men and tried again but with no better effect. Argyll next directed his horse against Moray's left but they could not break the levelled pikes. Battle was now joined in earnest all along the line, with the attackers struggling up the incline and losing cohesion in the garden enclosures.

For some time the issue hung in the balance, but the regent's foot gradually began to push their opponents off the ridge. Judging the moment Moray unleashed his highlanders in a downhill charge. Neither ground nor garden walls could impede the swift-moving clansmen, whose flashing broadswords carved a bloody swathe through Argyll's flank.

It was enough. The queen's army faltered and then broke, streaming away from the stricken field, leaving the wreck of her hopes behind. Moray, to his credit, refused to order a pursuit that could have converted the rout into a massacre. He was in no need to spill more Scottish blood than was necessary.[38]

Disheartened by this fresh and crushing reverse the queen gave way to despair and, at Dundrennan, despite advice, she 'resolved to go to England and throw herself on the mercy of Elizabeth, in hopes by her assistance to be repossessed again of her kingdom'.[39] The arrival of the small band of fugitives at Workington on Sunday 16th May proved both unexpected and something of an embarrassment to the English administration who had no inkling that so dramatic a happening was about to occur. The following day the queen, with a score of retainers including Maxwell, moved on to

Cockermouth where they were officially if somewhat uncertainly received by Scrope's deputy, Richard Lowther, and escorted to Carlisle where lodgings were provided within the castle.

Scrope had no real idea how to proceed; even Cecil had not foreseen such a contingency. Elizabeth's official position was cautious. She had not openly been able to approve of Moray's appointment, and could not be seen to support rebel lords against their lawful sovereign, however foolish that sovereign might have been. The queen had no doubts as to the folly of her royal cousin's liaison with Bothwell; after the earl's rigged acquittal in April 1567 she had written admonishingly to Mary:

> *O Madam, I would not do the duty of a faithful cousin and affectionate friend, if I thought more of pleasing your ears than saving your honour. I will not conceal from you what most people are saying . . . that you have no desire to touch those who have done you such pleasure . . . I exhort you, I council you, I beg you to take this event so to heart that you will not fear to proceed even against your nearest.*[40]

This was excellent and impartial advice and it could be suggested that had Mary taken heed she would not have been seeking lodgings in England the following spring. Within days of her arrival Mary's presence sparked dispute. The Earl of Northumberland, in whose liberty she had landed, demanded possession of the queen's person. Scrope cannily demurred, though it was soon obvious that his wardenry was altogether too close to the Scottish west march where the queen, supported by Maxwell, could still count on support.

This reality was not lost upon the regent who moved swiftly to consolidate his victory at Langside. By 13th June he was at Sanquhar complete with horse, foot and guns. Both Cesford and Hume provided light horse.[41] His ordnance was soon busily employed in reducing the castles of Marian supporters, and his tactics, if heavy-handed, soon proved effective. Maxwell was relieved of his post, with Drumlanrig installed as caretaker. Mary, now looking more and more like a captive rather than a needy ally, was shifted southward to Castle Bolton.

In August Elizabeth appointed her half brother Henry Carey, first baron Hunsdon, as east march warden.[42] Hunsdon was a bluff and responsible officer and his presence was to prove invaluable in the difficulties which lay ahead. He served his sister loyally and efficiently. Finding his wardenry subject to a rash of pinprick raids, ostensibly in support of Mary, the Scottish marches were observed to be as 'ready to go by the ears, for they are at catch that catch may'.[43] The regent appreciated the need for cross border co-operation and came to England at the end of the year. By January 1569 he was back north of the line and resolved upon a further exercise of his 'short, sharp shock' treatment.

In spring he moved against Jedburgh but the thieves had learnt from the dire consequences of their earlier laxity and the nest was bare. Moray's two thousand horse were complemented by two companies of foot drawn from the Berwick garrison and his treasury revived with a loan of £5,000. Undeterred, the combined force moved on to Kelso where they were joined by Forster and a select band of his own marchers before descending on Liddesdale and meting out more of the usual remedies. In the late summer Moray returned again to Kelso where he remained for over a month before shifting his base of operations westward to Dumfries in the heart of the troubled west.

Mary, in the meantime, had been moved again, southward once more, to Tutbury. Elizabeth, whilst probably still at a loss as to what she should do with her unhappy cousin, might at least have drawn solace in thinking her marches quiet. If so, she would have been quite wrong.

Notes

1 Quoted in Bingham, C., *The Stewart Kingdom of Scotland 1371–1603*, London 1974 p. 141
2 Ibid p. 141.
3 Ibid p. 141.
4 Fraser, Lady A., *Mary Queen of Scots*, London 1969 pp. 582–6.
5 Warwick, finding himself about to be redundant on the death of Edward VI attempted to install his fifteen-year-old daughter-in-law Lady Jane Grey as a Protestant alternative with tragic consequences.
6 MacDonald Fraser, G., *The Steel Bonnets*, London 1971 p. 281.
7 Quoted in MacDonald Fraser pp. 281–2.
8 Lord James Stewart was a bastard son of James V by Margaret Erskine, whom it was alleged the king had come close to marrying and it may be Lord James, a man of no mean ability, felt the throne should have been his though the taint of illegitimacy made this virtually impossible.
9 Lynch, M., *Scotland: A New History*, London 1991 p. 208.
10 Bingham p. 193.

11 Ridpath, Rev. G., *Border History*, Berwick 1858 p. 403.

12 Ibid p. 403.

13 MacDonald Fraser p. 284.

14 Ridpath p. 403.

15 Ibid p. 406.

16 Ibid p. 406.

17 Ibid p. 406.

18 A sconce; a small fort of timber and earth probably mounting a few guns.

19 Ridpath p. 406.

20 Quoted in Bingham p. 198.

21 The king was accidentally killed when he rode in the lists, having forgotten the elementary precaution of lowering his visor. A splinter from the opponent's lance pierced his eye and proved fatal.

22 Tough, D.L.W., *Last Years of a Frontier*, Oxford 1928 p. 190.

23 Quoted in Tough p. 190.

24 Ibid p. 191.

25 The existing medieval walls had been altered and strengthened to mount guns in the 1530s and traces of the Henrician rebuilding remain. In the reign of Edward VI the construction of a new and mighty citadel was planned but the work was never carried out. The loss of Calais in 1558 lent urgency to the modernisation and Sir Richard Lee was appointed as surveyor, his choice based on an Italian precedent, the walls of Verona, completed in 1530. This involved the construction of a series of projecting platforms or bastions, thrusting toward any attacker and linked to the curtain wall by a narrow neck or gorge. The bastions were artillery platforms which were angled so as to provide flanking fire along the line of the curtain and decimate any attempt at escalade. The walls were lower and battered outward at the base to improve strength and deflection whilst the ability to soak up the besiegers' fire was provided by the massive earthen embankments which supported the masonry. Though impressive, the works were never fully completed. The original concept involved the construction of a citadel at the southern end on the town and the old walls survive by the riverside. The Elizabethan enceinte was smaller by approximately a third and the castle, to the north, thus became isolated. Lee was eventually removed and the Italian master engineer Portinari was brought in, firstly in 1560 and again, this time in partnership with Jacopa Contio, four years later. The final cost amounted to £128,648. 5s. 9¹/₂d. (See Pevsner, Sir. N., 'Northumberland' in the *Buildings of England* series, London 1992 ed. pp. 175–7.)

26 Tough p. 195.

27 Ibid p. 195.

28 Ker of Cesford, a contentious grayne, one of the leading families of Teviotdale, frequently held the march wardenship and just as frequently featured as a major instigator of troubles, not infrequently at odds with the Scotts and their kin Ker of Ferniherst.

29 Quoted in Bingham p. 207.
30 Tough p. 206.
31 Quoted in MacDonald Fraser p. 290.
32 Ibid p. 293.
33 Bothwell had received a severe head wound in a fight with one of the Elliots, 'Little Jock of the Park' who, unlike the earl, is said to have succumbed to his wounds. The duel featured in a popular ballad: 'My name is little Jock Elliot, And wha dare meddle wi' me.' (See MacDonald Fraser note p. 209.)
34 Quoted in Tough p. 202.
35 Ibid p. 202.
36 Ibid p. 204.
37 Sadler, D.J., *Scottish Battles*, Edinburgh 1996 p. 90.
38 Ibid p. 91.
39 Quoted in Tough p. 206.
40 Quoted in Bingham p. 214.
41 Tough p. 206.
42 Henry Carey, Lord Hunsdon, was a natural son of Henry VIII by Anne Boleyn's sister Mary and a first-rate border official. Blunt and frequently contentious, both of his sons, John and Robert, were to become officers toward the end of the reign. Robert was to enjoy considerable success.
43 Quoted in Tough p. 200.

Chapter 20

Last Years of the Frontier

The vermin be fledd into a forrayn covert.

Sir William Cecil[1]

Verie ticklie

Sir John Forster[2]

Everywhere that Mary went trouble was sure to follow. This apposite comment was made by George MacDonald Fraser[3] and is by no means overly pejorative. The queen's fall from power and her subsequent confinement in England did not bring about the end of the disturbances linked to her cause. For a period quite the reverse situation obtained. Thomas Percy, 7th Earl of Northumberland, a Catholic recusant, had already attempted to gain control of the fugitive Mary and been rebuffed.

'Simple Tom' was scarcely the stuff of conspirators. A diligent if not unduly talented border officer, the glamour in his life was supplied by his vivacious Countess Anne. His younger brother Henry, a Protestant, had been widely active in the wars of the earlier, English Mary. The earl's zeal to pay court to the queen set alarm bells ringing. Cecil, who had no love for Percy, could already discern a whiff of treason.

Throughout 1568 Moray and Hunsdon pursued a policy of active co-operation. Both shared equally robust notions as to how border justice should be dispensed. The regent was fulsome in his praise of the warden when he wrote to Elizabeth. Moray needed all the assistance he could summon, for the west, in particular, continued to be exceptionally unsettled.

The Liddesdale men were riding unchecked and inflicting 'innumerabil slauchteris, fyre raisingis, herschipps and detestabil enormities'.[4]

In the spring of 1569 the regent summoned Ferniherst, Cesford and Buccleuch, supported by the English under Forster, for a major punitive raid against the troublesome dalesmen. The valley was thoroughly 'taken up' and Mangerton, the principal Armstrong hold, levelled. Assurances were taken and the exercise was repeated in October to curb the lure of those lengthening autumn nights.

This process of repeated hammerings, whilst draconian, produced short-term benefits and Moray was able to observe that 'thair wes sic obedience . . . as the lyk was never done to na king in na mans dayes befoir'.[5] At the end of the month a host of pledges were surrendered at Hawick. Moray and the Scots Privy Council had decreed that any marcher who persisted in offences against England could, at the third instance, forfeit his life. This shows a greater level of cross jurisdictional co-operation than had existed before but Mary's partisans still remained strong on the marches, ripe for mischief.

Quite when 'Simple Tom' contemplated a northern rebellion remains unclear but he was egged on by his two confederates, Charles Neville, Earl of Westmorland, and 'Crookback' Leonard Dacre. There had not been an alliance of the Percys and Westmorland Nevilles since the 1460s and the impetuous earl was no better qualified to lead than Northumberland. Dacre, on the other hand, that 'cankred suttil traitor',[6] was born to intrigue; his present disaffection arose from mercenary rather than religious sentiment. Disappointed when the Dacre inheritance fell to the Howards on the death by accident of his young nephew, he was ready to throw in his lot with the conspirators, whilst being equally ready to abandon them should expediency so dictate.

The finely tuned antennae of Cecil's intelligence network were already picking up intimations of treason before the rebels raised their flag in November. The earls had been in correspondence with both Spain and the Papacy; there was talk of an army of thirty thousand under the Duke of Alva being brought over from the Spanish Netherlands. Westmorland was the first to take up arms. Northumberland required further persuasion if not actual coercion and the riding names of Tynedale and Redesdale, ready as ever to support any venture that offered spoil, flocked to his banner. For a while it looked serious. The rebels marched to Brancepeth and openly held mass in Durham Cathedral. English bibles and Cranmer's liturgy were consigned to the flames. It seemed as though the Pilgrimage of Grace was to be re-enacted, a vast northern uprising with the captive Mary as their inspiration and objective.

Whilst Elizabeth's lieutenant in the north, the Earl of Sussex, was frantically trying to raise a levy in the south, the rebels secured both Alnwick and Warkworth. Mary was hustled to the greater remove of Coventry. The northern host marched confidently into North Yorkshire, feinting at the city of York itself before falling back to lay siege to Barnard Castle, a rather pointless exercise and symptomatic of commanders who really had little idea of what they were about. Hartlepool had been occupied as a handy port in the expectation of Spanish aid, though none came, and Mary's supporters throughout the marches prepared for action. In the English west march the recusant Forsters and Hetheringtons were preparing a descent on Rose Castle and the assassination of the Bishop of Carlisle.[7]

The English Queen was not without partisans of her own. Moray held the Scottish border in check whilst Hunsdon, Forster and Sir Henry Percy marshalled their forces in the rebel rear. The wardens were initially reluctant to act, being unsure of how widespread the disaffection might prove, but the old magic of the Percy and Neville names had worn thin. Even the earls' own tenantry proved unwilling to hazard their necks in so desperate a venture. Forster retook both Warkworth and Alnwick and, with Harry Percy, advanced to secure Newcastle. Having, after a fortnight, succeeded in taking Barnard Castle, the rebels moved swiftly eastwards to confront Forster and a skirmish was fought at Chester Dean.

The affray could not be described as a battle or a defeat but the rebel cause, already starting to unravel, collapsed completely. As their host disintegrated and appeals to their tenants fell on deaf ears, the earls found themselves suddenly on the run. With no more than four hundred riders they fled towards Hexham, their band diminishing steadily till they were left with barely a tenth of that number. Sussex's forces were now marching north, though they were to contribute little to the fight. Hunsdon was typically blunt when he noted: 'This lusty southern army would not have returned laden with such spoil, nor put their noses over Doncaster bridge; but others beat the bush, and they have the birds'.[8]

Desperate, the rebel earls sought sanctuary with their confederate Dacre at Naworth, only to find the door bolted firmly against them. Crookback

Leonard had seen which way the wind was blowing and wanted nothing more to do with his former conspirators. He was already at pains to exonerate himself, though his brother, Edward, received the earls kindly enough and did what he could for them before they scattered towards the illusory sanctuary of the border. As MacDonald Fraser also observes, this was not a good year for brotherly love.[9]

By 20th December the rebel earls, Northumberland's countess with a handful of loyal retainers stumbled into Liddesdale, a place as far removed from the comfort to which they were habitually accustomed as might be imagined. The valley was not the bland, smiling farmland seen today but a grim, remote fastness, trackless, lawless, guarded by the natural barrier of the hills, impenetrable forest and mire. To them it must have spelt despair, the woods stark and bare beneath lowering winter skies, sullen, frozen mosses, the only habitations the crude bothies of the names and their gaunt towers rearing like squat, primeval sentries.

Their hosts in this dreadful wilderness were Jock Armstrong of the Side and Black Ormiston, the latter strongly implicated in the murder of Darnley and as choice a brace of villains as might be found, even by the flexible standards of the locality. Liddesdale could never be described as a safe haven, not even for the inhabitants, and Sussex was soon appraised of the fugitives' hideaway.

Knowing where they were and lifting them were two very different matters. The earl knew that their present hosts would be 'very unwilling to deny aid to banished men . . . it [being] against their custom to deliver such as fled out of England, for that they many times in like manner receive succour in England'.[10] Sussex was, however, certain he could replace force with the equally effective expedient of bribery: 'Their whole trust is upon three or four mischievous thieves and men full of treason . . . they shall be had by corruption though the Queen pay dear for it.'[11]

Moray was anxious to oblige and detailed Martin Elliot of Braidlee, he who had so forcefully led his name against the Scotts in their recent feud, to act as his emissary. Elliot was under pledge to the regent and lost no time in spelling out current realities to Ormiston. The Elliots did not seek a vendetta but either the fugitives left their sanctuary within the day or violence would ensue. Braidlee was not the man to utter empty threats and the hapless rebels were promptly hustled west into the Debatable Land, that lawless abandoned waste, the threap disowned by both realms where only the truly desperate would ever venture.

Their new host was to be Hector Armstong of Harlaw who wasted little time in selling his most valuable guest, Simple Tom, to the regent.[12] Westmorland mounted a hopeless rescue to try to liberate the captive earl, but Percy's fate was sealed. For two years he was to languish in Lochleven Castle, where Mary herself had been imprisoned, before being sold on to Hunsdon on behalf of the crown and a traitor's death at York. His rebellion was very definitely over.

For Sussex only the business of retribution now remained and he set to with a will. Somewhere between six and seven hundred suspected rebels were hanged, many from Durham and Northumberland with the odd Redesdale or Tynedale rider, unlucky enough to be caught. John Knox, vituperative as ever, demanded Mary's head be added to the pile and Cecil probably agreed but Elizabeth was not yet ready for such drastic surgery. For the loyal victors rewards abounded. Forster did very well indeed[13] and Harry Percy now became earl in his brother's stead.

It had cost the crown some £200,000 to suppress the rebellion the failure of which owed as much to the incompetence of the leadership as to the swiftness of the government's riposte. The rebels had been driven into precipitate action by the discovery of their treasonable correspondence. They had then failed to secure both widespread support and, crucially, physical possession of Mary herself. Forster, Hunsdon and Harry Percy had reacted surely and decisively. It could be said Elizabeth owed her throne to her half brother and Forster, who whatever his failings as warden, never shirked a fight. She was to have need of both men again and soon.

In Scotland the regent Moray continued to cling to power. Given the difficult circumstances his job was never likely to be an easy one and the list of his enemies was legion. Plots against his life were commonplace and in January 1570 he was made aware that the Hamiltons were proposing to assassinate him in Linlithgow. Despite the warning Moray rode boldly through the teeming streets where Hamilton of Bothwell, concealed behind a line of drying washing, shot him down. Mortally wounded the regent managed to stagger free of the ambush but expired soon after.

There were many who rejoiced. The fugitive Westmorland, still skulking, is said to have thrown his hat in the fire, overcome with jubilation. The day that Moray fell, Buccleuch and Ferniherst, declaring their support for Mary, torched Hector of Harlaw's dwelling. On 31st January, together with Neville, they struck deep into Northumberland, raiding as far south as Morpeth.[14] 'The Regent is as cold as my bridle bit', Buccleuch joyfully expounded.[15]

Moray had been a hard man but was remembered after as the 'Good' Regent.[16] Whilst the young king spent his childhood in relative isolation behind the thick walls of Stirling, Moray had the job of trying to create a stable foundation for government in the uncertain aftermath of Mary's fall. The Hamiltons did not see their defeat at Langside as necessarily being decisive and though Arran had been Moray's ally in the farce of the Chaseabout Raid, the Hamiltons were now his inveterate foes. It was from the forestairs of a house belonging to Archbishop Hamilton of St Andrews that the regent's assassin fired and the Hamiltons facilitated their kinsman's flight from the scene.[17] By the time of his murder Moray had succeeded in making the king's party considerably the stronger and his death did not signal victory for the queen's faction.

The Marians' objective was to provoke a further Anglo-Scottish war and in this they had a powerful ally in Dacre. Though he had escaped reprisal in the immediate aftermath of his earlier treachery, Crookback Leonard was a marked man. In January Scrope had been ordered to procure his arrest but Dacre was not easily drawn, alleging a knee injury prevented him from answering the warden's summons. He utilised the breathing space to raise his own tenants and any that would ride with him on the pretext of opposing a fictitious Scots attack, soon he had three thousand lances at Naworth with the promise of thousands more from the Marian names, particularly Maxwell and Irvine in the west.

Scrope lacked the manpower to oppose him should he choose to advance on Carlisle. Once again it was Hunsdon, stripping the Berwick garrison and Forster with his dalesmen who reacted, by the night of the 18–19th February their combined forces lay at Hexham. Hunsdon determined on a bold night march to Naworth, his orders were to take the place despite a lack of ordnance – the whole countryside was in uproar, 'the beacons burned all night, and every hill was full of horse and foot crying and shouting as though they were mad'.[18]

Dacre's scouts would have kept him well posted as to his enemy's progress, he probably commanded something like two thousand horse and a thousand foot, outnumbering the wardens by two to one. Naworth was going to be too tough a nut to crack, Dacre had both men and guns, Hunsdon declined battle and decided to continue his westward march and link up with Scrope. South from Naworth the rebel forces shadowed the government brigade and, on the heath adjoining the confluence of the Gelt and the Hell Beck, some four miles south of Brampton, Dacre arrayed for battle.

Hunsdon was seriously at a disadvantage but his troops were the regular whitecoats, pike and shot, from Berwick, both he and Forster were bold and experienced leaders. Neither could be in any doubt as to the consequences of failure, if the rebels defeated them then Scrope would be hopelessly isolated at Carlisle and the way open for the Scots marchers to well Dacre's rebel host, the kingdom could yet be lost.

Hunsdon in his subsequent dispatch describes the fight which now ensued, 'in a heath where we were to pass a river [the Gelt] his foot gave the proudest charge upon my shot that I ever saw; whereupon, having left Sir John Forster with five hundred horse for my back, I charged with the rest of my horse upon his foot and slew between three and four hundred'.[19]

The wardens had thus deployed with their pike and shot in the centre, horse upon both flanks. Dacre's foot advanced against the government centre where they were held by the regular volleys of the whitecoats. Hunsdon led his horse in a flanking attack whilst Forster kept Dacre's wing occupied, the result was a rout. Over a hundred were captured and the proud Red Bull banner of the Dacres, born with honour in many a fight, was trampled underfoot until Hunsdon claimed it as a prize.

The slippery Dacre was nearly caught but succeeded in escaping the stricken field abandoning his followers to the wardens.[20] It is possible that many of those who'd followed him did so on the assumption they were indeed to fight the Scots not their own side and thus lacked the stomach for a rebel cause. It was, as Wellington might have said, 'a near run thing'. As Hunsdon marched on towards Carlisle his prickers spotted a large body of Scottish horse, Ferniherst and Buccleuch, barely hours away from the rendezvous with Dacre, had this meeting been effected the rebels would have been far too strong for the wardens. 'Had we tarried, he had been past dealing with'.[21] A close run thing indeed.

The battle had been won but this must have been scant comfort to the government. The margin was far too slender and, with Moray's strong hand no longer upon the borders, fresh disturbances might arise at any time. For as long as the Marians could seek shelter in the Scottish marches the frontier would never be secure and if the king's party in Scotland was too weak to administer the necessary correction then England must do it for them. Westmorland and Dacre were both at large fomenting trouble and the marchers knew well the opportunities that a state of anarchy offered. By the spring Liddesdale and Teviotdale were riding nightly. In the English middle march over a hundred-and-forty persons were kidnapped, and towns and vills were taken up with regular thoroughness.[22]

Sussex was thus furnished with instructions to cross the line and seek out rebels and malefactors generally. The means were provided by a levy of a thousand horse and three times as many foot. Despite the military nature of the proposed expedition this was a police action not an invasion. Sussex wrote to the regent and advised that this was not an act of war, not a repeat of the indiscriminate mayhem of the Rough Wooing. It would not, however, be surprising if the inhabitants of Teviotdale found the distinction to be a very fine one.

On 17th April Sussex, seconded by Hunsdon, led the main column out of Berwick, marching towards Jedburgh where they met with Forster who'd taken his marchers over the head waters of the Coquet and spread fire along the banks of the Oxnam Water. Buccleuch's lands were especially targeted and though the Teviotdale men hung on Forster's flanks there was no serious fighting. Hume was in the field with Dacre in tow but could not muster sufficient forces to offer battle. On the 19th the commander in chief divided his forces into two mobile columns, advancing in a broad swathe through Teviotdale and reuniting at Hawick having paused only to slight Ferniherst Castle.

The town was largely deserted, the inhabitants having fled but not before they had stripped the thatch and turf from the roofs of their cabins and set all alight in the streets, creating a dense and largely impenetrable cloud of dense, acrid smoke. Only Drumlanrig's Tower was held against the invaders. The foot were left in the town to complete the work of destruction whilst the horse, under Forster, spread ruin to the surrounding vills. Sussex and Hunsdon concentrated their efforts on Buccleuch's seat at Branxholm. The tower had been prepared with a packing of smouldering peat but such precautions were no proof against gunpowder which was liberally employed to slight the place in a thorough manner.

Sussex led the main body back to Jedburgh where they were joined by Forster on the 21st. The area around the town was now extensively taken up before, having again split into two columns, the army converged on Kelso, their passage marked by smouldering thatch, empty byres and the odd blackened corpse. The destruction was not entirely indiscriminate. Those who came in and offered submission, cemented by pledges, avoided harrying. With Hunsdon leading the left-hand column and Forster the right, Kelso was taken without a fight. Cesford came in and begged Sussex to spare East Teviotdale, though, as he refused to nominate pledges, these entreaties fell on deaf ears.

As Hume had failed to offer submission his castle was targeted, though the attempt to establish a leaguer was initially frustrated when the draught animals needed to drag the great guns were inexplicably sent back to Berwick. By the 26th April the investiture of the castle was complete and, horses having been procured, the artillery opened a bombardment two days later. The garrison soon decided they'd had enough, despite being some two hundred strong, and were swiftly replaced. On 4th May Fast Castle also capitulated and received an English garrison. Left defenceless the Merse was thoroughly wasted; over three hundred vills were torched before the invaders withdrew.

Whilst Sussex had been so busily engaged in the east, Scrope struck in the west. On the 18th he had crossed into Scotland and spent the first night at Ecclefechan. Two days later he detached Simon Musgrave with a commanded party, fixing a rendezvous at Cummertrees. In this instance the invaders did not go unchallenged. Maxwell with Johnstone and a substantial force from Dumfries, perhaps six hundred foot and four hundred horse, confronted Musgrave at Old Cockpole and a fierce fight ensued. For three hours the combatants remained locked in a swirling mêlée, the issue undecided till Scrope came up with the main body of the English, ably assisted by the Armstrongs and won the field. The Scots were driven back towards Dumfries and over a hundred prisoners were taken in the rout. Victorious, the English returned to Carlisle.[23]

In May fresh disturbances broke out when the Marians were seen to be massing their forces at Linlithgow, presumably for a move against Stirling. Sussex detailed Forster to feint towards Teviotdale and thus persuade the marchers to remain in their homes. The earl went further and sent both men and materiel to assist the king's party. By July the regent was begging further assistance and Sussex felt the need to chastise the west where Dacre was known to be skulking. A wet August saw him marooned in Carlisle whilst the marchers were given space to remove themselves and their goods from his intended path. It was not until the 22nd of the month that Sussex was able to take the field, leading four thousand men against Annandale. The town and castle were levelled; other holds, Dumfries, Caerlaverock, Hoddam and Cowhill fared the same.[24]

By the 28th the queen's lieutenant was back in Carlisle, his men loaded with spoil. Whilst he had been active in the west Forster and Hunsdon had kept both the middle and east marches fully occupied. It was enough: Ferniherst and Buccleuch offered their submissions and Westmorland slipped quietly into exile from Aberdeen. By the end of the campaigning season it seemed that the lesson had taken hold and the border remained relatively quiet. In any event Sussex was not able to keep large forces in the field and left for the south in November. Before long the names were back in the saddle and it was business as usual during the long winter nights.

It might seem as though nothing had changed and Sussex's raids of 1570 conformed fully to the dismal cycle of foray and reprisal. From the perspective of the average inhabitant of Dumfries or Hawick this must have seemed very much the case. Yet the border, in 1570, saw the last passage of armies across the marches. There would be no more large-scale actions, no more wholesale harrying and 'herschipp'. For the remaining three decades of the sixteenth century there would be a gradual, if halting, increase in cross border co-operation, a realisation that lawlessness affected both kingdoms in equal measure and that the wardens, if they were to do their jobs, must learn to work together. This was easier voiced than accomplished; several wardens, Forster, Cesford, Maxwell and Buccleuch remained as much a symptom of the disease as the remedy and there would be many setbacks – the Raid of the Redeswire, the murder of Russell, the affair of Kinmont Will Armstrong. But none of these led, as they almost certainly would have done in the past, to open warfare; relations were strained but never sundered. From the late 1580s onwards it became increasingly obvious that a union of the kingdoms was likely and James VI of Scotland had his eyes firmly fixed on the ultimate prize.

In Scotland, in 1570, Moray had been replaced as regent by the Earl of Lennox, Darnley's father and a man of limited capabilities. The real energy behind the king's party now came from James Douglas, Earl of Morton, a doughty fighter whose immediate objective was the reduction of those key bastions, Dumbarton, Doune and Edinburgh still held by the Marians. Moray had failed to recover any of these though, by early 1571, the first two had fallen. Edinburgh was an altogether different proposition, held by the capable Kirkcaldy of Grange, seconded by Maitland of Lethington. For a while they were supported by Arran and his son Lord Claude Hamilton.

The siege dragged on through the summer of 1571. The king's party, despite their ascendancy, did not possess the weight of ordnance to reduce so formidable a fortress. Grange, in an attempt to break the deadlock, proposed a daring night raid upon Stirling, where the Scots Parliament was sitting with the objective of capturing as many peers of the king's party as might be found. Such a haul would both weaken the government and provide the Marians with a clutch of valuable prisoners as bargaining chips.

Whilst the idea found favour it was decided Grange was too valuable to be hazarded and leadership of the expedition was shared between Lord Claude and Huntly (the Gordons, equally, had not accepted the débâcle at Corrichie as conclusive). As Grange might have feared, the raid, launched one August night, was a failure; some lords were taken but were soon rescued in a series of untidy and confused skirmishes. King James's tutor, the Earl of Mar, led a sally by the castle garrison which saw off the attackers but not before the Regent Lennox, in the thick of the fight, was shot in the back and mortally wounded. It is said the young king's introduction to the brutal realities of Scottish politics was the sight of his dying grandfather being carried back into the castle.

On being appraised of the raid's failure Grange may have been excused for raging against his subordinates. The queen's party had succeeded only in further weakening their position; the assault on Stirling and the killing of Lennox were bound to reduce their prospects of a negotiated settlement. Mar now became regent whilst the siege of Edinburgh dragged on through the winter. Huntly and the Hamiltons had been allowed to march out during a temporary truce in the summer; Grange and Lethington, the latter by now terminally ill, were left to cling to the defences. Mar died in 1572, ostensibly of natural causes. Poison was not ruled out as the banquet he attended shortly before his death had been given by Morton, who on 24th November became regent, the same day that John Knox died.

Morton, as his first priority, needed to bring the siege to a close. He made peace with the Hamiltons cemented by the Pacification of Perth in

1573. Arran finally retired and died two years later. In May the regent sought and received help from England; Sir William Drury with a train of twenty guns was sent north. The arrival of such an array of artillery spelt the end for Grange who surrendered on the 29th of that month. Lethington probably died before the castle fell; Grange, who would have known he could expect no quarter, was hanged at the Mercat Cross.

The Marian faction was now in eclipse but Morton was not to be free of opposition. With Knox dead the leadership of the kirk passed to Andrew Melville, recently returned from Genoa. A Calvinist like Knox, Melville directed the Kirk's increasingly Presbyterian and anti-Episcopalian stance. When Archbishop Hamilton had been executed Morton had appropriated the revenue from his diocese. Even when a successor was appointed the man was the regent's creature and accepted a mere wage for his office whilst Morton continued to enjoy a substantive income. Increasingly the kirk, under the governance of the General Assembly, took on the role of an official opposition.

Morton was careful to cultivate the English alliance without ever accepting any hint of subservience. Elizabeth's support was a resource to be husbanded while he struggled with the economy and, like most of his predecessors, failed. The constant debasement of the coinage throughout the late sixteenth century meant that the Scots pound, worth 5s. (25p) against the English in 1560, was worth only, at best, 2s. (10p) by 1600.[25]

By and large the regent ignored the young king at Stirling; the lad's education was strongly Protestant in character, his tutor, George Buchanan, an outstanding scholar if a strict and dogmatic teacher. He despised the boy's mother and all she stood for; he believed a prince was accountable to the people and whilst James followed his direction in certain areas, here they disagreed. The king believed in Divine Right, the special relationship between the prince and God, which absolved the monarch from accountability to earthly assemblies. This teaching James would pass on to his son and eventual successor Charles, and his assertion of his right would contribute, in no small measure, to the loss, firstly of his kingdom, and finally his head.

For most of 1571 the border was relatively quiet. Several lairds had been involved in the raid on Stirling. Buccleuch and Ormiston had been taken. Hunsdon was much occupied with negotiations for the handing over of Northumberland and frequently expressed the view that the marches would not be pacified until Mary was more closely confined. In May 1572 the warden concluded his transaction with Mar and Simple Tom was delivered for justice at a price of £2,000. His execution took place on 22nd August. Events in Paris that summer, leading to the frightful cull of Huguenots in the course of the Massacre of St Bartholemew's Eve,[26] hardened the religious divide and inevitably drove Protestant England and Protestant Scotland into a closer understanding.

After Drury's expedition secured the fall of Edinburgh, Hume and Fast castles were returned to the regent in October, though Elizabeth, with typical parsimony, held on to the captured ordnance.[27] In July Morton had proposed a levy at Peebles but did not, in fact, travel to the borders until August where he met with the wardens from both realms. Much business was transacted and, though none was executed, sureties were taken and the regent certainly made his presence felt. Morton was every inch a Douglas and the marchers can have been in no doubt as to the toughness of his character; his portrait shows a fierce uncompromising stare, glaring belligerently at the world.[28]

In November he returned, appointed new wardens and showed that a strong hand was never far away. Ferniherst, for one, took the hint and departed for France. Relations between the two kingdoms remained cordial through 1574 though the appropriation of the Scottish guns remained contentious. Nonetheless, Elizabeth was advised that the marches were sufficiently quiet to allow a company from the Berwick garrison to be drafted to Ireland.[29]

The burgeoning amity was disrupted in 1575 by the fray of the Redeswire which could so easily have triggered a war. (For detail see Chapter 21.) Each side blamed the other though both probably looked hard at Forster's role in the affair; 'selfish' was perhaps the kindest description of the ageing warden.[30] Elizabeth and Morton were equally anxious to maintain the peace and dispose of the matter as quickly as decency would permit. During the third week in August English commissioners met with the regent and the negotiations dragged on for nearly a month. Pledges, including Carmichael, who was Morton's cousin, were eventually delivered for a nominal term (the Keeper was home by the end of October) and with that the whole sorry business was laid to rest.

From Foulden the regent travelled to Dumfries where he was sitting by mid-November dealing firmly with malefactors and causing 'execution of justice to be made apoun certain of the offenders, and mony greit offence bipast to be redressit'.[31] In the following year he spent three weeks at Jedburgh dealing with bills and registering complaints against Forster. In the west Scrope and Maxwell had approached a better understanding and were co-operating with each other. The years 1576 and 1577 were relatively calm but early in the following year Morton fell from power.

The regent was not a popular figure. His single-minded ruthlessness had made many enemies and his general indifference to the young king meant there was no personal relationship to sustain his position. The crisis of 1578 was fomented by a dispute between the earls of Athol and Argyll. Morton summoned both to appear before him and be bound by his ruling. Their dislike of the regent caused both peers to forget, at least for the moment, their own quarrel and make common cause against him. The earls prevailed upon James to call a general assembly of the nobility, thus undermining the regent's authority. Stung by the monarch's failure to support him, Morton offered his resignation which was accepted. The king now embarked, some two years ahead of his official majority, on his personal rule.

Morton's fall ushered in a period of uncertainty and for the next nine years the polity of the realm was disturbed by shifting factions and a series of coups. The former regent was the first to seek to recover his authority; in alliance with the Earl of Mar, he was able to recover, at least in part, his position. Robert Bowes, the English ambassador, acted as honest broker mediating between the Morton–Mar and the Athol–Argyll factions. The result was a form of coalition in which Morton, though no longer regent, was *primus inter pares*. Athol also took a leading role though he died early in 1579; poison was again suspected and inevitably fingers were pointed in Morton's direction.

Having disposed of Athol the earl next set about reducing what little power and influence the Hamiltons still possessed; in so doing he unintentionally cleared the way for the rise of the Lennox Stewarts. Lord Robert, Bishop of Caithness, was head of the sept. On his death the mantle passed to the surviving son of the late regent's younger brother, Esme Stewart, who returned to Scotland from France in the autumn of 1579. Stewart possessed the charm and charisma which the dour Morton lacked and James, always engaged by handsome young men, became besotted. So great was his infatuation that the king was said to be 'in such love with him as in the open sight of the people, oftentimes he will clasp him about the neck with his arms and kiss him'.[32]

Stewart was soon elevated to the earldom of Lennox and was presently engaged in procuring Morton's final fall. A captain James Stewart accused the Douglas of complicity in the murder of Darnley and, on 31st December 1580, Morton was imprisoned. Elizabeth was prepared to use all diplomatic means to succour her ally but the former regent had too many enemies by far and went to his death six months later.[33] The queen contemplated providing military assistance to Morton and, at the end of March, Hunsdon was instructed to be ready to enter Scotland at the head of an expedition though, on 10th April, these orders were countermanded.[34] For his role in the affair Captain Stewart earned himself the earldom of Arran (notwithstanding the fact the existing incumbent was still alive) and Lennox climbed to a dukedom.

Although now unchallenged Lennox had neither the experience nor the necessary web of kin and allies to govern effectively. The nature of his relationship with the king and his suspected popish leanings (he was born a Roman Catholic but had cannily converted to Calvinism) did not endear him to the kirk. Despite his frequent protestations he was suspected of being in touch with Queen Mary. In the following year William Ruthven, first Earl of Gowrie (the son of Riccio's principal assassin), a fanatical Protestant, kidnapped the king under the pretext of a hunt, dubbed the 'Raid of Ruthven'. Lennox found himself suddenly without friends and was obliged to accept exile in France, where he died in 1583.

One of the charges laid against Lennox was that he had failed to maintain order on the marches. It was certainly true that, since Morton's first fall in 1578, the situation had deteriorated. The borderers' finely-tuned instincts quickly detected the vacuum once the regent's grip was prised free. Even when he partially recovered his authority, Morton was not able to prevent the names from riding: 'The broken estate of Scotland falling daily into dangerous condition by the great discords renewing still among the nobility, and presently threatening seditious effects'.[35]

The Marian faction also saw an opportunity to revive their flagging fortunes and create fresh disturbances. In August 1578 Hunsdon and Forster were conferring on the necessary measures not only to secure their own marches but to be ready to support James should the Marians look to be capable of moving from being an irritation to a threat. Hunsdon also undertook to issue dire warning to both Cesford and Hume should their sympathies waver. His bluntness appears to have had the desired effect.

In 1579 Ruthven was sent to the border as lieutenant general where he took steps to curb Maxwell who, after an enquiry, was dismissed and replaced by Herries. Morton's final purge of the Hamiltons created further tensions, yet Elizabeth felt sufficiently secure to dispatch a further three companies from the Berwick garrison to Ireland. Morton's final fall and Lennox's supremacy provided the spur for Liddesdale and Teviotdale both of which were soon riding in earnest. The queen was disposed to cast the blame for this on to Lennox, and Bowes was instructed to demand his removal from office. The taint of treason which hung over the duke, his suspected links, real or imaginary, with Mary, were sufficient to alarm the English administration.

Morton's Douglas kinsman Angus had sought temporary refuge in Carlisle from where he mounted a series of raids into the Scottish west march, even taking Langholm. Scrope, who must certainly have been aware, turned a blind eye and Johnstone, recently ousted from the wardenship and put to the horn by Maxwell, lent assistance.

In July 1583 the king gave his captors the slip and the Earl of Arran became his first minister. Sir James Melville described this new pseudo-regent in less than flattering terms, 'a scorner of all religion, presumptuous, ambitious, covetous, careless of the commonwealth, a despiser of the nobility, and of all honest men'.[36] James would never be as besotted with Arran as he had been with Lennox. However, he was wholly taken in by the man's masterful self-assurance and his willingness to take on the day-to-day business of governance, which allowed the king to devote time and energy to more rewarding pastimes such as hunting and poetry. As a result the court became the focus for a growing literary circle.

Throughout 1583 there was tension on the marches. Hume and Ferniherst were riding again and in Queen Mary's name; rumours of conspiracies abounded. Johnstone again replaced Maxwell, whose Catholic leanings placed him firmly in the Marian camp. James, with Arran, was playing a clever double game. Bowes was by no means certain of the king's continued amity with England and that he might yet prefer an alliance with France.

In August Walsingham came north on a fact-finding mission and concluded that the disturbances were not merely local but originated with or were condoned by the Scots government. He was shown the 'bluidy sarks'[37] of those allegedly slain by the reivers.

Gowrie paid for the Raid of Ruthven with his head in 1584 and the rising power of the kirk was curbed by the passing of the 'Black' Acts which sought to establish James's position as head of both church and state and the promotion of the bishops. This was anathema to the General Assembly which was firmly anti-episcopalian in sentiment and had no desire to be controlled directly by the monarch.

The survivors of Gowrie's affinity fled to England where they were given safe haven at the same time Mar and Angus were planning a coup of their own. This uncertainty offered fresh encouragement to the marchers; the Liddesdale names were soon foraying as far south as Hexham. The proposed coup proved abortive and the plotters joined the ranks of the exiles already skulking in England. Elizabeth refused to deliver and a fresh round of disturbances flared up.

Despite the rapidly deteriorating situation neither side seriously contemplated war. Though Hunsdon was sent north in July and the Yorkshire levies were summoned the warden was able, on 13th August, to meet with Arran at Foulden. Nothing was settled, however, and Forster was at odds with Cesford. In October Patrick, Master of Gray, was sent to Elizabeth to seek an accord against a pattern of escalating violence on the marches. The king was unhappy with the performance of his officers and sacked Johnstone, Hume and Cesford. The latter was replaced by Ferniherst who, despite being provided with both manpower and funds, was scarcely more successful.

The following year promised to be no easier. Whilst in the west Maxwell and Johnstone were bickering, Edward Wotton was sent as Elizabeth's ambassador with a brief to undermine Arran whilst the exiles in England prepared for more direct action. The creation of the Holy League in France emphasised the need for the two Protestant governments to work together. Part of Wotton's mission was to preach the concept of a counter league, a formal alliance between England and Scotland both defensive and offensive in nature. On 31st July the concept was agreed in principle and it was further decided that the state of the borders should be examined by a new commission.

Four days before this accord there was another serious incident when Lord Francis Russell was murdered by an unknown assailant at a truce day. Inevitably Forster, the victim's father-in-law, was involved and the warden's version of events went through several transitions; what began as very possibly an accident quickly degenerated into a conspiracy. Wotton was keen to use the killing as a pretext to further weaken Arran's position and to demand the rehabilitation of the exiles. The commission met in October but the exiles had resolved on direct action. Hunsdon was looking the other way when they rode north to a muster at Kelso. Forster kept the Tynedale and Redesdale men at home whilst the exiles' ranks grew to include Hume, young Cesford ('Fyrebrande')[38] Drumlanrig, Maxwell and James Hepburn, 5th Earl of Bothwell (the nephew of Mary's third husband.)

Having secured Jedburgh the exiles marched to Stirling to confront Arran. The king failed to raise a force to match theirs and the favourite wisely sought refuge in flight on 2nd November.[39] James was largely done with regents or quasi-regents and whilst Gray now came to enjoy the king's favour he was never to enjoy the same monopoly of influence as Lennox or Arran. As consideration for entering into the League with England James was to disavow any association with his mother's faction and, whilst Elizabeth was not yet ready to nominate him as her successor, he was to receive a stipend of £4,000 per annum, a very handsome sum. If the queen was not yet ready to name him she would undertake not to derogate from his rights unless he were to display 'manifest ingratitude'.[40]

Maxwell's support for the exiles guaranteed his further rehabilitation but his fondness for Rome soon cost him his position and, for a period, his liberty.[41] The warden was also said to be conspiring with Arran and the French. Against a background of these fresh uncertainties, Thomas Randolph was sent to urge the engrossment of the League. James undertook to make recompense for Russell's murder and his pension entitlement from the English crown was confirmed. Ferniherst, long an active adherent of Mary, died at Aberdeen in April 1586; his demise raised hopes that Teviotdale might remain quiet, though Liddesdale was active. It was not until June 27th that the commissioners finally met at Berwick to finalise the detail of the accord. Immediately there was disagreement, mainly over the dates from which mutual redress would be due, but the League was finally sealed on 5th July. Angus was confirmed as lieutenant of the Scottish border and held court at Jedburgh, where sixteen offenders received a capital sentence.[42]

One major impediment to the durability and success of the League was the matter of the king's mother. Her continued survival placed James in a difficult position; put quite bluntly, Mary was an obstacle in his path to the succession. A few months after the League was concluded the amateurish conspiracy, called the Babington Plot, was uncovered and this led to the queen's subsequent trial and execution. There was never any prospect that James would intervene militarily on his mother's behalf; he lacked both the means and the will, and her taking off was a boon.

He went through a show of diplomatic activity, Gray acting as ambassador and his comment 'the dead do not bite'[43] pretty well summed up his royal master's sentiment. Elizabeth was probably the more unwilling of the two; after Mary's head had rolled she had made a great show of declaring the thing had been done without her knowledge or consent. James, unconvinced, wrote to her in suitably reproving terms: 'Whereas ye purge yourself of yon unhappy fact [the execution] I dare not wrong you so far as not to judge honourably of your unspotted part therein, so I wish that your honourable behaviour in all times hereafter may fully persuade the whole world of the same'.[44] Clearly James and Elizabeth understood one another perfectly.

On the border there was only a muted response to Mary's death. Maxwell, the inveterate plotter, was said to be engaged in fresh, treasonable correspondence with Jesuit agents but Forster and Cesford met twice to transact warden business and the old rogue found time to travel to Newcastle and explain the many charges laid against him. Huntingdon was disposed to accept Forster's version whilst nonetheless advising him that it would be entirely appropriate for him to retire (he was, by now, in his late eighties, an age which the majority of his contemporaries failed to attain).

The summer proved a busy season with the Scottish names frequently in the saddle, their natural propensities exacerbated by a dearth of corn. Hunsdon, who was sent to make representations to James in August, was convinced the king was complicit to further his demands in relation to the succession and the idea of a grand northern duchy which he now coveted. The king showed willing by sending the doughty Angus in his office of lieutenant.

Hunsdon, meanwhile, was embroiled in fresh accusations against his old comrade Forster and felt obliged to deprive the warden of office, assuming the role himself whilst his investigations continued. Forster, once again, escaped censure, Hunsdon concluding that, as the warden alleged, these new allegations were wholly vexatious, engineered by the malice of Sir Cuthbert Collingwood.[45] The fact of the matter was that Forster, despite the weight of his years and misdeeds, was simply too valuable to put aside. Most of the gentry in his march were linked to him by blood, marriage or patronage and not a mouse stirred but that he knew of it. His understanding and knowledge of the Scottish marchers and the web of his contacts were irreplaceable.

James, despite the signing of the League, was possibly still flirting with offers from Spain, and despite his assurances to Huntingdon the marchers remained active. Buccleuch, Cesford and Johnstone were all riding. In November Huntingdon was once again sent north with a commission to raise an army ten thousand strong. The mere threat was sufficient for James who wrote, in placatory tones, to Hunsdon, intimating that he had 'byn gretly solycyted bothe by france and Spayne with many grete offers . . . yet he hath never yeldyd'.[46] Philip II had in fact laid claim to the throne of England himself, thus obliging James to stand by the League if he was to further his goal of attaining Elizabeth's crown on her death.

The year 1588 began in fever of anticipation. Philip II was known to have amassed his great fleet, his Armada, which was to transport a Spanish army from the Netherlands to invade England. In January commissioners from both sides met at Foulden to resolve a list of outstanding matters. Forster, despite the temporary cloud of his suspension, was included amongst the English. The wealth of his experience outweighed the extent of his malpractice – no mean achievement. Hunsdon, who was present for the latter part of the deliberations, was moved to recommend the old man's reinstatement.

In the west William, 5th Lord Herries, had been appointed as Maxwell's replacement though he was himself tainted by popery. In May Maxwell, who had returned from temporary exile in Spain, rebelled and Herries was unable to prevent his seizure of the key fortresses of Langholm, Lochmaben and Caerlaverock. This was no mere local disturbance for it was feared, at one point, that the south-west coast of Scotland might be the Spaniards' favoured beach-head. James reacted swiftly; by 28th May he had brought forces to Dumfries and sent Maxwell fleeing into the fastnesses of Galloway. All of the lost castles were immediately retaken except Lochmaben whose garrison continued defiant until the place was reduced by an artillery train borrowed from Carlisle.

Robert Carey, Hunsdon's swashbuckling son, acted as the facilitator whilst on a diplomatic mission to James. Maxwell was soon back in familiar captivity in Edinburgh, whilst a number of those who had journeyed from Spain with him suffered a traitor's death. The border was left in Angus's competent hands whilst Huntingdon maintained a full alert on the English side. Despite alarums the doomed Armada fled past the Northumbrian coast without serious incident. James received a cash bonus of £3,000 as reward for his prompt action and support. Carmichael was appointed as west march warden.

On 22nd October 1589 James departed for Denmark to claim the Princess Anne for his bride. He returned in May 1590 and the royal couple were married on the 20th August. In his absence governance of the border was entrusted to John, Lord Hamilton (Angus had died in July). The new lieutenant was based for part of the time at Jedburgh and in Dumfries for the remainder. His stipend was to be one tenth of the marriage tax, a substantial emolument.[47]

One of the more colourful and eccentric characters of the era was the Earl of Bothwell, something of a favourite and employed as Keeper of Liddesdale but with a wildness and instability that alarmed even his hardened contemporaries. In 1589 he was making a nuisance of himself on the border where he was always able to attract support from the more desperate elements but neither Hume nor any of the Teviotdale men wanted anything to do with him. Both sides were making efforts to promote justice, but throughout 1590–1 Bothwell was a constant irritation. James replaced him as Keeper with Buccleuch, a less controversial character if only marginally so.

A dramatic series of events which unfolded in 1590 implicated Bothwell in matters far more serious than reiving. That year witnessed the sensational case of the North Berwick witches. The heightened hysteria which accompanied the kirk's more inflammatory utterances promoted a climate of fear and suspicion. The king was by no means removed from this and the diabolical exerted a particular fascination for him. In 1597 he published his own treatise, 'Daemonologie', on the subject. Under the robust form of questioning sanctioned for use against the agents of the antichrist the witches named the earl as the leader of their infamous cult. Whether this was true or not the accusation was never entirely disproved and this, together with an estrangement from the king, translated Bothwell from troublemaker to terrorist.

Now an outlaw he pursued a vendetta against James. In December 1591 he mounted a dramatic night raid against Holyroodhouse. The following June he made an abortive attack on Falkland, and a year later a further attempt on Holyrood when, with a fine dramatic flourish, he is said to have laid his unsheathed sword at the king's feet. This would have been an uncomfortable experience for James, the least martial of men with a terror of drawn steel, clad only in his nightshirt and confronted in the half light of a summer's night by a lunatic peer in full harness!

In addition to being an alleged Satanist Bothwell emerged as the unlikely paladin of the reformed religion. The ministers seemed prepared to overlook his diabolical leanings for so long as he represented a counter to the perceived popish influence of Huntly and the Gordons. The king had shown favour to the Earl of Huntly despite his treasonable correspondence with Spain. James had also been minded to overlook the sanguinary outcome of his favourite's feud with the 'Bonnie' Earl of Moray. This reached its bloody denouement on 7th February 1592 when Huntly set fire to Moray's tower house of Donibristle and brutally cut down the younger man as he tried to flee. By the end of that year, however, the 5th Earl of Bothwell was implicated in a fresh popish plot, the affair of the 'Spanish Blanks'.[48]

After Bothwell's final abortive chevauchee in 1594 he sought refuge with Huntly in the north-east. This must have been something of a disappointment for his friends in the kirk – their paladin throwing himself on the mercy of a notorious papist and ally of Spain. The king's patience was finally exhausted, and though Huntly bested Argyll in the fight at Glenlivet, he was obliged, subsequently, to flee the realm. In the spring of 1595 the mercurial Bothwell followed Huntly into exile and whilst the latter returned a year later, Scotland had seen the last of James Hepburn.[49]

Throughout 1592 Bothwell was a presence on the marches. For a space he was at Lochmaben just prior to the raid on Falkland on 28th June. A couple of weeks earlier Scrope had died; a highly able and respected warden, he was succeeded by his son, a man of far inferior stamp. Bothwell could make little headway in the west for he was opposed by Maxwell who kept Johnstone in check. As reward for this loyal service the equally mercurial

Maxwell was made, for the second time, Earl of Morton and reinstated as warden, a position Carmichael was only too happy to relinquish. Bothwell withdrew to the refuge of grim Hermitage where he stayed till, in October, the king led a force of three thousand lances to Jedburgh to recover the castle. By this time the renegade earl had most probably fled into England.

On 6th December 1593 Morton's career came to an abrupt and violent end in the battle on Dryfe Sands, the final and bloody clash with Johnstone (see following chapter). At this time Bothwell was likely skulking in Scrope's march; he crossed the border after the turn of the new year and the king detailed Hume, Cesford and Buccleuch to bring him in but, once again, he slipped the net. He next appeared with four hundred riders at Dalkeith where his outlaws were worsted and put to flight. He sought refuge for a while at Hermitage but the border was now too hot to hold him and it was sometime thereafter that he sought refuge with Huntly and finally disappeared into obscurity.

In the English middle march Forster still clung tenaciously to his office though his great age prevented him from exercising his former control and the marchers did much as they pleased. The old man relied on his bastard son who was frequently rendered equally incapable through drink. Both Robert Carey and Rafe Grey were after his job. By now both Buccleuch and Cesford could prey upon Forster's march at will and the Council issued him a stark warning. In September 1595 Lord Eure was finally sent as his replacement and the ninety-four-year-old was packed off into involuntary retirement.

Running Forster's march proved an unequal challenge. Eure was both diligent and enthusiastic but he found the tangled, entrenched web of his predecessor's network impossible to penetrate and could make no headway. In March 1596 Scrope's officers seized the notorious Armstrong, Kinmont Will, and carried their captive to Carlisle. Regrettably the arrest was unquestionably illegal as it had occurred on a day of truce. This set in motion the celebrated raid on Carlisle when Buccleuch, with the aid of the English Grahams and the connivance of Scrope's own officers, broke into the castle and freed the prisoner. The English warden's humiliation, which some thought overdue, was complete. His rage paled into insignificance compared to that of the queen who delivered a withering blast to her would-be successor. James, as ever, was patient and allowed the storm to burn itself out. There was no war.

On 22nd July, Hunsdon, the queen's half brother and unfailingly loyal servant, followed the elder Scrope to the grave. The queen's parsimony prevented any immediate replacement and his two sons, Robert and John, were left to carry on in subordinate positions, lacking the means and the authority to fully carry on their father's work. Neither possessed the rank, therefore, to deal with Cesford or Buccleuch, both of whom were riding with impunity. In the middle march Eure was hopelessly out of his depth. In despair he wrote: 'the border groweth wylde and disorderlie since the delay of the commissione, our bills increaseth, justice decreaseth, corne fayleth, peoples hartes are gone, my discomforth in my charge followeth – these are the news of the Borders'.[50]

The commission, to which Eure refers, had been due to meet in 1596 but did not, in fact, convene until January. There was no shortage of business. Buccleuch alone stood charged with no less than twenty homicides and Cesford with sixteen.[51] The affair of Kinmont Will, colourful as it had been, had damaged the wardens' trust in each other; without active co-operation matters were bound to deteriorate, especially when two senior border officials, Buccleuch and Cesford, were themselves prime culprits. A further accord was signed in May but the raids continued. Matters became so 'ticklie' that the Earl of Essex in Ireland was instructed to send back the Berwick detachments.

In that October a further incident occurred at Norham Ford. Bowes, with perhaps half a thousand riders, met with Hume to conduct an exchange of pledges. On the Scottish side Buccleuch himself was by far the most important and kept the gathering waiting until late afternoon before making a grand entrance. Cesford also delayed handing over his Teviotdale pledges. In all probability it was he who engineered an incident when one of his company discharged his pistol and screamed murder. Things very quickly became ugly. The English were seriously outnumbered. Hume did his best to try and calm matters and shield Bowes from harm (several of his affinity were cut down by the English who took them for Cesford's men). In the confusion and gathering dusk the English pledges quietly disappeared.

The season continued in like vein. In November James sat in the west where he hanged 'three score or more' thieves and broken men. This failed to deter either Buccleuch or Cesford. The next month Robert Carey was appointed to the English east march and, in 1598, Eure gave up the forlorn quest and resigned his wardenship. There was an outbreak of plague in that year which produced something of a quietening effect and on 14th February Hume delivered Cesford as a pledge to Carey's brother John on Halidon Hill 'as the freinde in all the world he loved best, with great entreatie of letting passe former unkyndnesses, and to receyve him to his favourable custodie'.[52] Cesford was not inconvenienced for long; he was home by the spring, as was Buccleuch, exchanged for his young son on 21st March.

In March Sir Wyllughby d'Eresby took over from Carey, now Sir Robert, in the east whilst he accepted Eure's former role, not without misgivings. The middle march had degenerated into a free-for-all and it would take a very strong hand to curb the riding names. In August a body of some sixty Scots who, by their own account, were armed only for the chase and who had crossed into England, were set upon by a body of four hundred English riders, harnessed for battle. In the running fight that followed several Scots were killed, others injured or taken. Carey believed the Scots had been at least three times the stated number and a good four score were carrying firearms. In the season his march was sustaining twenty serious incursions a month and, of course, the Tynedale and Redesdale men were never slow to reciprocate.

1599 looked set to be a busy year. Liddesdale, Teviotdale and the English upland dales were all riding. Introduction to polite society in England had calmed both of the firebrands, Buccleuch and Cesford; perhaps they saw the shape of things to come. Elizabeth could not live for ever and King James would then have need of good officers rather than thieves and murderers. Their marchers were not convinced and it was business as usual on the frontier. Cesford was now zealous in his duties as he wished for the safe return of his pledges. In the west the English Grahams were busy and Carmichael was appointed as Scottish warden.

In the east d'Eresby was much troubled by the activities of Dunkirk pirates who were raiding along the Northumbrian coast, harassing and robbing the fishermen there. He found himself increasingly under pressure; differences with the citizens of Berwick and a falling out with Robert Carey added to his burden. His health was deteriorating and he died on 25th June 1600. John Carey took over his wardenship.

Another casualty of the new century was Carmichael. Always a zealous officer, honest but not overburdened with tact, he was ambushed by a body of sixteen Scottish and two English riders who shot him dead, 'slaine be the Armstrangis and Carliles, he doing and executing his office as Wardenrie'.[53] On November 14th 1601 one Thomas Armstrong was convicted of the murder and hanged; five years later another of the same grayne also swung for the crime. Despite this doleful beginning there was increasing co-operation between the wardens; only the Scottish west march remained fractious and Scrope mounted several punitive raids. James sat on the march in both February and September in an effort to curb the lawlessness.

It was Robert Carey who, on the evening of 26th March 1603, rode, exhausted and injured by a trick from his horse, to Holyrood. He greeted the king with the title of James I of England, and in that instant the Anglo-Scottish border, the old frontier, ceased to exist.

Notes

1 Quoted in Tough, D.L.W., *Last Years of a Frontier*, Oxford 1928 p. 208.
2 Quoted in Tough p. 241.
3 MacDonald Fraser, G., *The Steel Bonnets*, London 1971 p. 295.
4 Quoted ibid p. 297.
5 Quoted ibid p. 298.
6 Quoted ibid p. 299.
7 Quoted ibid p. 299.
8 Quoted ibid p. 300.
9 Quoted ibid p. 301.
10 Quoted ibid p. 301.
11 Quoted ibid p. 302.
12 'Taking Hector's Cloak' became an expression denoting perfidy thereafter.
13 Forster had garnered an estimated £4,000 in loot augmented by a generous stipend of £500 per annum, see MacDonald Fraser p. 303.
14 Tough p. 210.
15 Quoted in MacDonald Fraser p. 304.
16 Bingham, C., *The Stewart Kingdom of Scotland 1371–1603*, London 1974 p. 224.
17 Archbishop Hamilton was the most illustrious of the captives taken after the fall of Dumbarton and, for his part in Moray's murder, was executed on 7th April, 1571.
18 Quoted in Tough pp. 211–12.
19 Quoted in Tough p. 212.
20 Leonard Dacre made good an escape to Flanders where he died an exile in 1573.
21 Quoted in MacDonald Fraser p. 306.

22 MacDonald Fraser p. 307.

23 The Scots' version of the affray was somewhat different, they alleged their marchers had the better of the fight and harried the raiders back to Carlisle.

24 Tough p. 118.

25 Bingham p. 231.

26 Before dawn on 24th August, the Huguenot leader, Admiral Coligny, wounded in an earlier assassination attempt, was attacked in his lodgings and brutally done to death. This was the signal for a general massacre of Protestants in the capital, an atrocity which continued for three days of horrific bloodletting. The slaughter was repeated in Orleans, Lyon, Rouen, Bordeaux and Toulouse and with it any hope of a peaceful end to the Wars of Religion in France disappeared.

27 Tough p. 222.

28 The portrait by Arnold van Bronkhorst which now hangs in the Scottish National Portrait Gallery shows a fierce-looking Douglas, with a full red beard, soberly attired in black, glaring from the canvas, a 'wha dare meddle wi' me' expression. Esme Stewart, by contrast, appears effete, even effeminate, in a slightly later portrait, a sensuous face, wide eyes, long nose and trimmed, pointed beard, by an unknown hand, also in the National Portrait Gallery.

29 Scots' mercenaries found a ready market for their martial skills in Ireland throughout the sixteenth century. By 1539 two thousand were said to be serving there, known generally as 'Redshanks' (bare legs). Mostly drawn from the Western Isles, demand for these tough soldiers of fortune increased after the commencement of Shane O'Neill's wars in Ulster from 1561. By 1584 their numbers were reported as having swelled to seven thousand. The warband of Sorley Boy MacDonald in Ulster comprised a Scots brigade two thousand strong. Another three thousand landed in Antrim in 1594. James VI attempted, largely without success, to stem this tide of intervention. The Scots who were accounted as formidable opponents saw action at the key battles of the Yellow Ford in 1598 and Kinsale three years later. On the English side detachments of the Border Horse did good service. In terrain where heavy cavalry were largely ineffective, the borderers were in their habitual element. See Heath, I., and D., Sque, *The Irish Wars 1485–1603*, Osprey *Men at Arms* series no 256.

30 Quoted in Tough p. 226.

31 Quoted in Tough p. 229.

32 Quoted in Bingham p. 237.

33 Morton met his end, not by conventional beheading but on a device known as the 'Maiden'. This was a prototype form of guillotine which he had, with tidy irony, invented himself. The original survives in the National Museum of Scotland in Edinburgh. The blade is square rather than set at an angle as in the later, more famous French device.

34 Tough p. 232.

35 Quoted in Tough p. 229.

36 Quoted in Bingham p. 240.

37 'Bloody shirts.' These were taken and shown as proof of the owner's violent demise. In 1603 James was shown the bloodied shirts of Colqhuhouns allegedly killed by the MacGregors in the fight at Glenfruin. The slaughter was real enough but the evidence shown to the king was faked!

38 Robert Ker of Cesford, 'the Firebrand' (Scott of Buccleuch earned the same sobriquet), was a notorious reiver and abettor of reivers in his own right. His portrait shows him in his later years when he was lauded as a sober servant of the crown and his gaze is steady, almost benign.

39 Arran's career ended abruptly in 1595 when a Douglas, Morton's nephew, took revenge for his part in the regent's fall and execution.

40 Bingham p. 242.

41 Maxwell flaunted his popery to the outrage of the ministers of Dumfries. He was reported as having led a torchlit procession to the church where, on Christmas Day, he celebrated no less than nine masses and the same on New Year's Day, see Tough p. 240.

42 Tough p. 242.

43 'Mortui non mordent' see quote in Bingham p. 243.

44 Quoted in Bingham pp. 243–4.

45 Tough p. 244.

46 Quoted in Tough p. 245.

47 Tough p. 250.

48 One George Ker was apprehended carrying blank letters ostensibly to Spain. Although not directly incriminating, these were purportedly signed by leading recusants, including Huntly and, as the messenger was persuaded to confess under torture, were part of a fresh invasion plot.

49 Bothwell finished his career in Naples where he died in penury in 1624.

50 Quoted in Tough p. 264.

51 Tough p. 265.

52 Quoted in Tough p. 268.

53 Quoted in Tough p. 274.

Chapter 21

The Steel Bonnets

I curse thair heid and all the haris of thair heid; I curse thair face,
thair ene, thair mouth, thair neise, thair toung, thair teith, thair crag,
thair schulderis, thair breist, thair hert, thair stomok, thair bak, thair
wame, thair armes, thair leggis, thair handis, thair feit, and everilk
part of thair body, frae the top of thair heid to the soill of thair feit,
befoir and behind, within and without.[1]

The slaughter at Pinkie was the last full scale encounter between an
English and Scots national army. The half-century which followed
saw a mellowing in the turbulent relationship between the two sovereign
states to an extent which those who had survived the harrowing earlier
decades would not have thought possible. However this fruitful thawing
may have influenced diplomacy at the higher levels, the ordinary resident
of the border marches could easily have been forgiven if he or she failed to
detect any tangible sign in day-to-day life. The last half of the sixteenth
century saw the final, savage flowering of the riding clans, the border reivers,
the 'Steel Bonnets' of legend.

Later centuries reinvented the reiver. Scott created the image of 'Young
Lochinvar' – a dashing, chivalrous rogue pounding over moonlit moorland
with his stolen (but willing) bride upon his proud steed. A far more
objective analysis by more recent historians has rather dulled this bright
image and the reiver now emerges as a scruffy peasant farmer cum bandit
stealing over the mosses on his surefooted garron, bent on plunder rather
than honour. In fact the steel bonnets were not in the least romantic.

Theirs was a hard, brutal and bloody world of theft, murder extortion and corruption, where family mattered far more than nationality, where warfare and casual violence were endemic and where a man might habitually expect to settle a quarrel with his sword.

As a general observation the east marches of both realms were quieter than the middle and west. On the Scottish side the powerful Humes held sway for generations – the garrison at Berwick controlled the English east and the Percys remained virtually omnipotent. The English upland dales, Coquetdale, Redesdale and Tynedale were home to the riding names – Collingwoods, Forsters, Charltons, Milburns, Dodds, Robsons, Hedleys, Potts, Dunnes and Storeys. In the Scots middle march the Kers and the Scotts were prominent with lesser graynes such as the Burns, Pringles, Youngs and Taits. In the west, English Grahams, Musgraves, Dacres, Carletons, Bells and Lowthers faced Maxwell and Johnstone, Douglas, Beatties, Littles and the Liddesdale names – Armstrong, Elliot, Bell and Croser.

From an English perspective the border was a long, weary journey away from the seat of power and the crown was often content to rule by proxy, though the menace of the overmighty subject could be the consequence. Few noble families in England attained the level of power exercised by the Percys under the first earl in the late fourteenth century or the Nevilles later under the Kingmaker. Both threatened the monarch of the day, bloody civil war and rebellion the result. In the sixteenth century border wardens were often appointed from outside the area; this was only partially successful as local knowledge was an essential tool of the office. Over the border matters were somewhat different. The marches, on the eastern side, were only ever a good day's ride from Edinburgh and Scottish kings therefore played a more personal and active role in border affairs, though all too often this involved the ready employment of the noose. They tended, however, to appoint or at least acquiesce to the appointment of local magnates to the wardenship. The Maxwells were hereditary holders in the west as were the Humes in the east.

Reiving was by no means an all year round event, 'The season' lasted from late August to the following February. Sir Robert Carey, who had cause to know,[2] offered the following observations:

Border thieves will never lightly steal hard before Lammas for fear of the assizes, but being once passed, they return to their former trade and unless in such yeares as they cannot ride upon the wastes by reason of stormes and snowes, the last moneths are theyr chief time of stealing, for then are the night longest, theyr horses hard at meate and will ride best, cattell strong and will drive furthest; after Candlemass the nightes grow shorter, all cattell grow weaker and, oates growing dearer, they feed their horses worst and quickly turn them to grass.[3]

In the late summer the pathways and tracks through the spongy mosses were dried out. Cattle were well fed and strong as were the reivers' garrons. Long nights afforded the shroud of darkness. Such a clandestine trade was not without art. Indeed, the reiver needed several skills: he had to be a competent drover, a ready fighting man, bold but not reckless, with stamina and nerve. A foray might involve a dozen riders or half a thousand, with the graynes active every night the weather allowed, the bright reiver's moon their guiding star. So important was this lunar conspiracy that the image appears in border heraldry – the Scott's badge was a star and two crescent moons; mottoes such as 'we'll have moonlight again' were popular amongst the riding names.

The foray might cover a considerable distance. English riders scoured into the Lothians, the Scots raided as far south as Durham. Although the shaggy black cattle of the region were the favoured prize, horses, sheep and swine were never ignored, nor was any manner of portable loot or 'gear' . . . 'Dyverse Scottes to the number of two thousand or thereabouts . . . run a forrowe within England and have taken and driven away out of Tyndall about nine hundreth threescore and five kye and oxen and about a thousand sheep and goates, besides insight, clothers, gear and weapons'.[4]

The elements of a successful raid were favourable weather conditions, a well chosen company, energetic leadership, sound guides and a grasp of tactics. It was not uncommon for reivers to lay an ambush and fall upon their pursuers. When the company was divided between a raiding party and an ambush group, properly employed such tactics could be highly and murderously effective. There were few more accomplished exponents of the thieves' trade than Walter Scott of Buccleuch, the 'Bold Buccleuch'[5] who, notwithstanding his status as a high-ranking border official, was as tough, savage and not infrequently vindictive as any Armstrong, Elliot or Graham. A complaint was lodged against Buccleuch in 1588:

Captain Steven Ellies and the surnames of the Rowtledges in Bewcastle,
complain upon the said laird of Bucklughe, the laird of Chesame. the
young laird of Whithawghe, and their accomplices to the number of
120 horsemen arrayed with jackes, steil capps, speares, gunis, lancestaffs
and dagges, swordes and daggers purposely mustered by Bucklughe,
who broke the house of Wille Rowtledge, took 40 kye and oxen, 20 horse
and meares, and also laid an ambush to slay the soldiers and others
who should follow the fray, whereby they cruelly slew and murdered
Mr. Rowden, Nichell Tweddell, Jeffraye Narbie and Edward Stainton,
soldiers, maimed sundry others and drove 12 horses and meares,
whereof they crave reddress.[6]

Every 'heidman' (petty chieftain) and grayne had their particular mustering place and marks would be cut into the turf or etched into tree bark to guide any latecomers. Unkempt men on their ragged ponies, they steal over the mosses without trumpet or guidon, arguably the finest light cavalry of their day, traversing the silent moors by moonlight. Time has not really changed the border landscape but has tamed it. The hills are as majestic but many of the treacherous mosses have been drained and much virgin timber felled.

The unnatural ranks of forestry pinewood crammed symmetrically into vast ordered phalanxes of trees are a more recent aberration. The paths were little more than sheep tracks, a skilled guide, like the celebrated Hobbie Noble, an invaluable asset. Surprise was of the essence, for if the countryside were ready and armed then the foray was lost before it struck. The whole purpose was gain not confrontation, a successful raid was one that emptied byres rather than saddles.

The time of greatest peril was on the long ride home, slowed by lifted kine and sheep, possibly reduced to the shambling pace of protesting livestock, possibly even with injured men reeling in the saddle. Again we are indebted to Robert Carey who has left us this account contained in a letter to his master Cecil in 1596:

This night being abroad with 20 garrison men allowed me a watching,
it was our good happe to meet with the Burnes, the principallest theves
of Tyvidale, with goodes dryving before theme which they had stolen.
We kild twoe of them forthright, tooke the third sore wounded before he
would yeald, and the fourth, the night being darck, unhappelye scapte

away. Before winter passes, (he adds ominously), I expect many such morning works if I continue here . . . and either weary them of night stealing, or they me of watching.[7]

Watching was a vital function in itself. The reivers' routes were well known, the trick was knowing who was riding and by which road they would come. To deny the raider the key element of surprise a series of watches was ordained – bridges were chained or barred and fords guarded. From the 1st October to the 16th March a daylight watch was kept from the hilltops and known pathways were covered at night. This system was codified by the Earl of Sussex in 1570; 'searchers' organised the sentries and a posse of 'settlers' was on hand to carry out random inspections to ensure the sentinels remained alert at their posts. When intelligence indicated a foray was imminent the watch was reinforced, perhaps to as many as forty men – the 'plump'.

Warning beacons were an integral part of the defence mechanism. Lit when the raiders were espied, the response, at least in theory, was a zealous spilling of armed men to do battle with the intruders and see them off. In practice this did not necessarily obtain: the ties of blood, the tangled skein of cross-border alliances, fear of feud, and the whiff or corruption blunted many a watcher's appetite for confrontation. Nonetheless the denizens of the marches had a strong incentive to guard their own back doors. Ralph Lord Eure, who had the misfortune to take over the office of English middle march warden after the long, fabulously corrupt tenure of Sir John Forster, was clearly impressed by the qualities of the marchmen though he was, it has to be said, a singularly poor choice as warden:

The native countrymen are better at handling spears on horseback than the Yorkshire or Bishopric men, better prickers in a chase as knowing the mosses, more nimble on foot, and some keep 'slewe dogges' to serve the country which the country could not pay for. Also divers of them live in the 'High Streete' where the malefactors pass, not 4 or 5 miles out of Hexham, next the Waste, and few are landed or rich men and failing the pay, cannot keep horses.[8]

A man despoiled of his beasts and chattels could follow the 'hot trod'; lawful pursuit across the border, he must bear a lighted peat upon the point of his lance and the posse could demand assistance from those they encountered on the other side. Honest men were legally obliged to comply; again, this custom was likely to be more honoured in the breach than the observance though, in theory, to refuse was a heinous offence: '. . . Whosoever hydes from the fray or turns again so long as the Beacon burns or the bell rings shall be holden as partakers to the enemies and used as Traitors, and fra henceforth to be used as a fugitive and disobedient person'.[9] Invaluable in tracking thieves were the tracker dogs or 'slue' (sleuth) hounds that bounded ahead of the trod. The better of these dogs were a valuable commodity and their descendants are most likely the Cumbrian trail hounds of today.

The border rider was never a sartorial triumph. His mount, his weapons and gear reflected the nature of his trade, plain, workmanlike and without adornment. 'Wearing a steel cape, a coat of plate, stockings of plate, bootes and spurres; a short skottish sword and a dagger, a horseman's staffe and a case of pistolls.'[10] English survivors of Pinkie noted that the border gentry had suffered with their commons: their dress and accoutrement being equally plain, so devoid of finery they would be considered uneconomic for ransom.[11]

The military potential of these hard men from the upland dales, born to war, was appreciated, particularly by the Tudors. In 1546 Henry VIII had some 2,500 border horse in the royal service, as scouts, skirmishers, 'prickers' and, of course, freebooters. They had no equal . . . 'The most remarkable of the mounted men in Henry VIII's army were the Northern Horsemen who, called into being by the eternal forays of the Scottish Border, were light cavalry, probably the very best in Europe.'[12]

A body of riders, a 'Band', was usually commanded by a captain general and divided into companies, around a hundred strong, each under its own captain, petty captain and carrying its own flag or guidon. Officers were drawn from heidmen or other notables from the riding names and the military organisation would reflect the hierarchy within the grayne, not unlike the clan regiments of the Scottish highlanders. A mounted trooper was paid 8d. per day, a better rate than the foot levy whose daily rate was a mere 6d.; a petty captain or ensign might earn 2s. per day, a full captain twice that.[13]

Contingents of Border Horse fought in Flanders and the Low Countries. In 1544 the king ordered the recruitment of two picked companies of riders from Tynedale and Redesdale. Foreign service was, if nothing else, a useful means of keeping the hot blooded youth of Northumberland suitably employed away from home. Henry VIII considered his borderers to be something of an élite. A merchant from the capital who had given the king some offence found himself serving in the Border Horse, presumably on the basis that the harsh realities of frontier strife would teach the unfortunate subject humility![14] Scottish borderers fought for England from time to time and also saw much service in French wars. Each nation's riders proclaimed their loyalty by the wearing of armbands, the cross of St George for the English, St Andrew for the Scots. These armbands were useful in that they were easily detached and replaced one with the other if the wearer felt the changing shift of fortune on the field made such an alteration the most prudent option! Contemporary writers were quick to voice suspicion – thus Patten writing after Pinkie:

> . . . *Another manner they have among them is of wearing handkerchers rolled about their arms and letters broidered upon their caps. They said themselves the use thereof was that each of them might know his fellow, and thereby the sooner assemble, or in need to aid one another and such like respects. Howbeit there were of the army among us some suspicious men that thought they used them for collusion; and rather because they might be known to the enemy as the enemy are known to them, for they have their marks too, and so, in conflict, either each to spare the other, or gently each to take the other. Indeed men have been moved the rather to thinks so because some of their crosses were so narrow and so singly set on, that a puff of wind might have blown them from their breasts; and that they were found right often talking with the Scottish prickers within less than their gad's length asunder; and when they perceived they had been spied, they have begun to run at one another, but so apparently perlassent that they strike few strokes but by assent and appointment.*
> *I heard some men say it did much augment their suspicion that way, because at the battle they saw these prickers so badly demean themselves, more intending the taking of prisoners than the surety of victory; for while other men fought they fell to their prey; that as there were few of them but brought home his prisoner, so were there many that had six or seven . . . our prickers, if their faults had been fewer, their infamy had been less.*[15]

In Elizabeth's reign the protracted guerrilla campaigns waged in Ulster by the rebels under O'Neill and O'Donnell provided ample employment for the Border Horse whose skirmishing skills made them the perfect choice for operations in the unfriendly mosses of Northern Ireland, where conventional horse and foot struggled on the unfavourable ground.

The borderer's choice of weapons reflected his role as a specialist fighter: The 'staffe' or 'Jedhart staff' appears to have originated in the workshops of Jedburgh in the early sixteenth century. A formidable weapon, it had an elliptical blade, a haft of perhaps four feet in length, the head socketed and secured by long flanges or 'languets' extending down the oaken handle which prevented the timber being shattered by an opponent's blow. Iron stops or vamplates protected the owner's hands. It was a handy weapon for close-quarter fighting.[16]

The steel bonnet itself was a close-fitting, peaked horseman's helmet of the type known as a burgonet. Hinged cheek pieces covered the temples but the face was usually exposed. Infantry or 'foot loons', as they were known, wore the equally distinctive morion with its curving brim and raised, central comb. Those who possessed body armour might wear a simple breast and back or a half-armour. Most rode with only a leather or canvas 'jack' or brigandine, not infrequently worn with a mail shirt underneath.[17] Leg harness was rare: the reiver tended to prefer stout woollen breeches with thigh-high leather boots which still afforded a fair measure of protection against a slashing cut. He might sew chains on to his leggings to give added deflection. A surviving sixteenth century muster roll from the English west march described those appearing as having 'steel caps and jacks'.

The borderer, as a light horseman, would prove unbeatable on his own ground if unreliable in a charge. His main weapon was the lance, a steel spike mounted on an ash shaft, a dozen feet or more in length. This was generally held couched for thrusting but could be hurled overarm as a javelin.

English borderers continued to rely on their longbows till the close of the sixteenth century. Volleys of arrows were loosed in the affray known as the Raid of the Redeswire as late as 1575 and further evidence is provided by a muster roll from Northumberland nine years later.[18] The Scots reivers often carried a handy, diminutive form of crossbow, known as a latch. Matchlock muskets and carbines were ill-suited to the foray, slow, noisy and unreliable, essentially a one-shot weapon for a horseman whose presence could easily be betrayed by the tell-tale glow of the lighted match.

Regular foot from the garrisons at Carlisle or Berwick would bear muskets or trail the 'puissant pike'.

By the end of the century all who could afford or were able to acquire them would carry a pair of pistols, wheelock daggs, holstered on each side of the saddle. The wheelock was a sophisticated mechanism where the wheel had to be wound up using a key, not unlike a clock. A piece of pyrites was held in a jaw and this, when the trigger was released, sparked from the spinning wheel to ignite first the priming powder and then the main charge. Some very fine examples of these gentlemen's weapons have survived. The best are a triumph of the gunsmith's art: the sloping grip is usually finished with a heavy wooden sphere, allowing the pistol, once discharged, to assume the more basic function of a club.

Swords were carried by all who could gain possession of one. By mid-century a distinctive border fashion emerged, the 'Skottish short sword' which had a straight, single-edged blade of thirty inches or more, and a simple but graceful basket hilt described as 'Irish'. Few examples survive[19] but these backswords (so named as they were essentially a horseman's weapon designed for the downward cut) are both light and graceful whilst remaining deadly functional. A Scottish ordinance of 1540 records that 'unladen gentlemen have jacks of plate, halbriks, splents (greaves), sallet or steel bonnet with pesanor gorget and all to wear swords'.[20]

The reiver's trade demanded a specialised breed of horse. The shaggy border garrons or 'hobblers' were prized for their sure-footed stamina. Strong rather than fast these mounts were said to be capable of covering vast distances, eighty miles or more in the course of a foray. Horse-breeding was an area wherein the Scots excelled: Kings of Scotland imported stock from as far afield as Hungary, Poland and Spain. One of the repressive measures enacted by James VI when he became James I was to ban the ownership of any horse worth more than £30 Scots.

Horseracing was a very popular pastime. One of the borderers' main diversions, race meets were grand social occasions, when vast quantities of ale and spirits were consumed. Not infrequently mischief was also plotted under cover of the sport. Buccleuch and his confederates are said to have agreed the final draft of their strategy to lift Kinmont Will from Carlisle Castle at the races.

It was in the cold, clear nights of the autumn that the reivers rode out, the tracks through the mosses still dry from the summer's heat with the cloak of darkness around them. Their routes over the waste of moorland and rock girt hills were many and devious:

> *They sally out of their own borders, in the night, in troops, through unfrequented by-ways, and many intricate windings. All the day time they refresh themselves and their horses, in lurking holes they had pitched upon before, till they arrive in the dark at those places they have a design upon. As soon as they have seized upon the booty, they in like manner, return home in the night, through blind ways and fetching many a compass. The more skilful any captain is to pass through those wild deserts, crooked turnings and deep precipices, in the thickest mists and darkness, his reputation is the greater, and he is looked upon as a man of an excellent head.*[21]

The considerable burden of attempting to maintain some form of law and order fell on the shoulders of the wardens of the marches, those law officers who administered the legal system of each country and also the peculiar local code of the border laws – the 'Leges Marchiarum'. The office of warden was already long established by the sixteenth century, probably originating in the mid-thirteenth; certainly wardens were in existence by 1318. Each jurisdiction appointed three wardens, one for each march. These were supplemented by deputy wardens, land sergeants and bailiffs with a breed of lesser officers, 'Keepers', delegated to oversee certain troublesome areas. These included, Liddesdale on the Scottish side and, on the English, Tynedale and Redesdale.

The warden's role was far wider than that of law enforcement and local justice. He was expected to act as diplomat, general and, very often, spymaster. Although his powers were extensive his lot was by no means an easy one: the job was never a sinecure and more than one warden died violently whilst in office.[22] Excessive levels of remuneration were never an incentive. An English warden might earn between £300 and £1,100 per annum; his Scottish counterpart invariably less, on average around £100 Scots (or say £20 English).[23]

As part of his wage he was provided with forage and stabling for his personal retinue, though his officers and servants had to be funded from his salary. The job was by no means devoid of 'perks' – half of stolen goods recovered and a healthy proportion of fines were his by right. A number of wardens, perhaps most notoriously Sir John Forster and Sir Robert Ker of Cesford,[24] were as steeped in villainy as the meanest of their charges and maintained a healthy traffic in stolen beasts and gear, supplemented by thriving blackmail rackets.

On the English side there was, as a matter of policy, a trend to appoint southern gentlemen as wardens. This developed out of a mistrust for the unchecked power of the 'overmighty' subject which, in the fifteenth century, had seen marcher lords such as Percy and Neville abuse their offices to build private armies and settle local scores.

The daily office of the warden in apprehending malefactors often led to a summary form of justice, killing without trial or 'justifying' in the contemporary euphemism. Bloodshed could easily embroil the warden in the deadly violence of the feud or 'feid' – a tit-for-tat cycle of murder that could fester for generations. The distinguished English west march warden William, Lord Dacre, found himself at feud with the Maxwells from the opposite march when the Scottish warden, himself a Maxwell, handed over one of his kin who'd murdered an Englishman. Other members of the grayne took revenge upon Dacre by slaughtering his brother, hewing him 'in pieces', a form of savage reprisal that occurs time and again in the catalogue of internecine atrocities.

Law enforcement often sat uneasily with politics and espionage: the national government might choose to use its wardens as instruments of policy rather than as purely law officers. It might often be to England's perceived advantage to promote internal strife in Scotland, suborning and funding those very reivers whose activities south of the line caused so much loss.

In the unhappy reign of Mary Queen of Scots a deadly feud erupted between the Scotts and Elliots, the latter led by Martin Elliot of Braidlaw, a born guerrilla captain who offered to go as far as to secure and hand over Hermitage Castle in return for English gold to fund his vendetta. Forster and Dacre were happy to fund the feud as it served English political aims and had the added benefit of keeping the Elliot and Scott riders in their own marches. Mary herself was happy to invite Dacre to incite the English Grahams against Maxwells, with whom the queen was at odds. Forster worked hand in glove with a mysterious character called Ballard and/or Fortescue who was one of Walsingham's agents. Forster himself scored a noted intelligence coup when one of his patrols detained an itinerant dentist.[25]

The warden might find his authority peremptorily usurped if the monarch chose to appoint a senior officer or lieutenant to command all three wardenries. The débâcle at Solway Moss in 1542 was precipitated by such an affront when James V left orders for his favourite Sinclair to assume command over Maxwell, the warden. The unseemly row which followed contributed to the disaster which overtook the Scots army. Forty-five years later, in 1587, Lord Hunsdon made no bones about his position when it was proposed he would serve under the Earl of Huntingdon, '. . . one that never saw any servys,' he fumed, 'nor knowse yn any respecte what appertaynes too a capten . . . but I perceive yt ys a grete matter to be an Erle . . . I wyll ley yn pryson rather'.[26]

In order that the border laws might be enforced it was necessary for opposite wardens to work together in administering justice. No easy matter, given tension between the realms, personal animosities and the fact that most wardens considered themselves woefully inadequately resourced, and expected to administer the law on a largely lawless frontier, continually hamstrung by a distant and parsimonious Treasury.

The Day of Truce was intended as a monthly meeting between the wardens and/or their deputies; very rarely did these run so smoothly and often there were long lapses between truce days. Certain wardens like Forster or Cesford were notoriously difficult to pin down if a meeting did not suit their purposes.

For obvious reasons of security the meetings were commonly held on open ground on or very near the frontier when each warden should have no more than a hundred followers in his retinue. In practice a truce operated as much like a fair as a judicial proceeding. Custom dictated that any and all attending enjoy safe conduct from sunrise on the day to sunrise on the next. The business began with an exchange of correspondence, whilst the warden's clerk compiled a list of bills of complaint to be heard and agreed these with his opposite number. Once decided on, the date was published by proclamation and the location fixed. From east to west these could be at Wark, Carham, Coldstream, Cocklaw, Reidswire, Kershopefoot, Gretnakirk, the Lochmabenstone and English Rockcliffe.

On the day the two parties, often hundreds strong, would approach with some wariness till the other came in sight, often a difficult moment, the participants in today's peaceful exchange could easily be yesterday or tomorrow's raiders. Protocol then entailed an English emissary riding over to the Scots to formally seek safe conduct till the following dawn (or possibly longer if the caseload demanded). Having acquiesced the Scots warden sent one of his own to seek similar assurance. These matters then being agreed both leaders raised a hand in amity and the parties converged. So far so good.

In his train the warden was expected to hold not only those riders he had captured but those from his own march who were to answer complaints brought against them. The business of the day therefore involved a judicial process whereby each of the bills of complaint was decided. If a man was found 'clear' he was innocent but if the bill was 'filed' or 'foul' he was guilty. Numerous examples of bills of complaint survive. In one instance Armstrongs living on the English side in Gilsland accused Auld Wat of Harden (by no means an uncommon respondent) and others of instigating and leading a raid of some 400 riders and lifting some 300 cattle and oxen together with other stock and leaving a trail of burnt and empty dwellings in their wake.

Verdicts could be arrived at by a number of means. 'Avower' was the sworn testimony of a third party whom both sides could accept as a credible witness; 'Compurgation' was a communal form of oath-taking by three uninvolved and responsible persons; the word or oath of the warden or his deputy themselves who would 'speire, fyle and deliver' upon his honour after full and due enquiry; and lastly, the 'Inquest of Assize' delivered by a jury of twelve, six from each jurisdiction. On paper this seems admirable but the theory falls short of the harsh realities of border life where family arrangements, cross-border ties and dealings, fear of feuds and powerful neighbours, not to mention the warden's own illicit dealings, could combine to obfuscate the process.

One aspect of cross-border justice was the giving of 'assurances' or 'pledges' – the former was a form of generalised undertaking usually given by a heidman on behalf of his kin to keep the peace or adhere to an agreed course of action. The Tudor administration regularly sought assurances from Scottish borderers in maintaining a pro-English faction; such bonds were likely to involve payment or at least the promise of payment. In 1547 in the violent course of the Rough Wooing some 7,000 of Liddesdale's finest, together with inhabitants of the west march and Debatable Land, were induced to enter into such agreements.

The pledge was in effect a hostage, someone who was handed over into custody as a guarantee of good behaviour or as a surrogate for an absent offender. In the early years of the century the 'Bastard' Heron remained at liberty whilst his unfortunate half brother languished in the grim confines of Fast Castle. Disease, neglect and malnutrition shortened the lives of many of those handed over as pledges if they were unlucky enough to be lodged in one of the sorry fastnesses used as gaols. Their ordeal might be short lived or could drag on for years; they might simply be forgotten, 'written off' in the haphazard ledger of cross-border law enforcement.

The 'Border Laws' were a joint judicial effort to create a code which wardens from both sides could enforce, independent of their own legal systems, which were far from compatible. Again the origins of the Leges Marchiarum go back to the mid-thirteenth century when a joint commission comprising twelve knights from each realm was appointed to draw up the first body of laws. This original drafting was much modified and varied, often according to local custom, so that a single lasting definition proved elusive. The code included a kind of catch-all offence, known as 'march treason', and varieties of 'recetting' which related to both receiving stolen goods and harbouring wanted men.

Wounding could result in an award of compensation against the offender. The more serious offence of mutilation also incurred a six-month gaol sentence. Restitution was a remedy for theft and if the culprit did not appear, he was likely to be 'put to the horn' or outlawed. For generations custom allowed borderers on both sides to pasture their stock over the line, provided the beasts were herded back by sunset. This arrangement, however, was so open to abuse that it was eventually proscribed and a safe conduct required for cross-border travel – the exception which remained was that of the 'hot trod' or hot pursuit when the pursuer, bearing a lighted peat upon his lance point, could follow in the thieves' trail.

The lawis of marchis, or bordour laws, betwixt the realmis of Scotland and Ingland, in the time of peace, are common and indifferent to the subjectis of baith the realmis; the groundis and effect of the samis lawis ather being contentit in the contractis and treaties of peace past betwixt the Princes . . . or then they are ancient and lovable custumis, ressavit and standing in force as law, be lang use, and mutual consent of the Wardenis and subjectis of baith the realms.[27]

William Armstrong of Morton Rigg, known to border ballad as Kinmont Willie, was an experienced Liddesdale thug with a formidable record of raids, pillaging, blackmail and murder. He is undoubtably best remembered as the chief if unwilling protagonist in the celebrated raid on Carlisle Castle in 1596 – he was by then well into his middle years, a powerful and dangerous man, though not without a ready wit and the distinctive gallows humour of the true reiver. When Mary Queen of Scots was executed in 1587, her former subjects of Liddesdale, in a burst of righteous indignation, set about the business of harrying the English with a will. Kinmont, no doubt anxious to show his undying loyalty to his martyred sovereign and determined not to be outdone by his neighbours, planned a full-scale foray against the township of Haydon Bridge.

This was to be a serious affair. Some four hundred riders mustered for the raid, drawn from Liddesdale itself but also from the west, from Ewesdale, Eskdale and Annandale. These experienced reivers drawn from the élite of the riding names may have crossed the border at the desolate head of the Liddel water and followed the North Tyne Valley along the heights of Black Knowe, Rough Pike and the Rigg, then skirted Spadeadam Waste. It is equally likely that they came more from the west and traversed the wastes, avoiding the garrisons at Naworth, Askerton and Bewcastle – these were in any event by now in poor repair, victims of Elizabeth's parsimony. Langley, the nearest hold to Haydon Bridge, was likewise dilapidated and undermanned.

Nonetheless the Liddesdale riders did not pass undetected. Sir John Heron of Chipchase was Keeper of Tynedale and one of his sons, on patrol, reported the raid. The keeper, however, seemed disinclined to any sudden exertion and only the persistent urging of those around him, particularly his brother-in-law, Edward Shaftoe, finally goaded him into action. Even then he merely summoned a muster of horse: he did not dispatch them. Such sloth cannot be blamed on natural timidity: the Herons were a martial grayne, and it is far more likely that the Keeper's purse was already filled with reiver's coin.

The town was thus undefended though not by an means necessarily defenceless when the raiders struck. The inhabitants of border townships were hardly strangers to such incursions: witness a description of the villagers of Bywell:

> *These handy craftsmen whose trade is all in yron worke for the horsemen and borderers of that country . . . are subject to the incursions of the*

theaves of Tyndale and compelled wynter and somer to bryng all their cattell and sheepe into the strete in the night season and watch both endes of the strete; and when th' enemey approachith to raise hue and cry whereupon the town preparith for rescue of their goodes which is very populous by reason of their trade, and stoute and hardy by contynual practyse agenst th' enemy.[28]

The townsfolk resisted as best they could and may have broken a few heads, but the Liddesdale men were experts in their calling and the place was literally stripped bare with a liberal application of the torch to keep the people occupied whilst the reivers slipped away, driving everything on four legs before them. The riding names principally sought livestock, cattle, sheep, pigs, and horses but they would never overlook 'insight gear' – in short, just about anything that could be carried, including, from time to time, clothing and domestic utensils, furniture and door frames. At least once even burial shrouds were lifted. A tale is told of Auld Wat of Harden, a seasoned brigand, who is said to have remarked as he passed a haystack – 'if ye had four legs ye wouldn't stand there frae lang'!

Having now sacked and burnt the town the riders should have made good their escape whilst their good fortune held. Possibly they were overconfident or perhaps felt secure in the knowledge that the local law enforcement officer was suborned. Nonetheless they proceeded to divide their force, half driving the catch back the way they'd come, the remainder foraying further into the west march. This proved unwise. The first company were ambushed by Tynedale men, exasperated by their keeper's lethargy and probably divining the cause; seven Scots were taken and a score of beasts recovered. The second party fared even worse, running into a strong body of marchers. They were hounded clear to the border, returning with empty saddles and lost prizes.

This, then, was a border foray, ridden on the larger scale. Many more involved much smaller groups, perhaps even a handful. Equally, 'official' raids or warden 'rodes' led or sanctioned by the warden could take on the scale of a military operation. Such a raid was mounted by the English east march warden, Sir Robert Bowes, in 1542, aimed at Teviotdale and concentrating some 3,000 followers, mixed horse and foot. On this occasion the English were aided by the renegade Earl of Angus and his Douglas kin.

Bowes, no novice, sent a flying column of his Redesdale and Tynedale men under Heron to beat up the valley whilst the main body, including all the foot, stripped from the regular complements of Berwick and Norham, established themselves at Haddon. The Teviotdale men, by no means over-awed and led by Huntly, struck back, harassing the flying column and plac-ing a body of horse between them and the main body. The fight developed into the type of confused, running mêlée that so typified border skirmishing and, in this instance, the English were worsted and severely mauled; some seventy dead were left in the rout. Both Heron and Bowes were taken. Angus, who hacked his way clear, wasted no time in laying blame for the débâcle squarely on the dalesmen, accusing them of being far more con-cerned to garner and protect their loot than accept the hazard of battle.

Despite the growing *entente* between the two kingdoms evident in the last quarter of the sixteenth century, several incidents caused considerable diplomatic tension and might, in the earlier period, have led directly to conflict or all-out war. One such instance was the affray which occurred on a truce day at the narrow neck of land which runs between Catcleugh Shin and Arks Edge by Carter Bar. The modern A68, heading north, strains to reach the border and then finally offers an unrivalled panorama of the defiant hills on the Scottish side. On 7th July 1575 the English warden, Sir John Forster, a man who needed no schooling in the realpolitik of border strife, met with his opposite number the Keeper of Liddesdale, Sir John Carmichael. He was an officer of a very different stamp but, as a mere keeper, technically inferior in status to the warden.[29] This was a fact of which both men seem to have been acutely aware, engendering arrogance and condescension on the one hand and perhaps pedantic officiousness on the other.

> *The seventh of July the smith to say,*
> *At the Reidswire the tryst was set;*
> *Our wardens they affixed the day*
> *And as they promised, so they met.*
> *Alas that day I'll ne'er forgett!*
> *Was sure sae feard, ad then sae faire*
> *They came theare justice for to gett,*
> *Will never green to come again.*[30]

For several hours the business of the day appeared to progress smoothly. A number of bills were disposed of and, as was usual on these occasions, much liquor was consumed fuelling old tensions, particularly the enmity between the Fenwicks and the Liddesdale Crosers. Earlier in the year the English riders had descended upon Liddesdale, the excuse for the foray being a feud already a generation old. Forster's deputy, Sir George Heron, had been slow to co-operate with Carmichael, never the most patient or tactful of men; Forster was no better. Carmichael was, of course, well aware of the innumerable illegal 'rackets' sponsored by the warden and, as the ale flowed, the exchanges became a good deal less cordial.

Matters came to a head when a bill was laid against a notorious English reprobate named Farnstein. For some reason Forster chose to prevaricate, much to his opposite number's annoyance. Polite insistence bred further intransigence and frayed tempers flared. Insults and recriminations snapped the bonds of protocol.

> *Carmichael then spoke out plainlike*
> *And cloke no cause for ill or good;*
> *The other answering him as vainlie*
> *Began to reckon kin and blood*
> *He raise and raxed him where he stood*
> *And bade him match him with his marrows.*
> *Then Tindail heard them reasun rude,*
> *And they loot off a feight of arrows.*[31]

This hostility sparked the dry tinder of enmity between the Liddlesdale men and the Fenwicks. Blows and shafts were soon flying, and William Fenwick of Wallington went down. Sobered by this sudden upsurge of violence the wardens curbed their own ire and sought to calm their countrymen. Carmichael, at this point (or at least according to Forster, whose version of events was seldom if ever objective), had drifted apart from the English warden and his immediate entourage, who were immediately set upon by a body of Scots. Forster's deputy, Heron, was cut down but the Tynedale men surged into the fray and beat back the Scots who were looking defeat in the face till a party of the stalwart men of Jedburgh arrived, late for the truce but most opportunely for the fight.

> *With the help of God the game gald right*
> *Fra time the foremost of them fell;*
> *Then ower the know, without goodnight,*
> *They ran with mony a shout and yell.*[32]

In the end it was the English who were worsted and driven southward in rout. Forster and numerous others were made captive. The 'Raid of the Reidswire' as the fracas is remembered was scarcely a large affair; fatalities were few, pride, particularly that of the outraged English warden, was the main casualty. The whole affair was an embarrassment in Edinburgh and the captives were treated with every courtesy, soon being restored to their liberty with Carmichael himself handed over as a pledge. Forster protested loudly, volubly and at some length but the warden's reputation was not such as was likely to engender much sympathy and even the most partisan English official would be bound to treat any utterance of Sir John's with scepticism.

Ten years after this unfortunate incident, in July 1585, a similar disturbance arose on a truce day and, somehow inevitably, involved Sir John Forster, still obdurately clinging to office despite the weight of his many summers. On this occasion the Scottish middle march warden, Sir Thomas Ker of Ferniherst, was present. No stranger to mayhem, he was at feud with the entire citizenry of Jedburgh. The meet was at Windygyle, where the rolling sea of bog and grass fills the horizon and the cold wind whips over the tussocks like a keen edged blade. Forster was accompanied by his son-in-law Lord Francis Russell. The younger man attended despite the warden's warnings: Forster was convinced Ker bore Russell a grudge and the mere fact of a truce day was not likely to deter the Scotsman from seeking revenge.

The truth of what actually happened, as is not unusual when we rely on Sir John's testimony, remain unclear. What is clear is that the atmosphere was fraught with tension from the start and proceedings marred by a series of random scuffles. In the press of one a shot rang out and Russell fell dead – clearly no accident. The killing could have led, like the Reidswire, to a general mêlée but both wardens seem to have acted responsibly and calmed the situation. The day ended peacefully with an exchange of pledges.

Immediately afterward Forster changed completely his version of events, claiming the whole affair was stage-managed by Ker and that the Scots had turned out in numbers, armed as though for war. He alleged the fatal shot was the clarion for a massed charge by the warden's men and that he himself and his party has been chased four miles into England. No culprit was ever charged with Russell's murder. A rude cairn atop Windygyle now marks the spot where he is said to have fallen.

James VI referred to the most pernicious of the border customs as 'the auld detestable monster of deadly feid'. The king did not love his border subjects overmuch but he correctly identifies the very worst trait of the riding names. This was the feud, the vendetta, more savage than any Mediterranean squabble, murderous and protracted, that could haunt down through the generations, a legacy of violence that endured long after the source of the quarrel was forgot.

> *There is said to have been a tradition among the Borderers that when a male child was christened his right hand should be excluded from the ceremony, so that in time of feud he would be better equipped to strike 'unhallowed' blows upon his family's enemies.*[33]

> *And at the sacred fount, the priest*
> *Through ages left the master hand unblest,*
> *To urge, with keener aim, the blood-encrusted spear.*[34]

In 1526, Scott of Buccleuch, 'Wicked Wat', interfering in national politics, vowed to release the 14-year-old James V from the clutches of the Red Douglas. Having failed to lure the canny Angus into a hostile reception at Branxholm he reverted to more forcible means, laying an ambush at Bridge of Melrose with a thousand border riders, Scotts, Armstrongs and Elliots. The trap, when sprung, developed into a full-blown skirmish, the 'battle' of Darnick, and though the day appeared to be going against the regent he received a timely reinforcement of Humes and Ker of Cesford. The tide of battle now swung irrevocably against the Scott faction and they were soon dissolving in rout. In the pursuit Sir Andrew Ker was run through by one of Scott's Elliot allies at the spot known appropriately as Turnagain.

The Elliot in question soon felt his neck being stretched but Scott escaped and was eventually pardoned. If the king forgot the matter the Kers certainly did not and, a generation later, Wicked Wat was called to account on the High Street in Edinburgh when he had the misfortune to run into a party of Humes and Kers who savagely cut the old man down where he stood.

The feud was often ignored by the wardens, in part because they would have had no wish to become embroiled personally and also because they tended to regard such private murders as being outside the law, essentially where a private matter between the families was concerned:

The people of this country hath had one barbarous custom among them;
if any two be displeased, they expect no lawe but bang it out bravely, one
and his kindred against the other and his; they will subject themselves to
no justice, but in an inhumane and barbarous manner fight and kill
one another. This fighting they call their feides, or deadly feides, a word
so barbarous I cannot express it in any other tongue.[35]

This broadminded if pragmatic view was not calculated to stem the practice, for as one faction drew in its kin and allies, so did the other and the
first feud could spark a whole raft of murderous grudges. The prevalence
of the vendetta was undoubtably a major cause of the seemingly unstoppable
decline into anarchy which continued throughout the latter half of the
sixteenth century. As Robert Carey observed:

The country dare not kill such thieves for fear of feud, if they be but foot
loons and men of no esteem . . . it may pass unavenged, but if he is of a
surname, as a Davyson, a Young, a Burne, a Pringle or a Hall . . . then
he who killed or took him is sure himself, and all his friends (specially
those of his name) is like, dearly to buy it, for they will have his life,
or two or three of his nearest kinsmen, in revenge.[36]

Peebleshire, on the fringe of the marches, was the home of the Tweedys
of Drumelzier and their neighbours the Veitches – neither name features
extensively in the reivers' roll of infamy but these two families pursued
a savage feud in the late sixteenth century. The 'De'il o' Dawyck', chief
of the latter, pursued a vendetta against the Tweedys who retaliated by
ambushing and killing his son near Neidpath Castle. The 'De'il' sent
his kin to track down and murder John Tweedy the Tutor (guardian) of
Drumelzier who was followed to Edinburgh and there dispatched. The
Tweedys in turn hunted James Geddes, Dawyck's brother-in-law, to the
capital, gunning him down in the Kirk Wynd. The feud was still simmering
nicely as late as 1611.

In 1564 the Liddesdale Elliots descended on Teviotdale. At least one of
the Scotts was slain in the course of the foray which sparked a savage feud
between these two riding names. Some were taken and ceremoniously
beheaded by torchlight on Castle Hill in Edinburgh but the survivors were
by no means daunted. The feud coincided with a period of diplomatic tension between England and Scotland so neither Scrope nor Forster scrupled

to stoke the flames. Martin Elliot rode, his purse heavy with English coin, offering at one point to hand over Hermitage as consideration for more active support. Buccleuch struck back, however, carrying a torch through Liddesdale and killing seven Elliots.

The Northumbrian gentry were every bit as contentious as their Scottish neighbours. The Greys feuded with the Widdringtons, the Herons with the Carnabys. A particularly savage hate developed between the Selbys and the Collingwoods. The latter were an active name, already at feud with the Scotts. In 1586 Sir Cuthbert Collingwood accused Sir John Selby of march treason. Selby's son, another John, stung by the insult, ambushed Collingwood and a family party which included his wife, his brother-in-law, Robert Clavering, and around ten others at Stanton near Morpeth. When the smoke had cleared, Collingwood was wounded and one of the Claverings died of his wounds.

At the same time Collingwood was at feud with the Burnes, a small but viciously tough grayne. A decade after the first blows the Burnes retaliated in a foray that left no less than 35 of Collingwood's people dead. So savage did this enmity run that it was agreed that the only way to settle the matter was for a formal duel to be slogged out by six champions from each name. James VI, unsportingly, took the view that this was private justice taken a little too far and intervened to prevent the encounter taking place.

One of the most notorious feuds was that of the Scotts and the Charltons of Tynedale. The latter still hold, as a treasured relic, the sword of one of the Bold Buccleuch's forebears which was taken from him, a humiliation which fuelled the discord. Buccleuch spent three years, 1594–1597, diligently harrying Tynedale and killing Charltons without compunction whenever any might be found: 'Mary! He makes another quarrel, that long synce, in warr time, the Tynedale men . . . tooke his grandfather and killed divers of his countrye, and that they took away his grandfather's shworde, and would never lette him have itt synce. This sayetth he is the quarrel'.[37]

It might prove difficult for border officials to stand aloof from a feud that boiled up all around them; Fraser cites the instance of the murder by the Scottish Laidlaws of a son of Hobby Forster in 1585. The Forsters, big with vengeance, rode towards Scotland, a body of horse from Bewcastle shadowing them under the captain, Christopher Musgrave. Their purpose was ostensibly to ensure no violence occurred on English soil. It did not but the Forsters were soon in serious trouble on the Scottish side. Musgrave was simply incapable of standing by whilst fellow Englishmen were cut to pieces so he led his squadron into the attack, saving the day and discomfiting the Scots, forty odd of whom were taken in the fray.[38]

It was possible to call a halt to the feud once first blood had been spilt. The offender might pay cash compensation, a marriage alliance might be proposed, though equally such events could be utilised to foment and spread the feud. Where the marriage was proposed as a means of burying enmity the normal dowry or 'tocher' was not paid but a land grant, effectively compensation, was offered. A statute, the Arbitration Act of 1600, was introduced to provide a system of judicial review and arbitration, ending the feud through the courts rather than on the duelling ground or down a handy back alley.

In certain circumstances, if the parties were willing, the Church might intervene. An offender might be ordered to undertake a suitable penance or even go on pilgrimage. A particular ritual obliged both parties to attend their or a suitable parish church where he who had admitted fault should do so publicly before God and his enemy and seek the forgiveness of one and the forbearance of the other.

No more bitter rivalry existed between any of the riding families than the enmity between the Maxwells and Johnstones. As early in the century as 1528 Lord Dacre was reporting that a state of open warfare existed between the two graynes which had seen a tide of destruction spread through the west. The Maxwells had been leading gentry in the west march for centuries from their lordly base at Caerlaverock. The wardenship they assumed was theirs by right. By the 1580s the feud was at boiling point; Johnnie Johnstone clashed with John, 8th Lord Maxwell. A recusant and inveterate plotter, Maxwell was twice appointed and dismissed early in the decade, latterly he was imprisoned and Johnstone assumed the office both times. In 1581 it was Johnstone's turn to be ousted and Maxwell entered upon a third term; a year later the roles were once again reversed. Smarting under this fresh humiliation Maxwell effectively declared open season on his arch rival.

His fractious intransigence led to further reverses when Arran, the king's chancellor and kin to Johnstone, proceeded to strip him of the office of Provost of Dumfries, a prestigious and lucrative appointment. Undeterred Maxwell spread lucre to hire in English Grahams and other free lances to wreak havoc in Johnstone country. A virtual state of civil war now obtained. By the middle of the decade Maxwell's ruffians had wasted eighty Johnstone holdings and they, far from being cowed, responded in kind burning out Maxwell's township of Duncow. In August Maxwell scored a significant win when Johnnie Johnstone was taken. James, wearying of this internecine strife, took the easiest course and reappointed Maxwell to the wardenry!

A lesser man might have been content with this but Maxwell drew trouble like a magnet and his incessant plotting fuelled by his ardent catholicism soon landed him back in gaol. Johnstone, not unsurprisingly, seized the moment to wreak full revenge and also soon found himself incarcerated. The fury of the vendetta had taken its toll, however, and Johnstone died in 1587, a broken man. Maxwell proved more resilient: in exile he plotted with Spain to the detriment of England, this landed him back behind bars once again, and yet, despite his unenviable track-record, the king reappointed him as warden, this time for life, in 1592.

The years, however, do appear to have mellowed Maxwell, to a degree at least. Now fully in control of the west he appears to have exerted himself to bring the feud to an end. Johnstone's successor as head of the name was married to a Maxwell bride and, for a brief moment, it did seem as though the feud might wither. This happy prospect, however, did not endure for long: a petty skirmish born out of a minor theft served to reignite the whole mix. This time it was the Crichtons who clashed bloodily with the Johnstones and were badly mauled, fifteen of their number being left bereft of life on the field. Maxwell may have tried to avoid involvement at the outset but the Crichtons and their Douglas neighbours were shouting for redress. The Johnstones, fearing the inevitable, prepared to take on Maxwell and his allies.

This was no mean task. Maxwell outgunned Johnstone by a hefty margin. Even after he'd scoured Liddesdale and the Debatable Land for allies and mercenaries, a hotchpotch of Elliots, Irvines, Scotts and, inevitably, the English Grahams, Johnstone could muster no more than four hundred riders, perhaps a quarter of the numbers Maxwell could command. Having now abandoned all notions of reconciliation Maxwell had decided to finish the job. Summoning Johnstone to surrender he advanced upon Lochwood with a mixed force of horse and foot, perhaps two thousand strong.

On 6th December 1593 scouts from the two forces collided near Lockerbie, Johnstone leading the van with some forty or so riders. The warden's men, falling on, pushed these back in sharp retreat, a virtual rout. This was, however, no more than a ruse, for the main body lay concealed nearby and galled Maxwell's disordered prickers with a charge. The van recoiled upon the main body as they sought to close up and the Johnstones were on them like hungry wolves, tearing at the flanks, biting and wheeling, lances flashing in the pallid, winter light.

The mêlée sprawled over the low-lying ground known as Dryfe Sands, horses chewing up the soft ground, laced with spreading gore as the casualties mounted. The fight was short but ferocious. The Johnstones were fighting for their very lives, their homes, their families. The warden's force, paid men for the most part, simply dissolved. Men fleeing on foot through the streets of the little town suffered dreadful slashing wounds from sweeping backswords, called 'Lockerbie Licks'. Maxwell's long run of luck had ended. Burdened by full plate he had no hope of flight and was hacked down in the slaughter. It was the end of an era and the most savage clan fight in British history. Possibly as many as seven to eight hundred were killed or wounded. Some of the Johnstone riders were not even in their teens; for some it was their first and in many cases last battle.

It was not, however, the end of the feud. Johnstone was outlawed but eventually secured both a pardon and the wardenship. Fifteen years later a formal truce was arranged with both he and the current Lord Maxwell attending. It was hoped that this meeting might finally lay the anger to rest. It did not; Maxwell shot the warden down, a crime for which, on 21st March 1613, he made his final journey to the block.

Perhaps the most celebrated drama in the whole, violent history of the reivers occurred three years after Dryfe Sands, and one of the principal actors was Will Armstrong of Kinmont, the same 'Kinmont Willie' who took up Haydon Bridge six years before. In the spring, on 17th March, Will attended a truce day at Kershopefoot on the Scottish side. As the spring sun was setting, and doubtless after a fair day's 'sup', Will was exchanging banter with a body of English horse, riding parallel on the south bank of the Liddel Water.

Drink and the feeling of security afforded by the protocol of the truce prompted Will to be particularly creative and expansive in the range of insults he genially heaped on to Salkeld, the deputy west march warden and his company. Infuriated beyond all measure the English decided they'd had enough and swarmed over the shallow water. Digging in his spurs Will made a run for it but this time he had miscalculated. He was taken and carried furiously captive to Carlisle; '. . . seeing him ryding on his way and lyming for na harme, as that day fell, they brake a chace of more than two hundred men out of the English trayne.'

Whether Salkeld, 'the fause Salkeld' excoriated by the Scottish ballad, actually ordered the chase, condoned it or was helpless to prevent it, remains unclear. But, having secured so notorious a prisoner he was disinclined to meekly let him go, prudent as this might have been. Kinmont was not without friends. Most potent of these was Walter Scott of Buccleuch, Keeper of Liddesdale and senior Scottish law officer, with jurisdiction. In fact his was the only authority available, the wardenry of the west march was vacant after the carnage of the Johnstone–Maxwell feud and it was Buccleuch's deputy who had presided at the truce. Outraged at the incident the keeper wrote firstly to Salkeld and, receiving no satisfaction, to Scrope, the warden who had been absent at the time of the capture.

> And have they e'en ta'en him, Kinmont Willie,
> Against the truce of border tide?
> And forgotten that the bauld Buccleuch
> Can back a steed, or shake a spear?[39]

There was no love lost between these two men. Scrope, a peevish successor to his altogether more able father, cordially detested Buccleuch, who, dashing as he might be, was also violent, rapacious and vindictive, no stranger to the foray. When their correspondence descended into acrimony the keeper wrote to the English ambassador, Robert Bowes who, annoyed and alarmed, cautioned the warden to set Kinmont free. This advice was ignored. The matter had now become a clash of wills between two haughty and obdurate men. It is highly unlikely that Scrope ever intended to hang Will. No charges were laid and he was housed comfortably outside the forbidding bulk of the mighty keep within the outer ward.

Scrope, imagining himself inviolate behind the cyclopean walls of Carlisle, had gravely mistaken the character of his opponent. If Buccleuch could not release his man by diplomacy then he would not be daunted from seeking more direct means. He, unlike Scrope, knew the marches. He knew the Grahams who dominated the country between the Debatable Land and the city and they facilitated a meeting with the Carleton brothers. Thomas and Lance were related to the Grahams and, by marriage, distantly to Kinmont himself. More to the point they hated Scrope who had sacked Thomas from his sinecures of deputy warden and Constable of Carlisle. To succeed the raid had to be what might now be termed 'an inside job'.

Scrope feared he was surrounded by enemies and, to be fair, in this at least he was not mistaken. Thomas Carleton was also Land Sergeant of Gilsland and had a finger in every dishonest pie in the English west including a thriving blackmail racket in which he was partnered by Ritchie Graham of Brackenhill. Thomas, it may fairly be supposed, was able to suborn members of the watch and thus ensure the Scots would not run into any enthusiastic opposition once inside the walls.

On Saturday 12th April at Langholm races the final touches were added to the plan and the following evening, Sunday 13th, some eighty riders splashed over the Esk in the spring dusk, the welcome cloak of a foul Cumbrian evening around them. Buccleuch, Keeper of Liddesdale, led the raid. With him were a choice troop of cutthroats including four of Kinmont's sons, Auld Wat of Harden, other Scotts, Elliots and Armstrongs. With the Grahams as sponsors the riders could be sure all eyes were averted as they moved silently over the dripping mosses, eighty lances against the strongest fortress in the border, one that had defied the Scots' best efforts for several centuries. Reprehensible as his actions were it is not difficult to conceive an admiration for Buccleuch: the tale could come straight from the pages of Dumas or G.A. Henty.

The column moved forward through the night preceded by a vedette of scouts, a stronger party behind, the assault group and the main body as rearward. The ladders and grapnels they'd brought proved too short to surmount the walls. Access was gained via a postern which was either left unopened or was battered in without the alarm being raised. Once inside it was almost too easy: Kinmont was sprung, resistance from the garrison was either feeble or non-existent and the raiders were soon on their way north again – the impossible had happened, the walls of Carlisle were broached and not a man lost on either side.

Scrope was horrified, humiliated and outraged, betrayed by his own side, laughed at by the Scots and made to look the biggest fool in England. Had he been a more sympathetic character one might feel almost sorry for the man but his shrill protests did little for his cause. He quickly inflated the number of assailants to five hundred and wasted no time in blaming his own subordinates for their dereliction of duty: '. . . The watch, as yt shoulde seeme, by reason of the stormy night, were either on sleepe or gotten under some covert to defende themselves from the violence of the wether, be meanes whereof the Scottes atcheived theire enterprise with lesse difficultie.'

If he had disliked Buccleuch before he now hated him with passionate venom and the affair sparked raid and counter raid in the west, Scrope harrying north of the border and Buccleuch, Auld Wat and the Armstrongs retaliating with gusto. The diplomatic row simmered for months. Elizabeth, at the outset, shared her warden's thirst for blood but James played cannily. One suspects he was not entirely displeased with his officer's conduct: the arrest, after all, had been illegal, all peaceful avenues had been exhausted, and nobody had much time for Scrope. In the autumn of 1597, when the more vengeful protestations had mellowed, Buccleuch was sent south to explain himself and, in fact much impressed his hosts with his genial charm. Within a few months he was home again.

The experience of England, however, does seem to have sobered him. Now thirty, he could clearly perceive that the bad old days of the border were numbered and that men like his former self would soon run out of history. It is an ironic postscript to the most famous raid of all that Walter Scott of Buccleuch later became an active suppressor of the riding names after the Union of the Crowns.

'Now sound out, trumpets!' quo Buccleuch;
'Let's waken Lord Scrope right merrilie!' –
Then loud the warden's trumpet blew –
'O wha dare meddle wi' me?'[40]

In the increased prosperity and security of the Tudor age and with the former wealth of the monasteries redistributed into the ready grasp of secular magnates domestic architecture flourished as men of rank built magnificent houses commensurate with their aspirations. Montacute, Audley End and Burgley are but three examples in England. Indeed the trend away from the purely defensive towards the ornamental had begun even whilst the long enmities of the Wars of the Roses still smouldered. In Scotland Linlithgow and Falkland palaces were built or enlarged in Renaissance splendour. None of this affected the borders.

In Tynedale and elsewhere on the English side, the hillsides are still dotted with the remains of 'peles' or 'bastles', squat, solid blockhouses of massive rough-hewn stones that were the dwelling or refuge of yeomen and minor gentry. Most of those that remain were built in the latter part of the sixteenth century and, primitive as they may seem to us, represented a significant refinement of what had gone before.

Earlier defensive dwellings had consisted of log cabins, reminiscent of the movie image of frontier steadings from the American wilderness, with turf roofs and perhaps a timber palisade around. The stone bastle was a two-storey construction with either a stone-vaulted or timber-floored basement at ground level and a single storey above for living accommodation. Many examples remain: Black Middens, Gatehouse Bastles and the Bellingham Hole are notable survivors in Tynedale, though such towers are liberally scattered over Northumberland and parts of Cumbria. The lower level was entered by a single door and internal access to the upper level was by a timber ladder let through a trapdoor. The upper floor, likewise, was reached externally by ladder; the stone steps we tend to see now are later additions. The pitched roof had solid sandstone slates laid over oak trusses.

We have a reasonably good idea of the state of the defences on the English side as surveys were undertaken periodically, particularly in 1415 and 1542 when Scottish attack seemed imminent. A wealthier gentleman might aspire to a hall house or hall tower, such as Aydon on the Cor Burn or Thirlwall by the Tipalt Stream. The former was added to as the need for defence increased in the wake of Bannockburn with stronger and more extensive walls being built. Perhaps larger than a fortified manor, a kind of small castle was described as a 'fortalice'.[41]

In Henry VIII's reign his agents Robert Bowes and Ralph Ellerker reported on the strength of the North Tyne bastles '. . . very strong houses whereof for the most part the utter syddes or walls be made of greatt sware oke trees strongly bounde and joyned together with great tenors of the same so thycke mortressed that yt wylbe very hard without greatt force and laboure to break or cast down any of the said houses, the tymber as well of the said walls, as roofs, be so great and covered most part with turves and earth that they will not easyly burne or set on fyre'.[42]

Legislation passed in England in 1555 and again in 1584 provided for the need to ensure all defensible dwellings within twenty miles of the border were maintained in good repair. The East march was anchored by the fortress of Berwick and the west by Carlisle. Norham, Wark, Harbottle, Bewcastle, Askerton and Naworth all did service to provide border officials with garrison posts though Elizabethan frugality and cost-paring saw most of these fall into a fatal decline towards the end of the century.

The Scottish tower house was as distinctive as the English bastle, though generally grander, the residence of a laird and gentleman of substance. Again survivors abound, some still in use as functioning dwellings or museums, others battered and roofless, some as the mere broken remains of a doorway or gable. Of these none is more romantic than Smailholm, a Pringle hold, perched on its rocky eminence some six miles west of Kelso. Nowhere else perhaps offers a more dramatic and isolated setting, brooding over the moss and crag which surrounds it. As a boy Walter Scott spent some time at the farm which now stands nearby and the aura of conflict and romance clearly had its effect.

Typically a tower house is a well constructed edifice built of squared ashlar, perhaps 40 feet by 30 feet in plan and 40 feet to 60 feet in height. The ground floor is usually barrel-vaulted with living accommodation on the upper levels, the laird's hall with private chambers over. Internal access is by a newel stair which is turned so as to favour a right-handed defender obliged to retreat upward (it is said the stairway is turned around in any Ker tower as the family were famously left or 'ker' handed). Another hazard for the attacker was the trip stair inserted at random to afford the defender a further advantage. The external access was through a heavy oak door with a form of iron gate or 'yett' behind. The walls were from six to ten feet in thickness, confirming that impression of great strength which the elevations convey.

The roof, again finished with stone tiles, was steeply pitched with distinctive 'crow stepped' gables and a defensive parapet around where the watch might huddle by the chimney. Most were furnished with a beacon filled with pine roots and peat, used to light a warning to neighbours that a foray was underway. The curtain was pierced by tiny apertures or arrow slits with little provision for light or comfort. Internally the floors would be carpeted with heather and moorgrass, scented with the sweet fragrances of thyme and rosemary, masking the less pleasant smells of occupancy. Furnishings in all border dwellings were minimal, long settles and benches – 'crackers' with oak trestles and boards.

The tower was girded by a defensive rampart or barmkin and a cluster of domestic buildings, smithy, chapel and the bothies of the laird's tenantry. The bulk of the population lived in miserable cabins of turf and brushwood. There was little incentive to invest in more permanent or commodious dwellings when these could so easily and with depressing frequency be destroyed by fire and sword.

Both English bastle and Scottish tower proved highly defensible, proof against any random assault unless surprised. Artillery was hardly ever deployed in border warfare – the expense of the great guns and the labour in their transport, not to mention the time involved, rendered their use totally impractical. When threatened by overwhelming numbers the defenders could choose to abandon the works and withdraw to the shelter-ing mosses. In such an eventuality they would seek to protect the tower from damage or 'slighting' by cramming the interior with peat which was set alight, creating a dense, cloying shroud of smoke that was likely to prove impenetrable to the attacker.

If the assault party could approach undetected they might hope to surprise the defenders with a sudden rush, securing the doorway or break-ing down the iron yett. An eyewitness account of an assault on Lochwood, the Johnstone tower near Moffat, survives and gives a clear picture of how a successful attack could be made:

> . . . *We came thereabout an hour before day and the greater part of us lay without the barnekin; but about a dozen of the men got over the barnekin wall and stole close into the house within the barnekin and took the wenches and kept them secure in the house till daylight. And at sunrising, two men and a woman being in the tower, one of the men rising in his shirt went to the tower head, and seeing nothing stir about, he called on the wench that lay in the tower and bade her rise and open the tower door and call up them that lay beneath. She so doing and opening the iron door and a wood door without it. Our men within the barnekin broke a little too soon to the door, for the wench, perceiving them, leaped back into the tower and had gotten almost the wood door to, but one got hold of it that she could not get it close to; so the skirmish rose and we over the barnekin and broke open the wood door and she being troubled with the wood door left the iron door open and so we entered and won Lochwood.*[43]

Another method of breaking in if the element of surprise was lacking was to employ scaling ladders to gain access to the roof and then, ripping free the flags, descend through the rafters, 'to get to the top of the tower and to uncover the roof; and then some twenty of them to fall down together and by that means to win the tower.'[44]

If surprise could not be achieved then the attacker could always have recourse to 'scumfishing', the practice of stacking peat and other combustible material in the doorway and around the walls, seeking to turn the tower into a giant smokery. Heat and fumes forced the defenders to quit their refuge and capitulate, or run the gauntlet of the besiegers' spears.

It must have seemed that this dreadful way of life should continue for ever with tit-for-tat raid and reprisal, amply seasoned with bloodshed. Yet the end, when it came, was, in the circumstances remarkably swift. On the 24th March 1603 the unthinkable happened, when Elizabeth I died. Resolute to the very end she had, by sheer willpower, held off the grim reaper for some weeks, but even Gloriana herself was not immortal. As the queen breathed her last, Sir Robert Carey was in the saddle, galloping almost without a halt, till, filthy and bleeding due to an uncivil kick from his horse, he clattered into Edinburgh.

The king was roused from his well-earned slumber and though the sight of a comely male in his bedchamber was probably not unwelcome the news he was now King of England was even more so. Carey was hoping that his energy and zeal might light the path to advancement, in which he was to be somewhat disappointed but the Union of the Crowns heralded the death knell for the border reiver as surely as Judgement Day. And judgement was what James VI of Scotland, James I of England, had in mind, a drastic and permanent 'solution' to the problem of his troublesome borders. Borderers no more, their frontier was to become the middle shires of a united realm and there was no longer a place for the Steel Bonnets.

James, as Fraser points out, has not enjoyed a good press, being spindle-shanked, slack-jawed, pedantic, cowardly, deviant and deceitful. He was a man who could talk rubbish in a variety of tongues, who swooned at the sight of sword steel, never led an army and, in the final analysis, never really got on with his English subjects. They, in order to redraft their relations with the Stuart monarchy, were obliged to cut his son's head off and eventually expel his grandson into romantic exile. Nonetheless James had managed his troublesome and fractious northern kingdom with some élan. If nothing else, he had a better understanding of his border subjects than any English king since Richard III.

The plain fact of the matter was that, without a political frontier, the main recourse of the borderer was gone. Worse, their harsh uplands became marketable title again and a wave of 'carpet baggers' suddenly saw opportunities unrivalled since the Percys had exploited the earlier wars in the fourteenth century and bought up a sackful of unprofitable holdings. Principal amongst these was James's new lieutenant of the English marches, George Clifford, Earl of Cumberland. He was descended from a long line of warriors, notably John Clifford, known as the 'Bloody' who so savagely espoused the cause of Margaret of Anjou in the north, dying famously and bloodily in the skirmishing before Towton in 1461. Clifford saw particular attraction in the rich farmlands currently occupied by the English Grahams, a grayne that nobody was likely to miss.

The borderers themselves had scarcely boosted their cause. The queen's death was followed by an uproarious outburst of pillaging, 'Ill Week' as it was known, and the Grahams were prominent in the west, a grand finale on the epic scale. If James had ever doubted his resolve this two-fingered gesture would have quelled any reservations.

The king set to work. The office of the warden was abolished to be replaced by a single officer, one for each side of the line, Hume in Scotland, Cumberland for England. Each had a professional deputy who commanded a mobile mounted force designed and empowered to strike hard, fast and, all too often, without discernment or clemency.

The main period of mould-breaking or oppression, depending on which side of the line you stood, occupied the years 1603–7, though the border was not truly 'pacified' until some four or five years later. The methods employed were at best robust; hanging, deportation and conscription were the principal tools employed. Buccleuch, at the start of the reign, raised a brigade of 2,000 border horse to fight for the Dutch in their interminable war with Spain. Others, from Tynedale and Redesdale, were enlisted for service in conflicts as far distant as Ireland and Bohemia.

The business of law enforcement was begun in earnest, in 1603, with the setting up of a Royal Commission. This comprised ten members, five from each of the former jurisdictions and based at Carlisle. Hume had, as a deputy, Sir William Cranstoun and Cumberland appointed Sir Henry Leigh, hardbitten professional soldiers, and both were soon fully engaged. In November of that year 32 Elliots, Armstrongs, Johnstones and Batys were hanged, 15 were banished and 140 outlawed. This rather set the pattern for things to come. The Grahams, as mentioned, were singled out for special attention. As well as the rope and the drum many were forcibly exiled to the harsh pastures of Roscommon and Connaught where they signally failed to prosper.

The existence of the riding names for the best part of three centuries had been bleak, bloody, poor, savage, ruthless and cruel. The end of the era was every bit as bad: James was determined to use all necessary and available means to give substance to his ideal of the peaceable middle shires. By and large he was successful. A generation later lawlessness had much declined: A few gangs of mosstroopers skulked in the heather where the riding names had swaggered. Even the troublesome times of the Civil Wars in the 1640s did not open the floodgates to a sudden revival of the reiver's pernicious art, a factor that stalked each outbreak of hostilities for generations past.

The carrying of arms was forbidden, iron yetts were to be beaten into ploughshares and the ownership of a horse worth more than £30 was proscribed. There is an echo of this repressive regime in the measures that were enacted to suppress the Jacobite clans in the savage aftermath of their defeat at Culloden. The concept was not merely to rigorously enforce the law but to destroy the cultural fabric of a particular society for political ends. There is a very strong argument, in the case of the borders, that such rigour was justified, that the culture of violence had taken such deep root that only the harshest of measures would suffice.

The bad old days did not slip quietly into history in their entirety. A report of an attack on Carlisle Castle in 1648 has a distinctly familiar ring to it. A mixed body of horse and foot, 'cavaliers' and 'malignants of Scotland' descended on the fortress '. . . with ladders, scaled the walls, entered the castle, broke open the gaol, released Moss troopers and other prisoners, wounded the gaoler and all marched off together into Scotland'.[45] Surely the shade of Kinmont Will must have nodded approvingly.

The pacification of the border, though brutal and thorough, did not result in a wholesale depopulation, a version of the vile concept of 'ethnic cleansing' so familiar to us from our television screens. If one was to look in the telephone directory for Cumbria, there are still a great many Grahams. Tynedale and Redesdale remain brimful of Charltons, Robsons, Dodds, Ridleys, Storeys *et al*. Liddesdale, now a peaceful, gently undulating valley, almost disappointingly unrecognisable as a haunt of thieves, is still home to Armstrongs and Elliots.

At the eastern, remoter end of the valley Hermitage Castle still stands guard. Go there in the late autumn when the trees are stripped and the bracken bare, when the cold wind whips over the wet grass and that grim, dark sentinel stands foursquare and brooding. Then ponder how it must have been.

Notes

1 An extract from the Archbishop of Glasgow's 'Monition of Cursing' which is reproduced in full as an appendix to MacDonald Fraser's *The Steel Bonnets.*
2 Sir Robert Carey (1560–1639). MacDonald Fraser describes him as the 'beau sabreur' of the borders and this is by no means unjustified. A son of Lord Hunsdon he was also an accomplished courtier and something of a favourite of Queen Elizabeth in her later years, though she disapproved of his marriage. He was a deputy to Scrope in the west and served as warden in the east and middle marches. His memoirs are an invaluable first-hand account of the tribulations of a border warden. He hoped of high office from King James but never achieved his full ambition. In his later years he and his strong-willed wife became tutors to the young Prince Charles, who remembered his old mentor and created him Earl of Monmouth.
3 Carey's Memoirs as quoted in Durham, K., *The Border Reivers*, Osprey, London 1995 p. 17.
4 Ibid p. 18.
5 Walter Scott of Buccleuch – 'The Bold Buccleuch' (1565–1611), something of a swaggerer but equally a skilful reiver and often vengeful enemy, much addicted to feud and foray. Nonetheless he was Keeper of Liddesdale from 1594–1603, his most celebrated exploit the raid on Carlisle castle to free Kinmont Willie in 1596. After the Union he became a stiff adherent of the new policy of disarmament and retribution.
6 Quoted in Durham pp. 18–19.
7 Ibid p. 20.
8 Ibid p. 19.
9 Ibid p. 20.
10 The Bishop of Durham as quoted in Sadler, D.J., *Battle for Northumbria*, Newcastle 1988 p. 123.
11 MacDonald Fraser p. 272.
12 Durham p. 24.
13 Ibid p. 33.

14 Ibid p. 33.

15 Ibid pp. 34–5.

16 Sadler p. 124.

17 Ibid p. 125.

18 Ibid p. 123.

19 As pictured in Durham p. 19 – a fine original being housed in the Museum of Border Arms and Armour, Teviotdale.

20 Quoted in Sadler p. 20.

21 Bishop Leslie, quoted in Sadler p. 125.

22 These were Robert Ker in 1511, killed in a fight with the Bastard Heron at a Truce Day. Heron's two accomplices or seconds, Lilburn and Starhead, were pursued by the vengeful Kers and hunted to death. Starhead was in hiding in York when the revengers caught up with him. Anthony Darcy the 'Sieur de la Bastie' – he was appointed over the heads of the powerful Humes who, in 1516, murdered him, riding in triumph with their victim's head tied to the saddle bow in a grisly echo of ancient Celtic fashion. Maxwell, killed at Dryfe Sands in 1593 and Sir John Carmichael in 1600 (see note 29 below).

23 MacDonald Fraser p. 130.

24 Geordie Burne, the notorious son of a particularly savage grayne, was sponsored by Sir Robert Ker of Cesford, who despite being a warden ran his march more like a latter-day Sicilian 'mafioso' than an officer of the law. He and Carey clashed more than once though Cesford, like Buccleuch, became 'respectable' as he advanced in years, being created Earl of Roxburgh in 1616.

25 Forster's watchers arrested and then released an itinerant Scottish barber surgeon in 1582. Though the Scot rode free, having bought off the guard, his instruments remained confiscated and Forster discovered encrypted notes hidden amongst these which he sent to Walsingham whose codebreakers set to work and unearthed the beginnings of the 'Enterprise of England' – the Spanish Armada of 1588 (see MacDonald Fraser pp. 145–6.)

26 Quoted in MacDonald Fraser p. 137.

27 Ibid p. 149.

28 Quoted in Durham p. 19.

29 MacDonald Fraser pp. 141–2.

30 Quoted in Sadler p. 126.

31 Ibid p. 127.

32 Ibid p. 128.

33 MacDonald Fraser p. 169.

34 Watson, G., *The Border Reivers*, London 1974 p. 139.

35 Quoted in MacDonald Fraser p. 170.

36 Ibid p. 171.

37 Ibid p. 170.

38 Ibid p. 172.

39 'The Ballad of Kinmont Willie' – quoted in MacDonald Fraser pp. 386–91.

40 'Kinmont Willie' supra.
41 A 'fortalice' is nowhere clearly defined. It would appear to be something larger than a fortified manor house but perhaps less than a castle, see Long, B., *Castles of Northumberland*, Newcastle 1967 p. 10.
42 Quoted in Durham p. 21.
43 Ibid p. 23.
44 Ibid p. 23.
45 Ibid p. 42.

Glossary

Arbalest – A form of crossbow favoured by continental armies.

Arquebus – A matchlock musket, sixteenth century.

Aventail – A defence made from mail to protect the neck.

Ballista – A type of catapult, in use since classical times, which discharges a missile from a bow, tensioned by means of a windlass.

Ballock knife – A form of dagger, late fifteenth and sixteenth century, Scottish in origin, so named because of the kidney-shaped lobes at the base of the hilt.

Banneret – A military rank, the banneret was higher than a knight and entitled to carry a square banner rather than the knight's pennon.

Barbican – An outwork constructed to provide additional protection to a castle or town fortified gateway. This could be a permanent, stone construction (examples can be seen at Alnwick, Prudhoe and Dunstanburgh) or a temporary timber affair.

Bascinet – A conical helm of the fourteenth century, could be worn open faced or fitted with a pointed visor 'pig face'.

Bastion – A defensive feature associated with the development of sixteenth-century artillery fortifications, a fighting platform that projects outward from an angle of the walls.

Bastle – Possibly from the French 'Bastille' – used to describe a form of domestic, defensible building that became a feature of the English marches during the fifteenth and particularly the sixteenth centuries. Often interchangeable with **pele** or **pele tower** (possibly from the Latin 'pilum' – i.e. a stake or palisade).

Belfrey (Beffroi) – A wooden siege tower moved forwards on wheels or rollers.

Bill – A pole arm, born of a deadly fusion of the agricultural implement and military spear, a particular favourite of the English.

Bombard – Heavy siege gun of the fifteenth century of substantial but irregular calibre.

Brigandine – A form of protective doublet with metal plates sewn in.

Broken men – Akin to outlaws but not necessarily outlawed; having no chief or **heidsman**.

Buckler – A small, round shield, usually metal, held by a central grip, used primarily for parrying.

Caltrap – A rather nasty spike device, scattered on the ground and intended to maim horses.

Captain – The officer in charge of a particular place or area, responsible for that area but not beyond.

Chevauchee – A large-scale raid or expedition intended to devastate and strip enemy territory, to belittle the foe and, possibly, a means of goading him into giving battle.

Cleane – Innocent (or not proven).

Coif – A mail hood.

Constable – The man in charge of a lord's tenantry who might serve within the lord's castle or without, i.e. in the field.

Crenellation – The form of battlements on a castle parapet, 'licence to crenellate' being a form of medieval planning consent to be obtained from the crown before a castle or tower could be lawfully constructed.

Cuisse – Plate defence for the thigh.

Dagg – A wheelock horseman's pistol, usually carried in pairs, holstered on the saddle.

Destrier – A warhorse.

Dudgeon – A form of dagger related to the ballock knife, popular in the late sixteenth century.

Enceinte – A term used to describe the circuit of walls of a defended place.

Escalade – An assault against town or castle walls.

Falchion – A cleaver-like sword with a heavy blade.

Fief – Land held on military tenure.

Fortalice – A small castle or fort, never clearly defined in terms of size or importance.

Fosse – A defensive ditch.

Fyled – Proven, i.e. guilty.

Glaive – A pole arm not unlike the bill but with a heavier curved blade.

Gorget – Plate defence for the neck, normally hinged.

Greaves – Plate defences for the calves.

Halberd – A pole arm with a broad axe blade, much favoured by the Swiss.

Harness – Plate armour/mail and plate combined.

Hauberk – A mail shirt reaching usually to the knee, the shorter version is called a **habergeon**.

Helm – Helmet, the 'Great Helm' was the form of knightly, protective head gear in use at the end of the thirteenth century and the early phase of the Edwardian wars.

Herschip – A raid or harrying.

Hobiler(ar) – A border horseman, light cavalry who could fight as infantry.

Insight (Gear) – Household goods.

Jack – Similar to the brigandine but stuffed with rags, generally sleeveless.

Jupon – A heraldic tunic, close fitted and worn over the plate breast and back in the fourteenth century.

Kettle hat – A form of metal helmet worn by common footsoldiers, with a wide protective brim, very similar in appearance to British helmets of both world wars.

Lance – A tactical unit built around a knight's following, not fixed in terms of numbers.

Land–Sergeant – The principal law officer within a given area or district. His precise role is unclear and probably was never defined. He could and was perhaps expected to act with a fair degree of personal initiative.

Latch – A form of simple crossbow used by mounted troops, favoured by Scottish hobilers.

Leaguer – Siege or blockade.

Mangonel – An engine for throwing stones. The arm is held back under tension, the missile is launched when the arm is released to strike against a crossbar.

Merlon – The raised section of a battlement.

Mesnie – A household knight, i.e. of the lord's demesne or domain.

Meurtriere – Literally 'murder hole', the open space at the foot of the parapet walk where the battlements are extended beyond the wall head to permit the defender to drop the missiles of choice onto the heads of careless attackers at the foot of the wall.

Palfrey – A form of horse used for everyday travel, the destrier being reserved for use in battle or the lists.

Pauldron – A form of plate armour to protect the shoulders.

Pricker – Scout and/or light horseman.

Quillons – The bars at the base of the sword hilt, to protect the hands.

Reiter – German mercenary cavalry of the sixteenth century.

Ricasso – The flat and blunted section of the blade immediately below the hilt, enabling the swordsman to extend his grip.

Rode – Raid.

Rondel dagger – A fifteenth-century long-bladed knife, carried by men at arms and civilians, used often for dispatching an armoured foe.

Saker – Light field gun of varying calibre, sixteenth century.

Sallet – A fifteenth-century helmet with a swept neckguard and also often fitted with a movable or fixed visor. The lower face and neck were protected by a complementary piece, the **bevor**.

Surcoat – Flowing tunic of the thirteenth century worn over mail. Longer and much looser fitting than the jupon.

Tasset – Plate defence for the thigh.

Trebuchet – A large siege engine with a heavy throwing arm.

Vintenar – A type of NCO in charge of a platoon of twenty foot.

Bibliography

Anderson, R. and R.C., *The Sailing Ship* 1926.

Archibald, E.H.H., *The Wooden Fighting Ship* 1968.

Armstrong, R.B., *History of Liddesdale, Eskdale, Ewesdale, Wauchopedale and the Debatable Land* 1883.

Armstrong, W.A., *The Armstrong Borderland* 1960.

Bain, J. (Ed.), *Calendar of Documents Relating to Scotland 1108–1509* 1881–1884.

—— *Calendar of Border Papers* vols. 1 and 2 1894.

Baldick, R., *The Duel* 1965.

Barber, R., *The Knight and Chivalry* 1974.

Barr, N., *Flodden* 2000.

Barrow, G.W.S., *Robert the Bruce* 1965.

—— *Kingship and Unity; Scotland 1000–1306* 1981.

Bartlett, C., *The English Longbowman 1330–1515* 1995.

Bates, C.J., *History of Northumberland* 1895.

—— *Border Holds of Northumberland* 2 vols 1891.

Bennet, M., *Agincourt 1415* 1991.

Bingham, C., *The Stewart Kingdom of Scotland 1371–1603* 1974.

Black, C., *Scottish Battles* 1936.

Black, J., *Culloden and the '45* 1990.

Black, J.B., *The Reign of Elizabeth 1558–1603* (Oxford History) 2nd (Ed.) 1959.

Blackmore, H.L., *The Armouries of the Tower of London – Ordnance* 1976.

Blair, C., *European Armour* 1958.

Boardman, A., *The Battle of Towton* 1994.

—— *The Medieval Soldier in the Wars of the Roses* 1998.

Borland, Rev. R., *Border Raids and Reivers* 1910.

Brenan, R., *History of the House of Percy* 2 vols 1898.

Brown, J. (Ed.), *Scottish Society in the Fifteenth Century* 1977.

Brown, C., *The Second Scottish War of Independence* 2000.

Brown, T.C., *The History of Selkirkshire* 1886.

Bulmer, T.F. (Ed.), *Historical, Topographical Directory of Northumberland* (Hexham) 1886.

Burne, Col. A.H., *Battlefields of England* 1950.

—— *More Battlefields of England* 1952.

—— *The Agincourt War* 1956.

Carey, R., *Memoirs* 1747.

Cauldwell, D.A., *The Scottish Armoury* 1976.

Chandler, D., *A Guide to the Battlefields of Europe* 1989.

Charlesworth, D., 'Northumberland in the Early Years of Edward IV' *Archaeologia Aeliana* 1953.

—— 'The Battle of Hexham' *Archaeologia Aeliana* 1952.

Christison, Gen. Sir P., *Bannockburn* 1960.

Chronicles of London.

Clifford, A. (Ed.), *Sadler's State Papers* 3 vols 1809.

Complaynt of Scotland 1548 1801.

Curwen, J.F., *Castles and Fortified Towers of Cumberland and Westmorland* 1913.

De Commynes, P., *Memoirs for the Reign of Louis XI 1461–1463* Transl. M. Jones 1972.

Dixon, D.D., *Upper Coquetdale* 1903.

Dodds, J.F., *Bastions and Belligerents* 2001.

Douglas, Sir G., *A History of the Border Counties* 1899.

Douglas-Simpson, W., *Scottish Castles* 1959.

Drummond-Brown, R., *Brave Borderland* 1935.

Durham, K., *The Border Reivers* 1995.

Fisher, A., *William Wallace* 1986.

Forde-Johnston, J., *Great Medieval Castles of Britain* 1979.

Fraser, G.M., *The Steel Bonnets* 1971.

Fraser, Lady A., *Mary Queen of Scots* 1969.

Froissart, *Chronicles* Transl. Berners 1924.

Fordun, J., *Chronicle of the Scottish Nation* (Ed.) William F. Skene 1872.

Gauld, H.D., *Brave Borderland* 1935.

Gillingham, J., *The Wars of the Roses* 1981.

Goodman, A., *The Wars of the Roses* 1975.

Graham, G., *Condition of the Border at the Union* 1907.

Gravett, C., *Medieval Siege Warfare* 1990.

Gray, Sir Thomas of Heton, *Scalacronica* Transl. Sir Herbert Maxwell 1907.

Griffiths, R.A., 'Local Rivalries and National Politics: The Percies, The Nevilles and the Duke of Exeter 1452–1455' *Speculum* 1968.

Haigh, P., *The Military Campaigns of the Wars of the Roses* 1995.

Hayes-McCoy, G.A., *Irish Battles* 1969.

Heath, I. and S. Sque, *The Irish Wars 1485–1603* 1993.

Hedley, W.P., *Northumbrian Families* 2 vols 1970.

Hicks, M.A., *Edward IV, the Duke of Somerset and Lancastrian Loyalism in the North* Northern History.

Hodgson, Rev. O., *History of Northumberland* 7 vols 1863.

Holinshed, *Chronicles* 1808 edn.

Hume, P., *A History of Scotland* 2 vols 1911.

Humphrey, D., *Our Man in Scotland* 1969.

James, M.E., *The Murder at Cocklodge on 28th April 1489* Durham University Journal 1965.

Keegan, J., *The Face of Battle* 1976.

—— *Intelligence in War* 2003.

Keen, M. (Ed.), *Medieval Warfare* 1999.

Kendall, P.M., *Richard III* 1955.

—— *Warwick the Kingmaker* 1957.

Kightly, C., *Flodden and the Anglo-Scottish War of 1513* 1975.

Lander, J.R., *The Wars of the Roses* 1990.

Long, B., *Castles of Northumberland* 1967.

Lomas, R., *County of Conflict – Northumberland from the Conquest to the Civil War* 1996.

Loyd, A., *My War Gone By I Miss It So* 1999.

Lynch, M., *Scotland – A New History* 1991.

MacDonald, A.J., *Border Bloodshed* 2000.

MacDougal, N., *James IV* 1989.

McIvor, I., *A Fortified Frontier* 2000.

McNamee, C., *Wars of the Bruces* 1997.

McNeil, T., *Castles* 1992.

Mack, J.L., *The Border Line From the Solway Firth to the North Sea* 1924.

Mackie, J.D., *A History of Scotland* 1964.

—— *The Earlier Tudors 1485–1558* 1952.

Marsden, J., *Galloglas* 2003.

Middleton, A.E., *Sir Gilbert de Middleton* 1918.

Moffat, A., *The Borders* 2002.

Moorhouse, G., *The Pilgrimage of Grace* 2002.

Morris, J.E., *The Welsh Wars of Edward I* 1901.

Mortimer, I., *The Greatest Traitor* 2003.

Neillands, R., *The Hundred Years War* 1990.

Newark, T., *War in Britain* 2000.

Nicole, D., *Medieval Warfare Source Book* 1999.

Norman, A.V.B. and D. Pottinger, *English Weapons and Warfare 449–1660* 1966.

Norris, J., *Early Gunpowder Artillery c. 1300–1600* 2003.

Northumberland County History Committee, *Northumberland County History* 15 vols.

Nusbacher, A., *The Battle of Bannockburn 1314* 2000.

Oakeshott, R.E., *A Knight and His Weapons* 1964.

—— *A Knight and His Armour* 1964.

—— *A Knight and His Horse* 1964.

—— *A Knight and His Castle* 1964.

—— *European Weapons and Armour* 1980.

Oman, Sir C., *The Art of War in the Middle Ages* 2 vols 1924.

—— *The Art of War in the Sixteenth Century* 1924.

Pease, H., *The Lord Wardens of the Marches of England and Scotland* 1913.

Pevsner, Sir N., 'Northumberland' in the *Buildings of England Series* 1992 edn.

Pitcairn, R., *Criminal Trials in Scotland 1488–1624* 1833.

Platt, W., *Stories of the Scottish Border* 1919.

Pollard, A. (Ed.), *The North of England in the Reign of Richard III* 1996.

—— 'Percies, Nevilles and the Wars of the Roses' *History Today* 1992.

Prestwich, M., *Edward I* 1988.

—— *The Three Edwards* 1990.

—— *Armies and Warfare in the Middle Ages – The English Experience* 1996.

Ramsay, Sir J.H., *Lancaster and York* 2 vols 1892.

Reese, P., *Bannockburn* 2000.

Ridpath, Rev. G., *Border History* 1858.

Robert, Fabyan, *The New Chronicles of England and France*.

Rogers, Col. H.C.B., *Artillery Through The Ages* 1976.

Robson, R., *The Rise and Fall of the English Highland Clans* 1989.

Rollason, D. and M. Prestwich (Ed.), *The Battle of Neville's Cross 1346* 1998.

Rose, A., *Kings in the North* 2002.

Ross, C., *The Wars of the Roses* 1976.

Rothero, C., *The Scottish and Welsh Wars 1250–1400* 1989.

Runciman, Sir S., *The Fall of Constantinople* 1965.

Sadler, D.J., *Battle For Northumbria* 1988.

—— *Scottish Battles* 1996.

Scarisbrick, J.J., *Henry VIII* 1968.

Scott, Sir W., *Minstrelsy of the Scottish Border* 1892.

Seward, D., *Henry V as Warlord* 1987.

Seymour, E., *Battles in Britain* 2 vols 1975.

Sitwell, Brig. R., *The Border* 1927.

Smurthwaite, D., *Battlefields of Britain* Ordnance Survey 1984.

Tabraham, C., *Scottish Castles and Fortifications* 1986.

Talbot-White, J., *The Scottish Borders and Northumberland* 1973.

Talhofer, H., *Medieval Combat* transl. M. Rector 2000.

Tomlinson, W.W., *Comprehensive Guide to Northumberland* 1863.

—— *Life in Northumberland During the Sixteenth Century*.

Tough, D.L.W., *Last Years of a Frontier* 1928.

Tranter, N., *Fortalices and Early Mansions of Southern Scotland, 1400–1650* 1935.

Traquair, P., *Freedom's Sword* 1990.

Trevelyan, G.M., *English Social History* 1946: 1965.

Treece, H. and R.E., Oakeshott, *Fighting Men* 1963.

Tuchman, B., *A Distant Mirror* 1978.

Turnbull, S., *Book of the Medieval Knight* 1985.

Warkworth, J., *A Chronicle of the First Thirteen Years of the Reign of Edward IV 1461–1474.*

Watson, G., *The Border Reivers* 1974.

Weiss, H., 'A Power in the North? The Percies in the Fifteenth Century' *The Historical Journal* 1965.

White, R., *The Battle of Otterburn* 1857.

William Gregory's, *Chronicles of London.*

William of Worcester, *Annales Rerum Anglicarum.*

Wise, T., *The Wars of the Roses* 1993.

Year Book de Termino Paschae 4 Edward IV Surtees Society 1864.

Index

INTRODUCING PRACTICAL THEOLOGY

Mission, Ministry, and the Life of the Church

PETE WARD

Baker Academic
a division of Baker Publishing Group
Grand Rapids, Michigan

Published by Baker Academic
a division of Baker Publishing Group
PO Box 6287, Grand Rapids, MI 49516-6287
www.bakeracademic.com

Printed in the United States of America

Library of Congress Cataloging-in-Publication Data

Names: Ward, Pete, author.
Title: Introducing practical theology : mission, ministry, and the life of the church / Pete Ward.
Description: Grand Rapids : Baker Academic, 2017. | Includes bibliographical references and index.
Identifiers: LCCN 2017026064 | ISBN 9780801098192 (pbk. : alk. paper)
Subjects: LCSH: Theology, Practical.
Classification: LCC BV3 .W37 2017 | DDC 230.01—dc23
LC record available at https://lccn.loc.gov/2017026064

In chapter 4, in the section titled "The Four Theological Voices," an earlier version of this section appears in Pete Ward, "Seeing and Believing," in *The End of Theology: Shaping Theology for the Sake of Mission*, ed. Jason S. Sexton and Paul Weston, 145–70. Minneapolis: Fortress, 2016.

Scripture quotations are from the New Revised Standard Version of the Bible, copyright © 1989, by the Division of Christian Education of the National Council of the Churches of Christ in the United States of America. Used by permission. All rights reserved.